Praise for Jeff Madrick's

AGE OF GREED

"The timing could not be better for a book like *Age of Greed*. . . . A solid review of half a century of economic history. . . . A commendable compendium." —*San Francisco Chronicle*

"Excellent. . . . Straightforward. . . . We owe Madrick thanks for what he has done." —*The American Prospect*

"A compelling and worthy read. Madrick is an able journalist; an excellent and cogent storyteller in a field that often defies the straightforward plot or easy explanation—economics." —*Salon*

"Persuasive. . . . Vivid. . . . As a comprehensive survey of the way institutions work together to create wealth for a few individuals and destroy it for a mass of others, *Age of Greed* deserves attention." —*The Columbus Dispatch*

"Madrick pulls no punches. . . . Readers who want to understand where we are, how we got here, and some possible outcomes will repay their investment in reading time if they pick up this new volume." —*The Free Lance-Star* (Fredericksburg, VA)

"*Age of Greed* is lucid and compelling because of its character-driven nature." —*The Dallas Morning News*

"Meticulous. . . . Madrick makes a good case—and financial news junkies will savor it." —*Boulder Daily Camera*

JEFF MADRICK
AGE OF GREED

Jeff Madrick is a regular contributor to *The New York Review of Books*, a former economics columnist for *The New York Times*, and editor of *Challenge* magazine. He is an adjunct professor of humanities at The Cooper Union, and senior fellow at the Roosevelt Institute and at the Schwartz Center for Economic Policy Analysis, The New School. His previous books include *The End of Affluence* and *Taking America*, and he has written for *The Washington Post*, the *Los Angeles Times*, *Institutional Investor*, *The Nation*, and *The American Prospect*.

www.jeffmadrick.com

AGE OF GREED

*The Triumph of Finance
and the Decline of America,
1970 to the Present*

JEFF MADRICK

Vintage Books
A Division of Random House, Inc.
New York

FIRST VINTAGE BOOKS EDITION, JUNE 2012

Copyright © 2011 by Jeff Madrick

The Library of Congress has cataloged the Knopf edition as follows:
Madrick, Jeffrey G.
Age of greed : the triumph of finance and the decline of America,
1970 to the present / [Jeff Madrick].
p. cm.
Includes index.
1. Wealth—Moral and ethical aspects.
2. Financial crises—United States—History.
3. United States—Politics and government—20th century.
4. United States—Politics and government—21st century. I. Title.
HC79.W4M33 2011 330.9730092'2—dc22 2011003399

Vintage ISBN: 978-1-4000-7566-9

Author photograph © Dominique Nabokov
Book design by M. Kristen Bearse

www.vintagebooks.com

Printed in the United States of America
10 9 8 7 6 5 4 3 2

For Kim

Contents

Introduction

This book starts with a relatively unknown man named Lewis Uhler, a Southern Californian, who, like his father before him, hated the New Deal. He and others like him, who came of age in the 1950s, feared their personal liberty was in constant danger of being taken away by big government. Many of them were sincere, and most were angry—especially because in the 1950s and 1960s they weren't being heard. But they laid the foundation for a new age.

In those years, most Americans believed the federal government was good for them. Washington created far-reaching financial, social, and economic reforms in the Depression and managed the massive war effort in the 1940s. In the 1950s it built highways, set out to send men into space, and subsidized housing. In the 1960s, it created Medicare, expanded Social Security, adopted regulations to protect consumers and workers, passed long-awaited civil rights guarantees, and developed antipoverty programs. Progressive taxation to pay the bills was widely accepted as just. All the while, the American economy grew rapidly and wages doubled adjusted for inflation for workers at every income level.

Perhaps more than any other factor, punishingly high inflation in the 1970s changed all of this. Americans panicked. Well before incomes became highly unequal or the wealthy gained undue political power with outsize campaign contributions and well-financed lobbying organizations and think tanks, Americans came to believe that government had gone too far. The ideology of the Lewis Uhlers of America, long dormant, began to gain influence. Soon social programs were curtailed. Regulations were eliminated and weakened. Uhler among many others participated in a tax revolt that started slowly but then spread rapidly, well before Ronald

Reagan was elected president. The new persistent refrain was that big government held all Americans back. The narrative came to dominate the public discourse.

Greed will always be with us, but it rises and falls with the times. Some rebalancing between government and business may have been necessary by the 1970s, and some reworking of government programs was needed. But the reforms went blindly ahead. Vital purposes of government were rejected. An age of greed did not begin in the 2000s. It started decades earlier, and the crisis of 2008 was its culmination, and probably not its end.

This book is about how this shift came about, and how profound its influence has been. It contends that the rise of an age of greed since the 1970s was not the result of the inevitable forces of history or of a natural swing of a political pendulum. The new age was made by people, and how they reacted to crisis and change. Much damage was done along the way.

Part I tells the story of this revolution. Presidents, policymakers, and economists are critical to the history. But it is mostly a story of business pioneers who fought government regulation or, through innovation, escaped government oversight—all the while diminishing the power of government and reinforcing the changing national attitudes. The 1970s set the stage for a different America.

Once government was no longer a counterweight and a new political ideology cleared their path, financiers led the way. Wall Street changed radically. Part II tells these stories. Debt more than innovation and technological progress became the economy's driving force. Financial businesses doubled in size compared to the economy and profits grew still faster. Hundreds of billions of precious American savings were wasted.

The new age started with Walter Wriston, the most innovative, aggressive, and admired of the nation's commercial bankers, head in the 1970s of First National City Bank, later Citicorp. He was an adamant believer in laissez-faire economics—minimal government intervention. He revolutionized banking by circumventing and often ignoring New Deal regulations. Financial deregulation started with him, but three times in thirty years the bank he built nearly went out of business due to the hundreds of millions of dollars of bad loans it made, saved only by federal intervention. The story of Citibank runs through this entire history.

Not all those who are the principal focus of a chapter were blatant practitioners of greed—some not at all. Tom Peters, the famed management consultant, was much the opposite. Paul Volcker, the stringent chairman of the Federal Reserve, was mostly oblivious to financial gain. George Soros, the hedge fund manager, gave much of his fortune to causes that were detrimental to his personal financial interest. The age's philosopher, Milton Friedman, was not intent on getting rich. They all contributed importantly to this history, however.

These separate stories are integral parts of a large picture. Ultimately, they fit together. Most of the people in this book were not wholly destructive. History is never so simple. Some were not destructive at all. But most of those discussed here took the economy along an unfortunate, tragic path for their own purposes from which it may not be possible to turn back.

One

REVOLUTION

PROLOGUE

Lewis Uhler

BELIEVER

[handwritten margin notes: — Conservative — Runs National Tax Limitation Committee — Reagan's cabinet as Ser. to Health & Welfare Agency]

Ever since the Gold Rush of the mid-1800s, California seemed a promised land to Americans. The economy grew at prodigious rates, benefiting from the national expansion of the railroads, the discovery of oil, the birth of the movies, cheap plentiful farmland, and the appealing climate. New Deal policies helped during the Great Depression. After World War II, the underpinnings of the economy were agriculture and the defense industry, government the too easily forgotten partner to the region's prosperity. Businessmen created defense and aerospace giants with federal contracts to support the war in the Pacific theater. State and local governments financed critical public projects to bring invaluable water to the fertile farmlands of the south from the great rivers of the north and west.

The post–World War II American economy grew rapidly almost everywhere, but Southern California and, in particular, Orange County, grew faster still. The flood of migrants from the Midwest needed new subdivisions of affordable housing as well as new cars, appliances, supermarkets, and banks—and new roads, water systems, and sanitation. To many citizens of the region, life was good and hard work and talent paid off beyond expectations. Soon, to many of those who did well, prosperity was seen as the just reward of a determined and diligent populace. Government programs—defense contracts, highways, water works, sanitation projects, primary schools, and high schools—were accepted as a right, social programs and high taxes an intrusion on the marketplace and personal freedom. The seeds of America's future took root in the soil of these counties.

Lewis Uhler was born in the Los Angeles area in 1933 and raised as a teenager in one of its up-and-coming suburbs. His father, James, was a suc-

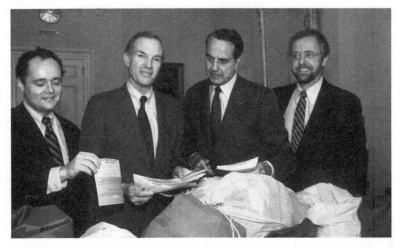

Lewis Uhler, second from left, with Senator Bob Dole and other members of the
National Tax Limitation Committee, opening sacks of mail addressed to his organization

cessful executive at Sunkist, whose principal suppliers were the politically
conservative growers in California and Arizona.

Lewis carried the conservative message inside him almost as a birth-
right. "My father was a political animal and he hated FDR," Uhler says.
"The whole New Deal thing was anathema to him." The farmers James
Uhler worked for feared nothing more than the unionization of labor,
and labor organizing, one of the New Deal's legacies, was now spreading
throughout the nation.

The foundation of American success was not the romanticized dream
of finding a pot of gold. Rather, it was the consistent rise in white workers' compensation, both blue-collar and white-collar, decade after decade,
even if one did the same work as, or its contemporary equivalent of, one's
father. Thus, it was not that the son or daughter necessarily got a better job,
but that wages after inflation went up for most kinds of work. Ultimately,
the typical white American thirty-year-old male earned significantly more
than his father had when he was thirty, a forty-year-old more than his
father had at forty. There were poverty and need in Southern California,
and bitterness and futility, as captured especially by some novelists and a
handful of filmmakers. But the lives of most in Southern California, if not
always ideal, improved materially and dependably. They participated in the
real and reliable American dream of fairly constant material improvement.

This was true of James Uhler's life. He made a good and generally improving living. Lewis Uhler, learning from his father, came to believe that public social programs interfered with the virtues of American life, in fact, trampling on Americans' rights, and, further, that the Founding Fathers fully agreed with him. The rise in power of the Soviet Union after World War II stoked a passionate fear that this freedom would be violated. The new superpower was both antireligious and anti-market, in his mind and in those of his like-minded friends deeply challenging the values of a free nation. In Southern California, anticommunism gained rapid popularity. Richard Nixon, the fresh-faced congressman from Whittier when Uhler was a teenager, based much of his early political career on it, and stoked it further.

Franklin Roosevelt was the natural enemy of these believers, his waywardness and dangerous ways, as they labeled them, frequent dinner conversation for many. High taxes were justified by the war, some conceded, but after Harry Truman's presidency these believers feared the spread of progressivism even under his Republican successor, Dwight Eisenhower. Desegregating the Little Rock, Arkansas, schools became the symbol of the misuse of federal power. These conservatives also felt that Eisenhower's program to build the interstate highways overstepped federal bounds.

For a while, the believers lost major elections: Nixon to John F. Kennedy in 1960, Barry Goldwater to Lyndon Johnson in 1964. California, a largely Republican state, even elected a Democratic governor, Edmund "Pat" Brown, in 1958. The believers eventually found a unifying voice for their philosophy in the economic writings of Milton Friedman and the novels of Ayn Rand. They found their national political leadership in Ronald Reagan. They found powerful allies in big business, who were relative latecomers to their cause, learning in the 1970s to organize themselves politically for fear the progressive country was turning against them. The views of a relatively small band of believers came, improbably, to dominate the nation.

Lewis Uhler was a good student and was accepted to Yale in 1953. He was wary of enrolling there. He believed the future publisher of *National Review*, William Buckley, when he wrote in his book *God and Man at Yale* (1952) that the school was disturbingly liberal, though it was among the more conservative of the Ivy League colleges. With the publication of *God and Man at Yale*, an undergraduate's diatribe, if an articulate one, against Yale professors for their religious agnosticism and support of Keynesian government intervention, the charismatic Buckley had become a household name. The book became a best seller, evidence that a conservative undertow existed in the United States despite the nation's politically liberal direction. Buckley, the son of a wealthy oilman, hailed personal freedom, hated the United Nations and the Soviet Union, and confidently started a new organization, Young Americans for Freedom, which attracted a large number of disenchanted men and women in the 1950s. By the time Uhler entered Yale, there was a congenial group of friends to be made at Yale who had similar political views about the dangers of big government. "We thought of ourselves as the successors to Buckley," he said.

Uhler was outgoing and optimistic and enjoyed himself immensely at Yale. He then won entrance to Boalt Hall, the law school of the University of California at Berkeley, where he earned his degree in 1960. After his service in the Navy, he joined the office of Congressman John Rousselot from Pasadena. Rousselot was proudly, unabashedly conservative and the only congressman who was an open member of the John Birch Society, the new right-wing extremist group. Robert Welch, a retired candy manufacturer (maker of Sugar Daddys), started the Birch Society in 1958 when he was nearly sixty, out of his home in Belmont, a handsome Boston suburb north of Harvard Square. The society soon drew tens of thousands of members, many in Southern California, where one chapter after another was opened in the early 1960s. Welch wrote a self-published book accusing not only Harry Truman but also Eisenhower and his secretary of state, John Foster Dulles, of being part of a Soviet conspiracy. He had also demanded the impeachment of Chief Justice Earl Warren, who wrote the Little Rock decision desegregating the public schools. Rousselot was an early and consistent supporter, but William Buckley, also an early member of the Birch Society, turned against it as extremist. According to Lou Cannon, Ronald Reagan's biographer, Uhler joined the Birchers, but only for six months.

In 1958, Governor Pat Brown started raising taxes and establishing ambitious government programs. A native of Northern California, Brown had been a moderate Republican early in his life. He switched parties as a young man and became the state attorney general as a Democrat, the only Democrat at the time in a prominent statewide office. A popular and energetic attorney general, he decided to run for governor against Goodwin Knight, a moderate Republican governor, and won the statehouse by a wide margin. He epitomized the rising national confidence in government. Nixon, hoping to launch a political comeback after his narrow loss to Kennedy in 1960, challenged Brown for governor in 1962, but lost badly.

With Nixon's career seemingly over, Uhler now placed his hopes on the more conservative Barry Goldwater, the Arizona senator who had come to national attention during the 1960 Republican National Convention. Goldwater published a literate book that year, *Conscience of a Conservative*, ghostwritten by William Buckley's brother-in-law, L. Brent Bozell, a close classmate of Buckley's at Yale (and a former political liberal). It became a best seller and showed supporters that there was life in conservatism even after Kennedy's victory. The book's central theme was personal freedom, the conservative philosophical warhorse. Goldwater advocated a vast reduction in government programs and sharply criticized Social Security, but the popularity of the book had greatly to do with his tough stance toward the Soviet Union. The book successfully bolstered his campaign for the Republican presidential nomination, which he won in 1964, beating back the moderate Republican governor of New York, Nelson Rockefeller.

That summer, President Lyndon Johnson was passing the first important legislation of his Great Society, the Civil Rights Act, which made illegal Jim Crow state laws that authorized segregation in public places throughout the South. Goldwater voted against the legislation in the Senate, insisting to widespread scorn his vote was not racist but simply reflected a desire to preserve the rights of states to make such laws. His decision may have made him more popular with the rightist diehards, but it reduced his chances against Johnson. Goldwater was an impatient candidate of little charm, and given his bellicose pronouncements about foreign policy, it was easy for his opponent to raise American fears he might launch a nuclear war in a stare down with the Soviet Union. Goldwater lost in a landslide to Johnson, and the Republican Party looked moribund.

There was, however, one shining light for conservatives at the 1964 Republican convention. Ronald Reagan, the actor and General Electric television host, not yet a professional politician, made an especially effective nationally televised speech that strongly supported Goldwater. Reagan had been making essentially the same speech around the nation as a spokesman for GE for several years, and political backers in California had taken note of a potential new Republican star. Reagan gave no ground to the liberal groundswell. In one stroke, he brought himself national recognition as a viable political contender, even as Goldwater lost badly to Johnson. Only two years after Goldwater's resounding defeat, Reagan defeated Governor Brown for the California statehouse.

The governorship was Reagan's first elective office and he was already fifty-five years old. Most observers thought his election was a political aberration and that his future was limited. But to people like Uhler, he was a talented, courageous, and honest "citizen politician," as Reagan called himself, with remarkable verbal skills and deep convictions. He was a former New Dealer who had seen the light, a man who was willing to exalt individualistic ideals and personal freedom, someone who seemed clearly unafraid to stand up to the Soviets.

Edwin Meese, Reagan's key legal staffer and his future attorney general, had known Uhler at Boalt Hall, and in 1968 invited him to join Reagan's gubernatorial staff. Uhler's first major assignment was to challenge California Rural Legal Assistance, a nonprofit organization established by Lyndon Johnson as part of the War on Poverty to provide legal aid to the poor, mostly agricultural workers, regarding housing, wages, and health care. The program was a thorn in the side of Reagan's backers, and especially the politically powerful farm community. Uhler wrote a report charging the program's legal staff with serious improprieties. "It was one of those new liberal agencies," Uhler said, "where you saw hammer-and-sickle banners drawn on the walls." Reagan wanted to shut the program down, and he thought Uhler's denunciatory report gave him the justification to do so. But the next year, Nixon, by then president, appointed a federal committee of former Supreme Court justices to investigate Uhler's charges. The investigation concluded that the Uhler report was "totally irresponsible" and a misrepresentation of key facts.

Nonetheless, Reagan took to Uhler's youth and enthusiasm and found his ideological faith congenial to his own. Uhler had been railing against the progressive income tax—one of Reagan's favorite themes—and the governor now appointed him to spearhead an effort to cut the tax permanently in California. "The Founding Fathers never foresaw such a progressive income tax," Uhler said time and again. He wanted to restrict any further increases in the income tax, but he believed it would require an amendment to the state constitution. Reagan welcomed the idea, despite the objections of some of his staff. He had raised taxes in his first term and, for all his talk about welfare abusers and coddling the poor, had failed to cut state spending significantly. If he sought higher office, he felt he would need an unambiguous conservative achievement such as this on which to base a campaign. Reagan had, with the help of a Democratic state legislature, cut property taxes moderately—house prices had risen so rapidly in the 1960s that the poor and the elderly were strapped—but this did not seem enough.

By 1972, Uhler had laid the groundwork for a statewide referendum on a constitutional amendment, which would reduce California income taxes and create a maximum level for future taxes. They called it Proposition 1.

If approved, it could only be changed by a two-thirds vote of the state legislature.

Following Uhler's advice turned out to be the worst miscalculation of Reagan's still evolving political career. The amendment, endorsed and supported by a group of prestigious right-wing economists, including Milton Friedman, who had served as Goldwater's chief economic adviser, and supported by Reagan in frequent speeches across the state, was decisively defeated by voters in 1973. Even as Americans began to distrust government, religious, business, and educational institutions—especially during the Vietnam War—California and most of the nation were not yet ready for Reagan or the conservative revolution. The campaign for Proposition 1 made him look irresponsible in the eyes of some California voters, an image the former actor had thus far ably countered. Reagan, characteristically sticking to his views, attributed defeat to other factors, including union opposition. He never wanted to appear that he was betraying his ideals, though in office he compromised pragmatically to maintain his popularity.

His political future, indisputably bright to that point, was now uncertain, as was the conservative political movement itself. Nixon, who became president in 1969, signed legislation to start the Environmental Protection Agency, the Occupational Safety and Health Agency, and the Consumer Product Safety Commission, froze prices and wages, provided generous funds to the War on Poverty, aggressively expanded Social Security, and spent federal funds prodigiously to stimulate economic growth. Even though he tried to limit civil rights in the South, Nixon was still not the conservative Uhler had hoped for as the next Republican president. But Reagan, like the army of the committed of which Uhler was a tireless member, kept sowing the truly conservative fields.

Uhler never relinquished his vision. He started an organization to support similar constitutional amendments in other states, and he later succeeded beyond his best hopes. More than half of America's state governments eventually adopted such a constitutional limitation. Uhler published a book in 1989 called *Setting Limits: Constitutional Control of Government,* and Milton Friedman, who sat on the board of Uhler's organization until his death in 2006, wrote an admiring Foreword. Uhler dedicated the book to his father: "To my late father James Carvel Uhler, who urged a mid-course correction long before it became clear to others that our Republic had lost its compass."

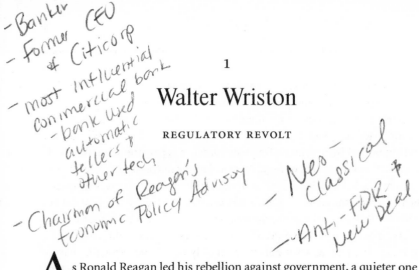

1

Walter Wriston

REGULATORY REVOLT

As Ronald Reagan led his rebellion against government, a quieter one was born in the business community. Its leader was Walter Wriston, a tall, slouched, deeply intelligent and taciturn man with unusual ambition, little regard for tradition, and a highly conservative political ideology that he had inherited from his father. Wriston wanted to transform banking into a business like any other, capable of increasing profits as rapidly as the most admired companies in the nation. The goal would require undoing the federal financial regulations established during the Great Depression.

Walter Wriston was born in 1919 in Middletown, Connecticut, his father, Henry, an eminent history professor at the town's prestigious university, Wesleyan. When Walter was five, his father was named president of Lawrence College in Appleton, Wisconsin, where Walter grew up until he entered Wesleyan in 1937. Despite the Depression, the Wriston family remained comfortable during Walter's adolescence.

Henry Wriston's reputation rose in these years and he was named president of Brown University in 1936, from which perch he was able to preach against FDR and the New Deal, convinced that the programs would lead to a planned economy. His heroes included Adam Smith, who, despite the complexities in thinking of the Scottish philosopher, he saw largely as the father of the invisible hand and laissez-faire economic philosophy. He also deeply admired the British philosopher Herbert Spencer, who a century after Smith had become popular for what was later called social Darwinism. Spencer, who beginning in the 1850s was philosophically opposed to government intervention in markets, was the popular author of the notion that human poverty was natural because the "survival of the fittest" (a phrase Charles Darwin borrowed from him) was a law of nature.

At Wesleyan, Walter Wriston studied history, his father's field. He entered the Fletcher School at Tufts University, one of the nation's most prestigious schools of diplomacy, just outside Boston, to pursue a graduate degree in foreign affairs. Wriston was married to a coed he had met at Connecticut College by the time he graduated in 1942. He was drafted into the Navy in 1944 and sent overseas but did not see combat. He returned to the United States in 1946, one of hundreds of thousands of other soldiers wondering what to do with their lives—and whether the economy would slide back into depression.

Walter Wriston as First National City CEO, 1971

Wriston said he did not want an academic career like his father's. "I knew I wouldn't do that because you'd have nothing but comparisons," he said. "My sister's an academic and a very good one. But I didn't want any part of that." Hostility toward his father surfaced when Henry remarried in 1947, only a year after his mother's death, at which point Walter stopped speaking to him.

Wriston at first had "very little" interest in business. It was his mother's doctor who suggested he go into banking. "If I stayed up all night, I couldn't think of anything more stupid to do," he said, but the bank "hadn't hired anyone new since 1933," and it badly needed recruits. Moreover, it was willing to pay salaries comparable to those in industry. So in 1946 he took a temporary job in New York with National City Bank, at that time a diminished version of its pre-Depression glory, when it had been the largest and most visible bank in the nation. He fully expected to leave in a year and return to his planned career in diplomacy.

When Wriston joined National City, banking was a stodgy and unimaginative business. Regulations had been imposed in the 1930s to prevent the excesses in finance that had buffeted America time and again. Overaggressive banks had been a serious national concern throughout the nineteenth and early twentieth centuries.

To attract savers, deposit-taking banks historically had to make good the promise to pay back a depositor's money at a moment's notice, which in the 1800s usually meant maintaining specie (gold and silver coins) against deposits and investing those deposits cautiously. The essence of banking was dependability. The banks redeemed deposits in specie when requested and some created paper currency they also would redeem in specie.

During good economic times ever more confident banks offered higher interest rates to attract depositors and made riskier loans to farmers and businesses at higher interest rates. They kept less in specie as reserves and paid back less in specie for their paper currencies, and the system of credit expanded rapidly to support speculation in agriculture and livestock, land itself, and countless new businesses. Regularly, speculative bubbles were created, then burst, and financial panic turned into severe recession. Banks went out of business by the hundreds, depositors lost money, and debtors went bankrupt—and, in the early years of the century, often to prison.

In its early years, the United States had had a national bank, the principal legacy of Alexander Hamilton (there had also been an earlier, informal national bank just after the Revolution), to restrain overspeculation, but it also tended to restrict lending to elite businesses and urban financiers. The bank's original charter was renewed under President James Madison in 1816 for another twenty years. But in 1836, President Andrew Jackson's veto ended the reign of the Second Bank of the United States. Jackson flamboyantly sided with the farmers and populists who believed the big Eastern bankers were corrupt and habitually made credit too scarce or expensive for them.

Jackson's anti-bank policies have been widely criticized by business historians, but the farmers were correct about often inadequate credit from the national bank for smaller borrowers. Looser banking standards did contribute to economic growth and the democratization of credit in these years. But a balance between adequate credit and overspeculation could not be reached. Big centralized banks favored elites, and overspeculation at smaller banks almost invariably had painful consequences, contributing to the uneven if occasionally exuberant growth of the nineteenth century.

In the wake of a devastating panic in 1907, the U.S. Federal Reserve was created in 1914 to avoid such unstable conditions. But the bankers who manned the new young central bank had neither the experience nor the will to do the job properly, and lacked some of the necessary authority. Flagrant abuse in the financial community was unchecked in the 1920s and the roaring stock market, supported by highly indebted speculators, burst in 1929. The real estate market, also supported by mammoth levels of debt, collapsed as well. By then, banks were not only making business and consumer loans in excess, but also selling stocks and bonds, running

investment management companies, and creating new and highly speculative investment vehicles for individuals—as well as promoting their own
stock prices.

Such a credit boom and bust alone may not have resulted in the Depression but it contributed substantially to its severity. Thousands of banks
failed in the early 1930s as savers withdrew their funds, fearing that the
banks had no assets with which to pay them—a classic bank run. By 1932,
one fourth of all U.S. banks had failed, and state after state imposed a mor-
atorium on banking. Franklin Roosevelt, on taking office as president in
1933, declared a bank holiday, closing the deposit and withdrawal windows
around the country temporarily. Roosevelt resisted pleas to nationalize the
banks, but he and his advisers established comprehensive new regulations.
Under Roosevelt, the federal government created the Federal Deposit Insurance Corporation (FDIC) to insure savers' deposits in case of bank failure, giving the government further oversight of member banks. The federal
government also restrained overly risky investments with insured deposits
by establishing limits on the interest banks could pay savers to attract their
money (Regulation Q of the new law), and eliminating interest entirely
on checking accounts. The fear was that competition for deposits would
drive rates up and encourage banks to make more risky investments to
earn higher returns.

FDR and members of Congress were determined to end the conflicts of
interest of the financial institutions. If a commercial bank owned equity in
a company, it had incentives to lend money to the company, disregarding
the risk of the loans. There were natural incentives to provide biased information to stockbroker clients about companies in which the banks had
investments or to whom they made loans. The Glass-Steagall Act of 1933,
named after its congressional sponsors, Senator Carter Glass and Congressman Henry Bascom Steagall, legally separated commercial banks,
which collected deposits and lent money, from investment banks and
stockbrokers, who could own parts of companies, raise equity for clients,
and advise investors on what investments to make. (The establishment of
the FDIC and Regulation Q were parts of the legislation as well.)

Wriston's bank, National City, was, before the Depression, the largest
bank in the world, and was an aggressive leader in many of the interde-
pendent businesses that eventually caused so much trouble, including
stockbrokerage. Its high-profile chairman, Charles Mitchell, was forced to
resign in 1933 in the depths of the banking panic, but the bank survived.
Under Glass-Steagall, National City, like other major banks, was required

to divest itself of its brokerage and underwriting arms, and do business only as a commercial bank, accepting deposits and making conservative purchases of government securities or cautious loans to business. The prestigious J.P. Morgan bank, run by the most influential financier of the age, was also separated from its investment banking arm, which took the name Morgan Stanley. The investment banks and brokerage firms were now regulated by the newly created Securities and Exchange Commission, whose first chairman was Joseph P. Kennedy, an aggressive financier himself and the father of a future president. The principal demand of the SEC was disclosure of far more information by investment banks about the firms for which they raised money, and other investor protections. America thus entered the post–World War II era with New Deal programs and state government regulations to control interest rates on consumer loans, which in sum regulated banking and the financial system far more thoroughly than at any time in its history.

The New Deal philosophically infuriated Wriston as much as it had his father. When he joined National City (it changed its name to the First National City Bank of New York in 1955), state law restricted it to operate branches in only the five boroughs of New York City. Regulation Q, with its limits on interest rates on savings and checking accounts, particularly frustrated Wriston. Since access to new funds was restricted, its lending policies were restrained as a result. Wriston felt the company he worked for could never thrive under the weight of such regulation, and might not even survive.

Wriston's effort to undo one regulation after another became a personal crusade, driven less perhaps by the desire for profit than by an almost inchoate anger against government intrusion. The desire to have one's way can rise to the level of greed, too. "There was something emotional about his drive," said Albert Wojnilower, a leading Wall Street economist of the time. "I felt Wriston wanted simply to dismantle the financial system as we knew it."

Wriston's early career was characterized by clever innovation, a useful willingness to discard tradition for its own sake, and considerable intelligence. He made small but rapid advances up the ranks at National City, soon becoming a lending officer. A year into the job, he was assigned Aristotle Onassis as a client. Onassis, in his early forties, was already a wealthy and glamorous Greek shipping entrepreneur, a conspicuous member of the new international jet set, who had been borrowing at National City for years. After World War II, he saw an opportunity to expand his operations. A postwar boom in energy demand, and a surge in oil discovery and production in the Middle East, would mean the world was short of ships to transport adequate petroleum supplies efficiently. Onassis needed substantial financing to acquire more tankers, and eventually the enormous supertankers that came to dominate trade on the seas. When Wriston's superiors passed Onassis on to him, Wriston was only twenty-eight.

In the past, the cautious banks and insurance companies had made collateralized shipping loans based only on the asset value—in other words, the resale value—of the ship itself. But just after World War II, a steep recession made the ships almost worthless, and undermined confidence they would recover their value. Onassis argued that growth of energy demand was inevitable, but bankers, who had money on the line, were not as confident in the future as he claimed to be. In his first encounter with Wriston, Onassis told him he was willing to pledge the income from the charter he was awarded to deliver oil for Texaco as collateral against a loan rather than on the resale price of the ship. Wriston was convinced, believing that such a loan, if unprecedented at National City, was less risky than it seemed. Wriston won quick approval from his open-minded boss, George Moore. Moore, a rare charismatic banker and then head of the lending department, encouraged Wriston's willingness to take risks and some observers credited Moore with the new entrepreneurial spirit at the bank, and with some of the innovations Wriston eventually implemented. While Moore alone would not have been able to accomplish what Wriston did, he gave Wriston the green light time and again, and approved of his aggressive instincts. Wriston would not have done it without Moore, as he readily acknowledged. "The rest as they say was history," said Wriston.

National City soon became the largest bank lender to shippers, often in tandem with Metropolitan Life, the insurance company that made the longer-term tanker construction loans. Since insurance policies had long-term payouts, it made sense for insurance companies to make long-term loans. Banks, in contrast, had to meet withdrawal requirements from depositors on short notice, so they typically tried to make short-term loans, at least if they were managing their funds prudently.

Shipping loans based on income rather than asset value became a model for loans to finance trucks, railroad cars, planes, and office buildings. The other major shipping magnate of the time, Stavros Niarchos, Onassis's brother-in-law, offered Wriston's counterpart at Metropolitan Life, Walter Saunders, a permanent job directing his financing. Saunders moved to Monaco, where both Onassis and Niarchos lived. Onassis then offered Wriston $1 million a year to come with him to Monaco. It was too bold for the modest Wriston, who was then living in Stuyvesant Village in Manhattan, a middle-income housing project, with his wife and daughter. Wriston, well paid by banking standards, would not earn more than $1 million in a single year until 1982, the first commercial banker to do so in the post-Depression era. Wriston remained friends with Onassis and his eventual companion, the celebrated opera singer Maria Callas, and later with the former first lady, Jacqueline Kennedy, who wed Onassis in 1968.

George Moore called Wriston the best employee he ever had. Wriston, in turn, both admired and feared the often abrasive Moore. "One time I brought him a loan," said Wriston. "It was Friday. He read the thing and said to me, 'You're an idiot. An absolute idiot. Idiot. Idiot. Idiot.' He said everything three times. So I went home despondently to my wife and asked where else would you like to live? And she said, 'What did George say to you this time?' So the next day was Saturday and we had a business gathering with clients from around the country. George was holding court in the middle of this group and I walked in not feeling too great. 'I want to introduce you to one of my future senior lending officers,' he said. I said to him, 'That wasn't what you said yesterday.' 'What'd I say, what'd I say?' I said, 'You called me an idiot.' 'Oh, if I didn't think I could teach you something, I wouldn't talk to you.' He would beat up on you one day and it would completely evaporate by the next. He was a teacher and a mentor, and he had vision."

There are two sides to the business of banking. One is using the funds a bank gathers to lend and invest. The other side is to gather the funds from individuals and businesses in order to increase lending and investing, and thus raise a bank's profits. To repeat, the New Deal regulations restricted both, but Wriston's desire to find new funding sources developed into an all-consuming passion. The most revolutionary of the bank's new ideas was a way to pay interest on something very much like a demand deposit, until then strictly forbidden by Regulation Q. "We looked at the data and it turned out that demand deposits in New York City had not grown for ten years," Wriston said. "You didn't have to be a rocket scientist to know we were going to go out of business." The government reported that demand deposits plus currency fell from 29 percent of all financial assets in 1946 to 16 percent in 1960.

Wriston and his colleagues' idea was that the bank would allow corporate and foreign customers to deposit $100,000 in what they called a "negotiable certificate of deposit." This CD would have characteristics of a savings and a checking account. Buyers would earn a higher interest rate on the negotiable CD like a time deposit (a savings account), but buyers could cash out by selling the CD at any time, as with a demand deposit. The CD would be sold into a secondary or after-market, where the price was technically "negotiable," as with any stock or bond. There was always the possibility a $100,000 CD would fetch slightly less when it had to be sold if interest rates rose in the meantime, or more if interest rates fell, but the company could thus tailor the timing of its cash needs with minimal risk. With the secondary market, Wriston was creating a checking account with interest for big investors.

But to create the secondary market requires someone to "make that market"—buy and sell the CDs—and that requires substantial capital. "The problem was that you had to have a market for it to be successful, and there wasn't any market," said Wriston. By then, 1960, Wriston was executive vice president of the bank, and head of the newly expanding international lending operation. "George and I went over to see the Discount Corporation [a government bond dealer]. We said, 'Would you guys make a market in CDs?' They said, 'If you lend us $10 million we'd do that.' We said, 'We don't lend unsecured to broker dealers like you.' They said, 'Well, in that case we can't make a market.' We went back and had a long conversation with the powers that be and we decided to lend them the money. That was pretty wild and it turned out to be a great decision."

Wriston's audacity was not fully appreciated in the press. Financing the secondary market through Discount Corp. was almost as if First National City were making its own markets for the CDs they issued, taking a substantial risk, and violating the spirit and perhaps even the letter of the New Deal regulations that prevented conflicts of interest.

Another banker would have asked the Fed's permission to create the negotiable CD, but not Wriston. "We had a debate on the CD," he said. "Do we go to the Fed? Well if we go to the Fed, they will probably say no as a matter of principle while they study it. So we agreed not to go to the Fed. That was a major decision. We got a legal decision from our lawyers and we went ahead. The Fed was not exactly pleased. But at the same time, the logic of trying to keep the banking system in funds weighed heavily in favor of the CD."

Wriston got away with it. In 1961, the Federal Reserve was concerned that banks have enough funds to prevent an economic slowdown then under way from getting worse. When interest rates rose in an overheating economy—or were raised by the Fed to forestall inflation—depositors put their money elsewhere because banks could not raise their own rates under Regulation Q. This diversion of funds was known as disintermediation, and the result was a credit crunch as bank lending to businesses would dry up.

Wriston realized that the Fed now feared disintermediation and the economy needed him as much as he needed the economy. But not all his competitors were in favor of the negotiable CD. Unlike Wriston, they feared challenging the Federal Reserve and were also concerned with a possible rate war, in which banks would keep raising rates competitively to attract depositors. Why pay for deposits when you get them for free? they wondered. Some economists also wondered aloud whether banks would have to make more risky loans at high rates to pay rising rates to depositors.

The negotiable CD was offered by First National City in early 1961, the Federal Reserve looking the other way. Within a year, outstanding CDs totaled $1 billion, as all major banks joined City in issuing them. So-called money center banks, like J.P. Morgan, which had only large depositors, found them especially valuable. By the mid-1960s, the volume of these CDs surpassed the volume of commercial paper, the short-term loans to large corporations, to cover immediate business needs usually due to fluctuations in sales, issued directly to major investors through investment bankers. Now, with CDs, banks could more effectively compete. There were still restrictions on the rates paid, and the minimum size of a CD was $100,000, but bank credit increased far faster than the economy in these years, lending rising from $30 billion to $200 billion between 1962 and 1965.

By the mid-1960s, new negotiable CDs were not adequate to ward off likely disintermediation and resulting credit crunches. Spending on the Vietnam War was pushing the federal budget into deficit at a time when the economy was growing strongly, new social programs were under way, and U.S. business was booming. The negotiable CDs actually contributed to higher inflation and interest rates, a fact that was not well recognized by either policymakers or economists. Even as rates rose, "banks began to bid for funds aggressively," wrote Salomon Brothers' influential former economist Henry Kaufman, "driving open market rates to the maximum allowable under Regulation Q." In 1966, rates on short-term Treasury bills reached more than 5.5 percent from well under 4 percent a year earlier. Lending did not dry up as usual. "The year 1966 was a dress rehearsal for disaster," according to one history of the period, reflecting the common view at the time. Inflation kept rising, doubling in 1966, to 3.5 percent.

The Federal Reserve, eager to staunch inflation, raised its discount rate sharply to suppress the ongoing business lending. When the banks raised rates to the maximum allowed to be paid even on the negotiable CDs, and market rates went still higher, disintermediation again began and a credit crunch was unavoidable. Large depositors fled the banks, and placed their money in commercial paper or in overseas investments. The volume of CDs shrank rapidly. Corporate lending and mortgage underwriting dried up, and the economy slowed down. A recession seemed likely.

In the tightening circumstances, Wriston, with Moore's encouragement, initiated another practice to find the bank more deposits, one that would soon be adopted industry-wide. When Americans bought products from overseas, or traveled there, the U.S. dollar payments accumulated in overseas banks. These deposits were called Eurodollars, and they were mostly free of American banking regulations—the most important of which was the Fed's requirement to keep reserves against domestically made loans. The deposits reached an enormous volume, as Americans bought more foreign goods. Facing the loss of funds in the United States, Wriston had his London branch issue certificates of deposit in Eurodollars to overseas buyers. Other banks followed Wriston's lead. The banks in turn lent the Eurodollar deposits at attractive interest rates to U.S. international subsidiaries, overseas borrowers, or foreign companies, the loans soon contributing handsomely to profits.

As U.S. bank lending nevertheless slowed, and the economy weakened, the Federal Reserve under William McChesney Martin, Jr., influenced by President Johnson's exhortations, eased monetary policy and pushed rates down in general. Funds flowed back into the banks as rates fell, but Wriston's Eurodollar deposits and loans became a profitable staple for American banks.

In 1967, Stillman Rockefeller, the staid chairman of First National City, frequently annoyed by Moore's energy, aggressiveness, and ebullient personality, appointed Moore chairman but did not name him the chief executive officer of the bank. "Moore never got along with Stillman," said Wriston. Instead, the lower-keyed Wriston, at forty-five, was named president, which gave him more authority than Moore had.

The negotiable CD and the Eurodollar CD were major victories for Wriston, and he wanted more. The strong economy of the late 1960s was making men wealthy on Wall Street and across the nation, stock prices hitting record levels. The Standard & Poor's 500 had soared by five times since the early 1950s. The stock market awarded those companies whose profits grew fastest with the highest price-earnings multiples—the stock price as a multiple of a company's earnings per share. (P-E multiples are the conventional way to measure a stock's value.) The average price-earnings ratios rose from 12 or 13 in the 1950s to 17 or 18 in the bull markets of the late 1960s. By the end of the 1960s, some companies were selling at multiples of 100 and 200 times earnings per share. The high prices led to a new wave of high-flying conglomerates, such as Ling-Temco-Vought, Litton Industries, ITT, and Gulf + Western, whose business objective was acquisition of other companies by exchanging high-priced stock for them. High stock prices were also the path to great wealth for the executives in these companies, who owned shares or options to buy shares. Wriston felt left out.

In 1968, after considerable internal debate, First National City decided to form a one-bank holding company (known formally as First National City Corp.), which could serve as an umbrella to acquire subsidiaries, not all related directly to banking. As a holding company, First National City could also apply for listing on the New York Stock Exchange, with the possibility that First National City might become a Wall Street favorite.

Wriston had one dream above all—for his bank to become a one-stop financial center for consumers, supplying them with not only traditional banking products like savings accounts and mortgages, but also credit cards, mutual funds, insurance, brokerage, and other investment services. Consumers were where the money was, he figured. One of his first acquisition targets as a bank holding company was the large insurance company Chubb Corporation, but the Nixon antitrust authorities, despite their sympathies toward business, believed the potential conflicts of interest violated the antitrust laws, and First National City abandoned the idea. Wriston's other attempts to make First National City a one-stop financial institution were also largely foiled by government regulators: he had to give up plans to sell mutual funds, and his decision to join the Master Card (then called Master Charge) group to sell credit cards also faced difficult legal obstacles.

But First National City was thriving. Wriston had expanded its lending operations boldly to include international clients. He was hiring MBAs from the best schools to run lending programs, encouraging them to develop new ideas for growth, and paying them well, if not Wall Street salaries. His foray into negotiable CDs turned out to be a gusher. "The negotiable CD was number one for us," said Wriston, "but commercial paper was number two." Banks and other corporations were also typically the buyers of these loans. Because they were issued only by major corporations, they were generally thought riskless in the 1960s. That would change.

In 1969 and 1970, another credit crunch descended on the financial community as the economy again overheated sending interest rates up. The amount of commercial paper outstanding more than doubled between 1968 and 1970 to some $38 billion. The Federal Reserve, still under William McChesney Martin, pushed rates up in 1969 to fight rising inflation, and soon the nation was sinking into recession. Stock prices had fallen sharply since early 1969. In 1970, the Federal Reserve, now under a new chairman, the economist Arthur Burns, and President Nixon's close friend and adviser, was being tested by the strained conditions. Then, in June 1970, the Penn Central, a major borrower in the commercial paper market, filed for bankruptcy because of the higher interest rates. The expansion of the highways and air travel had long been undermining the health of the nation's once essential railroads. The Grand Central Railroad and the Pennsylvania Railroad, the two lines that terminated in Manhattan, had merged in 1967 to reduce costs, but significant savings were hard to find. To meet its needs, Penn Central borrowed relentlessly from banks like First National City at low rates. The railroad had been given a high rating by Dun & Bradstreet, a leading ratings agency at the time. Characteristically, the aggressive First National City loan officer, more poorly informed than Wriston realized about Penn Central's fiscal affairs, and trusting the ratings agencies too well, had lent more to the railroad than anyone else. Wriston was about to take his biggest loss ever. Overall, Penn Central defaulted on $80 million of commercial paper. Wriston blamed Penn Central management, not his own loan officers, for disguising its problems, and demanded that the railroad's CEO resign.

The Penn Central announcement so roiled investors that they stopped buying the commercial issues, creating an unprecedented crisis. Businesses often simply rolled over commercial paper—they paid off one set of loans with another. Now they might not be able to pay back their creditors. Wriston, the free market evangelist, implored the Nixon administration to make an emergency loan to save Penn Central before it went bankrupt, but help was refused. Wriston then got on the phone to beg Federal Reserve officials—it is not clear whether he spoke directly to the chairman—to urge them to keep their discount window open over the weekend, an unusual practice, enabling banks to borrow reserves to finance their business clients (banks can borrow reserves from the Fed at the discount window, paying an interest rate, known as the discount rate). Without access to commercial paper, clients needed a lot of money quickly, Wriston made clear. Many companies were in jeopardy of not paying their bills, meeting their payrolls, or paying back their loans. If workers weren't paid, they would stop buying goods, which could throw the economy into a more severe recession. If bank loans were not paid, some might not survive. Burns, sensitive to the dangers, kept the discount window open that weekend, and continued to supply substantial reserves to banks the next week. Under pressure, Burns also eliminated the Regulation Q restriction on the low rate banks could pay on CDs of less than three months' duration. It was the first crack in Regulation Q. The government had saved the day. Money partially flowed back into the banks as they paid rates in line with other rates in the market.

The crisis passed without spreading to other borrowers, but another milestone was reached, as Wriston made a further serious dent in Regulation Q. Wriston was bailed out by the government on his reckless loans to Penn Central, and also won the ability to raise money on CDs with the change in Regulation Q. "It was the beginning of the end," said one banker, meaning the demise of Regulation Q.

The financial economists Henry Kaufman and Albert Wojnilower argued that the essential nature of finance had now changed as long-standing capital controls on lending were dismantled by Burns or circumvented through the negotiable CDs and Eurodollar deposits. The rationing of credit would be determined by rising and falling interest rates, not explicit financial controls. Unlike free market advocates like Wriston, both Kaufman and Wojnilower were skeptical that the level of interest rates alone could regulate and stabilize the system. Businesses in robust times were eager to borrow even as rates rose, and especially if inflation was raising the prices at which they could sell their goods and services. But the quality of the loans—their creditworthiness—would decline. Wriston, more reliant on the economic philosophy espoused by Milton Friedman, thought Kaufman and Wojnilower were dead wrong, and said so.

Kaufman and Wojnilower, who followed the credit markets closely at their respective institutions, Salomon Brothers and First Boston, believed interest rates would rise higher without slowing borrowing due to the weaker financial controls. The two economists gained legendary reputations by anticipating the rise in rates while traditional economists kept forecasting that these high and rising rates would slow economic growth and soon fall themselves. "Spread banking" had begun by 1970, said Kaufman, and both he and Wojnilower believed it would create inflationary conditions. Most economists, including academic economists, neglected this. Spread banking meant the price of credit was effectively indexed to inflation and credit would largely be available no matter how high interest rates and inflation went. Thus, demand for goods and services would not be slowed.

Eventually, Wriston published a book called *Risk and Other Four-Letter Words,* criticizing those who would limit the initiative of bankers. Wriston also started an economics department in his bank based on Friedman's economics, which produced a newsletter and gave advice to traders and investors. Looking back to 1961, Kaufman wrote, Wriston's negotiable CD was the "key development" that started it all. "These new money market instruments fundamentally altered the structure of financial markets, for they allowed the banks to bid for [funds] in the open market for the first time. Whereas before a bank depended on the wealth of its local community, now it could buy deposits [anywhere in the world] in order to increase its loans and investments, and thereby enlarge its role as a financial intermediary." There were still some regulations on interest rates, however, and Wriston was determined to eliminate them.

In 1970, Moore retired and Wriston was named chairman, more an honor than a new job, since he was already CEO. Once the Penn Central debacle was digested, with the help of the Fed, First National City was triumphant in the early 1970s. In deposits, it was larger than its old rival Chase Manhattan. Its stock was now trading as if it were an industrial or services growth company, earning a high price-earnings ratio due to the rapid growth of earnings—if not high enough for Wriston. And Wriston was the best paid banker in the country. He lived in the glamorous United Nations Plaza, home of Johnny Carson and Alan Greenspan, the future Federal Reserve chairman, who was something of a man about town and a prosperous Republican consultant. Wriston had married a lawyer twenty years his junior two years after his wife died in 1965, and was famously driving a red sports car—famous because it seemed out of character for the man.

In 1971, Wriston announced to Wall Street analysts that the bank's objective would be to increase earnings by 15 percent a year on average. This was unheard of for a bank, and many inside First National City thought it an impossible goal. By then Wriston believed in the impossible, however, and he knew it was exactly what Wall Street wanted to hear. Rapid consistent earnings growth could turn First National City into a full-fledged growth company, like Xerox, Johnson & Johnson, and IBM. He wanted nothing more. And a high stock price would enable him to acquire other companies for fewer shares in an exchange of stock.

But Arthur Burns worried that such goals would encourage Wriston's bank to take unwarranted risks, and he said so publicly and told Wriston himself. Burns knew that Wriston always had the government to bail him out, unlike nonfinancial companies, and Wriston surely knew it, too, though he preached otherwise.

Wriston was unfazed by the Fed chairman's chastisement. He increasingly cited free market economic theories to justify his aggressive ways. Increasingly, there were no bounds on how much banks could raise and lend, and Wriston's ambitions encompassed new territory. By 1980, Wojnilower concluded, the old economic rules no longer applied. Only a credit crunch truly slowed economic growth and dampened inflation, he wrote in an academic paper, and these were being eliminated as bank regulations were loosened and more sources of funds were being found. High inflation was partly the result of deregulation and the new spread banking, he said. This conclusion was much different than the one drawn by economists like Friedman, who blamed inflation entirely on a rapidly growing money supply. In more vernacular terms, Wojnilower said, "I thought the old regulations protected the market from runaway speculation. But the reduction in the regulations ultimately fed inflation. People did not realize the height interest rates now needed to go to slow the economy and inflation."

Wriston's ambitions, stock market gold in his sights, encouraged him to make expensive and risky bets on borrowers. First National City became a favorite of Wall Street and the press, and Wriston became the most admired banker in the world. He was providing needed funds, the lifeblood of business, to deserving companies, and eventually funds to undeserving companies—and nations—as well. Up to 1970 or so, his aggressiveness was partly justifiable. He provided a service to a growing economy. But then the light in his eye turned to a blaze.

The expansion of debt, facilitated by the commercial banks and then the entire Wall Street community, became the fulcrum on which the economy was levered for the next forty years. Nothing turned out to be as important to economic growth, including the new computer technologies, as the expanding capacity to lend and borrow. Personal and business debt rose more than two and a half times as fast as total income over the course of this history. Debt payments as a percentage of the nation's income grew accordingly. Wriston multiplied the risks of financial collapse of the entire financial system as he pursued his ambition to build his bank. Banking was simply not like any other business.

Financial institutions, including banks, brokers, and insurance companies, ultimately gained power not known to them since the 1920s, and set the stage for further expansion. The financial industry, which borrowed and lent money, and invested it as well, accounted for one in two and a half to three dollars of business profits in the 2000s compared to one in eight in earlier years.

Finance had rarely been the source of greatest personal wealth in American history until this new era. Traditionally it was handmaiden to the great industrial, transportation, chemical, communications, and retailing fortunes. Now this changed. By the 1990s and 2000s, financial companies provided the fastest path to fabulous wealth for individuals, directly producing 20 percent of America's nearly five hundred billionaires and having a central part in the wealth creation of most of the others. Moreover, corporate executives, once adversaries as customers of banks, were increasingly now aligned with Wall Street as their pay was dominated by the company stock, and their focus therefore turned mostly to short-term profits.

Wriston relished his role in diminishing the federal government's traditional role as overseer and regulator of finance, knocking down barriers through audacity and attracting competitors to join him in his freewheeling ways, and thus turning his bank into the biggest in the world. He was at the center of every financial storm in the nation during his tenure. Over these years there were many. For decades, First National City under Wriston walked an edge of illiquidity and even at times insolvency, making enormous profits and occasionally fantastic losses. But the health of the giant banks became so critical to the nation's financial system that Wriston learned to use it as political leverage, while, given his intense laissez-faire philosophy, denying his dependence on government all the time. This advantage he played like a maestro. While preaching the values of competition and unfettered markets, he created a bank that was too big for government to allow it to fail, and Citibank, its successor, needed rescuing several more times, most urgently in 1982 when its loans to developing nations went bad. Aggressive business gave way to vanity and greed.

Milton Friedman

PROSELYTIZER

After he had gained worldwide fame and influence, the economist Milton Friedman wrote in a 1982 preface to an earlier book, "Only a crisis—actual or perceived—produces real change. When the crisis occurs the action taken depends on the ideas that are lying around."

Friedman did not think he had the power to provoke crisis deliberately, but crisis is what brought Friedman's ideas to the foreground and made them popular. High unemployment of 9 percent and consumer inflation, which reached 12 percent in 1974 and rose even faster at the end of the decade, seemed to discredit prevailing economic theories and created demand for new explanations and policies.

Friedman had warned persistently about both inflation and government spending throughout his academic career, which began in the 1940s. Attempts to stimulate economic growth usually failed, he argued, often resulting in inflation—a conventional conservative argument based on the classical economics that prevailed before the Great Depression. Friedman revived the precepts of that economic theory, and turned them into an easily understandable theory known as monetarism. Inflation could only be created by the Federal Reserve's allowing the money supply to grow too rapidly, he said, and it could only be controlled by reducing money's rate of growth, but no government interventions could increase the long-term rate of growth of the nation's annual income itself—its Gross Domestic Product, including wages and profits. Crisis served him well. When inflation did rear its head in the 1970s as federal budget deficits increased, Friedman's views seemed correct and he got credit for his foresight. His relatively simple solution was also easy to communicate—stop money from growing—and he denied that tightening the grip on money would mean a serious and prolonged recession—that is, reduced investment, lost

Milton Friedman, second from left, and Arthur Burns, his former professor, flanking President Richard Nixon

jobs, and widespread bankruptcy. Receiving the Nobel Prize in economics in 1976, awarded in the midst of rising inflation, gained him international credibility.

His broader philosophical view was that government social programs and regulations, inflationary spending aside, were almost always damaging interference with the efficient workings of an economy. They undermined opportunity, social justice, and above all personal freedom, he felt. His economic views were indistinguishable from traditional libertarian political philosophies whose overriding concern was personal liberty. He sought to eliminate one social policy after another, including Social Security, unemployment insurance, the minimum wage, and a wide range of regulations governing labor organizing, pharmaceuticals, consumer safety, and job safety. Friedman, in effect, provided the intellectual map for a reversal of the progressive evolution of the nation.

He insisted he was not ideological, and adamantly claimed he based his theories on facts. In this, he exaggerated greatly. His public policy essays and speeches were well written and often ingenious but overly simple assertions of free market claims based on a straightforward interpretation of Adam Smith, disregarding Smith's many caveats and philosophical and psychological writings. Friedman's social policies as opposed to his work on monetary policy were rarely substantiated by empirical research or even historical examples. His academic research, sometimes usefully provocative, was controversial and usually not adequate to justify his many claims.

Throughout his career, one of his major goals was to undermine the rising reputation of John Maynard Keynes, who since 1936 had strongly advocated government spending as a way to support rapid growth, rising wages,
and low unemployment. Keynes elaborately argued that increases in public
spending could ease recession and increase the long-term rate of growth.
Friedman's constant critiques of Keynes became a personal calling, as he
devoted much of his more vigorous research to attempts at disproving the
Keynesian models.

Friedman's ingenuity, persistence, and articulateness were the sources
of his attractiveness. In the 1970s, there was no other intellectual force
comparable to him on America's right. This son of working-class Jewish
immigrants became an extreme political conservative at a time when those
brought up like him were mostly liberals. His main competitor for conservative attention, Ayn Rand, a Russian-Jewish immigrant, was more romantic than analytical—her reputation depended on her novels far more than
her philosophical essays. Friedman's popularity also eased the path toward
acceptability for complex analyses made by some of his controversial rightist economist colleagues, such as James Buchanan and Ronald Coase, who
also advocated minimal government regulation and oversight.

Friedman remained the avatar of the conservative cause, however. He
embarked on an intellectual adventure, doing seemingly fearless battle in
academia and the halls of political power with the best minds of his time.
Without him, the nation's newly harsh attitudes toward government would
not have become nearly as respectable or as popular.

Milton Friedman's parents were born in the Hungarian part of Austro-
Hungary and emigrated as teenagers to Brooklyn in the mid-1890s. They
met there, married, and had three girls before a son arrived in the summer of 1912, a little more than six months after Ronald Reagan was born
and a year before Richard Nixon. When Friedman was one year old, his
parents bought a building on Main Street in Rahway, New Jersey, near the
railroad tracks, where they would live and run a clothing factory and dry
goods store. Before that, his mother worked as a seamstress in a garment
factory—a sweatshop, as he later called it, about which, he proudly wrote,
she never complained. Friedman was unclear about the success of his parents' early business ventures. "Money was always a concern," said Friedman. Yet the family was able to buy a Model T by 1918 when few others as
yet could.

Friedman recalled being "fanatically religious" as a boy, abiding faith-fully, for example, by the dietary requirements of Orthodox Judaism. He once ran away from his Boy Scout camp because the boys were cooking hot dogs containing pork, which was forbidden to him. But as a teenager, Friedman turned against Judaism with as much determination as he had once embraced it, pronouncing himself an agnostic. He was attracted to rule-based systems, and even as a youth demanded intellectual consistency in himself. His resoluteness and commitment to purity of thought were hints of his future absolutist nature.

His religious agnosticism was tested when his father died. Friedman, then fifteen and the only son, was required by Jewish law to attend a syna-gogue and say Kaddish, a prayer of mourning, every Saturday for a year. He hesitated to do it, but at last relented, traveling by bus for well over an hour to a synagogue every Saturday morning. He was a dutiful son, but remembered it as a violation of principle.

His father died in the midst of the Roaring Twenties, before the progres-sive politics of the Depression. If his father had any political influence on him, he did not recall it, and his mother, he said, was more consumed with raising her family than with politics.

Friedman went to public schools in Rahway and was an excellent stu-dent. He won a scholarship to Rutgers, a dozen miles away in New Bruns-wick, New Jersey, and participated in school activities. Despite his bookish ways, he was naturally affable, served on the school newspaper, and started several business ventures, including a tutoring service for struggling high school students. Anyone who met the adult Friedman was immediately struck by his articulateness and the force of his unhesitant voice, in dis-tinct contrast to his diminutive stature; he stood about five feet tall. If his size bothered him, it hardly made him hold back, and probably propelled him. In later years, he wore his fame casually, but to those who had known him as a younger man, his ambition was everywhere evident.

His original college major was math, and he planned to become an actuary, but he met two persuasive economists in college who turned him toward his future interest. The first was Arthur Burns, the traditionally conservative economist, who would later head the National Bureau of Economic Research, teach at Columbia University, and eventually serve as President Eisenhower's chairman of the Council of Economic Advisers, the three-person council created in 1946 to provide economic information and guidance to the president, before serving as Nixon's Fed chairman.

Burns was never as conservatively doctrinaire as Friedman became, allowing greater room in his economic philosophy for government policy and regulation. Friedman, despite serious open disagreements with Burns about monetary policy in the early 1970s, remained devoted to him. "Save for my parents and my wife, no one has influenced my life more than Arthur—as my teacher, mentor, colleague, and friend," Friedman said in his eulogy for Burns on his death in 1987.

When Burns was doing his doctoral work at Rutgers, he asked Friedman and a fellow student to go over his dissertation line by line for accuracy. Burns's statistically oriented dissertation was called "Production Trends in the United States." "That seminar," said Friedman in the eulogy, "imparted standards of scholarship—attention to detail, concern with scrupulous accuracy, checking of sources, and, above all, openness to criticism—that affected the whole of my subsequent work." Burns also introduced him to the main work of the British economist Alfred Marshall, author of *Principles of Economics,* published in 1890, and a teacher of Keynes at Cambridge University in England. With Friedman's bent toward mathematics, he readily took to Marshall, who, among other pioneering contributions, helped develop more clearly the idea that the price of goods and services will change until the supply and demand for goods are equalized at a point economists call "equilibrium." A higher price will encourage more to be supplied and less to be demanded, and conversely, a lower price less to be supplied and more to be demanded. The maximum number of producers and consumers are satisfied at equilibrium.

Marshall's innovative supply and demand curves are a foundation of every economics textbook, and lend themselves to the sort of clarity of analysis that appealed to Friedman. He was especially attracted to the seeming stability of markets in Marshall's analysis—equilibrium could be achieved and it was ideal. The Cambridge University don believed his version was an abstracted model, and not itself a complete representation of the real world. Friedman thought Marshall's model, if not the real world, a close enough approximation to be taken more literally. Prices to Friedman were wondrous carriers of information that set the supply and demand for goods, services, jobs, and capital as efficiently as possible as long as they were left unfettered by government regulation or control. For Friedman, then, prices (including interest rates and wages, if set freely) were the key to competition and functioning markets. In this, he was a successor to an earlier school of Austrian economists led by Ludwig von Mises and a younger disciple of that school, Friedrich von Hayek.

Friedman eventually virtually ignored the power of business to raise prices in a market with limited competition or set a wage unrelated to the demands of workers. He also largely ignored the effects of speculation in financial markets, which may drive the value of stocks, or the willingness to borrow to unjustified and damaging extremes, claiming such distortions were in fact rare. He took little account of how consumers could be deceived in markets for complex products, from used cars to health care. What did bother him was when labor organized to negotiate for higher wages, which he believed was a distorting and unfair market intrusion. Burns remained more sensitive to institutional power and irrational market decisions.

The other persuasive conservative teacher Friedman met was Homer Jones. Jones had been a student of a brilliantly original, conservative economist, Frank Knight, of the University of Iowa, who later taught at the University of Chicago. Knight, a Midwesterner, was, as Friedman said, committed to the American ideal of self-reliance. The free market, unencumbered by government intervention, was consistent with this vision. "Like his mentor, Frank Knight, [Jones] put major stress," wrote Friedman, "on individual freedom, was cynical and skeptical about attempts to interfere with the exercise of individual freedom in the name of social planning or collective values, yet he was by no means a nihilist." Jones was the reason Friedman ultimately went to the University of Chicago for his graduate studies, turning down a scholarship offer in math from Brown.

The economy was in the steepest slide of the Great Depression when Friedman entered graduate school in 1932. The university faculty proudly represented a variety of intellectual views, but the prevailing philosophy of the economics department, led by Knight, and the other illustrious Chicago economics professors of that era, including Jacob Viner, Henry Simons, and Lloyd Mints, was unreservedly liberal in the nineteenth-century meaning of the word (that is, conservative in the modern American sense). It emphasized, as Simons put it, a traditional liberal political philosophy, "of dispersion of economic power and of political decentralization." This approach in a time when progressive ideas were ascending, wrote Simons, was "almost unrepresented among great universities, save for Chicago."

According to Friedman, the Chicago economists also believed that the Depression was the consequence of mistaken government policies, not the financial speculation of the 1920s or any other inherent weakness of free markets. "My teachers regarded the depression as largely the product of misguided policy," Friedman wrote. "They blamed the monetary and fiscal authorities for permitting banks to fail and the quantity of deposits to decline."

But what became known as the Chicago School was originally not, contrary to conventional wisdom, as pure a free market institution as it became when Friedman was its leading member in the 1950s. "Simons for example did not equate the ideal market with the actual market in this country," wrote one economist. The older guard also believed that short-term government spending could be necessary in some circumstances to support a falling economy and that monetary policy itself was inadequate at times—ideas that were anathema to Friedman. "Once a deflation has gotten under way, in a large modern economy," wrote Simons, "there is no significant limit which the decline in prices and employment cannot exceed, if the central government fails to use its fiscal powers generously and deliberately to stop the decline." Knight, the most prestigious member of the faculty, was in particular not involved with the evolution of the Chicago School in the early 1950s. A different sort of economics then evolved, contrary to the conventional views of Friedman himself and his acolytes. It was more purely devoted to laissez-faire, more reflexively antagonistic to government, and generally justified big business and monopoly far more enthusiastically than did the early Chicago economists.

Friedman completed his graduate studies at Columbia, where he polished his skills in statistics. Then in 1935, he took a research job with the Roosevelt government. Friedman later said he was not opposed to government social programs at that time. He was, in fact, a mild proponent of the New Deal. His future brother-in-law, Aaron Director, later an influential professor at the University of Chicago law school and eventual head of the economics research program, teased his younger sister and Milton's future wife, Rose, that Milton was too much of a New Dealer for him.

Friedman met Rose in a class they were taking at Chicago. Her brother, Aaron, a dozen years older, encouraged her to attend school at Chicago and she adopted Aaron's newfound conservative views. She and Milton began dating in 1932 and were married in 1938. After a difficult year as a young associate at the University of Wisconsin embroiled in faculty politics, Friedman returned to Washington to work for the Treasury in the early years of World War II. He helped develop the nation's tax withholding system, which made possible the rapid growth of government that he ultimately deplored. There is no greater irony in American economic history. He later said his experience in government reinforced his doubts about its efficiency.

Friedman received his Ph.D. from Columbia in 1945. His doctoral thesis already contained conservative claims. Written with the future Nobelist Simon Kuznets, it was titled "Income from Independent Professional Practice," and argued that state limitations on the number of entrants, even if the desire is to maintain a high standard, into professions like medicine, dentistry, and law raised fees artificially and reduced the accessibility of the professional services. With his degree at last in hand, Friedman sought a teaching position at a good university. Aside from the aborted Wisconsin offer a few years earlier, few invitations came his way until he was at last offered a position at the University of Minnesota.

There, he joined his fellow Chicago graduate George Stigler, already a professor, and together in 1946 they co-authored a stinging, ideological article criticizing rent control. The central thesis was that rent control restricted the supply of new housing and artificially kept the price (the rent) down. The article, like his graduate thesis, focused on the dangers that arise when government sets prices. The piece was based on skimpy data regarding rents in a single month in San Francisco after the 1906 earthquake (forty years earlier). Moreover, it was published by an advocacy organization called the Foundation for Economic Education, which was dedicated to "the explanation of the meaning of free private competitive enterprise. It seeks to demonstrate the difference between voluntary enterprise and coercion; between individualism and collectivism; between limited and unlimited government." One conservative staffer referred to the foundation as the "granddaddy of all libertarian organizations." The publication was a clear announcement of Friedman's conservative philosophy, which seemed to be formed sometime in the 1940s, perhaps not long after he married his libertarian wife.

In addition to his new views, Friedman already had a reputation as a highly competent economics statistician. When Stigler turned down an offer from the University of Chicago in 1947, Friedman, known to the faculty, connected by marriage to Director, and a credentialed conservative, was offered the job, which he accepted. The University of Chicago would become his intellectual home.

Rose's brother, Aaron, himself had converted from early left-wing views to Chicago-style conservatism. He had emigrated in his early teens from Eastern Europe with his family and entered Yale, where he was a politically active left-wing undergraduate and co-edited the school newspaper with the future Abstract Expressionist Mark Rothko (then Marcus Rothkowitz). After stints as a migrant farmworker and a textile factory employee, among other jobs, he went on to study for his doctorate in economics at Chicago in the 1920s. There, partly under the influence of Henry Simons and the especially persuasive Jacob Viner, he changed his political views.

The newly conservative Director took jobs teaching at various economics departments, including Chicago, and also worked for the government during World War II. Aaron found his way to London where Simons had made an introduction for him to his good friend Friedrich von Hayek, the Austrian economist, who was teaching at the London School of Economics. Director, like many others, became a devotee.

When Director returned to Chicago, he convinced the University of Chicago Press to publish the American edition of Hayek's new British best seller, *The Road to Serfdom,* for which Director wrote a favorable review for a journal. Hayek, a serious academic, turned *The Road to Serfdom* into a fear-inspiring polemic. Its central message was that a growing welfare state in Europe would inevitably lead to totalitarianism, the rise of Nazi Germany fresh in the public's mind. The welfare state would also weaken the nation's economy by undermining markets, which were the only means by which to send signals to producers about the quantities and quality of goods and services. This was accomplished through the "discovery" of the efficient price for goods and services, or in the case of credit, for the interest rate. As noted, this sanctity of freely set prices was a key part of Friedman's thinking.

Hayek wanted to establish an international cadre of influential intellectuals with like-minded ideas. He succeeded in finding the financing and attracted a formidable group of thinkers, including the Chicago economists Knight, Simons, Director, and the Friedmans, as well as the philosopher Karl Popper and the chemist and philosopher Michael Polanyi. They named the group after the small Swiss town in which they convened, Mont Pelerin, near Vevey, Switzerland.

The formation of the Mont Pelerin Society was financed by Europeans and a highly conservative tax-exempt American foundation, the William Volker Charitable Fund of Kansas City, founded by prosperous right-wing local businessmen. The fund also helped finance the Foundation for Economic Education, which published the Friedman-Sigler paper on rent control. After the remarkable success of *The Road to Serfdom,* the Volker Fund attempted to bring Hayek from London to an American university. The fund's president, Harold Luhnow, was determined to underwrite an Americanized version of the Hayek book—though there was already a condensed version of it published by *Reader's Digest.* But finding a suitable university position for Hayek turned out to be difficult, and he was not interested in rewriting his book for an American audience.

Hayek convinced Luhnow and the Volker Fund to support an economics program study at Chicago, to be headed by Director. The Volker Fund, with Hayek as its guiding hand, had a strong influence over the new direction to be followed by the Chicago economics department as well as the law school where Director taught. Hayek wrote the proposal for the new program, to be called the Free Market Study: "The free market [is] the most efficient organizer of economic activity—[the study will] emphasize and explain that the free market is systemic, rational, not chaotic or disorderly—, show how the free market performs some of the more difficult functions, such as allocating resources to their best use and distributing consumption through time."

Simons, Hayek's long-standing friend, was the original choice to lead the new program. But his less than extremist conservative views did not truly suit the Volker Fund executives. He had written in 1948, for example, "The great enemy of democracy is monopoly, in all its forms: gigantic corporations, trade associations and other agencies for price control, trade-unions—or, in general, organization and concentration of power within functional classes. . . . A monopolist is an implicit thief . . . because his possession of market power leads to the exchange of commodities at prices that do not reflect underlying social scarcities." This was a conventional argument in classical economics, which held that monopoly market power wielded by business as well as other institutions could distort prices (or wages or interest rates) by keeping them artificially high for more profit or keeping them low to drive off potential competitors. But the men who ran the Volker Charitable Fund were put off by any views critical of big business and it is possible that Hayek was dubious himself of Simons, having written that public regulation was more dangerous than private monopoly. Simons, for example, was also opposed to "squandering" money on advertising and marketing.

Simons died suddenly, possibly a suicide. Had he become the program's director, the Chicago School of economics would have had a significantly different outlook—conservative but less doctrinaire and absolutist. Aaron Director, on the law school faculty, was appointed to run the study. Director was an acolyte of Simons and devastated by his death, but where Director often agreed with Simons in the past, he was now reorienting his views. The most marked shift regarded monopoly, which like Simons he once thought destructive. A few years later, he clearly no longer believed that it was the problem Simons and others once thought it to be. In 1950, he wrote that competition would often naturally undermine monopoly. By 1951, Milton Friedman had also shifted his views of the dangers of powerful monopolies, claiming that monopoly was not even widely present in the U.S. economy. The power to set prices and wages of monopoly corporations, he wrote, was "considerably exaggerated." Director and Friedman argued that a monopolist in one market still had to respond to the competition from a company in a seemingly different market. Airlines compete with trains, for example, or in a more contemporary example, the Web competes with newspapers. With such a rationale, an economic theory could be devised that was far more tolerant of power waged by a single or a small group of large companies over a particular market. This claim was easily taken to extremes. In *Capitalism and Freedom,* written as noted in the 1950s but not published until 1962, Friedman said that in most cases he preferred private monopoly to government regulation, much as Hayek had suggested a few years earlier. It was also a view highly congenial to the executives of the Volker Fund.

As a member of the law school faculty, Director helped found the Chicago School of thought on antitrust law, which claimed the American application of antitrust laws to break up large companies was often misguided and restrained economic growth, and these ideas became the foundation of Ronald Reagan's weakened antitrust enforcement in the 1980s. Director's students at the Chicago law school included future outspoken federal judges Robert Bork and Richard Posner, whose conservative views later had wide influence.

Hayek was ultimately given a position on the university's Committee for Social Thought, not in its economics department. It is possible that the economics faculty, fully understanding how influential he was in redirecting their theoretical work, did not want to acknowledge him.

But the more extremist and overtly political turn the Chicago economics department had taken under Director and Friedman's influence disturbed the old guard, whom Friedman nevertheless ever after cited as his admired mentors. Frank Knight, the most highly regarded of the original group, was significantly more skeptical of laissez-faire economics than Hayek or Friedman and was concerned that some of Friedman's public policy proposals were doctrinaire and oversimplified. In private conversation, he told a friend that Friedman's criticism of government-run public schools was "foolish." Knight was also more sympathetic to the progressive writings of John Kenneth Galbraith than his younger associates. "Colleagues spoof at [Galbraith], but I find some truth in what he says, perhaps as much as in their position," he wrote to the British economist Lionel Robbins, referring in particular to Friedman. As economic historians Rob Van Horn and Philip Mirowski make clear, claims that the "neo-liberalism" of Friedman was a pure outgrowth of the highly respected Chicago pioneers like Knight and Simons were misleading.

Once securely at the University of Chicago, Friedman became a prolific researcher and writer, much of his work based on a Marshallian framework. Economists refer to this as partial equilibrium analysis—partial because it is focused on one market at a time, for autos or stockbrokers, for example, and not on how each of these markets interacts in the entire economy.

As noted, Friedman applied much of his energy toward pushing Keynes off the influential pedestal on which he had been recently placed by young American economists. Keynes had been a student of Marshall's when he was an undergraduate at Cambridge, and until the Depression largely a classical economist himself. But this economic theory, Keynes felt, could not make sense of the worldwide catastrophe of the 1930s Depression. In the United States, the nation's income fell by 25 percent, industrial production by half, and unemployment rose to 25 percent by 1933. Partial recovery in the mid-1930s was followed by a new recession. Keynes was at this point an exalted figure in British life, having first become internationally known when in 1919, as a junior British Treasury official, he published an angry, eloquent polemic, *The Economic Consequences of the Peace,* against the American, British, and French demands for reparations from Germany that were part of the Treaty of Versailles ending World War I. He wrote highly regarded economic treatises on money and related subjects in later years, mostly oriented along the lines of classical theory, and many influential political essays and journalistic pieces.

During the Depression, however, Keynes believed, as he once put it, that ideas had to change. In 1936, after struggling for years with his new concepts, Keynes published a complex theoretical book, *The General Theory of Employment, Interest, and Money,* which altered thinking about economic growth and employment more than any other work in the century.

Classical theory held that economies were self-adjusting. An overheated economy may lead to recession but when interest rates, prices for equipment and inventory, and wages fall far enough, business will start investing and hiring again. Through such adjustment, the ideal quantity of goods and services is produced, incomes generally rise as much as possible, and the maximum number of jobs is created—that is, unemployment falls to its lowest possible level.

But Keynes argued that economies could stabilize at much less than ideal levels of capital investment, incomes, and employment, and that this was precisely what had happened in the Depression. The central idea was a radical innovation in thought, and Keynes went a long way toward demonstrating it. Even if interest rates and prices fall, business may not invest, not for lack of access to bank loans, but because of lack of demand for their goods and services as consumers hold on to their money. In other words, businesses may not borrow because they have nothing to invest in profitably. Therefore, a nation's central bank could try to reduce interest rates and increase the supply of money, but these actions would often have little or no impact during deep recessions. Business would not invest without customers' buying their products. And, most revolutionary, the economy could stabilize indefinitely at this reduced level of activity—a direct refutation of the classical self-adjustment process. In economic terms, equilibrium could be reached at far less than ideal levels of employment and capital investment.

Roosevelt and President Herbert Hoover before him sought to balance the federal budget because, as classical economists argued, budget deficits reduced the savings available to be invested. Keynes argued this was exactly the wrong approach because, by cutting the deficit, the nation also reduced demand for goods and services, and could undermine capital investment, deepening any recession.

The solution, by contrast, was to increase government spending—"fiscal stimulus"—to create demand for goods and services and therefore the desire to invest by business. In other words, even as deficits may rise in recession, it made sense temporarily to create a bigger deficit. Keynes stood conventional economics on its head with these views and also became the most compelling target for the Chicago free market school. (Even the least ideological old-guard Chicago professors argued that any fiscal stimulus should be at most a stopgap, removed as soon as possible.)

Many American economists, who up to the Great Depression and even World War II were mostly avowed classical theorists, now quickly converted to Keynesianism. The converts included Alvin Hansen, an influential Harvard professor, who had earlier argued that the nation's technological advances were simply petering out, and also young newcomers to the profession like Paul Samuelson and John Kenneth Galbraith.

To Friedman, any views that promoted government spending as a way to stabilize economies and promote prosperity were not merely wrongheaded but seen as pandering to the majority by promising more social programs. Moreover, government itself had its own greedy expansionist motives, he believed. "Ever since the New Deal," as Friedman put it, "a primary excuse for the expansion of government activity at the federal level has been the supposed necessity for government spending to eliminate unemployment."

In the late 1940s and early 1950s, Friedman regularly wrote academic pieces criticizing Keynesian policies, international currency rates fixed by government agreement, and progressive income taxes. Friedman's early efforts typically met the academic standards required for publication in professional journals, and his originality and impressive statistical abilities won him a coveted award in 1951 from the American Economics Association, the John Bates Clark medal, as the most accomplished economist under forty.

To reinvigorate classical economics and show that Keynes was wrong, Friedman updated a theory about the quantity of money in an economy dating back to the seventeenth-century philosopher David Hume and in even simpler versions still earlier, one that had also more recently been refined by other economists, notably Yale professor Irving Fisher. The theory held that the quantity of goods and services an economy produced was equal to the size of the money supply and how rapidly the money was circulated, known as the velocity of money. Money circulation was held to be stable (or at least predictable); therefore, money was the only variable that could affect the economy.

This contention was a direct refutation of Keynes's main argument that government spending could affect the rate of growth. Keynes's budget deficit would be effective only if the central bank increased the money supply to compensate for Treasury's additional borrowing, claimed Friedman, but the increase would result in more inflation, not real economic growth—the benefit of any gains in income from more spending would be wiped out by the higher prices. If the central bank, in turn, did not expand the money supply to provide funds for government borrowing, the new Treasury debt would "crowd out" valuable private borrowing and growth would be unchanged—or, over time, even reduced.

To make his key point, what Friedman needed to demonstrate was that changes in the money supply caused GDP to rise and fall. His first efforts at documenting this were not promising. So, in 1948, with Anna Schwartz, a highly competent, dedicated researcher from Columbia University, he started an ambitious research project under the auspices of the National Bureau of Economic Research. He and Schwartz would reconstruct money supply data in the United States since the Civil War and compare it to changes in GDP, Schwartz compiling the data, a monumental task, and Friedman overseeing the project.

Friedman tried to marshal other evidence against Keynes. The success of Keynesian policies depended on how much of the money earned due to stimulative government spending programs, such as unemployment insurance, was spent. More money spent would mean more revenue for business, which in turn would mean more hiring and investment, and still more money spent. The round-robin of increased spending raised the level of GDP by a "multiple" of the original government spending. This "multiplier" was central to Keynesian analysis and policies.

Friedman gathered evidence to show that people did not spend as much of their increases in annual income as Keynes assumed. He reasoned that people based spending decisions on their expected earnings over time and would not increase spending significantly from a onetime boost in income. Thus, a government stimulus would not necessarily result in all the spending Keynes said it would. It was probably Friedman's most effective use of statistical evidence against Keynes. But it only dented the surface of the Keynesian edifice. Friedman showed that the multiplier was somewhat less than Keynes proposed, not that there was no multiplier. And Friedman's conclusions overstated the ability of people to foresee their future income accurately. Such alleged consumer prescience—his theories typically depended on prescience on the part of business and workers as well—became a hallmark of Friedman's thinking, and one of its weakest links.

In the 1950s, before Schwartz fully gathered the evidence, Friedman, sometimes with collaborators, promoted his new monetarist theories based on partial statistical analyses in a variety of academic essays. He had not yet come up with a definitive statistical foundation for the endorsement of the theory. He also began to write journalistic essays and make speeches about public policy mostly paid for by the Volker Charitable Fund. With Rose's considerable editing help, he organized these essays into *Capitalism and Freedom*, which when published in 1962 received little national attention.

The clarity of writing and breadth of subject matter made *Capitalism and Freedom* a compelling book, however. The central theme of the essays was that free markets not only can solve most of the problems of producing and distributing goods and services but also can solve most of the nation's social problems as efficiently as possible. Boiled down, Friedman proposed that most social goods, including secondary schooling, health care, and retirement savings, were no different than a box of cornflakes, a Buick, or banking. His fundamental assumption was that competition in free markets is the great regulator. Businesses produced goods and services to maximize their profits and people bought them to fulfill their needs and wants. The price arrived at by the interplay of supply and demand allocates the goods and services as efficiently as possible. Even speculation in stocks, bonds, and commodities will quickly adjust to sensible levels and capital will be distributed to where it can be invested most usefully. In direct refutation of Keynes, Friedman believed that stability would always return at high levels of prosperity: "The fact is that the Great Depression, like most other periods of severe unemployment, was produced by government management rather than by inherent instability of the private economy."

Above all, Friedman argued, no one will take advantage of others. "So long as the freedom of exchange is maintained, the central feature of the market organization of economic activity is that it prevents one person from interfering with another in respect of most of his activities." The consumer is protected from coercion, wrote Friedman, because there are other sellers; the seller is protected because there are other consumers; and the employer is protected because there is a pool of workers from which to pick.

Thus, Friedman summarized his moral philosophy. If individuals are given the choice, free of government rules and regulations, of where to work, where to invest their retirement funds, where to send their children to school, where to buy their health care, and where to rent or buy their homes, competition to supply the best goods or services will result in a greater number of cheaper and higher-quality options. In this way, Americans will have more high-paying jobs, a more secure retirement, schools of surpassing quality, a possibly cheaper but surely more efficient health care system, and more affordable housing. He argued further that with reduced government and lower taxes, the poor would be better off, inequality would be minimized, and discrimination eliminated; coercion would be minimized and material prosperity maximized. It was nearly a utopian or religious promise, and that was its broad appeal, a moral call for the protection of personal freedom. Economic freedom is also the way to achieve political freedom, according to Friedman.

Capitalism and Freedom was free of any doubts that might have been raised by a closer look at history, which would have suggested that its bold promises had not been achieved in past periods of limited government. Moreover, the American economy in the 1950s and 1960s grew rapidly as did the typical worker's standard of living, despite higher taxes, progressively applied, and the growth of government. America's public schools were considered excellent, its colleges were becoming unparalleled, its highway network expansive, measures of health first-rate, and its government research unexcelled.

Friedman did not bother with more than minimal statistical or empirical proof in *Capitalism and Freedom;* there were few studies he could have cited. Without offering evidence that American social programs were failing or inadequate, Friedman urged the United States to do away with Social Security, progressive income taxes, free public high schools, the minimum wage, housing and highway subsidies, and health care, even for the elderly (Medicare was passed a few years later).

Friedman conceded in *Capitalism and Freedom* that government had some justifiable if rudimentary duties. It should be in charge of the national defense, the enforcement of the laws, and the financing and administration of primary education. It should develop local roads but not national highways. He believed the poor deserved subsidies, advocating what he then called a negative income tax—a credit against taxes due when people worked—thus providing them incentives to work even at lower wages. In one of the few moderately technical pieces in the book, he argued that government should not fix currency levels but let them float, to be set by traders in a free financial market. Concerns about controlling the level of the currency distracted central bankers from their sole task, according to Friedman, which was to control the supply of money.

No major general publication reviewed Friedman's book when it was published. To sell, as Friedman suggested later, it required the economic crisis of the 1970s. Ultimately, it sold well more than half a million copies, however, and became the guide for anti-Rooseveltians like Lewis Uhler.

Barry Goldwater and his associates, familiar as they were with Friedman's writings, named him chief economic adviser for the 1964 presidential campaign. His talent for popular writing and equally for articulate public speaking, rare for most economists, raised his visibility in the media. In 1964, *The New York Times Magazine* asked him to write a summary of Goldwater's economic plans. In 1966, *Newsweek* offered him a column alternating with renowned Keynesians, notably Paul Samuelson. He made television appearances at a time when financial coverage on TV was scant. In particular, *The Wall Street Journal* editorialists exalted his theoretical powers and promoted his views time and again.

Almost every suggestion Friedman made in *Capitalism and Freedom* was taken up by serious proponents over the next forty-five years. Some were adopted by the nation. The call to privatize Social Security has frequently been sounded since the 1980s and 1990s; increases in minimum wage were successfully avoided for long periods of time; a version of a negative income tax for the poor rather than direct outlays (the U.S. Earned Income Tax Credit) was backed by both Republicans and Democrats; international currencies were floated in the financial markets in the mid-1970s; and there has been a sharp reduction in progressive income taxes, beginning with John F. Kennedy, and still more aggressively by Ronald Reagan and later by George W. Bush.

In this same period of Friedman's ascendancy from the 1970s to the present, while inflation declined, inequality rose steeply, and wages stagnated for many Americans and most males in particular; productivity except for the late 1990s and part of the early 2000s grew slowly; floating currencies fostered serious international imbalances in trade and flows of capital; and the level of poverty remained as high as it was in the early 1970s. In 1979, the Federal Reserve adopted monetarist targets only to discard them a few years later.

In 1963, *A Monetary History of the United States, 1867–1960* was at last published. For Friedman's disciples, the publication moved monetarism to the forefront of the economic discourse. Anna Schwartz had calculated changes over one hundred years in the quantity of money, which Friedman and she defined as currencies and checking accounts, as well as, in some cases, savings accounts.

It was a monumental statistical effort. In general terms, the research showed a broad relationship between changes in the quantity of goods and services—the GDP—and changes in the money supply. To the academic mainstream, even for those with political views opposed to Friedman's, the new data were fascinating. No one had produced such a detailed empirical re-creation of the money supply before.

But the relationship between the nation's income (GDP), inflation, and money was too loose to prove, or even strongly suggest, that changes in money caused changes in GDP. The quantity of money and incomes changed together but only in approximate precision. The only reasonable reading of the findings was that money supply changes sometimes affected business activity, and that business activity sometimes affected changes in the money supply. Economists referred to business activity's impact on money as the "endogeneity of money," which is to say that the quantity of money is the creation of the strength of the economy.

Friedman frequently overlooked or minimized questions about the causal relationships, however. In 1953, he maintained in one of his few philosophical essays that the accuracy of a model's assumptions or the details of its workings do not matter, only whether the model accurately predicts the future. Perhaps in anticipation of his future findings, he argued that if there was a statistical relationship between money and GDP, it would suffice for purposes of public policy, even if one couldn't explain exactly how it worked.

Money creation in a modern economy is too complex to fit the simple Friedman model, however. The Federal Reserve does not just press a button and produce more money. When original monetarism arose a few centuries earlier, new supplies of gold were often the driving force behind money expansion, not a complex banking system of reserves. Now, the Fed made securities available to banks, which they could use to meet the reserve requirements needed to make new loans. The loans appeared in the nation's checking accounts, raising the money supply.

But to create money, the banks had to want to make more loans, and businesses had to want to borrow more money. When do they do this? If business activity is strong, companies will typically want to borrow more and banks will be willing to lend more because there seems less risk of default. But if the economy is not strong, no matter how much in reserves the Fed makes available, loans may not be issued by banks and money not created. Even if the Fed limits reserves, business activity may be so strong that more loans are made anyway, thus raising the money supply. Friedman was unable to prove that money was independent of the economy, a point his acolytes often ignored. Yet Friedman himself wrote that the cause "may be in either direction."

There was another important slip in the data. The key to Friedman's theory was that the circulation, or velocity, of money—how often it was turned over each year to support the level of GDP—was stable or at least predictable. If the same amount of money produced different levels of GDP, it was not clear how the money supply either caused or controlled GDP—or inflation.

But *The Monetary History* did more to raise doubts about money velocity than it did to eliminate them. Velocity or the relationship between money and the economy was markedly different in the 1920s than in the 1930s and

1940s and then shifted markedly again in the 1950s. As the Nobel laureate James Tobin put it soon after the book's publication, "To me it seems strange to rely on a trend which regards the 1930s and 1940s as normal and the 1920s and the 1950s as abnormal." This early criticism still stands. Friedman and Schwartz had to be deeply disappointed that velocity was not more stable than they had discovered it was. The instability of velocity is what finally undid monetarism in the 1980s.

Thus, the data did not support the view that only money affected the economy or inflation, and that therefore Keynes was wrong. The big prize for Friedman would have been to show conclusively that the Great Depression was caused by a fall in the money supply—that is, caused by an error in Federal Reserve policy. Although Friedman and Schwartz claimed victory in this case as well, they made little advance over what was already known. No one had doubted, even before Friedman's commentaries on the subject, that the Federal Reserve made matters worse when it raised interest rates in 1931 by contracting the reserves available. (It was especially worried about the outflow of gold as dollars were cashed in for gold to be invested elsewhere, a large reserve of gold then being thought critical to maintaining the value of a currency.) Money supply did fall, as the Friedman-Schwartz data now corroborated. But this sharp reduction was largely due to falling demand for loans, not simply Fed policy. And the Fed fairly quickly reversed itself in 1932, a point Friedman from time to time conveniently ignored.

Friedman thus attributed much of the severity of the Depression to a brief contraction of reserves in 1931, which was quickly reversed. When reserves were added in 1932, money supply contracted anyway, as the British economist Nicholas Kaldor pointed out in a 1972 article. In the two preceding years, money supply contracted even though the Fed did not raise rates. Kaldor further pointed out that Friedman and Schwartz's data showed that the money supply of Canada generally dropped as sharply as it did in the United States but the depression there was not nearly as severe.

The Fed, though it clearly made matters worse, as non-Friedmanite economists conceded, almost certainly could not have forestalled the Depression once it was under way simply by making reserves available and cutting interest rates at that point. The money supply probably would not have risen and even if it had, velocity would probably have fallen due to lack of confidence and slow business activity.

Once the 1930s Depression was under way, Friedman could not academically dismiss inadequate Keynesian demand as the main problem.

In 2009, Ben Bernanke, the Federal Reserve chairman, and one of the most prominent of Friedman's admirers, strongly advocated Keynesian stimulus to raise the economy from deep recession. The administration of Barack Obama successfully got an $800 billion package passed to provide just that. Even at the time, many believed it was not enough.

Economists Abraham Hirsch and Neil De Marchi drew the fairest and least ideological conclusion about Friedman and Schwartz's widely cited work. *The Monetary History,* they wrote, was supposed to prove that money was an independent and primary determination of the economy. Rather, they rightly said, it had "the flavor of assertion without empirical basis." Hirsch and De Marchi wrote further, "What Friedman knew in 1963, therefore, was that the facts resisted attempts to dismiss Keynesian interpretations out of hand."

Nevertheless, one of Friedman's decided accomplishments was to return attention to the importance of monetary policy after its neglect in favor of fiscal policies—Keynesian spending. But the later attention was to be focused on interest rates, not money, as Friedman had sought. Keynesianism did not deny the importance of monetary policy, but Keynes believed it affected the economy through changes in interest rates, and in the Depression these were largely irrelevant. When the economy was strong again, and inflation an issue after World War II, adjusting the level of interest rates was a powerful policy tool, and more easily implemented than adjusting government spending. In the 1930s, when Keynes wrote his *General Theory,* monetary policy was not potent because business would, as noted, often neither borrow nor banks lend no matter how low interest rates fell. Keynes's view was simply conceived in wholly different economic circumstance when inflation was not a priority.

Friedman's major lasting theoretical contribution was his claim that there is a natural rate of unemployment below which inflation would be stimulated—a concept widely accepted by mainstream economists in later years. Again, it was a strategy to defeat Keynesianism. Before Friedman, Keynesians had assumed that the unemployment rate could be lowered by improving the rate of economic growth and creating jobs without causing more than a gradual increase in inflation. Businesses would only raise prices modestly to preserve profit margins if their labor costs rose more rapidly than output per hour of work. The relationship was known as a Phillips curve, named for the British economist who discovered a similar relationship. Slightly higher inflation was thought to be worth it if it meant more jobs.

But Friedman argued that there was no such thing as a slight increase in inflation as unemployment dropped below its normal, or as some later called it, natural rate. He also claimed there would be no more jobs. In an early 1967 speech as president of the American Economics Association, he argued that if the unemployment rate was pushed below the natural rate, as he noted Keynesians typically tried to do, inflation would keep rising to ever higher levels. Workers' wages would rise, but business would offset this by raising prices. Some workers perceiving that their wages were being eaten away when business inevitably raised prices would simply quit, pushing the unemployment rate back up, even as inflation increased. Thus, he argued, under Keynesians, the federal government would adopt more stimulative policies to get the unemployment rate down again, but inflation would rise again, eat away at worker wages, and some would quit again. The unemployment rate rose back to its natural level but now there was more inflation without new jobs.

At the time, the contention was regarded skeptically by most economists. Were workers really that sensitive to their "real" wage—the wage after inflation? The natural rate theory caught on, however, when inflation started to rise rapidly in the mid-1970s. The rising inflation rate, indeed, did not lower the unemployment rate as the Phillips curve predicted. Stagflation resulted—high unemployment and high inflation simultaneously, as Friedman seemed to predict. Even many economists who broadly disagreed with Friedman's politics considered it his finest hour. His theory seemed prescient.

In fact, Friedman's prescience was somewhat exaggerated. He gave his 1967 talk when there was a new inflation scare—consumer inflation had doubled over the previous year as the unemployment rate fell below 4 percent, and it kept on rising. And the unemployment rate did not rise, as predicted. There was little doubt that expectations of ever higher inflation were driving business, consumer, and worker behavior in the 1970s. The question was whether this was a permanent economic law or a result of the unusual circumstances of the time, especially because wages for so many Americans were automatically or informally raised when prices rose—indexed to inflation.

The bigger test of his theory came in the late 1990s. Before that, both Republican and Democratic economists, under the influence of Friedman, warned that the natural rate of unemployment was between 5.5 and

6 percent, below which inflation would rise to dangerous levels. In the late 1990s, many jobs were created and the unemployment rate fell to below 4 percent with no sign of renewed inflation. There seemed to be no natural rate of unemployment. The concept remained in the mainstream thinking and in the academic textbooks, however, most economists now argued that the natural rate simply shifted from time to time.

In the 1960s and even the early 1970s, Friedman was an outsider. Although his star was rising by then, and he was the leading conservative intellectual in the media, he had little influence in the Nixon administration, which took office in 1969. Arthur Burns, Nixon's closest economic adviser and former Friedman teacher, thought Friedman's theories were oversimplified and ignored the real-world influence of unions and big business. Nixon's chairman of the Council of Economic Advisers, Paul McCracken, avoided being characterized as a Friedman disciple, as did Herbert Stein, who was in charge of macroeconomic policy at the council.

Inflation brought Friedman front and center. But the causes of inflation were far more complex than the growth of money. Inflation began rising more rapidly in the late 1960s partly due to the increase in federal spending on the Vietnam War. Then Nixon pumped up federal spending in 1972 to ensure a strong economy before his reelection bid that year. Burns reduced interest rates significantly to strengthen the economy at the same time. When the OPEC oil countries first tripled prices in 1973, partly in response to rising American inflation, and then raised them again in 1974, the higher prices contributed to the inflation and also acted as a higher cost to business and a tax on consumers, driving the American economy into its deepest recession thus far in the post–World War II period. Due to two poor crops in a row, rising food prices added even more to inflation than did the oil price increases.

Friedman did not accept that such unique events more than momentarily raised inflation. He argued that other prices would fall to offset the increases unless the money supply rose too rapidly. This was Friedmanite fantasy—the assumption that all prices adjust very quickly. (Even he eventually allowed there could be a temporary rise in prices.)

Later statistical analysis did not bear out Friedman's claim that inflation was always a monetary matter. The economist Alan Blinder showed that changes in money did not nearly correlate well with rising inflation in the 1970s. Blinder found that changes in the money supply underestimated inflation in 1973 and 1974 by 3 percentage points and completely failed to anticipate the falling inflation rate in 1975. "The Great Inflation of 1973–74 was simply not a monetary affair," wrote Blinder. There has been so much corroborating research of Blinder's claim that the issue has been fairly settled.

Still, even Democrats adopted Friedman's natural unemployment rate hypothesis. Friedman turned the attention of the nation's policymakers to keeping inflation low and it became an unchallenged priority for them. Many economists hailed the resulting low inflation that began in the 1990s as the beginning of a new stable age of ideal growth—which became known as the Great Moderation. Much the opposite is more likely. The anti-inflationary policies were adhered to too firmly, and contributed significantly to slower rates of growth, higher levels of unemployment, the disappointing growth rate of productivity until the late 1990s, and stagnating wages. Extreme speculative excesses arose in other areas while Friedman's anti-inflation heirs were in charge—in high-technology stocks in the late 1990s and mortgage finance in the 2000s, to take but the starkest examples. Friedman's assurance that financial deregulation would work turned into an empty promise, with disastrous consequences. Since the early 1980s, the financial markets have been far more unstable than in the 1950s and 1960s. There had been dissenters among mainstream economists who thought the inflation target was too low, but their advice went untaken by those running policy. By 2010, this was changing. Economists at the International Monetary Fund, for example, suggested the annual target for inflation could be raised from 2 percent to 4 percent. "Nobody knows the cost of inflation between 2 and 4 percent," wrote the IMF chief economist and former MIT professor Olivier Blanchard, who once fully expressed his faith in the benefits of the Great Moderation. "So I think people could get used to 4 percent and the distortions would be small."

In 1980, the Friedmans published a simple version of *Capitalism and Freedom* called *Free to Choose,* which was the basis of a public television series. By then he was internationally known and respected and his criticism of government was carried across the world.

But Friedman, who claimed he was an empirical economist, never developed a political or moral philosophy. Rather, his social policy was driven by a simple moral claim, which was to exalt personal freedom and individualism. In his view, society had little role in the development of individuals; it was the individual who accounted for civilization, as he wrote in this revealing paragraph:

> The great advances of civilization, whether in architecture or painting, science or literature, in industry or agriculture, have never come from a centralized government. . . . Columbus did not set out to seek a new route to China in response to a majority directive of parliament. . . . Newton and Leibnitz; Einstein and Bohr; Shakespeare, Milton and Pasternak; Whitney, McCormick, Edison and Ford; Jane Addams, Florence Nightingale, Albert Schweitzer; no one of these opened new frontiers in human knowledge and understanding, in literature, in technical possibilities, or in the relief of human misery in response to government directives. Their achievements were the product of individual genius, of strongly held minority views, of a social climate permitting variety and diversity.

Capitalism, he believed, allowed people to pursue their creative interests without interference. "The great achievement of capitalism is not the accumulation of property," he wrote, "it has been the opportunities it has offered men and women to extend and develop and improve their capacities."

But dozens of events in Friedman's lifetime showed just the opposite. The martial technology of Germany, including the V2 rockets, were created under the directives of a central government. That most creative and dreadful product made by the human species, the atomic bomb, was the result of a U.S. government directive to J. Robert Oppenheimer and his colleagues. Radar was developed by government. It is now a commonplace that the Internet originated in the Pentagon. The space missions of the 1960s were successful. The advances sponsored and financed by the federal government's National Institutes of Health saved countless lives, and these were led by state and local government research, and preceded by the systematic dissemination of vaccines and the development of urban and suburban sanitation systems.

Consider the quality of American art produced by the federally subsidized painters during the Depression. Many writers, including Saul Bellow, Richard Wright, Ralph Ellison, and John Cheever, started to learn their craft while working for the Federal Writers' Project in the 1930s. Half a millennium earlier the creative consequences of intense government and church subsidy of art were visible in Florence, Siena, Venice, Padua, Milan, Rome, and later the Spanish Court. The craft guilds of these city-states had critical parts in training and organizing work. Newton and Einstein,

Shakespeare or Edison, or to broaden the selection, Michelangelo, George Eliot, Manet, Pasteur, and Marie Curie thrived in a social and political world of cultural, intellectual, and economic nourishment, for which government served as a critical foundation and organizing mechanism.

Government did not simply get out of the way of genius and let it thrive. There were the universities of Germany, the theater of England, the great craft guilds of Venice and Florence, the publicly supported scientific tradition of France. Did Friedman really believe genius arose in a vacuum of social development? I can only attribute so biased and simplistic a notion in an intelligent man to a strong emotional desire to service his main point: to minimize government.

Friedman expressed surprise that economists did not agree on more matters, and thought they would once the facts were known. In a passage in the autobiography he wrote with Rose, *Two Lucky People,* Rose herself raises doubts about his belief. "I have always been impressed by the ability to predict an economist's positive (meaning economically scientific) view," she wrote, "from my knowledge of his political orientation, and I have never been able to persuade myself that the political orientation was the consequence of the positive views. My husband continues to resist this conclusion, no doubt because of his unwillingness to believe that his own positive views can be so explained, and his characteristic generosity in being unwilling to attribute different motives to others than himself."

This, then, was the intellectual leader of the revolution in ideology that began in America in the 1970s. When the time was right, his ideas rose to dominance from obscurity and outright derision. They served the era more thoroughly than the ideas of most other intellectuals of any kind ever did. He helped turn the people against government in general, and he was probably most proud of this. His reputation as an economist rested on his prediction of the stagflation of the 1970s. But the economic crises of the 1970s were not the products of the policy mistakes he claimed they were. They were the consequence of political opportunism and failures of leadership, of society's moral exhaustion, of an international oil monopoly turned angry, of severe weather, of outdated labor institutions, of a sudden turn downward in the nation's productive capacities, of unchecked credit creation, and of the denigration of government itself that he did so much to encourage.

Richard Nixon and Arthur Burns

POLITICAL EXPEDIENCY

Richard Nixon, who became president in 1969, did not have an interest in economic policy. He believed foreign policy determined the course of nations, and he intended international diplomacy to be the mark he would leave on the nation. But his guiding political principle was expediency, and to such a man economic policy always had its purpose, which was to win elections. He undertook a reckless set of stimulative fiscal policies beginning in late 1971, designed to assure his reelection in 1972, that contributed as much as or more to inflation than Lyndon Johnson's often cited war spending. He adopted a freeze on wages and prices, hard to implement in a large modern economy at any time, but impossible to make work while stimulating the economy excessively at the same time; he tightened the lid on the kettle and then turned up the heat, making a burst of renewed inflation inevitable. He unhinged the dollar from gold but refused to reestablish a new fixed currency system. Unstable currencies led to immediate disarray in international trade, and the falling dollar added more to inflation for the rest of the decade.

Nixon could have blunted inflationary forces when it would have been less economically painful to do so. But he set inflation afire. Even as the nation was lashed by rising prices, there was a sharp rise in unemployment, wages for many fell, corporate profits plummeted, and business investment dried up. It was the worst economic crisis Americans faced since the Great Depression, and set the stage for Milton Friedman's ascent and a change in America's ideology.

Coupled with the Watergate scandal and the continuation of the Vietnam War, which Nixon had promised to end quickly, it was Nixon more than anyone else who undermined the nation's faith in what it could

President Nixon conferring with Burns, whom he appointed
Federal Reserve chairman, and other advisers

accomplish and pride in what it was. He not only created the conditions
that led to punishing stagflation but, by making the nation so distrustful
of government, he lay the groundwork for an age of greed freed of federal
oversight.

Richard Nixon's father, Frank Nixon, born in Ohio, had moved to California around the turn of the century to escape a dead-end job as a cable car
operator in the cold Midwest climate. He bought a small and poorly located
citrus grove and built the house of Richard's birth on his own twelve acres,
where he dreamed of striking oil in the California farmlands. It was Yorba
Linda, about forty miles into the farmlands southeast of Los Angeles.
Frank's miracle did not happen, and Richard, the second son of five, born
in 1913, grew up in relative poverty—two of Nixon's four bothers died as
children from tuberculosis. When Richard was nine, Frank Nixon, bitter
about not becoming rich, abandoned his hopes for a gusher and bought a
Richfield gas station near Whittier, a town a dozen miles from downtown
L.A. Frank was stern, ill-tempered, and voluble, and Richard often medi-
ated arguments between him and his brothers, avoiding the strappings
that his father liberally dispensed. Richard's mother, Hannah Milhous,
descended from a line of California Quakers, was by most accounts a ten-

der, religious woman, of whom Richard later wrote with compassion. Hannah had two years of college, while Frank only made it through the sixth grade, but Nixon wrote in his memoirs that Frank had the greater interest in politics and followed Richard's later political career closely. Frank had converted from Methodism to Quakerism when he married Hannah. Whittier was originally a Quaker town.

The Richfield gas station did well as Whittier grew, and a few years later Frank bought an abandoned church, moved it to the gas station lot, and opened a grocery store in it, called the Nixon Market. It blossomed in the booming 1920s, and the Nixons lived comfortably, but Frank Nixon still felt the market was a humiliating descent from his loftier ambitions. In later years, Nixon openly expressed shame at being the son of a grocer, inheriting the bitterness and sense of failure that would define much of his life.

With a thriving store, the Nixons comfortably survived even the Depression. Garry Wills wrote, "For Nixon, the thirties seemed not to have taken place. He lived through the Depression, studying, working, going to school. He was then at a formative age. Yet neither the Depression nor the New Deal, neither cause nor cure, had any discernible effect on him."

Nixon worked almost every day in the market from the time he was a boy until he finished college. Nixon was, in his own proud words, a diligent and disciplined worker, and he believed his success depended on this, not on any natural talents. He was invited to attend Harvard, having won an award for his academic achievements in high school, but his father could not afford the additional expenses, so Nixon went to Whittier College instead, the local Quaker school. He wanted to be popular and made the football team, acted in school plays, joined the debating team, and was elected president of his junior class. He helped form a new fraternity when he was not invited to join the school's leading one. Graduating number two in his class, he won a scholarship to Duke Law School in 1934. He was certain he did not have the ability to excel there, but working hard at his studies, graduated third in his class.

He was incapable of taking pride in this achievement—never having done well enough or attributing what he did do merely to hard work rather than talent—and his intense insecurities were reinforced when, despite his high ranking, he did not get a job at a major New York law firm (it was still the Depression). He was also turned down by the Federal Bureau of Investigation. He took the rejection by the New York law firms, and especially the FBI, as personal failures. (As president, he found out from an official at the FBI that he did not get a job there simply for lack of funding.)

His politics during law school were, according to friends, in the liberal tradition of popular Supreme Court Justices like Benjamin Cardozo and Louis Brandeis. His mother voted for Woodrow Wilson, while Nixon described his father as a populist who shifted his political allegiances often.

Nixon returned to Whittier to work as a local lawyer and entered the Navy in 1942, serving as an operations officer and never seeing combat. After the war, dissatisfied with his career, he decided to run for a seat in Congress in 1946 against the politically liberal incumbent, Jerry Voorhis, though he did not even vote in those years and probably still had moderately liberal political views himself. To run for office, however, he shed those leanings. With the advice of an aggressive political consultant, Murray Chotiner, he repeatedly accused his opponent of communist sympathies. Voorhis, a Yale graduate from a wealthy family, was indeed politically radical in his youth, but was a stalwart Roosevelt Democrat as a member of the House for ten years and certainly not a communist sympathizer.

Anticommunism was only just starting to find wide support in California in those years, and Nixon and Chotiner could not have anticipated the wave that soon arose. At a time when the United States was increasingly concerned about the growing power of the Soviet Union, Nixon's red-baiting contributed to the anticommunist passions. At thirty-three, Nixon beat Voorhis for the congressional seat. In his memoirs, he claimed that the main issue of the campaign was economic concerns, given the recent Depression and uncertain prospects after the war. The record does not match his memory.

On entering Congress, Nixon sought a seat on the House Un-American Activities Committee, and soon found a high-profile issue to which he could lay claim. Alger Hiss, a State Department official and outspoken proponent of the new United Nations, was accused by former communist and *Time* journalist Whittaker Chambers of being a secret member of the Communist Party. Nixon became the most voluble and caustic of Hiss's critics, and won himself a national reputation. Nixon had "a passion for taking on enemies and slaying dragons," as biographer Fawn Brodie wrote. Hiss's guilt for spying was never proved, but he was charged with and found guilty of perjury.

Nixon rode his reputation as a communist hunter into the U.S. Senate. In 1950, at thirty-seven, he defeated Democratic congresswoman Helen Gahagan Douglas. Nixon referred to Gahagan Douglas, a former actress and the wife of the well-known actor Melvyn Douglas, as "the pink lady."

In 1952, General Dwight Eisenhower, who had been head of the Allied forces in Europe during World War II, won the Republican nomination for president. He did not like Nixon but chose him for vice president to appease the more conservative wing of the Republican Party, who preferred Ohio senator Robert Taft. For some, the vice presidency is a path to anonymity—but Nixon was often in the news. During the campaign, he was accused of taking $18,000 in campaign contributions for his personal use. He went directly to voters to plead his innocence. In an unctuous but successful television performance, he denied the accusation, said his wife and two daughters were plain people, and admitted only that their dog, Checkers, was a gift from a donor and that the family was going to keep him no matter what the election laws said. The nation overwhelmingly voiced approval for Nixon in phone calls and telegrams following the speech, and Eisenhower kept him on the ballot. The popular Eisenhower easily defeated the liberal Democratic opponent, Adlai Stevenson.

As vice president, Nixon traveled widely, honing his expertise on the international issues he loved, all the while, he later wrote, reading extensively on foreign policy matters. He was stoned by angry crowds in South America, gaining him headlines at home and winning him more sympathy as America's defender. Late in his second term, he again made sensational headlines for a televised impromptu discussion in 1959 with the Russian leader, Nikita Khrushchev. The confrontation took place in the up-to-date American model home built for an exposition in Moscow. Captured on color videotape, the "kitchen debate" showed a still young Nixon strongly defending American material plenty and holding his own against the older, experienced Soviet head of state.

His critics resented his mix of opportunism and pandering, and Nixon was indeed easy to ridicule. Helen Gahagan Douglas had tagged him years earlier as Tricky Dick, and the name stuck. Stevenson, running against Eisenhower for president again in 1956, constantly ridiculed Nixon's anticommunist excesses. So pronounced was his nasty reputation that Duke University, Nixon's alma mater, refused to give him an honorary doctorate after alumni nominated him in 1956.

By 1958, he was actively planning to run for president. One of his vice presidential duties was to chair an economic policy committee on inflation. In this, he had little interest, but he made friends with Arthur Burns, Friedman's early mentor, and until 1956, Eisenhower's chairman of the Council of Economic Advisers. The serious and rather pompous Burns, born in the Ukraine in 1904 but brought to the United States by his parents, was by then one of the Republicans' leading economic advisers, invariably on a short list of those whose advice was sought. He had studied and then taught at Columbia and had become an expert in business cycles.

The economy sank into a serious recession in 1957 and 1958, and Burns, back at Columbia, urged Nixon to get Eisenhower to stimulate the economy by cutting taxes. Otherwise, Burns thought, the unemployment rate could again be high just as Nixon was launching his presidential campaign in 1960. Nixon made the request but Eisenhower refused. Eisenhower wrote in his memoirs that he had wanted to balance the federal budget to rid the nation of the inflationary psychology that seemed to be developing in the mid-1950s, a constant concern of his. The economy foundered again, as Burns had warned, and the unemployment rate stood at nearly 7 percent on the day of John F. Kennedy's inauguration, its highest level for the decade. In his 1962 memoir, *Six Crises,* Nixon bitterly attributed his narrow loss to the weak economy, which was likely correct. He would not let such a thing happen again.

Nixon, still restless, chose to run for governor against the popular Pat Brown in 1962. His loss reflected the rising tide of political liberalism, but Nixon's distasteful reputation for character assassination and public pandering affected the outcome. He was also, as usual, out of touch with economic issues. During the campaign against Brown, he discussed international affairs far more than the economy.

Nixon vowed he would never again run for office. But he kept making speeches for candidates and maintained his base of support in the party. After Barry Goldwater's embarrassing loss in 1964 to Lyndon Johnson, Nixon saw an opportunity in campaigning for Republicans in the South against incumbent Democrats who were now losing electoral support due to Johnson's integrationist policies, the political backlash Johnson had always feared. Nixon, though widely considered mean-spirited, was seen as more moderate and thoughtful than Ronald Reagan, who was testing his potential to win the nomination, and Reagan had little over the arch anticommunist Nixon as a cold warrior. Reagan, who had won the very California gubernatorial office in 1966 that had eluded Nixon, was still a political newcomer, even at age fifty-seven. Nixon won the Republican nomination for president in 1968.

As war protests grew, Johnson stunned a television audience by announcing he would not run for a second term. At the contentious, sometimes violent Democratic presidential convention in Chicago that summer, Hubert Humphrey, Johnson's vice president, won the nomination, but he had locked himself into support for Johnson's war policies, and was a compromised man. Nixon, meanwhile, promised to end the Vietnam War, alluding to a secret plan he had, which, if he did, never saw the light of day. In economic matters, he preached predictable moderate Republican principles about fiscal caution, but, throughout the campaign, he exploited racial anger in the South over poverty programs and efforts to integrate schools and other public places, the so-called Southern strategy. At the Republican convention, he had assured Southern delegates he did not agree with open housing laws and that he recognized the dangers of the federal busing of schoolchildren to integrate schools and communities. He was also countering George Wallace, the former governor of Alabama and aggressive opponent of school integration, who ran as a third candidate. Wallace almost surely took more votes from Nixon than from Humphrey, but Nixon nevertheless won by a comfortable margin.

Few could imagine the economic travails the nation would soon face. By the time Nixon took office in 1969, annual consumer price inflation was ratcheting up to 6 percent from 3 percent in 1967 and 4 percent in 1968. Blame, even by Democrats, was directed at President Johnson's refusal to raise taxes in 1967 in order to finance spending for the war. The federal budget deficit in 1968 rose to more than $25 billion, nearly 3 percent of GDP, which at the time seemed explosive, far higher than at any point since the years just following World War II.

Balancing the budget had been widely preached and overly praised as necessary fiscal medicine throughout the 1950s and into the 1960s. But it was true that the fiscal stimulus of war spending plus spending on new social programs had swollen the budget, raising demand more quickly than the economy could supply. Johnson finally supported a tax increase in 1968, but it was classically too little and too late. Keynesianism, now known as the New Economics, was designed to be applied in both directions, certainly as stimulant but also when needed as depressant. The latter was politically difficult to do. In 1968, Arthur Okun, a leading Keynesian economist and chairman of Johnson's Council of Economic Advisers, described the refusal of Johnson to raise taxes as the "defeat of the New Economics by the old politics." The Harvard progressive John Kenneth Galbraith, lamenting the political problem, wrote later, "It appears Keynesian policy is unavailable for limiting demand. It can expand purchasing power but it cannot contract it."

On taking office in 1969, Nixon's economic team, given rising inflation, believed the economy needed to be modestly reined in. The Federal Reserve chairman, William McChesney Martin, however, was more determined than the administration economists to stop the rise in inflation, and the Fed sharply raised the interest rate it uses as a target to set monetary policy (the federal funds rate). It is the interest rate on funds banks lend to each other to meet requirements for the reserves against bank loans required by the Fed. The Fed raised it from roughly 6 percent to 9 percent that year. Once the Fed started raising rates, the previously soaring stock market cracked almost immediately. As a consequence of the higher rates and the burst market bubble, GDP contracted toward the end of 1969 after nearly ten years of expansion, and the rate of unemployment began to rise. The stock market continued to plummet in the first half of 1970, and the economy officially slid into recession as the unemployment rate rose above 6 percent.

Until this point, economists believed the New Economics had largely solved the problem of serious economic recession. Keynes had explained how stimulus through expanded spending or tax cuts could mitigate recession and unemployment. Herbert Stein, as noted, a member of Nixon's Council of Economic Advisers, wrote that Kennedy's broad tax cut, proposed before his death in 1962, was the first explicit test and "a major event in the history of fiscal policy." When passed under Johnson in 1964, the highest tax rate was cut from the wartime level of 91 percent to 70 percent. And the economy grew strongly over the next four years, the unemployment rate falling to less than 3.5 percent.

Thus, in times of high unemployment, deficits were now entirely acceptable, and Nixon's team was open to a moderate amount of deficit spending at times. Only when full employment was reached should the budget be balanced, the economic consensus held, otherwise a deficit was appropriate. The head of Nixon's Council of Economic Advisers was Paul McCracken, an Iowa farmer's son from a deeply Republican region, who had been a member of Eisenhower's CEA. McCracken, a political conservative by temperament, had nevertheless studied with Alvin Hansen, Harvard's famous Keynesian, and accepted a moderate version of Keynesianism. The macroeconomic specialist on the CEA was Stein, who did his graduate studies at the University of Chicago in the 1930s, well before the Friedman revolution there, and accepted Keynesianism.

By 1970, the economy was possibly already in a steep recession, and Nixon's team now realized it had to stimulate demand. Two business failures added to the concerns. There was the Penn Central bankruptcy in the spring of 1970, and then Lockheed, the defense company and aircraft manufacturer, found itself on the brink of bankruptcy. Nixon refused to save the railroad giant but the administration engineered a $250 million loan to bail out the defense contractor on grounds of national security.

What disturbed the advisers, however, was that inflation wasn't falling as fast in the recession as they had expected. This seemed new. Inflation was embedded in the economy now. Unions had their wage increases indexed to inflation. If consumers expected prices to rise, they often bought more now, the opposite of what should occur because higher prices should deter buying. And oligopolistic American businesses could also easily raise prices to cover their costs because of their market power. Manufacturing and service giants in autos, steel, aluminum, machinery, retailing, communications, and other major industries could force price increases on their customers because there were so few competitors to undercut them.

The stubborn inflation rate made the Nixon economics team cautious and they did not recommend more than a modest stimulus. And preoccupied by the Vietnam War (and the secret bombing of Cambodia) as well as by domestic social issues, Nixon did not turn his full attention to the economy. Toward the end of 1970, the unemployment rate was still rising, the budget deficit was reaching levels as a proportion of GDP higher than in the Johnson years, and the Dow Jones Industrials had collapsed to the 600s in mid-1970 compared to nearly 1,000 just two years earlier. The next reelection campaign would soon begin, and Nixon could no longer blame the Democrats for economic mismanagement or the deficit. The memory of Eisenhower's refusal to stimulate growth in 1959 lingered.

One policy option to break embedded inflation was war-style restrictions on price and wage increases. If inflation was forced down, and wage increases were legally restrained, inflationary expectations might be reduced. But to the Nixon CEA, such government tampering with free markets was anathema. Arthur Burns, more influential over Nixon than anyone else on economic matters, was not entirely hostile to the idea. Nixon was similarly inclined to consider restrictions. As Stein wrote, Nixon did not believe corporations were powerless to set prices as they saw fit, which was classic free market doctrine. Nixon hardly regarded large companies "as chips floating on a tide of market forces but thought they were powers to contend with."

Nixon's dissatisfaction with his taciturn treasury secretary, David Kennedy, whom he found indecisive, was growing, and he had come to respect the outspoken tough-minded, former governor of Texas, John Connally, who had been a member of one of his presidential commissions. Connally, a flamboyant middle-of-the-road Democrat, had been with John F. Kennedy when he was shot in Dallas and was himself wounded. In a fateful move, Nixon replaced Kennedy with the highly pragmatic, seemingly fearless Connally in late 1970. As if to announce his more aggressive plans, Nixon told ABC's anchorman, Howard K. Smith, "Now I am a Keynesian." He was preparing his reelection bid.

Nixon's domestic policies to this point were an unusual mix. He taunted Democrats for their social programs for the poor, who were typically black, in appealing explicitly to Southern Democrats. One of Nixon's key advisers, the young Harvard law school graduate Kevin Phillips, denied the strategy was racial. He argued there was a new conservative majority emerging among the working class across America, north to south. Phillips insisted that his assessment of the shift was based on a cultural, not a racial, divide. Yet Nixon attacked many of Johnson's programs for the poor, among them Head Start and the Job Corps, fanning the racial fires with the accusation of "welfare dependency."

But Nixon felt he had to maintain good graces with a nation that was still on balance in favor of progressive social programs. As Ralph Nader said years later, he was the last president to be afraid of liberals. In 1970, Nixon supported and signed legislation that created the two powerful new regulatory agencies—the Environmental Protection Agency and the Occupational Safety and Health Administration. The next year, he signed legislation to establish the Consumer Product Safety Commission, another of the Washington agencies least liked in the business community, and soon after he signed a bill to index Social Security benefits to rapidly rising consumer prices.

Through 1971, the unemployment rate hovered around 6 percent, higher than at any time since the temporarily slow growth of the early 1960s. Consumer inflation had at last fallen, but only to 4.5 percent or so, high given that a recession had long been under way. According to Stein, Nixon at the time was still formally opposed to nationwide wage and price controls. On the other hand, Democrats were increasingly pushing such an incomes policy, as it was known. Controls imposed during World War II and the Korean War were considered by many to have been successful. When they were lifted after the Korean War, for example, inflation remained moderate. Congress voted the president discretionary authority to impose such controls the year before, placing the political onus on him.

As bad news gathered momentum, the balance of trade also turned negative for the first time. Americans were now importing more than they were exporting, which reduced U.S. GDP to the extent that goods were bought from foreign not domestic firms. It also placed pressure on the U.S. dollar. A high and stable U.S. dollar had been the cornerstone of international trade and enabled U.S. companies to expand foreign operations cheaply, as well as helping the U.S. government finance military bases around the world. But a deficit meant that a growing number of dollars were in foreign hands, and they were increasingly likely to cash them in for gold. What helped keep the dollar stable was that the U.S. Treasury agreed years earlier (in the Bretton Woods agreement signed by the victorious Allies in 1944) to buy back dollars from foreign central banks at a rate of $35 an ounce in gold in return. But America's reserves of gold were now dwindling rapidly—only some $10 billion worth, one third of the amount of dollars in foreign hands.

By late summer 1971, the adverse events were coalescing, in Nixon's always anxious mind, into a frightening crisis. Nixon wanted to respond strongly, with, as Stein wrote in an understatement, a "large political gesture." Political perception was his priority, and Connally, who understood the uses of political image, was just the man to carry the water. Nixon must have had this in the back of his mind when he appointed him treasury secretary only months earlier. "I can play it round or play it flat," one Nixon administration member after another recalled Connally saying. Said economist Arthur Laffer, who worked on the staff of budget director George Shultz, and was later a key adviser to Ronald Reagan: "I really loved the guy. 'You tell me what it is, and I'll get it sold,' he'd say."

There were members of the Treasury staff who also believed it was time to take a strong stand against embedded inflation, despite an unemployment rate of 6 percent. One was Paul Volcker, whom Treasury Secretary Kennedy had appointed earlier in Nixon's term as his undersecretary for monetary affairs. Volcker had served in the Treasury for Presidents Kennedy and Johnson and had been a staff economist at the New York Federal Reserve Bank. He was a protégé of, and key aide to, David Rockefeller, then president of Chase Manhattan Bank, the nation's second largest after First National City, before joining the Nixon administration. Six foot seven inches tall, he was as strong-minded as he was prepossessing.

Another Treasury member favoring a strong anti-inflation stand was Murray Weidenbaum, an economics professor at Washington University in St. Louis, who had gotten his Ph.D. from Princeton. Weidenbaum was a moderate Republican, schooled in Keynesian economics but traditionally averse to inflation and government spending. He reported to Volcker. Volcker and Weidenbaum had been working together on a plan to freeze wages and prices to staunch inflationary expectations, but this was politically precarious for a Republican administration.

On August 9, Britain suddenly requested $3 billion worth of gold in exchange for dollars, nearly one third of the nation's total gold reserves. If the United States decided against shipping so large a sum of gold, it would have to let the dollar drop, with all its inflationary consequences. For Nixon, in particular, it would be a harsh humiliation.

Nixon called his advisers to a meeting at Camp David the next weekend. Sixteen were asked to attend and felt themselves a privileged group on the brink of making history. Connally presided over the direction that policy would now take, not the economists. And it wasn't economic logic but the need for a strong political front that dictated what the administration labeled its New Economic Policy.

Connally convinced Nixon that convertibility of dollars to gold had to be ended temporarily—"the gold window had to be closed"—to protect the gold reserves that remained. What made it palatable was that the plan was to reopen the window soon, but at a different price for gold, the dollar moderately lowered in the process. (A temporary tariff was added as well.)

More significant, Connally argued that Nixon had to impose a freeze on U.S. prices and wages to stop inflation, partly because the lower dollar would add inflationary pressures and, more important, to stop building inflationary expectations. It was the Volcker-Weidenbaum plan.

No one expected this of a Republican. "We pushed controls strongly," said Weidenbaum. "We just couldn't figure out a way to meet our noninflationary goals without knocking out inflationary expectations. And then it was Connally who sold it to Nixon. Shultz and Stein took over managing the plan later." Both Stein and Shultz, the latter a devotee of Friedman, relented after some hesitation, and Stein later wrote that Burns's approval was probably the key reason Nixon agreed to it.

But more important to Nixon, the price freeze would enable him to stimulate the economy before the election by speeding up federal spending, stoking the economy with a powerful Keynesian stimulus without an inflationary impact due to the wage-price freeze. (The new policy also included modest tax cuts, another stimulus to the economy.)

The team of sixteen returned to Washington and Nixon announced his New Economic Policy in a televised speech that Sunday night, August 15. A discussion had taken place earlier over whether to preempt the popular TV

western *Bonanza,* and it was decided to do so—a measure of the importance of economic disarray to Americans.

Nixon promised the New Economic Policy would stamp out inflation,
reduce unemployment, and solve the gold drain problem all at once. Investors on Wall Street, impressed by the boldness, despite the anti-market
wage-price controls, sent the stock market soaring the next day, the Dow
Jones Industrials up at one point by nearly 6 percent or some 50 points (the
equivalent of 600 points in the 2000s).

Nixon then stimulated the economy aggressively to ensure his electoral
victory. He took no chances and pulled out all stops. In the remaining
months of 1971, Nixon raised Social Security benefits, increased business
tax credits on investment, and reduced personal tax rates for individuals.
He instructed his cabinet to spend as much as they could of their annual
budget by the middle of July 1972, and raised Social Security benefits again
just before the election.

After having resisted Nixon's 1970 entreaties, Burns also pushed interest
rates sharply lower. The federal funds rate was about 5.5 percent in the summer of 1971. By February 1972, Burns's Fed pushed it down to 3.25 percent,
and the economy was soon growing strongly again. There is no question
that Nixon asked him to do this; the request is on the Nixon tapes made
public in the wake of the Watergate scandal. Whether Burns did indeed
step harder on the throttle at Nixon's request alone is ambiguous. But the
evidence suggests Burns acceded to Nixon's pleas.

Most important, the wage-price freeze worked for the ninety-day
period. Inflation fell markedly, most consumer prices basically remaining
constant over the next three months. A less stringent phase of wage-price
controls was then implemented in December, to last roughly a year; this
Phase II was also a mandatory system, but with wider latitude for price and
wage increases, and, despite the stimulus, it also seemed to be working.
Throughout 1972, inflation rose at modest rates.

By election day in November 1972, the unemployment rate had fallen to
below 5.5 percent, and, more important, was trending lower. Stock prices
had shot up again, the Dow Jones Industrials piercing its former high of
about 1,000. The major blemish on the record for a Republican president
was the historically high budget deficit, necessary to stoke the economy.

Nixon's determination to win reelection was also reflected in the timing of other initiatives that interested him more. He traveled to China
in early 1972 to start normalizing relations with the former enemy, his
greatest presidential ambition. He worked strenuously to establish a cease-

fire in Vietnam before the election through secret negotiations with the North and South Vietnamese led by Henry Kissinger, his national security adviser. But the negotiations ground to a temporary halt.

Hell-bent on winning a second term, Nixon earlier that year had apparently approved a plan to have several men break into the Watergate headquarters of the Democratic National Committee to get information regarding the Democrats' campaign. In July, the burglars were caught, but too late to affect the election a couple of months away.

Facing Senator George McGovern, who demanded a quick end to the war, a man seen almost as extreme on the left as Barry Goldwater had been on the right, Nixon won reelection in a landslide.

Nixon had a second term in which to make history, unconstrained by election pressures and his gnawing politically insecure nature. He bombed North Vietnam intensively in December and forced President Thieu of South Vietnam to make concessions, thus bringing both parties back to the negotiating table in early 1973, where they agreed on a cease-fire at last. He brought the American troops home, but fighting among the Vietnamese continued for two more years.

As the economy grew rapidly, new inflationary pressures built. Now Nixon wanted to reduce the budget deficit. He raised payroll taxes to finance the more generous Social Security benefits he legislated and cut back social programs. He also wanted at last to unwind the wage and price controls and, in early 1973, he established a voluntary set of controls, Phase III.

The lid did not hold. It is one thing to freeze prices and wages when the economy is growing modestly, another when it has been stimulated to grow rapidly. Inflation rose quickly under Phase III of the controls program, and this put more pressure on exports and the dollar. The dollar had already been devalued further, and by October 1973 it was likely to be cut again. Finally, the fixed exchange rates of the Bretton Woods agreement were formally abandoned by the Nixon administration altogether. The United States would no longer redeem dollars for gold and the currency would float, as would most others, in an international financial market uncontrolled by government. This eventually led to further declines in the dollar, inflationary because it raised import prices.

With such inflationary conditions now sown, there was little tolerance for new price shocks. There would be two such inflationary events, however. In late 1972 and in 1973, a series of weather-related crop failures raised farm prices across the globe. Severe weather in the Soviet Union destroyed much of the fall 1972 harvest, forcing it to import millions of tons of grain from the U.S. and elsewhere. The effects were felt in early 1973, when U.S. retail food prices rose at a stunning annual rate of 20 percent. Overall consumer prices rose at an annual rate of nearly 10 percent between February and July, more than 4 percentage points of which were attributable to the leap in food prices. Crops failed again in 1973, and in 1974 food prices rose by 12 percent, adding 3 percentage points to the rate of consumer inflation.

With prices now soaring, Nixon, against the advice of his economics team, imposed a new two-month freeze on prices, though not on wages. Burns was, meantime, raising interest rates aggressively to stop inflation. Once inflation settled down again, Nixon anticipated he would then put a new set of voluntary controls in place, to be called Phase IV.

The second shock was the sharp rise in oil prices. In October 1973, Egypt and Syria launched an attack on Israel on the Jewish state's major religious holiday, Yom Kippur. Before the war began, the Arab oil producers and other members of the Organization of Petroleum Exporting Countries, OPEC, including Venezuela, had agreed to use their oil exports as a weapon in the combat with Israel. Oil was generally paid for in U.S. dollars, and as prices of goods rose in the United States, OPEC had also been seeking higher prices per barrel to pay the higher prices on their imports. Thus, inflation itself may also have been a provocation for OPEC to raise prices.

After the attack on Israel, OPEC embargoed oil shipments to the United States as well as Japan and several other nations. OPEC resumed shipments in the late fall, but unilaterally raised the price of benchmark crude oil to $9 a barrel from its former level of $3, then raised it again roughly another $3 a barrel in 1974. The hike added about 2.5 percentage points to consumer inflation that year.

By early 1974, gas prices at the pump had risen by 60 percent, from roughly 35 cents to 55 cents a gallon on average. Electricity rates rose commensurately. The cost of manufacturing soared for many industries. At the time, oil expenditures came to roughly 5 percent of GDP.

In 1973 and 1974, then, three unique factors were working to raise inflation to record levels. Crop failures raised food prices rapidly, adding the most to inflation; OPEC quadrupled oil prices, adding about half as much; and the end of the Nixon price freeze and the new voluntary Phase IV unleashed a wide range of price hikes. Alan Blinder computed that the explosion in prices in 1974 resulting from the relaxation of controls had about two thirds again the impact that the OPEC oil shock did. In the second half of 1973, consumer prices rose on average by an annual rate of 10 percent and, through most of 1974, they rose by an annual rate of 12 percent, almost half of which was due to these three unique factors.

Interest rates also rose rapidly. Those who bought homes had to pay 9 to 10 percent in interest for conventional mortgages in 1973 and 1974, not the 7 percent paid two years earlier or the 4 or 5 percent that prevailed in the 1960s. And the prime rate for business loans from banks rose from about 5 percent in 1972 to more than 8 percent in 1973 and more than 10 percent in 1974.

In the fourth quarter of 1973, U.S. consumers slashed their spending on food and cars, and by early 1974 the economy ground to a halt. Compounding matters, inflation had pushed Americans into higher tax brackets, increasing their taxes as a proportion of their income, and thus reducing the money they had to spend on goods and services.

In fact, the worst recession of the post–World War II era had begun, but few economists realized it. Among the least aware were the Nixon advisers, who remained preoccupied with inflation and budget deficits. William Simon, a successful Salomon Brothers bond trader and active Republican fundraiser, was now treasury secretary. Shultz, who had an economics Ph.D., had resigned the Treasury post in 1974 to return to teaching. Simon had been running Nixon's energy policy. Roy Ash, the former head of Litton Industries, one of the high-flying conglomerators of the 1960s, was now Nixon's chief budget officer.

Throughout the summer of 1973, the nationally televised Watergate hearings cast a pall over Nixon's second term, and in early 1974 the House of Representatives began impeachment proceedings. When Nixon resigned in August, the economy was contracting sharply, and the unemployment rate was beginning a relentless rise to 9 percent eight months later. Yet Nixon in his last economic speech in July of 1974 argued for more cuts in government expenditures to control the inflation he had done so much to create. The Federal Reserve under the persistent inflation hawk Arthur Burns had raised interest rates into August, the federal funds rate reaching nearly 13 percent that summer, even as the economy collapsed.

Under Nixon, Americans experienced the worst of both worlds— stagflation. It was the nation's first post-Depression bout with serious economic turmoil. The American economy now punished most Americans, and at this point, the nation's political attitudes toward government began to change. Economists offered no easy solution, but the ongoing focus on inflation, despite the severe recession, made matters worse. The seeming failure of wage and price controls eliminated them as a future tool to break inflation's back. Nixon's cynical economic policies, driven by politics, were the trigger.

Nixon's handpicked successor, Gerald Ford, the Republican leader of the House of Representatives, called a meeting of Nixon's economic advisers the afternoon of his first day in office, August 11. Ford, who pardoned Nixon a month later, had much on his mind, but inflation was at the top of his list. Although Ford decided to retain most of Nixon's economic team, it was a different group in spirit, theoretical understanding, and education from Nixon's original team, which had academic origins. The thoughtful and highly effective manager and conservative academic, Shultz, was succeeded by the bond trader and unmovable ideologue, Simon, who thought government spending was always and everywhere the cause of social ill. The only newcomer to Ford's group was Republican Alan Greenspan, a politically savvy fifty-year-old business economist from New York City. Nixon had appointed him to the Council of Economic Advisers earlier that year to replace Stein. Greenspan had deep libertarian views and was a close friend and follower—in fact, part of the inner circle—of the philosopher and novelist Ayn Rand, who referred to the sober Greenspan as her "undertaker." He was also, true to his Republican background, an earnest inflation fighter. Stein, far less ideological and better trained, had taken a teaching position at the University of Virginia.

Before Stein left, he asked the advisers at that first Ford meeting in August 1974 to submit a written synopsis of their views on the economy. "Everyone agreed that inflation was the great problem," he summarized later, with irony. Despite the evidence that the economy was softening rapidly, Stein wrote, Simon argued that inflation would remain in double digits in 1975. Stein himself thought inflation would fall from 10 percent or so to 7 or 8 percent, as did many private forecasters. (In fact, inflation fell to 5 percent by 1976.) Greenspan, though a professional forecaster, was noncommittal.

Greenspan wanted to cut government expenditures "as much as possible." Burns and Simon more vigorously urged cutting government spending; Simon was committed to a balanced budget as almost a religious doctrine.

As for unemployment, all believed the unemployment rate would not rise to much more than 6 percent by the middle of 1975. In fact, the unemployment rate rose to 9 percent, and the economy weakened far more than anticipated.

After the August meeting, Ford told Americans that inflation was "public enemy number one." He then called for a summit meeting to be held the next month, inviting leading business and union officials and economists to Washington to discuss how to fight inflation. The meeting produced more publicity about the economic dangers of government deficits than it did solutions. A couple of months later, Ford said in a widely watched speech that inflation was the equivalent of an enemy army that might, during war, strip the American people of their liberty and their property. All his key advisers endorsed the Friedmanesque hyperbole—or Randian, given Greenspan's association. Ford said he would ask Congress for a tax increase and cut federal spending significantly. He then urged Americans to compile a list of ten ways to fight inflation voluntarily and send the list to him. He called the program WIN, or Whip Inflation Now. WIN buttons were soon to be seen everywhere, including the president's lapel. Stein deeply regretted the easily ridiculed idea.

By the end of 1974, the GDP was plunging, and would continue to contract until the middle of 1975. Consumers reduced their spending sharply, corporate profits plunged, and capital investment was cut by roughly 35 percent from 1973 levels. The Dow Jones Industrials and the Standard & Poor's 500, a broader index than the Dow, dropped to levels first reached in the early 1960s, the Dow sinking to 578, somewhat more than half its 1973 high.

By early 1975, the Ford advisers began at last to understand the depth of the recession. With Greenspan's advice, Ford now reversed course and proposed a stimulus package of government spending and tax cuts. Even at this point, Bill Simon hesitated to support the proposal, claiming that the increased government borrowing that resulted would inevitably crowd out businesses borrowing. Agreement with Congress on a stimulus package was reached, however. Burns, in fact, had been cutting interest rates at last.

The recession had been severe, but it at least reduced consumer price inflation to an annual rate of 7 percent in 1975 and, as noted, to about 5 percent in 1976. But the unemployment rate remained stubbornly high at around 8.5 percent until the end of 1975.

With the government budget deficit rising in the depths of the recession—to be expected as tax revenues fell with lower incomes—Ford and his advisers tried to restrain policy. The federal deficit was likely to exceed $75 billion in fiscal 1976, more than 4 percent of GDP, and he proposed cutting government spending though inflation was falling and the economy was weak even as he proposed modest tax cuts. While advisers like Stein and Greenspan praised Ford's restraint, Americans were surely confused by his lack of clarity and repeated shifts in policy.

Nixon was the last president who could have stopped the inflationary surge with only moderate pain. Nixon's advisers, as did Ford's, chose to blame the inflation on big government, neglecting the unusual temporary forces at work—the oil cartel, the poor crops, and the institutional power of unions. Fatuous anti-inflation policies launched by Ford and constant policy shifts undermined confidence in government still more—after the tragedies of Vietnam and Watergate. It was in these years that America changed.

In 1976, an election year, as the economy grew strongly and inflation fell to 5 percent, the unemployment rate fell only slightly below 8 percent. Few economists could have imagined that consumer prices would rise so rapidly with unemployment so high. When consumer price inflation first rose to roughly 5 percent in early 1969, the unemployment rate was 3.5 percent.

When Ford ran for president against Jimmy Carter in November 1976, unemployment was above 7.5 percent, and the federal budget was deeply in the red. Still, Carter won the election by only a small margin. Some Americans had already begun losing faith in government solutions.

4

Joe Flom

Pioneer of mergers & acquisitions

Business innovation was by no means entirely halted by the stagflation of the 1970s. The semiconductor revolution was under way, and the desktop computer, the commercial personal computer still several years off, was already changing the way business operated. Satellite communications made it economical to broadcast television programs across the nation. Video games changed children's behavior. Many businesses successfully developed fuel-efficient products and manufacturing methods.

But for most companies, prospects had dimmed, reflected in persistently low stock prices. New competition from Japanese and European manufacturers particularly showed how vulnerable American companies were to innovation. American manufacturers were losing market share rapidly in many areas, including textiles, consumer electronics, appliances, machine tools, heavy machinery, and even steel production. By the mid-1970s, imports exceeded exports by a wide margin.

With recession, inflation, high interest rates, and foreign competition, the Dow Jones Industrials Average, which had risen to more than 1,050 in the Nixon boom of 1973, fell by almost half, and did not recover its old highs until the early 1980s, so raising money for new business through equities was not economical. Venture capital for new companies was nearly impossible to find. With stock trading slowing, traditional Wall Street firms were rapidly consolidating, and struggling firms were lucky to be bought up by the remaining strong ones, and the survivors searched aggressively for new investment products and sources of revenue as they cut personnel remorselessly.

The low stock prices of many well-established corporations looked like opportunities to some corporate executives and Wall Street bankers. With

Joe Flom, takeover lawyer, on right, with his son, a music executive,
and Ron Perelman, CEO of Revlon and takeover specialist, middle

their traditional markets slowing down or becoming obsolete, acquiring a company in a new field was attractive. As oil prices rose, the energy business looked especially appealing.

For the first few years of the early 1970s, mergers were relatively rare. There had been a merger movement in the late 1960s, led by conglomerates, which used their highly priced stock to acquire new companies, some absorbing hundreds of companies a year. They invariably claimed they could manage these companies better. But relatively few of the acquisitions worked as planned as the merger wave rose to unjustifiable levels, investors driving up stock prices, some of the conglomerates trading at stock prices one hundred to two hundred times earnings. The bubble burst in 1969 as it became clear the conglomerates could not generate the earnings promised.

The demise of the conglomerates in 1969 and then 1970 put the mergers and acquisitions practices of investment banks on hold. Not only was there widespread distrust of mergers, but stock prices were so low they could not be used as a medium of exchange, as they had been in the 1960s. However, it was dawning on some of the more adventurous bankers that low stock prices made it attractive to pay for the companies with cash, some and eventually most of it borrowed from banks or institutional investors like pension funds. The problem was that few executives would choose to sell their companies at such bargain prices. Not only was the purchase price likely to be low compared to values of earlier years, running the risk that shareholders would blame management if they turned down takeover offers even at small premiums to prevailing prices, but also the executives often lost their jobs when the acquiring company moved in.

But low stock prices were simply too tantalizing to be ignored for long by ambitious Wall Street bankers, increasingly desperate for profitable opportunities. Even as the recession reached its depths, a new takeover wave was started by merely a dozen or so lawyers and investment bankers on Wall Street. This movement was hostile: companies now regularly acquired target companies against the wishes of their current management. Whoever could borrow the most to buy a target company soon became a prime determinant of which company won a takeover battle.

The result was the beginning of a sweeping takeover movement that transformed the way American companies were managed. In 1974, paying $150–200 million for a company was considered a large transaction; by the 1980s, the size of deals reached billions of dollars, and in the 2000s, mergers valued at more than $15–20 billion were common, and some still larger. Over the course of the 1990s, several trillion dollars of mergers were undertaken, and globally there were several trillion dollars' worth completed each year in the late 1990s and again in the mid-2000s.

Some mergers were sensible business decisions. But when Wall Street soon found another money tap, it drove the corporate takeover to its unimaginable and insensible heights, companies paying enormous premiums over stock market prices to buy their target. The Wall Street specialists who took a percentage of the transaction price of the deals became rich. High fees for bankers, lawyers, and even public relations firms, and enormous profits for those who invested in takeover targets, particularly risk arbitrageurs who specialized in buying takeover targets, became the stimulant for ever larger mergers. Now CEOs made a fortune by selling out to acquirers, as did their immediate subordinates, because they were given stakes in the company. The allegiance of business management thus shifted from the long-term health of the corporations, their workers, and the communities they served, to Wall Street bankers who could make them personally rich, their compensation now mostly options for shares of their companies for which they paid nothing.

A company claimed it was taking over another because it believed the whole would be bigger than the sum of its parts—that operations could be merged to reduce costs or to optimize management. Time and again, however, the prospects for "synergy" due to combining operations were exaggerated. While academic research became a combat zone for competing schools of thinking—the Friedmanite Chicago School more typically supporting the view that mergers had value—the statistical research of Mark Sirower, a management consultant, formerly with the prestigious Boston Consulting Group, has been widely considered conclusive. He found that the shareholders of the acquiring companies usually lost value. "It is more likely than not that any given acquisition will fail," Sirower concluded, based on his own research and that of others in the 1980s and 1990s. While the shareholders of the target companies consistently gained in the acquisitions from the premiums paid over the prevailing stock prices, these gains were not adequate to offset the consistent losses in shareholder value of the acquiring firms. *BusinessWeek* later did a follow-up study in the early 2000s, confirming that stockholders of acquiring firms fared worse a year later on most deals. "So eager were they to snare a deal," wrote the magazine, "that the premium they paid gobbled up the merger's whole potential economic gain from the get-go." It would become the first of the great speculative bubbles of the age of greed.

To wring adequate cash flow from companies to meet the high levels of debt taken on by the acquirers to buy the companies, expenses were generally cut sharply, including R&D and especially payrolls. Business and Wall Street were no longer buyer and seller, with the natural tensions and competitive checks and balances that came with such a relationship, but on the same team. The CEOs running the merged ventures, now owners of stock, usually made a fortune. In 1986, when Edward Finkelstein arranged for a private buyout of Macy's, the retailing firm where he was CEO, for $4.5 billion, he became the envy of fellow CEOs. As an investment banker put it, "Suddenly, every CEO looked at what Ed Finkelstein stood to make on the transaction and what it had done to his organization to spread stock around to 300 executives, and all those CEOs said, 'I want to get in on this.' Then we had the start of a runaway train." Macy's went bankrupt in 1992, in part because Finkelstein borrowed a fortune to buy other retail chains (I. Magnin and Bullock's), and was bought in turn and restructured, eventually to survive as a scaled-down entity.

The man most responsible for the hostile takeover movement was neither young nor brash in the early 1970s. He was small and low-key and lived humbly even after he became wealthy, a brilliant connoisseur of the ins and outs of the law, and one of the most aggressive lawyers of his time. His manner partly disguised his consuming ambition. By the early 1970s, Joe

Flom had been plying his trade, hostile takeovers involving smaller companies, for twenty years. He eventually built the small law firm he joined after law school in the 1950s into the largest and one of the most respected in the world.

Flom was born in 1923 and raised in Borough Park, Brooklyn, a son of Russian Jewish immigrants. "My father was a union organizer," he said. "He couldn't provide for the family." His parents wanted him to be a "professional." "To them being a professional was a great thing," Flom said. "That meant either a doctor or lawyer." Flom qualified for admission to Townsend Harris, one of New York City's fast-track high schools. He knew he wanted to be a lawyer "right from the word go," and in high school wrote a review of a book on cases in constitutional law. True to his early ambition, Flom worked by day as a clerk in one of the few well-established Jewish law firms of the time, and went to City College at night.

He was drafted before he entered his junior year at City College. On returning, he wanted to get into law school as soon as possible, but had not finished his bachelor's degree. "Yale and Columbia looked at my record and told me I could apply but don't hold my breath," Flom said. "So I wrote a letter to Harvard about why I was the answer to sliced bread. They invited me up for an interview and they let me join the class." Flom excelled at Harvard, making the law review. Robert Pirie, who attended Harvard Law years later and worked for Flom's firm, said he was considered by the faculty one of the most brilliant students ever to have graduated.

Flom interviewed at several prestigious law firms, including Cravath Swaine and Cahill Gordon. "But I just didn't feel comfortable with them," he said. "I was a fat, ungainly kid with no social graces. Then the placement office told me there were these guys who were starting their own firm. They didn't have an office. They didn't have a client. The more they told me about the risks and the problems, the more I thought these were the guys I'd like to be with. And when I met them, I just liked them. I just thought these were the people I could be comfortable with."

Slate, Arps and Meager was not exactly a fly-by-night firm. The three partners were Ivy League graduates who had left a prestigious firm, the predecessor to Dewey Ballantine, to start their own. But they were struggling to find business when Flom joined them. He was paid $3,600 his first year, 1948, which was more than the three partners paid themselves. Fortunately, an airline lawyer from another firm passed business on to them when he had a conflict of interest, said Flom, which kept the firm barely alive.

There were many hostile acquisitions involving smaller companies in these early years, and Flom seized an opportunity to serve as legal adviser to one of the acquirers. Battles for corporate control then were often fought through proxy contests. Each shareholder is entitled to a vote for the board of directors in proportion to the size of his or her ownership. Usually the existing board proposes a slate of directors. But a shareholder can contest the slate or run for the board, or propose a different board and campaign for the proxies of shareholders to vote in its favor. Thus, someone seeking to acquire another firm can initiate a proxy contest to win control of the board of directors if a friendly offer is turned down.

In those years, hostile proxy contests were widely frowned upon in the polite society of major law firms and prestigious investment banks. The contests for control could quickly become inflammatory, bitter, and vindictive, and the conventional wisdom was that the hostilities only encumbered the management of the merged firm.

Flom willingly participated in hostile battles. His favorite tactic was to acquire shares of the target firm quietly without management's knowledge. To make victory likely, gaining control of 25 percent of the shares was often sufficient, he learned. With those votes in hand, the potential acquirer could more easily win over enough of the remaining shareholders to take the company. But buying a quarter of the shares meant a substantial investment, had to be done secretly, and usually required convincing a bank to finance the purchase in a secret collaboration. One tempting advantage was that the purchaser could make additional money on the investment because the share price of the takeover target almost always rose—an early version of what would later be called greenmail. "As the 1960s began," said Flom, "acquirers realized these expensive proxy contests didn't make sense. So they figured out, or we tried to convince them, that if you bought some shares, you could win the proxy contest and even make money once the share prices rose. But the banks were not familiar with this kind of approach. I had to go to them and convince them. I remember one $60 million deal. I had to swear in blood that if we got the money from the bank, we could win the deal."

As Flom and a handful of other lawyers and bankers won contests for their clients, public companies, fearful of being taken over, demanded government protection from the assault. In 1968, Congress passed a bill, sponsored by Senator Harrison Williams of New Jersey, that required any shareholder who bought 10 percent or more of a company's shares to disclose the purchase publicly in a filing with the Securities and Exchange Commission (Section 13d of the law). In 1970, the threshold was reduced to 5 percent.

Designed to make it more difficult to sneak up on an unsuspecting company, the Williams bill, said Flom, also served, paradoxically, to make hostile takeovers more acceptable to establishment companies by providing legal guidelines. The law prescribed not only what you could not do but also indirectly what you could do. A furtive and once disreputable maneuver was now legally sanctioned as long as the rules were followed.

Even prestigious Wall Street firms began to shed their objections to hostile takeover battles as their profits fell. The broader S&P 500 had reached a new high of 119 in 1973 (it rose more rapidly than the Dow in this period), but by the end of 1974 it had also fallen by nearly half to the mid-60s and, though rising sporadically since, finished the 1970s at only approximately 108—no gain over a decade. Adjusting for inflation, in fact, the investor in the S&P 500 would have lost about 1.5 percent a year on average. The traditional equity business was foundering.

Price-earnings multiples fell more steeply. The average P-E multiple for the S&P 500 was roughly 18 in 1969 and only 7 in late 1974. To those who were confident the economy would someday return with vigor, stocks looked like a fire sale. The stock price of a company was now often equal to or lower than the book value, or the value of the assets on the company's books less its liabilities. In other words, one could often sell off subsidiaries or plant and equipment for more than investors were willing to pay for a company in the stock market. In 1974, the average price of a stock in the S&P 500 was trading roughly 30 percent below such book value.

But the ignominious failure of the 1960s conglomerate wave made Wall Street especially cautious. "Certainly in the late 1960s they got excessive. The big crash took the fluff out of takeovers," said Flom. And corporate takeover waves had never followed each other so quickly in the past. There was such a wave in the 1890s, repeated again a generation later in the 1920s, but there was no similar takeover wave again until the 1960s.

The tool that made it all work was the cash tender offer. Unlike a proxy contest, an offer to buy other companies for cash—buying a majority or even all of their stock—had a critical advantage because it could be undertaken quickly, before the target company had time to respond. Flom became the leading advocate of the cash tender. "My approach is that if you take the job you do everything you can to win," he said, "including being creative and imaginative, within ethical limits."

The first hostile takeover by a first-tier company occurred in 1974, but it was not initiated by Flom or a Wall Street banker. The idea came from a bold chief financial officer, an articulate, charismatic ex-Marine named Charles Baird, who saw a good bargain in low stock prices generally. Baird, born in Long Island, rose to chief financial officer of old-line International Nickel Co., or Inco. He prided himself on his aggressiveness, and at sixty was a champion racquet ball player in senior competitions. "I had the fastest hands in the West," he said.

Based in Canada, Inco, the product of a merger early in the twentieth century, was the largest producer of nickel in the world. J. P. Morgan had helped found the company in an attempt to control nickel supplies, a commodity vital in steel production. As befit the century-old giant mining company, Inco's investment banker was the most prestigious of Wall Street firms, Morgan Stanley. They did not break with tradition lightly.

Although Inco's business suffered badly in the 1969–1970 and 1974–1975 recessions as demand for nickel fell, as did its price, like many natural resource companies in this period, it had excess cash—in this case $300 million, which it was willing to use to enter the energy business. The company wanted desperately to offset its cyclical downturns, and energy was now the world's most valuable scarce commodity. The company turned its attention to battery makers.

Inco's first choice for an acquisition was Britain's Chloride, Inc., which made car batteries. But the Chloride management resisted being taken over, and Inco executives believed making a hostile acquisition in England would be difficult to manage.

Inco's second target was ESB, formerly Electric Storage Battery, a maker of car batteries. ESB also had a dry cell battery, known as Ray-O-Vac, which Inco believed could compete with the popular Duracell and Eveready brands if the stodgy company invested more in marketing and research. ESB's price-earnings multiple had fallen to 6, its stock traded well below its book value, and, in fact, even below its net working capital per share—that is, its cash, inventories, and receivables less short-term liabilities. To aid in its pursuit, Inco was determined to acquire ESB, whether its management agreed or not. Inco approached Morgan Stanley, which had never managed a hostile acquisition before.

In the bear market of 1974, Morgan Stanley was hurting, and a respected partner, William Sword, along with his young, determined assistant, Robert Greenhill, both Harvard Business School graduates, were eager to represent Inco and encourage its hostile ambitions. Traditionally, the investment banker's fee was a percentage of the purchase price, which could be substantial. Frank Petito, the firm's managing partner, at first highly skeptical of sponsoring a hostile takeover, eventually gave in to Sword and Greenhill's persistence. Sword had worked with Flom on smaller deals, had come to respect him, and boldly chose to bypass the firm's usual counsel, another white-shoe firm with a long pedigree, Davis Polk & Wardwell, to hire Flom because of his experience with acquisitions. Inco now had prestigious Morgan Stanley to back its unsolicited offer, and Morgan had Joe Flom.

ESB was aware that, with its stock price so low, it was a potential target. But its banker, Merrill Lynch, did not understand how vulnerable it was. Goldman Sachs knew. The merger team at Goldman was headed by Stephen Friedman, a Columbia Law School graduate and former AAU college wrestling champion at Cornell. Friedman's familiarity with the environment was supplemented by Goldman's experienced risk arbitrage department, one of the most profitable and aggressive on Wall Street. Risk arbitrageurs invest independently in takeover deals when they are announced, and the practice had a long tradition at Goldman. The current head of the firm, Gus Levy, was once its risk arbitrageur. His successor, L. Jay Tenenbaum, had also been a risk arbitrageur. Now the department was headed by a Levy protégé, a young Yale Law School graduate, Robert Rubin. Goldman shunned initiating hostile takeovers but would defend clients from unsolicited bids.

Inco fired its first volley in July 1974 after ESB management turned down a friendly offer. On Morgan and Flom's advice, the nickel company announced it would pay all ESB shareholders $28 a share in cash if they tendered their shares by a certain date, a substantial premium over the current value of $19 a share. The total bid came to $164 million. The professional arbitrageurs bought up shares in the open market at the lower price, gambling that the deal would go through and perhaps even attract another bidder at a higher price. These risk arbitrageurs made substantial profits investing in such deals while their outcomes were still uncertain. If they were wrong, and a merger failed to be consummated for legal or financial reasons, they could lose a lot of money. Mostly, they succeeded. The "arbs" usually worked for larger, often private investment companies like Goldman; there were only one or two independent investment partnerships unaffiliated with large brokers that accepted individuals as investors. At the time, it was a mostly secretive and lucrative business, with a modest volume of capital chasing substantial opportunity.

Once an open bid was made, ESB's defense was to look for a friendly counterbidder. The arbitrageurs buying up so many of the existing shares would certainly sell to the highest bidder. ESB had had earlier merger conversations with Harry Gray, an aggressive acquirer who ran giant United Aircraft, later called United Technologies. Gray had been groomed on acquisitions in the 1960s as an executive at the conglomerate Litton Industries, under Roy Ash, Nixon's chief budget officer. ESB hired Goldman to defend it and told Steve Friedman about Gray's potential interest. Friedman immediately approached Gray, who was willing to join the bidding fray. Friedman thought $34 a share would chase Inco away—and Gray obliged—but he also realized the bidding could go higher. Inco, with the guidance of Flom, Sword, and the young, aggressive Greenhill—and cash in the bank—was hardly about to surrender. It countered with a bid of $36 a share. The next morning, now just one week after Inco's first bid, United matched the Inco offer of $36 a share. Inco raised its bid to $38 a share. Later that afternoon, United matched the offer. Inco was ready for United's matching bid, and upped it to $41 a share, and United at last folded its hand. The battle became the standard for dozens that followed.

With traditional underwriting almost dormant, the investment bankers were especially delighted with their fees, which grew with each higher bid. The arbs may have enjoyed the bidding contest the most, their profits far greater. Inco had agreed to pay more than twice ESB's original value in the stock market, $226 million in cash, $70 million above the original bid. Morgan Stanley earned a fee of $1–2 million. Goldman's fees were probably comparable.

The model for future takeover battles was now set. Morgan Stanley, Wall Street's premier investment bank in effect opened the door for all bankers. Flom was available to any and all for the right price and could quickly make any smart investment banker into a takeover expert. Soon, investment bankers, enticed by ever bigger fees that could be earned in a matter of weeks, were urging acquisitions on their clients and abandoning their former delicate principles about hostile contests, and potential target companies signed up with investment bankers to prepare defenses. "M&A [mergers and acquisitions] was always an adjunct to the underwriting business in the past," said Flom. "But once it got started, the banks realized it was a good source of income. Instead of just reacting, they went after the business." This understates the reality. The new stars of the investment banks were in M&A. Greenhill, thirty-five, became Morgan's leading corporate merger specialist, perhaps the most aggressive of his time. Friedman, also thirty-five, was his counterpart at Goldman, and the two would be rivals ever after. Ultimately Friedman and Robert Rubin became co-heads of Goldman. Joseph Perella, thirty-one, another Harvard MBA, started a mergers department at First Boston, also an old-line institution. He would later be joined by lawyer Bruce Wasserstein, four years his junior, who had degrees from Harvard's law and business schools. Martin Siegel, another

Harvard MBA, like Wasserstein just twenty-seven, developed a defensive practice at relatively small Kidder Peabody. The veteran and also the most admired of the group was Felix Rohatyn, of Lazard Frères, a couple of years short of fifty, who had built his expertise as an acquisitions specialist for the 1960s conglomerator Harold Geneen. Geneen had turned his company, ITT, into one of the nation's largest conglomerates during the late 1960s.

Flom was everyone's first choice as a lawyer, but soon he had an equally aggressive and skilled opponent in Martin Lipton, a graduate of New York University Law, almost a decade younger. Flom and Lipton had dueled against each other a few times in the 1960s and Lipton was now learning from Flom. In the 1950s and 1960s, Flom had similarly found an older mentor in his chief competitor, a proxy lawyer named George Demas. Arthur Fleischer, another Harvard Law graduate, of Fried Frank Harris, eventually became a third prominent takeover attorney. As these deals paid off, commercial bankers like Walter Wriston were willing to put up more money to finance them.

Professional takeover tacticians began to engineer acquisitions themselves. The most prominent of the early practitioners was T. Boone Pickens, a former geologist and Oklahoma oil wildcatter, who would buy some shares of a company, then bid for it, hoping to sell out to a higher bidder and pocket the profit on his initial purchase of shares. Thus, he put companies "in play," and earned "greenmail" in the process. Carl Icahn used Boone Pickens's tactics to launch still bigger attacks.

For Wall Street, the profitability of takeovers increased as the number and size of deals grew. The Wall Street investment bankers and the new takeover "artists" like Pickens and Icahn, who provoked hostile bidding contests, accrued more capital to make higher bids as they engineered more deals. Because the largest and most respected companies were also increasingly willing to attempt hostile takeovers, almost every major industry was swept into the new wave, and all but the nation's largest companies were vulnerable to an unsolicited offer.

The mere threat of takeovers changed corporate values. Vulnerable companies were desperate to raise the value of their stock to make them less attractive and avoid a takeover, which usually required focusing on improving profits in the short run, often by cutting wages and jobs, just as if they had been taken over. Others bought entities they did not necessarily want or need in order to use up their idle cash in the bank, which otherwise made them tempting targets for hostile acquirers. And often the best-run companies were takeover targets, not failing ones. Thus, American businesses did indeed become lean and mean—far too much so. It became a narrowly focused revolution and the gains, when made, were short-term. The takeover movement did not create an environment that was propitious for new ideas and more risk taking—that came from more traditional breakthroughs in technology.

The takeover targets changed over the decades. In the 1970s, buying energy companies or companies that specialized in commodities seemed an appropriate hedge against inflation. A seminal acquisition was made in 1976 by General Electric, the machinery and consumer products company, long considered one of the best-managed companies in the nation, and the fifth largest company in America. Even this long-standing American giant was being pressured by the conditions of the 1970s. Its admired chairman, Reginald Jones, was determined to find a company that could protect GE's principal businesses from inflation. Jones decided to acquire Utah International, a highly profitable company that mined coal and to a lesser extent uranium, and whose earnings had been rising rapidly for a decade. When Jones announced the plans in late 1975, the proposed acquisition surprised the investment community. GE was diversified, but it never went this far afield. The friendly merger—the Utah chairman had suggested the deal to Jones—was completed toward the end of 1976 for an exchange of GE shares worth $2.2 billion, the largest merger thus far. The fees earned by advisers were enormous.

Oil companies, swimming in profits, sought to diversify. In turn, Mobil tried to put its new profits from oil prices to work by diversifying into retailing. In 1976, it paid $900 million in stock for Marcor, the newly named Montgomery Ward chain. Atlantic Richfield bought Anaconda, the copper company, to reduce its dependence on oil.

By the late 1970s and early 1980s, as inflation rose higher once again, oil-based acquisitions accounted for one third of mergers. But these giant mergers did not pay off. As inflation subsided in the 1980s, not only oil prices but most commodities prices fell. General Electric sold Utah International at a loss. Atlantic Richfield sold Anaconda. And the notion that an oil company could run a giant retailer was debunked as Mobil sold Marcor in 1985 with great relief. Companies lost but the Wall Street firms made their fees—even on the sales.

New takeover tactics were devised over these years, as acquirers and targets tried to seize the advantage. There were legal battles amid changing state and federal laws, and new, usually more aggressive bidding practices. There were intense public relations campaigns to embarrass opponents about their professional records. These new practices were given bellicose names that reflected how aggressive the hostile takeover environment had become, and perhaps the joy the protagonists took in their rough-and-tumble ways. The "Saturday night special" was a late-night cash tender for all shares; the "bear hug" was a letter to the board of directors pressuring it to find a higher bidder or risk a shareholder suit; the "scorched earth" defense publicized embarrassing information about opposition CEOs.

Even when stock prices rose in the 1980s and there were fewer bargains left, Wall Street had grown so powerful and access to cheap tax-deductible debt financing so easy that the wave of takeovers continued with only occasional pauses. In 1975, the year after the first hostile takeover, there were $12 billion in takeovers; by 1976 there were $20 billion; and by 1979 the volume had leaped to well more than $40 billion. In succeeding decades, deals would get much larger. There were deals of $10 billion in the early 1980s and as much as $25 billion in the late 1980s.

Leveraged buyout (LBO) companies led the wave at this time and raised men like Henry Kravis and George Roberts, who ran the largest LBO partnership, Kohlberg Kravis Roberts, to the Forbes 400 list of the nation's richest people. These were not acquisitions by other companies but management buyouts financed by the LBO partnerships. In an LBO, a publicly traded company is taken private by borrowing against the company's assets or future cash flow to pay off the shareholders at a handsome premium. Finkelstein's buyout of Macy's in 1986 was such an LBO.

Proponents of the LBOs generally claimed that by making the executives who ran them substantial owners in the company, they were run more efficiently. Leverage referred to the debt taken on to supplement that cash or equity and thereby multiply the size of the investment made—much like a homeowner taking a mortgage to supplement the down payment. These LBO partnerships bought the targets from shareholders, borrowing enormous sums from banks, insurance companies, and eventually through the junk bond market (junk bonds are risky securities that must pay high interest rates to attract individual investors and institutional investors like pension funds). They then either generously compensated the existing management with stock or installed new management. But debt levels were so high for LBOs, management almost always sharply reduced annual expenses, especially labor and research investment, or sold subsidiaries, to pay the annual interest rates and amortization. Academic studies of LBOs alone, where the levels of debt were typically higher than on even hostile takeovers, found that profits on average rose in the short run but fell over time, research and development funding was cut substantially, and the level of debt remained high.

Low interest rates in the late 1990s and most of the early 2000s led to a renewed boom in these LBOs. Institutional investors, from pension and trust funds to university endowments, replaced individuals as the leading investors in the partnerships. These LBO partnerships became known by the more innocent-sounding name "private equity firms." The intention, however, had always been to buy up all publicly traded shares and then take the acquired company public again by issuing new stock at higher prices.

In the late 1970s, there was more than $1 billion in fees to divide among investment bankers and lawyers. By the late 1990s and early in the new century, there was $10–20 billion in annual fees. The size of individual deals reached nearly $50 billion. A leading firm, Blackstone Group, earned enormous returns over these years from fees and the equity they themselves had in their companies, and made billionaires of its principals, Steve Schwarzman and Pete Peterson, when they took their partnership public in the spring of 2007 at nearly $30 a share. In the recession of 2008, many of Blackstone's companies' cash flows had sharply declined. Blackstone's stock plunged to $5 a share by the end of the year, only twenty months after it went public.

Flom was at the center of almost all the innovations, with Martin Lipton a worthy opponent who specialized more in defense. It was Lipton who devised the "poison pill," a tactic in which a new issue of shares was triggered making a potential takeover more difficult and expensive.

Flom remained the merger movement leader for the next thirty years. He was unrivaled in his knowledge of the technicalities of pertinent law, his judgment about how courts might rule and competitors react, and his creativity. In one year, Flom recalled, there were eighteen hostile deals and he was involved with seventeen of them.

His influence spread beyond his own firm. He urged a young, ambitious Marty Siegel, for example, who was struggling to find an opening in the market for his relatively small investment bank, Kidder Peabody, to sign up companies that seemed likely targets. Siegel got such companies to pay Kidder $75,000 a year as a retainer. In return, he would devise a takeover defense beforehand. Kidder thus became a key participant in the market.

Flom, in building one of the largest law firms in the nation, diversified far beyond takeovers. His success was the triumph of content over style. He was generally diffident, but at work he was relentless. Sometimes investment bankers would get the credit for Flom's ideas. But, as one dealmaker said during an intense negotiating session, Flom, the lawyer, was invariably the best banker in the group.

Corporations would not have been nearly as aggressive about acquiring other companies had Wall Street and the legal community led by Flom not provoked them. It was not a healthy economic process on balance. Wall Street did not otherwise provoke much constructive investment in these years, but rather discovered more certain and immediate profits by dismantling what already existed. Flom, who claimed he was just doing the bidding of the marketplace, was like all members of this small community motivated by high fees. These men were making the marketplace, not merely obeying the signals it sent out, in the efficient way Friedman and others suggested such markets worked.

Ivan Boesky

WANTING IT ALL

I nvestment bankers and corporate management made ever increasing fortunes in these years, but for much of the 1980s, it was the risk arbitrageurs who made the most money from the takeover movement that Flom had so much to do with starting. They invested in the takeover targets aggressively even in the 1970s and 1980s when few fully understood the potential for profits. As they made more profits, they provoked takeovers themselves by buying shares of likely target companies or pushing prices far higher than initial bids for these companies. Once stock prices rose due to the the arbs' buying, shareholders demanded that management find a so-called white knight to make a higher counterbid to keep the prices from falling back to their old levels. The profitability of investing in takeover targets also created a strong demand for secret corporate information—inside information—about who the next takeover target would be. A company whose stock was selling for $15 could suddenly explode to $20 or $25 on public news of a hostile bid. But trading on inside information was illegal—it amounted to stealing from unsuspecting pension funds, insurance companies, or other investors who sold stock at $15 not knowing about the takeover offer to come.

Ivan Boesky always wanted to make money, and risk arbitrage, he discovered, was the surest path to it. When an arbitrageur invested in prospective mergers and acquisitions, the risk of loss, though high, could be calculated, and the rewards enormous, especially with leverage. Boesky boldly formed a private partnership to do just that. Until then, risk arbitrage had been practiced almost only in long-standing, well-capitalized firms on Wall Street. Outsiders typically didn't want to put money at risk to invest in a process they did not fully understand. Access to information about the activity and interest of investment bankers was also an impor-

Arbitrageur Ivan Boesky, center, after sentencing for insider trading

tant advantage, even if it wasn't explicit knowledge of bids to come. Outsiders did not have access to such informal signals about corporate intentions. The degree to which the established firms traded on inside information was harder to determine. Some argued that trading on inside information did no harm, because there were no victims, but this claim was specious. As noted, an unsuspecting investor who sold shares to someone with secret information about a merger deal lost the potential profit. Inside information about takeovers was similar to the advantage real estate barons and railroad entrepreneurs had in the late 1800s when they bought land from farmers because they knew—and the farmers did not—the railroad was planning to come through.

In their defense, many major investment firms argued that they kept from their arbitrageurs pertinent information that their underwriting and research departments might have. Such so-called Chinese walls, however, were likely porous. In practice, many of these arbitrageurs talked directly to the CEOs and bankers involved in the deals. And valuable information itself was not necessarily explicit. It could be the shake of a head, the lilt of the voice, or access to a trading desk in which it was obvious that unusual volumes of shares were being bought in a particular stock. Such questionable avenues to big profits added incentives to encourage corporate acquisitions. Almost no company but the very largest was safe from acquisition by the 1980s.

Boesky, hungry for a fortune, was aggressive in his search for information to enable him to compete with, and even better, the established Wall

Street firms. He was certain they had access to inside information he did not and knew more about possible deals due to their firms' relationships on Wall Street and with corporate America.

Before Boesky came on the scene, the financial media rarely reported on risk arbitrage, and it was little understood. Traditional arbitrage began in international equity and commodities markets and was ideally riskless. The arbitrageur looked for minute discrepancies in the price of a stock that was traded internationally—say, Royal Dutch Shell—priced at one level in New York City and slightly differently in London. Risk arbitrageurs sold the high-priced shares in one market and bought the low-priced in the other. They leveraged those gains by borrowing money. Arbitrage opportunities were found in other kinds of securities as markets developed, especially in options and futures contracts on government bonds and international currencies.

Mergers gave rise to this riskier form of arbitrage. An arbitrageur could lock in a profit when one company offered shares at a premium for another. The arbs could buy the target company's shares and sell the acquirer's shares, thus locking in the spread. (They typically sold short—that is, sold shares they did not actually own but merely borrowed at an interest cost with the promise to give them back even if the price of the shares rose.) The risk was that the deal might fall through if, for example, antitrust authorities stopped the proposed merger. This was one of the questions that arose in 1975 when General Electric bid for Utah International. The proposed merger took a year to consummate while the Justice Department decided whether the merger violated the antitrust laws because GE made nuclear reactors and Utah International mined uranium. The arbitrageurs had sought legal advice and were convinced the authorities would not raise antitrust objections and therefore invested heavily in the deal. But such delays nevertheless reduced profits because they tied up valuable capital on which arbs were likely paying interest. The essence of risk arbitrage was assessing the likelihood that mergers would be consummated, when, and at what price.

Deal after deal, with few exceptions, was completed in the 1970s because stock prices were so low, management so determined, cash plentiful, more and more bank loans available, and Wall Street professionals like Flom and the persuasive battery of young ambitious investment bankers were hawking deals day and night—and making fortunes themselves.

Ivan Boesky had little else on his mind but to be rich. He became famous for saying to a college audience that greed is "healthy," a line paraphrased more famously in the movie *Wall Street*. Boesky, however, was nothing like the debonair Michael Douglas, who played the lead role in the movie. Few if any on Wall Street were. Boesky in particular was socially awkward, had a grating, artificial smile, and usually wore identical black suits; he had a dozen or so. Nor did he quite mean what the scriptwriters put in Douglas's mouth; Boesky was adapting Adam Smith's postulate about the benefits of self-interest. Milton Friedman was by then widely preaching the same virtues, as was Alan Greenspan. But Boesky was the quintessentially greedy man of his time. He wanted more money because he believed it conferred esteem and glory, and he had a bottomless need for both. He never felt he had enough money.

Boesky was born in 1938 and raised in Detroit. He was not poor as a child, but his father, William, struggled with a slowly dying business. William had once owned several restaurants, where Ivan often worked through his teenage years and into his twenties. But Detroit's inner city was running down rapidly in the 1960s as the middle class moved to the suburbs, local mass transit was reduced, and those left behind were poor, culminating in racial confrontation in 1967 during which more than forty African Americans were killed. William struggled to keep his last downtown Detroit location open, turning the dining room into a nightclub in the evenings. Eventually, he had to close this last of his outposts as well.

Nevertheless, the family was able to send the young Boesky for a year to the Auburn Hills, Michigan, prep school, Cranbrook, his mother having social ambitions for him. Boesky was dyslexic and schoolwork did not come easily, but he ground it out. He transformed himself from an overweight teenager into a winning high school wrestler, through, as one classmate and later a close friend put it, "unrivaled self-discipline." Boesky attended Clarke University, but did not graduate, and eventually earned a law degree at night at Detroit College of Law while working at his father's restaurant and club. Boesky, though, was not interested in practicing law, never seeing it as the path to wealth he was seeking.

Boesky married Seema Silberstein, an attractive and wealthy Jewish socialite. She was the younger daughter of Detroit real estate developer Ben Silberstein, who owned one of the largest office buildings in the city, among other properties. Silberstein, at the urging of his ambitious older daughter, Muriel, had also bought the Beverly Hills Hotel from a flamboyant hotelier, Hernando Courtright, who had made it glamorous before

World War II. After the war, however, it was available at a bargain price, and Silberstein rebuilt it into perhaps the most prestigious hotel in Beverly Hills in the 1960s and 1970s. Silberstein's ownership of the Hollywood jewel burnished the social image of his daughters back home in Detroit, and attracted the eager Ivan.

Seema had been smitten by Boesky's ambition and energy, and perhaps the intense attention he paid her. He found his way into the securities business in Detroit, but he felt he was not comfortable with the risks of traditional investment management or analysis, especially after the 1969 crash, because in his mind you could be right about everything in a stock, but if the market went the other way, it didn't matter. Boesky, visiting New York City, had a meeting with a boyhood neighbor and prep school classmate, who was making a lot of money in the risk arbitrage department of Bear Stearns. Returning to Detroit, Boesky told his wife how impressed he was with his friend, though at that point he had little idea of what general arbitrage involved, no less risk arbitrage. He and Seema went to the Detroit public library to research the subject.

Boesky quickly made up his mind to make risk arbitrage his profession; the rewards could be large and the risk subject to serious analysis. He got a job in 1971 on sheer brashness at a medium-sized brokerage firm, Edwards & Hanly, convincing the management he could develop a risk arbitrage practice. Most important, Boesky had found an expert tutor, Steve Sherman, an iconoclastic and brilliant head of risk arbitrage at Paine Webber, who could advise him daily on how to invest in deals. Sherman had a volatile personality, constantly shouting at his assistants, and was determined to thumb his nose at Wall Street traditions, sometimes wearing orange suits to the office, for which he was tolerated because he made so much money for the firm. Boesky also became a shouter at work. Sherman, Boesky's age, had been trained at Goldman Sachs by his mentor, the future head of the firm, Gus Levy. Sherman said he liked Boesky, one iconoclast attracted to another.

During the bear market of 1974, Edwards & Hanly, like many other brokerage firms, went out of business. But Boesky had always wanted to be independent and set about raising money from his wife's well-off family and from her many Detroit friends, promising to open the door for them to the closely guarded moneymaking secrets of the best Wall Street firms. This, in fact, was true. He raised enough to open a partnership mostly consisting of Seema's contacts.

The key to Boesky's future wealth was the way he structured the partnership. As the lead, or general, partner, he kept half of the profits for himself, returning half to his partner investors. He earned no money if the firm did not make a profit. But even so, a 50 percent share was more than audacious. In investment partnerships, the managing firm typically took only 20 percent. More to the point, Boesky did not share in the losses, and was thus motivated to take substantial risk.

In the early years of the 1970s takeover movement, risk arbitrage profits were the low-lying fruit of Wall Street, partly because there were still few firms doing it and because the collapse of conglomerates in the 1960s also thinned the ranks of risk arbitrageurs. The GE takeover of Utah International was the investment of a lifetime for Boesky. GE offered stock worth $61 for every share of Utah, but Utah's stock rose only to $49. The difference would be profit if the deal went through. There was the risk that antitrust authorities would kill the deal, as noted, but legal advisers thought it unlikely. The shares GE offered totaled $2 billion and there was simply not yet enough investment capital to drive the price closer to the GE bid.

Boesky frantically tried to raise more money to buy up shares. He tried to borrow as well. GE and Utah signed an agreement to merge for the equivalent at the time of $65 in GE stock in May 1976—making the deal a near-certainty—but Utah still only traded at $50. Boesky kept raising money as best he could to invest in the Utah shares, certain he would cash in near $65. And he was right. He made a fortune, but if he had had more capital, he would have made much more. He thought there might never again be a deal as profitable. In later years, such easy opportunities dissipated as the possibility of making almost certain money attracted much more capital.

By 1975 and 1976, bidding wars became common. With stock prices still low, target companies often sought a friendly counterbid to keep hostile management from taking over the company. The investment banks lined up potential white knights before bidding contests even began, and sometimes the arbs themselves suggested possible counterbidders. The more frenetic the bidding was, the higher the likely takeover price, and the bigger the profits for the arbs. In these years, Bethlehem Copper made a hostile tender for Valley Camp Coal, only to be outbid by the white knight Quaker State Oil Refining, which Valley Camp's management favored. MCA, the entertainment company, bid for Sea World but lost to a higher bid from book publisher Harcourt Brace Jovanovich.

The most profitable bidding contest for Boesky was between Harry Gray's United Technologies and J. Ray McDermott, an oil firm, which were in combat for Babcock & Wilcox, a nuclear reactor maker—again an energy-related target. There were eleven bids over six months, McDermott finally emerging as the victor by making a bid totaling $750 million, twice the value of Babcock before the contest began. A large part of this was profit to the arbs. Now the investment banks scoured lists of companies for potential suitors, white knights, and takeover targets.

The larger firms had particular advantages that Boesky did not. Goldman Sachs was an example of how interrelated operations could help each other. As we have seen, Steve Friedman actively defended takeover targets, and Robert Rubin ran the risk arbitrage department. The firm had an enormous trading desk, making it privy to the buying and selling trends on the Street. The firms, to repeat, insisted information of a critical nature was not passed around the firm, from one department to another, but communicating more informal information was difficult to stop.

In the 1980s, as the size of takeovers dwarfed the deals of the 1970s, the new risk arbitrageurs were key members of the network that enabled the takeover movement to expand far beyond anyone's expectations, and as all the participants made more and more money, there was in turn more money to finance bigger and bolder mergers.

The arbs themselves bought shares to force up a target's stock price above an initial offer. They thus raised shareholder expectations, and, as noted, if a new bidder was not found at a higher price, shareholders were easily dissatisfied. The arbs were not neutral bystanders and they contributed greatly to the increasing activity and growing size of mergers. Management was often forced to do its best to find a higher bidder to appease shareholders. Ideally, they would drive the company into the hands of a friendly suitor who would retain top managers, and give them substantial stock options. Sometimes the arbs would buy shares of potential takeover targets before any bid was announced, trying to put them in play, and forcing management to seek a bidder or be renounced by shareholders as not seeking an opportunity for stock price appreciation. As the arbs made more money, they could drive still more hostile contests at ever higher bids.

Many independent arbitrage partnerships were created following Boesky's lead. An increasing number of established firms started new risk arbitrage operations. Several other firms besides Goldman, including Salomon, had both large merger banking departments and aggressive arbitrage departments. Commercial banks, with funds to lend, due partly to Walter Wriston's aggressive maneuvers, became generous lenders to companies making bids, especially since they could charge handsome interest rates and high fees per loan. In the 1980s, Michael Milken almost single-handedly developed the junk bond market—where the bonds of riskier companies traded—which was used to finance the largest takeovers to that point.

In the 1980s, Boesky hit jackpots in the oil mergers in which giant firms like Conoco, General America, Gulf, and Phillips Petroleum were bought for billions of dollars each. The price paid for Gulf alone was $13 billion. The Reagan administration essentially gutted the antitrust units of both the Justice Department and the Federal Trade Commission, and there were few inhibitions to consolidate giant oil companies or firms in other industries, either. RJR, the former R.J. Reynolds, bought Nabisco, and Philip Morris, seeing a limited future for their tobacco business, bought General Foods. Sears bought the brokerage firm Dean Witter, lighting the glow in Wriston's eye that one-stop shopping for financial products had arrived. In 1984, there were roughly $120 billion worth of mergers, in 1985 there were more than $150 billion worth. For Boesky, the vein of money he tapped had become far deeper than he could have imagined.

One set of mergers in particular stood out. Few believed a television network could ever be taken over if the Federal Communications Commission had anything to say about it. Broadcasting rights were given free to the networks and considered a national treasure. But in the 1980s and 1990s even NBC and ABC were bought by Disney and GE respectively at handsome prices. Reagan's FCC approved the acquisitions.

Boesky's determination and self-discipline defined him. He gained weight easily so he hardly ate all week, drinking endless cups of coffee. According to his wife, Seema, he then gorged himself on Twinkies and Devil Dogs on the weekends. For a headache, he took at most half an aspirin. Dressing precisely the same way every day in his custom-made London suits was part of this self-discipline. His personal ambition kept growing and he never satisfied it. He was constantly calling CEOs, analysts, and traders to come up with any morsel of information that might give him an edge.

Boesky was ultimately caught paying investment bankers outright for valuable information about forthcoming deals. Boesky's downfall began with a young investment banker, Dennis Levine, who had difficulty at first finding a job in the alluring takeover business. He was finally hired in 1981 by Lehman Brothers, despite an unimpressive background by the firm's standards. He had not attended a graduate business school, let alone a prestigious one, but the Lehman executives were impressed by his eagerness.

Levine apparently never had any intention of playing by the rules. He secretly started buying shares based on inside information at Lehman and passed on tips to a handful of others on the Street, from whom he got tips in return. Levine then talked himself into a job at Drexel Burnham in 1985 where Milken had developed his junk bond business. There, he made contact with Boesky, a regular Drexel client. Boesky had previously refused to take his calls, but he was now eager for Drexel information, and Levine was ready to pass along valuable tips to the legendary man who traded with little hesitation before any announcement of a deal, seemingly oblivious to the chances of ever being caught by the SEC. For insurance, Levine built up a secret $10 million getaway fund in a Bahamian account.

At Levine's request, Boesky made an explicit arrangement to pay him for his tips: 5 percent of Boesky's profits if Levine informed him about a takeover target in which Boesky had as yet bought no shares, having had no idea the company might be in play, and 1 percent on a tip in which he was already a buyer. If the merger fell through, Levine would pay back some of the losses Boesky incurred when the price of the target fell.

By 1985, Levine's frequent trading on inside information, and the related trading of his insider associates, could no longer be easily hidden from the authorities. In the spring of 1986, he was arrested, and when he saw how strong the government case was, he made a deal to name those to whom he gave tips in exchange for a lighter sentence. The biggest catch was Boesky. Levine was sentenced to two years in prison, paid a substantial fine, and returned $11.6 million, substantially all his profits, to the SEC.

When Boesky was subpoenaed that fall of 1986, he, too, immediately named others in exchange for leniency. He agreed to wear a wire recorder and meet with those he had named to acquire more direct incriminating evidence. Among the most prominent was the former Kidder Peabody banker Martin Siegel, now with Drexel. On arrest, Siegel admitted to taking $700,000 in cash on street corners from a Boesky messenger in return for tips since 1981. Siegel also agreed to implicate others in order to reduce his sentence, naming an arbitrageur at Goldman Sachs, Robert Freeman, a protégé of Robert Rubin's, and colleagues at Kidder. Freeman pleaded guilty to one felony count, and in his statement to the court, as recounted by financial writer James Stewart, Freeman described a sordid Wall Street world in which information unavailable to others was readily passed on, even at prestigious Goldman.

Boesky served three years, but the biggest catch was Michael Milken, whom Boesky implicated for securities law violations. Milken, who had by then become the richest man on Wall Street by selling junk bonds, ultimately pleaded guilty on six counts and was sentenced to ten years in prison. Boesky's penalties came to $100 million, and Milken paid approximately $1.3 billion in fines and restitution of profits. For his cooperation, Martin Siegel was sentenced to only two months in prison, but was banned from the securities business forever, as were Boesky and Milken. Siegel moved to Florida, Boesky to California.

The year before scandal toppled Boesky, *Financial World* reported that he earned $100 million, more than anyone else on the Street. That year, he also made the Forbes 400 list of the richest men and women in America, worth according to some estimates $200 million. But he was near the bottom of the list. At home that evening, he hung his head low, resting it on the dining room table for a long time. Finally, he told his concerned wife that he would never let her down like that again, never again be at the bottom of the list.

Boesky was widely disliked on Wall Street, but not merely for his aggressive personality and publicity seeking. He opened up risk arbitrage to outside competitors and brought sunshine to a Wall Street practice many preferred to keep in the dark. With no advantages, this man made a fortune on his own; this, too, generated envy. But he was a bandit, and just because he was caught, banditry did not die on Wall Street, even after Boesky's activities alerted the authorities. Meantime, much financial damage was also done in the open, under the glare of increasingly negligent regulators.

6

Walter Wriston II

The takeover movement was the most aggressive response to the strained conditions of the economy and persistently low stock prices of the 1970s. But new ideas flourished in other areas and would change the way Wall Street made money radically. Inflated commodities prices and volatile interest rates, as well as the newly floating international currencies, created opportunities in derivative securities—futures contracts and options that would enable buyers and sellers to lock in future prices of all kinds of assets, including, gold, silver, wheat, soybeans, petroleum, and now interest rates, currencies, and stocks. Businesses could thus hedge against rapid, damaging movements in the prices of bonds, commodities, and currencies, and investors could speculate in their price movements. These transactions were completed for a small cash down payment (the rest of the money borrowed) or at a fraction of the actual purchase price of the asset, which led to the development of new investment strategies and techniques to facilitate these activities. These securities were called derivatives because they were based on prices of other securities, currencies, or commodities.

Derivatives quickly became popular and exchanges were formed to trade them. In 1972, the International Monetary Market was founded to trade futures contracts in currencies, establishing trading rules and making the price of transactions visible to market participants. The Chicago Board Options Exchange was opened in 1973; previously options had been traded over-the-counter. Agricultural futures had long been trading on the Chicago Mercantile Exchange, enabling farmers and food processors to lock in prices. Now financial futures were also traded on the "Merc"—futures contracts on Treasury bonds, for example, in which an investor could speculate on the direction of interest rates or a business could lock in

Walter Wriston, at far left, with President Ronald Reagan and his economic advisers, 1980, including Milton Friedman, second from the left, and Alan Greenspan, to Reagan's left

a future borrowing cost. So popular did derivatives trading become compared to trading in traditional stocks that, in 1973, a seat on the Merc sold for $112,500, far more than a seat on the New York Stock Exchange, which now sold for only $95,000 compared to more than $1 million in earlier years.

There were other thriving innovations that changed the nature of the financial industry. Mutual funds, which bought portfolios of stocks and bonds, in which even small investors could place their money, were also expanding into new areas of investment. Established before World War II, new mutual fund companies such as Dreyfus and Oppenheimer now had many different kinds of funds under one roof. The creation by the federal government in 1974 of tax-advantaged Individual Retirement Accounts (IRAs) made mutual funds a still more popular investment as individuals sought places to invest for their retirement. Among the most important innovations were index funds, which provided a way to buy a piece of a stock market average, like the S&P 500. This was a way around the perennially bullish and often wrong recommendations by Wall Street professionals to buy individual stocks. Most of the new index funds, usually computer-driven, charged low management fees and eliminated the high upfront sales charges.

An especially effective innovation was the money market mutual fund, which provided savers with much higher interest rates than were available at banks, ultimately circumventing Regulation Q. As interest rates rose during the credit crunch of 1966 and again in 1969 and 1970, as we have seen, the banks were prevented by Regulation Q from passing on the higher rates to smaller savers. The negotiable CDs launched by Walter Wriston in the 1960s, and now by other banks, required a minimum investment of $100,000, prohibitive for most investors. Treasury bills were also subject to a minimum purchase and a broker's commission, and were not easy for a small and infrequent investor to buy or sell. With interest rates high, two investment bankers, Henry Brown and Bruce Bent, saw an opportunity. At first, they looked for small banks around the country that weren't, for local technical reasons, subject to Regulation Q, and channeled savers' money to them. But this was a laborious and low-profit business. As Bent put it: "I said to my partner, 'Why not start a mutual fund?' And he answered, 'I know nothing about them.' " They had struck on a far better idea: a new fund to provide high interest rates to small savers by pooling deposits and buying high-interest bank CDs and Treasury securities in bulk. The fund passed on the higher rates to its small investors for an annual management fee. Savers could also use the funds like checking accounts.

Brown and Bent started their new fund, the Reserve Fund, in 1972. It had no retail organization, neither branches nor salespeople, and at the outset got few takers. An article describing the fund in the business section of *The New York Times* in early 1973 made the difference. Small investors could earn as much as several percentage points more than in a bank for little risk, according to the article. The deposits were not federally insured but the Reserve Fund placed the money in major banks or Treasury bills. Within a week of the *Times* article, the Reserve Fund had $1 million in deposits, within two months, $10 million, and by the end of 1973, a year in which interest rates rose sharply, they had $100 million.

Many bankers were furious that the Reserve Fund took low-cost savers from them, restricted as they were by Regulation Q. At a dinner at the Waldorf-Astoria in New York, John McGillicuddy, the chairman of Manufacturers Hanover, "had to be physically restrained from attacking me," recalled Bent. But Wriston saw an opportunity. For one thing, such funds invested in his large CDs. More important, the growth of the Reserve Fund and the quick entry into the market of other money market funds encouraged some bankers at smaller institutions to join Wriston's lobbying efforts against Regulation Q. Until then, small banks supported Regulation Q because it limited the large big-city competitors, which might be willing to pay more for depositor money than the smaller banks could afford.

The impact of another major new development that profoundly changed the financial community was not clear until the 1980s. Bankers at Salomon Brothers experimented in ways to package conventional home mortgages into simple bonds that appealed to pension funds, investment managers, insurance companies, and other investors around the world. The government-sponsored enterprises Fannie Mae and Freddie Mac were already doing a version of this with their high-quality mortgages. Salomon, however, began buying mortgages from thrifts or specialized mortgage brokers, packaging them into simple-seeming new vehicles (including Fannie Mae and Freddie Mac issues), and selling bonds with the mortgages as collateral. The ratings agencies awarded most of these new bonds high ratings yet the yields on these mortgage-backed securities were higher than equivalently rated corporate or government bonds. Over time, "securitization" grew dramatically, making banks and thrifts obsolete as providers of mortgages, drawing literally trillions of dollars more into the housing markets. In the 2000s, it was abuse of this procedure, the apotheosis of the age of greed, that led to the financial collapse of 2008.

Despite the growing competition, Wriston was riding high. It seemed as if all the new innovation energized him, even when it increased competition for the bank. He pursued new avenues and government was responding to demands for more bank alternatives. State banking authorities soon allowed some savings banks to issue NOW accounts, a negotiable order of withdrawal, which paid interest on the equivalent of a checking account, and they were soon legalized nationally. Arthur Burns had already loosened some restrictions on Regulation Q during the Penn Central crisis, and more loosening came in the late 1970s. Wriston pushed his Eurodollar financings aggressively, and made raising money for foreign companies and even nations a key profit center for the bank, often joining with other banks to provide large loans. The first such syndicated financing was for the Shah of Iran.

Meantime, the bank holding company (an umbrella corporation) for First National City, Citicorp, whose name was changed in 1974 from First National City Corp., was able to buy a management consulting company, banking operations in England, a consumer finance company in the United States, and banks in other parts of New York State. Some of these were folded into the bank itself, a subsidiary of the holding company. Wriston pushed hard into consumer banking, hoping to make profitable personal loans, even with rates high. Ideally, he wanted branches everywhere, but banking laws prohibited interstate branches. He also let the bank's prime lending rate float to ward off constant criticism whenever he raised it. Now, he pegged this rate to a Treasury bill rate, letting the market decide.

His currency trading desk was making substantial profits as well. Wriston had a part in convincing the administration, with the support of his friend George Shultz, then treasury secretary, to unfix the U.S. dollar. Like another of his friends, Milton Friedman, Wriston insisted that changing prices would not affect exchange of goods because widespread currency trading (with the use of derivatives) would stabilize the price of the currency. The more buyers and sellers there were, the less volatility in price there would be, he argued.

Wriston also lent more aggressively to domestic entities, including real estate companies (especially real estate investment trusts, a real estate version of a mutual fund). He ran the amount of capital the bank held against assets to unusually low levels to improve his return on equity, maintaining that banks did not need minimum capital requirements set by government because his bankers knew a lot more about the riskiness of their loans than government examiners did.

At first, more risk turned into more profit—in 1973, some $200 million, an all-time high and more than any other bank in the nation. The stock price rose to more than $51 before the stock market slid sharply later that year. Although some observers were already worried about the quality of his loans, the business magazine *Dun's Review* named First National City one of the five best-managed companies in the country. Before Wriston, it was unimaginable a bank would be on a list of best-managed companies. In the first half of the 1970s, Wriston's bank was achieving the level of profits he had earlier promised Wall Street, an annual growth rate of 15 percent.

Wriston scored another major victory in 1974. Arthur Burns began to raise rates again in 1973 to suppress inflation. But as usual, funds dried up rapidly the next year, with likely recessionary consequences. So Wriston took the opportunity to launch something entirely new for a commercial bank. He would issue a five-year note with a rate of interest not limited by Regulation Q but floated with other market rates, reducing the risk for First National City because the rate it paid would go up and down with the rate at which it could invest or lend. The initial plan was to raise $1 billion in amounts as little as $1,000, meant to attract small investors. As he was wont to do, Wriston issued the notes first and asked the Fed for its approval afterward. There was a congressional uproar, but eventually, in light of the recession, Wriston won Fed approval, and congressional criticism quieted down. Investment bankers did not fail to notice that Wriston's commercial bank was effectively underwriting its own loans. Wriston now had a foot in the door once slammed shut by the Glass-Steagall legislation of the New Deal that separated underwriting from commercial banking.

Burns continually raised red flags about the adequacy of Wriston's bank capital, and Wriston kept fending him off. Ralph Nader, the consumer critic, complained about the number of bankers in general, including at First National City, who sat on the boards of the companies to which their banks lent money, as well as how few women and African Americans worked for them. Wright Patman, the Democratic head of the House Banking Committee, an old-fashioned populist, was particularly concerned about the growing power of banks, especially since they now managed so much pension fund money, again investing in the very companies to which they lent.

But Wriston was undeterred, and his greatest victory was about to come, one that would create hundreds of billions of dollars of new debt, funneled through his and other banks. The Arab oil embargo and oil price increases of 1973 and 1974 severely strained the international financial system. As much as $100 billion a year now flowed from the United States, Japan, Europe, and South America into a relative handful of coffers belonging to the oil sheiks, a few Arab governments, and Venezuela. The petrodollars, as they were now called, had to be recirculated. If they stayed uninvested, under, so to speak, a nation's mattress, the world's economies could collapse. Alarm spread that the oil cartel countries had too much power.

The developing and poorer nations were severely penalized by the higher oil prices, and some proposed that the Arab oil countries finance the long-term economic development of the poorer nations with loans and investments on low-cost terms. Furthermore, many thought the World Bank, the International Monetary Fund, central bankers, and the government treasuries of the developed world should also help arrange the massive recycling to the developing world—known as less developed countries or LDCs. Paul Volcker, still serving in the Treasury Department, helped set up a group at the World Bank to do so. Even Gerald Ford's chief of staff, Alexander Haig, advocated U.S. government involvement in the recycling of the money.

Wriston argued vehemently that the large private banks had the capacity to handle the task of recirculating the tens of billions of dollars more efficiently than government-sponsored international institutions could. Burns, though privately derisive of private banks' recycling, publicly supported the idea. ("Recycling. Blah. These are bad debts," he privately said to a colleague more than once.) The Arab oil nations seemed uncomfortable making long-term loans to LDCs, and would not do so without a strong commitment from the White House, while many Arab investors and heads of state preferred the security of America's largest banks. As one International Monetary Fund economist later conjectured, they knew the U.S. government would not allow any of these commercial banks to fail if the LDC loans went bad. The U.S. banks also believed that ultimately their government would help them collect their money from the LDCs if necessary.

Wriston had strong support for private recycling from Treasury Secretary Shultz, with whom he often discussed the issues. In a brazen act, Shultz unilaterally ended official government limits on making U.S. bank loans to these nations just before he resigned from the Nixon administration in early 1974. The decision opened the floodgates. "After that, you could hardly find a banker at home," said one economist. Bank lending to the LDCs quickly soared. William Simon, Shultz's replacement, showed only contempt for those at the World Bank and within the administration who wanted the government to have a part in the recycling.

The dominance by private banks of the recycling of the petrodollars was a historic event—a triumph of free market ideology over practical good sense, then and later—and it came about largely because Wriston started the process before government gathered the forces to stop it. With Haig and Volcker, and perhaps Burns, against it, it was not a sure thing. The approval of Wriston's good friend Shultz was decisive, but Wriston was already pushing the lending limits before Shultz's decision, and had the in-house capability to expand rapidly. He had branches around the world, as well as a strong team of international lending officers. "We were ready to go," said one of Wriston's bankers. "Having set up the machinery, he was pleased to see it in operation."

Wriston took Arab deposits and lent them out aggressively to corporate clients in the poorer nations but mostly to their governments, especially in South America. The bank not only made money on the substantial spread between the cost of money it received from the oil exporters and the interest charged the developing nations, but it also made large fees immediately on each loan it closed, and these flowed unencumbered to the bottom line.

The paperwork for the loans was usually drawn up before Wriston's bankers arrived in the nations' capitals. Officials only had to sign on the dotted line.

The other banks now had to catch up. David Rockefeller, chairman of First National City's main rival, Chase Manhattan, at first wanted to proceed cautiously, warning that the banks would make bad loans. Wriston had heard this before, and said time and again his lending officers knew better than to make bad loans. Never mind that colossal errors of judgment concerning Penn Central had been made so recently. And the poorer nations needed the money quickly. Yet even First National City employees believed some of the projects they backed were fanciful. Borrowing nations like Zaire, Bolivia, Turkey, and Argentina were soon in trouble and could not repay. Wriston had to reschedule their loans. But by 1976, as growth in Western economies and Japan rebounded, economies in most of the LDCs also improved, allowing them to meet their repayment schedules. Inflation was enabling them to sell their minerals and other commodities at higher prices. So, for the time being, LDC lending stayed profitable. For the thirteen largest U.S. banks, international lending accounted for one third of profits in 1973, nearly half by 1975, and three quarters of profits in 1976. Foreign lending accounted for an even higher proportion of Wriston's profits than for other banks. As competition in LDC loans increased, the spread between the cost of funds and the rate charged the borrowers narrowed, but fees charged per loan were so high that, as Paul Volcker later said, aggressive lending was undiminished.

Many of Citibank's domestic loans made earlier in the 1970s were coming up bad, however, even as the U.S. economy started to grow again by mid-1975 and into 1976. Wriston, who had lent more to Penn Central than anyone else, had been still more aggressive in making bad loans. In particular, the loans to the formerly hot citizens band radio makers, to tanker owners whose business had boomed and now collapsed as the quantity of oil used fell with higher prices, and especially to high-flying real estate companies now come down to earth, were turning sour. In addition, several other large creditors went bankrupt, including the retail giant W.T. Grant and the controversial investment firm Equity Funding. New York City nearly went bankrupt as well. Despite the stronger economy, in 1977, Citibank reported its first loss since the Depression. In 1977, *BusinessWeek* announced that Citibank had already seen the end of its headiest days. It was largely true. Wriston's brilliant run was over. Far more difficult days lay ahead.

Volcker was surprised that the aggressive petrodollar recycling of the mid-1970s had been going fairly smoothly. Through the late 1970s, Wriston insisted that sovereign nations did not go broke and that they fully understood they had to pay back their debt in order to retain access to international financing. Wriston paraded this most famously self-interested of his comments in a *New York Times* op-ed piece. Treasury Secretary Simon praised the U.S. banks for their gallant efforts to recycle the oil debt. In 1974, foreign loans to developing countries by private banks totaled only $44 billion. By the end of 1979, lending totaled some $233 billion.

But the main reason the lending of the petrodollars initially went better than expected, as mentioned earlier, was rapidly rising inflation, which reduced the burden of debt payments. The prices LDCs received for their exports of commodities and occasional manufactures went up at a faster rate than the interest rate they paid on their loans. The record of repayment, therefore, did not reflect the health of these nations, or the perspicacity of the Citibank loan officers. The second round of international lending that began in 1979 soon put the banks into a serious hole.

In late 1978, local strikes curtailed the flow of oil from Iran, the world's fourth largest producer, evidence of growing anger at the Shah's rule. Gas lines formed in the United States, shocking Americans. The Shah was forced from government in January 1979. Over the period, the price of oil more than doubled to roughly $18 a barrel, adding another upward dose of inflation in America, where gasoline prices rose accordingly.

Beginning in 1979, the banks, led as usual by Citibank, enthusiastically lent the new cycle of petrodollars to the LDCs. After all, the first round that began in 1973 and 1974 had gone fairly well. Now, however, the loans were becoming more reckless. In some cases, as with Brazil, Western and Japanese commercial banks were lending so that the countries could merely pay the interest they owed them. Then, inflation turned down sharply, no longer carrying these countries along.

In 1979, President Jimmy Carter named Volcker chairman of the Federal Reserve. Volcker vowed above all to stop the inflation that was now running at double-digit annual rates. Few, including Wriston, and his young executive vice president, John Reed, believed Volcker would persist. They had heard this rhetoric before. Even if Volcker succeeded, no one anticipated the height of the interest rate hikes to come.

At first, Wriston supported the battle against inflation, but the Friedman sympathizer, who believed the Fed should keep the money supply growing at a slow and steady rate, had no idea that it would result in an unprecedented rise in interest rates. Neither did Friedman. He had all along thought any recessionary effects would be minor, as did his more extreme disciples in the new rational expectations school, who stressed that people so well anticipated government policy that they neutralized its worst consequences. Volcker himself later said that he did not realize rates would rise as high as they did. For a while, economies grew even as the rates rose. But finally the high rates created the deepest recession in the United States to that point since the Great Depression.

The extreme bank irresponsibility that occurred in 1979 and the following two years can only be explained by a combination of the greedy pursuit of profits and the simplistic assumption that the past success with recycling would repeat itself. The banks failed to realize that a global economic collapse could damage all the LDCs simultaneously, an analytical error that would be repeated time and again in different markets in years to come. "We had set limits, long and short, on each country," said Lewis Preston, the head of J.P. Morgan. "We didn't look at the whole. That clearly was a mistake." Now most of the LDCs were defaulting at the same time.

It took time for observers to notice. The February 1980 issue of the respected magazine *Euromoney* called Citibank's 1979 performance "a triumph." A Citibank executive insisted to *The Wall Street Journal* a year later that recycling is still "a very manageable picture overall."

Citibank had again lent irresponsibly at home in the late 1970s, driven by Wriston's mandate. In 1977, the bank established a profit-sharing program based on the company's stock price and everyone seemed determined to add to the bottom line. The result was a new level of bad loans and, in the early 1980s, the risky domestic loan portfolio started producing losses. Some foreign loans were at last beginning to produce losses as well, although the worst was still to come. In 1980, Citibank lost a stunning $450 million. In 1981, Standard & Poor's downgraded Citicorp's debt rating (the rating of the bank holding company) from triple-A. Moody's followed suit a few months later.

But it was Mexico's troubles that broke the dam. By late 1981, oil prices were falling, and consumer price inflation was receding in the United States. Mexico, in particular, a highly indebted oil exporter and one of Citibank's favorite lending clients, looked like it would soon be in dire trouble. Brazil's so-called manufacturing miracle no longer benefited from high and rising export prices, and it was also a major Citibank debt client.

In 1982, the developing nations found themselves in a serious squeeze. Their exports were fetching sharply lower prices and the global recession reduced worldwide demand for their goods. In August 1982, Mexican treasury officials visited Washington to inform their American counterparts that they couldn't meet their debt payments. Volcker immediately cut interest rates (he claimed he had started to do so before the crisis), and put together a rescue package of loans with Jacques de Larosière, head of the International Monetary Fund, the organization created in 1944 under the Bretton Woods agreement to make loans to distressed nations. It was an admirable feat. Volcker was able through complex manipulations to make well more than $1.5 billion available to Mexico—a bridge loan to stave off immediate collapse—in expectation that the major private banks that were now facing enormous losses would put up a substantial amount of longer-term funding. De Larosière threatened that the IMF would not contribute to the initial rescue unless the commercial banks promised to put up $5 billion in additional funding. After haggling, the banks ultimately agreed. They had little choice—economic collapse in South America and widespread defaults would have endangered the survival of some of them. Because of Volcker's bailout, and de Larosière's ultimatum to the banks, a catastrophe was avoided. But LDCs' economies did not recover until the next decade, the banks holding bad loans on their books all the while rather than reducing terms for repayment, even as Volcker kept cutting interest rates in light of the steep recession.

Volcker was determined to take emergency measures in 1982 and 1983 because the LDC debt, not large in itself compared to the world economy, was concentrated in a dozen or so large commercial banks. He feared the bad debts in a few of them could take down the entire banking system. The commercial banks were in his mind "too big to fail."

Wriston had long bridled at the regulations that kept him from offering a wider array of consumer services. In 1981, Ronald Reagan now president, there were major alliances made among brokers, insurance companies, and traditional retailers, confident the weakened antitrust departments of the Reagan administration would not challenge such mergers. Sears bought the Realtor Coldwell Banker, and multi-branch retail stockbroker Dean Witter. Prudential Insurance bought Bache Securities. American Express bought Shearson Loeb Rhoades. Wriston saw all this as the beginning at last of a true one-stop shopping revolution, but all these mergers ultimately failed to work out.

Wriston retired in 1984 and named John Reed, his protégé, to replace him. He had put Reed in charge of consumer business in the 1970s, but Reed had only made a major success of the ATM machine. As Reed lost a lot of money in the other consumer ventures, he nevertheless remained Wriston's favorite. Wriston was proud that he did not seek employees whose first interest was to make a personal fortune. Although Wriston was the first banker to make more than $1 million a year, he was never comfortable with the Wall Street investment bankers to whom this was a pittance. He specifically wanted Citibank executives to put the company first and principally to enjoy the adventure in entrepreneurial free market banking on which he had embarked. Reed, thoughtful and unflashy, was like him, he thought. But Reed was not truly interested in the bank's bread-and-butter business, lending, and knew little about LDC debt.

Wriston lived a free market charade at Citicorp's helm, strongly opposing the federal bailouts of Chrysler in 1978 and Continental Illinois in 1984, for example, while his own bank was saved by timely and often urgent government interventions. The Fed frequently lowered interest rates and opened the doors to enable the banks to borrow needed reserve when the banks were in trouble, in particular during the Penn Central crisis of 1970, the New York City crisis of 1975, in which President Ford hesitantly provided funds to the city, and the 1982 Mexican crisis. In later years, Wriston insisted the LDC debts worked out, but they in fact weighed heavily on his bank profits for years after he left until Reed finally took a hefty loss on the books.

As we have seen, Wriston had won battle after battle with the government. In another such battle, he successfully fought SEC attempts in 1974 to force banks to put loans on their books at market value, then called current value accounting and later "mark to market." If the SEC had won the battle, Wriston would have had to mark down the value of his domestic and LDC loans, taking substantial losses. He claimed no one would make risky loans if the accounting rule were in place. According to journalist Phillip Zweig, he even helped "orchestrate" the removal of the SEC chairman Sandy Burton, who had supported the changes.

The battle of his life was over the New Deal's Regulation Q, and before he retired, he had a complete victory. He strongly lobbied the Carter administration to eliminate what remained of Regulation Q, and, in 1980, the Democratic president supported a bill to end what remained of the regulation gradually over a six-year period. The Depository Institutions Deregulation and Monetary Control Act of 1980 was passed by a strong majority of a Democratic Congress. Two years later, Volcker's high interest rates so hobbling banks and savings and loan associations (thrifts), Regulation Q was eliminated entirely to save the thrifts. That year, Congress passed the Garn-St. Germain bill, named after Republican senator Jake Garn and Democratic representative Fernand St. Germain, to end altogether these New Deal restraints on interest payments paid to savers to help replenish the thrifts by allowing them to pay higher interest rates to attract savings accounts and in turn enable them to invest in areas other than mortgages.

President Reagan had offered Wriston the position of treasury secretary, but he turned it down. He had previously turned down the position in 1974 during the Ford administration. He knew he had more power as an outsider than as an insider—he was, in fact, an outsider who truly was an insider. He strongly favored Reagan's early tax cuts and believed in supply side economics, claiming deficits would fall, not rise, as taxes were cut, because tax cuts would generate so much income growth that additional tax revenues would compensate for initial losses. Like Friedman, he wanted to stop inflation above all else, and supported Volcker's efforts to do so. When interest rates soared, however, and Citibank's own survival was at stake because borrowers couldn't meet their interest payments, he turned against Volcker and did not support Volcker for reappointment in 1981.

It was Wriston's luck that 1983, his last full year in office, was a strong year for the economy and Citibank generated handsome earnings. He left much admired throughout the country, while Reed inherited a hobbled company, many of his borrowers struggling to survive. After the Volcker rescue package of 1982 and 1983, the LDC debts remained heavy burdens for Reed. The Reagan Treasury did not try to force the banks to write down or reschedule the debt to make it easier for the LDCs to repay it, but allowed them to wait it out, hoping, as were the major banks, that eventual strengthening of the economies abroad would turn the lingering debts into solid financing without harming the banks. The LDC debt festered and, in 1987, Reed decided to get Wriston's monkey off his back by taking the large loss on the LDC debt that his predecessor had resisted. It was a $3 billion write-off, and it shocked the banking community. Only in 1989 did George H. W. Bush's treasury secretary Nicholas Brady demand a successful reduction and rescheduling of LDC debt, partly at the banks' expense.

Least noticed was the plight of the LDC borrowers themselves, especially in Latin America. They had been driven into steep recession, plagued by enormous unemployment and countless bankruptcies, forced to make critical cutbacks on public investment in health and education—all to meet their outsize debt service requirements. These were the countries Wriston insisted he was helping to grow. The income per person after inflation in almost all the LDC countries with high levels of debt was lower in 1989 than in 1981.

Citibank under Reed fell in line with most of the new financing fashions. It made large risky loans to finance LBOs in the late 1980s. Many of these acquisitions failed. It lent to the most glamorous real estate investors of the period, including Donald Trump and the Reichmann family of Canada, then real estate crashed. In 1990, the U.S. economy sank into recession and some of Citibank's own bonds were downgraded to junk status. In 1991, Reed took other write-downs for bad debts and reported an $850 million loss for the year.

During the recession, Reed had slashed expenses, fired tens of thousands of employees, and made Citibank a more cautious and conservative lender, but Alan Greenspan cut interest rates sharply beginning in 1991, producing an economic recovery. Citibank returned to profitability. Now profits returned with economic recovery. By the mid-1990s, Reed had remade his reputation and saved the bank's independence, but he was still not certain the giant bank could survive without a major partner.

Ronald Reagan

THE MAKING OF AN IDEOLOGY

I n the 1960s, Ronald Reagan, well into his fifties, became the political
leader of the conservative movement. To almost everyone's surprise, the
former actor won election as governor of California in 1966, even as political conservatives were defeated around him. One of his main strengths had
been his understanding of the needs and fears of working people, of which
he never lost sight. Sympathizing with them, he could convince them of his
views, even if his policies ultimately conspired against them. But Reagan
made economic want and frustration a moral issue in ways only Democrats had before him in the twentieth century. To this, he added religious
rhetoric and blind conviction in an American providential land. Early in
his life, big business was the simple, undiluted enemy of the American
working man; he was a fully committed advocate of the New Deal. By the
early 1950s, big government had become in his mind the equally simple
enemy, and the New Deal one of the nation's great blunders. In the 1960s,
he became a Republican leader. In 1981, shortly before his seventieth birth-
day, he became the most politically conservative president of the United
States at least since the 1920s.

Reagan, born in 1911 in Tampico, Illinois, the second of two boys, moved
with his family from town to town as his father sought work. Jack Reagan,
of Irish Catholic descent, spent much of his early working life as a shoe
salesman, dreaming of someday owning his own big store. He rarely made
financial ends meet and, for Reagan, bread-and-butter issues were central
to the American experience. Jack was likely a full-fledged alcoholic when
Reagan was growing up. Reagan told of an episode in both his memoirs in

Ronald Reagan with his wife, Nancy, at a victory celebration after
winning the governorship of California

which as a teenager he had to drag Jack, passed out drunk in the snow, into
the house—an event that was apparently common in his life. His Protestant mother, the do-gooder, as he described her, assured them that they
should understand alcoholism was simply a sickness. Reagan's memory of
his father was frosty and distant, while he openly professed his love for
his mother, who raised him as a Disciple of Christ. But Jack may have left
deeper emotional, intellectual, and political marks on the son, while from
his mother he got his religiously oriented optimism.

According to Ronald Reagan, Jack was an angry citizen, lashing out constantly against injustices to the working man, even injustices to Negroes,
for which he blamed the Republicans, and taught his sons about righting
the wrongs done to men like them. Unlike Richard Nixon, Reagan understood both the value for a typical worker of even a modest material gain
from year to year and also the worker's natural distrust of the elite, any
elite.

Ronald did not seem to contract Jack's debilitating bitterness, perhaps
because he had gifts his father did not. Jack was big and handsome, but
Ronald was taller and especially handsome. Jack could talk up a storm, but
his son had an even greater talent for it. Ronald Reagan easily won social

approval from those around him. Being athletic, graceful, good-looking, and smooth-talking, he knew he could depend on appearance and charm to help him make his way.

Jack said Ronald looked like a little Dutch boy when he was born, and Ronald adopted the tougher-sounding name as his own when he grew older. "Dutch" Reagan acted in high school plays, was an admired lifeguard in the community, and worked hard to become a lineman on his college football team. He went to Eureka College in Illinois, affiliated with the Disciples of Christ, graduating in 1932. Both his father and his brother were hired by Roosevelt's New Deal programs, saving them from extreme poverty. Reagan got a temporary job as a radio sportscaster. He had a gift for vivid play-by-play commentary, making compelling fictional narratives out of skimpy details of the baseball games that came across the telegraph wire. He quickly became well known in the region.

His movie career started as suddenly as had his sportscasting career. He visited a California talent agent on the recommendation of a friend, and the agent immediately called up Warner Bros. to tout him as the next Robert Taylor. On the basis of one screen test, he was signed to a movie contract. "He succeeded in everything he tried," wrote his most knowledgeable biographer, Lou Cannon. But this claim is overstated. His was a charmed life compared to most, but he paid his dues in Hollywood, and as his expectations rose, they were ultimately not met. He was known to be docile when around his powerful superiors, which often enabled him to get ahead, but some thought that this determined affability undermined his screen presence. He showed little of the deeper emotion or wit of those who rose higher. He would forever think of himself as a B-movie actor, and aspired to Errol Flynn's success, though few considered Flynn a full-fledged A-actor, either. But he made a few A-movies, like *Knute Rockne,* about the Notre Dame football coach, which was apparently his idea, and played in the well-received *King's Row.* He admitted to Cannon that he regretted never getting the girl in the movies the way Flynn did.

Reagan retained his father's interest in working-class politics. He was a committed Democrat, FDR his idol. He even considered joining the Communist Party in the depths of the Depression. He became active in the Screen Actors Guild, joining the board of the actors union in 1938.

World War II interrupted his movie career. Serving in the Reserves, he was assigned to the Army Signal Corps because he was nearsighted. (That he needed glasses in high school was indeed eye-opening for him, for then he discovered he was actually a good athlete; before glasses, he couldn't see the ball.) After the war, he joined protests against nuclear proliferation and remained a Democratic supporter. Like almost everyone else, he worried about a new depression. He blamed business for the economic crises of the 1930s, and became head of the Screen Actors Guild in 1947. When Arthur Schlesinger, Jr., John Kenneth Galbraith, and Reinhold Niebuhr, among others, founded the leftist Americans for Democratic Action in 1947 to fight extreme-left Soviet ideology, Reagan signed up at the Hollywood branch. In 1948, campaigning for Harry Truman, Reagan made a speech on what was his favorite theme. "The profits of corporations have doubled while workers' wages have increased by only one quarter," Reagan wrote. "In other words, profits have gone up four times as much as wages." In 1950, he campaigned for Helen Gahagan Douglas against Nixon.

It was around this time that his views shifted. His change of heart was the principal theme of his book *Where's the Rest of Me?*, which he wrote with Richard G. Hubler, a screenwriter, in 1964 as a potential campaign aid for a run for national office on a decidedly antigovernment program. During his time in the service, as he later described it, he had become distrustful of government because the Army played favorites. As he began to make a better living in the 1950s, he wrote, he became conscious of the high tax rate the government imposed on him.

The rise of communism in Hollywood was, he said, a deciding factor. A confrontation with organizers of a union insurrection in his first year as president of the Screen Actors Guild showed him, he later claimed, what the communists were really like. The set makers wanted to break away from SAG, demanding higher compensation from producers. Reagan fought to keep them in the union when they called a strike, and he considered many of them Communist Party members. Someone associated with the strikers threatened Reagan by phone, a threat sufficient, he felt, that he carried a firearm.

Garry Wills argues persuasively that Reagan's main interest in fighting the set makers was to rid the union of communists. It was the early stages of his new ideological turn. Stopping communists had become an obsession among Hollywood producers and company executives. (The principal leader of the breakaway strikers was almost certainly not a communist; it was simply convenient to portray him as one.) Reagan prevailed over the union rebellion and negotiated the new contract. Fifteen years later, Reagan wrote about the experience in *Where's the Rest of Me?*: "The Communist plan for Hollywood was remarkably simple. It was merely to take over the motion picture business. Not only for its profit, as the hoodlums had tried—but also for a grand worldwide propaganda base."

Reagan, it turned out, was also an FBI informant. He had publicly resisted the communist witch hunts undertaken by the House Un-American Activities Committee in Hollywood in 1947, the year he became SAG's president, and he refused to name publicly those he thought might be sympathizers. In private, however, it was a different matter. It was later discovered that he had been in communication with the FBI all along, and had a secret identity, T-10. Based on FBI documents requested by the *San Jose Mercury News*, he had passed on names of suspect SAG members to the FBI. It is likely his actress wife, Jane Wyman, did as well.

Movie offers were fewer after the war, and his role at SAG, including his anticommunist battles, facilitated his making friends of powerful men in Southern California, most of them political conservatives. In 1952, his longtime agency, MCA, founded by Jules Stein and largely run by Lew Wasserman, who were active Democrats, wanted to start its own television production operation and hire its own stable of actors. The union had firm rules that actors could not hire producers as agents. Agents negotiated with producers on behalf of actors. How could agents be producers themselves? But Reagan had SAG provide MCA a waiver from the rules (later made permanent)—"the brainchild of Stein and Wasserman," according to Lou Cannon—allowing MCA to become in the 1950s one of the most powerful TV producers in the nation. Only MCA was given the waiver. Ten years later the Justice Department investigated MCA for monopolistic practices as both a producer and agent, filing a civil indictment against MCA and naming SAG as a co-conspirator. Reagan was called to testify and claimed he could not remember the terms of the agreement. But it solidified his relationship with Stein and Wasserman, who would one day make him far richer than by getting him movie roles.

Reagan's political transformation may have become complete when he married actress Nancy Davis in 1952. She was the stepdaughter of a wealthy doctor from Chicago, an active political conservative. In the presidential election that year, Reagan headed Democrats for Eisenhower in California, the first time he worked or would vote for a Republican.

In 1954 he took a two-week job as a nightclub host in Las Vegas. Then MCA landed him a life-changing job as host of an hourly TV drama sponsored by the corporate giant General Electric, to be called *General Electric Theater*. He would be paid the handsome salary of $125,000 a year, and act in some of the TV pieces as well.

The show soon had the highest viewership ratings for its time slot. Reagan also gave politically oriented speeches to GE employees at most of its 135 plants. He spoke at countless Chambers of Commerce and

Republican-oriented political groups, sharpening his politically conservative points. His speeches were homilies, frequently using *Reader's Digest* for facts and ideas. He was unusually good at delivering these talks, polished and casual, articulate and down-to-earth, never condescending and always sympathetic to the working American. His central theme now was that big government was the nation's main problem. "Since the beginning of the century our gross national product has increased by thirty-three times," Reagan, still nominally a Democrat, said. "In the same period the cost of federal government has increased 234 times, and while the workforce is only one and one-half times greater, federal employees number nine times as many."

He and Nancy had bought a lovely new house in Pacific Palisades and GE furnished it with its latest appliances. He occasionally hosted the program from the house, proud of his possessions. It is hard to imagine Richard Nixon proud of a GE refrigerator. Nixon never lived the American way of life he extolled in the kitchen debates with Khrushchev. Reagan did, and admired it.

The former liberal critic was turning into a full-fledged outspoken conservative. A decade later, he wrote that he was greatly relieved he had recovered from the liberal disease. He had been, as he put it in *Where's the Rest of Me?*, a "near hopeless hemophilic liberal. I bled for 'causes.' " He now had only contempt for his former life. But unlike some others who made similar conversions to laissez-faire economics, justifying as did Milton Friedman the pursuit of their own self-interest and profit, for Reagan self-reliance, not self-interest, defined the moral character of mankind: one lived and succeeded or failed by one's own abilities.

Reagan was a moralizer, and that required preaching less about selfishness or self-interest and more about selflessness. If one did well materially by being selfless, so be it. His religious rhetoric turned Milton Friedman's competitive self-centeredness into a higher goal. If America did not return to the right path, "a thousand years of darkness" lay ahead, he said, with biblical overtones. In a speech first delivered in 1952, he said, "I, in my own mind, have thought of America as a place in the divine scheme of things that was set aside as a promised land."

Martin Anderson, a principal economic adviser during his presidency, wrote that he gave Reagan Hayek's *Road to Serfdom* and Friedman's *Capitalism and Freedom,* and that he read these, among other books. Some claimed they saw copies of the Hayek and Friedman books dog-eared in his library. But Lou Cannon wrote that Anderson was exaggerating when he implied that Reagan read broadly. Still, he clearly took ideas from Hayek, notably the danger to individual liberty of growing government, and the inevitability of Nazi-style dictatorship under a welfare state. "Today," Reagan said in a speech in 1959, "there is hardly a phase of our daily living that doesn't feel the stultifying hand of government regulation and interference. . . . This power, under whatever name or ideology, is the very essence of totalitarianism."

Aided by Friedman's short essays, Reagan attacked Social Security, Medicare, aid to the poor, housing subsidies, and taxes of almost any kind. This list may have suggested how unoriginal Friedman's public policy views truly were, that Reagan's agenda coincided with his. As Robert Dallek wrote, "To Reagan . . . there are striking similarities between a Communist Russia and a welfare-state America that [he sees] as abandoning its traditional spirit of rugged individualism." Reagan agreed with Friedman that unfettered capitalism gave people the freedom to find their own way; this was its greatest benefit.

As for communism, he was surely influenced by Whittaker Chambers's *Witness*, published in 1952, his self-lacerating account of his renunciation of communism and turning government witness against Alger Hiss. Reagan mentioned his fellow convert admiringly in *Where's the Rest of Me?* For Chambers, it was not communism versus capitalism but communism versus freedom. "At heart," wrote Chambers, "the Great Case was this critical conflict of faiths . . . the two irreconcilable faiths of our time—Communism and Freedom." Ultimately it was a religious battle, for communism was godless. Chambers went on: "Other ages have had great visions: the vision of God and man's relationship to God. The communist vision is the vision of Man without God." It was "the sin of the Garden of Eden."

The transformation of a political and economic message to a moral one was Reagan's strength. In the 1950s, Reagan had warned of the Soviet Union's "evil" dozens if not hundreds of times in his GE speeches. "We are faced with the most evil enemy mankind has known in his climb from the swamps to the stars," he told audience after audience. It should not have come as a surprise, then, that in 1983, as president, Reagan famously pronounced, in a speech to the National Society of Evangelicals, that the Soviet Union was an "evil empire." "Let us pray for the salvation of all those who live in that totalitarian darkness. . . . Beware the temptation . . . to ignore the facts of history and the aggressive impulses of an evil empire, to simply call the arms race a misunderstanding and thereby remove yourself from the struggle between right and wrong, good and evil."

For a president, it was a thunderous faux pas. But he used the word many times before he was president. In the same 1983 "evil empire" speech, he also said that the inalienable rights of individuals are "God-given," and that this individualism "puts us in opposition to . . . a prevailing attitude of many who have turned to a modern-day secularism." To not believe in the supremacy of the individual was that most outrageous of things, secular—that is, irreligious.

The story he told Americans was one of good and bad, a narrative suitable for Hollywood—the point emphasized repeatedly by Garry Wills but also acknowledged by Lou Cannon. "The basis of the dramatic form of entertainment is the emotional catharsis," Reagan himself wrote. Many observed, particularly Cannon, that Reagan had trouble discerning the truth from a good story. He exaggerated what he had done in World War II. He pretended his first marriage, to Jane Wyman, was a loving one. He made his childhood sound happy, except for the occasional bouts with his father, and it mostly was not. "Reagan's capacity for self-denial in personal matters was extraordinary," wrote Cannon. Cannon believed Reagan simply thought in narratives, often highly simple ones.

Reagan said he worried about the same deprived American as his Democratic father had. To Reagan, however, the new parable was that the working man was now "forgotten" by government, not protected by it; he was the hardworking, middle-class person who paid high taxes but saw them go to those who shirked their work or held fancy government jobs. He wrote in a later memoir, *An American Life*, that he thought FDR would have scaled back his New Deal if he had not been distracted by the war. Economic issues, adviser Martin Anderson wrote, were as important to Reagan as fighting communism, but his appeal to working Americans offered salvation to the weary and troubled.

With John F. Kennedy as president, and the country returning to its former progressive thinking, GE may have worried Reagan had become too conservative. He had lambasted government programs so often—one of his favorite whipping boys was the indebted Tennessee Valley Authority, which provides electricity to the large region on the Mississippi—that the company thought he was now giving GE a bad name. Reagan had claimed the company was upset that he had endorsed Nixon for the presidency. More likely, *Bonanza*, the new "adult" western, in color, had replaced the Reagan program as the ratings leader in its Sunday evening TV time slot. Garry Wills, however, argues that the government action against MCA based on the waiver Reagan granted it was the decisive blow; GE did not want to contend with the controversy. Cannon leans toward the *Bonanza* explanation.

The company dropped both the program and Reagan's GE contract in 1962. But MCA landed him another television job as host of *Death Valley Days,* and he also made a movie in 1964, his last, a well-done thriller called *The Killers.* His entertainment career was clearly running on empty but now, at least moderately financially secure, his interest in politics was dominating his life.

In 1960, Reagan wrote Nixon that he was frightened by Kennedy's ambitions for government, and Reagan supported Nixon in his losing 1962 run for California's governorship. Reagan campaigned hard for Goldwater to win the 1964 nomination. As Goldwater lost ground in the opinion surveys, wealthy and frustrated California Republicans, who by now regarded Reagan as a talented up-and-comer, wanted to put him on national TV in a paid advertisement to rally support for the flagging candidate, so confident were they in Reagan's speaking abilities. The talk he delivered was basically the speech he had given time and again for GE, and an earlier, lengthier version was included as an appendix in *Where's the Rest of Me?* the following year. Reagan called it "A Time for Choosing," and later it became known simply as The Speech. One week before the election, the producers gathered a small audience for Reagan to address in a studio where they filmed the speech. "I have spent most of my life as a Democrat," he began. "I recently have seen fit to follow another course." The speech touched on his main themes: high taxes and the size of government; the failure of anti-poverty policies; criticism of Social Security; and accusations of cowardice against those who would appease the Soviet Union.

As was often the case, Reagan's relationship to the facts was exiguous. He said no nation ever survived if it collected 37 cents of every dollar a taxpayer earned, as America, he claimed, was doing. In 1964, however, America's total federal, state, and local spending came to approximately 25 percent of the economy. A British writer and theater critic, Kenneth Tynan, wrote that he would rather get down on his knees than die fighting communism. Reagan made it sound as if Tynan were not British but an American-born appeaser. He ended the speech ironically with a line from FDR, who in turn borrowed it from Abraham Lincoln: America was "the last best hope of man on earth," he said.

Reagan delivered his message thoughtfully and calmly. He could raise alarm without raising his voice. He avoided self-destructive rhetoric like

Goldwater's proud and famous assertion that "extremism in the defense of liberty is no vice." Money from viewers poured into Goldwater's campaign coffers. Young columnist David Broder wrote that it was the most impressive political debut since William Jennings Bryan's Cross of Gold speech. Reagan had won a national reputation.

Johnson's landslide victory over Goldwater was an embarrassment to the Republicans. "Goldwater had become a cause to giggle at across most of the country," wrote Reagan biographer Edmund Morris. "Only in those spacious, mainly sun-baked enclaves where Holmes Tuttle and his friends holed up and teed up—Montecito and La Jolla, Palm Beach and Palm Springs, Scottsdale and Jupiter Island—was there no sound of mirth. Over margaritas and screwdrivers in dark freezing desert restaurants, yesterday's power Elite set about transforming itself into tomorrow's Silent Majority."

These men, led by Tuttle, who made a fortune in car dealerships, saw in Reagan a serious contender against Governor Pat Brown in 1966. In his second memoir, published in 1990, Reagan wrote that he did not want to run for office but was pressed to do so. (He also claimed such reluctance regarding the Republican presidential nominations in 1968 and 1976, and finally even for the nomination he won in 1980.) It was more likely a stance than true hesitation. When "the Friends of Reagan," led by Tuttle, hired political and psychological consultants to help remake him, he was amenable to their tutoring. Their advice was predictable: keep answers short, avoid the hot-button issues, learn more about local California concerns. The one demand he made of his supporters was to ensure his complete financial security; he couldn't keep up his home. His agents at MCA obliged (the Democrats Stein and Wasserman handed him over to their leading Republican executive), arranging for Twentieth Century Fox to pay $2 million for the ranch, as he called it, he and Nancy bought in the Santa Monica Mountains for $65,000 a decade earlier. (It was consummated a month into his term as governor.) When Fox went to sell it soon after, it could only get about $500,000 for the property. While Reagan was governor, Jules Stein arranged for him to buy a still larger property in the Los Angeles area, which Reagan eventually sold secretly at more than double the purchase price. Stein also helped him reduce his federal and state tax bill with shelters devised by a member of his family. According to *The Sacramento Bee,* Reagan paid no state income taxes one year while governor. Reagan, financially secure before, got rich while in office.

Reagan now developed the themes and the electoral approach that would eventually take him to the presidency. Governor Brown's own great society in California was taking its toll, Reagan persistently argued. Welfare policies were resulting in ever-growing numbers of people on the dole, who were lazy and taking advantage of working people. It happened that they were often black Americans. In addition, migrant workers were being effectively organized by César Chávez, raising still more racial fears. Crime was rising because criminals seemed to have more rights than victims. "We must return to a belief in every individual being responsible for his conduct and his misfortune." And taxes were too high.

Two major events moved the state Reagan's way. The first was the Free Speech Movement at the Berkeley campus of the University of California, which began as a civil rights protest in late 1964, but grew to include criticism of the Vietnam War and related social issues. The ingrates, as Reagan saw them, had taken over the administration building in the fall of that year. It was the beginning of rolling crises on campuses across the nation. Reagan had a perfect campaign issue in which to mobilize public anger and he promised to "clean up the mess." ("If it takes a bloodbath, let's get it over with," he said, one month before the National Guard killed four demonstrators at Kent State University in Ohio in 1970. He knew enough to back off his hard line after that.)

Then there were the tragic riots in Watts, the South Central L.A. district in which thirty-four African Americans were killed in the summer of 1965. Reagan said he would reestablish order, and stopping crime became a major campaign theme.

Reagan lost few opportunities to blame the state's growing financial problems on welfare recipients. "Welfare is the greatest domestic problem facing the nation today and the reason for the high cost of government," he said. Reagan typically defined welfare to include Social Security, unemployment insurance, and Medicare, thus pushing up the costs by his definition of "welfare" well beyond the costs of programs for the very poor. Lou Cannon insisted Reagan was not personally a racist, but the racial appeal to the frustrations and fears of white working-class citizens was unambiguous. He enjoyed setting the "tax takers," as he called welfare recipients, against the "tax givers," working Californians. Like Goldwater, he had opposed the Civil Rights Act of 1964.

Pat Brown did not take the former actor seriously, nor did much of the state. "We never thought he would last," said Walter Shorenstein, a real estate investor and prominent Democratic fundraiser from San Francisco. Brown took his political support for granted. Reagan understood the voter he wanted to reach. Reagan won in a stunning upset, with 58 percent of the vote.

On taking office in 1965, Reagan sent in the National Guard to quell the "upstarts" at Berkeley. He instituted tuition for state colleges and universities and reduced the college budgets. He proposed welfare reforms and made plans to cut taxes. He supported the death penalty and demanded stricter sentencing guidelines.

But he was also surprisingly pragmatic. While his rhetoric remained conservative, he compromised frequently with the Democrats who controlled the state legislature. Rather than cutting taxes, he sponsored the largest tax increase in the state's history early in his first term, effectively blaming the tax hike on the financial hole he claimed Governor Brown and the Democrats had left. State spending generally increased under Reagan.

Reagan handily won a second term in 1970, beating California House speaker Jesse Unruh, even in a year when California elected a progressive senator, John Tunney, a Kennedy-like liberal, who took the Senate seat from the conservative former actor George Murphy.

Reagan once again compromised willingly to get bills passed. He and the Democrats jointly agreed at last to tighten requirements for welfare recipients, but, as Lou Cannon wrote, it was a less stringent bill than Bill Clinton's twenty years later. He and the Democrats also agreed on a bill to reduce property taxes moderately.

Government spending kept rising under Reagan. By midterm, he wanted to leave California a more decided conservative legacy, and, most important, one that might help him improve his image for a presidential run. A decisive cut in taxes would be ideal.

Reagan formed the Tax Reduction Task Force in the fall of 1972 under Lewis Uhler. But Uhler said he would do the job only if he were able to fly across the nation to gather the support of "the best free market minds in the country." Given a free hand, he conscripted economists whose voices would dominate the conservative political dialogue in coming years. They included William Niskanen, who later served as Reagan's chairman of the Council of Economic Advisers; John Buchanan, a future Nobel Prize winner; several prominent economists from Stanford's Hoover Institute; and a relatively obscure law professor, Anthony Kennedy, who became a decisive figure as a Supreme Court justice.

Uhler's first stop in his national tour was to have dinner with Milton and Rose Friedman. Also at dinner was George Stigler, who then ran the Chicago economics department. Milton Friedman immediately agreed to join Uhler's task force, but Stigler did not, saying he doubted it would help.

As we've seen, Uhler proposed an amendment to the state constitution to reduce taxes permanently. "Laws control men but only constitutions control government," Uhler said. Getting Friedman's support was a coup, Uhler believed. "I'd read a lot that Milton had written," he said. "There was the book *Capitalism and Freedom.* He was writing his *Newsweek* column." Uhler's direct contact with the governor, he said, was usually blocked by Reagan aides who did not approve of him. Indefatigable, he said he tracked the governor down at his father-in-law's vacation house in Phoenix to discuss and develop the tax proposal at length.

In December 1972, Uhler presented a complete proposal to Reagan in a two-hour meeting at the Century Plaza Hotel in Los Angeles, and Reagan embraced it enthusiastically. At the time, California was running budget surpluses and Reagan thought it was the right moment for a permanent tax cut. The main provision of Proposition 1, as they named it, reduced state taxes from 8.3 percent of personal income to no more than 7 percent by year-by-year reductions of one tenth of 1 percent, and the rates could not be raised again. A constitutional ceiling, if adopted, could only be overturned by a vote of two thirds of the people.

Uhler kept a log of his time with Reagan, calculating that the governor spent a total of twenty-six hours on the details of the complex plan. "When he had something important, he got involved in the nitty gritty," said Uhler. Ultimately, according to Uhler, Proposition 1 underwent more than forty drafts. Uhler not only won Reagan to his side, but Edwin Meese and communications adviser Michael Deaver, mindful of Reagan's potential for national office, were also strong advocates of the amendment. Proposition 1 was finally put before the California people in November 1973. Reagan had a year left on his second term. He campaigned aggressively for the amendment and it became completely identified with him and his ideology. Friedman campaigned with him once, despite a recent heart bypass operation.

But neither California nor America was as conservative as Reagan had believed, or as susceptible to his charms. Despite the growth of government that Reagan had constantly criticized, the typical family's income in the United States—the median, at which half of families earned more and half less—had more than doubled after inflation since 1950.

In the early 1970s, Lyndon Johnson's social goals were still favored by most Americans. A Gallup poll found that in 1966 more than 60 percent of Americans favored a nationwide antipoverty program. In a 1972 survey, the year that Reagan began his campaign for Proposition 1, Louis Harris in his poll found that 56 percent of Americans still favored antipoverty and other social programs. According to one 1972 survey, only 12 percent of Americans favored reducing spending on public housing, a constant refrain of Milton Friedman's, while 80 percent wanted either to increase federal spending or maintain the same level. Roughly four out of five Americans also favored rebuilding inner cities, and a large majority wanted to increase funds for programs for children and the elderly. Federal welfare programs for the poor were the least popular, yet even in this case only one out of four Americans wanted to reduce or eliminate funding for them, according to the 1972 survey.

The defeat of Proposition 1 was decisive—54 percent to 46 percent. Reagan's unquestioned place as a strong Republican presidential contender was shaken by the defeat. Uhler attributed the loss to the lavish spending by the teachers union. Some claimed the proposal was too complex for the electorate. Ultimately, as Senator Tunney said, it made Reagan seem as irresponsible as many suspected he was.

But Reagan refused to retract his views on the constitutional tax limits. To the contrary, he wrote a piece defending a constitutional tax limit for *National Review,* claiming the opposition exaggerated the dangerous consequences of the proposal. Reagan did not feel he was finished as a national candidate. He watched as Nixon resigned and Ford floundered. His attempt to wrest the Republican nomination for president from Gerald Ford in 1976 had too little support. But he won Southern state primary battles with his brand of conservatism, and turned in a sudden and surprising win in North Carolina by taking a hard line on America's return of the Panama Canal Zone to Panama, which he persistently characterized as a display of American weakness.

Some of Reagan's advisers remained bitter toward Uhler, perhaps Reagan himself did. References to Uhler are almost nowhere to be found in insider accounts of Reagan's governorship. Meese himself mentions him only once in his memoir. Reagan did not mention him at all in his 1990 memoir, *An American Life,* though he wrote that the time for the proposal was simply not yet right.

In 1976, America elected Democrat Jimmy Carter to replace Ford. Carter promised to put the nation back to work, as Kennedy had a decade and a half earlier. But Reagan continued on diligently shaping and reshaping his message. He made approximately six hundred radio speeches in the late 1970s, becoming for a time more crusading journalist than politician, not knowing whether he would have an opportunity again to run for office, but familiarizing himself on a wide variety of issues. Meantime, the economy was lurching from one problem to another. Americans were losing their confidence, increasingly frustrated and confused, but still clinging to the notion that all could return to normal.

It bears repeating that Reagan mostly avoided making economic self-interest the centerpiece of his economic program. His was not the controversial morality of Smith's invisible hand, or of the free market economists some of whom were his advisers, but rather something more like the opposite. It was the selflessness of hard work, self-reliance, and courage associated with an American Protestant ethic. Material success was its by-product, not its objective. He believed the rich earned what they made and he castigated those who saw a fat man and a skinny man together and blamed the fat man for the travails of the thin man. But he also said in a 1967 speech, "The world's truly great thinkers have not pointed us towards materialism; they have dealt with the great truths and with the high questions of right and wrong, of morality and of integrity. They have dealt with the question of man, not the acquisition of things." And he once warned, "Free enterprise is not a hunting license."

He told the people time and again that government had become the principal obstacle to their personal fulfillment. "I want to help get us back to those fiercely independent Americans," he said as president years later, "those people who can do great deeds, and I've seen them robbed of their independence . . . because of these great social reforms." It did not matter to him that he got rich, not due to rugged individualism, but due to the gifts of rich men. The facts of his own life, as many of his biographers, including Cannon and Wills, document, were reconstructed according to his own needs—to create his own myths. He planted a visceral distaste for government in the American belly, justifying to many, and even making moral, runaway individualism and greed.

8

Ted Turner, Sam Walton, and Steve Ross

SIZE BECOMES STRATEGY

I n the 1970s, imports rose to 12 percent of the U.S. economy from less than 5 percent a decade earlier, and old-line industries became subject to intense competition. But other older industries were being radically transformed, partly through innovation, but also, and more importantly, by the growth of the dominant companies into competitive giants. In particular, banking, defense, retailing, and entertainment, including the news media, became bulwarks against foreign incursion and mainstays in the American economy, partly because they were naturally shielded from foreign competition but largely through rapid consolidation and sheer size.

Ironically, this occurred despite the spreading conventional wisdom among academic students of the economics of the firm that size was no longer the advantage it was earlier in U.S. economic development. How this happened tells much about how the economy worked in these years. Microsoft, Apple, Cisco, Intel, and others like them were, relatively speaking, mere green shoots in the 1970s, but they and a handful of others rode a wave of new technology to become remarkable mass production and distribution giants by the late 1990s. They were classic examples of the American business tradition, turning innovation, new technology, and entrepreneurialism into complex but standardized and affordable products that could be mass-produced and distributed—modern examples of Henry Ford's mass production model. Thus, what economists call economies of scale—where the quantity of goods and services sold leads to lower costs per product—were revived and accounted for a lot of the nation's renewed productivity growth.

But the consolidation and growing marketing power of older-line businesses was also the result of changes in corporate finance that made mergers

Sam Walton giving a pep talk to Wal-Mart employees

Ted Turner at the debut of his
company, CNN

Steve Ross of Warner Communications with his
socialite wife, Amanda Burden

far easier, the relaxation of antimonopoly laws by the Reagan administration, and new managerial methods that emphasized tough bargaining with
suppliers and employees. A relative handful of ambitious entrepreneurs
reoriented older-line companies as well, by adapting new technologies in
ways that created market power through sheer size. The principal competitive strategy was to grow ever larger. Through mergers, the financial community had a central part in these consolidations. But success came often

at a serious price to competition, the livelihood of American workers, and the nation's social values, as we've had a glimpse of already. The stories tell much about the new age.

Three entrepreneurs were representative. Sam Walton built the discount retailer Wal-Mart into America's largest company and the largest retailer in the world, and raised inventory management and distribution, through computer technologies, to a level of efficiency that enabled him to minimize worker pay and place immense pressure on suppliers for low prices. Steve Ross raised the entertainment conglomerate to new heights, building Warner Communications into the most enterprising company in its field. Ross, who began by running funeral parlors, showed that anyone could now buy almost anything because the new Wall Street structure could finance outsize deals. Ted Turner built the new, novel, independent-minded, twenty-four-hour news channel CNN, but this most important new information-gathering innovation of its time was acquired from him in a period when to survive meant becoming a corporate giant. The news content of CNN was radically changed, as entertainment, news, and book publishing were consolidated and homogenized.

Walmart

Sam Walton was born in 1918 and raised in modest circumstances in the Midwest. "I have been overblessed by drive and ambition since I was a boy," wrote Walton of himself. Said Sam's brother Bud, "From the time we were boys, Sam could excel at almost anything he set his mind to." Sam was president of his college class, a member of countless other clubs at school, and a ferociously competitive tennis player. After finishing college, he got his first job at a J.C. Penney store in Des Moines. Walton stayed at Penney's for only a year and a half, learned its ways thoroughly, and left determined to make merchandising his future. World War II was under way and he was drafted, but did not see combat. Once discharged, he was eager to embark on the trade he learned at Penney's.

He soon married the valedictorian of her high school class, the daughter of a well-off rancher and lawyer in Oklahoma from whom Walton borrowed enough money to buy a franchise in a five-and-dime variety store chain, Ben Franklin. The store was located in a small town in Arkansas. It was 1945 and Walton was twenty-seven.

From the start, Walton was obsessed with cutting costs. Instead of buying from the Ben Franklin wholesaler, he violated the company's strict protocol and bought directly from the manufacturers themselves—and passed on all the savings to consumers through reduced prices. His business model was to cut costs, sell at a low profit margin, and make it up in volume. He came to think of himself as being like Ben Franklin, for whom frugality was a cornerstone value. His attention to costs in business was matched by his stingy personal style.

He demanded the same frugality and dedication of his employees. He typically got to work at 4 A.M., drove his employees almost as hard as he drove himself, and traveled relentlessly (soon with his own plane) to examine his stores and investigate his competitors' practices.

What offset and softened his stern demands for his employees was his natural friendliness. He eventually ran Wal-Mart like a family operation, paying attention to employees and creating group activities for them, even as he paid poorly—indeed, to make up for paying poorly.

After his first purchase, Walton bought other Ben Franklin franchises in small towns, reduced their costs, sharpened their focus, kept wages low, and used the profits to buy still more. One of his first stores was opened in Bentonville, Arkansas, where he set up the company headquarters, partly because his wife wanted to live in a small town. By 1962, he had sixteen stores, several as large as twenty thousand square feet. He called the bigger ones Walton Family Centers.

He also became aware of the discount store revolution in the United States, led by E.J. Korvette and K-Mart, among others, and was determined to join it. The Ben Franklins and Family Centers charged low prices, but were not true discount stores, and Walton feared the large discount chains might put him out of business. He raised more money with help from his wife's trust fund, and opened the first large Wal-Mart Discount City, matching and even beating prices at Korvette's and K-Mart. By the end of 1969, Walton had fourteen variety stores like Ben Franklin and eighteen Wal-Marts, located throughout Oklahoma, Missouri, and Arkansas.

But Walton was still short of financing, not yet personally rich, and determined to expand further. In 1970, he successfully brought the company public, raising $4.6 million through the Wall Street firm White Weld, later acquired by Merrill Lynch. Another public offering in 1972, when stock prices temporarily strengthened, brought in more expansion money. Walton's personal shares were now worth $15 million.

His early successes were built on the rapid expansion of the American economy. Wages grew rapidly across the board until the early 1970s, unemployment rates were historically low, and people in the Southwest were rapidly moving from the farms to the towns where he put his stores. In the

1970s Walton bought entire small retail chains with his Wall Street money, transforming the stores into serious profit makers. Acquisitions became his path to rapid expansion.

His later success, however, was partly built on a troubled economy. With high unemployment rates in the 1970s, Walton had a large and increasingly pliant labor pool from which to hire workers. His shoppers were also looking for bargains in tough inflationary times. His obsessive emphasis on low costs and tight management allowed him to underprice his main rivals, K-Mart and Sears (Korvette's went bankrupt), and provide more product choice as well. As he grew larger, he could manage inventories more efficiently and buy in greater volume than his competitors, combining purchasing and shipping operations.

Walton tried to get away with below-par wages even in his very first Ben Franklins, justifying paying less than the statutory minimum by claiming he was exempt from the laws because the company was so small. The Labor Department ordered him to raise pay to the minimum wage. Later, in the first Wal-Mart in 1962, the cashiers were paid 50 cents an hour when the federal minimum wage was over $1. Even his wife complained that he didn't pay the workers well enough.

In the early 1970s, there were attempts to unionize his workers at several stores and he hired a tough union-busting lawyer. After he stopped the unions, he and his lawyer devised a plan to create the more friendly and caring environment he became well known for—without paying the workers any more. Walton was a talented, committed cheerleader, walking the aisles of his many stores as often as possible, remembering clerks' names, creating a newsletter, and establishing a modest profit-sharing plan for the employees, whom he now called "associates."

In 1978, Walton made a key decision to invest aggressively in computerized inventory and distribution methods. He had resisted such technological investment in the past, but his mind was changed by one of his key executives. In 1979, his sales and inventories were computerized. Satellites had become commercial only in the mid-1970s, but Walton was quick to act, and by the early 1980s he had invested in an elaborate satellite communications system that was up and running so stores could communicate swiftly with suppliers everywhere, and make the purchasing and distribution of the goods highly efficient. By 1988, the company had the largest satellite communications system in the world, enabling Wal-Mart to reduce what the company spent on transportation and warehousing to 2 cents per dollar compared to K-Mart's 5 cents. Bar scanning to keep track of sales was raised to a high art and Wal-Mart even minimized the use of warehouses, arranging that trucks merely meet on schedule at depots and goods be shifted from one to the other, rather than stored in warehouses.

Along with these efficiencies, Wal-Mart also enforced disciplined and often stern labor practices and produced a much higher sales volume per employee than its competitors. It didn't share the savings with employees, but instead cut the prices of its goods to shoppers—the Walton business model.

Even as it expanded rapidly, Wal-Mart was still a regional chain. In 1979, Wal-Mart's 229 stores in ten states were producing $1 billion in sales, but K-Mart and Sears were many times bigger, and the Walton legend would not be truly spun until the late 1980s, when, through acquisitions, new store openings, intense cost controls that included low supplier prices and rock-bottom wages, and still more advanced computerized methodologies, he overtook K-Mart and Sears. In the 1980s, he became America's richest man with a personal fortune estimated at $20 billion in 1985, based largely on the shares he owned in his company.

Walton contracted leukemia in the late 1980s and died in 1992. His successors intensified his devotion to controlling labor costs. As criticism of Wal-Mart's low pay, long hours, and scant benefits grew, the company defended itself by noting that nearly three quarters of its employees worked full-time and earned twice the minimum wage. But it defined full-time as working thirty-four hours a week, and even for a forty-hour worker, that meant less than $1,300 of income a month after taxes. Few families, no less individuals, could live on that anywhere in the United States. Wal-Mart was simply not set up to pay a worker a wage that alone could support a family. To the contrary, it assumed that many workers would have their health care paid by Medicaid and that they would become regular users of food stamps. Turnover rates of workers were unusually high at Wal-Mart and worker abuse became a virtual managerial requirement.

Over the years, there were many allegations of much harsher and sometimes illegal practices. Workers were locked in stores at night, underage workers were regularly hired, workers were forced to work more hours than Wal-Mart reported and were paid for, and illegal workers were hired below minimum wage (though they are legally entitled to the minimum wage). As Wal-Mart bought more goods from China, researchers documented that some of the manufacturers physically abused their workers.

Labor laws were increasingly poorly enforced in this era, starting with the Reagan administration. The number of government labor inspectors was not increased even as the nation's workforce grew vastly in number, and the number of professional "union avoidance" consultants (union busters), often private lawyers or public relations experts, grew from about one hundred to two thousand. Across the nation, a rapidly growing number of workers were illegally fired when they tried to organize fellow workers into unions. Congress also deliberately kept the minimum wage down, raising it rarely, so it fell compared to inflation.

It is doubtful Wal-Mart would have met similar success in an earlier period of American economic history, or in a different social and political environment. Even as it became the largest employer in America, its profit margins were so low, due to managerial efficiency, technological methods, and its power to extract low prices from suppliers, that if it had to pay workers more, it would have had to raise prices. And if it raised prices, it would not have become the phenomenon it has become. It bullied its way to profits by squeezing both suppliers and employees and built a business model it probably could no longer change even if management had wanted to.

Wal-Mart earned almost as much as Microsoft in the mid-2000s, about $11 billion in profits, but from a far higher level of sales. It had roughly 1.1 million employees, full-time and part-time, compared to Microsoft's forty thousand workers. To put it another way, even if Wal-Mart paid out all its profits to workers, the work was so labor-intensive each worker would make only slightly more.

Overseas retailers did not invade America. There were no great European or South American retail chains in the United States. But Wal-Mart became the largest retailer in Mexico and Canada, and the largest seller of groceries in Britain. It was even opening stores in China.

In its later years, Wal-Mart bought goods liberally from China, importing 10 percent of everything China sold to the United States. Thus, it got another enormous boost from the rise of Chinese manufacturing capacity and the deliberate policies of the Chinese government to keep its currency low, and therefore prices to the United States low as well.

Many claimed, despite the low wages, the nation benefited from Wal-Mart's low prices. American consumers had voted with their pocketbooks. Ninety percent of Americans lived within an hour's drive of a mammoth Wal-Mart store, half of Americans lived within a ten-minute drive. By the 2000s, the chain sold 20 percent or more of all consumer items bought. More than seven billion shoppers passed through a Wal-Mart worldwide in a single year.

In the 2000s, for the first time, more Americans were working in retailing than in manufacturing and the pay on average was far less. This was the business environment of a new age. Some companies went against the trend, such as Costco, which emphasized more service for customers, paid higher wages, and offered better benefits. But it was not nearly Wal-Mart's size.

McKinsey, the consulting firm, estimated that Wal-Mart's productivity gains accounted for one fourth of the productivity gains of the entire nation between 1995 and 2000. Yet in the past, higher productivity of industrial giants was usually associated with high wages—even as the prices of products fell. The great entrepreneurs of an earlier era created jobs that paid good wages. The price of a Model T fell from roughly $1,000 to $300 in the early 1900s, and Henry Ford fought vehemently against unionization, yet he paid his workers up to $5 a day, an extremely high wage in those times. This had become the classical example of capitalism at work. Now productivity was losing its historical meaning in a political environment that tolerated low wages and worker insecurity. It was not a model that a prosperous nation could depend on indefinitely.

Steven J. Ross was in most ways the opposite of Sam Walton. Walton stuck to his knitting in classic entrepreneurial style, while Ross moved rapidly to the latest fad or fashion. Ross was a big-city sophisticate, and proud of it. Few entertainment executives were as bold—some argued careless, others fearless—as Ross. He developed a model that other entertainment companies followed over the next three decades. His supporters argued that the entertainment business now had to be large and powerful to compete in the world entertainment playground, and that his strategy was eminently sensible. But what drove Ross was ambition and glamour, and, as with so many conglomerators of the time, the value of a larger company was not only marketing power and capital for new ventures but more compensation and bigger perks. Competition grew among the entertainment giants, turning into internecine conflict, with costs and individual compensation rising higher with no discernible improvement in the quality of what was being made. Those who ran these companies got rich, famous, and ever more determined to grow larger.

Ross was born in 1926 and brought up in a rough neighborhood in the Flatbush section of Brooklyn. His mother had been the daughter of a successful businessman, but he lost his job in the Depression, and Ross knew for several years what it was to be truly poor. He survived the streets of

Brooklyn, the family recovered financially, and, his mother's social ambitions still intact, he was sent to a private prep school in New York. Eventually, he attended a small junior college in upstate New York, where he played football.

Tall, handsome, with an infectious personality, classically the most popular boy in the class, and a good athlete (and reputedly a good ballroom dancer), Ross got his start in business in 1954 by marrying Ellen Rosenthal, the daughter of a successful funeral parlor owner. The father-in-law brought the son-in-law into the business, and he eventually ran the company, whose primary property was the Riverside Chapel on Manhattan's West Side. But his ambition was not so easily satisfied.

By the 1960s, the financial markets were making it possible for almost anyone aggressive enough to buy almost anything through an exchange of stock if the company's stock price was high enough. From his modestly profitable core business, Ross emulated giant conglomerators like Ling-Temco-Vought and ITT and built a small diversified company. At first, he stuck to less glamorous businesses: the cornerstone of his company was the purchase of Kinney parking garages. But he also bought a cleaning business and started a car rental company after taking Kinney National Services public in 1962.

Soon, Kinney was generating enough profit to allow Ross to extend his reach, and in 1967 he turned to entertainment. The year before, Charles Bluhdorn, who ran the conglomerate Gulf + Western, which mostly owned auto parts distributors, bought Paramount Pictures for $125 million. Now, Ross's far smaller Kinney National Services bought Ted Ashley Famous Artists along with DC Comics. Next, Ashley, an influential and well-connected entertainment agent, urged Ross to buy Warner Bros.-Seven Arts, which included the old-line motion picture company Warner Bros., now a shadow of its former self, and a much more profitable music company, which included Atlantic Records, founded by Ahmet Ertegun, and Frank Sinatra's Reprise Records. A takeover battle ensued with the banker Felix Rohatyn of Lazard Frères heading Ross's strategic team and Allen & Co. representing Warner Bros.-Seven Arts. Ross eventually won with an exchange of his stock worth several hundred million dollars at the time. Sinatra had such a large ownership position in the company that to do the deal, he had to agree. Ross went to Sinatra's mother's home in Fort Lee, New Jersey, to meet with Sinatra, where they signed the deal for nearly $25 million in cash. (Sinatra told Ross not to let his mother see the size of the check because she would demand he save the money.)

It was not obvious that the movie business was an intelligent investment in those years. The rise of television had undermined its market, and studios were floundering and mismanaged. But Ross believed that leisure time would only expand in America and filling it would be a growth industry. That was the conventional wisdom of the day, except that it was not yet obvious owning a movie studio was the answer to consumers' leisure needs. Ross immensely enjoyed being with the actors, directors, singers, and iconoclastic producers, however, and this was to serve him well. They in turn responded to his charm and enthusiasm. "He was a guy who inspired belief very quickly," said Warren Beatty on Ross's death in 1992. He was in many ways like them, and in such a world, Ross remade himself, whether by honest effort or easy lie. He even claimed he had played football for the Cleveland Browns, as reported in a profile done by *The New York Times* in 1972. He had not. Hollywood may have been his natural home.

Under the cloud of a financial scandal, Ross separated Kinney (and started selling some of its operations) from the entertainment company operations in 1971, and renamed what was left Warner Communications. Ross did indeed strike gold as the American film business blossomed in the 1970s after its long sleepy period in the 1950s and 1960s. It turned out to be a new golden era of moviemaking with hits by first-rate directors. Ted Ashley was put in charge of the movie company, and given free rein by Ross, which was to be Ross's managerial approach. Ashley, in turn, picked able executives who developed a run of hit movies, including *Klute, Dirty Harry,* and *A Clockwork Orange.* Later in the decade Warner released *The Exorcist, All the President's Men, Superman,* and many other successes. Most of the old-line studios were doing well also and American cinema enjoyed a renaissance.

Meantime, videocassette recorders were creating a new "backend market" for films. It turned out the VCR did not cannibalize turnout at movie theaters, as was initially feared, but added more sales revenues for films, even those that weren't hits. Foreign sales for American movies also grew strongly. In addition, people like Ted Turner were creating a market for old films through cable distribution. No one could truly pick future hits, it was conceded, but by investing in a package of well-conceived commercial films, it was likely several of them would "break out," and the "backend" sales of videocassettes, foreign rights, and TV syndication rights would help compensate for the costs.

Warner's music business also soared, including Elektra/Asylum Records. When the American economy suffered in the 1970s, entertainment kept doing well, as it had to some degree in the Great Depression. Ross's movies generated $353 million in revenues and nearly $60 million in profit by 1977, and Ross's collection of record companies did as well.

With so much money coming in, Ross could now make more acquisitions. The most profitable of these was the video game maker Atari. Video game popularity suddenly exploded, and Atari, which began with *PONG* and eventually licensed *Space Invaders,* produced huge profits for Ross's bottom line. Ross's purchase of Atari made him the stuff of legend.

Ross was now lavishly spending money on himself, and paying his key executives well also. Limousines and private jets became the Warner Communications norm, expense accounts enormous. For Ross, it was large houses as well, much of the extravagance subsidized by Warner as a business expense. And Ross began dating Amanda Burden, perhaps the nation's most prominent socialite.

Ross's true obsession in this period was the relatively new cable TV business. He thought cable was a natural bet on the future and he became, as was his way, overenthusiastic about it. Laying cable across America was similar to laying railroad track in the nineteenth century. There was no serious market yet for the product but entrepreneurs bet fortunes that there would be one day soon. The cable operators made deals with local governments for the franchise to supply the cable to homes and they contracted for programming in hopes of attracting households to subscribe. Ross thought he would have it both ways: buy up the cable operators and supply programming through his movie production company. Cable at this point was in its infancy, and most homeowners were simply buying cable to improve their TV reception, but with profits from movies and music, Ross invested heavily in cable, becoming one of the largest such operators in the country. It was an expensive bet.

By the end of the 1970s, Ross was at the top of the changing entertainment industry. He made well-publicized mistakes, including an abortive attempt to introduce professional soccer in America with the creation of the New York Cosmos team, made up of near-retirement-age stars from Europe and South America. He also invested in an expensive innovation for cable television, called QUBE, which enabled viewers to interact, through a handheld box, with their cable television, among other things, to shop, play games, and participate in quiz programs. The system did not work efficiently nor did it interest many viewers, though QUBE did help Ross win more cable operators to the Warner system because they believed QUBE would attract new subscribers. On the other hand, Ross started MTV and Nickelodeon, future successes.

Because of the expense of cable operations, and the fact that they were not yet generating adequate revenue, Ross with the help of investment banker Rohatyn persuaded American Express to invest in Warner's operation in 1979. Ross rarely was satisfied to be an equal partner with anyone, even the powerful Amex CEO James Robinson III, and he managed to keep Robinson from involvement in the important decisions of what was now called Warner-Amex Cable. By 1979, he had also attained the social status to which he always aspired. Amanda Burden, daughter of the famed hostess Babe Paley whose husband was CBS founder William Paley, at last agreed to marry him.

Other ambitious men were also now buying into movies and the entertainment business, partly following Ross's lead. They were rich entrepreneurs, usually with no pedigree in entertainment, but they had access to financing and a hunger for glamour. The result was a radical consolidation of entertainment and news in America just as the markets for entertainment grew rapidly and expanded into new areas, from TV syndication to videocassettes, cable TV, and music.

Columbia Pictures, controlled by investment bankers from Allen & Company, which had a long financial relationship with Hollywood studios, was run by one of Allen's own financial experts, Alan Hirschfield (who helped sell Warner Bros.-Seven Arts to Ross). Confident in the future of movies, Hirschfield sold Columbia's profitable TV stations to invest more in film and then expanded quickly into the music business, hiring Clive Davis to start Arista Records. In 1982, Allen & Co. sold the company at a large profit to Coca-Cola, which was then determined to diversify its soda operations.

Marvin Davis, an oil magnate from Denver, who made a fortune off the rising price of oil in the 1970s, bought all of Twentieth Century Fox Film Corporation in 1981. He had bought the company jointly several years earlier with commodities trader Marc Rich, but after having been charged with financial fraud, Rich became a fugitive from U.S. justice. Davis was able to buy Fox for a mere several hundred million dollars in the late 1970s. The asking price rose to the billions in the 1980s as the studios added more operations, as more investment bankers became media specialists, encouraging deals and pushing up prices—and as domestic and international markets expanded as American filmmakers continued to make hits.

Sony, the Japanese giant, flush with profits, bought Columbia Pictures for $3.4 billion from Coca-Cola in 1989. The long-established entertainment professionals like Lew Wasserman (once Ronald Reagan's agent) of MCA, which owned Universal Pictures, traditionally among the lesser of the movie studios until it produced Steven Spielberg's early hits, like *Jaws,* successfully avoided the merger race but found himself forced to sell the company to Matsushita Electrical, the giant Japanese manufacturer, in 1990 for a hard-to-refuse $7 billion. Seagram eventually bought Universal from Matsushita, then sold it to the French conglomerate Vivendi, which in turn sold most of it to NBC.

Sumner Redstone's Viacom, originally a theater chain company and the owner of Showtime, the smaller rival to premium cable station Home Box Office (HBO), bought Paramount Pictures in 1993 for $10 billion from Gulf + Western. It was hard to believe that ten to twenty years earlier, such studios were selling for a small fraction of the 1990s prices. Bluhdorn, as noted, paid only $125 million for Paramount in 1969.

Television networks also became fair game, a surprise at first because they were large and owned by companies dedicated to remaining in the business. They were also protected by the Federal Communications Commission, which had been cautious about who could own the public airwaves, until the Reagan administration. Capital Cities, a highly profitable owner of TV stations, bought the much larger ABC Television in 1985 for $2.5 billion, with substantial financial help from Warren Buffett's Berkshire Hathaway. Ten years later, Walt Disney bought ABC/Capital Cities for nearly $26 billion, a record price for a network. Ted Turner, whose CNN was by then highly successful, but was still small compared to the networks, bid $5.5 billion for CBS in 1985 with junk bond financing from Michael Milken but failed when no major investment bankers would support the upstart's bid. The Tisch brothers, financial men who had years earlier acquired Lorillard, the tobacco giant, bought CBS in 1986, only to sell after several disappointing years to Westinghouse. Rupert Murdoch, the Australian newspaper baron (who had first threatened Ross at Warner Communications with a takeover bid) bought half of Twentieth Century Fox in 1985 and then TV stations from Metromedia, preparing to start the Fox TV network. Later that year, General Electric bought RCA, the parent of NBC, for $6.3 billion. Viacom, which already owned Paramount, bought CBS during the roaring bull market of 2000 for more than $37 billion, the biggest communications acquisition yet, breaking the record set by Disney's takeover of ABC/Capital Cities. Only five years earlier, Westinghouse had paid $5 billion to buy the struggling network from the Tisch family. Many of these deals were for exchanges of shares; others included financing from investment and commercial banks.

Television news, print and magazines, movies, TV networks and production, and music were now completely intertwined under a single management. And the businesses were now huge. The only foreign owners were Sony and Murdoch's News Corp., but they bought American operations, and hired American managers for the most part. Everything was up for sale, and the prices paid kept rising. Television news was controlled by only a handful of men now. Newspapers, magazines, and book publishing were virtually consolidated into a few entertainment conglomerates. In this age of free market ideology, the homogenization brought only mild criticism. All was made possible by the development of finance: everything was in play, financing was there to be had, and legal and financial expertise was available and cheap compared to the financial stakes.

In the early 1980s, Ross's luck temporarily ran out. He was dogged by scandal over a Westchester music theater, having always been linked to organized crime since his ownership of the Kinney parking garages. Amanda Burden left him. His movie company was no longer making hits.

Most important, Atari collapsed after generating almost absurdly high profits between 1980 and 1982, led by *Space Invaders*. Atari accounted for more than half of Warner's profits, and the Warner stock price rose to record heights solely on the basis of its video game profits. The stock market had faith the good times would last forever.

Ross knew that Atari was likely to start reporting losses and he began selling his own Warner shares, in total $21 million over the course of a year. When the sharp downturn in earnings was announced in late 1982, Warner's stock plunged. But the Reagan SEC did not investigate Ross for insider sales. Shareholders did sue, however, and on the stand Ross denied knowing anything about Atari's collapse beforehand. The company settled the suit for $17 million.

Atari lost nearly $1 billion over the next two years, and with Warner's stock now well down, the company was vulnerable to a hostile takeover. Many observers believed Ross's run was over, and in 1982 Rupert Murdoch hired Allen & Co. to investigate a takeover. Ross resisted and sought a white knight in businessman Herb Siegel, who owned Chris-Craft and had bought a large piece of Warner, making it difficult for Murdoch to launch a hostile acquisition.

Then Ross pulled a rabbit out of his hat. He bought out American Express's half ownership in Warner-Amex, the cable joint venture. When Ross first got Robinson to buy in five years earlier, the Amex chief had paid several hundred million dollars, reimbursing the full cost to Ross of his total investment in cable thus far. So Ross had already had half of the cable operation essentially for free. To pay for the purchase, Ross had to sell some valuable properties, including Showtime. But now he had the giant cable company to himself.

The cable subsidiary's losses remained substantial, however, until a new deregulatory bill supported by Reagan removed controls on the prices charged for subscriptions, allowing Warner Cable and others to raise them significantly. Before this, the local franchises had been treated like the monopolies they were and their prices were regulated, like those of utilities. The company worth about $800 million when Ross bought out Amex's half in 1984 was worth $4 billion by the early 1990s.

With Ross back on top, his enthusiasm turned to his biggest potential deal, a proposed merger with Time Inc., the magazine empire. The old-line, white-shoe publishing company was dubious about aligning itself with a man once associated with the mob, the subject of several legal investigations, and so well connected in entertainment he could overpower the more staid executives of its own company. But as entertainment companies grew ever larger, even Time Inc. executives believed the company was now too small and vulnerable and needed to expand beyond print and HBO to cable television and movie studio production. Ross, as usual, was ecstatic to merge with such a prestigious company, anticipating synergies between the prestigious magazines and entertainment production. The merger was completed in 1989, a $20 billion exchange of stock.

Ross, diagnosed with cancer, soon weakened, and he died in 1992. Gerald Levin, a former HBO executive who had fought for the merger, was named CEO. Seeking competitive size, he bought Turner Broadcasting Network from Ted Turner in 1995. In 2000, he went on to merge Time Warner with AOL in one of the most costly business mistakes of the time as AOL's profits fell sharply. Running entertainment companies was high finance in the new age, and men made fortunes trading movie and other entertainment companies like baseball cards, creating ever bigger enterprises with which to keep the competition at bay and bid ever higher for everything from the rights to broadcast the Olympics to big-name television and movie stars. In this environment, even Ted Turner was swallowed up.

Turner was born in 1938 in Cincinnati and raised in Atlanta, son of a self-made but emotionally fragile man who had built a successful billboard advertising company. Ed Turner was an alcoholic and drug addict, as well as a depressed man with large dreams and frustrated ambitions. When

Ted was twenty-four, his father killed himself. Young Ted took over the company in 1962, and completed the acquisition of a far larger billboard company that his father had backed away from. Now Ted was running one of the ten largest billboard advertising companies in the nation, but he was not easily satisfied. Several years later he bought a handful of radio stations and eventually an Atlanta UHF TV station, Channel 17.

His initial interest in television was not to raise its quality but to clean it up morally. On his TV station, he played cartoons, TV reruns like *The Mickey Mouse Club,* and old Hollywood movies. Ted, like his father, was a conservative, and had supported Barry Goldwater in 1964.

In 1976, Turner had a bold idea. The year before, Gerald Levin, then a young Time Inc. executive, had made Home Box Office, already a high-quality service offering recently released movies, into a nationwide operation. RCA had just launched America's first commercial satellite and Levin bought time on it. He could then send his signal across the nation to local cable operators who would pay a fee to show HBO programming to their subscribers. The cable operators badly needed programming, and Levin provided them high-quality Hollywood movies.

Turner was inspired. He bought time on the satellite and made his Channel 17 in Atlanta available to any cable operator with a satellite dish. His edge was that he didn't charge them a fee, but sold advertising time himself to the New York agencies, and kept the proceeds. Cable entrepreneurs like John Malone of Tele-Communications in Denver and Ross of Warner Cable were beginning to buy cable systems long before they were profitable, anticipating that once a threshold was crossed, money would roll in. What they needed was programming, even the poor quality of Turner's Channel 17, which was soon called the Superstation, "a revolutionary insight," according to one media writer. Turner made a lot of money. He bought the Atlanta Braves to fill air time and later he bought the Atlanta Hawks basketball team.

But Turner always had a moral mission. He wanted to undermine the monopoly of the three networks. Still a politically conservative programmer in those years, he was opposed to the lurid movies of Hollywood and the "negative" news of the networks. In 1978, a veteran newsman, Reese Schonfeld, brought Turner the idea of a twenty-four-hour television news service, which Schonfeld, for one, had been trying to start for some time. Levin at Time Inc. had tried but failed to convince his fellow executives to start one in 1977, especially with all of Time Inc.'s newsgathering capabilities. The Superstation having made Turner rich, he warmed to the idea immediately, and put Schonfeld in charge. Their relationship was difficult from the beginning, but the Cable News Network, though it drained Turner's money for several years, was on the map in 1979 and fully running by 1980.

Turner's politics changed radically as he became more intimately involved with news around the world. He also became friendly with President Carter, also from Georgia, who often invited him to the White House. CNN had a vitality that was lacking in conventional network news, and viewers gravitated to it. While most thought its success was based on news being broadcast twenty-four hours a day, in fact the news on CNN was more daring, less predictable, more relevant, and usually more honest.

Turner also started a cable entertainment network, TNT, which mostly ran old TV programs already out of syndication, and another network, Turner Classic Movies, which featured the old Hollywood films he loved. He had bought MGM's movie library, the most coveted of the studio's old films, but the expensive transaction hamstrung him financially ever after, leaving him with so much debt, even with CNN's profits, that he had to find financial partners. The largest stake went to John Malone, whose Tele-Communications was the biggest cable operator in the country.

By the mid-1980s, Turner felt hemmed in as he competed head-on with the mammoth TV networks. He had CNN and TNT, but he did not have the broad TV distribution that could give him the leverage to invest in ever more expensive programming, whose costs were being driven up by the larger networks. ABC, CBS, and NBC could bid far more for professional football or the best Hollywood movies, or even for movie stars to make TV series. Turner wanted to bid for CBS in 1985, but only Michael Milken supported him, and the deal fell through.

CNN kept growing and its twenty-four-hour coverage of the 1990 Iraq conflict raised its reputation to an unassailable peak. Ironically, Time Warner was also beginning to feel left out again. Rupert Murdoch was a newspaper owner across several continents and now had a movie studio and a TV network and was competitively breathing down everyone's neck, bidding aggressively for the rights to programming, while driving up its costs. Time Warner had an international newsgathering capability, the profitable HBO, and Warner Bros., but it had nothing like CNN or a TV network.

Both Levin and Turner were also concerned because the Federal Communications Commission rules that limited TV and newspaper ownership had been loosened in the 1990s. Formerly, networks could own only a limited number of local TV stations. Cross-ownership of newspapers and local TV stations had also been limited. Now, government concerns about the dominance even of news by a few organizations were disregarded as free market economic thinking grew in influence. A principal beneficiary was the ever-expanding Murdoch, who was a major owner of a New York newspaper, a New York local television station, a twenty-four-hour news channel on Fox cable TV, and a national TV network (not to mention the movie studio and TV production operation).

Turner knew by the 1990s he could not survive on his own. Levin at Time Warner felt the same way about his already mammoth organization. "You needed to control everything," Turner told journalist Ken Auletta. "You want to have a hospital and a funeral home, so when people die in the hospital you move them right over to the funeral home next door. When they're born, you get 'em. When they're sick, you get 'em. When they die, you get 'em."

It was classic tasteless Turner, but he summed up what was now driving entertainment executives across the nation. They had to buy up whatever operations were still independent and they were willing to pay ever-higher prices to do so. Wall Street bankers were there as handmaidens, urging them on, and providing the financing and expertise.

Levin bought Turner Broadcasting in 1996 for $7.5 billion in stock. Turner himself got about 25 percent of that, and as the share price of Time Warner rose, he became even richer. "I'm tired of being little for my whole life," Turner told *The New York Times*. He was assured that CNN would keep its independence. But its edge was softened, its courageous reporting mostly a memory, and it began to lose ground to the growing competition. Turner was tired and eventually he resigned from the company. Levin went on, as noted, to merge with AOL in 2000, determined to get bigger and bigger.

In terms of content, all news channels soon spoke with one middle-of-the-road voice, including CNN, avoiding controversy, except for the openly conservative Fox News. There were always sparks of creativity, but the movie companies followed similar principles to make hits. The television networks kept losing audience.

The concentration of the industry was mostly not criticized in a time when deals like these seemed natural and a man like Turner felt tiny and picked on by the men who created nothing comparable to what he did. This was not always how it was.

Entertainment, news, and communications were now run according to financial criteria, and size inevitably became the most important criterion for survival. When there are strong financial incentives to homogenize news and entertainment, and government stops demanding independence and variety of ownership, the dangers are evident. There were more movie channels and sports coverage, and eventually cable TV did original programming. But the shows were generally similar. As for movie entertainment, the common denominator became violence. Movies for mature adults became rarer. There were occasional bright spots, but TV series stuck to formulas.

Serious news in particular was discarded in favor of entertaining and titillating stories. There were no longer locally produced documentaries on TV, nor did network news divisions provide serious hour-long fare for prime time. Features replaced hard news on front pages. Serious issues were covered less regularly and far more briefly. Print stories were shorter and sound bites in TV news were reduced literally to a few seconds from the thirty seconds to a minute of earlier times. The number of foreign bureaus was cut back sharply in both print and TV news operations. In general, the range of political views on major news channels narrowed, with the exception of the overtly conservative Fox News and liberal MSNBC. In the name of size, marketing power, and efficiency, dependable information became scarcer and informational and cultural diversity narrowed.

9

Jimmy Carter

CAPITULATION

Jimmy Carter was a fresh face in American politics, idealistic, a Southerner, and seemingly open to new ideas. A religious man, the Democrat was modest and private about his faith. A governor of Georgia for only one term, he had little national record to criticize. Some felt he had the answer to the economy that the old Washington professionals did not. He promised as much, confident that in office he could assess the pros and cons of policy proposals and arrive at a right answer.

His image of frankness and honesty, and the promise of change, more than any concrete set of solutions—few details of which he presented in the campaign—appealed at a time when the nation had been stung by harsh economic conditions, the Watergate scandal, and demanding foreign policy issues. Carter had attracted national attention as governor of Georgia for his strong stand against segregation, becoming known as one of the South's New Governors, according to *Time* magazine. He captured the presidential nomination, not in the political backrooms, but by taking his message directly to the people and winning key early electoral tests—the Iowa caucus and the New Hampshire primary. America was willing to give this Democrat who promised more jobs a chance. He beat the incumbent, Gerald Ford, by a narrow margin,

Rather than providing a new direction, Carter, despite his evident intelligence, offered more of the same. He reinforced the prevailing fears of government size; started a broad deregulatory revolution, some of it useful, much of it not; and shifted economic policies even more often than Gerald Ford. His well-meant but frustrating international efforts regarding nuclear disarmament and Mideast peace also provoked his detractors. In economic matters, he was soon known more for his vacillation than

President Jimmy Carter with his economic advisers, from left to right: Council of Economic Advisers chairman Charles Schultze, Federal Reserve chairman Arthur Burns, Treasury Secretary Michael Blumenthal, Budget Director Bert Lance

his conviction, at one moment worried about unemployment, at the next inflation, all the while reinforcing the nation's lack of confidence in government. The result was still more inflation and only modest growth to go with it.

Carter, it turned out, did not comprehend what a difficult, nearly intractable set of circumstances he was facing, a domestic agenda more complex and perplexing than any post–World War II president faced before him and with an inflationary environment to which the well-learned lessons of Depression economics did not seem fully to apply. His was not a time for dithering, but he seemed to America to dither. He did not offer serious economic change but relatively small gestures. He scolded America for its lack of will rather than leading it assertively down a new path.

Among new economic issues to be dealt with were a falling dollar, a rising trade deficit, high oil prices, federal controls on domestic oil prices, serious crop failures, another Arab oil embargo, the clash of economic theories at the best universities, and far higher levels of both inflation and unemployment. Most important was a sudden reduction in the rate of productivity growth, the amount the economy could produce per hour of work, that no one anticipated, including Milton Friedman and his sympathizers, and few even perceived at first.

Finally frustrated with inflation, he appointed the strong-minded Paul Volcker as head of the Federal Reserve in 1979, late in his presidential term, and Volcker ultimately adopted a severe policy of high interest rates to combat rising prices, causing the worst recession of the post–World War II period a couple of years later under Ronald Reagan. Carter was ambivalent about Volcker's approach but did not criticize him. It was Reagan who later enjoyed the political benefits of Volcker's anti-inflationary policies, enthusiastically supporting him, and at the same time winning popularity for his deep tax cuts, despite causing enormous potentially inflationary budget deficits. Carter's policies led to a long period starting in the 1980s whose policy priorities were restrained wages and minimal inflation. This was an environment in which financial markets thrived as interest rates fell—both stock and bond prices rose sharply—but new investment remained tepid. Wall Street prospered as American doubts about the purpose and uses of government only grew.

Jimmy Carter was born in Plains, Georgia, in 1924, the son of a prosperous peanut farmer. Carter could, however, remember the earlier years when his father struggled to build the business. He graduated from the Naval Academy at Annapolis in 1946 and later took advanced courses in nuclear engineering in the Navy. He wanted to make a career in the armed services, but when his father died in 1953, he resigned to run the family business, which he successfully grew.

As a politician, the businessman in Carter promised to end waste and inefficiency in government. He had a visceral dislike for deficit spending. Charles Schultze, Carter's chairman of the Council of Economic Advisers, later said that in economic matters Carter was a fiscal conservative who was eager to balance the budget.

But he was torn. He was sympathetic with working people and strongly supported the civil rights movement. He was not easily about to have the poor, the disadvantaged, and black people bear the burden of subduing inflation. He ran for president partly on a platform to create new jobs, but had little idea how that contradicted his fiscal conservatism. When *BusinessWeek* asked him what his economic philosophy was after he won the presidency, he said he had none.

He brought to office a set of experts and friends with contradictory views, some of them cronies from Georgia, whom he valued as much as he did the Washington professionals. His close confidant, the lively lawyer Bert Lance, an economic conservative, was put in charge of the Office of Management and Budget. Another aide was a young Atlanta lawyer, Stuart Eizenstat, his informal chief of staff, who was politically liberal. Carter named Michael Blumenthal, chairman of the Bendix Corporation, as his treasury secretary. Born in Germany, he was a trained economist, with a Ph.D. from Princeton, but he was skeptical of theory and determined to subdue inflation.

Charles Schultze, his chief economist, was a conventional Democratic economist. Born in 1924, Schultze was more Washington insider than academic economist, though he was well trained. He went to college at Georgetown University, graduating in 1948, and later earned a master's degree there. He got his Ph.D. in 1960, studying nights at the University of Maryland, which like most respected economics departments of the time had a Keynesian orientation. Schultze was on President Eisenhower's CEA staff in the 1950s and later the budget director for Lyndon Johnson. He was an acolyte of the influential Keynesians of the Kennedy and Johnson administrations. He was there when Johnson refused to raise taxes and he was chastened later by the inflationary experience of the 1970s. The respected academic Keynesian theorist Lawrence Klein had been Carter's principal economic adviser when he was running for the presidency. Klein developed one of the first econometric models of the economy, largely based on Keynesian principles, for which he later won a Nobel Prize. But when Carter offered him the policy job, he turned it down. Carter then offered it to Schultze, for whom it would be the crowning achievement thus far in his career.

The increasingly centrist Schultze, the moderate conservative Blumenthal, and the more conservative Lance (who was forced out of office a year later due to a banking scandal) served as Carter's economic troika. Tempering them from the political left was both his labor secretary, Ray Marshall, a liberal economics professor and an outspoken defender of organized labor, and also Vice President Walter Mondale.

Carter deliberately diversified his team of advisers and did not lean heavily on any one of them. He himself participated in most of the policy debates, as his advisers put it, the hub of the wheel while they were the spokes. "Carter promised almost everyone a say in economic policy after he won," said Schultze. But in later years many said Carter was simply arrogant, believing he could come up with the right answer if he gave it enough thought. Schultze complained that Carter never gave him the power to say no to anyone. Others believed Schultze could have pressed his economic views more forcefully on Carter. Instead, Schultze shrank from the role of firm decision maker, preferring to enumerate the pros and cons of various policy alternatives and let Carter decide, as seemed to be the president's preference. "Carter was very bright but he often sent inconsistent signals," said Barry Bosworth, the former Johnson official brought in by Schultze to head Carter's voluntary wage and price controls. In taking on so many decisions himself, Bosworth said, Carter developed no coordinated strategy.

The man likely to hold some decision-making power was Eizenstat, who was closest to being Carter's chief of staff, but he was given no such responsibility. He wrote summary memos to Carter that typically presented not just two or three but many options. Carter's economists failed to develop a consistent strategy or set of answers, as their guiding Keynesian principles were increasingly challenged by the alternative theories of Friedman and others in a new, confusing, and finally frightening inflationary environment.

Carter held within himself the contradiction that he would contend with ever after. He believed that rising prices had developed a forward momentum due to excessive spending, including by government, placing pressure on its limited capacities and resources, and that the American people had to reduce their expectations. He thus became known for talking more about what America could not do than what it could. "We have learned that more is not necessarily better, that even our great nation has its recognized limits, and that we can neither answer all questions nor solve all problems," he said in his inaugural address. He did not consider that perhaps the nation could expand its capacities to produce goods and services and someday again meet its high expectations.

His first economic policy initiative on taking office in 1977 was to keep his campaign promise and stimulate the economy to get unemployment down, which Schultze fully supported. Reflecting Carter's ambivalence, however, the administration proposed a timid fiscal package of spending and business tax cuts totaling $15 billion in stimulus, and an additional $15 billion in 1978, significantly less as a proportion of GDP than Ford's last stimulus and far less than Nixon's in 1972. Schultze got Carter to include a $50 rebate for every American and a tax credit for business investment. The Democratic Congress, more liberal on balance than the president, wanted the business tax incentives to be linked to the creation of jobs.

Labor Secretary Marshall and Congress also demanded that the administration double the number of public service jobs the federal government created under the Comprehensive Employment and Training Act, CETA, which had been passed several years earlier under Nixon. Thus, a jobs program was included.

But Carter wanted to suppress inflation at the same time, and his advisers led by Schultze agreed. On this matter they were only slightly different from the Republicans they replaced. As Schultze put it in an early 1977 memo, "Inflation has continued at around a 6 to 6½ percent rate not because aggregate demand has grown too rapidly, but because the momentum of inflation is so strong." They paid relatively little attention to the temporary nature of the OPEC oil price hikes, the crop failures, the after-effects of the Nixon price freeze, and the overstatement of housing inflation. The Schultze CEA described the momentum of inflation created by expectations in their first Economic Report of the President:

> Inflationary momentum becomes built into the structure of the economy in several ways. Expectations of inflation and workers' desires to maintain their real wages lead to indexing of wage rates to price increases in both a formal and informal fashion. . . . Widespread belief that inflation will continue also leads businesses to accede to cost increases in the expectation of being able to pass the costs forward into higher prices. These price increases become the basis for still further rounds of wage increases.

The explanation was essentially identical to the one that Volcker and Weidenbaum subscribed to when they developed Nixon's wage-price freeze.

Schultze might have advised outright wage and price controls, but the failure of Nixon's ill-conceived program made that politically impossible. Instead, the Carter advisers proposed a voluntary system of wage and price restraints for business and labor starting in April 1977. Barry Bosworth was put in charge of the Council on Wage and Price Stability, the commission that had been formed earlier under Nixon, which would administer the new voluntary restraints.

By the time the program went into effect in the spring, Carter backtracked on his stimulus proposal. The economy, he thought, seemed to be reviving, as retail sales strengthened in April and inflation rose slightly for a couple of months. Carter's reaction to the short-term data reflected his oversensitivity to inflation and his overmanagement; a little patience would have served him well. He now wanted to scrap Schultze's proposed

$50 rebate. Lance and Blumenthal, the administration's inflation fighters, supported Carter's decision, but Schultze and Eizenstat still wanted it, as did Walter Mondale. The modest $50 rebate became a battleground. "Bert, Mike Blumenthal and I were more conservative than anybody else among my advisors," Carter said in an interview years later. "The test came with the fifty-dollar rebate." Carter maintained his position, the rebate was dropped, and the proposed fiscal stimulus was reduced. No one in the administration seemed capable of pressing the notion that the administration could deal with inflation better over time, stabilizing the economy at perhaps an unemployment rate of 5 to 6 percent rather than 4 percent on one side or 7 percent on the other, as inflationary expectations were reduced. There was a characteristic urgency to solve the deeply entrenched problem too quickly, and certainly before the next congressional election.

The most damaging long-term change in the economy, in fact, was not inflationary expectations but the slowdown in the rate of growth of productivity, not yet noticed, even by the astute Schultze, though he suspected it before most others. If businesses could not produce much more per worker, they could not give the same raises as in the past without raising prices to maintain profit margins.

In the recent past, productivity increased at an average 3 percent a year, adjusted for the ups and downs of business cycles, and now it was increasing at only 1 percent a year—a momentous fall-off if continued over the long run. And America was indeed about to embark on just that—a long period of slow productivity growth. Schultze, however, did not yet think the low productivity growth rate was permanent, but he had come to believe that pushing the unemployment rate even to 5.5 percent, when most Democrats still believed 4 percent was possible, might now have been inflationary. Still, even 6 percent was a serious improvement over the current rate, which was well above 7 percent.

One anti-inflation policy initiative undertaken by Carter, and ultimately a far-reaching one, was the deregulation of formerly fixed prices for several industries. As a former businessman, he believed such regulations led to inefficiencies and higher prices. He was joined by the traditional liberal Senator Ted Kennedy, his Democratic rival, who saw controls as favoring the monopoly power of airlines and truckers. Deregulation would help bring down prices, Kennedy believed. Carter brought the affable, even charming Alfred Kahn to his administration as head of the Civil Aeronautics Board, a rare economist who could handle himself with wit and grace publicly. Kahn, who had first worked in the New Deal, had developed an expertise in government regulation as head of the New York Public Service Commission, where he introduced market-oriented reforms. Under Kahn, and with Kennedy's support, airline fares were deregulated in 1978, and by 1980 trucking and railroads were also deregulated. Guided by the same principles, Carter also wanted to deregulate banking by eliminating Regulation Q. Wriston's ultimate wish was coming true under a Democrat. Although Kennedy did not support financial deregulation, the Democratic Party was turning into the political party of high finance. Carter was consistent about this deregulatory ideology, and he prevailed.

The economy suddenly appeared to be weakening again toward the end of 1977. Now Schultze, largely endorsed by Carter, urged a new stimulus, a $25 billion set of tax cuts, three quarters of which would benefit individuals. The proposal also sought to close tax loopholes for upper-income taxpayers, a favorite concern of Carter's.

By this time, the administration was well aware that there was a growing groundswell of public opinion in favor of tax cuts. Proposition 13, which called for sharp reductions in the property taxes that supported public education, was gaining adherents in California and a federal bill to cut income taxes by one third over three years, co-sponsored by the charismatic representative Jack Kemp, was making headway in Congress.

In early 1978, the administration replaced the Nixon appointee at the Fed, Arthur Burns, who had been keeping interest rates too high for their purposes. Carter's new chairman was the CEO of Textron, William Miller. Miller, it was widely believed, would be more sympathetic with helping to boost employment as the congressional elections approached and therefore not as eager to raise interest rates.

In a year and a few months, the Carter administration had already switched the direction of policy three times. But in May 1978, Carter switched again as both inflation and the federal budget deficit started to rise. Now he wanted to cut his stimulus plan and postpone any tax cuts as well. The administration also suppressed the Humphrey-Hawkins bill, named after its Democratic sponsors, Hubert Humphrey and a veteran African American congressman, Augustus Hawkins, which would have required the Federal Reserve to make a low unemployment rate an explicit objective, perhaps as low as 4 percent. Schultze was convinced that would be inflationary. At his urging, Carter removed the teeth from the bill, and a more innocuous version passed in October 1978.

The fourth switch in tactics was again an overreaction by Carter to the short-term data. The spurt in measured consumer inflation in early

1978 was largely due to yet another poor crop, the third of the decade, and the inaccurate way of measuring housing costs. The Bureau of Labor Statistics, the federal agency that gathers and computes the inflation data, significantly exaggerated housing costs because it recorded costs of new housing—current mortgage rates and house prices—as if these were the costs that all homeowners paid. In an inflationary time, as rates rose for new homes, this method gave an especially distorted picture. In the 1980s, the methodology would be changed, but that was two years away; it now added more than 1 percentage point to the reported inflation rate, and the failed crops considerably more than that.

Then, early in 1979, food prices exploded upward again due to yet another poor crop yield. Mortgage rates, measured incorrectly, were also rising. The Shah of Iran, long supported by the United States, was overthrown in early 1979. Oil exports were cut off and the price of crude was doubled. By the summer of 1980, the cutoff of oil exports closed half of the nation's gas stations, and the costs of energy to consumers—electricity, gasoline, home heating oil—tripled. In 1979, the government reported that consumer inflation rose to an annual rate of more than 13 percent. In 1979, Treasury bills were paying an interest rate of almost 11 percent a year, the typical mortgage rate approached nearly 12 percent, and the banks' prime lending rate to their best borrowers reached nearly 13 percent. In early 1980, reported consumer inflation temporarily reached an annual rate of almost 15 percent.

Under the influence of Milton Friedman, all the talk was now about the rapidly growing money supply, as well as the rising budget deficit and inflationary expectations, especially the role played by the unions that had their wages indexed automatically to inflation. But core inflation was actually much lower than the reported rate; few were of a mind to take notice. Economist Alan Blinder later found that the growth in the money supply could not have caused the high inflation rate. The money supply didn't rise nearly fast enough to explain the inflationary spurt attributed to it by the Friedmanites and much of Wall Street. According to Blinder's estimates, in 1978, after energy and food price increases were removed, and housing measured properly, the core inflation rate was 7 percent. In 1979, the core inflation rate was 9 percent, as noted earlier, much lower than the reported rate of 13 percent.

No one in the Carter administration was willing to make the case strongly at the time that much of the increased inflation was temporary and that the right policy was patience. Certainly Schultze did not press on

Carter a policy of waiting inflation out. The nation had been convinced by policymakers and the preachings of Friedman, his followers on Wall Street, and support in the media, that inflation was intractable, except by reducing budget deficits and sharply tightening monetary policy.

Nor did the policymakers recognize that because banks had new sources of funding, higher interest rates were not nearly as restrictive as they once were, the points repeated continually by economists Henry Kaufman and Albert Wojnilower. They would have to go much higher to bite.

As the inflation rate rose, the value of the dollar also fell further, which raised import prices and added still more to inflation. The gold price kept rising as investors sought a safe haven for their money, reaching $400 an ounce by the end of 1979, compared to roughly $125 an ounce when Carter took office. The supposedly prescient bond traders drove interest rates up as if the reported inflation data were accurate as well. Consumer confidence, according to the University of Michigan index, fell from 87 when Carter took office to 60 in 1979. Carter's overall approval rating fell to about 25 percent from 47 percent a year earlier. This president was not about to disabuse the nation of its inflationary fears. Instead, he, like much of Washington, panicked.

Most of the political pressure to stop inflation now fell on William Miller at the Fed. Schultze and Blumenthal both publicly argued that monetary policy should be tightened more, but Miller told *The New York Times* that he resisted tightening further because he believed the economy was weak. In fact, he had been raising rates rapidly by any historical standard—the federal funds target rate up 3 percentage points in a matter of months. But with inflation so high and lenders and borrowers almost immune to the restrictions once imposed by rising rates, a far higher increase than in the past was, in retrospect, called for to have the same dampening effect.

In July 1979, a frustrated Carter took his key advisers to Camp David to discuss the issues, much as Nixon had done eight years before. When Carter returned from the weekend, he made a speech watched by two thirds of the television public. He told the nation it faced a deep-seated crisis not so much because of new circumstances but because of a national attitude that needed adjustment. "It is a crisis of confidence," he said. "It is a crisis that strikes at the very heart and soul and spirit of our national will. We can see this crisis in the growing doubt about the meaning of our own lives and in the loss of a unity of purpose for our nation. The erosion of our confidence in the future is threatening to destroy the social and the political fabric of America."

This religious man, who had always kept his faith out of politics, seemed to attribute the nation's plight to a loss of personal meaning. By any presidential standard, it was an intelligent speech. But he asked the nation to accept sacrifice and lower its sights when the nation wanted action and someone to blame. An aide said that the speech suggested America suffered from "malaise," and so the speech was dubbed, even though Carter had not used the word.

At first, judging by calls to the White House and television news departments, the public reacted positively. But the stock market fell when trading opened on Monday. On Tuesday, Carter asked for the resignation of all of his cabinet members, only then to decide who would stay. Treasury Secretary Blumenthal, Health Education and Welfare Secretary Joseph Califano, and Energy Secretary James Schlesinger were let go, the rest retained. (Carter had created the Energy Department to deal with the energy shortages.)

Carter had trouble finding an immediate replacement for Blumenthal. David Rockefeller of Chase Manhattan Bank, Reginald Jones of General Electric, and Irving Shapiro of DuPont reportedly turned down the job. So Carter moved his Federal Reserve chairman, William Miller, into the Treasury job, removing Miller from a hot seat.

Carter now appointed as Fed chairman Paul Volcker, who after serving in the Treasury had become president of the New York Federal Reserve Bank. Volcker was far better schooled in economics than Miller. He was also determined to stop inflation, now well into double digits—more determined to meet his objective than many had thought. In their meeting, Carter liked his strong stand and his willingness to speak his mind. Given his strong anti-inflationary views and his frank discussion with Carter, Volcker was surprised that he got the job.

Howard Jarvis and Jack Kemp

Disappointment in the Carter presidency added to the concerns
about the economy and contributed to the building tax revolt in
the nation. But the worry was more over inflation than over employment.
A University of Michigan survey found that every year since 1975 (even
when the inflation rate fell sharply in 1976), consumers said they were more
worried about rising prices than jobs. In the years under Nixon and Ford,
America changed. Wages adjusted for inflation grew much more slowly on
average in the 1970s than in the 1950s and 1960s. Men's wages in particular
grew extremely slowly if at all. Understandably, Americans sensed that it
was inflation eating away at their paychecks, not a lack of job prospects,
that was keeping them back.

In California, the unfinished business of Reagan's governorship—the
failure of Proposition 1—was being finished without him by Howard Jarvis. Jarvis had been working the conservative political fields of California
since the 1930s. From early adulthood, he was obsessed with big government and taxes. Born in 1903 in a small town near Salt Lake City, he idol-
ized his strong-willed, strict father, who worked as a carpenter during the
day and studied law by mail at night. Eventually the senior Jarvis became a
respected Utah judge. Jarvis's mother's family had moved from Illinois to
Utah before she was born because "they were sold on Mormonism," wrote
Jarvis, and his mother attended the Mormon church for the rest of her life.

After graduating from the University of Utah with a law degree, Jarvis
did not want to follow his father into the profession. Instead, he bought a
weekly newspaper called *The Magna Times* in 1925, named after the tiny
Utah town in which the family lived. Journalism excited him more than
law, and he had a talent for selling ads. Jarvis bought more newspapers

Howard Jarvis, right, with Paul Gann,
campaigning for Proposition 13

in the region. He particularly liked muck-raking journalism and published stories on corrupt government officials and fraudulent stockbrokers. Soon he was prosperous, running some fifteen papers in all, and playing golf every day, besides. He was actively involved in local political organizations like the Lions Club, the Chamber of Commerce, and the Young Republicans.

He was pugnacious and competitive, a fighter in many ways. Small but stout, he indeed won money as a prizefighter as a young man. He wrote that he had a golf handicap of two and was a first-rate ballroom dancer. With money in his pocket, he was now even more confident, and his gregarious personality won him constant attention.

Politics inspired Jarvis. Early in his life he came to prefer the Republicans, though his father was a traditional Southern Democrat. He was not devout, but he admired his mother's Mormon church. The Mormons were what "Americanism" was all about, he wrote in his 1979 autobiography. Comparing Salt Lake City to Detroit or San Francisco, he went on, is like comparing a temple to a stable.

Such politically conservative outspokenness characterized him. He became an ardent antigovernment conservative by his thirties, developed an intense hatred for Franklin Roosevelt, and praised Winston Churchill, whom he said he had met. His autobiography reads like a folksy yarn and he claimed Gary Cooper and Clark Gable as friends.

Jarvis moved to California in 1935 at the urging of a friend, Earl Warren, then a conservative himself but later the liberal Supreme Court chief justice. In California, Jarvis invested in one business after another, built profitable manufacturing companies, and became, by the 1950s boom, one of California's largest industrial employers. He was active in politics, serving as the California manager of Nixon's 1960 presidential campaign, and ran for several offices himself, entering the Republican primary for Senate in 1962. He never won. In 1962, not yet forty, he essentially retired from business and turned his attention to his greatest concern, high taxes.

He hit pay dirt in the late 1970s when he teamed up with another relentless antitax businessman, Paul Gann, far less flamboyant but more organized than Jarvis. Gann had transplanted himself years earlier from Arkansas to California, where he became a real estate salesman. He had switched from Democrat to Republican in the 1970s. Though the diffident Gann was no match for the explosive Jarvis in capturing attention or creating public enthusiasm, he had built a solid political organization of volunteers and activists whose support he could mobilize. Jarvis needed Gann's people to gather enough signatures to put Proposition 13 on the ballot. The goal was to reduce property taxes permanently.

Milton Friedman, by now far more visible than in 1972 when he first campaigned for Reagan's Proposition 1, was easily persuaded to support the new initiative, and appeared in television ads for the bill. "During our fifteen year struggle against property taxes," wrote Jarvis in his autobiography, "we were never even able to gather enough signatures to qualify our tax initiatives for the ballot, until the end of 1977, when we succeeded in collecting 1.5 million signatures of registered California voters—the most in the state's history." His rallying cry was, "I am mad as hell," and it touched a chord he hadn't been able to reach until then. He made it the title of his book.

Since Reagan had lost his tax reduction referendum in 1973, property values in California had risen rapidly, pushed up by inflation, which in turn led to higher property taxes as appraised values shot upward. For example, home prices in the San Francisco areas rose by 18 percent a year on average between 1973 and 1978, and rose still faster in Los Angeles. Property taxes on a $45,000 home in Los Angeles increased from $1,160 in 1973 to $2,070 a few years later. The increases were especially hard on the elderly, whose incomes were often low and fixed.

Less severe reforms than the Jarvis-Gann amendment, which would limit taxes to only 1 percent of the cash value of a property instead of the prevailing average of 2.6 percent, could have ameliorated the burden, but by 1978, anger stoked by Jarvis and others was high. In 1963, only 49 percent of Americans, traditionally resistant to taxes, thought taxes in general were too high. By 1976, 72 percent believed they were too high. Even though income tax rates had been cut under Kennedy and Johnson, inflation in the 1970s now seemed to drive up the taxes paid. As wages were increased to keep up with prices, ordinary taxpayers were pushed into higher federal tax brackets, known as "bracket creep."

After years of disappointing economic policies, compounded by the long Vietnam War, Watergate, social change concerning sexual mores, the role of women and minorities, and Great Society programs meant to aid the disadvantaged, skepticism about government ran high. Two social scientists devised an index to measure distrust of government. The "antigovernment" index began to rise in the late 1960s but then much more rapidly, increasing by 139 percent from 1958 to 1980, when it reached its highest level. Americans were also increasingly distrustful of business over this period, but the rate of increase in a similarly designed index to measure attitudes toward business was not nearly as great, up one third as much.

In June 1978, Proposition 13 was affirmed by 65 percent of voters. In addition to lowering the property tax rate, it limited future increases. Property taxes in California had been 50 percent higher than the national average and now were, under the new law, 35 percent below the national average. Jarvis became among the best-known personalities in the nation. (So well known, he made a cameo appearance in the Hollywood hit *Airplane!*) In total, Proposition 13 reduced California government revenues by roughly $7 billion in its first year, or 40 percent.

Other antitax efforts gained ground as well. In 1978, personal income taxes were lowered in New York, New Mexico, Maine, and Minnesota. Other taxes were reduced in Vermont, Colorado, and Mississippi, among thirteen states.

By early 1978, Lewis Uhler was gearing up constitutional amendments to limit income taxes, and was succeeding. In the November elections in 1978, Michigan, Hawaii, Arizona, Illinois, and Texas passed referendums favoring limits on state spending. Twenty-two states in association with the National Taxpayers Union asked for a nationwide constitutional convention to adopt an amendment to limit taxes. And Jake Garn successfully sponsored Proposition 4 in California, which called for a constitutional amendment to limit any increase in income taxes to the rise in the cost of living. A stunning 74 percent of voters approved the amendment in 1979.

"California Vote Seen as Evidence of U.S. Tax Revolt," said a *New York Times* headline after the vote for Proposition 13. But the story was buried on page 23. The extent of change was not yet understood.

The widespread disenchantment with taxes gave rise to another strong-minded and convincing political figure whose main agenda was cutting taxes. Jack Kemp, handsome former star quarterback, was now a Republican congressman representing a heavily unionized district in Buffalo, New York. His popularity with working people, traditionally loyal to Democrats, was a harbinger of changing times. Kemp had been working on a tax reduction bill since 1974, and found a supportive Hoover Institution economist, Paul Craig Roberts, who had developed a "supply side" analysis of tax cuts that claimed such cuts would not result in a large budget deficit. Traditional Republicans balked at Kemp's ideas out of fear of large deficits, but Roberts argued that lower taxes would create such powerful incentives to invest and work that the growth rate of the economy would increase and incomes and tax receipts with it, offsetting the reduction in rates.

Kemp claimed he could now justify deep cuts in income taxes without demanding equally deep reductions in government spending, continually citing the success of the Kennedy-Johnson tax cuts a decade earlier as an example of the rapid growth and higher revenues tax reductions could generate.

But Democratic economists argued that it wasn't incentives due to lower tax rates but increased demand for goods and services that made the Kennedy-Johnson cuts effective. This was precisely the lesson of Keynesianism.

Roberts went to work for the House Budget Committee, and Kemp recruited former Nixon economist Arthur Laffer to help his cause. He famously created something called the Laffer curve to illustrate how tax revenues could increase—or at least not fall very much—when taxes were cut, not for Keynesian but for supply side reasons. Kemp introduced a massive tax cut bill in the House and Delaware senator William Roth introduced the bill in the Senate. The Kemp-Roth bill proposed cutting personal income taxes by 30 percent over ten years. The top tax bracket would be reduced from 70 percent to 50 percent (the Kennedy cut reduced the top bracket from roughly 90 percent to 70 percent), and the bottom bracket from 14 percent to 8 percent. The dramatic proposal was unthinkable only a few years earlier.

As inflation rose ever higher, Kemp and Roth had been rounding up congressional supporters, but it was the overwhelming passage of Proposition 13 in June 1978 that gave the Kemp-Roth bill the political boost it needed. The bill went before the Senate Finance Committee in July, where Herbert Stein and Alan Greenspan both testified in its favor. Ultimately, it was defeated in the Democratic-controlled House that August, but not before Ronald Reagan had made it a key part of his campaign for the White House.

Paul Volcker, Jimmy Carter, and Ronald Reagan

REVOLUTION COMPLETED

I t's not likely that President Carter thought carefully about the consequences of appointing Paul Volcker as the Federal Reserve chairman
or understood the extent of Volcker's determination to stop inflation. Nor
did the president fully understand the power of the Fed office or the reach
of its influence. By driving interest rates to record heights, he cut inflation to 4 percent by 1983. But Volcker ultimately delivered a major blow to
the U.S. economy in his single-minded quest to end inflation. He was so
widely admired for it that few ever criticized afterward the severity of the
medicine he administered—a deep recession, an unemployment rate of
11 percent, countless bankruptcies, low levels of investment, government
loan defaults around the world, and near bank failures at home. Volcker's
reputation grew so large, in fact, that Alan Greenspan, his successor in
1987, felt only one obligation, which was to show that he could be as tough
an inflation fighter as Volcker. Volcker became the heroic man of action
to Milton Friedman's man of ideas, and did as much or more to make low
inflation the nation's policy priority for the next thirty years, regardless
of the costs paid in persistent slower economic growth, high levels of
unemployment, and stagnating wages.

Volcker was not an ideologue or a Friedmanite. He adopted Friedman's monetarist policies when it suited his purpose—using them, without admitting it, as a cover for creating a steep recession to stop inflation.
He never fully endorsed monetarism: that growth of money alone caused
inflation, the monetarists' view that all that needed to be done to halt inflation was slow the growth rate of the money supply. But citing monetarism allowed him to administer the age-old recessionary medicine in a new
bottle. About one thing, however, Volcker was not flexible, and that was his
desire to place a stake in the heart of the inflationary menace.

Jimmy Carter shaking hands with new Federal Reserve chairman Paul Volcker, left, with newly designated Treasury Secretary William Miller at his side

Volcker never endorsed Friedman's view on deregulation or reduced government size, either. Friedman approved of almost any tax cuts, even if they caused federal budget deficits, because over time, he argued, such tax cuts forced governments to shrink in size, a policy that became popularized as "starving the beast." Volcker, in fact, was unnerved by Reagan's growing budget deficits because he thought them inflationary and debilitating on the grounds that they denied private borrowers capital and drove up interest rates. In turn, he favored strong government intervention, when necessary, such as when he rescued the banks in 1982 after the Mexican default, or to control overspeculation. He was closer in temperament and political ideology to a European statesman than an American banker.

In politics, however, he was no match for President Reagan, who reappointed him to office. Reagan praised Volcker's stern policies, thus acquiring Volcker's anti-inflation luster. But then Reagan cut taxes deeply while raising military spending, creating enormous budget deficits—far higher as a percentage of GDP than under Johnson, Nixon, or Carter. Volcker vehemently warned against the budget deficits and, even after the 1982 recession, kept rates higher than the Reagan advisers preferred as protection against what he thought would be the deficit's inflationary consequences.

By getting inflation down, Volcker enabled Reagan's revolutionary tax cut, which would otherwise have been inflationary. Volcker also supported Reagan's anti-union campaigns, because he thought rigid wage contracts were inflationary. Due to Volcker's efforts, Reagan kept his reputation as an inflation fighter even as budget deficits soared to 6 percent of GDP, and never fell below 3 percent of GDP during his second term, higher than in Carter's last year.

Once economic recovery was in sight, stock prices started to soar, winning support for Reagan from the financial sector. Though slow to back Reagan at first, and ambivalent about the budget deficits, some Wall Street financiers learned to like a Reagan administration that was lenient about restrictive regulations on banking and underwriting, and was willing to fight labor. Big business had been organizing more aggressively since the 1970s to raise its influence in Washington. The Business Roundtable, a group of CEOs from the nation's largest companies, was founded then. The Chamber of Commerce focused its activities on Washington lobbying. Conservative think tanks like the American Enterprise Institute produced economic research in favor of lower taxes and reduced regulations. Though the organizations were started or refocused in the 1970s, their conservative views did not fully congeal until the late 1970s and early 1980s. The Business Roundtable opposed the Kemp-Roth tax cuts and was skeptical of a Reagan candidacy, for example. Events would solidify their conservative policies, however, and their influence only rose.

Born in 1927, Volcker was the son of the town manager of Teaneck, New Jersey, and politics was dinner table conversation. He studied economics at Princeton, where he graduated Phi Beta Kappa. He had already been working summers at the Federal Reserve in Washington. Volcker went on to Havard, where he completed his course work toward an economics Ph.D. but did not do a dissertation. In the early 1950s, he went to the London School of Economics, completing a thesis on central banks. He found the British cultural atmosphere congenial and perhaps discovered role models for himself in the dedicated British government officials he met who saw government service as an admirable and long-term career. Back in the United States, he got a job as an economist under Robert Roosa in 1952, head of research at the New York Federal Reserve Bank.

In 1957, after serving Roosa, Volcker took a job offer from Chase Manhattan Bank, one of his few forays into the private sector, where he won the attention of the bank's president, David Rockefeller, who named him his assistant on congressional matters. But the rewards of the private sector apparently did not hold his interest. Imposingly tall, Volcker had little interest in sartorial splendor, his suits usually ill-fitting. The ashes of a ubiquitous cigar were often evident amid the pinstripes, definitely not the look of a classically polished aspiring investment banker. He always lived modestly, even after he had made some money as a private banker.

His serious work in Washington began under John F. Kennedy. Roosa became undersecretary of the treasury for monetary affairs and hired Volcker to do long-term planning. Volcker admired Roosa. "He was an intellect with a substantial body of writing on domestic monetary policy," wrote Volcker, "but he was also very much a doer with a richly inventive mind capable of spewing out ingenious technical approaches to strengthen and protect the monetary system." Volcker saw himself in Roosa's mold, a believer in government action to regulate and influence the markets. For example, Roosa conceived of the controversial interest equalization tax on interest earned by Americans who invested abroad to earn higher returns. The objective was to slow the outflow of dollars. It was an idea that a market purist like Friedman would have found objectionable, and Wriston railed against it; Volcker helped draft the legislation.

After a second stint at Chase Bank with David Rockefeller, David Kennedy, Nixon's Treasury secretary, asked Volcker, a Democrat, to join the Republican administration in 1969. By this time, he was caring for a wife with diabetes and two teenage children, but the smaller government salary did not deter him.

The forty-two-year-old Volcker was given Roosa's powerful old position. The Nixon administration's call for strong economic action appealed to him, and, as discussed, he and Murray Weidenbaum, who reported to him, eagerly developed their plan for the ninety-day freeze on wages and prices. He also became central to the Nixon plans to rewrite the rules of Bretton Woods.

Volcker later wrote that he regretted that the Nixon administration did not have a better strategy to follow the ninety-day freeze. He also regretted dismantling the Bretton Woods system since he was more comfortable with a fixed-rate currency system than the floating rates that followed. Though a Democrat, he was not especially liberal, but he also did not trust the financial markets to sort out the complexities of currency values on their own, and did not believe, as Wriston vehemently did, that unregulated interest rates would result in the most efficient allocation of capital.

Having managed the country's open market operations—the buying and selling of Treasury securities—as president of the New York Fed branch since 1975 and with years of experience at the Treasury under Democrats and Republicans, he was a highly qualified candidate for Federal Reserve chairman. Carter put Walter Mondale in charge of the search for a replacement for William Miller, and his chief of staff, Richard Moe, kept coming across Volcker's name as he called dozens of people for recommendations.

Carter's advisers knew they had reason to worry about Volcker. They had worked with him as New York Fed president and he favored harsher steps to counter inflation than they were willing to take. He was convinced inflation stayed unmanageably high because of inflationary expectations, the same view he had back in the Nixon administration. As economics writer William Greider put it, Volcker believed that "as long as people believed that rising prices were inevitable, then they would be." Even Bert Lance, who thought of inflation as the economy's worst problem, warned Carter that Volcker's appointment could cost him reelection. But his trusted confidant could not change Carter's mind.

Miller at last called Volcker to ask him to meet with the president, and Volcker was not at all confident after the meeting that he would get the job. He frankly told the president that inflation was out of hand, monetary policy had to be severely tightened, and the price to be paid would be higher unemployment. Carter was not put off. The annual consumer inflation rate rose to 13 percent in 1979 and his approval rating fell. In fact, as economist Alan Blinder later showed, and as earlier discussed, consumer inflation was only 9 percent when temporary and mismeasured factors were eliminated, but few were paying attention, including bond traders on Wall Street who typically set interest rates based on expected inflation rates. Carter called Volcker a couple of days later and asked him to accept the job offer.

On taking office in August 1979, Volcker did not immediately rush to raise interest rates. He had to win over the other governors and Federal Reserve branch presidents who served on the Federal Open Market Committee, which had to vote on major changes in monetary policy. Not all of them were convinced, even in light of much higher reported inflation, that rates had to be raised. After all, the target federal funds rate was already pushed up by Miller to roughly 10.5 percent from 7.5 percent the summer before. Volcker convinced them to raise the discount rate—the rate banks paid to borrow reserves from the Fed—at least modestly. The increase was barely noticed in the markets and Volcker believed a brighter line had to be drawn.

Up to now, the Federal Reserve kept its eye on both interest rates and the rate of growth of money. By September, Volcker had fully decided to focus only on money growth—that was what now mattered most in slowing the economy, he was going to claim, and inflation with it. That way, he could let interest rates rise sharply, and thereby fend off criticism that they were deliberately doing so. He could argue he was merely following the new Friedmanite prescription. In discussions more than ten years later at the Brookings Institution, a Washington think tank, economist Paul Krugman asked Volcker just that: whether his adoption of monetarist goals was a "stealth tactic" merely to pursue a traditional anti-inflation strategy of recession. Volcker denied it. At the time, he said, it seemed common sense that too much money led to inflation, and the Fed governors had frequently been hearing it in the media. The explanation was hardly convincing. He also conceded it was easier to talk to the public about the money supply than about the other factors affecting inflation. Oversimplification was precisely why Friedman's influence was powerful, but it was not a reason for Volcker to oversimplify the issues for the public as well.

In the same Brookings discussion, Charles Schultze said that it would have been much harder to convince the public to accept such a high interest rate target than to talk about controlling the supply of money. To the monetarists, any resulting recession would be mild and discussing the money supply seemed nonthreatening. To traditionalists, only a harsh recession would end double-digit inflation decisively, yet such a stance was not politically practicable.

Volcker faced a difficult task trying to convince other members of the board to support the shift to money targets. Even former Yale professor Henry Wallich, who feared that the nation could be overcome by hyperinflation, like Germany after World War I, believed following a Friedmanite monetary rule "was a pact with the devil." It was too destabilizing, he told Volcker, and could lead to frighteningly high interest rates.

But inflation was high and rising, and panic was spreading. As Volcker gathered support among the Fed board members, he had not yet told the Carter economists of his desire to shift to monetarist goals. On a flight with Schultze and William Miller to Belgrade for the annual conference of the International Monetary Fund, he made his intentions clear. This confirmed Schultze's worst fears about Volcker's independence. He told Volcker he was opposed to the idea—it would surely lead to recession by election time. But the Federal Reserve is legally independent of the president, and Schultze and Miller knew they were helpless.

Volcker returned early from the meetings in Belgrade, having received some encouragement for his plan from European leaders, particularly Helmut Schmidt of Germany, a country with a strong traditional fear of inflation. When Miller and Schultze returned a week later, they pressed their case against the new policy, visiting the president to ask for his opposition. But Jimmy Carter refused to oppose Volcker openly.

On October 6, 1979, a Saturday, the Fed board approved Volcker's plan and Volcker dramatically told the press of the adoption of monetarist goals that afternoon. The announcement was labeled "the Saturday night special." Volcker said the central bank would start targeting only money supply growth, focusing on controlling the supply of new reserves to banks, and the Fed funds ceiling was immediately raised as rates rose. In addition to the new monetary controls, the central bank adopted Volcker's suggestion to raise the amount of reserves needed against loans by another 8 percent. It was currently 16.25 percent, and much less on some kinds of borrowing. Being unable to lend an additional $40,000 of a $500,000 deposit was substantial. It was "a new regime," said Barrie Wigmore, a former Goldman Sachs partner.

Six months later, the first dose of monetarism had still not worked. The money supply grew more slowly, but consumer inflation kept rising, reaching for a time an annual rate of more than 15 percent. In addition, the dollar fell again, adding still more inflationary pressure as import prices rose, and gold climbed to more than $800 an ounce. The unemployment rate rose as well, heading to more than 7 percent.

As previously discussed, one reason the higher rates did not at least partly suppress inflation was that Wriston and the other banks now had so many sources of lendable funds that higher interest rates had much less bite. They would simply borrow at higher rates through CDs or in Eurodollars—and in domestic markets to the degree Regulation Q had already been partially loosened by Burns—and raise the rate they charged to lend, so that the flow of loans went unimpeded. "The October [1979] spurt in interest rates and change in the Federal Reserve's mode of operation" had no retarding effect on the economy or inflation, recalled economist Al Wojnilower, because interest rates now had to rise to very high levels to have an impact.

In early 1980, Carter had other serious troubles. Americans had been taken hostage in Iran. The Soviet Union mobilized troops in Afghanistan. But inflation remained high on the list. The fiscal conservative decided that cutting government spending should be a major goal for him in the election year of 1980, the objective being to bring the fiscal 1981 budget deficit down to a mere $13 billion. He also proposed restricting credit for banks and consumers to hold down excessive borrowing. The credit controls were strongly supported by Alfred Kahn, who had been named the inflation czar after his success deregulating the airlines, but the controls also required implementation by the Federal Reserve. Volcker, whose instinct usually favored government action, was a reluctant convert to the idea, but he decided that he had little choice but to do Carter's bidding on this issue.

In March, Carter made a speech asking the American people to stop borrowing. The nation listened and obeyed their president. In a sign of how frightened they were, Americans reduced their spending so sharply that, coupled with the credit restrictions that Volcker agreed to impose, the economy immediately plunged into a steep recession. GDP fell at nearly an annual rate of 10 percent over the next three months—a stunning collapse—as borrowing and lending slowed to a virtual halt, and the money supply contracted sharply.

Volcker was now frightened—a typical recession drives GDP down by only 2 or 3 percentage points over a year. Now it was all happening in three months. He immediately undid the credit restrictions and pumped up bank reserves aggressively. He drove the federal funds rate down from nearly 14 percent in October to 10 percent by June. And by midsummer, the GDP revived. The nightmare ended almost as rapidly as it had begun.

In light of the coming presidential election, Volcker's sudden stimulus was suspect, and he was accused of playing politics with the economy as Burns had in 1972. By September 1980, as the economy strengthened rapidly, the Volcker Fed now reversed course and raised rates aggressively. By October, a month before the presidential election, the federal funds rate was nearly 13 percent, surely recessionary. The unemployment rate had risen that year to around 7.5 percent and stayed there. To counter Reagan's promise of steep tax cuts, Carter now proposed modest tax cuts shortly before the election.

Polls showed the contest was still close, but Reagan clearly scored points with his famous question, "Are you better off today than you were four years ago?" Another comment was possibly more influential. "We don't have inflation because the people are living too well," said Reagan in his only election debate with Carter. "We have inflation because the government is living too well." After the debate, Reagan's popularity rose sharply and he won the election by a wide margin.

———

After Reagan's election, reported inflation was still high, running at about 12 percent a year. Volcker pushed up the federal funds rate more sharply to 19 percent at the end of December, to counter it. Blinder's core inflation rate was several percentage points lower than 12 percent .

Despite Reagan's public support, some of his advisers were more skeptical of Volcker's tough policies, particularly Donald Regan, former head of Merrill Lynch and now Reagan's treasury secretary. Regan knew a recession was the likely result, but Reagan was already planning to sponsor the large cut in income taxes. His economics team had been working on the tax legislation almost from the moment he won the election.

Reagan's supply side advisers, led by Arthur Laffer, insisted deficits would not rise substantially because the economy would be so stimulated by the tax cuts, tax revenues would rise with expanding incomes. But more conventional Reagan advisers, like Charls Walker and David Stockman, argued deficits would rise, and Walker later claimed the influence of Laffer and his staff was exaggerated by the press.

No doubt at the back of Reagan's mind was Friedman's advice to starve the beast; tax cuts would eventually force government to contract. Reagan was rarely interested in details, even when the consequences could be large—in this case, creating an enormous budget deficit. He had always been able to entertain contradictory ideas, and even espouse them with his customary optimism and, in Lou Cannon's view, ability to deny facts. Yet Reagan had talked of large budget deficits as an American nemesis in almost all his GE speeches, as well as in The Speech itself, delivered for Goldwater, and he continued to do so throughout the 1970s. To ignore this was a substantial feat of denial. Reagan perhaps realized, however, that Volcker would inflict the pain required to stop inflation and he would win political popularity with his tax cuts and likely economic recovery—which is what happened.

The tax cut was passed by a Democratically controlled House of Representatives, largely due to Reagan's popularity and well-organized lobbying from the business community. Reagan had the support of Southern Democrats who were now rebelling against the traditions of the party, but his win had also swept enough Republicans into office for them to give the party control through the early 1980s. Meanwhile, Republicans won a majority in the Senate for the first time since 1954. One of the more surprising upsets of the election was Birch Bayh's loss, the traditional liberal senator of Indiana once highly popular in his state. Reagan also now had the support of some Northern Democrats in the Senate, including the influential Daniel Patrick Moynihan of New York.

In August, Congress passed the historic tax cut, which reduced income taxes by a total of 25 percent over three years, the top rate cut from 70 percent to 50 percent. It also adjusted rates for bracket creep so that as inflation raised worker income, it no longer moved workers into higher tax brackets. Business also got a major benefit in a more generous depreciation allowance, the main objective of the Business Roundtable.

Moderate social spending cuts were also approved by Congress, but Reagan's rapid run-up in defense spending more than offset the cuts. How he would manage a rise in government spending and the largest tax cut of the post–World War II era (more in total dollars after inflation but less as a percentage of GDP than the Kennedy-Johnson cuts) was a detail he did not yet face. The supply side tax cuts did not generate nearly the rapid growth in tax revenues promised. Reagan's economists estimated that the budget deficit in his first fiscal year (ended September 1982) would be $45 billion; it turned out to be nearly $130 billion.

Meanwhile, Volcker had pushed interest rates to record levels, not only to reduce money supply growth but also in response to the much higher budget deficit. It was shock therapy. The rate of GDP growth slowed significantly in 1981, but reported inflation fell only moderately, so Volcker kept up his tight policy. The bank prime lending rate exceeded 20 percent in the spring of 1981 and remained well above 15 percent until the fall of 1982. The interest rate on conventional mortgages hit 18 percent by the end of 1981 and hovered around 17 percent until mid-1982.

Political criticism of the Reagan tax cuts and ensuing deficit came swiftly, and, with his popularity quickly falling, even he accepted the need for a compromise. He backtracked, advocating several rounds of moderate business tax increases. As Reagan continued to support Volcker publicly, some of his advisers seethed at Volcker's continuing high-rate policy. Midterm elections would be upon them in 1982 and they could not afford to lose the Senate due to a recession. Wriston had also started to criticize Volcker as he became aware that the high rates on his loans, especially to less developed nations in South America, placed the bank in jeopardy of loan defaults. Volcker did not budge.

In July 1982, there was a downturn in the rate of money growth and the inflation rate, and Volcker at last started to cut interest rates. But it was too late to prevent severe damage, both at home and, more threateningly to the banking system, overseas. The U.S. economy contracted sharply. And in August, Mexico announced it could not pay the interest on its debt. With the Mexico emergency, Volcker immediately cut rates sharply. He also put into place the Mexican rescue package in cooperation with the International Monetary Fund (see Chapter 6), bolstering Mexico's ability to pay while saving the American banks that lent to it. The target federal funds rate slid from 14 percent in June to 8.5 percent in December.

The result of Volcker's harsh monetary policy until August 1982 was the worst recession since the Great Depression in the United States and still deeper ones in many of the less developed nations that took loans from the American banks. The unemployment rate stayed above 9 percent for nineteen months, topping out at nearly 11 percent in December 1982. Stock prices had fallen nearly to their lowest levels in a dozen years. Capital investment plunged.

But inflation was at last subdued, falling to just under 4 percent in 1983, and the American electorate was pleased. Voters did not rebel, and left the Senate in Republican hands after the November 1982 elections. As we have seen, reducing inflation to the public in general was more important to them than lost jobs, and the Reagan tax cuts were the added bonus. A sharp economic recovery then began and the unemployment rate fell to 8.3 percent by the end of 1983.

Reagan continued to raise taxes, however. He proposed, in fact, a substantial increase in payroll taxes that fell largely on the middle class and working Americans. Reagan focused on projected Social Security deficits, and the tax hike was well disguised as a Social Security matter. A serious gap between benefits to the elderly and Social Security tax receipts was forecast. Reagan had wanted to cut Social Security benefits to close the gap, but it was politically impossible, and he appointed a bipartisan commission headed by Alan Greenspan and Senator Moynihan to arrive at a joint solution. The bill agreed upon was passed in 1983. It included a reduction in some benefits—for example, the retirement age was to be gradually raised from sixty-five to sixty-seven—but payroll taxes were raised substantially from a total of 12.3 percent, half paid by workers and the other half by employers, to 15.3 percent by 1990. The tax is applied equally to workers of all income levels up to an income of $107,000 (as of 2010), above which there is no further payment. It was a decidedly regressive tax: earners in the middle fifth of Americans would now pay 9.8 percent of their income in payroll taxes, while those in the top 1 percent now paid 1.4 percent of their income in payroll taxes.

The tax was passed with the alleged intention of using the revenues only for Social Security payments. But the Social Security taxes were comingled with general tax revenues to pay for all government programs, and have been ever since. On balance, including the income tax cuts and payroll tax hikes, Reagan cut taxes for middle Americans only marginally. The rate of actual federal taxes of all kinds on the middle fifth of income earners in America (households) fell by only .7 percent between 1979 and 1989, but for the top 10 percent it fell by 3.3 percent, and 8.1 percent for the top 1 percent of earners.

Thus, Americans paid lower taxes, but the cuts for the well-off were far greater on a percentage basis than for those in other brackets. All the while Reagan claimed he was benefiting the "forgotten" American, the typical worker who got too little back from government to justify his taxes. It was, in truth, very much the opposite.

Under Reagan, defense spending rose rapidly from 5 percent to about 6.5 percent of GDP in the late 1980s. The other major federal spending increase was interest expense, due to the growing debt burden, also up by 1.5 percent of national income. Spending on social programs from Social Security to welfare also rose but not by as much. Meantime, business did not spend on productive investment the way it once did. Business investment remained significantly weaker as a percentage of GDP than in the 1960s and 1970s.

In fiscal 1983, the budget deficit exceeded $200 billion, more than 6 percent of GDP, and remained above 5 percent of the economy until 1987. The lowest point the Reagan deficit fell to was slightly more than 3 percent of GDP in 1987 and 1988, far higher than in Carter's final years as president.

Tax cuts were the spearhead of Reagan's revolution. But soon after he took office, he also set the tone for his first term by abruptly firing 11,500 striking air traffic controllers, who had refused a pay offer from the Federal Aviation Agency. Reagan announced in August that he was obliged to fire them, and disband the union, because they were federal employees and therefore legally forbidden to strike. America was ready to take on the unions, which were thought to have contributed to inflation by demanding high wages. They were a main target of the newly energized business lobbying organizations, like the Roundtable and the Chamber of Commerce. The traffic controllers were a relatively easy target, earning a good deal more than the average American. Though the union was one of the few to support Reagan for president, the nation saw their demands as selfish, inflation as the graver problem. Other airline unions, including the pilots union, ignored the striking picketers, crossing their lines to work. The union never revived, and Reagan, the master of his image at this point, sent another signal to the public that he was a hard-nosed inflation fighter even as he produced large deficits. (Volcker supported Reagan's decision to fire the controllers.)

With less fanfare, in 1981 Reagan seriously began to weaken the enforcement of federal regulations. Deregulation of airlines, trucking, and finance had started with Carter. The 1980 Carter financial bill not only began formally unwinding Regulation Q, but also preempted state usury laws long on the books that limited the interest rates banks, credit card companies, and thrifts could charge consumers (see Chapter 9).

More quietly, however, the Reagan administration undid regulations and significantly weakened their enforcement almost across the board. By then, the business lobbyists were actually providing suggestions, backed by their own research, of unnecessary regulations. Reagan and his economics team claimed they were carefully streamlining the system. Others saw little method in what was being done. It was "an antiregulation approach rather than meaningful regulatory reform," wrote one regulation expert.

Full-time positions at the National Transportation Safety Board, the Food Safety and Inspection Service, the Consumer Product Safety Commission, and the Occupational Safety and Health Administration were all cut by half or more from 1980 to 1989. The penalties assessed by OSHA on business were sharply reduced, as eventually were penalties for labor violations imposed by the National Labor Relations Board on companies.

The staff and financial appropriations of both the Federal Trade Commission and the antitrust division of the Justice Department to investigate the monopolistic implications of mergers were cut in half over the course of the Reagan administration. Large size and market share were no longer standards for judging abusive monopoly power. "Antitrust bashing was fashionable rhetoric through the rest of the 1980s," wrote an antitrust lawyer. The door was thus opened for the enormous takeover wave.

In 1982, with the support of Reagan, perhaps the most ill-considered deregulation bill ever was passed into law, the Garn-St. Germain Act, designed as discussed earlier to help failing savings and loan associations (the thrifts that mostly wrote mortgages). The bill allowed the thrifts to invest nearly half of their assets in almost any area they chose with deposits insured by the federal government through the Federal Savings and Loan Insurance Corporation. It also eliminated Regulation Q entirely, as mentioned earlier.

After forty years of stability since the Great Depression, there were two major financial crises in the 1980s under Reagan. The first was the failure of the petrodollar loans made by Wriston and other bankers to less developed countries. Volcker prevented domestic catastrophe when he rescued the banks in 1982, but the commercial bankers were generally hampered for the rest of the decade by the unprofitable LDC loans left on their books. And as inflation fell, the export-oriented economies of the LDCs performed poorly for the decade, with punishing results for their populations. Despite Volcker's rescue of the U.S. banks, Continental Illinois, one of the nation's largest and allegedly best-managed banks, almost went out of business. It was rescued by the federal government in 1984.

The second was the thrifts crisis of the late 1980s, the direct consequence of the Garn-St. Germain Act. No one had bothered to stop the thrifts from making these bad investments when it would have been far more economical to do so. Some two thousand such banks went under between 1985 and 2002 compared to seventy-nine in the 1970s. After Reagan left office, the federal government formed the Resolution Trust Corporation to rescue dozens of thrifts at an estimated cost of $150–200 billion. In tandem with this, the junk bond market built by Mike Milken, essentially unregulated, came undone, and the economy fell into recession in 1990.

Not only had the monetarists, and their like-minded offspring, the rational expectationists, badly underestimated the depths of the recession the policies caused, but also, in the early 1980s, measures of money growth had shown no relationship to changes in GDP or inflation. In fact, the money supply grew rapidly in this period, and Beryl Sprinkel, the first doctrinaire monetarist to hold a high-ranking Treasury position, warned Reagan and Volcker that such rates of money growth inevitably meant a quick return of high inflation. Nothing of the sort happened. Annual consumer inflation remained below 4 percent.

Even as nominal interest rates began to fall after the 1982 recession, they remained high compared to inflation, as noted, holding back capital investment. High rates also pushed the value of the dollar up sharply in the early 1980s, leaving American manufacturers at a serious cost disadvantage internationally, and harming manufacturing workers further. In 1985, James Baker, appointed Reagan's treasury secretary, and well aware of the dilemma, arranged to meet with other financial officials around the world at the Plaza Hotel in New York, and successfully got their support to push down the dollar's value. The deal, known as the Plaza Accord, helped temporarily revive manufacturing.

The imbalances in the Reagan economy were now starkly clear. Inflation was down, but the trade deficit kept rising. The invasion of imports was well under way. The U.S. domestic market was weak partly because of high real interest rates (nominal interest rates compared to inflation), but also because so much debt capital was taken on in the new wave of takeovers. The federal budget deficit did not fall below 5 percent of GDP until 1987 and 1988, Reagan's last two years, and then it remained high as a percentage of GDP. In October 1987, the stock market crashed under the weight of the nation's economic imbalances, only to be saved by rapid monetary expansion under the new Federal Reserve chairman, Alan Greenspan.

By the president's second term, Volcker was losing Reagan's support. Reagan's advisers blamed Volcker for keeping interest rates too high, taking little responsibility themselves for creating huge budget deficits with the Reagan tax cuts. Philosophically, Volcker was not the free-spirited laissez-faire optimist that Reagan was and the natural friction had at some point to take its toll. Volcker was skeptical of some financial deregulation and the growing takeover wave. When later asked whether he agreed with the movement toward deregulation of interest rates and the end of Regulation Q, Volcker answered, "Oh, by and large, I think that we needed some freeing up here. I get restive about it now and then because it comes out partially in interest rates higher than they otherwise would be."

Among his new concerns was that the banks he regulated were making risky loans for leveraged buyouts and hostile takeovers, and he wanted to limit the ability of investors to borrow from the banks to acquire other companies by buying their stock on the open market. He wanted to do this by applying the Fed's margin rules on stock trading, requiring that more capital be posted to buy up shares in a company. Volcker, however, was outvoted by Reagan appointees to his board. He also frequently let it be known that the administration had to get the federal deficit down, sounding a highly sensitive chord. Volcker resigned in 1987, saving the Reagan administration the trouble of asking for his resignation.

History accorded Volcker full credit for his anti-inflationary stand, but the shock therapy was taken very far. For all Volcker's firmness of thought and independence of opinion, he was caught up in the panicky environment. There were calmer and less punishing alternatives—a more patient strategy of only moderately high interest rates coupled with reduced fiscal stimulus would have likely worked with far less economic disruption. The task, even if Volcker had entertained it, was made especially difficult by Reagan's extreme tax cuts.

Reagan's defenders claim that after the 1982 recession, growth was strong. But no economist measures the rate of growth from the bottom of a recession. It must be measured over the course of a full business cycle, and thus measured, it was in fact mediocre. All the while, the unemployment rate remained historically high, suppressing the growth of wages. This would remain true until the mid-1990s. Wage growth slowed again in the 2000s, despite, and perhaps because of, a new round of tax cuts.

Most important, adjusted for the business cycle, productivity, the source of a rising standard of living, under Reagan or George H. W. Bush did not resume the rapid average rate of growth of a hundred years of American industrial history. This was the ultimate goal, and it was not attained, productivity growing at a historically torpid rate until the mid-1990s.

As for American workers, who so strongly supported Reagan politically, their wages, as noted, generally stagnated or at best grew slowly. Male wages were especially weak. In this period, income inequality started to climb to the levels reached in the 1920s. Typical family incomes rose only because spouses went to work. Female incomes rose consistently, but not robustly, and a typical woman of the same age and experience as her male counterpart still earned far less. Meanwhile, the public goods of America were neglected. Under Reagan, investment in public transportation infrastructure was reduced from 0.5 percent of GDP to 0.3 percent—a sharp drop. And more and more Americans had no health insurance.

Reagan's revolution was sweeping, but the sharp reduction in income taxes truly marked America's ideological transformation, the nation wholeheartedly renouncing its willingness to support government at former levels of taxation. After the Tax Reform Act of 1986, the top income tax rate was just 28 percent. To advocates of low taxes like Reagan, government had become big, wasteful, and, most important, exploitive of working Americans. To his most loyal supporters, government was worse—it was menacing, as he had been saying for years.

The Reagan tax cuts dominated all these policies. Even as the economy performed poorly, Americans were now apparently comfortable with shedding their sense of obligation to a larger community. (Volcker's defeat of inflation provided popular cover for the profound change.) Reagan ended the traditional sense of citizenship among Americans. The obligation of government was to benefit them individually or they would not pay for it. The regressive increase in payroll taxes, even if it burdened working Americans more than those with high incomes, was acceptable to them because it qualified workers for future Social Security; it was seemingly not paid to help others.

Antigovernment attitudes were strong, and even though America was tiring of Reagan—by the time his second term ended his star was not nearly as high as it once was—these attitudes remained in place for two more decades with serious consequences. Individuals should take of their economy what they could. Reagan had promised morning again in America, but delivered more in image than substance. Still, a new ideological anchor had been sunk by Reagan and a few strong adverse currents would not unloose it. The ideological revolution was complete.

Two

THE NEW GUARD

THE NOW DIARO

Tom Peters and Jack Welch

As the 1980s began with unprecedentedly high interest rates and the highest levels of unemployment since the Depression, Americans believed business, not just government, was in crisis. The loss of American corporate dominance was starkly apparent in everyday consumer products. Americans bought Toyotas, Volvos, and BMWs rather than Chevys and Cadillacs; Sony TV sets rather than RCAs or Zeniths; Krups appliances rather than GE; and Armani rather than Brooks Brothers. Everyone knew you had to get rid of your American car in three years, that you had to know a good TV repairman, and that American cameras were second-rate. American products simply broke down. American makers of steel and machine tools and tractors were losing market share to Japanese, German, French, and Italian manufacturers. There was no increase in the number of American manufacturing jobs in the 1970s for the first time since the Depression.

"The storm that flickered on the horizon for American industry during the 1970s came ashore with a rush in the 1980s," wrote three Harvard Business School professors.

> Torrents of imported products flooded our markets and eroded the profitability of domestic suppliers. The U.S. balance of trade in manufactured products went negative for the first time this century in 1971, recovered briefly in the late 1970s, and then plunged into increasing deficits after 1981. In 1986, American imports of manufactured goods exceeded exports by almost $140 billion. West Germany displaced the United States as the world's mightiest exporting nation.

By 1980, NBC News already decided the problems were of such widespread concern that it aired a prime-time news special called "If Japan

Management consultant
Tom Peters

GE's Jack Welch with President Bill Clinton

Can . . . Why Can't We?," a passionate complaint about American business, which had repeatedly attributed Japan's rise to that country's low wages and not the inadequacy of American business. In truth, said NBC, Japanese companies focused on quality and long-term growth while American business had focused for too long on maximizing the quantity of goods sold to reduce costs per unit. The NBC producers were reflecting a theme developed in the business press in the late 1970s. Articles in *The New York Times Magazine, Fortune, Time, Newsweek,* and *The Atlantic* increasingly blamed poor business management as much or more than inflation, government deficits, OPEC oil price hikes, or low-wage foreign competition for America's seeming decline. "When Detroit changes its management system," wrote *Fortune,* "we'll see more powerful American competitors." The NBC special got high ratings. "There was simply a profound hunger at the time for an answer to the failure of American business," said one management professor.

Tom Peters provided such a compelling explanation of the U.S. decline that he became a cultural hero—America's single pop star of management. Big business, the management consultant argued, had to become entrepreneurial again, and the path to doing so was by respecting workers, consumers, and the creative process. He blamed the militaristic, conformist management style of big American companies for the spreading failure, and its overemphasis on financial returns. There was a revolutionary streak in this view, which called for breaking down old formulas and past traditions, subverting the discipline of pyramidal bureaucracies, and resurrecting an egalitarian respect between workers and their bosses. Fully valuing workers would lead to higher quality, lower production costs, and more innovative products. Peters was profoundly optimistic and humanist. Americans liked what they heard.

America's seeming business failure had arrived almost suddenly. Only a decade earlier, in 1967, Jean-Jacques Servan-Schreiber, a French journalist and publisher, wrote a book, *The American Challenge,* that became an international sensation, in which he argued that American business methods were unassailable as American multinational companies set up shop around the world. Servan-Schreiber preyed on the growing fear of the American incursion. He warned that Europe was being threatened by the rise of the American multinational company—not because of America's technological advances, but because of its organizational discipline. It could produce the lowest-cost products, distribute them worldwide, and market them aggressively, winning market share across the world. Costs were cut sharply through repetitive assembly-line techniques at rapid speeds, and the adoption of the so-called scientific management principles of Frederick Winslow Taylor. Taylor's major work, *The Principles of Scientific Management,* had been published in 1911. Time and motion studies were Taylor's early tools and became the butt of many a future joke, including in silent movies featuring Charlie Chaplin and Buster Keaton. Workers were cogs in a machine, and even executives were above all conformists, implementing preset formulas and directions from above.

After World War II, sophisticated financial controls were added to this management model and Harvard Business School's famous course, "Managerial Economics, Reporting and Control," became a template for financial management by high-level executives. Its most illustrious student, Robert McNamara, ran Ford Motor as a young man and then brought the same financial controls to the Pentagon under President Kennedy. A symbol of the ascending power of financial control emerged when Roger Smith, General Motors' chief financial officer, was appointed its CEO in 1970. In the past, the CEOs of major auto companies were typically engineers. Now, big businesses were managed like a portfolio of assets, each part generating a rate of return that could be accurately measured. Control was asserted through the capital budget—determining which division and product lines were provided more funding, which less.

Tom Peters thought these methods were the cause of American competitive weakness. Heir to a variety of original thinkers, he believed American managerial strategy was frozen in time. The company that produced at the lowest price was usually the winner, which usually meant that bigger was always better due to economies of scale and marketing. Employees were treated as cogs in a machine and consumer satisfaction was taken for granted or was sufficiently molded through advertising or dominance of distribution channels. As a result, there was high tolerance for defects and inferior performance. Volume of sales and large marketing budgets were considered more important than maintaining quality, the power that came with an enormous volume of sales was a key to negotiating the best prices from suppliers and the best deals from distributors and retailers. If existing businesses did not grow fast enough, according to the financial criteria used to run the firm, or were not large enough to produce units at the lowest cost or confer adequate marketing power, the executives closed down product lines or bought other ones, even if they were far afield from the management's areas of expertise. "Strategy" became all-important— the strategy of a general choosing his theaters of war.

There had been early rebellion against the business rigidity. Narrative literature in America, such as the fictional works of John Cheever and John Updike, focused on the stultifying life of middle America. The journalist William Whyte in 1956 wrote a best seller about American conformism, *The Organization Man.*

Academic scholarship critical of accepted management principles also grew. An Australian-born psychologist, Elton Mayo, a researcher and professor at the Harvard Business School, started a humanist school of industrial psychology in the 1930s. Mayo demonstrated that the attitudes of workers affected their productivity. Simply painting and repainting the walls different colors, no matter what the color, made workers feel they were being noticed, and the attention itself improved performance.

Further studies corroborated these effects: workers wanted attention and acknowledgment. Douglas McGregor, an MIT management professor, took the new ideas further, arguing in the early 1960s that the authoritarian management theories of the early century had a deep flaw. They assumed that people did not like to work, that they could not take responsibility for their efforts, and that they had to be threatened with punishment to be motivated. He called this managerial approach Theory X. His own view, which he termed Theory Y, emphasized personal creativity and independence, posited that work was both natural to human life and valuable to those who did it. In a 1960 book, McGregor married Mayo's principles to the influential work of another psychologist, Abraham Maslow, who in the 1950s had emphasized people's strong desire for self-esteem. If work could provide such self-esteem, businesses would get the most out of their workers.

Peters and his co-author, Robert Waterman, absorbed this alternative tradition. In 1982, they published their findings in a book that became a landmark, *In Search of Excellence*. The book sold some twelve million copies.

Peters was more outspoken, effervescent, and provocative than his co-author and quit his job to become the proselytizer of the faith. Waterman stayed at McKinsey & Co., the big management consulting firm. Born in 1942, Peters had been trained as an engineer and served in the Navy in Vietnam and elsewhere, working on construction projects. People generally think of the military model as highly regulated and hierarchical, he said. "But the military model is not what you think it is. It was doing it on the fly, catch-as-catch-can." What succeeded was pragmatic and ad hoc.

After the Navy, Peters was not certain what he would do. He had become an engineer because in his generation that was often what one did, but in 1970, "business school was hot." The economic boom of the late 1960s created the first wave of demand for MBAs, especially in finance and consulting, and Peters went with the fashion. He was accepted at Stanford Business School, then the major competitor to Harvard. When he entered, he still did not know what he would pursue, but he took a course in organizational behavior, and was intrigued. His professor was James March, a leading academician in the field. March emphasized the complexity of organizational processes, and advocated stimulating individual talents and entrepreneurialism in big corporations. To March, "messiness" was superior to the streamlined managerial functions emphasized at Harvard, because it eliminated the boundaries on thinking, enterprise, and originality.

Peters joined the Ph.D. program and with his degree in hand, got his first job in the mid-1970s at McKinsey's San Francisco office. A new managing director, Ron Daniel, was looking for fresh ideas to interest clients since the firm was now losing ground to a rising consulting firm, the Boston Consulting Group. BCG thought devising sweeping business strategies about the choice of businesses to enter and the amount of debt taken, measured by precise financial calculations, was the key to managerial success. General intelligence, BCG believed, was what mattered in running a company, not experience, closeness to the manufacturing process, a relationship with the workers, or hands-on knowledge of products or clients. Both Peters and Waterman distrusted financial yardsticks devised in executive headquarters. To Peters, as the 1970s advanced, the reliance on financial tools seemed almost comically intricate with projections about the future that were detailed and unrealistic. Peters and Waterman were skeptical of "strategy," and for their views were not highly regarded at McKinsey.

They later wrote:

> Professionalism in management is regularly equated with hard-headed rationality. We saw it surface at ITT in Harold Geneen's search for "unshakable facts." It flourished in Vietnam, where success was measured in body counts. Its wizards were the Ford Motor Company's whiz kids, and its grand panjandrum was Robert McNamara. The numerative, rationalist approach to management dominates the business schools. It teaches us that well-trained professional managers can manage anything. It seeks detached, analytical justification for all decisions. It is right enough to be dangerously wrong, and it has arguably led us seriously astray.

Two prominent Harvard Business School professors had already turned against their financially oriented colleagues in the late 1970s. Harvard B-school's scholarship at the time, even as the academic home of Elton Mayo, had emphasized the quantitative business controls discussed earlier. To William Abernathy and Robert Hayes, enough was enough. American management had to get out of the financial office and back to the shop floor. In 1980, they published an irreverent piece in the *Harvard Business Review* called "Managing Our Way to Economic Decline." Peters and Waterman deeply admired them.

Daniel at McKinsey was also getting interested in how the behavior of and relationship between managers and workers affected business success. Others were speaking the same language. W. Edwards Deming, an engineer who was the centerpiece of NBC's news special, had gone to Japan years earlier to advise Toyota and others about high-quality methods. The Japanese workers were central to the new processes, actively involved in altering manufacturing methods; they were given more decision-making authority on the production line, mostly unheard of in American business.

Daniel handed Peters and Waterman a small project: to "analyze the anthropology of how an organization gets things done," as Peters put it. To them, it was clear that most of American business was not creative, not exciting, and not even interested in its customers. It had become automaton-like. But there were many exceptions, and Peters and Waterman set out to discover why. They made a list of the best companies in the United States and Europe, and the project was under way.

Theirs was not a scientific procedure. Some like Harvard professor Jay Lorsch believed they simply discovered what they wanted to discover, fitting their preestablished management theory to real-life examples. And many of their choices failed later, or were successful by sheer good fortune. Warner Communications was on their list, for example, because of its investment in Atari. Yet Atari's profits disappeared and what lasted was Warner's cable systems. Wal-Mart was also on the list because Sam Walton truly cared about people, they claimed, walking the aisles of his many stores, but this was a calculated policy to suppress union activity (see Chapter 8). But Peters and Waterman uncovered and reported on common threads of success in many other companies.

The best companies, they found, were those with lean staffs, not top-heavy. They fostered entrepreneurship at many levels of management, from the worker to the foreman to the general manager and higher. They listened to their customers, did not dictate to them, and changed with them as the customers' desires changed. They stuck to their knitting, and avoided business in which they had little experience or about which they had little knowledge. They acted quickly to fix problems. They understood that workers were the "root source" of new ideas and quality improvements. As Texas Instruments' chairman said, every worker was "seen as a source of ideas, not just a pair of hands." Profit was important but was thought to be the outcome of good management. Striving only for size could be self-defeating. This was a constant theme for Peters. For him, the good companies seemed to understand that beyond a certain size, inefficiencies set in.

Perhaps most important, they wrote that "the numerative, analytical component has an in-built conservative bias. Cost reduction becomes priority number one." Cost reduction should not be the goal of business; revenue maximization should be, they argued. Ideas, people, and passion were the source of more sales. *In Search of Excellence* was to a degree a cri de coeur—a humanist plea for big business to change by recognizing the contribution of its workers. That was the source of its immense popularity.

Among the people Peters and Waterman singled out for farsightedness and gutsy entrepreneurial attitude was Jack Welch of General Electric. A common strategy in successful companies good at innovation was to assign a small team of people to work under what Peters and Waterman called a "champion." The champion was the company's innovator, motivating his staff to be bold and protecting them from stifling conservative bureaucracy. Such teams led to successful new products time and again, they found, at companies like 3M, Johnson & Johnson, and General Electric. "Young Jack Welch was the classic champion," they wrote. As a rising executive, Welch headed a group that developed GE's Noryl, a new plastic material that became one of the company's fastest-growing businesses. In 1980, while the authors were doing their research, Welch was named GE's CEO.

Peters said that the most important influence he and Waterman had was not the revitalization of manufacturing but the renewed emphasis on product quality over cost and volume. Companies devoted much more energy to producing workable, attractive, innovative, and durable products. Others like Abernathy and Deming contributed to the movement. But in the end, Peters lamented that the humanist principles he espoused, including devotion to the workers, research into new, higher-quality products, and sticking to the businesses one knew, were seriously practiced only among the new computer and software companies. "The flip," as he put it, "was with the new entrepreneurs" in electronics. Peters himself moved his consulting practice to Silicon Valley.

Most of the rest of America's major companies returned with a vengeance to stressing the importance of size through takeovers, focused on reduced costs by keeping wages low, and emphasized short-term profits over long-term research and innovation. Finance was the driver, the employee little thought about. The bull market in stocks that began in 1982 affected the way CEOs managed more than any managerial theories, even as they continued to pay lip service to the principles Peters advocated. Short-term profits drove stock prices, and increasingly executives became rich on their stock options. Jack Welch claimed he cared about workers but ultimately mostly inspired fear in them. He was the avatar of the new guard.

On the way up, Jack Welch believed in the Peters philosophy—manage like an entrepreneur or owner, stick to your knitting, cherish workers, and don't overemphasize market share and size. When Peters and Waterman cited him as one of their most admirable "champions," he had proved himself a rebellious middle manager who could upend corporate bureaucracy to create and commercialize exciting new products within a giant company.

But by the time he was named GE's CEO in 1980, he had seen how vulnerable companies were to hostile takeovers, and in the 1980s he learned that the best defense was to become a Wall Street favorite and boost GE's stock price. Even at the height of popularity of *In Search of Excellence,* American business was adopting a business strategy based on maximizing profits, large size, bargaining power, high levels of debt, and corporate acquisitions. As management consultant Walter Kiechel wrote, "What's striking about the merger wave of the 1980s is how much of it was carried out in keeping with the basic principles of strategy, specifically its emphasis on treating your company as a portfolio of businesses that might be bought or sold, placing your bet on where you had a competitive advantage, and using debt to finance the effort."

What particularly focused this managerial view was the rising stock market, which increasingly rewarded a fast pace of profit growth with a high stock price. "The goal for corporate managers had become clear," wrote Kiechel, "to increase the value of the company as reflected in its stock price. Strategy was taking on ever greater urgency." Cutting costs boldly, especially labor costs, was a central part of the strategy. To modern American management, managing size and reducing costs was easier than managing innovation and people. Peters's extraordinary popularity, it eventually turned out, was mostly a distraction—and for many, Welch among them, a pretense.

Welch was named CEO near the bottom of a long bear market and retired near the top of the longest bull market in history. GE's profits rose ten times over these years to $13 billion in profits on $130 billion in sales. But its stock price rose by thirty times. When Welch took over GE in 1980, it was the ninth most profitable company in the nation. Now it was first, second, or third. Shareholder value reached $500 billion, more than any other company in America. The stock price was Welch's personal measure of achievement, though he later denied it. The boom of the late 1990s on balance sent the wrong message to American managers: cut costs rather than innovate. Despite its appeal, *In Search of Excellence* had little true staying power.

———

Welch was born in 1935 in Peabody, Massachusetts, and was brought up in the pretty coastline town of Salem, where his parents moved when he was nine. His father was a conductor on the Boston & Maine commuter line, and Welch later said he loved his work. He was an affable man of Irish descent, who, reminiscent of "Honey Fitz," the Irish mayor of Boston and grandfather of John F. Kennedy, chatted endlessly with strangers. But his was a dead-end job and, despite Welch's claim, took its toll on his morale. Welch's reverence is entirely for his mother. He credits her for his self-confidence, competitiveness, and work ethic. Welch had a bad stammer but his mother assured him it was because his mind worked too quickly. He was born when she was thirty-six (late for the time, notes Welch), and she lavished all her hopes, attention, and demands on her only child. Excessive confidence, his later colleagues would say, was Welch's most noticeable quality, and to his mother goes the credit.

He was fiercely competitive from a young age, Welch wrote in a 1998 autobiography called *Jack: Straight from the Gut* (co-authored with the journalist John Byrne). He thought he was too small to play football or baseball, but became captain of the high school hockey team, where he worked hard to excel, insisting he was not a truly natural athlete.

By his own account, he was easily humiliated. He had caddied at the old-line country club in town and came to love golf. When "one of the stingiest" members of the club demanded he wade into the pond to get a lost ball, Welch refused. It cost him the club's caddie scholarship for college.

Welch did not get into Dartmouth or Columbia, his first choices, and he settled, as he put it, for the University of Massachusetts at Amherst. It turned out to be a lucky break, he later claimed, because his professors took a special interest in him, which he attributed to lack of competition.

With their encouragement, he went to the University of Illinois for a graduate degree in chemical engineering and ultimately a Ph.D. He did well in school not because he was smarter than the others, he said, but because he was focused and willing to work harder than they.

Welch also liked a good time. He became an altar boy to make his devout Catholic mother happy but regularly skipped preparatory lessons. After his mother died, he left the Church. He wrote of rowdy times at his college fraternity house, getting caught once by the police with a girl on campus (then strictly forbidden), for which he was severely scolded by school officials.

Welch knew early that he wanted to make the money his father never could and his mother never got to enjoy. In his high school yearbook he wrote that his ultimate desire was "to make a million." One of the only emotionally revealing moments of his autobiography is his memory of being an outsider. He recalled how he often went to an amusement park with friends, where they usually ran out of money quickly and picked up stray bottles for the refunds to pay for more rides. But they never found enough bottles to continue, and watched from afar the better-off kids continuing to take more rides. "My early years were spent with my nose pressed up against the glass," as he put it.

After he earned his engineering Ph.D., Welch had several research offers from corporations, but he signed on with GE in 1960 to develop a new product at the company's plastics division, located in Pittsfield, Massachusetts, near his old college. When he joined GE, plastic was among the materials with most promise. GE had invented and successfully marketed Lexan, an especially hard plastic that could substitute for glass and metal. Welch was hired to manage the development and commercialization of another new discovery that promised to be nearly as successful.

Welch immediately saw his problem—the GE bureaucracy. If he needed more researchers to develop Noryl, he had to go through an elaborate process to bring them on. If he needed more money for the lab, there were red tape and constant delays. But the "champion" was quickly making progress on the new project and had other smaller successes in the division. He broke the rules repeatedly. Welch simply appropriated researchers from other departments and, later, had Noryl and Lexan marketers compete with each other for the same customers. Though he was voluble and hot-tempered, progress on the products and rising profits in his division quickly made him a budding star.

Now up for an annual raise, he got no more than other colleagues, $1,000 for the year. Already married and with responsibilities, he quit. GE simply did not vary the raises at his managerial level because, to the company, the egalitarian practice promoted teamwork. To Welch, the tireless competitor, this was ridiculous. "You build strong teams by treating individuals differently," he wrote. "Just look at the way baseball teams pay 20-game-winning pitchers and 40-plus home run hitters."

His boss convinced Welch to stay at GE by adding $2,000 to his salary and giving him more authority. Tom Peters and Robert Waterman generally praised his irrepressible competitiveness, perhaps not knowing of his sometimes wrathful style. He criticized and reprimanded subordinates relentlessly, and fired them easily, mixing praise with tough and sometimes demeaning demands—a hot-and-cold style he later boasted was effective.

The results spoke for themselves. He had successfully brought Noryl and other products to market, and made a lot of money for the company.

By 1968, at thirty-two, Welch was named general manager of the plastics business. He was the youngest general manager ever at GE, and the job came with handsome stock options.

In the following years, Welch promoted Lexan and Noryl especially aggressively and sales soared. He doubled sales of the plastics division in three years, and by 1971 he was named head of the chemical and metallurgical division. By 1973, he became group executive of the division, with sales of $2 billion. These were still the headiest days of American business as the nation's middle class expanded rapidly, and wages and salaries rose handsomely for workers at all levels. GE was no longer the technological leader it had been in its first fifty or sixty years, but Welch's corner of the empire in plastics and other businesses was still dependent on innovation, and his aggressive plans both to create and market new products were successful enough to make him stand out in the giant company in just the way that Peters and Waterman admired most. One of his victories was a significant advance in CT scanners, first developed by Europe's EMI. The medical services operation became highly profitable in future years, specializing in X-ray, scanner, and MRI technologies—rightfully his proudest achievement.

Reginald Jones, the venerated chairman of GE and a national business figure, realized that these were transforming times. The stalwart appliances business—toasters, irons, lightbulbs, refrigerators—was fading with increasing competition. Prices for what were once the cornerstones of middle-class life—the pride of Ronald Reagan in his GE-supplied house in Pacific Palisades—were harder to raise with new competition and the saturation of the market. Consumer electronics were the next horizon, but GE could not manage to find a toehold as Japanese and European dominance of these markets grew. And in the 1970s, inflation was hurting its sales, motivating Jones's decision to merge with Utah International.

Jones recognized that GE needed a more thorough overhaul, and had to get its bureaucracy under control. He was wary of, but also attracted to, Welch's brash and sometimes ruthless managerial methods, so unlike his own. More to the point, Welch got formidable results. He might be able to generate the degree of change the company needed, Jones figured.

In 1977, Jones named Welch one of a half dozen sector executives. He was only forty-two and managing businesses with sales of $4 billion, about 20 percent of GE's total. As a result, he was in the running for Jones's job, along with ten or so others who were being watched closely. Under Welch were appliances, including televisions and radios, TV stations, and GE Credit Corporation, among other divisions.

Welch made one of his landmark decisions in 1977. The team running appliances wanted to expand the business aggressively. Welch saw a future that was inevitably fading. Profit margins were "paper-thin" and prices had fallen with competition. "These ambitious plans reflected the company's conventional view of the business's potential. It had been driven by the glow of the postwar era," he wrote. "My new associates . . . tore apart the numbers and the conventional assumptions. Our look said growth would slow."

So Welch aggressively cut the operations of this revered part of GE, and proceeded to lay off workers. When he began slashing the workforce, GE's appliances had 47,000 workers. When Welch left the company, twenty years later, it had fewer than twenty thousand. "These downsizings are awful," he wrote, "as hardworking people get hammered by competitive change. . . . I can't tell you how often I was asked in the early 1980s, 'Is it over?' Unfortunately, it's never over."

Welch did find several businesses he liked in the portfolio he was handed. The TV broadcasting companies were appealing. They generated profits, had solid market share, and did not require substantial capital investment. Welch tried to acquire Cox Communications, an owner of local TV stations and a cable TV operation. He liked the prospects for cable, but made a mistake when he backed out of the deal when the asking price rose. Cox, like Malone's Tele-Communications and Time Warner Cable, went on to thrive.

GE Credit was a second appealing growth area under his domain. It started out as an adjunct to the equipment business for GE customers to finance their purchases, and it financed small business and real estate as well. Welch immediately liked what he saw. "My gut told me that compared to the industrial operations I did know, the business seemed an easy way to make money. You didn't have to invest heavily in R&D, build factories, or bend metal. . . . The business was all about intellectual capital—finding smart and creative people and then using GE's strong balance sheet." In 1977, GE Capital, as it was later called, generated $67 million in revenue with only seven thousand employees, while appliances that year generated $100 million and required 47,000 workers. He hired better managers and supplied GE Credit with a lot of capital, and he had built-in scale—meaning large size—due to GE's assets size and triple-A credit rating. In time, GE Capital became a full-fledged bank, financing all kinds of commercial loans, issuing mortgages and other consumer loans, and becoming a leader in mortgage-backed securities. By the time Welch left in 2000, GE Capital's earnings had grown by some eighty times to well more than $5 billion, while the number of its employees did not even double. It provided half of GE's profits.

As Jones's retirement approached, the list of candidates to succeed him was cut to three. Welch was the youngest. As a final challenge, Jones asked each of the three to write a memo on the future of GE. Since Welch was already known for laying off workers in the company, he defended such firings vigorously in his memo, saying they created job openings other employees eagerly sought. But his insight about appealing to stock market investors probably got him the job. He said GE was so large, even the prospective acquisition of Cox, and the later collapse of the deal, did not affect its stock price. He believed GE had only one choice if it was to push the stock price up. "What we have to sell as an enterprise to the equity investor is consistent, above-average earnings growth through the economic cycle," he wrote to Jones. "Our size may dictate that as the only option. The discipline to balance both short and long term is the absolute of such a strategy."

This was a turning point for GE. The harsh economy and poor stock market of the 1970s deeply influenced Welch. Despite respectable earnings, GE's stock languished with the rest of the sour market. It had once traded at twenty-two times earnings per share, but was now hovering around ten times earnings. Company after company was being acquired in the new hostile takeover environment. Could GE be a takeover target? It was likely much too large, but ever-larger deals were being made. Managers were watching stock prices more closely—scouting for acquisition opportunities or fearing they might be a target and lose their jobs if they were taken over by a hostile acquirer. The best defense, as noted, was a high stock price. Making acquisitions was itself a good defense against a takeover because it made a company a larger, more expensive target and also used up excess cash, making it less attractive to cash-hungry hostile acquirers.

Until then, GE had given much less prominence to short-run profits, more to long-run payoffs. If earnings weakened during a downturn, so be it. Management assumed that the value of the company would ultimately be recognized by investors, who would drive up share prices. The poor stock markets of the 1970s cast that faith in the long run in doubt.

In a few brief sentences, Welch had defined a new age for big business. He introduced short-run profit management to GE, understanding that stock market investors trusted little so well as rising profits every calendar quarter. It became the best indication of a company's quality, making it stand out in good times and bad.

Welch had additional support for his candidacy from several members of the GE board, notably Walter Wriston, who liked Welch's aggressiveness and who was among the most enthusiastic of his advocates. "He was with me from day one," wrote Welch. Jones told Welch he was the new CEO ten days before Christmas in 1980.

"He never stops bothering us," the wife of one of Welch's leading subordinates said. It was a characteristic of Welch's management style. He was intrusive and demanding, more of a one-man show, if such a large company could ever be one, than his managerial principles professed. He talked fast and dominated conversations. He liked to put people down and then build them up. He rewarded those who performed well while conspicuously penalizing those who did not. But there was no denying his charisma and ability to motivate people. Welch wanted his managers to act like owners. This was one of the lessons of the takeover movement, advocates claimed. Push out stuffy lackadaisical management and replace it with hungry managers who owned a healthy piece of the company through stock options and were unafraid to close struggling operations and fire workers to get profits up. In its simplest form, it was also one of Tom Peters's key precepts, to get managers to act like owners. A high stock price had many advantages. As noted, it made acquisitions cheaper by requiring fewer shares to be exchanged to complete a merger, kept away unwanted acquirers, and stock options could make CEOs and their immediate underlings rich.

When Welch took over GE, he told his managers that the company was in poor shape, stuck in old ways of doing business. GE was a classic command and control company and it had to become more entrepreneurial, with fewer layers of management and more decentralized authority. Welch sounded like Tom Peters: break down walls between divisions and between managers and workers; let ideas flow freely; bring passion to the businesses.

Welch also adopted new managerial approaches designed to disrupt bureaucratic inertia and let good ideas rise to the top, including regular training, open discourse (gripe sessions), and an emphasis on eliminating product defects. For these he was widely lauded in business schools and business magazines.

But, in reality, Welch almost immediately started thinking like a takeover artist, not a long-term manager. He would run GE as if it had been taken over by hostile management. This was not the Peters philosophy.

As stock prices rose over this period, the stock market became an obsession for much if not most of business. By the mid-1980s, serious academic literature maintained that the stock price rationally reflected the company's long-term value—known as the efficient markets theory. If CEOs managed well, the result should be reflected in the stock price. In fact, stock prices ran in fashionable cycles, often independent of company performance, and by the 1990s investors focused on reported quarterly earnings, which could easily be manipulated. The advocates of efficient markets theory, closely aligned with Chicago-style economists, remained an influential force, however. Times were never better for CEOs with stock options and such academic theory was especially appealing to them, not least to Welch.

One of his first important public appearances as CEO was a speech he made to Wall Street analysts at the Pierre Hotel in New York in December 1981, about a year after he took his job. He told the analysts that GE businesses would have to be number one or number two in their markets or he would cut them. It was management by size and power. Even if a company had a good idea, without such dominance, he felt it might never make it to market.

In justifying his shuffling of the business, he cited the management consultant Peter Drucker, who told him that you should decide whether you would buy into the businesses you already had if you weren't already in them. "And if the answer is no," Welch wrote, citing Drucker, "face that second difficult question: What are you going to do about it? The management and the companies that don't do this, that hang on to losers for whatever reason—tradition, sentiment, their own management weakness—won't be around in 1990." Welch was managing a conglomerate like a portfolio of companies—the strategic approach preached by so many management consultants. Managerial experience and expertise in a specific business had less and less to do with his acquisitions. Financial results became all. Business strategy was everything to Welch.

To angry outcries at the company, he sold GE's classic appliances business of toasters and irons to Black & Decker rather than try to remake it. He had long before sold Utah International, probably a wise decision. "The $2 billion divestiture of Utah didn't raise an eyebrow," he writes. "But selling this $300 million low-tech, tin-bending housewares business brought out unbelievable cries. I got my first blast of angry letters from employees."

In three years, Welch sold more than one hundred businesses. Some of these needed selling, others might have been saved with good innovative management. But with the stock market in mind, the fastest way to increase profits is to cut costs, and in his first two years, he laid off more than seventy thousand workers, nearly 20 percent of the GE workforce. Quickly, Welch earned the nickname "Neutron Jack" for ridding businesses of people while retaining the operations. Within five years, roughly 130,000 workers of GE's 400,000 were gone. In fact, he institutionalized layoffs by requiring that 10 percent of the workforce of each division be replaced every year. In 1984, *Fortune* named him the toughest boss in America.

He drew deserved criticism. During his tenure, Welch dropped good businesses, such as semiconductors. He failed to get into cable television, letting Cox go. He was not able to break into the consumer electronics boom.

But mostly he drew admiration. Welch delivered on his promise to Wall Street of consistently rising earnings. Investors came to trust the consistency, which he said was based on good management and the market dominance of his business.

Early in his tenure, Welch built a lavish $75 million "management development center" in Crotonville, New York, and added a glamorous guesthouse, a fitness center, and a conference area. Only the upper management of GE was invited to the center and used the gym. Now Welch, the kid who pressed his nose up to the window of life, was on the inside, most GE employees figuratively looking in. In light of the layoffs, Welch was roundly criticized for the expenditures, but the investment was small for the returns in better management that it would reap, he said. If people did not understand, he wrote, he did not care.

The sales of operations he disliked allowed him to build up a large pool of cash with which to make acquisitions, and as early as 1981 he established a group to find the best targets for his growing ambition. His first major acquisition was a large insurance company, General Reinsurance. He and his staff successfully incorporated it into GE Capital, and went on to make many more small acquisitions of financing companies for equipment, aircraft, and credit cards. By 1992, GE Capital had $200 billion in assets, almost as big as some of America's major banks and larger than the General Motors Finance Corporation. Lending to business and consumers was now one of America's major growth industries.

Welch was willing to go much farther afield. In 1985, GE bought RCA for $6.3 billion. RCA's main business was NBC, the television network. Welch liked it, he wrote, because broadcasting was protected from foreign competition. But it was an odd pick for a CEO determined to produce consistent earnings growth. Television, like all entertainment businesses, invariably has good years and bad, hot shows and busts. Still, Welch convinced himself that he wanted NBC. One obstacle was the TV stations GE already owned. A regulation still prohibited ownership of more than a handful of stations by a network. But under Reagan, this regulation, too, would be weakened, opening the door for Welch.

Welch had also thought he could beat back Sony by building up RCA's television production in combination with the small television manufacturing operation GE still owned. The task was difficult, expensive, and long-term. Welch liked quick results, and he became intrigued by a foreign medical services operation of Thomson, the French company. He believed it could be a good fit with his own medical services division. Welch was also impressed by the head of the Thomson medical services operation, an elegant, articulate Frenchman who seemed to be making enormous profits. So he sold Thomson the combined TV set manufacturing operations of RCA and GE in exchange for Thomson's medical services.

Welch was convinced he had made a brilliant move, only to discover when it was too late that the French manager had been issuing misleading financial statements. Welch in fact had bought a company with low earnings and little potential. And, ironically, Thomson, willing to do the hard work of TV manufacturing, made the combined manufacturing operations with RCA work. Welch did not write about the episode in his autobiography.

Welch turned his attention to NBC. First, he applied new cost controls and demanded severe budget cuts that were foreign to the business until then. He named Welch loyalist Robert Wright, a lawyer by training but with experience running Cox Broadcasting, and now head of GE Capital, to run NBC. Despite his faith in the loyal Wright, Welch got deeply involved in decision making at the company, dismissing the long-standing head of news, for example, and even participating in the decision to hire Jay Leno as Johnny Carson's *Tonight Show* replacement.

The network business proved unpredictable, occasionally producing enormous profits, at other times little. Some of his executives had been rightly skeptical of the decision from the beginning, to which Welch had a simple and frequently used response. He wrote: "I kept asking, 'Ten years from now, would you rather be in appliances or broadcasting?' " Many believed Welch simply loved the spotlight.

In 1986, he acquired another company far from his field of experience, the old-line investment house Kidder Peabody. Wright, when head of GE Capital, had been actively looking for a brokerage company. In the rush of the takeover wave, and the rise of the bull market in stocks and bonds (interest rates had fallen sharply), investment houses were making huge profits again. When times were good, the return to capital was excellent. Welch particularly liked that the primary asset was labor, and compared to revenue, there were relatively few employees.

Dependence on a few employees could be a potential problem, however. Kidder was a relatively small firm and the young banker Martin Siegel was making a large share of its profits in the bulging takeover movement. He was the highest paid employee of the company.

Michael Milken's operation at Drexel Burnham was now churning out enormous revenues and Drexel was becoming a major firm. The Drexel chief executive, Fred Joseph, reasoned that the smooth and attractive Siegel would be an ideal co-head of investment banking, and Siegel accepted the opportunity to work with the bigger firm and the intense, money-generating Milken. GE pressed its offer for Kidder despite Siegel's departure, Welch perhaps not fully understanding the value of key personnel to the business, and, panicked at the loss of Siegel, Kidder management eagerly accepted. In all, it cost GE about $600 million. Wriston, always skeptical of Wall Street even as he tried to engage in the same businesses, had warned Welch that the securities business was mercurial and that the talent was all you had and hard to keep. But the easy profits were too tempting to Welch.

In fact, the discovery a year later that Siegel regularly passed on inside information to the relentless Ivan Boesky in exchange for suitcases of cash threw GE's purchase of Kidder into turmoil. In cooperating with the authorities, Siegel named two Kidder Peabody employees as having been involved. GE made a financial settlement with the SEC and the New York attorney's office, headed by Rudolph Giuliani. Welch appointed a GE manager from a tooling subsidiary to shape up the company.

The late 1980s began a difficult period for brokerage firms, beginning with the stock market crash in 1987, followed by the thrift and junk bond crisis at the end of the decade, the sharp fall of stock prices in late 1990, and a recession in 1990 and 1991. When both debt and equity markets started to climb once more in 1992 and especially 1993, Kidder finally did well again, generating enormous profits in the early 1990s. Welch was in a business he had no understanding of at all, but the cash flow was plentiful. One of Kidder's traders, Michael Vranos, a leader in mortgage-backed securities, the Street's fastest rising business, took home a $15 million bonus in 1993.

However, in 1994, the Federal Reserve under Alan Greenspan raised interest rates in fear that inflation was returning, and markets turned down. Vranos, seemingly invulnerable, suddenly lost a couple hundred million dollars. About the same time, it was discovered that a trader, Joe Jett, had falsified $350 million in profits in bond trades. In 1993, his bonus had come to $9 million. When the stock market turned down in 1994, Jett could no longer cover up his false trading profits. It would have taken a $500 million capital injection to get Kidder back and running, and Welch wasn't about to do it. He had his comeuppance and he now wanted to wash his hands of the industry altogether. At the end of 1994, he sold what remained of Kidder to Paine Webber, claiming GE still made a small profit on the transaction. This was true only in the narrowest sense, by not calculating what else Welch could have done with his hundreds of millions of dollars of investment. Suddenly, in the eyes of the press, Welch was no longer the great manager. But disdain would be short-lived as GE Capital's fortunes were about to soar in the Clinton boom, as would many of Welch's other businesses, and stock prices kept rising to new heights.

Even before Welch's rise to the top of GE, he had been involved with GE's most persistent scandal. The company had dumped PCBs (polychlorinated biphenyls), a poisonous by-product of chemical processes, into a variety of locations on the Hudson River and elsewhere back in the 1960s and 1970s. Although GE had stopped the process before Welch became CEO, it was Welch who signed a $3.5 million settlement with New York State authorities for damage to the Hudson River when he was a lower-level executive, thus limiting GE's liabilities.

Congress passed the Superfund law in 1980, administered by the Environmental Protection Agency, which required that the companies at fault clean up PCB sites, but the law was weakly enforced under Reagan until public clamor resulted in additional funding in 1986. Welch marshaled as much evidence as he could that the health threats of PCBs were exaggerated, underwriting scientific studies to prove his point. His fear was that the costs of cleaning up the large Hudson River area could rise to $750 million, and that GE would then be required to do the same at the many other smaller Superfund sites for which it had been responsible. Welch successfully fended off the efforts by the EPA during his tenure, and passed the concerns on to his successor, Jeffrey Immelt. Despite Immelt's more sincere efforts, no resolution of the issue was reached by the end of 2010.

So strong was the economy, and in particular finance, that the Kidder debacle, the PCB battles, the ups and downs of NBC, and other miscues were not enough to divert GE from its course as America's most admired company. GE Capital's profits grew so rapidly it soon accounted for half of GE's total. It was a central participant in the debt boom of the 1980s and 1990s, and enabled Welch to retire in 2000 at the top of his world. "In 1980," Welch wrote, "GE Credit had 10 businesses and $11 billion in assets and was based only in North America. By 2001, GE Capital Services had 24 businesses and $370 billion in assets in 48 countries."

GE Capital also enabled GE to manage its quarterly earnings, engaging in the last couple of weeks of every calendar quarter in various trades that could push earnings up on the last day or two before the quarter's end. It was an open secret on Wall Street that this was how Welch consistently kept quarterly earnings rising for years at a time. "Though earnings management is a no-no among good governance types," wrote two *CNNMoney* financial editors, "the company has never denied doing it, and GE Capital is the perfect mechanism."

GE was now the most highly valued company in America. In the late 1990s, its stock was trading at a price-earnings multiple about 25 percent higher than the average stock in the Standard & Poor's 500 index. Welch had produced earnings increases for fifty-one straight quarters, nearly thirteen years.

But he was no longer the manager of the 1970s, fighting tooth and nail to produce a new, exciting product. Early in his career he tried to develop other new products—a long-lasting lightbulb, a factory of the future, a ceramics operation, and a new refrigerator technology, among them—but they did not succeed. Afterward, he turned mostly to the easier route of acquisitions and divestiture. Over his tenure, he cut back significantly on research and development—by some 20 percent in the 1990s. In 1993, he told *BusinessWeek*, "We feel that we can grow within a business, but we are not interested in incubating new businesses." GE Capital itself was built through countless acquisitions. As the *CNNMoney* writers put it, "Consider first what the company really is. Its strength and curse is that it looks a lot like the economy. Over the decades GE's well-known manufacturing businesses—jet engines, locomotives, appliances, light bulbs—have shrunk as a proportion of the total. Like America, GE has long been mainly in the business of services. The most important and profitable services it offers are financial."

The *CNNMoney* writers got it slightly wrong. GE was not exactly like the American economy. It was even more dependent on financial services. In the early 2000s, GE was again riding a financial wave, the subprime mortgage lending boom; it had even bought a subprime mortgage broker. GE borrowed still more against equity to exploit the remarkable opportunities, its triple-A rating giving it a major competitive advantage. By 2008, the central weakness of the Welch business strategy, its dependence on financial overspeculation, became ominously clear. GE's profits plunged during the credit crisis and its stock price fell by 60 percent. GE Capital, the main source of its success for twenty-five years, now reported enormous losses.

By this point, Welch was retired. Under Jeffrey Immelt, GE made an emergency deal to sell a package of securities to Warren Buffett for $3 billion to bolster its capital. Its greatest good fortune was that a couple of months later the Federal Deposit Insurance Corporation agreed to guarantee nearly $140 billion of its debt because it owned a small federal bank. Welch, the great competitor, saw his firm bailed out by the federal government much like his admired friend Walter Wriston. GE's industrial companies, at least, were still earning modest profits, but overall profits kept declining into 2009.

"Jack always argued he was a great innovator," said Tom Peters, understatedly. "I am afraid I don't agree with him there." When he got to the top, he quickly reverted to the old maxims. He didn't remake businesses, he sold them. He did not save American manufacturing but abandoned it. He didn't raise American workers to a new level of respect but ultimately demeaned them. He mostly stopped trying to create great new products, hence the reduction in R&D. He took the heart out of his businesses, he did not put it in, as he had always hoped to do. What made his strategy possible, and fully shaped it, was the rising stock market—and the new ideology that praised free markets even as they failed. Much of this he denied. He was, in microcosm, the new American economy.

In the 1980s and early 1990s, Welch was widely criticized for his harsh labor practices. He was belittled for closing down countless manufacturing operations, some deservedly, but he rarely sought to save such businesses when there was an easier course. The criticism became muted later in the 1990s as stock prices rose. In the fervor of the bull market, *Fortune* magazine named him Manager of the Century. He had risen to the Forbes

400 list of richest Americans, personally worth at least $680 million at the height of the boom when he retired in late 2001. America accepted and celebrated such men. The time was driven by the prospects of riches on Wall Street—and finance determined business strategy. Welch made GE into a bank; he did not save American business. Seven years later, the banks in America nearly collapsed.

Michael Milken

I n the poor economy of the 1970s and the early 1980s, financing for risky companies was especially difficult to raise. A young, independent-minded man, Michael Milken, stepped into the breach to provide money for many of these kinds of companies, and later in the 1980s became the key financier of among the largest takeover contests of the decade. In doing so, he became by far the richest man on Wall Street at his peak, almost single-handedly creating and controlling a $200 billion market for junk bonds—the high-interest-paying debt of risky companies. No single person ever wielded as much power in the post–World War II period. By 1988, junk bonds amounted to one fourth of outstanding corporate debt. Three fifths of it was for takeover transactions of one kind or another. Milken had enormous influence over both buyers and sellers, and this enabled him to set the prices of the junk bond debt. He took a piece of these deals every step of the way, often secretly. Even when other major investment banks were competing with him, Milken typically controlled well more than half the market.

Quiet and publicity-shy, he had a towering ambition to become one of the richest people in America. Like many others in the age of greed, he made some constructive contributions, financing new or growing companies. On balance, however, he got rich by making bad loans or convincing others to do so—and he did it superbly. Some thought Milken was unstoppable until he was snared in the Ivan Boesky insider trading scandals. But by the late 1980s, he had already underwritten the sorts of loans that would likely have toppled his empire had the government not caught him.

Milken's financial ambition was hidden by an unassuming demeanor. He wore a cheap-looking toupee, lived with his wife and children in a fine but modest house for a man of his wealth, and, like many introspective people, was uncomfortable socially. He dwelt mostly in his considerable mind, and that mind since college and before was dedicated to making money. Even in his thirties and forties, he reminded acquaintances of an eager eleven-year-old who knows the batting average of every baseball player in the majors—and in Milken's case a lot more. Milken, folders under his arms, would meet a client in a diner and recall the details of many complex deals, knowing which of three hundred financial institutions and investors owned what proportion of individual stocks and bonds. He would suddenly promise to raise perhaps $500 million, and eventually much more, for a client to make a bid for an uncoop-

Junk bond giant Michael Milken, after being arraigned for securities law violations

erative target company—a promise he almost invariably made good on. By 1986, he and his family had at least $2 billion of their own, probably more. "The first thing you noticed was his intensity," said Martin Siegel, the banker who was also undone by the same insider trading scandal. "That was hard to miss."

It seems odd that Mike Milken would be elected to be head cheerleader at Birmingham High School in Van Nuys, California, in his senior year. Milken, self-absorbed, obsessive, uninterested in the glamorous life, did not seem to be socially oriented. But for all his introspection, he was aware of his public image. College classmates at the University of California at Berkeley said he deliberately made getting As look easy but in fact was working relentlessly at his studies almost secretly, and earning a Phi Beta Kappa key. Wanting to be rich was also somewhat unconventional at a time when social concerns and progressive reforms were campus rages.

His father, who died before Milken achieved his financial success, was an accountant with a small practice and raised Milken and his brother, Lowell, in middle-class comfort in Encino. At Berkeley, Milken was already investing for himself and his father and friends in the bonds of companies that were having financial difficulties. The cash flow of these companies often had fallen sharply and existing bondholders were uncertain they would receive interest and principal. Some of the companies had defaulted on the debt, driving the prices down. The yields on these bonds rose—the interest rate paid as a percentage of the cost of the bond—to levels that were much higher than on the bonds of more solid companies, and became known generically as high-yield bonds. The ratings agencies usually downgraded these bonds from "investment grade" to "speculative"—from triple-A or double-A to below triple-B. The young Milken believed that investors systematically exaggerated the risk of default by selling the bonds too quickly when the companies ran into difficult times. He also believed it was possible to analyze these companies in depth to find investments that were underpriced. The bonds could be selling for 40 or 50 cents on the dollar, or even less. If the troubled company improved its prospects, and eventually paid off even 75 cents per dollar of its debt, the investors could make a gain of 35 to 50 percent and more in addition to the high-interest income. Some paid off the full 100 cents on the dollar (a bond is usually denominated in $1,000 units).

Despite the potential bargains, Wall Street generally neglected these bonds, especially the major firms, which were leery of staining their reputations by recommending investments in dubious companies. Because serious and professional analysis of the bonds of these troubled companies was rare, these markets were likely to produce bargains—in academic terms, they were "inefficient." Milken came across a study in a course at Berkeley that he believed proved him right. An economist, W. Braddock Hickman, analyzed returns on corporate bonds issued between 1900 and 1943 and found that an investor who bought a highly diversified selection of these bonds and held them for the long run would earn a higher return than an investor who bought investment grade bonds only.

In fact, Milken may have misinterpreted (or misrepresented) the study. The strategy depended on buying large numbers of differing bonds, building a well-diversified portfolio, not picking a handful of potential winners, which was Milken's objective. But Milken, whether he understood the full implications of the study or not, was emboldened by the research. It is interesting that Wall Street accepted Milken's interpretation that financial markets were inefficient when it was profitable to do so; when it gave CEOs outsize stock options based on the stock price of the company, Wall Street generally argued that markets were so efficient the stock price truly reflected the long-term value of the company.

Milken graduated from Berkeley in 1968 and married his high school girlfriend. He then went east to Philadelphia to study finance at the Wharton School of the University of Pennsylvania, but didn't complete the final paper and failed to graduate with his class. Eventually he did do the paper, but he had also discovered additional research at Wharton that he believed corroborated his idea that high-yield bonds were regularly undervalued, and he used the studies as sales tools.

Milken had taken a job while still at Wharton with a white-shoe Philadelphia firm, Drexel Harriman Ripley, which once had ties to J.P. Morgan. There were few employees of Jewish descent at the firm, and none who wanted to have anything to do with the arcane and disreputable universe of high-yield bonds. While working part-time, Milken impressed his superiors with his moneymaking abilities and was offered a full-time job in 1970. The young Jewish man accepted. He was shunted off to the side of the trading room, but he seemed not to mind as he started selling the bonds to investment clients; with the small amount of capital Drexel provided, he bought and sold some himself. He thought he knew what the others did not, that analyzing high-yield bonds was a surer way to make profits than the stock market.

As he later told financial writer Connie Bruck:

> The opportunity to be true to yourself in high-yield bonds is great. It is not like buying a stock. With a stock, its value is generally dependent upon investors' collective perceptions of the future. No matter how much research you have done regarding a particular stock, you don't have a contract as to what the future price will be. But with a high yield bond there is a date certain in the future when it matures, and if you hold it to maturity and your analysis is correct, you will be correct in your calculation of your yield—and you do have a contract as to future price. One is certain if you're right. The other is not.

The 1960s stock market boom had given rise to too many firms, and when the bull market crashed in 1969, Drexel was one of those that did not survive. Also, brokerage commissions on large trades were being reduced significantly; by 1975, all trading commissions would be negotiated rather than fixed at formerly high levels (see Chapter 6). In 1973, a small, still profitable brokerage firm, Burnham and Company, bought the struggling Drexel, and the head of the firm, I. W. "Tubby" Burnham, wanted the new company to become a more serious participant in investment banking and brokerage.

Burnham understood Milken's value; he was one of the few making money for the firm. Always an outcast at Drexel, Milken had earlier threatened to leave because it wouldn't give him more capital to invest in his bonds. But the more pragmatic Burnham happily increased capital for his operation. If anti-Semitism or mere snobbishness was an issue at Drexel, it wasn't for Burnham, who was himself Jewish, as were most of his partners. Moreover, Burnham let Milken keep 35 percent of the profits for himself or to distribute to his employees. Milken demanded autonomy, including the authority to hire his own traders and sales force, and Burnham gave it to him.

The high-yield bonds, soon referred to as junk bonds, a name Milken himself inadvertently gave them, according to one of his best clients, Boone Pickens, typically paid 2 to 4 percentage points more a year in interest than did investment grade corporate bonds. Milken seemed to be able to pick the good companies, the ones whose earnings might well recover, giving them the ability to meet their debt payments, or come close. Not only would the investors earn the higher returns safely, but often the market would come to have more faith in these companies and bid up the price of their bonds.

Milken became close to the executives of many of the large companies whose junk bonds he both bought and recommended to his growing list of investment clients. In turn, Milken asked these companies to buy the bonds of other companies he liked. As he made money both for investors and the companies that issued the bonds, they became more beholden to him, willing to buy when he asked them to, so he was both buyer and seller, or controlled the buyers and sellers, and was effectively setting the price for these securities.

By now, Milken was also trading junk bonds for Drexel's "own account," which often produced profits for the company. He was selling the bonds to brokerage customers, earning commissions for each trade. And he was making markets so that customers could trade his bonds with confidence, enabling him to make money on the spreads, the difference between what price a buyer bid for a bond and what price a seller asked—the spreads and prices of which he often set himself. All the while, he cultivated a set of loyal and dependent investors, often the junk bond issuers themselves. In the 2000s, investment and commercial banks made an independent and unseen market for trillions of dollars of mortgage securities that was similar to Milken's original junk bond market, fraught with conflicts of interest and noncompetitive pricing power.

Milken was not yet thirty and had this market mostly to himself, but attracted little scrutiny from the SEC in Washington or the rest of Wall Street. The bonds were traded over-the-counter, so there were no public prices for the securities. In stocks, the New York Stock Exchange and the Nasdaq were self-regulating institutions, establishing rules for trading, which, if they existed in junk bonds, would have eliminated or seriously reduced Milken's advantages. And Milken had no serious competition.

Gradually, Milken's interlocking web of clients who bought and sold his bonds became the source of his power to control billions of dollars. These men came to trust him—and to depend on him. They were often self-made men of scant education with hard edges and a cynical view of the straitlaced practices adopted in older and more established businesses manned by Ivy Leaguers. These clients were also single-mindedly devoted to making fortunes, and many ran up against the rules and regulations. Carl Lindner was the most active of Milken's early clients, and soon one of the wealthiest men in America. He built a dairy store chain into a financial conglomerate through the acquisition of banks, thrifts, and insurance companies financed by debt. In 1974, however, the traditional Drexel executives decided not to do business with him, in part because he was under investigation by the SEC. Milken was not deterred, and by 1974 Lindner's conglomerate, American Financial Corporation, an issuer of junk bonds, also became Milken's best customer for bonds. (In 1979, Lindner settled with the SEC, when the federal agency questioned his compensation.)

The fortune of Victor Posner, another early client, who had built a conglomerate of industrial companies, was founded on controversial real estate investments in Maryland. Meshulam Riklis, who had a well-publicized life as a bon vivant, built a conglomerate, Rapid American, on aggressive use of debt, buying companies like Schenley and Lerner Shops. In the 1960s, Saul Steinberg became rich in computer leasing and insurance before he was thirty and in 1969 tried but failed to launch a takeover of Chemical Bank, several times the size of his own company, Leasco. In the late 1970s, both Riklis and Steinberg eventually had to sign consent decrees with the SEC, neither admitting nor denying guilt on charges of financial misconduct, but agreeing to discontinue the practices.

Milken's junk bonds were severely tested in the 1973–1975 recession, and most held up. When the economic expansion started in 1975 and 1976 again, the junk bond issuers generated more cash flow and many investors made handsome profits on the bonds' rise in value. Junk bonds began to look more like trustworthy investments to a widening circle of investors.

Milken had mostly traded in the fallen bonds of once healthy compa-nies. Now he wanted to expand his business into investment banking by underwriting new issues of junk bonds for risky companies. In the past, such companies had to borrow from banks or insurance companies—loans that were heavily collateralized by assets or capital and almost always hard to get.

Fred Joseph, a Harvard graduate from a blue-collar background, had been hired by Burnham in 1975 to build up traditional investment banking at the firm. Joseph was a straight arrow compared to the rest of the group, and his goal was to bring Drexel into the establishment, without rejecting Milken's dubious clientele.

In 1977, Lehman Brothers, a respected old-line institution, ironically took the lead before Milken got started, but it needed his help to sell the bonds. Lehman issued new high-yield bonds for Pan American, the airline, which was doing poorly, and LTV, the struggling conglomerate, flounder-ing companies forced to pay a high interest rate for the money. The ques-tion for the Street was whether it could convince pension funds, mutual funds, and individual investors to buy. It was Milken's ability to sell a high proportion of the Lehman bonds to his growing list of junk bond investors that enabled Lehman to underwrite the deal successfully.

After the Lehman deal, Milken had no doubt he could be underwriting junk bonds, and Joseph agreed. Why give away lucrative fees to Lehman? Drexel could keep 3 to 5 percent of the proceeds for itself, nearly impos-sible in more competitive established markets for equities, investment grade corporate bonds, and government bonds. Thus, a deal for $50 mil-lion brought $1.5–2.5 million to its bottom line, and there were additional advisory fees collected by Milken. Often he bought part of the offering for Drexel's own account, sometimes to ensure that the deal worked, but sometimes just to pocket more potential profit.

By 1978, after a slow start, Drexel was taking many new junk bonds to market. The major Wall Street firms were still hesitant to tarnish their reputations by dealing with the clients who had to issue high-yield bonds, and Milken largely had the field to himself. Lehman remained a tepid par-ticipant for a while.

With the underwriting going well, Milken wanted more capital from Drexel to support trading and underwriting. Burnham obliged, finding a foreign investor, Bruxelles Lambert, to invest. One man, Michael Milken, was buyer and seller of junk bonds, and consultant, underwriter, and ana-lyst. According to traditional practices of investment banking and financial brokerage, these were serious conflicts of interest. Most disturbing, as noted, Milken often demanded that the companies for which he raised money also invest in his offerings for other firms. With control over buyers, he could set the price of the bonds. He had essentially cornered the market.

With his growing power at Drexel Burnham, Milken decided in 1978 to move his entire operation to his home city, Los Angeles. Burnham and Joseph resisted, but Milken was unstoppable. By one estimate in the late 1970s, he and his brother, who worked with him, were already worth between $25 million and $50 million, and the figure was probably too low. After several years in a conventional office building in Century City, Milken moved to a building he and his brother bought at the corner of Wilshire Boulevard and Rodeo Drive, the heart of the business and shopping district of Beverly Hills, a flashy step for the outwardly modest Milken.

Milken worked notoriously long hours and liked the idea that he could start his day at 4:30 in the morning, which was 7:30 New York time, and be finished by 2:00, which would provide him quiet time to study more companies. He expected similar hours from those who worked with him.

While at Century City, Milken did a deal that raised his profile substantially. Until then, he had brought only relatively small companies to market. But Steve Wynn, a young Las Vegas casino operator, convinced him that it was time to build a major hotel and casino in Atlantic City, which had voted to legalize gambling in 1976. The first complex built there, Resorts International, was a runaway success. It took two years after their final meeting, but in 1981 Milken raised $160 million in junk bonds for Wynn, all with Tubby Burnham's approval. A few years later, Wynn sold his casino in Atlantic City, the Golden Nugget, at a profit of nearly $450 million, his personal stake now $75 million on a $2 million investment. With Milken's financial help, Wynn went on to build other giant and successful casinos in Las Vegas, eventually including the famed Bellagio. The Wynn deals were typical of the way Milken did business, raising money, often investing himself if it was needed, or taking a participation, sometimes unknown to investors. In turn, he reportedly raised more money for clients than they needed so that they could reinvest these funds in his other deals.

Over the years, Milken raised $6 billion for Wynn, his first true investment client. Wynn thought of it as venture capital disguised as debt financing. Financial writer Connie Bruck reported that Milken's compensation included hefty underwriting fees of up to 3 percent of the value of the deal, a proportion of the bonds for Drexel's and often his personal accounts, consulting fees, and also warrants or other so-called equity sweeteners, which were supposed to go to investors to make the bond offering more attractive. Milken did not always tell his clients he was keeping the warrants for himself or a variety of family partnerships, a tactic that was likely illegal. Thus, Milken came as close to outright market manipulation as he could. At the least, it was a classic case of monopoly price setting with many investors not fully informed of what was actually being done.

Milken pushed up the debts of many of these companies so high that when interest rates rose sharply in 1981 under Fed chairman Paul Volcker, followed by the severe recession of 1982, issuers of junk bonds were especially vulnerable. Some of Milken's companies did not survive. But Milken demonstrated his power by getting investors in the risky companies to convert the junk bonds, which pay interest, into new stock that does not. Thus, Milken eliminated much or all of the interest payments on the debt, enabling the companies to ride out the recession. For the most part, Milken's coterie of close clients, like Wynn, was willing to oblige. They took the so-called cramdown without protest. A less closely knit and dependent group would not have done so.

By law, the SEC demands full disclosure and a complete registration statement when new equity is issued, as should have been the case with the cramdowns. This procedure would have taken valuable time, time the struggling companies did not have if they were to ride out the recession. What made circumvention possible was that Milken's lawyers claimed they found a legal loophole to avoid registration, and rapidly went ahead. Teddy Forstmann, who ran an LBO firm, Forstmann Little, told journalists the Milken cramdown was outright unethical.

Milken survived the turbulence and emerged stronger after the 1982 recession, with some of his early investors grown much larger. Fred Carr, a money manager in the 1960s who now ran an insurance company, First Executive, had been investing in Milken's array of junk bonds since the late 1970s and by the early 1980s had a total investment of several billion dollars in them. S&Ls became favorite customers of Milken's when the Garn-St. Germain bill was passed allowing them to buy junk bonds liberally. Thomas Spiegel had built his company, Columbia Savings & Loan Association, into a giant, investing heavily in Milken's bonds. Charles Keating of Lincoln Savings, who eventually spent time in jail for allegedly defrauding his investors, was a key Milken investor.

By 1983, Milken had built a juggernaut of enormous financial power. Some $40 billion of junk bonds were floating in financial markets, paying a yield of 13 to 15 percent compared to as little as 10 percent on traditional bonds. And the investors were not only his early friends. Soon, a couple of dozen mutual funds specialized in investing in junk bonds. Many pension funds and investment managers put clients' money into these investments. The majority of these deals passed through Milken's trading desk.

Milken and Joseph now looked for fresh opportunities. They saw potential in the growing takeover movement, led by the mega–oil deals. Joseph badly wanted to participate. Old-line firms like Morgan Stanley, First Boston, Lehman, and, as a defender, Goldman Sachs, turned their full attention to the highly profitable deals, and were dominating the business. With so much funding under his control, Milken was eager to find a niche, and, as usual, money opened doors.

Boone Pickens of Mesa Petroleum was a financial upstart who appealed to Milken. Pickens maintained that the oil companies were run poorly, and as noted he said he started bidding for them for their own good—always stressing his moral concerns. A wildcatter from Oklahoma and a former geologist, he had bid in 1976 for an oil company about the size of Mesa called Aztec. He did not buy shares of Aztec beforehand, as Joe Flom had urged acquirers to do years before, in order to pocket a profit if someone else bid the company away. When a white knight bid much more for Aztec than Pickens was willing to spend, he lost the bidding contest. Not buying shares in the target beforehand, he said, "was the dumbest mistake of my life," and he never made it again. In 1982, Mesa bid for Cities Service, which had three times as much in oil reserves as did Mesa. This time he had bought a substantial block of Cities Service stock ahead of his bid. Eventually, his bidding drew a much higher bid from Gulf Oil. When Gulf eventually dropped out of the bidding, stunning investors and even the sophisticated arbitrageurs like Ivan Boesky, who had taken huge positions in Cities Service, Pickens was already out, having made $40 million for Mesa, an enormous sum at the time, and letting the arbs like Boesky take the losses. Eventually Occidental, a smaller company, bid for and took over Cities Service.

Pickens became America's best-known greenmailer. No one thought Pickens ever truly wanted to take over a company, for all his talk of bad management. He just provoked bidding contests and took the profits from the higher bid as a payoff for backing away.

The $40 million from his Cities greenmail venture gave Pickens money to gamble with and in 1983 he started buying shares of Gulf Oil itself, one of the largest oil companies in the world. Soon he bid for it, a remarkably bold move. For the first time, Milken was at his side, a coup it turned out for both of them. Milken put together an anonymous financing proposal for his investors, called the Gray Memo, to keep the name of the target secret. The memo provided cash flow estimates and a proposal to sell oil reserves to finance a hostile bid, but gave no further details. On the basis of this informal, anonymous investing document, Milken's investor group signed on almost immediately. They included Carl Lindner, Fred Carr, and Tom Spiegel, among others. Milken was able to guarantee Pickens a war chest of $1.5 billion, enough to make the far smaller bidder credible. Thus, Milken demonstrated he had financial power no one else had achieved.

Ultimately, a white knight, Standard Oil of California (Socal), bought Gulf at a higher price, and Mesa made roughly $500 million in greenmail. Milken's own group pocketed an estimated $20 million in fees. Under Ronald Reagan as president, two of the largest oil companies in America were allowed to merge without a sign of public concern. The combination of Gulf and Socal made it the third largest oil company in America and the single largest gas retailer, even bigger than Exxon. Such a deal could probably not have happened in any prior administration, Republican or Democrat.

Greenmailing was soon overshadowed by leveraged buyout partnerships. LBOs were not a new concept. Some form of them had existed at least since the early 1950s. As discussed, in an LBO, the goal is to find a company with a low stock price compared to the value of its assets and with a substantial, solid cash flow from sales that could cover the higher levels of debt service—interest and principal payments—on the funds borrowed to take it over. A company's own assets essentially financed its takeover by outsiders.

But who provided the debt financing? The LBO partnerships were able to raise capital from wealthy investors and a handful of pension funds, enough to get the ball rolling, perhaps 10 percent of a bid, which was equity. They would then borrow from banks to provide roughly 60 percent of the debt, which was known as a senior obligation and the least risky portion of the financing because it got paid off first. This business was increasingly attractive to the banks like Citibank, now under John Reed's leadership. The LBO firms also needed what was called mezzanine or junior financing—a 20 percent layer of riskier debt that was paid only after the senior debt obligations to the banks were settled. Most often, this higher-risk junior financing was provided by large and demanding insurance companies, which expected high rates of return and equity sweeteners to do the deal—options, warrants, or additional shares of stock. Citibank became one of the few banks that was also now placing money in these riskier tiers to reap the higher returns.

In the 1960s, an early LBO practitioner was a Bear Stearns banker named Jerome Kohlberg, who completed several buyouts, even though most of the buyout deals were friendly. Kohlberg's expertise began to pay off in the 1970s when stock prices fell to levels that made borrowing to buy shares especially attractive and prices so low that hostile LBOs made sense. Kohlberg started working with two new Bear Stearns employees, George Roberts from Texas and later his cousin, Henry Kravis, from Oklahoma, both some twenty years younger than Kohlberg. In 1976, he left Bear Stearns and asked Roberts and Kravis to join him in their own firm, Kohlberg Kravis Roberts.

In 1979, after completing some modest deals, they succeeded with a $350 million leveraged buyout of a Fortune 500 company, Houdaille, a conglomerate that made car bumpers, machine tools, and other industrial products. Everyone did well in the Houdaille deal except the company and its workers. Japanese competition, the brief recession in 1980, and the severe one in 1982 battered its sales, and with high debt service to meet, there was little fat in the company. Under KKR supervision, the Houdaille executives sold subsidiaries, fired hundreds of workers, and cut salaries. The machinists union was powerless to protect jobs and wages. As the 1980s economy eventually strengthened, the executives paid themselves very well indeed, and benefited from their stock ownership positions, while the machinists who were not fired earned less per hour than they had a decade earlier. KKR's buyout of Houdaille attracted many imitators. The KKR trio put up only $1 million of partnership money to make the $350 million acquisition. Soon new companies like Forstmann Little and Adler and Shaykin were competing with KKR for deals. In 1981, there were 99 such LBOs, in 1982, 164, and in 1983, 230. In 1984, a KKR buyout of Amstar Corp., the former American Sugar Co., resulted in a $46 million profit for the partners on an $830,000 investment.

LBOs were an obvious opportunity for Milken. He realized that junk bonds could supply mezzanine financing, which was always difficult to raise, significantly more cheaply than could insurance companies or the occasional bank like Citibank. In 1984, Milken financed an LBO for John Kluge's Metromedia, which owned radio and TV stations, a cell phone business, and the Harlem Globetrotters. Kluge, who lived grandly and paid workers poorly, wanted to take the company private. He believed the stock price was low but he could not raise the $1.6 billion the shareholders wanted. Milken provided junk financing to make it possible.

KKR was always in search of elusive mezzanine financing, especially if it was cheaper than insurance company funds, but the partners were at first hesitant to deal with Milken. The reputation of clients of his like Pickens, Lindner, and Kluge would not help attract the capital of established institutions to KKR's deals. But KKR had already lost the bidding contest for Gulf in a battle with Pickens and Socal. And it was hard to ignore Milken's financial capabilities in helping Pickens make a credible bid.

In the summer of 1984, KKR had almost completed a $300 million buyout of Cole National, a retailing company, when one of its banks suddenly dropped out of the financing. KKR needed to fill a $100 million hole quickly. One of Milken's bankers invited KKR and Cole executives to a meeting at Milken's Beverly Hills office with investors who included Carr of First Executive and Spiegel of Columbia Savings. Roberts and Kravis represented KKR and Milken ran the meeting. When Milken asked if the investors would put up the money, they almost immediately said yes. Milken was able to assure KKR before the meeting was over that the $100 million was theirs. The KKR partners were stunned. "It was the damnedest thing I'd ever seen," said Kravis. This was the Milken magic. He could now almost create money, enormous sums of money, at a moment's notice. By 1984, Wall Street was put on notice that he had a buyout fund of billions of dollars that he could make available almost immediately to takeover impresarios.

It was the beginning of a historic relationship between Milken and KKR, which went on to dominate LBOs, culminating in the largest to that point, a $25 billion takeover of RJR Nabisco that made headlines daily in 1988 and early 1989. As noted earlier, almost always the takeovers resulted in large layoffs, reduced wages and overhead, and the sales of subsidiaries. Almost always, the financiers and the executive who managed the downsizing at companies like Safeway, Owens-Illinois, and Beatrice Foods made fortunes. To defenders of the LBOs, radical reduction of expenses was necessary to restructure the U.S. economy. Some cited occasional instances of more R&D investment. But rather than reviving the company operations by taking risks on research, innovation, and new products, management more typically lopped off frail subsidiaries with little thought. It became the corporate strategy of the age, not only practiced by the takeover artists but, as we've seen, by leading managers like Jack Welch. Some of these discarded subsidiaries and operations no doubt might not have succeeded over time, but others would have. With Milken's critical help, corporate debt levels exploded in America.

Milken also financed other iconoclastic takeover artists who, like Pickens, rose to prominence on the basis of his financial power. Carl Icahn became a more successful greenmailer even than Pickens. In 1982, Icahn made a bid for the department store chain Marshall Field, driving the company into the hands of the British retailer Batus. The Icahn group, which had bought a substantial portion of the shares beforehand, made $100 million in greenmail. He made other successful greenmailing bids for companies like Anchor-Hocking, Dan River, and American Can, and built a substantial fund with which to bid for more companies, while his personal fortune reportedly rose to above $100 million.

In late 1984 and into 1985, Icahn launched his largest bid ever, for Phillips Petroleum, this time with financing from Milken's group. His greenmailing was becoming controversial, drawing the attention of the U.S. Congress, and some at Drexel did not want to deal with Icahn, but for Milken the public controversy was not a deterrent.

Drexel provided Icahn with a "highly confident letter"—a tactic that Icahn himself thought of—which said that Drexel could quickly raise more than $4 billion for the bid. Icahn balked at the fees Milken wanted to charge, but nevertheless took $1.5 billion of the offer. With the "highly confident letter" in hand, Icahn made a credible hostile bid. Phillips managed to ward off the $8 billion Icahn bid and remain independent, but Icahn made another $50 million in greenmail. In ensuing years, a "highly confident letter" issued by Milken was nearly as good as cash in the bank.

Icahn proceeded to do larger deals but without Milken, due to high fees. He took over TWA, and bid unsuccessfully for USX, the former U.S. Steel, pocketing greenmail along the way. To justify his actions publicly, he wrote a piece for *BusinessWeek* claiming the rapidly expanding takeover movement was the best way to improve American management and dismantle bloated bureaucracies. His bid forced CEOs to act like owners, he argued, and entrepreneurs were always sources of prosperity.

The respected Harvard Business School historian Alfred Chandler disagreed: business managers, not owners, made America prosperous. Though entrepreneurial owners were often brilliant, with their aggressive energy and innovativeness at starting businesses, he argued, they were usually poor at running them.

Milken's financial clout made giants of businessmen formerly on the fringes. In 1985, Nelson Peltz's company Triangle Industries had sales only a sixth of National Can's when, with Milken's funding, Peltz took it over. That same year, Ron Perelman, who had bought the supermarket chain Pantry Pride when it was in bankruptcy, decided to bid for the legendary Revlon company, ten times its size. Perelman approached Michel Bergerac, the chairman, and told him he would make him rich if he approved of the takeover. Bergerac refused and one of the classic takeover battles of the time ensued, on one side the upstart Perelman backed by Milken money, on the other side more establishment financiers.

The Milken group usually had one notable member of the takeover industry on its team, Joe Flom of Skadden Arps. Other attorneys, like his rival Martin Lipton, avoided some hostile deals, believing that hostile deals were strong-arm tactics practiced by a few self-interested men, whose financial payoff usually required undermining the target companies. Lipton, however, was active in defending targets. Flom made no such moral claims.

Perelman won the bidding contest for Revlon with Milken's full financial support, beating back a counterbid by Bergerac financed by the LBO firm Forstmann Little. The Revlon victory was a crowning achievement but that same year Milken was scoring success after success outside the hostile takeover arena. On average, Drexel launched a new junk bond issue each week. With his success in hostile takeovers, there was no one on the Street generating profits like Milken.

The Revlon deal produced stunning fees for the bankers and lawyers. Flom's firm billed $7–8 million, Lipton's in defense of Revlon some $10 million. The various bankers together took some $100 million. With its many ways of participating in deals, Drexel earned more than any other single firm, roughly $65 million. The incentives for ever larger takeovers were obvious.

In these years, KKR did nearly forty such LBOs, Milken participating in many of them. Drexel financed KKR's takeover of Storer Communications, from which Milken collected $55 million in fees and commissions for the firm and his personal partnerships. Drexel raised $2.5 billion in financing for KKR's acquisition of Beatrice Foods. The banks, lawyers, and investment bankers split up fees of more than $240 million—$10 million to Siegel's Kidder Peabody, $20 million to the law firms that worked on the deal, $45 million to KKR partners. On its takeover of RJR Nabisco, with Milken's financing, KKR earned about $75 million.

Milken took money wherever he could, and earned still more than is recorded. He often kept for himself and his partners the warrants, which are rights to receive stock, he insisted KKR add to its financing package to attract investors to the Beatrice deal. KKR was led to believe that the warrants went to those pension funds and others who put up the money. Milken pocketed them, some for his personal accounts. When Kravis and Roberts found out about the warrants, they chose not to complain; they had, after all, captured their prey. And Milken's ability to raise money was too valuable.

In 1986, *Institutional Investor* published an admiring story about Milken called "Milken the Magnificent." It discussed Milken's central place in the takeover movement and detailed his financial power without questioning his aggressive techniques. It was only one of many such articles at the time. Milken was the most lionized man on the Street in the high-flying mid-1980s, when greed became institutionalized.

In 1977, Drexel's revenues were $150 million, in 1985 they were $2.5 billion, and in 1986, $4 billion, with more than $500 million in after-tax profits, more profitable at this time than any other firm on Wall Street. Milken's total personal take was probably $100 million in 1985. In 1986, *Forbes* figured Milken personally earned an astonishing $550 million, his total net worth some $2 billion, making him the 133rd richest American, according to the magazine.

While the RJR Nabisco deal was under way, a three-way battle among KKR, Shearson Lehman, and Forstmann Little, Milken was indicted. Would Drexel still be good for the bonds promised to KKR? Milken's serious troubles had begun. Once Ivan Boesky's dealings with Dennis Levine were uncovered, the key for Boesky to win leniency was to hand over Milken. Most important were accusations that Milken asked Boesky to park stock illegally for him. By parking stock of takeover targets secretly, Milken's corporate acquirers could get an advantage on their prey, one explicitly outlawed by the Williams Act, which as noted earlier required making public holdings of 5 percent or more of a company's stock. Boesky said Milken agreed to reimburse him for any losses on the stocks if they fell while he was parking them.

Milken vigorously denied the charges. But to him, and others, such rules and regulations seemed to be more like parking violations. They had their purpose, however, which was to give others a chance to bid and move share prices higher. It was shareholders who lost out. In fact, Milken's near total control of the markets through his domination of buyers of junk bonds was a far bigger concern than such infringements, but not necessarily a violation of the murky financial fraud laws—or very hard to prove criminal intent if they were. On such lesser charges, however, Rudolph Giuliani, the U.S. attorney in New York City, could make a case. Boesky provided one key piece of evidence: payment by Milken of $5.3 million to cover losses for the parked stocks if they fell in price. Milken claimed the payment was for other purposes and he got corroboratory support from his subordinates, who at first maintained a united front, refusing to testify against him. Eventually, however, two came forward and weakened his claims. Even while Milken was awaiting legal proceedings, Drexel was able to provide the financing for KKR's victorious takeover of RJR Nabisco. The RJR deal, completed in late 1988, was the largest to date, and Milken was indicted by a grand jury in the spring of 1989. He had already left Drexel to fight the case, and started his own firm in the meantime.

Finally, Milken agreed to plead guilty to six felony counts, for which he was sentenced to a stiff ten years in prison, given the nature of the charges, and fines and restitution of $1.3 billion. The sentence was reduced to two years after Milken at last cooperated in investigations of colleagues and for good behavior. The cooperation apparently did not lead to any new convictions. Even after fines, estimates of his and his family's fortune in 1992 left them with $1.2 billion. Once out of prison, he started a charitable foundation dedicated to economic research and contributed significantly to medical research, having survived prostate cancer.

By the time of Milken's plea in the spring of 1990, the junk bond market was collapsing. Deals financed by Milken and others had now clearly been done at unjustifiably high prices. The profits of the early junk bond issuers Milken sponsored were around six times annual debt service, but in the late 1980s, they were often less than debt service. A Harvard Business School study found that ratings on junk bonds had fallen sharply since the early 1980s, those with the lowest rating tripling in number. Many could not meet their debt payments when the economy slowed.

By 1987, in part due to Milken's raising billions of dollars of debt for his clients, and in general financing the enormous wave of takeovers, interest rates had risen, in fact, they were high throughout the 1980s compared with inflation. Rapid growth in these years was financed by high levels of government and business debt. The Volcker Fed raised rates in 1987, worried that the economy was overheating, with stock prices doubling in two years, and the new Fed chairman, Alan Greenspan, had begun to raise interest rates as well, contributing to the steep stock market crash in October. While Greenspan's Fed pushed rates down to calm financial markets in late 1987 and early 1988, he again started raising them later that year. Economic growth slowed again, and by 1988, nearly two in five new junk bond issuers were defaulting on payments, and their prices were generally collapsing. The nation sank into full-fledged recession by 1990. Highly indebted junk bond issuers and LBOs struggled to survive, and many failed. Contrary to Milken's reputation for brilliant investing, Drexel's own portfolio of junk bonds generated enormous losses by late 1989.

By this time, many of the great LBOs had begun to collapse. Robert Campeau's retail sales empire of Allied and Federated stores blew up in the fall of 1989, bringing down almost $10 billion of LBO debt. Revco, Fruehauf, Southland (7-Eleven stores), Resorts International, and many other LBOs went into Chapter 11 proceedings. Other KKR deals began to implode: SCI-TV, a spin-off of Storer Broadcasting, announced that it could not service its $1.3 billion of debt, and forced the holders of $500 million in junk bonds to settle for new stocks and bonds worth between 20 and 70 cents on the dollar. Hillsborough Holdings, a subsidiary of Jim Walter, went bankrupt, and Seamans Furniture put through a forced restructuring of its debt.

Among Milken's other major clients, Integrated Resources in New York, which wrote tax shelter investments, went under. Columbia Savings and Loan and First Executive went under, in large part because they had bought so much junk bond debt.

Some claimed that had Milken not been preoccupied with court proceedings, he could have brought the collapsing market to order through equity cramdowns (forcing bondholders to take stock for their bonds) and similar tactics. This tactic artificially held down the actual default rate of his earlier underwritings, which some academics touted as an indication that junk bonds were safer than widely perceived. It was highly unlikely it would have worked this time. By then, the number of indebted companies was too great, and the band of investors he had on call to supply money when needed were in financial trouble themselves. Milken had simply encouraged investors to make too many bad loans. Drexel's capital plunged and by early 1990 it was out of business. Junk bond financing would come back when the economy expanded again, but not before serious damage had been done to the many pension funds and other investors who bought them.

The ostentatious lifestyles of Wall Street's new rich were coming under closer scrutiny. HBO made a playful but generally accurate movie of the RJR Nabisco deal based on the account in the book *Barbarians at the Gate*. The RJR executives had spent shareholder money lavishly on themselves, and deserved their comeuppance. Henry Kravis of KKR, and his wife, society fashion designer Carolyne Roehm, lived a particularly opulent life by the standards of the day, with Park Avenue, Southampton, and Connecticut residences, major pieces of art, riding stables, a Vail, Colorado, ski lodge, and a jet. Roberts and Kravis were listed in the 1988 Forbes 400 with a net worth of $300 million each. Kohlberg had retired from the firm, which he believed had become too aggressive. The KKR executives maintained in their own defense that they had spent their own money, not the company's.

For years, there were complaints about the fees KKR earned. They charged their partners an annual management fee of 1.5 percent and took full investment banking fees on their deals. They also had major equity participation in their buyout targets.

KKR's crown jewel, RJR Nabisco, was also struggling to survive. The partners hired Louis Gerstner, a former McKinsey consultant and American Express executive, to straighten matters out as CEO. But the company could barely meet its debt service and had to raise more capital, KKR itself pitching in. Doing real business at RJR Nabisco was basically on hold due to the excessive debt payments, but Gerstner finally got the company to a point in 1992, once the economy was coming out of recession, where he could invest and expand again.

In the end, this aggressive era of corporate acquisition, high levels of debt, and paring of employment did not produce a seriously more innovative and competitive economy. Despite claims of renewed vigor, investment by business was historically weak for most of the decade. Out of dozens of financings, Milken could claim a few successes. Notably, he helped Ted Turner buy the MGM library of movies. MCI and the Wynn Las Vegas empire thrived. But the high interest rates, major investment losses, and misallocated capital took a heavy toll on the economy. With a few exceptions, Milken did not create an opening in the clouds for beleaguered business. If anything at all helped, the determination of the Reagan administration to reduce the value of the dollar restored profit rates some-what as exports became more competitive. Even so, in the 1980s, America's productivity did not begin to grow again at the rapid rates it had achieved through most of its industrial history. The Reagan revolution produced no economic revival. Productivity did not begin to grow rapidly again until 1996, more a consequence of the rise of the Internet and very powerful computerized inventory methods than other factors.

All the while, Washington looked the other way. In 1985 and 1986, Paul Volcker, as the Fed chairman, was worried about the LBOs. As discussed earlier, Volcker wanted a new Fed rule to establish margin requirements on loans made by banks to buy the equity of companies, in order to limit these loans (see Chapter 11). But the Reagan administration and its new Fed appointees opposed Volcker's suggestion, and Milken and other Drexel executives lobbied aggressively against it. Only a watered-down version was adopted, and it was easy to circumvent.

Later attempts by Congress to restrict LBOs and similar takeovers were generally thwarted by the succeeding administration of George H. W. Bush and active lobbying by buyout leaders. Rather than tightening financial regulations, Washington loosened them further in the next two decades, even when new crises arose. In Alan Greenspan, nominated by the Republican Reagan, but strongly supported later by Bill Clinton, the vested interests of the financial community were well served in the name of narrow free market ideology.

Alan Greenspan

IDEOLOGUE

In early 1985, Alan Greenspan wrote a long letter to federal regulators in support of Charles Keating of Lincoln Savings & Loan, who had been a client of Michael Milken's, later imprisoned for securities fraud. Greenspan had returned to his profitable economic Wall Street consultancy, Townsend-Greenspan, in 1977 after serving as President Gerald Ford's chief economist. Washington regulators occasionally tried to restrain the thrifts after the 1982 Garn-St. Germain law had opened avenues for them to make speculative investments. Almost always, the regulators were beaten back or circumvented by the industry, in part because President Reagan did not fully support the decisions of the thrift officials or had appointed industry-friendly people who overrode former regulators' findings. In the most glaring case, Danny Wall, head of the Federal Home Loan Bank Board, refused in 1989 to close down Lincoln despite efforts by San Francisco thrift examiners to do so. Wall, a Reagan appointee, had worked for Senator Jake Garn on the misconceived Garn-St. Germain legislation. "If the allegations the committee has heard so far are true," Congressman Jim Leach said of Keating, "Charles Keating is a financio-path of obscene proportions—the Rev. Jim Bakker of American commerce."

Since his return to Wall Street, Greenspan had become a favorite informal adviser to Republican politicians, including serving as co-chairman of Reagan's Social Security Reform Commission in his first term as president. At the request of Keating's lawyers, Greenspan examined Lincoln's financial statements and wrote a letter to the Federal Home Loan Bank, the thrift regulator, urging that Lincoln Savings should be exempted from a new rule limiting a thrift's investments in nonmortgage investments to 10 percent of assets. By the mid-1980s, when Greenspan wrote the letter,

Federal Reserve Board chairman Alan Greenspan, right,
with Treasury Secretary Robert Rubin

and after only a few years of deregulation, these investments were raising alarms, although the banks' widespread demise was still several years off. The thrifts like Lincoln invested in a wide range of risky assets, including junk bonds, shopping malls, ski resorts, and even uranium mines. Since deregulation, Lincoln, Columbia, Vernon in Texas, Silverado in Florida, and others were offering very high interest rates to attract depositors, occasionally over 12 percent, when traditional savings accounts were paying 6 or 8 percent. Deposit brokers gathered individuals' savings and placed them with the high-paying institutions. And the ordinary savers, insured by the federal government, took no risk. Some local Federal Home Loan Bank offices, like the one in San Francisco, were trying to control the risky uses of depositors' money, knowing full well by the mid-1980s how risky much of the investment was.

Greenspan wrote the FHLB that the "new management" of Lincoln "effectively restored the association to a vibrant and healthy state, with a strong net worth position, largely through expert selection of sound and profitable direct investment." Greenspan's service in Washington and his growing reputation got Keating his waiver. Four years later Lincoln was virtually insolvent, costing the federal government $3.4 billion to pay off its debt and depositors. Along the way, Keating, in a desperate attempt to shore up his failing company, induced many savers to buy the uninsured CDs of the parent firm of Lincoln. Few savers had any idea the investments were not insured and Keating did not make it clear to them. When the parent failed, it cost many their savings. One regulator later wrote that Keating's act was "one of the most cruel and heartless frauds in modern memory." When the regulators finally caught up with Keating's many abuses, five U.S. senators came to his defense, four Democrats and Republican John McCain, asking the authorities to be lenient with him. All had received substantial campaign contributions from Keating. In explaining his support for Keating, McCain cited Greenspan's complimentary letter, the opinion, after all, of a respected expert. Keating, as noted, ultimately went to jail (released on a legal technicality after four years but later pleading guilty on four charges) but the Keating Five, as they were called, were lightly reprimanded after a Justice Department probe. Greenspan, already Federal Reserve chairman when the letter was made public, went uncriticized by any government body.

In his memoir, *The Age of Turbulence*, Greenspan apologized for the four-page letter, which only came to public attention when the Senate investigated the Keating Five. His book claimed that the liquid assets of the firm were strong at the time he wrote the letter and he could not anticipate any future insolvency. He made a point in the book of noting that he had admitted his error to *The New York Times* only a few years later. "They struck me as reasonable, sensible people," as he put it to the *Times*. But the federal government was already wary of the thrifts' adventures in investing and some of the thrifts were, by then, reporting sizable losses. Greenspan remained, for whatever reasons, oblivious. There was no evidence he did any serious research. He reportedly received $30,000–40,000 for his quick analysis of the Lincoln balance sheet and his letter to the FHLB. He did not justify the fee in his memoir, or deny receiving it.

Greenspan's disposition to free and unregulated markets became increasingly acceptable in America in the 1980s and now he was about to step onto the right side of history. In 1987, when he was appointed by Reagan to be Federal Reserve chairman and took office, few then thought he could live up to Volcker's record or match his reputation. Volcker had, after all, stopped inflation with a brute policy that most believed could not be politically implemented until he did so. But inflation had come down sharply from annual rates above 13 percent to below 4 percent in the 1980s. Monetary policy—the control of interest rates—had become widely accepted, even by Democrats, as the main economic lever, replacing the dominance of the old Keynesian fiscal tools that seemed inadequate in the inflationary 1970s. By the time Greenspan took office, the primacy of both monetary policy and of fighting inflation were almost unquestioned. The Fed chairman and the Federal Open Market Committee (composed of Federal Reserve Board members and the heads of the regional Federal Reserve banks) were all-powerful and legally independent of directives from the president or Congress, whose only direct control was exercised when the chairman and the governors came up for reappointment.

Greenspan's philosophy on inflation had been formed much earlier. It was his central economic concern and, though not a monetarist, he was in complete sympathy with Friedmanite emphasis on reducing government spending and eliminating deficits. Government spending was the source of inflation, he believed—a lesson he learned from Arthur Burns, one of his professors, as Burns was one of Friedman's.

Unlike Volcker, Greenspan, it is fair to say, was also a free market ideologue—that is, he took market efficiency and rationality as givens. He had more influence than any other figure over the direction the nation took over the next two decades, not merely in fighting inflation, but also in government's role in the economy, effectively diminishing it. He repeated time and again that unfettered markets were best. A few weeks before the fall of the nation's largest hedge fund, Long-Term Capital Management, in 1998, which collapsed from borrowing extreme amounts, Greenspan argued that such hedge funds were already effectively regulated—by their lenders. Lenders wouldn't provide dangerous levels of debt to the clients because it was irrational to do so. But LTCM's lenders were mostly caught unaware because the hedge funds were not required to make their loan positions known. In 1999, when arguing against the proposal of the head of the Commodities Futures Trading Commission to regulate financial derivatives, Greenspan claimed that unrestricted derivatives trading would stabilize finance, not disrupt it. He had no idea how dangerous the new mortgage-based collateralized debt obligations were, as we shall see, the principal source of overly risky investment in the 2000s. It never occurred to him that investment banks were now creating loans just like the commercial banks he oversaw, but this shadow banking system was not regulated by the one agency designed to make sure U.S. credit was strong, his own.

Writing a letter in support of Keating, apart from the outrageous irresponsibility and suspiciously easy payday, was simply an ideological reflex of his at work. This philosophy was familiar Friedmanite social policy, but Greenspan did not cite Friedman's writings on these matters, or any theoretical economists. His philosophy reflected his long-held personal views. In fact, he discarded completely the use of money supply data to determine policy by 1993.

By the late 1990s, Greenspan became the most widely admired Federal

Reserve chairman in history, credited with both stopping inflation and creating conditions for stable, rapid economic growth. His shining hour was his willingness to let interest rates remain low in the late 1990s, when the unemployment rate fell to what almost all economists thought was too low to be sustained without creating inflation. For much of his tenure, however, he suppressed growth too much in his battle against inflation while neglecting employment and ignoring the rampant overspeculation in high-technology stocks and housing that low-interest-rate policies supported. Under Greenspan, banks and other banklike financial institutions were far more free from government oversight and regulatory enforcement than at any time since the 1920s. A large body of American opinion supported this development, and was mostly uncriticized by mainstream economists and the media.

The acquiescence to ideology occurred even when markets lurched from financial crisis to crisis under Greenspan's tenure—a stock market crash in 1987, a thrifts crisis in 1989, the collapse of junk bonds by 1990, a derivatives crisis in 1994, the Mexican peso collapse of 1994, the Asian financial crisis of 1997, the failure of Long-Term Capital Management and the Russian default on debt in 1998, and the severe stock market crash of 2000.

Speculative binges enabled by both stimulative monetary policy and regulatory neglect preceded all these collapses. Levels of speculation rose to ever more dangerous heights each time. In the 1980s, the takeover movement built on soaring levels of debt, much of it ultimately bad, rose to unmanageable levels. In the 1980s and 1990s, international capital flows pushed markets up irrationally in Mexico and Asia, partly due to deregulated flows encouraged, in the 1990s, by Greenspan and the Clinton administration economic advisers Robert Rubin and Lawrence Summers. In the early 1990s, a new round of speculation in derivative debt instruments almost undid Wall Street, when the Fed surprisingly raised rates in 1994. The higher rates also contributed to a financial crisis in Mexico, which owed American and other Western and Japanese banks billions of dollars. The U.S. Treasury bailed out Mexico with a $40 billion package, enabling it to pay its debts.

In the later 1990s, hedge funds with little regulation borrowed aggressively and American capital chased high interest rates across Asia. In the late 1990s, U.S. high-technology stock prices reached unjustifiable levels by any historical standard, again due to Federal Reserve forbearance. And in the 2000s, housing prices rose faster than at any time in modern history in a deliberate attempt by Greenspan to restart a flagging economy and avoid deflation after the high-technology collapse. Greenspan did not temper his monetary policy with regulatory vigilance, which would have been Volcker's predilection. He took little notice that, on average, consumer debt, business debt, and government debt were all consistently rising more than twice as fast as the nation's income.

Yet in an age of free market ideology, to which even Clinton subscribed, Greenspan's determined noninterventionist and deregulatory philosophy attracted little criticism during his twenty years of service. A comprehensive academic analysis of economic policies of the 1990s written by both Democratic and Republican economists did not even discuss government regulation, while a similar analysis of the Reagan years had several chapters on the subject. By 2008, two years after his retirement, Greenspan's ideological principles almost brought the nation down.

Alan Greenspan was born in 1926 in Washington Heights, the northernmost part of Manhattan, then a middle- and working-class Jewish enclave. Greenspan's father was a businessman and a politically liberal self-taught economist, but he and Alan's mother divorced by the time Alan was five, and he thereafter saw him infrequently. Greenspan's father, who became a stockbroker, was a New Deal supporter in the 1930s and wrote a book, *Recovery Ahead!*, which claimed that the New Deal policies would end the Depression. Alan and his devoted mother, Rose, moved in with her parents in a one-bedroom apartment in Washington Heights. His father was seemingly replaced in Greenspan's affections by his mother's brother, a prosperous businessman, who took Alan and Rose away for summers in Rockaway Beach in Queens. His uncle argued that the New Deal was bad for the country.

Alan was a good if not uniformly outstanding student in high school. As a boy, he was an avid sandlot baseball player, and a dedicated Brooklyn Dodgers fan; in high school, he was president of his home room and a member of the orchestra and dance bands. Rose's family was musical and Greenspan's early ambition was to be a professional musician. He became a competent clarinetist and was accepted at the Julliard School of Music, which he attended rather than conventional college. He quit the demanding program, coming to grips with his limits as a musician, according to biographer Justin Martin, and joined a professional jazz band as saxophonist and clarinetist. He was exempted from service during the war for medical reasons. In 1945, he entered New York University at the age of twenty, graduating summa cum laude in 1948.

After NYU, Greenspan attended Columbia in graduate economics, where he studied with Arthur Burns. The Columbia department, and especially Burns, was statistically oriented, which appealed to Greenspan. Moreover, Burns, one of the faculty's political conservatives, was the first authoritative economist Greenspan met who was a critic of John Maynard Keynes. Greenspan was himself a mild Keynesian in college at a time when Keynes was the ascending figure in the field. Burns's teaching released Greenspan from Keynesian influence.

Greenspan left Columbia partly because of the high tuition and took a job with an economics consulting organization, the Conference Board, where he researched industry data for corporate clients, delving into the minutiae he came to love. At the time, he also met an intelligent, pretty painter in New York City, Joan Mitchell (not the celebrated Abstract Expressionist), who soon became his first wife. She introduced him to Ayn Rand and her circle. Greenspan's ideology was more deeply ingrained in him by the charismatic writer and philosopher than by his economic education. Rand was the Russian-born self-declared "objectivist" philosopher who vehemently advocated laissez-faire capitalism, and had a profound, passionate distaste for government. Her best-selling romantic novels, *The Fountainhead* and *Atlas Shrugged*, whose masculine heroes were individual icons, extended her influence and made her wealthy. In the 1960s, Greenspan wrote several essays for the Rand publication, *The Objectivist*. In these extremist essays he called for linking the dollar only to gold and he scathingly criticized both consumer protection and antitrust laws because they interfered with the free market. In 1985, Ivan Boesky was mocked for telling a group at Berkeley in 1985 that greed was healthy. But Alan Greenspan wrote twenty years earlier that "It is precisely the 'greed' of the businessman, or more precisely, his profit-seeking, which is the unexcelled protector of the consumer." Ultimately because of policies based on this ideology, the American economy foundered in 2008.

Greenspan's marriage did not last, but Greenspan found comfort and camaraderie in Rand's cultish circle. Rand welcomed and admired the scholarly and intelligent young man, whom she became close to as a friend. In this period, Greenspan formed a partnership with the Wall Street veteran William Townsend, whom he had worked for. In 1958, Townsend died. At thirty-two, Greenspan inherited the firm and made it profitable during the bull market of the 1960s. He developed a computerized model that simulated the economy, an outgrowth of the pioneering econometric work of several economists—in the United States, notably the Nobel Prize winner Lawrence Klein. As was customary, Greenspan tinkered with his model's conclusions because outputs from all these models were crude. Greenspan thought the model provided a disciplined and consistent way of thinking about the economy, but not a technically reliable forecast. In fact, Greenspan's forecasts of economic conditions were not considered among Wall Street's best and he was criticized for his forecasting errors when testifying before Congress much later. He was more comfortable ferreting out data on steel shipments or scrap metal or paperboard deliveries, which gave him a picture of the current strength or weakness of the economy or particular industries, but that often had little bearing on events a few months ahead. Townsend-Greenspan—he never deleted the founder's name—prospered, adding many Wall Street clients to his list. Greenspan became a rarity at the time, a competent Republican economist when most successful economists were Keynesian Democrats.

Greenspan first became active in politics when he joined the Nixon presidential campaign in 1967. He started writing a conservative, laissez-faire-oriented economics textbook with Martin Anderson, who later became one of President Reagan's domestic policy advisers, and Anderson, in turn, asked Greenspan to become an adviser during the campaign. But when Nixon won, Greenspan, who considered Nixon unusually bright but disliked his profanity and volatile temperament, refused to join the White House staff, and chose to return to Wall Street to nurture his successful business.

However, Greenspan traveled to Washington often, providing informal advice to the Nixon administration, while publicly berating the president for the 1971 wage and price freeze. When Nixon's Council of Economic Advisers chairman, Herb Stein, lukewarm at best to wage and price controls, wanted to leave the faltering administration for a teaching post in 1973, the Nixon team aggressively sought Greenspan to replace him. Given the Watergate turmoil, Greenspan at first resisted, but Arthur Burns, then Federal Reserve chairman, insisted it was his patriotic duty to accept, and Greenspan did so shortly before Nixon's resignation.

Greenspan succeeded Stein as head of what was now the Ford CEA. In office, he provided more anti-inflation rhetoric for the Republican strategy and no especially insightful analysis. (Ayn Rand and her husband were two of only a few guests invited to his swearing-in ceremony.) As the steepest recession of the postwar era swept through the economy, Greenspan showed little prescience or originality and kept urging Ford to fight inflation almost into 1975, at the lowest point of the economy. By early 1975, as noted in Chapter 3, Greenspan could no longer ignore the rising level of unemployment and he switched course, encouraging Ford to adopt a tax cut to stimulate the economy in time for the election campaign of 1976—a Keynesian intervention. It wasn't enough of a stimulus to keep the unemployment rate from rising further. When challenged in October 1976 on why Ford was letting the economy slow down, Greenspan told a *Face the Nation* audience that the best way to get people to work was to get inflation down further, that the rise in unemployment was merely a pause in the upswing. The comments damaged Ford's reelection prospects, reinforcing the view that the Republicans were all too willing to sacrifice workers in the name of reducing inflation.

In Washington, Greenspan's low-key and comfortably engaging personality made him many friends, including Ford himself. Greenspan was frequently at the town's most coveted dinner parties and also enjoyed the company of women. After Ford lost, Greenspan returned to New York. With his reputation enhanced by his Washington experience, and his constant contact with the powerful in Washington, his business flourished. In the late 1970s, he earned roughly $300,000 a year. He was frequently quoted in the press, a reliable source who would always return phone calls and provide good copy. He genuinely enjoyed journalists and dated a few, notably celebrity newscaster Barbara Walters. In 1997, he married NBC News correspondent Andrea Mitchell.

He also finally got his Ph.D. from NYU. He had completed his course work years earlier, but did not write a thesis. Possibly because he was not comfortable with theory, nor is there any evidence he was conversant with new complex statistical techniques, Greenspan submitted as a thesis business analyses he had completed for clients or published mostly in business journals, and NYU accepted them as adequate. It is unlikely another established economics department would have done so, or that NYU would do so today. The Ph.D. was granted in 1977.

In the 1980s, as he developed his business further, he gave informal advice to the Reagan administration on a variety of issues, and spoke regularly to Democratic politicians as well when asked. Reagan called him formally to Washington in 1981 to address the prospective deficit in Social Security benefits. According to long-term Social Security administration forecasts, benefits would exceed tax revenues sooner than expected. Reagan wanted to cut benefits sharply, as we've seen, but Congress, including many Republicans, would not agree. Greenspan and New York senator Pat Moynihan headed the bipartisan commission that raised payroll taxes substantially and cut benefits mainly by raising the retirement age. Thus, as discussed earlier, a regressive tax—above a specified level, there is no further payroll tax on income—was raised markedly, while the progressive income tax was cut significantly in the early 1980s. On balance, Reagan reduced overall taxes modestly but made them more regressive.

Greenspan was still more businessman than Washington insider in 1985, when he signed the Keating letter. That year, he did a television commercial for Apple. His service on the Social Security commission further raised his stature on both sides of the political aisle. With access to Washington, a good analytical mind, a strong understanding of where to find data, and an ideology congenial to business and Wall Street, his client list grew. He expanded his ties to the media and he would argue sincerely about his principles with novice journalists and powerful businessmen, without arrogance or snobbery. All the while, his Republican credentials were burnished.

In 1987, Volcker was finishing his second term as chairman of the Federal Reserve. His reputation as an inflation fighter had been established. By 1986, however, Volcker was concerned the economy was growing too rapidly again and that debt levels, including Milken junk bonds, had become excessive. As discussed earlier, he was particularly disturbed by the use of the debt to fund ever larger and more aggressive corporate takeovers and LBOs. Unlike the Reagan appointees now on the board of governors, Volcker did not want to keep reducing interest rates, as he had been doing since 1982. The target federal funds rate had already been cut further, from 8.5 percent in the spring of 1985 to less than 6 percent in the summer of 1986. With the unemployment rate still near 7 percent, Reagan's economists wanted to spur growth still more. But Volcker was concerned that the federal deficit was still running high even five years into an economic expansion and that it would cause inflation. The size of the federal deficit remained the major economic issue until the 1990s—to resume again in the 2000s. In 1986, it exceeded $200 billion, 5 percent of GDP.

Volcker, also at odds with Reagan's deregulatory policies, decided to leave as his second term was coming to an end. It was clear that the Reagan administration wanted someone more in agreement with their views.

Greenspan was a like-minded friend to Republicans. He would not worry about restraining the amount of tax deductible debt available to fund the purchase of stock to make takeovers, for example. On monetary policy, the Reagan advisers believed he was more flexible than Volcker. James Baker, Reagan's treasury secretary, had been in frequent contact with him about the possibility that the position would open up and Greenspan did not deny his interest in the nation's highest economic office. In May, Baker called to tell him to expect a personal phone call from the president. He received that call in his doctor's office—the secretary thought it was a prank—and told the president he would take the job.

Democratic senators, who were in the majority, questioned Greenspan closely at his confirmation hearings. William Proxmire, head of the Banking Committee, noted that in the 1980s Greenspan consistently overestimated the level of inflation. Greenspan's extremist criticism of the antitrust laws, while writing for Rand's *The Objectivist,* were also questioned. He assured the senators he would be pragmatic about the antitrust laws as they related to the banking industry. The Fed was the nation's principal bank regulatory agency as well as custodian of monetary policy. Senator Bill Bradley worried that Greenspan would deregulate the financial community too assiduously, given his theoretical views about government intervention. Bradley ultimately voted against Greenspan on these grounds, but all but one of his colleagues voted to confirm, including Proxmire.

Greenspan became chairman in early August 1987, when inflation had started to rise faster and the unemployment rate had fallen to 6 percent, which many economists, abiding by Friedman's view of the natural rate of unemployment, now thought was as low as it could fall. Greenspan wanted to show the market professionals that he was as determined to hold inflation down as was Volcker, and he immediately pushed up interest rates further, easily winning over the other board members and continuing the shift in policy Volcker had started a few months earlier. To Greenspan, unlike Volcker, inflation was almost all the Fed had to focus on because a free market would otherwise adjust on its own, setting prices on goods and services, so they were distributed fairly and efficiently, as well as on capital, so that it was allocated to the appropriate areas of investment. Higher inflation would distort such rational decision making.

The narrow view was also increasingly held by mainstream academic economists, who eventually asserted that the Fed should explicitly target a low rate of inflation and do little else. One of its leading academic advocates was Ben Bernanke, the Princeton professor who eventually succeeded Greenspan. Maintaining a low inflation rate often meant higher interest rates and slower economic growth than many politicians thought ideal. Here, went the conventional wisdom, courage to stay the course was key. Implicit in the fight against inflation was the belief (clearly held by

Volcker) that federal budget deficits had to be minimized; they, too, were typically sources of inflation by creating too much demand for goods. Appeasing workers by reducing the unemployment rate and encouraging higher wages was seen as a sign of weakness.

Greenspan was the man for this job. If he was going to make mistakes, they would be to suppress economic growth and employment too much in the battle against inflation. As in foreign policy, economists had claimed they found the enemy, and such clarity was comforting. Meantime, deregulation of the financial markets was also widely supported. Here again, Friedman's ideas won out.

A month later, the stock market collapsed for fear higher interest rates would lead to recession. On October 19, on what became known as Black Monday, the Dow Jones Industrials fell by more than 20 percent, a record drop of more than 500 points. The next morning, international stock markets fell sharply. The sudden collapse was triggered by the use of computerized insurance programs, which failed to work when everyone was rushing to sell at the same time. The insurance was supposed to protect investment managers against larger losses.

Greenspan was away that Monday in Dallas and the health of the markets was in the hands of Gerald Corrigan, the New York Fed president, who had little doubt about what to do. With Greenspan's approval, the Fed announced early Tuesday morning that it would provide the liquidity the nation needed. Corrigan started buying short-term Treasury securities to provide funds to banks. This was precisely how the Fed cut interest rates as well, which fell. He also called all the major banks to be sure they were lending the reserves the Fed now made available.

International central banks also supplied liquidity to the markets and, within a few months, markets were rising solidly around the world—though not nearly as yet to their old highs. By spring of 1988, Greenspan's Fed was again tightening policy. Not only was inflation rising slightly, but the Reagan budget deficit of $150 billion, some 3 percent of GDP, remained high.

Even though 1988 was also an election year—and the Reagan administration had hoped Greenspan would be stimulative to help Vice President George H. W. Bush's candidacy—the new Fed chairman held his ground. The Greenspan Fed pushed up the federal funds target rate from 6.5 percent in early 1988 to well above 8 percent late that year. Greenspan's reputation as an inflation fighter, unafraid of the political consequences, grew. And despite the Fed's action, Bush solidly defeated the Democratic nominee, Michael Dukakis. The higher rates were taking their toll on the economy soon enough, however, and Greenspan started to cut rates in late 1989, but only moderately, as the inflation rate of roughly 4 percent still concerned him.

Recession was now likely, but Greenspan disagreed, still more worried about inflation. In August 1990, he told members of the Fed's Open Market Committee, "those who argue that we are in a recession . . . are reasonably certain to be wrong." It turned out that the nation was already officially in recession at that point, according to the later calculations of the National Bureau of Economic Research, the nonofficial arbiter of such matters. Once again, Greenspan overestimated the threat of inflation and underestimated the damage done to the economy and jobs. Only in mid-1991 did the Greenspan Fed start pushing down rates more rapidly and not until 1992, a presidential election year, did it push them down sharply. It was too late to save Bush. Bush had even gotten a tax increase on upper-income Americans passed, but Greenspan remained unmoved by the benefits to the federal deficit. It generally takes a year or more for the economy to react fully to interest rate cuts, and GDP recovered only sluggishly from recession in 1992, while the unemployment rate stood at nearly 7.7 percent on election day. Bush blamed his failed reelection bid on Greenspan and was probably right. In Bush's four years in office, GDP grew more slowly than in any other presidential term since World War II, certainly due to Bush's attempts to reduce the Reagan budget deficit, in part by raising taxes, and Greenspan's actions.

For all Greenspan's concern with forecasting details, he made decisions in large part by paying close attention to bond traders. As he read the signals, interest rates on bonds were still high in 1990, which meant that investors and traders were expecting high inflation—therefore, they demanded high rates to lend money to compensate for higher prices in the future. Greenspan took this as the key sign that inflationary expectations were still entrenched, and he was determined to drive inflation from the minds of the traders. He may also have thought the traders were good forecasters. Later research showed that they were more sensitive to an increase in inflation in the 1990s than they were in the past, which was more likely a result of habit than rational forecasting. Bond traders were wrong too often about future inflation to be trusted.

Only with recession under way and interest rates on bonds falling did Greenspan cut rates. To restart the endangered economy during Bill Clinton's presidency, Greenspan maintained the low-interest policy he started in 1991. The federal deficit remained a problem in the minds of most policymakers, reaching nearly $300 billion in the recession. As economic recovery began, the deficit fell, but hovered between 3 and 4 percent of GDP.

Under the influence of Robert Rubin, the former Goldman Sachs co-chief, who was now head of Clinton's Economic Security Council, Clinton and Greenspan agreed that reducing the federal deficit was a priority. Rubin, a former risk arbitrageur and securities trader, believed federal borrowing was an impediment to private borrowing, effectively pushing the latter aside. Clinton's first treasury secretary, former Texas senator Lloyd Bentsen, was even more concerned with the deficit than was Rubin, who eventually succeeded him.

Greenspan had a long private meeting with Clinton soon after he became president during which they discussed the dangers of the budget deficit, which was now approaching 5 percent of GDP. According to Greenspan's account, he was delighted that Clinton listened approvingly, which indicated Greenspan had allies in this administration. In his memoir, he termed Clinton's advisers "fiscally conservative centrists."

The first budget Clinton put together indeed bore the marks of Bentsen, Rubin, and Greenspan. Clinton had promised an increase in public investment during his campaign—particularly transportation infrastructure spending. But he decided to postpone such spending and, instead, proposed a substantial income tax increase on upper-end earners, making deficit reduction his first priority. It was one of the most significant decisions of his presidency. To Clinton, it all seemed to be working. The economy was growing strongly again due to the very sharp fall in interest rates across the board. Unemployment had fallen almost a full point to 6.5 percent at the start of 1994. Moreover, Greenspan had kept the federal funds target rate very low for nearly two years (zero if reduced for inflation, in fact).

Then Greenspan abruptly shifted policy. In February 1994, the Fed suddenly started raising rates—to almost everyone's surprise, because there was simply no increase in inflation at the time. The new Clinton appointments to the Fed board of governors in mid-1994, Princeton's Alan Blinder, the vice chairman, and the University of California at Berkeley's Janet Yellen, were disturbed. But in terms of influence over the decisive Federal Open Market Committee, composed of governors of the Federal Reserve and the regional Federal Reserve bank presidents, as noted, Blinder was no match for Greenspan.

In August 1994, at the annual meeting of Fed bankers, policymakers, and economists sponsored by the Kansas City Federal Reserve Bank in

Jackson Hole, Blinder argued that the Fed should be as concerned about high unemployment as high inflation. Robert Samuelson, a *Newsweek* columnist, made it a matter of character and courage, venomously writing that Blinder lacked "the moral or intellectual qualities needed to lead the Fed." If more extreme than most in the press, he reflected the general conviction of the time.

Greenspan had feared, as did many other economists, that any fall in the unemployment rate below 5.5 percent would be inflationary. Maybe more important to Greenspan, bond traders were pushing up interest rates again. Greenspan struck with force. In November 1994, he fired two shots against inflation that, Greenspan must have realized, would unquestionably make him the peer of Volcker as an inflation fighter. The Fed raised the federal funds rate that month in total by three quarters of a point; even a half-point increase then was considered large.

One side effect of the suddenly higher interest rates was the Mexican financial crisis, requiring a $40 billion rescue package put together by Lawrence Summers and backed by Greenspan. Otherwise, Robert Rubin, newly named as treasury secretary in 1995, and the guiding force of the rescue package, feared debt crises could erupt elsewhere—and investors in the United States as well as developed nation lenders would be left holding a bag of bad debt with a worldwide recession a possibility. The Mexican situation did stabilize quickly, for which Rubin, Summers, and Greenspan were given credit. But once again, private markets were bailed out by the federal government. (The banks had a lot of Mexican debt but less as a proportion of their capital than during the Mexican crisis of 1982.)

Greenspan, his eye still on U.S. inflation, raised the federal funds rate by another half point early in 1995; he had gone from 3 percent to 6 percent in a little more than a year, despite Clinton's tax increase.

To Clinton, it looked as if his hard-won tax increase, designed to cut the budget deficit, had no effect on Greenspan. He was privately furious. But Rubin convinced him not to criticize Greenspan and the Fed, and many economists later argued that the forbearance was one of the Clinton economic team's major achievements. Rubin strongly sympathized with Greenspan's policy. Blinder also voted for the increases and, in later years, fully justified them. The rate increases amounted to shock therapy similar to Volcker's.

Economic growth slowed sharply in 1995, at last mollifying bond traders, who started to push interest rates down on the longer-term bonds. The rate on the ten-year bond, for example, fell from nearly 8 percent to under

6 percent that year. With economic growth slowed to an annual rate of 2.5 percent in 1995, consumer price inflation fell to under 3 percent and bond traders apparently were convinced the back of inflation had been broken.

It turned out to be the beginning of a new era. The economy was growing handsomely again in the second half of 1995 and the unemployment rate had fallen to 5.5 percent. Yet Greenspan persisted in holding rates steady, rather than raising them. Many economists, both Democratic and Republican, were still arguing that the "natural rate" of unemployment was as high as 6 percent. Greenspan did not flinch in the face of the criticism, and held the line against some Open Market Committee members who were still hawkish about inflation.

Some Democratic economists believed he could have cut rates faster, as there was still no sign of rising inflation. Among them was one Democratic Wall Street star, Felix Rohatyn, the Lazard Frères partner who had directed the rescue of New York City from bankruptcy. With Greenspan's reappointment coming up, Blinder—who could never get out from Greenspan's shadow, especially given the sort of criticism Samuelson had directed at him—resigned as vice chairman, certain he would not get the chairmanship, but leaving an opening for someone else. Clinton wanted to balance Greenspan with a strong advocate of looser policies and there were reports that Rohatyn would have liked the job. But Clinton, under Rubin's strong influence, did not back him for fear his appointment, despite Rohatyn's Wall Street credentials, would reignite the inflationary expectations of the bond traders. Rohatyn, who would have been a powerful counterbalance to Rubin, withdrew from the fray. Clinton nominated the more moderate economist Alice Rivlin to replace Blinder.

By now, Clinton Democrats could hardly be distinguished from moderate Republicans. Earlier that year, in his January State of the Union address, Clinton had announced proudly that it was the "end of the era of big government." He also renominated Greenspan for a third term, proof to Wall Street that he understood their concerns. It was, after all, a presidential election year.

But Greenspan had a new worry. In October 1996, the Dow Jones Industrials exceeded 6,000, compared to roughly 4,000 in early 1995. The Yale economist Robert Shiller, a stock market historian, had warned repeatedly that stock prices were running at historically high levels. If stock prices were forming a speculative bubble that was likely to burst, it could jeopardize the economic expansion. Both business and consumers would reduce their spending. Raising interest rates to subdue the stock market might diminish the market enthusiasm, but it might also weaken the economy. In a speech in December 1996, Greenspan suggested that the stock market might have reached a stage of "irrational exuberance." It was a Sunday, but markets then open in Australia and New Zealand immediately fell, leading to a cascade of falling prices around the world. Would the Greenspan Fed now raise interest rates to burst the stock market bubble? The Dow Jones Industrials fell sharply the next day, and Greenspan was chastened by the market response. The Fed did not raise rates and calm quickly returned.

Despite rapid economic growth at an annual rate of 4 percent or more, inflation fell below 3 percent in 1997 and below 2 percent in 1998. Greenspan was convinced that computer technologies were at last taking hold across American business, meaning that the nation could get rising output per worker—more productivity—and pay substantial raises without raising prices. He became the leading government advocate of a New Economy. In fact, in 1997 the unemployment rate fell to 4.5 percent, far lower than economists—even Democratic economists—believed possible without stoking inflation. And long-term interest rates were falling sharply.

From mid-1998 to the end of 1999, the Dow Jones Industrials rose roughly 4,000 points from about 7,500 to 11,500 on the conviction there was a New Economy, and the unemployment rate fell to nearly 4 percent without stimulating inflation. The extreme government deficits turned into sizable surpluses, as tax revenues rose with incomes and the capital gains taken on the rising stock market. Greenspan's reputation soared.

Greenspan's willingness to ease interest rates, even as unemployment fell so low, however, was not only the result of his prescient discovery of a New Economy, as some had claimed. It was at key moments a response to major international turmoil. In 1997, a crisis suddenly erupted in major Asian nations that threatened the world. First, Thailand's currency dropped sharply, and as international investors withdrew money, the currencies collapsed in other nations including Korea, Malaysia, the Philippines, and Indonesia. The International Monetary Fund came forward with a rescue package, supported by Rubin, who also urged all central banks to loosen monetary policy. The Fed, according to economists Alan Blinder and Janet Yellen, was "poised" to raise rates in 1997, but now Greenspan cut them instead to limit the crisis.

A cause of the crisis was the deregulatory policy of the Clinton administration, which had insisted that nations like Korea end capital controls, which had until then restricted the inflow of international capital. This policy once again reflected the free market attitudes now ascendant in the major rich nations and international agencies like the International Monetary Fund, policies generally known as the Washington Consensus. But the capital flows reached speculative heights because interest rates offered in these nations were so high and, because their currencies were pegged to the dollar, there was no currency risk. Some $250 billion of foreign money was invested in 1996 alone, an increasing amount going into spurious real estate projects. Greenspan was in full agreement with these deregulatory policies. He and Rubin had a weekly meeting, typically breakfast, in which Rubin's deputy, Lawrence Summers, often participated. The "hot" money, as it was later called, rushed out of these countries when the bubble burst and it seemed the Asian nations would have to devalue their currencies—let the values fall—meaning losses for investors.

In testimony before Congress in 1997, Greenspan took no blame, nor did he cite deregulation of capital flows as a cause. He said that investors simply made mistakes from time to time, implying that lack of transparent and open deal making in these foreign countries had more to do with the crisis than did any deregulatory policies pushed on them by the United States and other rich nations. The Asian economies collapsed into severe recession, with high unemployment and countless failed companies.

The financial crisis subsided in Asia, but not without enormous damage to the economies of those nations. The following year Russia defaulted on its interest payments, and Brazil followed. The Greenspan Fed—formally, to repeat, decisions were made by the Open Market Committee, which Greenspan now effectively controlled—had again been ready to raise rates before this new crisis, but Greenspan now cut rates instead. Rubin again strongly urged the world's central bankers to loosen policies. In October, the highly indebted hedge fund Long-Term Capital Management failed, in part due to the Russian default. Hedge funds, too, were mostly free of regulation or even disclosure requirements about their levels of debt. Only weeks before the LTCM collapse, as noted earlier, Greenspan said that the banks themselves "regulated those who lend money" and would provide the surveillance necessary. The funds also traded actively in unregulated derivatives markets, which enabled them to borrow still more against capital. The Fed gathered the major investment bankers on the Street to bail LTCM out, worried that its failure could spread catastrophically. *Time* put Greenspan, Rubin, and Summers on its February 15, 1999, cover, calling them the committee to save the world.

Clearly, the turnabout in Greenspan's policy from inflation fighter to pro-growth Fed chairman, on which his reputation had reached rather dizzying heights, was not a simple matter of economic analysis. As Blinder and Yellen wrote: "No one should think the FOMC's [the Open Market Committee] 'experiment' of allowing unemployment to drift down to thirty-year lows was a deliberate policy decision. It was largely inadvertent."

Neither Greenspan nor Rubin sought any new regulations after the LTCM turmoil and the Asian crisis. Rubin later wrote that he favored higher capital requirements on investments in volatile derivatives. But nothing was done. It appeared that Summers convinced him they were not necessary. "Larry thought I was overly concerned with the risks of derivatives," Rubin wrote. "His argument was characteristic of many students of markets, who argue that derivatives serve an important purpose in allocating risk by letting each person take as much of whatever kind of risk he wants." Greenspan made similar arguments.

Before the LTCM debacle, Rubin, Greenspan, Summers, and Arthur Levitt, Jr., head of the SEC, had stopped Brooksley Born, head of the Commodities Futures Trading Commission, from regulating derivatives before the LTCM failure. As director of the CFTC, the former securities lawyer had the authority to regulate many of the derivatives contracts—they were largely futures contracts—and decided by 1997, given the amount of trading in newer kinds of financial derivatives, mostly over-the-counter and hidden from sight, it was her responsibility to do so. She was a regular member of the Financial Markets Working Group, high-level policymakers who met regularly to discuss financial matters, and Greenspan, Rubin, and Summers scolded her at one of the meetings in patronizing ways. But neither Rubin nor Greenspan had direct authority over her, so when Born tried to proceed, they had to persuade Congress to stop her. They were successful, and eventually Born resigned. Even after the LTCM catastrophe, Greenspan told Congress, "I know of no set of supervisory action we can take that would prevent people from making dumb mistakes." Congress then passed legislation to take the authority to regulate derivatives away from the CFTC. As Born warned back then, derivatives would live to do more damage.

Despite speculative excess on Wall Street and around the world, Greenspan had been convinced the economy was in superb shape in 1998 and 1999. Inflation was around 2 percent, growth fast, the unemployment rate heading to 4 percent. Capital investment in new technologies was unusually strong. Wages were rising, if not at a torrid pace, at all income levels.

"This is the best economy I have ever seen in fifty years of studying it every day," Greenspan told Bill Clinton in August 1998, a comment he repeated elsewhere. The federal budget deficit was also moving into surplus for the first time in thirty years, that year reaching nearly $70 billion. It grew to a peak of $236 billion in 2000, Clinton's last year in office.

But there were many factors going wrong that might have deeply worried someone with a broader view of his duties and economic events. The costs of computer chips fell at the astonishing rate of 25 to 30 percent a year between 1996 and 1998, twice as fast on a yearly basis as in the preceding fifteen years—meaning computer speed and power could increase rapidly. These falling prices reduced business costs sharply and generated a steady flow of significant innovation, making the rapid spread of the Internet and PC ownership possible, for example. But such astonishing cost reductions in computer power were likely to end soon, and they did. Oil prices had also come down significantly, reducing inflation generally, but low oil prices did not last.

Stock prices had reached levels so high that Wall Street was claiming that the prospects for the New Economy were unlimited and that stocks had lost much of their riskiness. More sober observers like Henry Kaufman wanted Greenspan to raise margin requirements on stocks to moderate the excesses. It was an era in which the prices of new issues of dot-com stocks doubled in an afternoon before the companies earned a dollar of profit. Greenspan told Congress that raising margin requirements was futile. He even provided justification for Wall Street's "exuberance." He testified before the Senate Budget Committee in January of 1999 that "the size of the potential market is so huge you have these pie-in-the-sky type of potentials for a lot of different vehicles . . . it does reflect something good about the way the securities markets work; namely, they do endeavor to ferret out the better opportunities and put capital into various different types of endeavors, prior to earnings actually materializing. That's good for our system . . . more plus than minus."

More to the point, consumers were supporting the economy by reducing their savings or borrowing in light of their newfound—if temporary—wealth in the stock market. Personal savings as a percentage of GDP was around 8 percent in Greenspan's early years as Fed chairman, and 12 percent at the start of the 1980s. By 1998, the rate had fallen to 4 percent and was heading to 2 percent in 1999. Even the federal budget surpluses were the result to a significant degree of temporary increases in capital gains tax collections. The soaring stock market led to outsized profits for investors, who took them, and paid more taxes to the federal government. This bonanza would soon end.

The other disturbing factor was a rapidly rising dollar. Rubin had publicly advocated a strong dollar, as did Clinton, and Greenspan favored it as well, because it kept import prices down and therefore inflation low. Largely as a result, the value of the dollar rose rapidly in the second half of the 1990s, putting U.S. manufacturers at a disadvantage and leading to a sharply expanding trade deficit. Manufacturing jobs were cut sharply in these years. The rising dollar, meantime, attracted capital to the U.S., especially as Asian nations built up reserves of the U.S. currency to combat future financial crises (after their 1997 experience). Wall Street, therefore, had far more money to lend to high-technology companies, telecom companies, and mortgage holders at low interest rates. While Wall Street did well, middle-class America lost good jobs. Some traditional economists insisted the rising dollar merely reflected international confidence in America's economic strength and that a rapid reduction in manufacturing sales was simply an inevitable step in the economic evolution of a sophisticated economy. Years later, Greenspan wrote in his memoir that he placed worries about America's trade imbalances "way down on the list."

By June 1999, Greenspan's Fed was ready to fight inflation again. The unemployment rate was heading down to 4 percent, a thirty-year low. Consumer prices were not rising any faster but longer-term interest rates were beginning to rise again. The bond market was always Greenspan's main indicator of future inflation. Greenspan was at last also apparently worried about the overpriced stock market.

In June, the Fed raised the federal funds rates by .25 percent, the first increase since early 1997, followed by five more increases, the last a major hike of .5 percent. In total the federal funds target was raised from 4.75 percent in early 1999 to 6.5 percent in May 2000.

The rate hikes took their toll. The stock market bubble burst in midyear. By the end of 2000, the Nasdaq index had fallen from a high of 5,000 to 3,500 on its way down to nearly 1,000 in 2003. By early 2001, the Dow Jones Industrials lost 1,000 points from its high above 11,000, revived slightly, and then headed to below 8,000 two years later. The long period of growth, overspeculation, and overinvestment in high technology and telecommunications was coming to an end, and lower stock prices and rising interest rates brought on a serious recession as George W. Bush took presidential office.

In early January 2001, Greenspan recognized that the economic weakness at the end of 2000 could worsen, and the Fed initiated its first cut in interest rates in more than two years. Greenspan also stepped far from the traditional duties of a Federal Reserve chairman. He endorsed President Bush's income-tax-cut proposal of $1.6 trillion over ten years, despite his long-held concerns about budget deficits. Nearly 90 percent of the benefits of the Bush tax cut went to the top 5 percent of earners in the nation, justified by Bush because they bore so much of the tax burden. Greenspan said his main concern was that the government might meddle in the private economy by using the surpluses to buy stocks and bonds and by supporting mortgages, all of which to him would be intolerable. Clinton had already recommended that the current surpluses generated from Social Security taxes be "locked away" and perhaps put into the stock market, for example, to earn returns over time. And Clinton had agreed to use the surpluses to pay down federal debt rather than invest in, say, transportation infrastructure. Paying down debt, Greenspan now claimed, might also prove to be a problem. If the Treasury debt was paid down, he did not know how the Fed could conduct its monetary policy because there would be no more Treasury securities. "I came to a stark realization: chronic surpluses could be almost as destabilizing as chronic deficits. Paying off the debt was not enough," Greenspan wrote in his 2007 memoir. He stipulated that the Bush tax cuts should be rescinded if the budget again fell into deficit, a politically meaningless proviso, as he must have realized. This was, in fact, a transparent rationalization on Greenspan's part to support the Bush tax cuts.

The tax cuts were passed, just as the surpluses shrank more rapidly than anticipated. As feared, capital gains tax collections dwindled by as much as $175 billion. Greenspan professed being caught by surprise by the immense capital gains shortfall, yet there had been explicit warnings from some economists. President Bush reappointed him to a fifth term in 2002.

After the attacks on the World Trade Center in September 2001, the Fed, already trying to restart the economy, cut rates faster, three reductions in a row of a half point each. By the end of 2001, the target federal funds rate, some 6.5 percent only two years earlier, was now only 1.75 percent. But the economy was not expanding at a healthy rate. And with tax collections cut due to recession, on top of the loss of former capital gains collections, the federal budget fell into a $150 billion deficit. It was a stunning reversal, and expensive incursions into Iraq and Afghanistan were looming.

In 2002 and 2003, the economy was still not recovering adequately despite the extreme rate cuts the Greenspan Fed initiated. Now Greenspan thought deflation—an overall decline in prices—was a far greater worry than inflation, which could result in financial turmoil. Debtors don't pay back their loans because dollars are more valuable—they can buy more. Creditors take large losses. Greenspan always believed he could recharge the economy by cutting rates sharply. The financial markets had come to depend on this ever since his rescue in 1987, and it became known as the "Greenspan put"—a floor Greenspan would always place under securities prices. But now the lower rates were not working. As economist Mark Zandi said, Greenspan realized the only way out was to push interest rates even lower to ignite a housing boom. Perhaps he believed he could this time pull the plug just short of its becoming a housing bubble. If housing was stimulated, higher house prices in turn would encourage consumers to spend—the "wealth" effect, as it was called. Greenspan cut the target federal funds rate to 1 percent and kept it there until mid-2004, the lowest since the early 1950s.

The low rates between 2000 and 2004 were the lifeblood of the housing boom. Thousands of new mortgage brokers, and twenty or so giant ones, were vying with one another to sell mortgages to lower-income Americans, relying in particular on adjustable rate mortgages, or ARMs. Buyers paid low interest rates in the first two years of the mortgages after which rates rose, usually substantially. But with house prices rising relentlessly, the homeowner could refinance with another ARM, or pay down some of the mortgage and reduce the monthly payments. A rapidly growing number of these were subprime mortgages, sold to home buyers with poor credit. But middle-income Americans also often took ARMs, to buy homes once out of their reach. With rates so low and no federal oversight, mortgage lending practices, long suspect, became widely abusive. Even the FBI warned in 2004 of an "epidemic" of fraud in subprime mortgage writing, but it had devoted so many of its resources to antiterrorist activities, it had little left to pursue unscrupulous mortgage brokers.

Greenspan knew about these loans, and was warned by associates at the Federal Reserve that abuses were mounting. He had the authority to investigate but chose not to. In 2004, remarkably, Greenspan himself spoke favorably of the ARMs. "Many homeowners might have saved tens of thousands of dollars had they held adjustable-rate mortgages rather than fixed-rate mortgages." As economist Zandi wrote, such a comment was essentially an endorsement of the practice.

At last, the economy started to grow strongly again, based on the housing boom, and Greenspan began to raise the federal funds rate in mid-2004, eventually by more than 4 percentage points. Inflation was increasing only moderately, but Greenspan's other great concern, the federal deficit, now enlarged by war spending, was about to exceed $400 billion, some 4.5 percent of GDP.

The rising federal funds rate, which reached 5.25 percent by the end of 2006, did not dampen the flow of mortgages, since Wall Street was now the most important source of mortgage money, not the thrifts. Packaging mortgages into securities—securitization—had made such institutional investors as pension funds and insurance companies the major providers of funding for mortgages. Hundreds of billions of dollars of new money found its way to homeowners each year. When Greenspan raised rates, it did not staunch this flow because mortgage brokers, which now included giant mortgage specialists like Countrywide Financial, big commercial banks like JPMorgan and Citigroup, and the major Wall Street investment banks, like Lehman Brothers, pushed ever harder to sell the ARMs with the low initial rates or mortgages known as Alt-A that required no verification of income. They knew that Wall Street had an almost bottomless pit of demand for the new securitized debt from pension and investment managers as well as financial institutions around the world. Greenspan just could not get long-term interest rates to rise much.

Greenspan, based on his firm market principles, approved strongly of securitization and most derivative products as a way to spread risk—a view traditional market economists like Summers shared. But even when crisis struck in 2008, it was clear the Federal Reserve economists in Washington and New York did not understand how excessive and risky the borrowing now was. In particular, the relatively new collateralized debt obligations (CDOs), a way of packaging risky mortgages for investors willing to make only low-risk investments, was not understood or even investigated. Greenspan's ultimately naive and dangerous faith in competitive markets showed itself nowhere as damagingly as in the Fed's failure to be vigilant about the CDOs. Not only did his interest rate increases fail to dampen the financing, but they encouraged Wall Street to take more risks and mortgage brokers to write more bad loans because their profit margins had narrowed. They made up in quantity what was lacking in quality. The high dollar coupled with the trade deficit, which put even more dollars in foreign hands, which they in turn confidently invested in U.S. securities, provided ample funds. Between 2000 and 2005, according to Wellesley economist Karl Case and Yale's Robert Shiller, house prices rose faster than at any time in modern history, and the number of mortgages being written exploded.

But when Greenspan raised rates in 2004—on which adjustable rate mortgages were based—the clock began to tick. The rates on tens of billions of dollars of ARMs would be reset upward in 2006. That year, default rates on mortgages started to rise rapidly and home prices for the first time started to fall. In 2007, two hedge funds at Bear Stearns went broke and the worst credit crisis since the Great Depression got under way. In early 2008, Bear Stearns was saved from bankruptcy in a distress sale to JPMorgan Chase. In September, Lehman Brothers collapsed altogether and the Bush Treasury initiated a $700 billion bailout of commercial and investment banks. Many observers blamed Greenspan's extreme monetary easing in the early 2000s for the debacle, making credit too cheap. But regulatory vigilance could have prevented the excesses. Greenspan would have none of it.

Greenspan retired at the end of 2006. In congressional hearings in 2008 before a House committee chaired by Henry Waxman, Greenspan testified that he "made a mistake in presuming that the self-interest of organizations, specifically banks and others, were [sic] such that they were best capable of protecting their own shareholders and their equity in the firms." He found, he went on, a "flaw in the model that I perceived is the critical functioning structure that defines how the world works . . . I was shocked because I've been going for forty years or more with very considerable evidence that it was working exceptionally well."

His admission was welcome but misleading. His model of economic behavior and government policy resulted in profound financial instability every few years and subpar economic performance for the nearly twenty years he was Fed chairman. The boom of the late 1990s, the one exceptional period, was highly dependent on spending encouraged by the stock market bubble and benefited from low inflation due to falling oil prices, a high dollar, and plunging computer prices. In the 2000s, he traded a boom in housing for the boom in high-technology stocks.

In his memoir, Greenspan wrote, "assisted by the wave of deregulation since the mid-1970s, today's U.S. economy remains the most competitive in the world, and American culture still exhibits much of the risk taking and taste for adventure of the country's earlier years." Yet, in more regulated times, America exhibited the very same entrepreneurial behavior and risk taking that it did in Greenspan's time, and perhaps more. In the 1950s,

with the rise of Xerox, Kodak, IBM, Sears, Syntex, Merck, Johnson & Johnson, Hewlett-Packard, and others, innovation and regulation went hand
in hand with financial stability, rising wages, and income equality. Had he
achieved that record, he would have deserved the praise he had received.
The unleashing of unregulated self-interest since the 1980s, he believed,
was a sufficient condition for prosperity.

George Soros and John Meriwether

FABULOUS WEALTH AND CONTROVERSIAL POWER

U ntil the mid-1980s, the takeover movement was the way to make the most money on Wall Street. Men like Henry Kravis, George Roberts, Boone Pickens, and Carl Icahn built enormous fortunes, and by the 2000s all were billionaires. Icahn was frequently listed among the twenty-five richest Americans, eventually with some $8–9 billion in personal wealth, and Kravis and Roberts were reported to have about half that.

Starting in the mid-1980s, managing hedge funds made more great fortunes for more people than the takeover movement did, and replaced them at the glamorous pinnacle of the financial community. By 2009, thirty-nine of the nation's four hundred richest people were hedge fund managers, according to *Forbes*. What made this possible was the many new kinds of securities that had been created since the 1970s, the global reach of financial markets, and the light federal oversight of banks and investment firms endorsed so strongly by Alan Greenspan. Greenspan in particular encouraged regulation-free trading by new participants of all kinds.

Hedge funds were investment pools that were restricted to a hundred or fewer wealthy investors. Because these investors were presumably sophisticated, and could hire expert advisers, they were free of most SEC regulations about disclosure of information, or limits on debt. Unlike mutual funds, which usually emphasized stocks or bonds, they could invest in almost anything anywhere—financial and commodities derivatives, options of all kinds, currencies, and silver and gold. They could sell short to benefit from falling prices, borrow aggressively to multiply their potential returns, and invest in any country they deemed appropriate.

The hedge fund managers got so wealthy because they could borrow aggressively against their assets and they took a large share of the annual

Hedge fund pioneer George Soros

Long-Term Capital Management founder
John Meriwether

investment profits—usually 20 percent, as well as 1–2 percent of the asset value annually. They had to convince wealthy investors to agree to the terms, of course, and this they did in growing numbers. In the 1980s and early 1990s, the returns in some hedge funds far outpaced the returns of the more conventional vehicles. In the late 1980s, hedge funds managed less than $100 billion in funds, in the late 1990s, some $400 billion, and in the mid-2000s, $2 trillion. When they borrowed multiples of that, their buying capability became enormous.

George Soros, a Hungarian immigrant who arrived in America in the 1950s, became the unquestioned leader among hedge fund managers and remained so for twenty-five years. According to an estimate by *Financial World* magazine, Soros earned $200 million in 1987, second only to Michael Milken's unprecedented earnings that year of $550 million. In 1992, Soros personally made $650 million, and in 1993 he made $1 billion, when such compensation levels were almost unimaginable. In the 2000s, the success of hedge funds only grew. By 2007, hedge fund manager John Paulson earned nearly $4 billion, while Soros, who had returned from retirement, earned nearly $3 billion. The top twenty-five hedge fund managers earned nearly $900 million on average that year. Soros's successes in the 1990s did more than anything else to attract eager new money managers to start hedge funds.

The hedge funds could provide a useful market service. When they looked for under- and overvalued securities and other investments, as noted, they may have uncovered information about companies, commodities, and government financing that was obscure or unknown. By buying and selling undervalued and overvalued securities, they could sometimes make the prices of securities adjust to the new information and analysis—perhaps add more rational analysis as well. Such balancing acts were generally the benefits that came from having many kinds of participants in a market.

The beneficial influence of such a balancing act was controversial. There were many crashes during the rapid growth of these hedge funds, after all; they clearly did not offset speculative irrationality sufficiently. Others argued that they added liquidity to markets as well, making price changes smoother. Again, to what degree such liquidity was useful was controversial.

But with their wealth also came power that could be abused. As the hedge funds grew in size collectively, their single-minded pursuit of profits led to attacks on stocks and on currencies and the bonds of smaller governments that contributed to financial crises in Europe in the early 1990s, Asia in 1997, and Wall Street in 1998—and perhaps Europe again in 2010.

Their currency attacks in Asia encouraged nations, including China, to build huge reserves of dollars to fend off future currency forays. This had policy implications for the United States. The foreign demand for dollars pushed the level of the dollar higher, placing American exports at a disadvantage. These nations then invested the dollars in U.S. debt instruments, thus encouraging consumers and business to borrow excessively.

The funds also launched attacks—sold bonds aggressively—on the debt of nations, during what may have merely been temporary shortfalls of tax revenues. As a consequence, governments often had to reduce social spending sharply, inducing recession. Such selling sometimes turned into uncontrolled panic.

For their part in these panics, the hedge funds offered a single, sometimes justifiable defense. They claimed that market panics would happen without them, as would the necessary changes in government policies, and they helped correct, not distort, market prices—often forcing government policies to change for the better. Government policies to protect currencies could indeed be misguided and damaging. But speculative attacks also often made matters far worse than necessary, driving interest rates to heights that assured steep recessions in some nations. "Speculation can be very harmful, especially in currency markets," admitted Soros to *The*

Times of London soon after making enormous profits by selling $10 billion worth of the British pound in 1992. In a 1995 book, Soros went on about his big winnings: "I consider [speculation] a necessary evil. My defense is that I operate within the rules." Despite the power of hedge funds, they remained largely unregulated. Many if not most were domiciled in Caribbean islands with especially light regulatory oversight and valuable tax advantages.

Their high levels of borrowing created potential instability as well. In the early 1990s, some hedge funds had grown so large, and had borrowed against assets so aggressively, they themselves jeopardized the financial markets. Many went broke when Alan Greenspan suddenly raised interest rates in 1994, unsettling their lenders and resulting in congressional hearings, but resulting in no new federal restrictions. Markets settled down again, and hedge funds regained their popularity.

In 1998, John Meriwether, one of the most admired of the managers at the time, had taken on so many liabilities at his firm, Long-Term Capital Management, that when markets turned against him, he almost brought Wall Street down single-handedly. A dozen other Wall Street firms paid off his creditors at the last minute, orchestrated by the Federal Reserve. The firm, which many thought impregnable to serious losses, was later dissolved. Again, no new regulations for hedge funds were adopted.

The hedge funds accelerated a growing trend on Wall Street emphasizing short-term speculation in derivatives, currencies, and commodities instead of long-term investment in stocks and bonds. In emulating the hedge funds, traditional Wall Street firms took on similar, and soon much greater, amounts of debt. Ironically, it was the fact that the huge commercial and investment banks indebted themselves even more than many hedge funds and used similar trading techniques that led to the 2008 collapse.

Even with Meriwether's success and fiery failure, Soros remained the most fascinating person in the field in the 1990s and 2000s, partly because of his contradictory nature. His political values defined him almost as much as did his wealth. On the one hand, he was a contributor to and exploiter of financial excesses. On the other hand, he was Wall Street's conscience as well, a harsh critic of many of the same values and practices that enabled him to become wealthy. "I believe our concept of freedom changed [since the 1980s]," he wrote in his 1995 book. "It was replaced by a narrower concept—the pursuit of self-interest. It found expression in the rise of geopolitical realism in foreign policy and a belief in laissez-faire in economics. . . . I believe these doctrines are inadequate and misleading. They emphasize the importance of competing within the system, but pay no attention to the preservation of the system itself. . . ."

He used his money for political causes in which he deeply believed, his annual charitable contributions making him one of the leading philanthropists in the world. But the public philanthropist and journalist he became belied the hard-nosed financial risk taker and opportunist he was. In 2009, despite many years of retirement and then a return to active investing in 2007, *Forbes* calculated his net worth at $13 billion, second only to Warren Buffett among financial specialists on the list. If market opportunities existed, he told anyone who listened, he'd benefit from them if he could, even as he worked politically to end, restrict, or regulate such opportunities because they could destabilize the economy.

Because his manner of public speaking was halting and dry, it was not readily obvious how confident a person Soros was. This self-confidence was enhanced by his wealth but did not begin with it. He oddly admitted in his first book, *The Alchemy of Finance,* to having had a messianic sense as a boy. What deeply influenced his life was the Nazi occupation of his hometown in Hungary.

Soros learned the arts of survival and the necessity of taking risk, he said, from his pragmatic, talented, and some thought unscrupulous father. Tivadar Soros had survived both the Russian Revolution and the Nazi occupation of Budapest. Soros often spoke about his father's pragmatic values, which boiled down, he said, to one principle: survival required breaking the rules. "The Russian experience shaped his outlook on life," he said. The Nazi occupation of his hometown deeply influenced Soros's young life. "My father was not a normal bourgeois person. He had a different set of values. He brought us up with a different set of values. When the Germans came and occupied Hungary, he arranged false names and everything." Soros said there was no doubt they did the right thing in hiding their Jewish background. "If you play by the normal rules you don't survive. If you play by the rules you die. So if you want to survive, you've got to break the rules. I really learned to break the rules. My brother also learned to break the rules."

Tivadar Soros wrote a book with the telling title *Masquerade: Dancing Around Death in Nazi-Occupied Hungary,* in which he proudly claimed that survival was his main achievement. "This is what set me apart," George said. "When you are fourteen years old, if you don't break the law you die. That's pretty shocking. It's a traumatic experience."

Coming to America required adjustment. "I had to reeducate myself in America to stop breaking the law," he said. "That's not that unusual for immigrants." His colleagues at work typically noted how hard-nosed Soros remained. Soros, given how indelible youthful experience can be, probably continued to sense survival was at stake, even when he had billions of dollars. "As with anyone who went through what he did as a boy, there is a point at which you cannot push him," said one of his former money managers, Gerard Manolovici. "If he was American, he wouldn't have been as hard as he was."

George Soros was born Dzjchdzhe Shorash on August 12, 1930, in Budapest. Tivadar was a lawyer and his mother was from a well-to-do family. Both owned property and lived well on a holiday island near Budapest for much of the year. George went to school in Hungary in the 1930s, a dutiful student but not an outstanding one. Friends from that period remember him as social and a good athlete. When World War II broke out, few in Hungary fully appreciated the threat to their lives, even those in the Jewish community. Tivadar was more apprehensive. By 1943, when George was thirteen, the threats became real. Tivadar wanted George to cater to the Germans and never tell them he was Jewish. In fact, he ordered him to help the Germans hand out deportation notices to Jewish attorneys. He created formal papers with Christian identities for the members of the family, and hid them in cellars and other out-of-the-way locations to escape detection by the Nazi soldiers—eleven locations in total, according to George's count.

The young Soros left Hungary for London in 1947 to live and study, but not before he had lived through the Hungarian inflation of the post–World War II years—worse, he said, than the German inflation of the 1920s. He learned how fleeting the value of money could be, the importance of interest earnings, and how to calculate in varieties of currencies. In London, he worked in several menial jobs, including as a waiter, a house painter, and a railway porter. In 1949, at nineteen, he registered at the London School of Economics, where he was drawn to philosophy and there completed his undergraduate degree. In particular, he absorbed the lessons of one of London's celebrated philosophers, the Austrian-born Karl Popper, regarding the value of an "open society," where public discourse and free speech were tolerated and encouraged. Soros, if interested in philosophy, was not especially studious. Instead of pursuing it, he found a job at a London brokerage firm as a trainee, where he discovered a talent for trading gold stocks. The London firm specialized in arbitraging securities. Soros's prospects in London seemed limited, however, and in 1956, with no particular career as yet, he left for New York, where his older brother already had relocated. Both his parents later joined the brothers, Tivadar opening a coffee stand in Coney Island.

Because Soros was familiar with European stocks, he was able to gain a foothold on Wall Street with a firm founded by Austrian and Hungarian financiers. He started, naturally enough, as an international stock arbitrageur—selling stocks priced slightly higher or lower in one market, say, London, compared to their prices in another, say, Amsterdam or New York. He later joined Wertheim, an American firm also with European roots, where he researched European stocks. He was already earning substantial money when in 1964 the U.S. government established the interest equalization tax on European securities in order to stem the flow of dollars overseas. Soros's business in European stock arbitrage was effectively ended.

In this period, Soros took time off to write a philosophy book he titled *The Burden of Consciousness* that had been obsessing him. But on rereading his first draft, even he found it difficult to follow, and he abandoned it to devote full attention to his financial career. With international equity arbitrage essentially obsolete for the time being, he focused on U.S. stocks. He developed a conventional investment portfolio of U.S. stocks at Wertheim as a model, whose performance the firm tracked and used to attract clients. When after a while the model produced consistently good returns, Soros was invited to take a job with Arnhold & S. Bleichroeder, a better-financed Wall Street firm also with roots in Eastern Europe. There he started a fund to invest in his Wertheim model portfolio, which he called the First Eagle Fund. His fund did well. Soros, meanwhile, became friendly with a handful of hedge fund managers, then a small interconnected group. In particular, A.W. Jones, one of the largest funds at the time, and the pioneering hedge fund started in 1949 by a former *Fortune* writer, was one of his customers at Bleichroeder. Soros's First Eagle Fund could only buy stocks and hold cash or bonds, not sell short or borrow. Soros was intrigued by how selling short, which, as noted, hedge funds were allowed to do, opened up possibilities for investing. The age-old technique enabled investors to sell shares (or bonds) they didn't own by borrowing them in anticipation that those shares would fall in price. When they did, the investor bought the securities on the open market and returned them to the traders who lent them, paying an interest rate on the borrowed amount but having likely made a far greater profit on the decline in price.

Soros was eager to emulate his newfound friends and, in 1969, Bleichroeder decided to sponsor a hedge fund at his urging, called the Double Eagle Fund, with Soros running it. The next year, Soros hired Jim Rogers, an innovative, hardworking analyst recently out of Yale and Oxford, to be his principal researcher. The high fees charged investors were the most compelling reason to start the fund. Like other funds, the Soros fund charged an annual management fee of 1 percent of the value of assets invested as well as 20 percent of the annual profit. "It was simple. You got one and twenty," said Rogers. "You could make a lot of money." Furthermore, the managers did not participate in the losses, so they were motivated to take substantial risks. By comparison, mutual funds, which were growing rapidly in the bull market of the 1960s, led by companies like Dreyfus, Fidelity, and Oppenheimer, received only an annual fee of 1 percent or so, though many charged an upfront sales load of up to 8 percent.

Mutual funds are poorly designed, said Soros. They don't provide an incentive to managers to make money for their clients but rather an incentive only to keep up with the average performance of stocks—say, the gains on the S&P 500—or to better them only slightly to keep their investors.

Though many academic and a few professional investors doubted that market averages could be regularly "beaten," even by the studious, often obsessive hedge fund managers, Soros fully believed a good investor could consistently outperform the market averages by a wide margin. Hedge funds opened all kinds of opportunities. Shorting enabled managers to "hedge" investment positions to narrow risks. For example, an airline stock considered undervalued could be bought and an overvalued airline stock simultaneously sold. If the entire industry is badly affected by a major unpredictable event, such as a steep rise in fuel prices due to political turmoil, a hedge fund manager can still make money because the undervalued stock bought will probably fall less in price than the one sold.

What appealed most to Soros was the ability to borrow money to leverage investments. "The attraction of hedge funds from my perspective," said Soros, "was that I was more interested in making money than in collecting management fees. Although one and twenty was very attractive of course, I saw the hedge fund more as a leveraged construct. In a conventional portfolio, you just have a certain number of stocks or cash. But with hedge funds you are also using leverage. You can build more on the same equity. It struck me as a much more efficient way of managing money because the equity could support more debt. So it was the use of that leverage that attracted me most. It was a more aggressive, complete use of money."

Most Americans take advantage of the same principle when they buy a house. The homeowner need put up only 10 percent of, say, the $100,000 cost in cash, or $10,000, and borrow the rest from a bank. If the value of the house rises by 15 percent to $115,000 and is sold, the homeowner will earn $15,000 on a $10,000 investment less interest—or almost one and a half times the cash investment. A hedge fund can multiply profits in the same way.

In these early years at Bleichroeder, Soros and Rogers focused mainly on American stocks. Generally, Rogers came up with ideas about appealing stocks or groups of stocks and Soros made the investment and timing decisions, and executed the trades. "That is an oversimplification," Rogers said, "but broadly, it is true." Their track record in these years was exceptionally good. They bought airline, defense, high-technology, and conglomerate stocks, among others, usually on leverage and with hedged positions. When in their view stocks got too high, they sold aggressively. Selling short the once soaring stocks of conglomerates in the early 1970s, after having bought them on their way up, was especially profitable for the fund. "That was the ideal," said Soros. "When you see both the boom and the bust. You identify the flaw. After the conglomerate boom came the REITs [real estate investment trusts, in essence a real estate mutual fund]. Then came the early tech stocks."

The claim that no one could regularly beat the markets was based on the academic theory that financial markets were highly efficient. The efficient markets theory held that new information was digested so rapidly by investors there was no way to get ahead of the pack. The theory was backed by strong evidence that few if any mutual fund or pension fund managers ever outperformed stock market averages consistently. This theory had no influence on Soros. To him, the prices of securities in the markets were pushed and pulled in a variety of irrational directions, optimism and pessimism feeding on themselves. He called his version of the idea "reflexivity." Others referred to roughly the same concept as "positive feedback" or the "herd instinct." For example, a rising price of securities might well encourage rather than deter demand because investors come to believe the companies are more valuable simply because prices are rising. "His greatest key to success is his psychology. He understands the herd instinct," an early partner of Soros's said. "He understands when lots of people are going to go for something, like a good marketing man." That the nation's most prestigious academic economics departments, including the Massachusetts Institute of Technology, Harvard Business School, the University of Chicago, and Stanford were denying that there was a herd instinct anyone could anticipate and profit from was foolish in Soros's mind.

In 1973, Soros and Rogers left Bleichroeder and took their fund with them. The Double Eagle Fund had already been domiciled offshore to avoid U.S. income taxes for investors, since his shareholders largely remained European; Americans were not allowed to invest in such a tax-free fund. The conflict between an investment fund that did not pay taxes and Soros's belief in strong government did not raise doubts in him. As manager and the largest investor in the fund, Soros paid taxes on his gains as an American citizen (which he became in 1961). When he left Bleichroeder, the fund had approximately $20 million in assets.

The hedge fund managers often talked with one another about what they were buying and selling in the early days, which was dominated by the conglomerate boom of the late 1960s and early 1970s. "The conglomerate boom was largely financed by the hedge funds. This was the go-go hedge fund," said Soros. "They were buying letter stock [stock given to management that is authorized for resale only after a waiting period]. They had inside info. They were sleeping with the management."

A.W. Jones was lauded across Wall Street and by *Fortune* for its consistent gains. Jones, the hedge fund pioneer, was indeed in some ways the Soros of his time, attracting many imitators. But Barton Biggs, later a prominent investment adviser with Morgan Stanley, worked with Jones as a young man and was dubious about the sources of his success. Of *Fortune*'s accolades, he wrote simply, "I think that was a bunch of baloney. Basically, Jones used commissions to develop an informational advantage and hired smart young guys to exploit it." These analysts recommended stocks for the client of the brokerage firms for whom they worked. But they were encouraged by Jones to develop model portfolios of stocks for him to consider buying and, as Biggs put it, nothing stopped the analysts from making their recommendations to their clients after Jones took a position—a version of what became known as front-running. If the portfolios then went up in price, Jones paid them well. The law was more ambiguous about the legality of such activities then. "Lucky Eliot Spitzer was still in diapers," Biggs wrote, referring to the aggressive New York State attorney general who prosecuted Wall Street wrongdoing in the late 1990s and early 2000s.

But Jones was not alone in exploiting the markets. One pioneering hedge fund manager described the early years of the hedge funds this way: "We had a gentleman's agreement. Some hedge funds would buy a stock and promote the others to come in. [They] basically shared info on the understanding that whoever originated the idea was allowed to buy it first. It was very helpful to have a few friends kick the tires and point out what was wrong with the stock. We had these informal pools."

"There was always this element of trying to make money where you could," said Soros. "Yeah, there was inside information. I'd say I probably used inside information less than most. I wasn't sleeping with management. But through this coterie I got the benefit of the others who had the inside information." Soros added, "I have always played by the rules but the rules were not tight back then."

As we've seen, in 1973, during the worst recession to date of the post-Depression era, stocks collapsed. Most investors did poorly as stagflation suppressed investor appetites for equities. But in this environment, the record of Soros and Rogers was impressive. In one of the predictions of which he was most proud, Soros anticipated the rise of large commercial banks as aggressive profit-making companies, led by Wriston at First National City. The worst the Soros fund did in any year in the 1970s was to rise by 30 percent. Compared to traditional mutual funds and pension fund managers, his performance seemed to be nearly a miracle.

Soros now widened his grasp of world financial markets, marking a new stage in his thinking. He began to invest in U.S. bonds as interest rates rose and became more volatile due to inflation. "That was the first time that interest rates started to move more than normal," he said. "That was the beginning. And investing in currencies came later."

He started to hear inadvertently about British government bonds, called gilts, as well as foreign currencies. "I was already pretty successful—in fact making enough money," he recalled. "It must have been 1979. I wanted to use the money for a philanthropic purpose. I wanted to set up a sort of Brookings Institution in England. So I went to Brookings and they said, 'Why do it [with someone] there, why not do it with us?' So I [financed] a Brookings study of Britain's future with the North Sea oil discoveries. We had the conference at Ditchley. It was the most expensive weekend of my life and the most unproductive. It was methodology running rampant. They used all this analysis and didn't have anything to say. But I got to know the British Treasury and the bank loan officials. Then Margaret Thatcher raised interest rates and their Treasury bonds fell in price tremendously. And I knew enough that I got on to those Treasury bonds. What I thought was the most expensive weekend of my life turned out to be one of the most profitable because I got involved in those gilts."

Soros sold British gilts, making his fund roughly $100 million on a $1 billion leveraged investment, when he anticipated accurately that Britain would raise rates. Did Soros get information from British banking officials under Thatcher? Even if he did, it would most likely not have been definitive or illegal. Inside information regulations in the United States mostly covered only corporate stocks and bonds. Their applicability to buying and selling currencies and government bonds (and derivatives on those) is far more ambiguous.

Soros was now the hedge fund industry's pioneer, daring to go where others had not yet. He became an active investor in gilts and the pound sterling. He turned his attention to broad analysis of macroeconomic conditions in the world, learning how changing economic conditions could create opportunities in foreign bonds and currencies.

One investing coup followed another. Soros's new strategy eventually became known as "macro investing." By 1980, Soros's share of his funds was worth $100 million and he had only a handful of rivals, perhaps the most prominent of which included Michael Steinhardt, who had partnered a hedge fund with Jerrold Fine and Howard Berkowitz since 1967. Some brokerage firms, such as Oppenheimer & Co., a mutual fund pioneer, were also making investments in ways similar to hedge funds for the accounts of their partners.

The lesson on Wall Street was clear. A hedge fund could make money in bad times as well as good, and few decades were as bad as the 1970s for traditional equities. The Soros Fund rose by 61.9 percent in 1976 (based on the net asset value of a share), by 31.2 percent in 1977 (a year in which the Dow Jones Industrials fell by more than 13 percent), by 55.1 percent in 1978, and by 59.1 percent in 1979. On balance, stocks were up only modestly over this period. The only rivals to such performance were investors who specialized in commodities like oil and gold, whose prices rose with the rapid inflation of the time—and such strategies became outdated when inflation fell in the 1980s. By 1980, his fund, whose name Soros changed to the Quantum Fund in 1979, was up 102.6 percent and valued at nearly $400 million, compared to $6 million a decade earlier.

In 1980, many new hedge funds were started. The most startlingly successful of the new managers was Paul Tudor Jones, who had specialized in commodities trading just out of college, and started Tudor Investment Management at only twenty-six. It grew as large as Quantum. Julian Robertson, a veteran investor, almost Soros's age, started a new hedge fund as well, Tiger Management, with $8 million in assets. His fund would eventually rival Soros's in size. The two managing partners of Oppenheimer, Leon Levy and Jack Nash, at last sold their mutual funds and brokerage firm and transformed themselves into a hedge fund as well, called Odyssey Partners. Several analysts from traditional investment banks like Goldman Sachs soon left to start independent hedge funds that became successful.

The hedge fund now became the vehicle of choice for managing money in an era of global capital flows, floating currencies, easily available credit, and loose regulations. "It is a superior mousetrap," said Soros. "Even for the investor, after the fees, it's superior if you have a good manager." For a while, this seemed indisputably true. But as the 1980s moved on, Soros had begun to lose interest in running his fund. He had more money than he could have imagined earning, and was bored at fifty years old. He and Jim Rogers parted acrimoniously after more than a decade of productive collaboration. Soros was now dating an attractive twenty-three-year-old woman, Susan Weber, and he wanted to travel and enjoy himself. At the back of his mind was his father's love of an easygoing life.

The bond markets of 1981 also became unpredictable for Soros. As interest rates rose to unprecedented levels under Paul Volcker, the cost of the debt that Soros took on to maintain his enormous investment exposure generated risk of substantial losses. Bonds collapsed in value in 1981, as did stocks, and the Quantum Fund suffered its first major loss in 1981, about one fifth of its value. Coupled with withdrawals by investors who rapidly lost faith, the fund's size was reduced by nearly half from $381 million to $193 million. The experience was a "disaster," said Soros. But Soros did not shy away, investing aggressively in stocks after their sharp downturn, counting on a strong recovery once the recession passed and inflation fell. He was again willing to invest against the pack, even in uncertain times. Stocks indeed came back strongly, and the Quantum Fund made back much of its loss in 1982, up about 60 percent. For many hedge fund managers, making a bold purchase was not necessarily personally risky; if wrong, they did not share in the losses. But Soros had almost all his personal wealth tied up in the fund.

Soros married Weber. He still wanted to take time off. He hired a new fund manager to take over many of his duties. He did not stay away for long, however, and returned to the fold in 1984 to score his biggest coup yet. He was increasingly certain the rising dollar would soon fall in value; high export prices were taking too much of a toll on American manufacturing. He positioned the Quantum Fund to take advantage of it. He shorted the dollar and bought the deutsche mark, the yen, and the pound. He also sold oil short. And he did all this aggressively, by borrowing to extend his positions to levels significantly greater than the size of the fund itself. The strategies did not immediately yield results, but in September of 1985, Treasury Secretary James Baker got finance ministers to agree at the Plaza Hotel to push down the dollar's value, and Soros scored. In 1985, the Quantum Fund rose by 120 percent, to more than $1 billion in assets. In 1986, Soros added another $500 million. He earned himself nearly $95 million in 1985 and another $200 million in 1986. Soros's results were spectacular by any standard. His reputation rose still more.

Soros's run ended temporarily when the stock market crashed in October 1987. He had just invested heavily in the U.S. stock market, transferring funds from Japan, which he believed was more vulnerable to a dramatic fall. It was a major error. The Quantum Fund lost $350–400 million in the market rout. Both Julian Robertson and Paul Tudor Jones anticipated the U.S. collapse correctly, piling up hundreds of millions of dollars for their investors, and their own legends were now made as Soros found himself defending his poor investment call. Soros, tireless, made back much of the loss before the end of the year, with the Quantum Fund up on balance by 14 percent. Soros still made $75 million personally.

Soros's first book, published in 1987, *The Alchemy of Finance,* described his investment philosophy in detail. It is a fine book. The major theme is that markets are frequently irrational, tend toward unjustifiable booms, and feed speculative excess, creating selling opportunities. Busts often follow booms, and these become buying opportunities. "Markets are always biased in one direction or another," he wrote, and "markets can influence the events that they anticipate."

Hedge fund managers like Soros had generated such superior returns that there were continued accusations of trading on inside information or market manipulation. Soros, for example, was accused by the SEC of trying to manipulate the stock of Computer Sciences in 1977 by asking a broker to sell a large volume of shares to reduce the price before he bought 165,000 shares. The SEC charge was made public and widely covered in press accounts when Soros signed a consent decree in which he neither denied nor affirmed the charges. Soros was also later accused of insider trading in France in 2002 for purchasing shares in Société Générale, then a take-over target. The French argued he had inside information. Soros denied it, claiming he bought several bank stocks at this time. But he was found guilty and required to pay a $2.2 million fine. In 2010, he started proceedings to have the charges reversed.

Insider information laws did not generally apply to currency and government bond trading, as noted, yet the sudden decisions of central banks often moved markets dramatically. Even informal information about their intentions could be valuable.

Major money managers and traders also had access to information about the flow of trading in stocks, bonds, currencies, and commodities that could easily give them an advantage. Traders could invest with the pack or front-run it by placing smaller orders before the large ones were executed. As Wall Street investment banks developed their trading departments, often operating like hedge funds, they could take advantage of such information as well. One large hedge fund manager said off the record he would never hire a fund manager from Goldman Sachs, for example, because his or her record reflected access to information about Goldman's enormous order flow, Goldman among the largest trading houses in the world. Frank Partnoy, a lawyer who worked in trading at Bankers Trust and since has written books on Wall Street, said traders at his firm were frequently front-running orders.

Financial writer Sebastian Mallaby concluded after interviewing Michael Steinhardt and his trading partners that he "pushed the bounds of what was legal." Steinhardt often bought and traded large orders of individual stocks—a block, as it was called. One of Steinhardt's advantages was that, due to his size, he "could expect special information." For example, a broker might tell Steinhardt his order was the first of several more sales to come, thus warning him not to buy. As Mallaby quoted one trader, these were "not collusive but were just honest attempts to protect each other." Even the sometimes credulous Mallaby found this claim hard to swallow. Mallaby inexplicably defended Steinhardt on the grounds that he was adding liquidity—buying power that smoothed price changes—to the market. But such liquidity came at the cost of buying shares low from unsuspecting investors, or selling high. Moreover, as one analyst put it, such "fair-weather liquidity" was only there when you didn't need it. When markets were falling, Steinhardt was often not there to supply buying power.

Steinhardt reminisced about these years with Mallaby, whom he apparently considered sympathetic to his exploits. "I was being told things that other accounts were not being told," Steinhardt told him. "I got information I shouldn't have. It created a lot of opportunities for us. Were they risky? Yes. Was I willing to do it? Yes. Were they talked about much? No."

A disturbing case of market manipulation involving Steinhardt came to light in the early 1990s. He and another hedge fund manager, Bruce Kovner, who ran Caxton Corporation, were accused by the SEC and the Justice Department of coordinated purchases of a Treasury note in 1991 in an attempt to corner the market. Their total positions came to $20 billion, far more than the actual quantity of bonds issued (technically possible through purchases of short sales). The objective was to inflate the prices artificially and then sell. So difficult is it to prosecute such potential abuses that it took investigators three years to make their case. The hedge fund managers were still able to settle the case without admitting guilt, but had to agree to pay $76 million in fines and the disgorgement of their profits.

Paul Tudor Jones, with enormous buying power and a big reputation, told Mallaby he moved market prices repeatedly with his purchasing power. In 1987, for example, he aggressively bought silver, suddenly pushing up the price, which created the impression there was a disruption in the physical supply of the commodity. Prices soared and he made a fortune on his holdings. "I can go into any market at just the right moment, by giving it a little gas on the upside, I can create the illusion of a bull market. But, unless the market is really sound, the price is going to come right down." Jones claimed such power was only temporary, but a short-term advantage was all that was needed. As Mallaby wrote, "If he could judge a market's potential for a move, Jones could set off a chain reaction at a time of his choosing—and be the first to win from it." How often were such tactics repeated on Wall Street?

Soros's strength as a hedge fund manager was to avoid being wedded to a single strategy for too long. He understood that investment conditions changed. "I used to say that I'm not the best at any one game but I'm the best at learning what rules of the game apply," he said. "I was more interested in the changes than playing the same game as well as possible. So instead of playing one game I was moving on from one to another. It started with stocks and eventually moved on to macro trading." As one of his former money managers put it, "George used to say, 'Don't try to play the game better, try to figure out when the game is over.' "

Since the mid-1980s, Soros divided his time between managing money and personal philanthropic interests, especially in reforming the totalitarian regimes with which he was familiar from birth. He started a foundation in Hungary and expanded over the years to Romania, the Soviet Union, and elsewhere, placing his foundations largely under one roof, the Open Society Institute. His philanthropic activities, politically liberal (in the American sense of the word), expanded with his wealth. Over the course of his life he gave away what he estimated is $5 billion, one fourth to one third of his net worth. In the late 1980s, given his expanding interests, he wanted to spend less time managing his funds and hired Stanley Druckenmiller, who had a formidable money management record at Dreyfus, to take over everyday duties. It would be a durable relationship, Soros staying closely involved and making many of the final major decisions.

The 1990s became the most profitable and controversial decade thus far for the hedge fund managers, gaining them celebrity and worldwide attention, but also calling into question their power to move markets against the interests of nations. Between $100 and $200 billion of such money was under management in 1990, much of it invested the way Soros did—canvassing the broad range of currencies, stocks, and bonds around the world for opportunities. In the following years, hundreds of new funds would be founded, some three thousand already by 1993 after Soros and others made their biggest profits yet. In these years, hedge funds grew large enough to move currency and government bond markets. "They could even overpower governments," wrote Mallaby.

In 1992, Soros and several other hedge fund managers realized that the new European monetary union was creating investment opportunities. In particular, the British Treasury was digging itself into a serious hole. To join the new currency mechanism, which was designed to stabilize the value of currencies in Europe before a single currency, the euro, was adopted, Britain agreed in 1990 to maintain the pound at an agreed-upon level. This was known as the Exchange Rate Mechanism (ERM). To make the system somewhat flexible, the pound and other currencies were allowed to fluctuate, but only in a narrow band of a couple of percentage points up or down from the agreed-upon rates.

But the value of the pound was hard to hold up because the British economy was weak. Traders started selling the pound aggressively. To keep it within the band, Britain had to buy pounds itself with its reserves of foreign currencies and to raise interest rates to attract foreign capital into their bonds as well. Meantime, Germany was raising its rates to restrain what it feared was escalating inflation as its economy strengthened, attracting money into the German mark in competition with the pound. More investors were selling pounds, pushing its value down, to buy marks for the higher rates. As Britain raised interest rates to keep the pound from falling more, it weakened its economy still further. The higher interest rates dampened home buying and business investment, and a high pound also raised the selling price of exports. The nation, meanwhile, was running low on foreign currency reserves to buy the pounds.

Certain Britain would let the pound fall rather than run out of reserves and accept a punishing recession, Druckenmiller also sold the pound furiously. Other hedge funds as well as trading desks of commercial and investment banks were doing the same. Once Soros saw the logic of Druckenmiller's position, he wanted to sell even more pounds. Though Soros rarely borrowed more than an additional 100 percent of his equity to invest—in this case, to sell short—now he borrowed much more. Soros, like others, realized it was almost a riskless investment. Even in the highly unlikely case that Soros and the others were wrong, and Britain stayed in the ERM, any rise in the pound would be no more than a couple of percentage points—the band within which the currency was to stay by the agreement with the ERM. Any loss would be small.

The investors, led by Soros, piled on, and Britain had no chance. The British political leaders aggressively resisted the pound's fall for a while, foolishly draining the nation's reserves of foreign currencies in the process and risking recession all the while. The investors kept selling the pound, forcing Britain to put up interest rates more, with the benchmark central bank rate eventually reaching 15 percent. Finally, in mid-September, the British government relented, dropping out of the ERM. The pound plunged in value and the Quantum Fund made a billion dollars almost overnight. Another billion of profits was to come, leaving Soros with a personal gain of roughly $650 million that year.

It took more than a month for the British papers and *Forbes* magazine to report the news of the "killing" made by the hedge funds, and Soros himself voluntarily gave an interview to a leading newspaper, where he openly explained his trading strategy. Other hedge fund managers and many currency traders made the scores of their careers as well, but not to the degree

Soros had. Soros was now an international celebrity, admired by some and vilified by others.

Soros denied that he and other hedge fund managers caused the crash of the pound. But the trading battle with the hedge funds had caused the British officials to panic, pushing up interest rates dramatically. In fact, a devaluation was necessary, and Britain managed its affairs poorly. But the correction could have been more orderly and less costly without the piling on by the hedge funds. "I didn't do it to hurt England," Soros told *The Guardian* newspaper. "I did it to make money." But England was harmed.

All the money Soros made was now attracting widespread attention. The Quantum Fund now had nearly $4 billion under management. In 1993, with more money to invest, Soros personally earned another $1 billion by correctly anticipating a sharp fall in interest rates. Robert Slater, a Soros biographer, pointed out that eight of the highest paid professionals on Wall Street were hedge fund managers in 1993 and they accounted for almost half of the top one hundred earners in the financial community. An investor who put in $10,000 when Soros started his fund in 1969 would have had $21 million in 1993. A similar investment in the Standard & Poor's 500 would have come to only $122,000.

As the hedge funds gained attention, so did their high fee structures, especially because the managers did not share in the losses. Soros claimed he had almost his entire personal wealth in the fund, so he did indeed take losses. "Even real estate investments are in the fund, even private investments are in the fund," he said. "That is not true in many other funds." Congress held hearings on the hedge funds, but there was no constituency in the SEC or the Clinton Treasury for regulating them.

The rest of the 1990s turned out to be more difficult for Soros and the other traditional hedge funds. For one thing, many new hedge funds were formed, and far more money was chasing the same opportunities. These hedge funds were also charging even higher fees, up to 2 percent of assets compared to 1 percent at Soros and Steinhardt. A more competitive problem for the hedge funds, the rapidly rising stock market of the mid- to late 1990s enabled investors to make a lot of money in more traditional equity investments, spearheaded by a new high technology boom. The NASDAQ index, which was dominated by high-technology issues, rose by three to four times in the second half of the decade and mutual funds specializing in high-technology stocks outpaced the performance of even the best hedge funds in such an environment. Soros could not make any sense of the high-technology boom. To him, those stocks seemed like the story stocks of the 1960s, which rose for no analyzable reason, and he prevented Druckenmiller from buying in. Quantum could not even keep up with the S&P 500 in these years, no less NASDAQ, and could not justify its management fees. Soros also took enormous losses in an investment in Russia, both in loans to the government and in private investments. When Russia, its citizens increasingly refusing to pay taxes, defaulted in 1998, Soros's funds (by then he had opened more funds) lost up to $2 billion in direct Russian investments and another $2 billion on the Russian ruble. The Russian investment was driven more by Soros's political views than by his financial acumen.

The year before, however, Soros made hundreds of millions of dollars in the Asian financial crisis by selling Asian currencies in much the same way he sold the British pound. The Asian currencies had pegged their levels to the U.S. dollar, and held the peg far too long. The nations attracted an enormous amount of capital because they paid high interest rates, but ultimately the lid would burst, Soros felt. In one day, for example, the Thai baht fell 16 percent. The Malaysian ringgit also fell rapidly. Most hedge funds profited from the fall, as did Soros, though he had not been as aggressive a trader as he had been with the British pound or as aggressive as many of his competitors. By now, his conscience may have been bothering him.

Soros, the most prominent and visible of the hedge fund managers, was quickly blamed for the new Asian currency crisis and ensuing deep recessions, which occurred because the countries had to raise their interest rates sharply and the International Monetary Fund forced them to cut social spending to reduce their budget deficits to qualify for IMF loans. The Malaysian prime minister, Mahathir Mohamed, claimed the Jews were the culprits, led by Soros. As usual, his friends said, Soros was unperturbed by the public accusations, firing back that Mahathir should be removed from power. "It didn't touch me," he said. "I learned that the public values are not necessarily right. And I have a very strong sense of right and wrong, which is my own sense."

In the early 1990s, many hedge funds bet that interest rates would stay low, and in 1994, they had their first major shakeout when Greenspan suddenly raised rates to staunch inflation. Many hedge funds failed, and the banks that lent to them lost enough to arouse the interest of Washington. Steinhardt was among the biggest losers and went out of business.

Congressional hearings about the damaging hedge fund losses and unpaid loans to banks brought no changes in regulatory oversight, as noted, but out of the 1994 ashes, a new style of investing soared. Its rise soon overshadowed Soros's traditional hedge fund strategies. Fund managers now took advantage of discrepancies in the prices of a widening array of investment vehicles, including in particular the ever-growing volume of derivatives, the contracts that enabled investors to take positions in stocks, bonds, and commodities with little down. The most prominent of the newcomers was John Meriwether of Salomon Brothers, who had perfected the new strategies, or so he thought, in the 1980s.

To Meriwether and others like him, most of them trained at graduate business schools or in mathematics, Soros's macro trading was based on mythology—the ability to forecast economic trends and asset prices and beat the market. Meriwether basically believed that markets were too rational for Soros's investment style, yet there were nevertheless many attractive discrepancies in prices to exploit. The new trading-oriented funds uncovered minuscule but sometimes long-standing "inefficiencies"—mispricings—in the market, with the help of complex computerized techniques. The potential gains on every trade were small, but the managers believed with near certainty that over time these discrepancies would be corrected and they would profit. Because they were certain, they borrowed aggressively to invest and any gain that could be made was significant as a multiple of equity. Meriwether borrowed much more on trades than those characteristically made by Soros and most other hedge funds. Time was the key, however; you had to be able to hold the position long enough for it to revert to normal, like a gambler in poker who waits for his luck to even out. Hence, Meriwether would name his future firm Long-Term Capital Management.

Meriwether was born in 1947 in Chicago. He attended Catholic primary and high schools, where he was an excellent student, and set out to be a math teacher, after earning his bachelor's degree at Northwestern. One year's teaching was enough for him and he entered the MBA program at the quantitatively oriented business school of the University of Chicago. This is where he learned that, because financial markets worked rationally, stocks and bonds, not to mention derivatives, always returned to sensible values when shocked into misalignment by events—they "converged" to a norm over time.

After graduating from Chicago, Meriwether joined Salomon Brothers in 1973, and started a bond arbitrage department four years later. That year the Chicago Options Exchange created options contracts based on Treasury bonds. The new vehicle made buying or selling bonds easier and cheaper to do, if riskier unless hedged. (A Treasury option was a simple contract to buy or sell a bond at a given price before a certain date, after which time it expired worthless.)

Meriwether's characteristic trade was to buy a temporarily underpriced bond and sell a highly similar but overpriced one in anticipation that these prices would return to their natural historical norms. Traders called this "relative value trading." Whichever way interest rates or currencies moved, they would theoretically make money as values converged to the norm. Forecasting, which was unreliable, was not necessary.

To those who had faith in efficient markets, the more trading there was, the more stability there would usually be. If more people were offering their opinions about prices, they would reflect more available information and analysis. There was also more "liquidity"—a seller could more easily find a buyer if there were more traders in the market with more money.

The advent of more investment alternatives, including international currencies and bonds of developing nations and the increase in derivatives contracts, in particular, created more opportunities for hedge funds to exploit small inefficiencies—that is, to find bargains. Derivatives were no longer simply ways for them to stake out inexpensive positions in the underlying securities, but ends in themselves, to be traded against each other when prices were out of line. At Salomon, Meriwether wed these opportunities to newer computerized techniques made possible by faster computers. In effect, Meriwether was running a hedge fund with Salomon's capital.

Meriwether displayed early the character trait that made him among the most admired traders on Wall Street, a trait many of the most successful traders shared, including Soros. He did not seem to flinch when an investment was losing a lot of money. The first major test came in 1979. The markets were in disarray that year, when Paul Volcker first took office as Federal Reserve chairman. Meriwether bought a large hedged position in Treasury bills from a struggling trading house. The position included Treasury bills and a futures contract against them, but Meriwether computed that their prices were out of line and would have to converge to historical norms over time. In the 1979 market turmoil then, Meriwether's huge position was not yet converging as expected, costing Salomon a lot of money because it had to put up more capital as the price fell to satisfy lenders. It looked as if Salomon could lose tens of millions of dollars on one trade—a substantial portion of its entire capital of $200 million. Some traders would have closed out the trade before the losses got even worse. But Meriwether insisted Salomon hold on through a tense few weeks, even under pressure from his powerful boss, John Gutfreund. Eventually, the prices converged as theory suggested they would and Salomon made a large profit.

Meriwether's sangfroid won him widespread admiration. Gutfreund, the firm's relatively new managing partner, following William Salomon's retirement, named him a partner the next year at the age of thirty-three. As financial writer Roger Lowenstein put it, Meriwether became "the priest of the calculated gamble."

By the early 1980s, Meriwether embarked on a more aggressive phase, having won the respect of, and therefore independence from, Salomon management. He hired mathematically oriented experts with Ph.D.'s in economics, finance, and physics who were more skilled than he. These men built computer models and teased out relationships within complex securities that others had not found. The computations were often based on an estimate of the value of a stock option first published by economist Myron Scholes of the University of Chicago and mathematician Fischer Black of MIT. The Black-Scholes model, based on estimated fluctuations (volatility) of securities prices, became the basis of derivatives trading and the measurement of portfolio risk. Mispricing in the markets was, with refinements, basically a deviation from the Black-Scholes price.

Meriwether was able to understand these advanced models sufficiently and bridge the gap between his intellectual hirees and the more rough-and-tumble traditional traders at Salomon. His group of Ph.D.'s, seated in the center of Salomon's famed trading room in downtown Manhattan, became a highly profitable island unto themselves and were as intensely loyal to Meriwether as he was to them. "Meriwether cast a spell over the young traders who worked for him," wrote Michael Lewis, who worked at Salomon at the time.

Other investment banking firms were also beginning to hire "quants," the mathematically trained newcomers to Wall Street. But Salomon remained the leader. In the past, trading securities was more seat-of-the-pants, based on a "feel" and an extensive network of trading clients. Salomon's specialty had long been trading in bonds, but trading securities in general was considered inferior to highly profitable investment banking on Wall Street, led by such firms as Morgan Stanley and Goldman Sachs. It was blue-collar versus white-collar. In the 1970s, with low stock prices, this relationship began to reverse, as underwriting volume and profits fell. By contrast, high inflation made bonds more volatile, which, coupled with new derivatives products, created a new and rising tide of profitable opportunities.

In the 1980s, Meriwether hired several leading academic economists as consultants. They included Robert Merton, of MIT and then Harvard Business School, who had been a professor to several of Meriwether's traders, and also Myron Scholes, who was at the University of Chicago. Fischer Black took a full-time job with Goldman Sachs. Scholes and Merton won the 1997 Nobel Prize in economics for their statistical theories (Black, who died in 1995, would have been named as well had he lived).

After the stock market crash of 1987, most traditional hedge fund managers, including Soros, lost heavily (as noted, Paul Tudor Jones and Julian Robertson were conspicuous exceptions). Meriwether's group also lost, but in adversity he encouraged his team to generate new investment ideas and redouble their bets if they still believed in their former trades. The conventional wisdom at the time was that the crash was likely to throw the economy into turmoil and interest rates would fall as recession engulfed the United States. Buying current bonds, therefore, made sense because their prices would rise with falling rates. (When interest rates rise, the prices of existing bonds fall; when rates fall, the prices of existing bonds rise.)

The government bond traders at Salomon, who sat not far from Meriwether's team, took the more conventional route and bought enormous quantities of the long-term Treasury benchmark bond (the latest thirty-year bond), as did most of their peers on the Street. But Meriwether did not believe he or his team could forecast interest rates. Rather than buying the newly issued benchmark bond like the traditional bond desk, Meriwether's group sold it—a new one was issued every six months—and bought an almost identical one due in twenty-nine years and roughly six months because it was slightly cheaper. It was a classic hedge. The new thirty-year issue always received a lot of investor attention, and the earlier one was typically neglected, usually selling at a very slightly lower price than it should. Meriwether's group figured they would make money whether rates rose or fell. If rates rose, the price of the thirty-year bond would fall more than the cheaper twenty-nine-year-plus bond. Meriwether would make money because he sold the thirty-year short. If rates fell, the thirty-year bond would rise less than the cheaper twenty-nine-year-plus bond. He'd make money because he owned the twenty-nine-year-plus bond.

The approach worked far better than Meriwether could have expected.

Alan Greenspan force-fed credit into the markets after the market crash, and the economy recovered rather than falling into recession. As a result, rates rose rather than fell, stunning Wall Street traders. The investment made by Salomon's government trading desk lost tens of millions of dollars on the thirty-year bond, but Meriwether made Salomon $50 million.

Gutfreund had new stars, but the traditional government bond trading department was humiliated and did not believe Meriwether's returns were honestly made. Craig Coats, head of bond trading, insisted that Meriwether's group overheard his own department's plans to sell and sold before they did at the high prices, then bought the bonds back as the government desk drove prices down—classic front-running. The claim did not save Coats's job. Meriwether was put in charge of all bond trading.

As Meriwether made a lot of money for Salomon, he demanded a portion of the profits for himself and his group of roughly one hundred traders and staff. In 1989, the arrangement was formalized, so that Salomon paid the group 15 percent of the profits it generated annually, which in 1990 came to $1 billion. One of Meriwether's star traders was paid $23 million that year. At this time, Salomon had $150 billion in assets—investment positions—and only $4 billion in capital. Most of the leverage was created by Meriwether's bond arbitrage group.

Implicit in Meriwether's investing techniques was the assumption that at times his group would lose money, but eventually would make it back. If they were using borrowed funds, they might also have to meet higher margin or other collateral requirements if assets took longer to recover than they thought likely. It was necessary to have enough capital on hand to cover those temporary losses. Experts at Bankers Trust and J.P. Morgan had developed a new measure, based on past price behavior, the volatility of securities, and the mix of securities held, that they argued could determine how likely losses on a portfolio were on any single day. They called it Value at Risk, or VAR. For example, VAR might find that a loss of 25 percent of a portfolio of assets would occur only once in twenty-five times. If the investment firm had more than enough capital to cover the maximum likely to be lost, according to VAR, it could feel comfortable borrowing still more to raise investment levels. For portfolio managers, VAR became invaluable. If VAR was too high, it could sell assets, or specifically, the more volatile assets. Diversifying assets was also thought to be a key way to reduce VAR, because different kinds of securities—say a California state bond and a Michigan state bond—rose or fell at different times; mixing securities usually meant less volatility overall. The managers could also buy hedges—offsetting investments—to reduce VAR. International regulators also placed their faith in VAR. The Bank for International Settlements (BIS) headquartered in Basel, Switzerland, in what were known as the Basel Agreements, set capital requirements for bankers according to the VAR of their portfolio of assets. Commercial banks, too, now trading actively for their portfolios, used VAR.

The Meriwether group used VAR to calm concerns of Salomon management that they were leveraging too aggressively. If the quants had a sure way to measure the risk they were taking, they could justify borrowing still more. All seemed entirely under control in the late 1980s and early 1990s, even as the economy entered another recession and federal budget deficits reached new heights.

But VAR also had drawbacks that were neglected in periods when markets were generally operating predictably. VAR worked when history repeated itself fairly closely. If markets moved sharply up or down due to an economic shock like a deep recession or a default on a major nation's debt, VAR could seriously misstate risk. In particular, the diversification of various assets may not be sufficient at such times to reduce volatility, as most fall together in price in a temporary atmosphere of uncertainty. But Long-Term Capital Management tested its analyses in many different ways and believed that if it could hold on to positions long enough, it could ride out such storms—this was the central tenet by which the partners managed the company.

While Soros was finding unprecedented levels of profits in sharp currency moves and interest rates in the late 1980s and early 1990s, Meriwether was starting to make Salomon enormous sums of money with his more scientifically based and supposedly low-risk techniques. He was also now making more than enough money to indulge his personal passions, the most important of which was golf. He became rich enough to buy himself a golf course in Ireland. He also bought a stable of thoroughbred horses in northern Westchester. The Irish Catholic South Side of Chicago, where he grew up, had produced a tycoon.

Gutfreund had long encouraged aggressive trading practices at the firm, which he had brought public, making himself and other partners wealthy. In 1985, *BusinessWeek* named him "King of Wall Street." Meriwether was now the likely successor to Gutfreund. Then Meriwether became involved in a firm-threatening scandal at Salomon that almost cost him his career and did cost his boss his. More important, it opened a window to the reckless nature of trading in ways that the press rarely captured.

Determined to minimize potential manipulation of bond prices so that the American public gets the best price (pays the lowest interest rate) possible, the Treasury carefully regulates the bond dealers who are allowed to bid at auctions for government bonds and then sell them. Officially designated dealers were allowed to buy only 35 percent of any Treasury issue to prevent a single firm from owning so many bonds they would have undue influence over the price—cornering the market. The limit was established in the late 1980s precisely because Salomon, Wall Street's leading bond house, too often dominated the bond auctions.

In late 1990 and early 1991, Paul Mozer, a key Salomon bond trader, tried to skirt the Treasury restrictions by placing orders for the Treasury bonds in customers' names without informing them, enabling him to control more than 35 percent of the auction. The New York Federal Reserve, which handles bond sales for the Treasury, formally asked Mozer to explain why he made a second bid under someone else's name; he replied it was a clerical error. Then the U.S. Treasury asked him for a response. In April, Mozer confessed to Meriwether, who brought the issue to the attention of Robert Strauss, Gutfreund's number two, and to the general counsel. Salomon's counsel told Gutfreund that Mozer's action was a serious violation, and possibly even a crime, and should be reported.

But Gutfreund did nothing, sweeping the violation under the rug, and did not inform his other directors. Strauss also let it pass and Mozer was not dismissed. All later claimed they believed someone else was handling it. Meriwether, who similarly claimed later that he assumed Gutfreund was addressing it, did not follow up either. Neither Meriwether nor Gutfreund made any attempt to scrub Salomon of such practices and Mozer, only a couple of months later, managed to bid illegally again for almost all the bonds in at least one other government offering. Competing firms complained about Mozer's practices, instigating an SEC investigation. Gutfreund knew about the next Mozer infraction but again did not report it or even inform the rest of the firm for several months. When the Fed sent him a letter of concern, he failed to tell his board. Only in August of 1991 did Gutfreund start talking to the federal government, after a Salomon investigation had turned up at least four Mozer infractions. By then, the press had the story. Mozer was let go, but the bad publicity now jeopardized Salomon. Its share price was falling and its bondholders demanded that the bonds be bought back by the firm, costing it hundreds of millions of dollars. Most alarming, Salomon's status as an official government bond dealer was now at risk and, without that, the firm would all but surely go under.

Gutfreund and Strauss resigned when the Fed threatened that it would suspend Salomon as a government dealer. (The general counsel resigned later.) Warren Buffett's Berkshire Hathaway had had the controlling shareholder interest in Salomon since 1987. At that time, Gutfreund had asked him to come in as a white knight and save the firm from the clutches of takeover specialist Ronald Perelman, who was armed with junk bond money from Mike Milken. Gutfreund asked Buffett to succeed him as CEO, and Buffett appointed Salomon's leading investment banker, Deryck Maughan, to run the company. Buffett also demanded that its reckless trading practices change.

Buffett also called the secretary of the Treasury to plead with him not to suspend Salomon as a bond dealer. Buffett used the classic warning that if Salomon went under, it could start a domino effect of collapsing firms and freeze the financial markets. The Treasury relented, and Buffett preserved his large personal investment. The SEC investigated Mozer, Gutfreund, and Strauss and banned them from the securities business for life, a shameful fall for the once high-flying Gutfreund. Meriwether was also investigated and then banned from the securities business for three months and fined $50,000. Salomon had to pay fines and compensation to shareholders of $200 million.

The scandal made headlines but its full implications—the cynical trading culture on Wall Street, which could operate oblivious to the law—were quickly forgotten. A stunned Gutfreund sued Salomon for a much more lucrative settlement package than the $8 million he received; he lost. Meanwhile, Meriwether bided his time, entertaining the hope that he would return to Salomon. He played golf and managed his stable of thoroughbreds. The rest of his arbitrage group stayed in place and continued to make enormous sums for Salomon in 1992, some $1.4 billion. Between 1990 and 1993, they made nearly 90 percent of all of Salomon's profits.

Buffett did not welcome Meriwether back to the firm and he finally resigned. But it was the beginning of an extraordinary new chapter for him. Soros's widely publicized profits in 1992 and 1993 made it a practical possibility to raise hundreds of millions of dollars to start an independent hedge fund. Bob Merton, now at Harvard Business School and still a consultant to Salomon, had always argued that the trading techniques he endorsed and that Meriwether used did not require the reach or even the deep financial pockets of a major investment house. Hedging techniques were so sophisticated, he argued, the risk was more limited than realized. Meriwether's team, with Merton's and Scholes's theoretical inputs, and new refinements of VAR, ensured the risk they took could accurately be measured and enormous amounts of leverage therefore employed. The Meriwether group would be able to invest ten times its capital and eventually twenty-five times because, they argued, they controlled risk more closely through these arbitrage and unique hedging techniques. They soon produced a string of strong profits, convincing many observers, including themselves, that they were right.

With Merrill Lynch's help, Meriwether raised money from business chieftains like Laurence Tisch of Loew's, Donald Marron of Paine Webber, Richard Fuld of Lehman Brothers, and many financial institutions, including Paine Webber and Bank Julius Baer. By early 1994, Meriwether had more than $1 billion to launch his fund and lured several of his key colleagues from Salomon to join him, including consultants Scholes and Merton. LTCM locked in its own investors so that they could not redeem their positions for three years, the key to success, they told them, being the ability to hold on to investments even when they went temporarily bad. The fund opened its doors in February in Greenwich, Connecticut, cheaper than and also a considerable distance from the clamor of Wall Street.

Now specialized trading strategies that emphasized "convergence" and "relative value" would be open to public investment—if a rarefied set of wealthy investors. Long-Term Capital Management audaciously charged a 2 percent management fee and 25 percent of profits, well above the average for hedge funds. Soon another round of talented traders in Wall Street firms started abandoning the security of the large firms to start their own hedge funds. In the mid-1990s, these men made enormous sums of money. For this wealth, they claimed they provided America valuable financial liquidity—which they also argued resulted in a lower cost of capital to invest in plant, equipment, research, private homes, and the stocks and bonds to support a handsome retirement for many. Some, maybe most, may have believed what they said, but the value of so much liquidity was exaggerated. No credible academic studies analyzed and determined what contribution such high levels of liquidity made to the economy.

In its first few years, the fund Meriwether and his partners created traded all around the globe and in almost any asset that could be traded. In 1994, a bad year for almost all on Wall Street when Greenspan sharply raised rates, LTCM, after a setback, earned more than 40 percent. In 1995, it earned nearly 60 percent and in 1996 nearly 45 percent. Many on the Street emulated LTCM, not just hedge funds but the trading desks of the investment banks, and eventually commercial banks and international merchant banks.

LTCM was now profiting not only by following its computerized models, however. In particular, it had also learned to take advantage of regulatory discrepancies in England, Japan, and especially Italy, where the central bank of Italy itself was an investor in LTCM.

But by 1997, after three years of strong profits for LTCM, the opportunities were drying up. There was too much money chasing the same investments. Secrecy was at the core of Meriwether's strategies; the price advantages were small, and if competitors knew them, the advantages disappeared quickly. Many were trying to find out what LTCM was doing and copying it outright, exactly as some hedge fund managers and others on Wall Street tried to emulate Soros and Paul Tudor Jones. In 1997, the financial devastation created by the Asian financial crisis also took its toll and LTCM made only 17 percent on its capital that year, its historical relationships no longer holding. In 1997, by contrast, the S&P 500 was up 31 percent as high-technology stocks were taking off.

In early 1998, LTCM decided to give a large portion of its capital back to its original investors because profitable opportunities were so hard to find. At the end of 1997, LTCM had nearly $7.5 billion under management, compared to $1 billion when it started, and it now returned $2.7 billion of that to investors. The partners also figured that they could, if necessary, simply leverage their portfolio further to compensate for the loss of capital, which would compound their personal gains. Greed was at the heart of what turned out to be a disastrous decision. At this point, one of Meriwether's key traders was estimated to be worth $500 million and Meriwether himself $300 million.

Unable to reproduce the returns of the first three years, LTCM took increasingly more risk, abandoning its purer arbitrage for the kinds of "directional" investments Soros made and LTCM had so long disdained— such as trying to forecast interest rate and currency movements. More and more of these trades were unhedged. For example, it sold options outright, meaning that it was gambling heavily that its forecast of a particular stock's price or the interest rate on a certain bond would be right. Such forecasting had been scorned at LTCM until now. One of the partners also used a substantial portion of capital to invest aggressively in risk arbitrage, with positions in some thirty takeover targets, an inherently risky business demanding a lot of research and experience.

As new hedge funds multiplied, and wealthy investment banks put up tens of billions of dollars of capital to trade like LTCM did, the Street became more interconnected. Such "tight coupling" raised the risk that if something went badly wrong, all assets could plunge in price together. LTCM believed religiously that VAR or sophisticated newer versions of it adequately measured the risk of its portfolio. Ironically, what undid LTCM in 1998 were not its far-flung and nontraditional bets, or even buying take-over candidates, on which it did on balance lose substantial money, but its core strategy. It ultimately placed too much faith that its trades would always return to historical norms within a reasonable time. Any warnings from their Nobel Prize winners that this would not always be the case were faint at best. To repeat, according to LTCM's long-term view, if you waited long enough, the odds would eventually turn in your favor. Unusual instability—volatility in Wall Street's terms—was always temporary historically and you could make a lot of money by not being afraid of it. In early 1998, after the Asian crisis, LTCM loaded up on what seemed to others like risk and to LTCM like opportunity. The prices being offered seemed too good to pass up. Others were selling risky, naturally volatile securities because it seemed during the crisis that volatility would stay high, and LTCM was buying them (or vice versa), betting that future volatility would fall, returning to normal faster than the market anticipated. LTCM became known as the bank of volatility.

In early 1998, markets had temporarily calmed. The fallout from the Asian crisis had settled, and the financial markets seemed back on track. LTCM's long-term investment performance was still strong, up a total of 185 percent in the four years since it started—a return of about 30 percent a year once compounded to investors after the high management fees.

But, in fact, LTCM's risk models—VAR and related statistical tools, one in particular called the Risk Aggregator—were misleading. The LTCM computer models suggested the fund could lose as much as $45 million only one third of trading days, as much as $105 million only 5 percent of trading days, and as much as $339 million only one out of one hundred trading days. It predicted that a loss of 50 percent of its portfolio of assets would occur only once in an unfathomable amount of time—several billion times the life of the universe. This absurd number should itself have sent signals to management that there were mistaken assumptions in their calculations. At the time, their capital was nearly $5 billion, and given the VAR computations, LTCM management believed that their debt (with which they loaded up on risky assets)—now some twenty-five times capital or $125 billion—was not outsized.

But they did not take into account the possibility that investors outside LTCM would rush to the doors at the same time, causing a general disaster. Diversification was little protection at such times. Analyst Joe Kolman wrote a widely cited summary of LTCM's decline based on presentations by LTCM partners after their fund's demise. In the spring of 1998, markets again became shaky, as mortgage-backed securities started to tumble. The Asian financial crisis was also still fresh in everyone's memory. Then, Sandy Weill, whose Travelers Insurance company had recently acquired Salomon Brothers based on its remarkably profitable run, discovered he had little taste for the risks of the arbitrage desk that was still operating there and losing up to $100 million. He and Jamie Dimon, his young adviser, who was also averse to such risk taking, decided to unwind the arbitrage desk. Winding down the big Salomon desk meant extra selling pressure on the assets that LTCM owned, pushing down prices further.

Losses at LTCM were mounting. In August of 1998, LTCM still had $3.6 billion in capital, down roughly $1.3 billion since April. Forty percent of the capital belonged to the partners, which was most of their personal net worth. In five weeks, they would lose almost all the rest.

The immediate cause was the Russian default on its debt. On August 17, Russia announced that it would temporarily halt interest payments on its debt and no longer support the value of the ruble. It also requested that its banks honor contracts in rubles, making LTCM's hedges almost worthless; they would not be paid off. But the Russian investments themselves did not bring LTCM down. It was the domino effect they precipitated in an investment community that was now tightly coupled. Almost all fixed income assets fell sharply in value; diversification, it turned out, did not matter. The finely calculated relationships on which LTCM was built and which the firm always believed would hold started to come apart. VAR could not account for such an unlikely but sweeping event—an event in which everyone wanted out at the same time and almost all investments fell significantly in price. The use of VAR itself precipitated much of the selling. As markets became more unstable, VAR rose—the estimate of prospective losses—forcing firms to sell assets to raise capital. Commercial banks under the jurisdiction of the Basel Agreements, which as noted set capital requirements based on the level of VAR (the lower the VAR, the lower the capital required), were forced to sell assets to raise capital. All the selling forced prices down further.

In the poor markets earlier in the year, LTCM had sold assets to raise capital, especially given how leveraged it was; it had little leeway. But in one of the more stark examples of greedy overconfidence, the partners sold the assets that were most liquid—easiest to sell because they were safest. As always, LTCM believed the markets would correct and become stable again, so if they sold the less safe and illiquid assets, they would be giving up the most profitable opportunities once markets returned to normal. This was classic LTCM thinking. Meanwhile, as many investors rushed out of the market, they invested in Treasury bills for safety, forcing prices up on the very low-risk assets that LTCM sold short as a hedge. (Treasury bills were often what LTCM sold short as a hedge.) Such a flight to Treasury securities—a flight to quality—had happened in 1994 also, causing big losses for hedge funds. Why didn't LTCM anticipate this possibility?

When Fed regulators looked over LTCM's complicated books, they found that its thousands of trades were not in fact nearly as diversified as their traders thought. They were highly correlated even in nonpanicky times—they moved up and down together. Meantime, LTCM's competitors generally knew which securities LTCM had to sell to raise collateral, and they sold ahead of it either to reduce their own losses or to make profits on LTCM's misfortune. LTCM took still more losses.

Most hedge funds lost money that August, but LTCM lost $1.9 billion. On August 21 alone, LTCM lost more than $550 million. Meriwether and his partners, who had been seeking more capital all along, now became desperate. (Meriwether knew events were precarious for him personally, and transferred ownership of a Pebble Beach house he owned to his wife that week.) Buffett and Soros were consulted and expressed interest in purchasing a portion of the fund, but the terms of a deal were not appealing. Buffett did ultimately put together a lowball offer with Goldman Sachs and AIG, the giant insurance company, but the deal presented legal hurdles, Meriwether was cool to it, and it fell through.

The Fed officials calculated that the total financial losses for other major banks and financial institutions due to the market debacle could come to another $3–5 billion, about equal to what LTCM was losing. Spread over seventeen major banks, this loss could be absorbed; LTCM could sell its assets slowly. But if the market stopped functioning altogether for a few days, there was no way to estimate the potential consequences. On September 21, LTCM had capital of only $1 billion and investments of $100 billion, a leverage ratio of 100 to 1. How would unwinding $100 billion in assets unsettle the markets? The Fed did not want to take the chance of finding out.

Finally, fourteen banks, organized by the Fed, put together loans of more than $3.5 billion to purchase 90 percent of the firm. Of those asked, only Lehman Brothers refused to participate. Meriwether and his partners lost their personal fortunes, and their stake, which once totaled more than $1.8 billion, was now a mere $28 million. They still had their jobs, but their task was to wind LTCM down in a stable way in order to pay back the $3.5 billion to the banks. Meriwether and his team were disturbed by the terms. They complained about how the other bankers, once shown LTCM's specific assets, sold ahead of LTCM, reducing further the value of its collateral. Meriwether told the Fed that Goldman in particular was front-running. The Fed did not investigate. LTCM did not do well over the next year, but it did manage to sell down assets in an orderly fashion and by early 2000 it was essentially out of business.

Had LTCM deeper pockets, or retained more capital—or indeed borrowed less—perhaps it would have survived intact. But its computer models, as Meriwether and his colleagues interpreted them, appeared to make such capital depth unnecessary. Firms that imitated LTCM or traded with it reported enormous losses, including Citicorp (which Weill's Travelers, Salomon in hand, had since merged with) and countless major investment banks. Merrill Lynch's stock, for example, fell by three quarters, Lehman's by almost as much. Goldman Sachs had to cancel its planned initial public offering.

Two days after the LTCM bailout was agreed to in 1998, a worried Alan Greenspan, leaning toward raising rates at the time, cut the federal funds rate. It was not enough to calm the markets, and he cut it again three weeks later. At last, stock prices began to rise and credit markets to settle down. In November, the Fed cut rates for the third time for a total of three quarters of 1 percent. As noted, these cuts were not precipitated by Greenspan's faith in the New Economy, as so many had assumed in retrospect.

Now the stock market turned up strongly, led by a new round of speculation in the high-technology stocks, as it became clear Greenspan was determined to loosen monetary policy to avoid a credit crunch and recession. (It was another example of the so-called Greenspan put.) The Clinton economic boom continued, and stocks rose higher and higher. It was not the self-correcting powers of the markets but aggressive central bank intervention plus a new round of irrational speculation that provided a floor under the downward financial prices and the calamitous consequences of bad Wall Street decisions. It was not even the LTCM rescue alone by private banks that saved Wall Street; to repeat, it was the central bank interest rate cuts and a new set of story stocks that saved the markets from the overleveraged investing of Wall Street, both by the hedge funds and the investment and commercial banks.

The alleged good done by such hedge fund investing—the liquidity of markets, the supposed reduction in interest rates—was overwhelmed by the risks. Reason, on which LTCM was allegedly built, did not prevail at Long-Term Capital Management; greed did, and greed did not work this time.

President Clinton named a blue-ribbon panel to investigate the events. It cautioned about the use of leverage and the unbridled derivatives market, but demanded little in the way of reform. Congress, which held hearings, did not press for new regulations. Alan Greenspan learned no lessons from these events about the inherent instability of a completely free market in finance. He still insisted markets regulate themselves. In October, despite the frightening hedge fund losses, Greenspan told Congress, "What is remarkable is not this episode, but the relative absence of such examples over the past five years." Neither the Clinton administration nor Greenspan even asked for more disclosure requirements for hedge funds, let alone restraints on leverage or regulation of derivatives. And before his term was up, Clinton supported the bill to end federal regulation of derivatives.

As we've seen, Soros and Julian Robertson had trouble competing in these years when high-technology stocks soared inexplicably. Soros, who long resisted Druckenmiller's pleas to invest in high-tech, then finally relented. For a few months, his funds prospered, then the floor fell out from under him. The Soros funds, led by Quantum, lost several billion dollars in the last few years of the 1990s, including on his investments in Russia. Still, Soros's initial investors would have earned more than 30 percent a year between 1969 and 2000. Druckenmiller left the company and Soros turned his hedge funds into conservatively managed investment vehicles. The troubled Tiger Fund closed in 2000, also with an enviable long-term record.

By the early 2000s, as interest rates fell and stock prices rose, hedge funds were revived. The amount of money attracted to them approached $1 trillion by 2004 and $2 trillion by 2007, as new funds churned out exceptional returns compared to conventional vehicles. As a result, hundreds of hedge fund managers were making huge fortunes with a wide variety of strategies. Mostly, however, Greenspan's low interest rates, coupled with the fund managers' ability to borrow aggressively, accounted for their big returns, not remarkable prescience.

Quantitative strategies were even more popular. LTCM's pioneering work was already outdated. Firms like James Simons's Renaissance had raised quantitatively based investing to new heights, seeking small repeatable if temporary patterns in trading on which to profit. He and several others like him were producing handsome gains on giant portfolios. To the quants, it seemed as if a holy grail had been found. Far from being discredited for its oversimplifications, a somewhat improved VAR was also used more widely than ever before to assess a portfolio's risk.

In the credit crisis of 2008 and its aftermath, however, most hedge funds lost money and many went down in flames, some 1,500 closing their doors. Few were smart enough to anticipate the debacle. But some did. These earned billions of dollars, forecasting the collapsing mortgage markets, including funds led by John Paulson and Soros (who had returned to active management because he thought opportunities to short mortgage securities were too appealing to ignore). Smaller, astutely run companies like FrontPoint Partners and Cornwall Capital made a fortune selling mortgage obligations short. These gains offset many of the losses of other hedge funds.

There were again now many critics of the hedge funds but there were many defenders as well. The defenders pointed out that on average the funds outperformed stock price indexes and deserved their outsize remuneration. Over the years, even in the 2000s, sophisticated statistical analyses suggested that the vast array of hedge funds produced, on average, more profits for the risks they took than did other investors like mutual funds or even the private equity funds that borrowed money to take public companies private. To these defenders, Soros's contention seemed right. It was a better mousetrap.

In fact, the superior performance for hedge funds on average may have reflected more controversial factors. In the early years of hedge funds, an intuitive case could be made in defense of superior hedge fund performance. With only $100 or $200 billion in assets, there may well have been many opportunities in the markets to be exploited by intelligent, fast-moving investors. Even when Soros bet against the pound, there was only $200 billion or so in hedge fund assets. But with $1–2 trillion in assets, the likelihood that there were so many market anomalies was diminished substantially.

The accumulated anecdotes about market manipulation, privileged information, and front-running by hedge funds, especially as the funds got large, makes the longer-term performance suspect. Steinhardt's admissions and Tudor Jones's "power to cause avalanches," as Mallaby put it, are probably but a couple of examples. A former Goldman Sachs trader, Christian Siva-Jothy, who started his own hedge fund, SemperMacro, characterized one of the central advantages for those in the know this way: "I remember in the 1990s, everybody knew who the players were—Tiger and Soros. They had billions of dollars under management and they could drive markets. Even if they were wrong, they could still move the market 5 percent or more in some instances."

That the SEC and Justice Department had not brought more cases against the industry was probably a result of lax attitudes since the 1980s and how hard it is to gather evidence and make an adequate case of fraud under current financial laws. After the credit crisis of 2008, however, a newly energized SEC initiated investigations of inside information at several large funds.

Meanwhile, hedge fund investors were not protected by the investment company laws the way mutual fund investors were. There is some evidence that despite their supposed sophistication they needed more federal protection. One academic study showed that hedge fund investors on average bought into hedge funds at the wrong time. They tended to buy when funds were high and sold when they were low, reducing their average returns to less than they would have earned had they simply bought the S&P 500.

For all the attention garnered by Soros, he was relatively untainted by financial scandal or persistent accusations of wrongdoing by regulators or competitors. To his defenders, this suggested strongly that he operated well within the boundaries of the law.

Whether hedge fund activity was on balance good for the economy was another matter. The growth of the hedge funds raised a key and disturbing question about the financial evolution of Wall Street. There was an implicit contract in free market economics that men and women could make great fortunes as long as they were contributing commensurately to the prosperity of the nation. In the classic case, Henry Ford perhaps deserved his fortune because he created many good jobs and cheap, highly utilitarian cars. The same assumption was made about financial dealings—that those who made fortunes produced commensurate gains for their investors and the economy. It was hard to imagine that the amount of liquidity supplied by hedge funds justified these personal fortunes. Damage done by over-speculation and extreme leverage was hard to deny. Even it hedge funds made better returns with less risk, evidence suggested their investors needed more protection to benefit adequately. Moreover, if above-average returns were the result of manipulation, front-running, and inside information, profits came out of the hides of other investors. As the age of greed matured, it became clear that Wall Street did not give back as much as it took—indeed, when balanced out, Wall Street often did great harm.

Sandy Weill

Whard hen Walter Wriston was building what became Citicorp from the 1960s to the 1980s, he could not have imagined that almost all the regulatory obstacles to his corporate ambition would one day be leveled, as they had been by the end of the twentieth century. He could not have imagined that he could have a branch almost anywhere in America, as a 1994 federal law now made possible, resulting in mergers of major banks across the nation. Or that a commercial bank with access to reserves at the Federal Reserve and federally insured deposits would someday be allowed to put its own or its customers' money into almost any kind of investment, and borrow aggressively to do so. He could not have imagined that his institution could make loans to customers by systematically violating regulations and by hiding assets or liabilities off the balance sheets of the borrower or the lender. A generation later, maybe he might have done the same, but it could not be done during his time as Citicorp's leader.

By the late 1990s, his eventual successor, Sanford Weill, finished the task that Wriston had begun. Anger at government on principle along with personal ambition combined to cause Wriston to charge straight into the fortress of government regulation. Weill had neither his vision nor his larger passion. He wanted to earn money and the prestige it brought. Because of Wriston's early efforts, and the rise of a new deregulatory ideology under Reagan, Weill was able to do that, and in fact was fully confident he could. If there was a wall of regulation, he tore it down with far less opposition than Wriston encountered. Finance had endured. Wriston started up or entered new business areas. Sandy Weill's career was based on empire building through acquisitions, usually of existing but vulnerable institutions. He was best at cutting costs at ailing operations and wringing profit from remaining businesses. His talent was singular and narrow.

Already by the late 1980s, there were fewer regulatory obstacles to obstruct Weill's ambition to consolidate financial services into one enormous firm, and during the 1990s regulations were eliminated almost entirely under the watch of Bill Clinton, partly due to Weill's influence. To Weill's advantage, the stock market became a dependable wealth-generating machine over the course of his career, rising by ten to twenty times, depending on the measure, from the early 1970s to the early 2000s. The short-term increase in earnings his managerial approach was designed to produce was more than amply rewarded with higher stock prices in these bull markets. Weill talked often of a vision of a financial conglomerate delivering one-stop shopping to all of America, as had Wriston before him—all financial products sold through his salespeople. He paid himself very well, usually through generous stock options. A personal fortune was the reward for his work and, in the logic of the time, proof of business achievement and even, it was eventually claimed, social good.

Sandy Weill in 1989, ten years before he took over as CEO of Citigroup

Weill had little taste for the sort of Wall Street risk taken by John Meriwether or the other hedge funds. His talent was for selling traditional investment vehicles, particularly equities, and, as noted, for acquisitions. Ironically, his avoidance of risk served him well during the crises of the late 1990s. He was more feudal lord than business entrepreneur. He surrounded himself with a relative handful of key lieutenants, thus keeping management intimate, despite the size of his empire.

Wriston managed his company more like an army, with chains of command and clear measures of success and failure, but with respect for his hundreds of lieutenants, and room for innovation and new strategies. Weill was more personal and subjective, his strategic thinking and even managerial techniques limited. He demanded intense loyalty to the point of obsequiousness from his employees and enraged those he pushed aside. In his autobiography, Weill demeaned two key aides, Peter Cohen and his longtime favorite, Jamie Dimon, without whom it is unlikely he would have risen to such heights. "He was so weak, needed love so badly, if he thought someone disloyal, he cut them down," said one member of his board of directors.

He was disparaged as ruthless for years, and picked on for his portly figure, his coarse bearing, and his indulgence in cigars, expensive wines, and martinis at lunch. But his creation in 1998 of Citigroup, the largest financial organization in the world, was considered by many the decade's greatest financial achievement. In 2002, he was named Chief Executive of the Year by *Chief Executive* magazine, and in that same year, he came close to losing it all. By 2003, Weill had left his position as Citigroup CEO under a cloud of suspicion about conflicts of interest, although he remained chairman of the board. Until 2007, his creation was a great profit machine, but it allocated capital carelessly and wastefully, and paid enormous government fines for its errant ways. Fines and billions of dollars in litigation settlements in the early 2000s did not deter it from further abuses in mortgage markets a few years later. By 2008, the enormous banking conglomerate Weill had proudly pieced together and believed was impregnable to serious risk was on the brink of collapse.

Sanford I. Weill—Sandy, as he was universally called—did not grow up poor, as some biographies imply. His parents were Polish-born Jews who as children moved to the United States with their parents in the early 1900s. They settled in Brooklyn, where Weill was born in 1933, the older of two children. His maternal grandfather did well in the dress business and owned a hotel and a farm in upstate New York. His father, Max, joined his father-in-law's business, and then started a moderately successful dressmaking operation of his own. During World War II, Max Weill branched into the steel importing business as demand soared to meet wartime needs, and turned a handsome profit. He liked spending his money, and began to drive fancy cars and wear showy clothes; Weill's mother, by contrast, remained comparatively modest.

The family lived in a fine house in the Flatbush section of Brooklyn. In his autobiography, Weill described his father as domineering, ebullient, a show-off, and a man from whom he consistently shied away. His father's overbearing nature, he believed, contributed to his own intense shyness and personal insecurities. Even as a CEO, he had stage fright. When his father suddenly left his mother about the time Weill was graduating from college, he was angry and never forgave him. By then, his father was modestly wealthy, but he had been convicted of fraud for selling products on the wartime black market. Weill showed little sympathy and wrote that his father was a "negative role model."

Weill was kept back in grade school. At Peekskill Military Academy in Peekskill, New York, however, where his parents had decided to send him, he found that he had a gift for sports and became a competitive tennis player, winning the Westchester County singles championship for private and parochial school students. From this success, he gained confidence, performed far better academically, and was accepted by Cornell. His father bought him a yellow Plymouth and gave him a credit card, which, he wrote, made it easy to get dates. He was an indifferent student, something of a bon vivant, and temporarily dropped out of school. On a visit back home, he met his future wife, Joan, and his devotion to her helped him focus his life. At her urging, he returned to Cornell to finish his bachelor's degree, and they married in 1955. Estranged from his father, he did not invite him to the wedding. Marriage further stabilized him after college, but he feared that Joan's parents, who were better off and unshowy compared to his father, did not approve of him. For many years, he felt he had to prove himself to Joan and her family.

At first he held only low-paying jobs, but, he wrote, when he passed a Bache & Company office in Manhattan he was attracted to the frenetic moneymaking activities inside. He landed a job as a securities runner, delivering certificates from brokerage firm to brokerage firm as the securities were bought and sold. A more credible account, according to other biographers, is that he looked hard for a job in the stock market, which was becoming a highly profitable business in the mid-1950s, where one could make a good living, and perhaps even a fortune, and was repeatedly turned down before he got his first offer at Bache. To his credit, he did not think twice about starting at the bottom. Hardworking and able, he rose quickly from messenger to margin clerk, recording trades and payments, the back-office routines he learned he enjoyed. Within a year, he applied for his own stockbroker's license at Bear Stearns, where he had moved. He failed the broker's exam on his first try, but passed on his second, and began searching for clients among friends and neighbors. Both the economy and the stock market were generally rising strongly in these years, creating profitable opportunities to uncover neglected stocks, as economic growth outpaced expectations. By the time Weill retired in 2003, the S&P 500, excluding reinvestment of dividends, had risen thirty times since the day he started as a broker.

Weill worked assiduously to cultivate clients and find stock market bargains. He left Bear Stearns to work at Burnham & Company, then larger than Bear, where he felt his prospects were better. He was now generating handsome commissions in an era of high fixed commissions on each trade (set by the New York Stock Exchange). But Weill always wanted to start his own company, like his father and grandfather; moreover, at the time, many new firms were being started. He and Joan moved to a small apartment in East Rockaway, Queens, at the end of a long subway ride on the A train. A neighbor in the apartment building, Arthur Carter, also harbored dreams of starting a brokerage firm. Carter already worked for Lehman Brothers, which afforded him the credibility and access to wealthy and influential people Weill sought. They found two other broker friends, Roger Berlind, who later became a successful Broadway producer, and Peter Potoma, whose Italian roots, they believed, would compensate in the eyes of the Wall Street establishment for their Jewish backgrounds. Each contributed $60,000 of personal and family money to buy a seat on the New York Stock Exchange in 1960 and they opened Carter, Berlind, Potoma & Weill that year.

This venture required more than a little patience, as they watched other friends buying fine new homes on Long Island's prestigious North Shore with their savings while Weill and his partners placed whatever extra they had into their company. The partners were energetic and committed, however, and acquired many new clients, including sports and show business celebrities. Weill was a highly persuasive salesman and early on acquired clients like Johnny Carson and Sonny Werblin, the owner of the New York Jets. Eventually, the firm gained a reputation for doing solid company research. Weill liked the nitty-gritty analysis and was good at poring over balance sheets.

By the mid-1960s, stocks were rising rapidly, and the firm was ready to expand. By then, Potoma had been the subject of a New York Stock Exchange investigation and in 1962 left the firm. In 1965 the remaining partners hired Arthur Levitt, Jr., a graduate of Williams College, whose father had been the state comptroller for many years. Levitt had wealthy connections and a winning, establishment style. They also hired Marshall Cogan, a fast-talking Harvard Business School graduate, who attracted institutional clients, particularly mutual funds, also often run by fellow B-school graduates, and built connections to the fast-growing conglomerates of the late 1960s. Arthur Carter, strong-minded, analytical, intelligent, and, if anything, overconfident, was the informal head of the firm and began developing investment banking business. In particular, one made larger competitors take notice. Saul Steinberg, still in his twenties, had in a few years built Leasco, a small computer leasing company, into an industry leader. Now he wanted to make a major acquisition and Weill's firm supplied him with an idea for a target: the much larger Reliance Insurance. With Carter, Berlind & Weill as one of his investment bankers (though more established underwriters got a larger share of the offering), Steinberg made a successful hostile bid for Reliance in the summer of 1968, stunning Wall Street. Weill's firm earned $750,000 in fees.

Moderate success was changing the partners. Carter pushed his authority to the limit and asked for a bigger share of the profits than the others. As friction grew, Berlind and Weill, with encouragement from Levitt, forced Carter out. Now Cogan was their main rainmaker, and they called the firm Cogan, Berlind, Weill & Levitt—CBWL for short. But they could not shed their reputation as uncouth Jewish outsiders. They now had fifty employees, but the Street derogatorily referred to them as Corned Beef With Lettuce. Reputation aside, they were earning a lot of money as the bull market gained strength, and Weill and Joan were able to move into a large home at last on the prestigious North Shore.

The excessive expansion of Wall Street during the bull market of the 1960s left many firms stretched thin as they neglected back-office documentation of orders. When stock prices began to fall in 1969 and into 1970, some one hundred member firms of the New York Stock Exchange went out of business or were acquired by others as revenue fell below overhead; many could not even tally their losses accurately. Because of Weill, CBWL had focused on accurate bookkeeping and close control of costs. Weill and a new employee, Frank Zarb, had built a state-of-the-art back office. This left CBWL in a position of strength and able to acquire former competitors. In this period of consolidation, Weill's strengths turned out to be invaluable.

Because Weill mastered the intricacies of the back office and the costs of operations, he could apply his knowledge of the numbers to CBWL's first coup, a takeover of the far larger Hayden Stone, which was now nearly failing as commissions sank. CBWL had already absorbed the old-line McDonnell & Co., with some twenty-six retail offices. Hayden Stone was nearly eighty years old, a "Waspy firm," as Weill had called it—the firm at which Joseph Kennedy, the father of JFK, had once worked—and had a customer base of wealthy individuals. Its likely demise during the bear market of 1970 frightened the Wall Street establishment, and a crisis com-

mittee, established by the NYSE and headed by the investment banker and
stock exchange board member Felix Rohatyn to monitor firms' finances,
was eager to find a buyer for Hayden. Weill was reluctant to attempt to buy
a company so much larger than his own, but Berlind urged the firm to go
ahead. Because Weill knew the costs of operations so well, he was chosen
to do the negotiating.

Hayden was in a weak bargaining position and Weill found that he
could be a tough negotiator. CBWL acquired twenty-eight offices and took
on some five hundred stockbrokers with fifty thousand customers, but
none of the firm's liabilities, which were absorbed by the NYSE to facilitate
the deal. The exchange also injected $7.6 million in cash into the combined
firm. Hayden Stone shareholders received new shares, and CBWL added
Hayden Stone's name to its own. The small fish swallowed the larger one,
the upstart run by men of little polish buying up the old-line traditionalists. In 1970, CBWL–Hayden Stone had $12 million in annual revenues,
compared to CBWL's $400,000 in 1960, and some $420 million in capital.

The partners immediately made plans to raise money through a public
share offering. "Going public" was still new for Wall Street firms. The first
to do so was the innovative partnership Donaldson Lufkin Jenrette, which
in 1970 had to convince the NYSE to change the rules in order for a public
firm to retain membership on the exchange. DLJ, run by three Harvard
Business School graduates, was glamorous and so widely respected that it
got its way, leaving the door open for the less prestigious Weill firm and
others as well. In mid-1971, CBWL–Hayden Stone successfully sold one
million shares to the public, 400,000 of which were owned by the four
partners. They announced before the deal they intended to cash in a portion of their shares immediately. After overcoming resistance from the
SEC, which looked askance at partners' selling shares while they raised
money from the public, the deal was approved, and the four partners each
pocketed more than $700,000 in cash. And CBWL–Hayden Stone had $7
million in new capital with which to expand.

With their sudden riches, Weill and Joan spent $500,000 on a
fourteen-room apartment on Fifth Avenue and 65th Street in Manhattan,
where, once they were ensconced, they threw a large party for the firm.
This, too, became a pattern for Weill. Frugal at first, he learned to live lavishly. He enjoyed chic hotels, big houses, and the best wines. Soon after the
CBWL–Hayden Stone offering, the stock market sank again, and the shareholders of the newly public company were already losing money. Weill and
his three colleagues had sold their shares just in time. Meanwhile, many
Hayden Stone brokers left the combined firm out of a mixture of pride,

humiliation, and probably anti-Semitism. But another reason they left was Weill's harsh cost cutting; he reduced the firm's expenses by half, firing hundreds of brokers and staff.

Weill was determined that the combined firm make money quickly to show the world he could manage the company. He didn't mind losing many Hayden brokers, but he worked hard to hold on to those he thought were valuable, who he knew were the true assets of the firm. CBWL–Hayden Stone willingly took on poor deals it should have avoided and sold offerings of questionable companies to the public that drew investigatory reviews from the SEC. Weill "would take almost anything that paid a commission," claimed one of Hayden Stone's brokers. Later, Weill blamed Marshall Cogan for the sale of shares of the dubious firms to the public, though he admits to questionable decisions himself. The most controversial of the firm's underwriting clients, Topper Toy Company, was his own. CBWL–Hayden Stone helped underwrite an offering of debt for the toy company but it turned out the CEO had grossly inflated sales; when this chicanery was uncovered in 1972, Topper Toy quickly folded. Underwriters are required to do due diligence on firms they sponsor and, even if they err about business prospects, at least the accounting should be aboveboard and reflect the firm's true sales. Moreover, Weill served on the board and bought shares himself. Two years later the SEC charged CBWL–Hayden Stone with violations of the securities laws. The American Stock Exchange also censured and fined CBWL–Hayden Stone. Weill pleaded ignorance. Finally, Weill's firm settled investor suits against it for a total of $1.7 million. Weill took a large personal loss on Topper Toy as well.

But CBWL–Hayden Stone survived in the bear markets of the early 1970s, the toughest business conditions Weill later said he had ever experienced. As he gained more power within the firm, largely managing the consolidation of Hayden Stone, his personal traits were less inhibited. He turned into a picky, scolding boss with a severe temper. He was sometimes a near hysteric, yelling across rooms at people, cursing at them, calling them "idiot" or "son of a bitch." The temper reflected an obsessive concern with details and his own nerve-racking drive to succeed. If an emergency arose in the firm—a loss on securities, a client complaining—he rushed to the broker's side and badgered his workers for information, explanations, and solutions. Anger was often his first reaction to any problem. Those co-workers who stayed with the firm learned to let these fits of anger pass, which they typically did—he often apologized afterward—but most people were scarred by them.

In early 1973, another prestigious firm, H. Hentz, more than a century old, Jewish in tradition and once run by Bernard Baruch, was on the brink of insolvency. An earlier deal had fallen through, and the New York Stock Exchange was eager to find a buyer. If not thriving, Hayden Stone was in the black with a positive cash flow at the time and the NYSE wanted it to absorb Hentz. Weill led the negotiations for the four partners. The combined operations doubled the number of retail salespeople and increased revenues by 50 percent. Weill's insecurity was so intense that an uncontrollable fear rose in him that the Hentz employees might steal stock certificates from the Hentz vault. He and a couple of colleagues ran over to empty the vault themselves. The takeover was completed by mid-1973, and Weill embarked on his customary round of intense cost cutting.

The acquisition of yet another retail firm specializing in brokerage business with individuals began to cause friction among the partners. Weill was always most comfortable with retail companies that sold understandable, straightforward securities to individuals. But he was not comfortable with the loftier business of investment banking, raising money for major companies from sophisticated financial institutions like large pension funds and insurance companies. Marshall Cogan had different ambitions, understanding that more profit could be made on big investment banking deals and he was generally more comfortable with fellow MBAs at major financial institutions. Finally, in a heated management confrontation, Cogan left under pressure from the other partners. Levitt and Berlind agreed Weill should take over as CEO, and among his first moves was to drop CBWL from the firm's name, burying, he hoped forever, Corned Beef With Lettuce. He also kept Cogan's assistant, Peter Cohen, twenty-six, an eager, energetic Columbia Business School graduate who was working for Hayden Stone when CBWL acquired it.

The tireless Cohen became Weill's key assistant, a fruitful but trying relationship due to Weill's temper, impatience, and constant demands, yet it would last, with one serious interruption, for fifteen years. The Hentz acquisition was "the turning point of my career," said Weill, who was running Hayden Stone on his own by then. "I was forty years old and it was time for me to see if I could do it."

The sharp demarcation in American finance, created by rising inflation and deep recession, played out uncomfortably on Wall Street for the rest of the decade. As we have seen, stock prices fell in 1974 and did not recover to former highs until the 1980s. Traditional stock brokerage and underwriting were no longer highly profitable businesses. Derivative contracts on commodities and interest rates were displacing stocks as enticing areas of opportunity, and as we have seen, mutual funds ventured into the money markets while real estate investment trusts were developed to invest in similar ways on property and buildings. The investment banks sought new business in mergers and acquisitions. Bank lending, led by Wriston at First National City, expanded rapidly, especially internationally. Weill, unlike most other traditional Wall Street CEOs, made an opportunity of bad times. Falling profits and rising insolvency on the Street served his principal skills well. His attention to costs continued to leave Hayden Stone in a position of relative strength while much of Wall Street foundered.

In the dire bear market of 1974, while other firms waited to see if the market turned up, Weill characteristically acted immediately. He cut salaries by 40 to 50 percent for much of the staff over two years—"a decision I regret to this day," he wrote later—including his own compensation and had to sell his Fifth Avenue apartment to make ends meet.

But cost cutting enabled him to take his next step. In 1974, Shearson Hamill, a far larger retail brokerage house, nearly seventy-five years old, was in desperate need of capital. Weill decided to stalk the larger prey again. The NYSE was on Weill's side, eager to avoid the collapse of the firm, fearing that if Shearson closed, others would fail along with it as shareholders sold their stock and creditors closed ranks. Hayden Stone was one of the few firms that could credibly make an offer. And Shearson enticed Weill. It had more retail offices than Hayden Stone and earned more in annual revenue. Due to Shearson's desperate condition, Weill was able to negotiate a low purchase price. Once he acquired the company, he let almost half of Shearson's employees go, some 1,200 people, mostly back-office workers. Shearson Hayden Stone, as Weill immediately named the new entity, was now the fifth largest brokerage firm in the financial industry, competing with Bache & Co., E.F. Hutton, and Merrill Lynch.

Weill had become the manager of adversity and his reputation for ruthlessness now spread rapidly. But he had defenders who insisted he was one of the few who understood the changing nature of the business and anticipated the end of fixed commissions, which had long been set by the NYSE at high levels, driving many large investors to reduce costs by making trades off the exchange at far lower commissions. Congress recognized that fixed commissions could not be maintained, despite intense support from brokerage firms, and passed a bill gradually outlawing them. On May 1, 1975, all brokerage commissions for NYSE member firms became negotiable. Weill's tight management and low costs now gave him a further advantage over his competitors. He could charge lower commissions than most of them and still turn a profit, and Shearson began winning market share.

With low brokerage commissions, a far more aggressive environment replaced the patrician world of Wall Street, more profit-minded and increasingly opportunistic, one well suited to Weill's managerial approach. He lost less money than most in 1974, and then set his sights on buying an old-line investment banking house. With his large retail operation, Weill believed he held an edge on other firms because he could sell offerings to so many individual clients. In 1977, he approached the investment banking partnership Kuhn Loeb, a long-standing member of the elite German-Jewish Wall Street establishment, called "Our Crowd," by Stephen Birmingham in his 1967 book of that title. Though Kuhn Loeb was struggling to survive, the partners rejected Weill's bids and sold out to a larger and better-heeled member of Our Crowd, Lehman Brothers.

Weill took the rejection personally, as he did most matters, his insecurities easily aroused. Some of his key employees were leaving. Arthur Levitt, who served as president, left the firm to become president of the American Stock Exchange. Frank Zarb, who had left to join Nixon's administration and then returned, now left again to become a partner at Lazard Frères (his stint with Nixon having raised his profile and expanded his contacts). In that same year, Weill also lost Peter Cohen, the aide he had so depended on to watch over the details of his strategies. Cohen had simply had enough of Weill's constant demands (which included buying Weill's son a college wardrobe), and when Levitt left, and Cohen was not offered the presidency of the firm, he accepted a key job with the wealthy Lebanese banker Edmond Safra, who controlled Republic National Bank. At Cohen's farewell party, a hurt Weill told a group of people Cohen was a "traitor," and the party abruptly ended.

Stock prices began to rise steadily again in 1978, though they still did not reach the peaks of the early 1970s. Many traditional securities firms, especially those with back-office troubles, continued to suffer. At Shearson, however, profits tripled in 1978 to nearly $6.5 million. Weill by now had a modest war chest, and the strains at so many Wall Street firms provided him a chance to acquire a prestigious investment banking house.

The following year, another old-line firm, Loeb Rhoades, run by John Loeb, one of the crown princes of Our Crowd, who was married to a Lehman, was teetering on the brink. It had acquired Hornblower, Weeks, a retail firm, in late 1977, in an attempt to broaden the firm's revenues, but the merger of the two culturally different firms—an investment house and a retail operation—proved unmanageable. Loeb Rhoades, founded in 1931 by Loeb himself, lost a lot of money in 1978 and Loeb felt he had no other choice. Loeb, now in his mid-seventies, was open to a bid even from an upstart like Weill and he approached the younger man to inquire about his interest. Weill needed Peter Cohen back to handle the endless details of the possible merger, and invited him and his wife to Passover dinner. When determined, Weill, the talented salesman, was persuasive, and he convinced Cohen to return. Once Cohen agreed, Weill set about acquiring Loeb Rhoades. Negotiations culminated in May 1979 at Weill's new estate in Greenwich, Connecticut.

Shearson Hayden Stone paid roughly $90 million in shares to Loeb Rhoades' partners. Weill became the CEO of the new entity, John Loeb taking a titular role as chairman. Loeb held the most shares but Weill had 5 percent of the merged firm. It was one of the largest mergers in Wall Street's history, the combined capital now some $250 million. The two firms were of equal size in terms of employees and offices, thus Shearson doubled again with the takeover. And the merger was an instant success. Weill cut about 20 percent of the workforce, and profits reached $56 million in 1980, compared to $20 million for Shearson the year before. Shearson's stock price rose from $10 in 1979 when the deal was struck to $37 in 1980. And Weill was now running the second largest brokerage firm in America, behind only Merrill Lynch. He sat atop an industry that in a decade of change was transformed from an enclave of smaller entrepreneurial firms to dominance by a handful of giant entities. With the Loeb Rhoades merger, Weill's personal shares in the company were now worth $15 million.

Weill now liked being a major player, and also believed that only the big would survive, so he continued to think about further acquisitions. (His personal wealth would rise with the size of his firm as well.) Insurance attracted his attention. In some states, especially New York, insurance companies were subject to more stringent regulations than financial firms. But why shouldn't stockbrokers sell insurance also? Walter Wriston had asked the same question. The acquisition of a giant insurance company, many of which had deep wells of unused cash, and whose cash flow grew at predictable rates, could triple or quadruple the size of Shearson. A few years earlier, Weill had approached Orion, a midsized insurance company based in New Jersey, but the insurance company chairman said cross-selling of stocks and insurance wouldn't work and serious talks were never begun.

A more exciting possibility was forming in Weill's mind: a combination with the credit card giant American Express, which also owned Fireman's Fund, mostly a property and casualty company. An independent investment banker named Salim Lewis approached Weill with the possibility of linking with Lewis's friend James Robinson III, CEO of American Express. "Visions of brokers selling credit cards and insurance danced in my head alongside the notion of trolling American Express's vast customer base for new brokerage clients," Weill wrote. Amex presented the ultimate fantasy in cross-selling synergies. At the time, it was also one of America's most respected companies—its credit card a status symbol—and one of America's most recognizable brand names. Moreover, American Express had $20 billion in assets; Weill's Shearson Loeb Rhoades had $2.5 billion. Even Weill knew he couldn't take over American Express, but the benefits of a combination were so great that he was willing to sell Shearson and accept a role secondary to Robinson's. Shearson Loeb Rhoades shareholders could make a substantial profit on the sale, as could Weill personally. It was a sign of the changing times that American Express may have been willing to acquire Shearson Loeb Rhoades, run largely by Jewish newcomers (though Weill had added former president Gerald Ford to his board). Robinson believed that in the expanding world of finance he had to make American Express a corporate titan that offered all major financial services. In finance, too, size now became strategy. In Shearson, Robinson saw a tightly run firm that generated nearly $60 million in profits. An international financial conglomerate that stood in no one's shadow would be his legacy.

Negotiations between Robinson and Weill got under way, but by Weill's timetable they were going slowly. Suddenly, Prudential Insurance, one of America's largest companies—it managed $20 billion in investments, more than any other firm in the nation—announced in March 1981 that it had agreed to buy the brokerage firm Bache Halsey Stuart Shields & Co. Bache feared an unfriendly acquisition attempt by the wealthy Belzberg brothers of Canada, whose fortune was made in real estate; the Belzbergs already owned a substantial portion of the company and had demanded seats on its board of directors. Bache saw in Prudential a friendly buyer. And there was no fear of regulatory resistance from the Reagan White House.

Weill was in Japan when the Bache news was announced. He immediately called Peter Cohen, who was traveling in Israel. "This will change the face of business," Weill told him. "We need to do something." He then told Cohen about his idea to merge with American Express. "It's a home run," Cohen replied immediately. Robinson, too, felt a rush of urgency when he heard of the Prudential offer.

The merger between Shearson Loeb Rhoades and American Express was approved in the late spring. American Express exchanged a little more than one of its shares for each Shearson share, bringing the total price of Shearson close to an astonishing $1 billion. Shearson stock was at $34 before the merger was announced and topped out at $65 shortly thereafter. On paper, Weill's shares were worth roughly $30 million, making him the largest shareholder in the new AmEx, with many times the shares that Robinson had.

One large merger had provoked another. That followed in industry after industry in a new decade of hands-off antitrust regulation. Sears, the giant retailer, bought Dean Witter, and Bank of America bought the discount stock brokerage firm Schwab & Co. The story all these executives told themselves was the same one that misled Wriston—one-stop shopping for all kinds of investment services would be the future of finance. That banking, insurance, and securities products were inherently different, sold in different ways, and bought by different people did not deter them.

Weill knew he would not be in charge of the new AmEx, but he expected to be second in command. From that position, he and his Shearson colleagues were certain he would eventually be able to achieve the top position, outmaneuvering the slower-moving executives at American Express. Wary of Weill's ambition, however, Robinson and his top executives gave him a nonoperating position at the firm. Even when he was promoted to president two years later, his duties were circumscribed. He had no authority to make a major decision without Robinson's approval, and he had earlier relinquished control of Shearson to Peter Cohen, his deputy, who had been named its CEO. Weill was not talented at bureaucratic management; his style—personal, abrupt, and involving minimal planning or paperwork—was hardly suited to the American Express establishment. Robinson was the son and grandson of prominent Atlanta bankers and had a Harvard MBA. Cohen, short and unimposing, had an MBA from Columbia. Weill was treated like an outsider.

Weill's strong suit was acquisitions, however, and he proposed several new ones to American Express as a way to establish his power base at the firm. One was the Minneapolis mutual fund firm Investors Diversified Services, which sold investments to middle-income clients through a large door-to-door sales force. The IDS people were "the Avon ladies and Fuller brush men of financial services," as one Weill chronicler put it, and the firm was not sufficiently prestigious for the American Express executives. But Weill was so determined to make his mark that he was willing to offer an unusually high price for IDS, unlike his hard bargaining when he ran his own companies. Influenced by Cohen, Robinson and the board refused to agree to Weill's $1 billion proposal. He was furious at Cohen's "disloyalty," but in 1984 Cohen, who thought IDS an attractive business at the right price, finally put together a deal for 25 percent less money.

In the meantime, the Fireman's Fund began losing money in 1983. It was a blemish on Robinson's record and losses there affected the American Express stock price. Weill was the one executive Robinson had who knew how to fire people, trim the company, and perhaps turn it around, and Weill eagerly took the reins. With his new key aide, Jamie Dimon, Weill moved to San Francisco, where Fireman's was headquartered, knowing full well that by leaving New York he was weakening his own position in the company, though he commuted home every weekend.

Weill had hired Dimon in 1982. He was the son of a successful former Shearson broker with whom Weill and his wife had become friends. Weill had known Jamie as a teenager and once gave him a summer intern job when he was a student at Tufts before he went to Harvard Business School. Dimon admired Weill, who to him was both uncle and mentor. With Cohen occupied at Shearson, Weill needed someone to run the numbers and flesh out his general plans. The Weill who had once pored over financial statements seemed no longer to have the time or interest. As one associate said, "Sandy was not a detail guy at all. He would get a conceptual grasp of the issue, move on to the concept, and leave the details to all sorts of other people. Ultimately, the details had to match his thinking."

Weill did what he knew how to do best at Fireman's. He cut 15 percent of the workforce and lopped off many operations, and the San Francisco press excoriated him for the ruthlessness for which he was now well known. When Fireman's began showing a profit, Robinson and his new number two, Louis Gerstner, wanted to sell it. Weill, at Dimon's urging, offered a leveraged buyout with Warren Buffett's financial help. The American Express board—according to the proposal, American Express would have retained 40 percent of the company—turned down the offer, possibly out of hostility toward Weill. The board had grown tired of Weill; many actively disliked him and did not want to have an ongoing relationship. His main rival, Gerstner, a former McKinsey consultant and Harvard MBA, who was the more likely successor to Robinson, did not want to keep Fireman's either and was ill-disposed toward Weill as well. American Express sold Fireman's Fund in 1990.

Weill knew he could soon be forced out of American Express, and

Peter Cohen's rising star made it more likely. Cohen had been seething since Weill failed to get him a seat on the American Express board. He clashed frequently with Weill, and successfully kept him from interfering with how Cohen handled Shearson. He now proposed to Robinson and the board that they buy one of the last of the Our Crowd firms, Lehman Kuhn Loeb. Lehman Brothers and Kuhn Loeb, recently merged, could not make the combination work. As with many of the traditional firms, costs were out of line. In the case of Lehman, feuds among partners had been vitriolic. The firm had little choice but to seek a buyer. Cohen negotiated a price of $380 million, one Weill thought far too high for a firm with so much internal friction. To Cohen, however, Weill's criticism seemed like sour grapes; here was the large prestigious investment banking arm that had always eluded Shearson. The agreement to buy Lehman Kuhn Loeb was reached in April 1984.

After American Express turned down Weill's offer for Fireman's Fund, they halfheartedly offered him ways to stay on, which would have left Weill well outside the mainstream of the business and further humiliated. Weill now fully realized they wanted him out. He had in fact been selling his stock for a while. He decided to resign, and at a final press conference, he said, "Whatever I do next, I will want to be the top person." In 1985, he was out of a job.

In 1985 and 1986, still in his early fifties, with an estimated $50 million in net worth, substantial but not nearly enough to lift him into the Forbes 400 list of richest Americans, Weill turned some of his energy to charities, including the refurbishment of Carnegie Hall in New York City.

But his business ambition was hardly satisfied. He set up an office with Dimon in the Seagram Building on Park Avenue, upstairs from his favorite lunchtime restaurant, the Four Seasons, and kept looking actively for takeover candidates. Bank of America was now struggling, like Citicorp and other large commercial banks, with rising losses on bad loans to Latin America, and Weill saw a chance to take it over. He even lined up financing from his old firm, Shearson, where, despite Cohen's rancor, he still had contacts. But Bank of America turned down the offer, and Weill would not consider a hostile bid.

He now lowered his sights significantly. An article in *Fortune* praising his managerial abilities piqued the interest of two executives at Commercial Credit Corp., a large consumer finance company in Baltimore that was foundering as a subsidiary of the computer company Control Data. Commercial Credit made small loans to lower-wage consumers at high interest rates from hundreds of storefront offices around the country. In one of the many odd pairings of the late 1960s, Control Data, once a daring and innovative technology company, bought Commercial Credit to help it lease its computers. As competition from IBM overwhelmed Control Data, it wound up borrowing funds from the CCC subsidiary, draining it of resources. The two CCC executives, worried about the company's future, nervously called Weill at his office and were stunned to get him on the phone immediately. Weill had once looked over the books of CCC for American Express, but deemed it unworthy. It had some $1 billion in annual revenues, hardly a small company, but was no longer one of the larger firms in the industry. It was also far from the sort of prestigious businesses American Express liked, a business widely thought of as exploiting lower-income workers. But now he had a new perspective and different objectives.

He instructed Dimon to research the consumer finance business and Dimon found it fragmented, profitable, and, most attractive, largely unregulated by Washington. If either was worried about whether CCC exploited poorer Americans by encouraging them to take high-cost loans, they did not hesitate. CCC was underperforming the industry benchmarks and Weill and Dimon realized they could pull off an impressive earnings turnaround. Weill knew there would be snickering on Wall Street if he took over such an unprestigious company, but he saw it as the vehicle for his return. He had the temerity to try to build not merely a company in a second-tier business, but a second-tier company in that business—and this distinguished him from many of his peers. Control Data, eager to unload the company, made a deal to spin it off and give control to Weill, who then prepared it for an initial public offering, the first sale of a company's stock to the public. As usual, Weill worked quickly and it turned out to be one of the largest IPOs yet, raising nearly $900 million, enough to pay the $600 million promised to Control Data and leaving $300 million to reinvest in the company. To show his confidence in CCC's future, Weill invested more than $5 million of his own money—only an estimated 10 percent of his net worth, but more than enough to impress the employees of the firm.

The deal was completed in October 1986 and Weill and his staff moved themselves to Baltimore, returning home only on weekends. By December he had fired 125 people from the corporate staff and soon fired a total of 2,000. He found it unbearable that the employees left work at 5 P.M., and he soon stopped that. He took away the free executive cars, the free daily

Wall Street Journals, and the earned vacation time not used. He also ended the program that paid the medical expenses of retirees, many of whom retired before they were eligible for Medicare. He commandeered the $50 million surplus in the pension fund to help generate a profit in 1987. To motivate workers, he ended bonuses for the lowest performing salesmen and offered as much as 100 percent bonuses to the best performers. "The work ethic of employees was a huge issue," he wrote, "but we soon found more evidence of an alien socialist corporate culture." What Weill angrily called "socialist" was a program at CCC for leasing automobiles to former prison inmates who were now on parole. Weill ended that.

All the while, he and his key executives feasted every night in the restaurant of the best hotel in Baltimore, eating its most expensive food and drinking its most expensive wine. He started controlling his tirades better, but few were entirely spared his temper and his humiliating behavior. With Dimon by his side, his cost cutting increased the bottom line. The company earned $10.8 million in 1985 before the takeover, $37.7 million in 1986 (Weill took over late that year), and $101.5 million in 1987, his first full year in control. Weill had gained the trust of shareholders and the stock price rose rapidly in the strong 1980s bull market, stopped only temporarily by the October 1987 market crash.

Because profits were so strong and Commercial Credit's stock relatively high, Weill was in a position to bid for another brokerage firm. The October crash devastated one firm after another but had hurt consumer finance far less than the securities business. As a result, there were bargains to be had. He first sought to buy E.F. Hutton but he was outbid by Peter Cohen, still at the helm of Shearson Lehman and still reporting to Jim Robinson. Again, as with Lehman, Weill felt Cohen overpaid. But another firm, Smith Barney, a venerable and unaggressive company with two thousand brokers, was for sale. It had been bought by Gerald Tsai less than a year earlier. Tsai was a star money manager in the "go-go" 1960s, founder of the Manhattan Fund, which rode the stunning bull market of that time by investing in future growth companies. The Manhattan Fund went under after the 1969–1970 market crash, but Tsai, who had already sold out of it, started another financial firm, which he quickly sold to American Can Co., which itself was trying to diversify away from its core manufacturing business, a popular business strategy for manufacturers at the time. By the early 1980s, Tsai was an executive at the company, holding a large part of its stock. His specific assignment was to diversify further, and he moved boldly into new arenas. He sold some of the manufacturing operations, and bought retail companies like record chain Sam Goody and the Coronado, the hotel in San Diego where the Marilyn Monroe movie *Some Like It Hot* was filmed. He became CEO in 1987 and changed the company's name from American Can to Primerica. Then, near the market high in May of that year, he bought the sleepy brokerage firm Smith Barney for $750 million, much of the money borrowed.

Smith Barney was not in any position to withstand the October market crash only a few months later. It lost $93 million in 1987 and more than $50 million in 1988 and Tsai was desperate for a buyer. Weill wanted only Smith Barney, but he agreed to buy all of Primerica for $1.7 billion, mostly for Commercial Credit stock. Primerica included a profitable life insurance company, A.L. Williams, and a large struggling mail order business, Fingerhut.

Once again, it was the minnow swallowing the big fish. Primerica had 25,000 employees and nearly $14 billion in assets compared to CCC's 3,700 employees and $4.4 billion in assets. And once again, Weill adopted the target's name, Primerica. He was back in his element. At his first meeting with Smith Barney, he told the partners that most of them were overrated. When a Smith Barney executive later told him that the meeting did not go well, Weill went into a tirade, calling the Smith Barney workers "a bunch of goddamn babies." Weill cut costs and made it clear that if the brokerage sales staff did not raise their sales volume significantly, they would be fired. He also began to sell other operations of Primerica. Weill conveyed the impression that his single-minded cost cutting was necessary and almost always benefited the bottom line; only fat was cut. But the A.L. Williams sales force reacted badly to what they saw as Weill's imperious cost cutting and the way he set explicit sales targets, and in the first two years, sales plummeted until new incentives were in place. The other Primerica businesses did well enough to compensate for Williams, however.

For Weill, there was a double standard about expenses. At an executive retreat in 1990, Dimon was going over the costs of Primerica. The first of the categories he examined on the alphabetical list was aviation. Weill's private plane, Dimon pointed out, with its full staff, was very costly. According to one biographer, Weill leaped off his couch and screamed, "If I don't have that many people, the plane will crash. Why do we have to pick on aviation?" "Sandy, because aviation starts with A," Dimon answered. Weill, who had ended first-class travel for almost everyone else when he took over Smith Barney, kept his plane. The executives called him the "imperial chairman."

His perquisites notwithstanding, Weill's approach generated profits overall at the firm, and he also enjoyed the good fortune of a strong bull market, which paused only relatively briefly when the nation entered a moderate recession in 1990. Smith Barney's profits rose rapidly, and the Primerica stock price increased 33 percent from $21 to $28 in 1989 alone, and reached into the $40s a year later. (In this period, he also bought sixteen branch offices from the now defunct Drexel Burnham at a bargain price.) *Fortune* reported that Weill had found his "green thumb." *Business Week* put him on its cover with a headline proclaiming "Sandy Weill Roars Back." One of Weill's executives explained the strategy for the *Harvard Business Review:* "We're operations people. Our heroes have been those who cut costs, who increase margins, and who run a tight ship. For the most part, our talented people are not marketing people, not new product people, but operating people." It was on tightly run operations, rather than on new products or innovative ideas, that many of the billionaires of the age of greed made their fortunes. Mostly, Wall Street admired Weill. He generated earnings and higher stock prices; he made them money.

Weill was of course soon prepared to make new acquisitions. He considered an offer for Kidder Peabody, the brokerage firm that had caused enormous problems for Jack Welch. But he and Welch couldn't agree on a deal. Then Weill was told by an investment banker friend, Bob Greenhill, the M&A pioneer, that Travelers Insurance, one of the largest insurance companies in the nation, was looking for financial support. Though Weill liked the stability of earnings that a well-run insurance company could provide, Travelers was losing ground, a "wounded" company, as he put it, and it was asking too much money for its operations. Then, Hurricane Andrew hit Florida and Travelers was in more desperate need of financial help. Now a bargain might be struck. The management quickly agreed to sell a substantial minority portion of the company to Weill for $700 million, and Weill and Dimon took seats on the board. Weill reasoned that if he and Jamie liked what they saw, they could someday buy all of Travelers.

By 1992, Weill had multiplied the earnings of Commercial Credit by ten times to $500 million, through acquisitions, cost cutting, and stern managerial practices. "He always wanted to be king of the world," said one Lehman banker. But he was not there yet, and the Weill zest for cutting costs had few limits. In 1992, even as the company generated enormous profits, he forced American Can retirees to pay for their own health insurance, canceling the former retirement plan (a replay of his earlier efforts at CCC), since a new regulation required companies to charge a part of the future costs of health care benefits payments to their earnings. Other companies had also cut the benefits, but more companies continued to keep their promises to workers. Weill saved the company $8.7 million by eliminating the health care benefits; he paid himself a total of $13 million that year.

Despite the improving stock market, Shearson Lehman, still run by Peter Cohen, was suffering. The company had not only been damaged by the 1987 crash but it had also taken on high levels of debt to grow, including the costly acquisition of E.F. Hutton. Cohen also became entangled in the takeover wave of the late 1980s that was dominating the headlines and making glamorous, wealthy people of takeover and LBO leaders like Mike Milken, Henry Kravis, George Roberts, Teddy Forstmann, and some investment bankers like Bruce Wasserstein of First Boston. Cohen wanted to compete at this level and reached too far. Shearson ended up on the losing side of the tumultuous $26 billion takeover battle for RJR Nabisco. The publicity tarnished Shearson American Express further and Robinson finally fired Cohen. In all, Shearson had lost nearly $100 million in 1991 and more in 1992. American Express was also suffering from increased competition for its core credit card business from MasterCard and Visa. Harvey Golub, whom Weill had helped make head of IDS, the Minneapolis firm American Express ultimately acquired, had been named president of the parent company in 1991, pushing Robinson upstairs. By early 1993, Robinson was gone and Golub was running it all.

Weill approached Golub to talk about buying Shearson back, and, with American Express in trouble, they quickly came to terms. In the spring of 1993, Weill paid $1 billion for the brokerage services, but didn't want Lehman, where there was still managerial turmoil. It was more than a small victory, Weill's winning back his old firm on his own terms. When the announcement was made, *The New York Times* headline read, "Building a Wall Street Empire, Again." Weill had sold Shearson for about $930 million in 1981 and was buying back a firm with many more salesmen and branch offices for just a little more money. His new firm could almost compete shoulder to shoulder with giant Merrill Lynch. Weill's shares in Primerica were now worth $100 million.

Weill did not yet have an investment banking presence, but with Shearson and Smith Barney combined, he felt he had a sufficiently strong sales base on which to build a first-tier investment banking operation almost from scratch. He hired his friend Bob Greenhill, the investment banker who got Morgan Stanley to break the code of honor and manage hostile takeovers back in the 1970s. Greenhill was trim, a sportsman, an experienced pilot, flamboyant, fast-talking, and sharply dressed. Weill was inarticulate, overweight, and did nothing more daring than hit a tennis ball, though he did that well. To hire the nearly legendary Greenhill, who had fallen from grace at Morgan, where he lost a power struggle to run the company, was a feather in Weill's cap. "World-class" was the word Sandy and others liked to use in talking about Greenhill and the new role investment banking would have in their firm. The hard-nosed Weill had developed an Achilles' heel as he got more established: he was susceptible to glamour. It was the same sort of unconsidered instinct that led him to hire Bob Rubin when he left the Treasury, and to offer Tim Geithner, the New York Federal Reserve president, the CEO position at Citigroup a decade later.

Greenhill brought in a big client right away, Viacom, which had purchased Paramount Communications (formerly Paramount Pictures). But there were few after that. He spent lavishly on new hires from Morgan Stanley and on his personal expenses; he had negotiated an exorbitant compensation agreement with Weill at the start. But Smith Barney Shearson did not break into the ranks of serious investment banking. Greenhill's poor managerial abilities and his excessive spending particularly irked Dimon, who was now the chief operating officer of the securities subsidiary. Weill was hard on everyone, even Dimon, his capable protégé, but not on his flashy superstar. Dimon's complaints about Greenhill, though they turned out to be right, began to irritate Weill.

According to their plan, Weill and Dimon, as minority shareholders, were analyzing the potential at Travelers. As aggressive members of the board, they induced Ed Budd, Travelers' CEO, to fire thousands of employees and Travelers profits began rising. Weill now decided he wanted to buy Travelers outright because he saw so much wasteful spending there. Such an acquisition would make Primerica one of the largest financial companies in the world. Primerica stock was now high, around $100 a share, making a purchase with an exchange of stock practical, and Budd was eager to sell. The marketing-savvy Weill also understood that the Travelers logo, the red umbrella, was one of the best-known symbols in the nation. (Once the merger was completed, he wore a red umbrella pin on his lapel every day.)

The Travelers CEO agreed to terms after only a few meetings with Weill. The $4.2 billion acquisition was consummated in the fall of 1993, less than a year after Weill first entered talks to buy Shearson back. Weill quickly renamed the company The Travelers, as he had done time and again after an acquisition, and moved into its downtown headquarters. The acquisition doubled the company's assets. Along the way, Weill also bought a large, complementary insurance subsidiary from Aetna.

Remarkably, Weill had a major position in both the securities and insurance business almost overnight. Stocks had started to rise rapidly after a hiatus in 1994, and Travelers was carried along with the tide, and then some. It was the Clinton boom and the era of Greenspan's easy monetary policy. Weill was in an excellent position to make still more mergers. He knew he was missing two or three major pieces to complete his empire and his ambition was relentless.

In early 1996, Bob Greenhill finally left the firm, not wanted any longer even by Weill. Dimon was vindicated, and at forty was named head of the brokerage subsidiary, but he had to deal with a larger problem that could affect his future. Weill wanted both his children to work for his firm. Marc, his son, was a senior vice president at the company, and would later have problems with drugs. But his daughter, Jessica, married to an architect Weill used to redo some of the company offices, was an intelligent and strong-minded businesswoman who had formerly run the marketing department of other mutual fund operations and was given the Travelers mutual funds division to manage. Sales in the division had been mediocre, however, and Jessica wanted to pay her sales force higher commissions; she saw it as a sales problem. Dimon, her direct boss, thought improving the investment performance of the funds, which had been poor, was the solution. A year later, escalating friction with Dimon caused Jessica to leave the firm against her father's wishes. Thus, a permanent wedge was lodged between Weill and his invaluable aide, Dimon. Weill later tried to minimize the issue over Jessica, claiming that "Jessica was a sideshow in my deteriorating relationship with Jamie."

The bull markets in stocks of 1995 and 1996 led to more underwriting and still larger mergers. But Shearson Smith Barney had only a minor investment banking operation. It also had little international business, even though capital flowed in ever greater volumes across borders. Since investment and corporate clients were now located all over the globe, securities firms like Salomon and Goldman were earning enormous profits trading global fixed income and equity securities and currencies. They also had aggressive trading departments that specialized in derivatives, turning themselves into virtual hedge funds. The stock market delivered the message. Travelers was missing out on major sources of growth; its price-earnings multiple was low compared to other major financial services operations.

Then in early 1997, Morgan Stanley merged with the retail firm Dean Witter. Shearson Smith Barney was in danger of becoming the only large brokerage firm with no significant international presence. Weill's impatience with the missing links in his operation, despite its enormous size, now turned to alarm. "The announcement shook me thoroughly," he wrote. Again, mergers drove others to make still bigger mergers in an ever-widening circle.

Earlier that year, Weill and Dimon approached J.P. Morgan to inquire about their interest in a possible merger with Travelers. J.P. Morgan was posting mediocre results. This time, for a change, Travelers was the bigger firm. But there was at least one obstacle, the New Deal Glass-Steagall Act, which legally separated insurance, commercial banking, and investment banking. Weill was determined to make such a combination work, and the Dean Witter acquisition made him all the more impatient. His law firm, Wachtell Lipton, suggested there might be a way to merge with J.P. Morgan if the Federal Reserve would agree not to undo the merger immediately but grant a two-to-five-year window while the merger was reviewed. Meantime, Weill and his lawyers worked on the Fed and Congress to change the Glass-Steagall restrictions on the insurance-banking combination. In these times, under a sympathetic Democratic president and a free market Fed chairman, Weill had every reason to be optimistic; Glass-Steagall had already almost entirely undone the prohibition on investment banking for commercial banks. Weill went to visit Greenspan, who agreed that the Fed would grant a waiting period, but could promise nothing beyond that. It was opening enough for Weill.

There was another significant obstacle. J.P. Morgan's chairman, Douglas Warner III, was deeply uncomfortable with the merger. He told Weill repeatedly that the two institutions had different "cultures." The message was clear: Weill was an upstart, Morgan an elegant old company with historic roots. Warner proposed such an impractically high price that Weill knew the deal was dead. Even Dimon, less thin-skinned than Weill, was incensed at the way they were treated.

Soon after, however, Deryck Maughan, the CEO of Salomon Brothers, appointed by Warren Buffett during the Paul Mozer scandal, called Weill. Salomon was for sale. Weill knew and liked the articulate, British-born investment banker. Years earlier he had asked Maughan to join the board of Carnegie Hall, where Weill had been serving as chairman. Weill knew that Salomon had been at the forefront of trading innovations for decades and that its mortgage-backed securities business and arbitrage operations were among the most profitable on Wall Street. But Maughan had been trying to change the mix of business at Salomon. He was less dependent on risky trading profits than in Meriwether's years, but the trading operation still accounted for half of the firm's profits and could eat swiftly through capital. Maughan was determined to build a first-tier investment banking group, and linking with Weill's retail operations and large capital base could make the difference.

Weill was immediately intrigued, but wanted to get a firmer grasp of how risky Salomon's trading was. He sent Dimon to study the trading operations firsthand. Dimon was more impressed than he anticipated, and concluded that big losses could be contained. Weill also visited the credit rating agencies, which confirmed that the merger would not damage Travelers' ratings. But once the merger was final, Weill did not put Dimon in charge, as he had expected. He decreed that Dimon share CEO duties with Maughan, whom Dimon thought an ineffectual manager, more concerned with polish and image than results. Dimon's relationship with Weill had already been deteriorating badly but now Dimon was incensed, though he swallowed his pride and accepted the co-CEO position.

The deal was announced in September 1997 for $9 billion in stock, the new Travelers subsidiary to be called Salomon Smith Barney. Three weeks later, the Asian financial crisis struck. "I am not sure we ever really enjoyed a honeymoon with Salomon Brothers," wrote Weill. In October, Salomon lost $50 million almost overnight. Then the risk arbitrage department got stuck on the wrong side of a major investment, and lost $100 million, when British Telecommunications pulled out of a deal to acquire MCI. (LTCM made a similar wrong bet, as did many others on the Street.)

Alarmed by such swift losses, Weill immediately began to limit the exposure of the trading desks at Salomon. He didn't have the stomach for the kind of risk trading that was now common at hedge funds and the largest investment banks, but he did not yet eliminate Salomon's famed arbitrage desk, the one started by John Meriwether. Even with Salomon's losses, the other operations at Travelers held up, and the price of Travelers' stock rose nearly 80 percent as stock prices resumed climbing in 1998. He was ready to do more deals.

With his stock strong, and Salomon absorbed, Weill was on the hunt again. By 1997, Citicorp had risen from the ashes at the start of the decade to become the most successful bank of its time. John Reed, its chairman, had been thinking about a merger; he believed his businesses were still not as stable as he would have liked, and he also thought he needed still greater exposure globally. He had ridden out the serious failures at Citicorp, particularly the devastating loan losses in developing nations in the 1980s, which continued to take a toll through the end of the decade, and then followed by real estate losses as the 1990s began. At one point in 1990, Citicorp's prospects were so poor that Reed hoped J.P. Morgan would buy it. Some of the ventures he initiated also failed, including his purchase of Quotron, the electronic stock quote terminal company, investments in consumer banking, and lending for LBOs. Citicorp's troubles had once almost seemed terminal: the company lost nearly half a billion dollars in the recession of 1991. But with the economic expansion in 1994, Citicorp rebounded, earning a record $3.5 billion in 1995. Reed's next goal was to build a still greater consumer brand for the company, making Citicorp, he said, the equivalent of Coca-Cola or McDonald's to customers around the world.

Reed was a thoughtful, intellectual CEO and in most ways the opposite of Weill. He wrote long memos and regularly held staff meetings. But he admired the Travelers chairman's energy and daring, sought the stability a large insurance company could provide, and also wanted to be much larger. In 1998, Citicorp and Travelers were valued about equally in the stock market, and when, in February 1998, Weill approached Reed about a possible merger, Reed was ready to talk. It may have helped that Reed lost money toward the end of 1997 in the Asian market turmoil, undermining some of the confidence he gained from the successes of the prior three years.

Weill wrote in his autobiography about his first formal meeting with Reed: "I launched into a monologue on why the Citicorp and Travelers franchises would complement one another and played up how a merger would be an ideal marriage of product and distribution while offering market positions and financial strength that would be the envy of our competitors." No surprise, he emphasized one-stop shopping: how Travelers could benefit from Citicorp's hundreds of thousands of credit card customers by selling them stock, mutual funds, and annuities. Citicorp could sell its checking services and credit cards through Travelers stockbrokers and insurance salespeople. In turn, Citicorp would be able to provide its corporate lending clients underwriting services and M&A advice from

Salomon Smith Barney, which would profit from the new loan clients Citi-
corp would bring to the investment bank. In terms of geographical reach,
Travelers was everywhere in America, while Citicorp was concentrated in
New York. And Citicorp had the international reach Travelers lacked.

There was one remaining impediment, Glass-Steagall. Weill had already
tested a J.P. Morgan merger on Greenspan, proposing the two companies
could combine and operate legally for two years, awaiting a ruling and
working on changing the law. Weill had access to the Fed chairman. But
Reed and his legal staff were skeptical that the New Deal restriction could
be so easily circumvented.

Weill, the nonintellectual, had a better sense of the political direction
than did Reed, and perhaps of his own influence on Congress and the presidential advisers. The loosening of New Deal regulations restricting banks
had been under way for a long time and was now nearly complete. Increasingly, the media supported it. The changes included the complete elimina-
tion of Regulation Q restrictions in 1982 by Congress; the Fed's granting
permission in 1987 for banks to underwrite commercial paper, municipal
bonds, and mortgage-backed securities; the Fed's loosening of restrictions to enable commercial banks to underwrite equities up to 25 percent
of business in 1989; and the refusal by Congress and President Clinton in
both 1994 and 1999 to regulate derivatives. Since the 1980s, Bankers Trust, a
commercial bank, had almost transformed itself completely into an investment bank, creating and trading in derivatives, and using basic complex
transactions known as swaps to enable corporate clients and municipalities
to manage their liabilities and reduce interest rates. In 1985, financial lobbying also took a major step forward, with the creation of the International
Swap Dealers Association, to ward off the establishment of new regulations. It only got more powerful in the 1990s, adding the word "derivatives"
to its name. Weill was a key supporter.

The argument the bankers like Weill made in favor of deregulation
was twofold. There was now an effective SEC overseeing securities underwriting and trading, the private ratings agencies were sophisticated, and
investors themselves were knowledgeable. The second argument was that
international competition forced banks to offer all services under one roof
and build enormous assets to compete and survive; Glass-Steagall was
therefore a dinosaur.

More important, Weill had Greenspan on his side. Once Reed agreed
to explore the issue with his lawyers, Weill called Greenspan and set up a
meeting for the three of them the following week. With their two general

counsels, Reed and Weill visited the Fed by the back door to avoid journalists. Being seen together would have amounted to a public announcement of their intention to merge. Such a secret meeting was also a stark example of the ease with which the powerful on Wall Street got the ear of key policymakers and also how easily the Fed, through its rulings, could bypass the intentions of Congress. "I have nothing against size," Greenspan told them. America's chief banking regulator could be confident his view would prevail. "It doesn't bother me at all."

Weill also talked to the SEC, and called President Clinton and Treasury Secretary Rubin to update them on the proposed deal. The largest merger of all time up to that point was announced in April of 1998, the exchange of stock valued at $73 billion. The stock prices of both Citicorp and Travelers rose immediately on the announcement, the total value of the deal soon exceeding $80 billion. Weill's shares in the merged entity would be worth $1 billion. Weill readily gave up the Travelers name for the better known Citicorp. Soon he and Reed would change it to Citigroup.

"This is really about cross marketing and providing better products for clients," Weill told the press corps when the deal was announced. *The Wall Street Journal* credulously reported Weill's claim in a piece titled "One Stop Shopping Is the Reason for the Deal."

Reed and Weill agreed to become co-CEOs. Reed, nearly sixty, had thought they would retire together in a few years, Dimon their natural successor. Reed in particular liked Dimon, in whom he found intellectual qualities similar to his own. Meantime, Weill, who just turned sixty-five, concealed whatever his true ambitions were during the negotiations, but retiring soon was not one of them.

Few believed that the amity between Reed and Weill could last. And there were natural conflicts between the two organizations. Because commercial bankers at Citicorp earned far less than did investment bankers and traders at Salomon Smith Barney, coordinating their activities was fraught with conflicts.

Though the firms were being integrated and Weill and his staff were already working at 399 Park Avenue, Citicorp's headquarters, the deal was not yet legally consummated as they awaited formal Fed approval for the two-year window to begin. While they waited, Weill threatened to pull the plug entirely on Salomon's quant trading operations—the old arbitrage desk. It had been losing money on and off throughout 1998, as had LTCM and other similar operations. In July, he finally acted, roiling the markets by unwinding the Salomon positions. A month later, the Russian default occurred, ultimately bringing down LTCM. Salomon's trading operations lost $360 million that quarter. Citigroup reported a decline in overall earnings of 53 percent from the same quarter a year earlier.

At last, on October 8, the Fed gave its okay for them to operate legally as a merger for two years to see whether Congress dismantled Glass-Steagall completely. The two-year window gave Weill until the fall of 2000 to persuade Congress to end the restrictions. With the market in turmoil after the LTCM and Russian collapse, and the shares of both Citi and Travelers falling sharply, the deal was worth only $37 billion, half what it had been the day it was announced six months earlier. In addition, some were uncertain Congress would reverse Glass-Steagall.

Now the losses at Salomon due to the Russian default and the LTCM failure created the final tensions between Salomon's co-CEOs, Dimon and Maughan. After a heated confrontation between them at a company party, Weill and Reed agreed to force Dimon, Weill's main lieutenant of fifteen years, to resign. The break was a deep personal shock to Dimon, who had essentially grown up by Weill's side and to whom Weill owed more than he acknowledged.

An unbridgeable breach also grew up between Weill and Reed over Weill's determination to cut costs sharply and orient the firm to short-term profit making. Reed was consistently more focused on longer-term profits and such relatively abstract ventures as the future of electronic banking. Reed increased the friction when he bluntly told the press it was a mistake to lose Dimon. Then, at a Wall Street analysts conference, several months later, after a strong quarterly showing, Reed talked frankly of his future concerns about overspeculation and global collapses like those in Asia and Russia. Weill, stunned by Reed's candor—this was not his way—remained effusively optimistic, claiming the merged company and its business model were already victorious after only a few months and were just beginning to generate even more business. The salesman's optimism, true or false, was one of the sources of his success.

Partly to make peace, Weill hired Robert Rubin in October 1999, a few months after he left the Clinton administration, to serve in a newly created office of the chairman and to be the co-CEOs' go-between. Not only did Rubin have an international reputation for effectiveness as Clinton's boom-time treasury secretary, but he was also low-key and had no ambition to run Citigroup. But by now, the differences between Weill and Reed were too serious to reconcile. In early 2000, the board of Citigroup was forced to decide between them. Characteristically, Reed told the board that he and Weill should both resign and a new CEO be appointed. Equally in character, Weill told the board he should be the one to run Citigroup, not Reed. A key vote in Weill's favor was delivered by board member Mike Armstrong, head of AT&T, which Salomon analyst Jack Grubman had just recommended as a buy to his brokerage clients, some conjectured at Weill's request. He needed Armstrong's vote. The board also asked Rubin's opinion, and he sided with Weill, who was chosen, and Reed became a has-been almost overnight, formally resigning in April 2000.

Meanwhile, Weill had been working hard to end the Glass-Steagall restrictions. He organized the most powerful allies, including Morgan Stanley, Merrill Lynch, MetLife, and Prudential, to lobby Congress and the president. He enjoyed close relations with Gene Sperling, one of President Clinton's high-level economic advisers, whom he talked to about the benefits of the merger. But there were jurisdictional disputes between the Treasury and the Fed about the legislation. Rubin had wanted more control to reside in the Office of the Comptroller of the Currency under the Treasury's jurisdiction. Greenspan wanted jurisdiction at the Fed. When Lawrence Summers took over Treasury from Rubin, Summers let Greenspan at the Fed have his way. The Republican House had long been ready to abolish Glass-Steagall entirely. In late 1999, the Gramm-Leach-Bliley bill, named after its Republican congressional sponsors, Senator Phil Gramm and Congressmen Jim Leach and Thomas Bliley, was passed with bipartisan support in the House but only along narrow party lines in the Republican-controlled Senate. Glass-Steagall was no more. Much of the media was on board for both the bill and financial deregulation in general. A *New York Times* editorial had enthusiastically praised the Citicorp-Travelers merger the year before, calling then for complete repeal of Glass-Steagall. "Congress dithers, so John Reed of Citicorp and Sanford Weill of Travelers Group grandly propose to modernize financial markets on their own," wrote the *Times*. "Some consumer advocates oppose the merger because, they fear, financial behemoths inevitably threaten ordinary consumers. But one-stop financial shopping could actually protect naive investors. . . . The fact is that Citigroup threatens no one because it would not dominate banking, securities, insurance or any other financial market."

The legislation was signed into law by Bill Clinton in 2000. Weill had beaten the Fed deadline by many months. No federal regulations would limit the size of financial conglomerates in the foreseeable future.

The economy resumed growing in 1999 and Citigroup's earnings rose rapidly again. Breathing easily now that the merger would not be challenged by the government, Weill continued to make new acquisitions, including in Mexico and Poland. His largest was the takeover of Associates Capital in Texas, another consumer finance firm with the sort of fat overhead and underperformance Weill loved to fix. It added to Citigroup's earnings that year, which now reached $13 billion. Citi would combine it with the former Commercial Credit into CitiFinancial, soon to become one of the largest subprime mortgage originators in the nation.

Weill was also fabulously rich now due to the stock options he had handsomely paid himself over the years. "He talked about reloading all the time," said one banking client. Reloading was the term that described Weill's approach to executive compensation. If you cashed in some options, the company replaced them with an equivalent set of new options. In 2000, Weill exercised options on twenty million shares of Citicorp and received nearly eighteen million in their place. In that year, his total compensation, including the exercise of options, was more than $224 million.

But the year 2000 would be the last happy one for Weill. Reality descended as the stock market bubble burst, and then Enron and WorldCom, two major Citigroup clients, went bankrupt. Weill was soon under investigation by the New York attorney general, Eliot Spitzer. The ties to Jack Grubman, his most influential research analyst, came back to haunt him. Grubman, who had evolved into a telecommunications guru, had raised his rating of AT&T just before Weill needed the vote of the Citigroup board member and company CEO Mike Armstrong to assure his election as CEO.

Weill survived scandal and investigation, suspect loans to Enron and WorldCom, huge fines and drawdowns to settle civil suits, and the stock rose again in 2002. He was worth $1.4 billion now and listed on the Forbes 400 at last. In 2003, seventy years old, he resigned as CEO, free of criminal charges, but under a dark cloud of suspicion.

In Weill's view, he had created a financial services company that could compete with any in the world and contribute to America's economic strength. He and others like him deserved the money they made. Weill biographers Amey Stone and Mike Brewster argued that Citigroup was now so large it could absorb serious risks with minimal damage. This was indeed Weill's claim—so large it could take the outsize risks that often were rewarded by enormous profits. The biographers merely reflected the conventional wisdom of the time. In an interview in 2004, Wriston agreed that such broad diversification was beneficial.

Weill was a classic representation of the times, a man who built a business not through innovation, new products, or entrepreneurial wit but by combining ever bigger companies. This was an extreme example of the very "strategy" the most respected consulting firms preached as the right way to manage contemporary business giants. Run big business like a portfolio of assets, grow through consolidation, and use size itself to your advantage. With size, a business could control the prices it charged, the wages it paid, and the costs of its inventory. As we have seen, size became strategy. Jack Welch was the classic practitioner in the so-called real economy, Weill in the financial community. By 1999, when Weill created the fully merged Citigroup, the top ten largest banks controlled 45 percent of all banking assets compared to only 26 percent ten years earlier. Almost all of it was the result of mergers or acquisitions.

For the banks, growth through consolidation and diversification could have meant more stability, but in fact for Weill and most others it meant they could take more risks to raise short-term profits. The banks, as economists put it, "spent" whatever stability they derived from diversifying their assets by risking it on trading, securitizing, and so on. "The goal was to be big *and* [my italics] to take on risk," wrote economists Simon Johnson and James Kwak. Size did not protect against the risks Sandy Weill's financial conglomerate was now taking. Citigroup had not been chastised by scandal, fines, and government investigation. To the contrary, the risks it would take at the start of the new century jeopardized the giant firm's existence, and badly damaged the financial community as a whole.

Jack Grubman, Frank Quattrone, Ken Lay, and Sandy Weill

DECADE OF DECEIT

S andy Weill's plan to cross-sell financial products to consumers never worked—insurance could not be sold readily to brokerage clients, stocks to credit card holders, nor credit cards to mutual fund investors. "The history of one-stop shopping is dismal," said one of Weill's colleagues. American Express was never able to integrate Shearson Hayden. Sears rid itself of Dean Witter. But cross-selling was an effective rationalization for building a financial empire and adding one large piece to the others, fiefdom to fiefdom.

The part that did generate enormous profits was the cross-selling of corporate bank lending, underwriting, and securities research for brokerage clients. Weill pointed proudly to his cross-selling success as if it proved his point. "The one you read about, which has worked out really well, is the connectivity between our Citibank commercial banking business and the corporate investment bank [Salomon]," he said proudly. A client company could borrow from Citibank, raise equity and debt through Salomon, and have its stock recommended to institutions and individuals by a Citibank or Salomon securities analyst or broker. Sophisticated Salomon traders went further, creating products for bank clients that were very much like debt, yet skirted capital requirements and did not have to be placed on the balance sheet. "Cross-selling doesn't work in a lot of other cases," said one former Weill executive after he left the firm. Mixing commercial and investment banking was the exception, he said.

But this model was better described as cross-promotion than cross-selling. Banking clients were implicitly promised a good deal when it came time to raise money publicly, investment banking clients an attractive interest rate on a loan, and all could be promised a sympathetic ear from

Telecom analyst Jack Grubman testifying
before Congress

Investment banker Frank Quattrone, left,
on the first day of his trial

Enron CEO Ken Lay citing his Fifth Amendment
right to refuse to testify before Congress

the purportedly objective analysts who rated the companies for investors. Such activity was in the long run a bad business model for the company and the economy. The lure of short-term gains led to bad loans, bad financing decisions, and bad advice to investors.

Though Weill was not alone in running an empire of such conflicts of interest, some potentially illegal, he led the way. Conflicts led to excessive leverage and intense promotion of stocks to investors. Bad loans, often hedged by complex derivative investments, plus misleading stock research, directly fed the high-technology and telecommunications stock bubble that emerged in the late 1990s. Conflicts of interest among the financial firms, accounting firms, and law firms led to the artificial growth and accounting chicanery of companies like Enron and WorldCom. The nation thus wasted hundreds of billions of dollars of savings on misdirected and meaningless corporate investment—in particular, in high-technology and telecommunications companies. Financial firms made billions of dollars, and their workers were paid unimaginably well.

The 1990s through 2002 was the most corrupt "decade" since the 1920s—and one of the most corrupt in American business history. An infrastructure of corruption, whose seeds blossomed with Mike Milken, Ivan Boesky, and the savings and loan entrepreneurs in the 1980s, spread in the 1990s across the American establishment into elite professions, including commercial and investment banks, accountants, lawyers, consultants, ratings agencies, and mutual funds as well as newer hedge funds. The nation did not fully comprehend or reflect upon the excessive degree of business corruption in the 1990s. New York state's attorney general, Eliot Spitzer, brought suits and gained settlements against the most prestigious of investment firms and mutual funds in the early 2000s, but Washington regulators did not follow his lead. The SEC tightened some regulations, but inadequately. Its Fair Disclosure regulation of 2000 required open dissemination of market research to all analysts, not just the favored few, but the law was passed after the worst of the abuses and penalties were brought to light. Blatant corruption in several enormous companies served by the Wall Street financial infrastructure momentarily stunned the nation, notably at Enron, WorldCom, Global Crossing, Tyco, and Adelphia, leading to criminal convictions of some of their executives and moderate congressional reforms, particularly the Sarbanes-Oxley legislation, named after its sponsors, Senator Paul Sarbanes and Congressman Michael Oxley, which increased requirements for disclosure and legal responsibilities for corporate officers and their boards. But by the mid-2000s, the outrages of the 1990s and early 2000s were forgotten as stock prices rose again and housing prices rose still faster. The federal regulators enforced the rules with more laxity. Old, discredited statistical tools such as VAR were still used to make seemingly simple judgments about how much could be safely borrowed by firms. Off-balance-sheet partnerships were used with even more vigor than was the case with Enron. The uproar over Enron, WorldCom, and the stock market debacle passed, and extreme free market ideology retained its hold for another decade.

A first marker for the unethical decade was an internal memo written by a high-ranking financial officer of Morgan Stanley in 1990 and uncovered by *The Wall Street Journal* in 1992. The officer, Clayton Rohrbach III, recommended that the pay of research analysts at Morgan be directly linked to how much underwriting, brokerage, or asset management business the company they were covering did with Morgan Stanley. Research analysts were supposed to be independent and objective. Their alleged loyalty was to the firms' brokerage clients who bought and sold stocks and bonds based on their recommendations. Trust and independent thinking were expected and were the basis of their influence. Morgan was now explicitly urging the analysts to serve a different master, the investment banking client or corporate borrower, and thus they had an explicit financial interest in distorting their research to encourage investors to buy shares and raise the stock price of the investment banking or corporate loan client. Such practices existed in the 1980s, but as the 1990s began, they became common and abuse of research became widespread and brazen. A stock analyst's compensation was tied by contract to a percentage of the investment banking business they brought in; positive recommendations generated a high payoff for analysts.

A measure of this practice was the increase in the number of buy recommendations. At the end of the 1980s, after a long run-up in stocks, buy recommendations exceeded sell recommendations by a large and suspect margin of four to one. By the early 1990s, buy recommendations exceeded sells by eight to one. By the late 1990s, only 1 percent of analysts' recommendations urged an outright sale. The low percentage remained unchanged even when stock prices were falling and the investing community was pessimistic.

After the stock market collapsed in the early 2000s, securities analysts started to admit to what was happening inside these firms. Ronald Glantz, a veteran, respected analyst from Paine Webber, testified before Congress in 2001 as follows:

> Now the job of analysts is to bring in investment banking clients, not provide good investment advice. This began in the 1980s. The prostitution of security analysts was completed during the high-tech mania of the last few years. For example in 1997 a major investment banking firm offered to triple my pay. They had no interest in the quality of my recommendations. I was shown a list with 15 names and asked, "How quickly can you issue buy recommendations on these potential clients?"

As Glantz pointed out, the commission a brokerage firm received for trading $300 million worth of stock was perhaps $300,000—or one tenth of 1 percent of the value of the trade. An analyst who encouraged clients to buy or sell a stock through the firm's brokers would generate a modest commission for the firm and relatively little compensation for the analyst. But an analyst who could bring in a client who raised $300 million in a new stock offering through an underwriting handled by his firm could earn the firm $10 million and receive a personal fee of perhaps $1 million. Said Glantz: "Bankers thought nothing of a million-dollar fee to the analyst responsible for the business."

Analysts began to fudge what they actually meant. Glantz went on:

"It is an open secret that 'strong buy' now means 'buy,' 'buy' means 'hold,' 'hold' means that the company isn't an investment banking client, and 'sell' means that the company is no longer an investment client."

Rising stock prices made overly optimistic recommendations seem correct and reinforced the practice. Most stocks rose in the first half of the 1990s. But from 1994 on, they soared. It was what economist Robert Shiller, as noted, a historian of stock trends, labeled "the biggest historical example to date of a speculative upsurge in the stock market." The economy's prospects improved markedly. But they did not improve as rapidly as the market did. From the end of 1994 to 2000, stock prices roughly tripled while corporate profits rose by only one and a half times. High-technology stocks rose faster still, often before the companies produced any earnings. By 1998, price-earnings multiples reached levels last reached in 1929, and surpassed them by a wide margin in 1999 and 2000.

As the payoff for exaggeration and deception rose, seeming to prove that those who warned about rising prices were Cassandras, prices rose still higher. Alberto Vilar, a hugely successful manager of a high-technology investment fund, Amerindo, produced average returns of nearly 40 percent a year over twenty years starting in 1980. By the end of the 1990s, his buy criterion no longer required that a company make a profit. He believed he couldn't pick the winners in advance, so the best strategy was to develop a portfolio of potential winners, before the fact—before they made a profit. "I have twelve or fourteen favorite stocks," he said, "half will go up by ten times, the others not, but I don't know which half." He persuasively told clients the nation was merely in the first inning of a nine-inning game of technological revolution. Amerindo folded and Vilar, convicted for security fraud in 2009 for using business funds for personal use, was sentenced to nine years in jail. He is still encumbered by civil suits by former investors. A major benefactor to opera companies around the world, including New York's Metropolitan Opera, he reneged on his grand promises.

What made Vilar's investment strategy credible was that the nation's business was in the midst of substantial change. In 1990, the ten largest companies in America were mostly industrial or natural resources companies, like General Motors and Exxon. In 2000, six of the top ten were in high-technologies. Said one analyst: "Stocks for a new industry have never risen this quickly, and a new industry has never emerged this quickly." In 1996, Alan Greenspan called it "a new era economy," according to *Business Week*.

Yet there were many historical analogies to the current period. Similar nationwide speculative surges go back in the United States at least to 1817, which was followed by the panic of 1819. Yet the myth was widespread that there were no precedents for the rapidity of the rise of Internet-related business. Rapid takeoff is the norm for breakthrough products. Such technological advances arrived every twenty to thirty years—the mass production surge of autos, washing machines, record players, and radios that accompanied the spread of electricity in the 1920s; the development of television, jet travel, plastic consumer products, computers, new drugs, and nuclear power in the 1950s and 1960s. The commercialization of radio in the 1920s and 1930s and television in the 1950s were every bit as rapid as the spread of the Internet.

The financial media were swept up in the speculative fever. In 1996, references to the "New Economy" of the Internet were relatively few, but by 1997, these references grew rapidly and by 1998 they were ubiquitous. *BusinessWeek, Fortune,* and *Forbes* were all advocates. *The Economist* wrote in 1999 that "this is not just a matter of accumulating extra capital. The new economy is about the specific potential to change the way businesses work and thereby yield a quantum shift in productivity." The increase in the rate of productivity growth rose almost to the rates reached in the 1950s and 1960s, but any "quantum" shift remained starry-eyed myth. As late as 2000, just before the market crash, when the Nasdaq index, the best measure of high-tech stocks, fell by three quarters, *Wired,* the industry's leading cheerleading publication, published a widely applauded story called "The Long Boom." Peter Schwartz and Peter Leyden, the authors, headlined the piece "We're Facing Twenty-five Years of Prosperity, Freedom, and a Better Environment for the Whole World. You Got a Problem with That?" The Nasdaq index never again rose to even 60 percent of the high reached in 2000.

The motives for the business press's overenthusiasm were not entirely a matter of reporting what they were told by their Wall Street sources.

There was broad support of the New Economy from Wall Street analysts, many economists, and the much honored Alan Greenspan, who not only called it a new era but claimed the advances were "historically rare." But high-technology companies also poured money into media advertising. The dollar value of advertising pages promoting the Internet rose by 183 percent in 2000 over 1999. High-technology advertising rose in 1999 by 34 percent at *BusinessWeek*, 49 percent at *The Wall Street Journal*, 86 percent at *Fortune*, and 83 percent at *Forbes*. The media paid growing attention to the New Economy to provide editorial content into which ads could be placed, and the incentive grew for the media to produce enthusiastically optimistic stories.

What may have made the media credulous was that corporate earnings were rising strongly, though not nearly as rapidly as stock prices. But the consistent earnings growth that resulted in high stock prices was increasingly a fiction, and research analysts, influenced by their compensation, did not adequately challenge the figures. General Electric's persistent earnings increases were a leading example of how earnings were manipulated to produce consistent gains. *Fortune* analyzed how Jack Welch used both pension fund reserves and reserves at GE Capital to supplement quarterly earnings in order to make them rise consistently. As noted, they rose every quarter for almost thirteen years. GE stock roughly tripled between 1990 and 1995 and then quintupled between 1995 and early 2000.

The analysts' waiting game was to see which companies would exceed the consensus forecast by even a few pennies per share. In the 1990s, the deception often reached absurd proportions, but analysts mostly went along with the charade, and stocks typically rose whenever companies beat the analysts' consensus. One way to estimate the amount of overstated earnings was to compare what companies reported in their financial statements to what they reported as earnings to the tax authorities. The gap grew throughout the 1990s and was enormous by the time the market crashed in 2000. For example, Enron reported earnings of $1.8 billion to shareholders in 1999 but reported losing $1 billion to the IRS. Such discrepancies were common. (Corporations will normally minimize taxable earnings, of course, but the discrepancies were far larger than could be explained by tax planning.)

In 1994, matters were made worse when the Supreme Court ruled that accountants, lawyers, and investment banks could not be sued for participating in a fraud perpetrated by a client. They were liable only if they were primary perpetrators of the fraud, making the bar for criminal conduct higher. "It was a radical decision," according to law professor Frank Partnoy, largely ignoring "hundreds of judicial and administrative proceedings over sixty years." The court now worried about abuses of litigation, not abuses by Wall Street or its handmaidens.

The situation was exacerbated when Congress passed an act that limited suits against investment firms by securities clients the next year. Such litigation had become common and at times was abused. But the bill raised effective barriers even to legitimate litigation: punitive damages were limited, as were legal fees to plaintiffs' attorneys. Plaintiffs were required to prove that defendants acted with reckless intent; periods for statutes of limitations were shortened; and companies could not be held liable for incorrect earnings projections. SEC chairman Arthur Levitt supported the bill as did all Republicans and many Democrats in Congress, even over President Clinton's veto. Some argued Clinton vetoed the legislation not to protect shareholders but rather to appease the trial lawyers, a political support group for him. In congressional testimony several years later, the outspoken hedge fund manager Jim Chanos attributed much of the deceitful behavior between 1995 and 2001 to the new law, which, he told Congress, "emboldened dishonest management to lie with impunity."

Major accounting frauds became common in the mid-1990s. Waste Management's was one of the most brazen. Its CEO, Dean Buntrock, took over his father's garbage collection company in 1955 and later merged it with the garbage collection business of a cousin by marriage, Wayne Huizenga (who went on to build Blockbuster video and other large firms). The merged garbage company went public in the early 1970s and Buntrock went on a spree buying hauling and landfill companies at a pace of up to two hundred companies a year, as local governments eagerly turned over the cleanup to private companies. As Waste Management grew to become the largest waste service company in the world, it developed a reputation for disregarding the law, repeatedly violating environmental regulations, and forfeiting millions of dollars in total fines (likely less than what it would have cost to abide by all regulations). It was also sued for antitrust violations a half dozen times.

In the 1990s, it started aggressively manipulating its accounting. The growth of its business was slowing and earnings became harder to generate, and Wall Street investors rewarded only consistently rising earnings. Waste Management systematically postponed recording expenses. It took questionable onetime profit gains on trumped-up transactions. Arthur Andersen, the accounting firm, did not challenge the accounting tricks.

Andersen was also a Waste Management consultant, for which it received lucrative fees—a practice that was a conflict of interest but repeated by Andersen time and again, including consulting and accounting services for Enron. In 1994, the accounting errors were so blatant, Andersen at last requested that Waste Management redo the books and correct the misleading accounting. Though Andersen's requests were ignored, even as Waste Management's accounting became more distorted, Andersen approved the 1994, 1995, and 1996 auditing statements without qualification (thus, supposedly assuring the public that the company abided by generally accepted accounting principles). By now, serious accounting manipulation was rumored at Waste Management and the stock price was falling. The board at last forced Buntrock out and invited former SEC chairman Roderick Hills to join it. Hills conducted a special audit and concluded that Waste Management had overstated its earnings by $1.7 billion, which became, when corrected, the largest accounting restatement in corporate history. Andersen, which had signed off on all these accounting gimmicks, was still retained by the company, and gave its unqualified approval to the restated books. The SEC sued Buntrock and other high-level executives but reached a settlement requiring him to pay $20 million personally without having to admit wrongdoing. It was a modest fine, given his wealth. The SEC also fined Andersen $7 million, only about one year's worth of the firm's earnings from Waste Management.

There were dozens of accounting frauds in these years, and Andersen was involved with many of them. Only a few of the CEOs who perpetrated the major frauds served jail time or were severely fined compared to their substantial wealth. A conspicuous exception was Walter Forbes, who in the 1990s oversaw earnings overstatements at his firm CUC International (later merged with Cendant) of $500 million. Forbes fought the charges in court, but was eventually convicted by a jury in 2007 and sentenced to twelve years and seven months in prison. The firm was also forced to pay a settlement of $3.275 billion in restitution to shareholders.

Walter Forbes's punishment came too late to have a deterrent effect. Between 1990 and 1994, 216 companies were forced to restate their earnings properly. By the mid-1990s, the number had risen, with more than one hundred restated earnings in 1996 alone. In 1997, Arthur Levitt, the SEC chairman, at last realized he had to take more aggressive legal action and the SEC started to bring suits, including those against CUC and Waste Management. But the campaign almost completely neglected the newer, more innovative kinds of accounting manipulation made possible by soaring stock prices, complicit Wall Street and accounting firms, and the growing derivatives market. Securities law professor Frank Partnoy argued the SEC focused largely on simple fraud cases because the new forms of fraud were so complex they were difficult to prove. Companies such as Enron and WorldCom were obviously managing earnings, but were not a target of investigations. Following the Enron scandal in 2000, approximately four hundred companies a year would be required to restate earnings.

Unethical accounting standards were, in large part, a consequence of the outsize personal compensation CEOs could earn because compensation was linked to rising stock prices through generous stock options. Theoretically, if they managed the company well, share values would rise and options with them. As the stock market rewarded consistent quarterly earnings increases, however, the incentive to focus on short-run performance overwhelmed other objectives.

The potential wealth that could be earned quickly by a CEO was new. In former bull markets, CEO compensation was less tightly linked to stock price. This situation had changed with the takeover movement of the 1980s. LBO managers particularly rewarded the CEOs they appointed to take over the companies they bought with generous shares of stock and options. By the mid-1990s, granting of stock options was widespread. High-technology companies, including Apple Computer and Dell Computer, granted stock options that, it was discovered, were illegally backdated so that the price at which the shares could be bought had already been exceeded when they were issued. The practices did not fully come to light until 2006, and the SEC then fined some executives, including at Apple, while in some other cases criminal charges were brought. Approximately one hundred companies were involved in cases brought by the SEC. By 1996, average CEO compensation among the Standard & Poor's 500 companies was 210 times the level of average pay for production workers compared to roughly one hundred times in 1990. It was only twenty-five times higher in 1970. The largest component of the CEO compensation by far was stock options. By another measure, at the height of the bull market in 2000, a CEO's compensation, including stock options, rose to more than five hundred times that of the average worker compared to forty in 1980. In the mid-1990s alone, CEO compensation in the finance and manufacturing industries soared, rising in just four years, 1992 to 1996, by more than 50 percent after discounting for inflation. It rose still faster in the late 1990s and early 2000s, comprising a significantly higher proportion of company profits.

The tying of CEO compensation to the share price was widely lauded by some academic economists as the best way to make business executives— known in academic literature as "agents"—act as owners. But research did not support the claim. Increased stock option incentives did not result in improved performance of the stock price, and often total pay went up even when performance was poor. Some economists claimed the share price accurately reflected the earnings prospects of a company, or at least all the publicly known and perhaps some nonpublic information about the company—the central assertion of efficient markets theory. If the manager made good decisions, the share price should reflect them. But CEOs also benefited simply when there was a general rise in stock prices that had nothing to do with their managerial abilities. The CEO compensation contracts could have easily been adjusted so that they benefited only when their company's stock performance exceeded the market average, but few companies bothered to do so. Two law school professors found that most of the compensation based on stocks was earned because of such bull markets or mere short-term rises in stock prices. Many CEOs profited handsomely from the roaring bull market of the late 1990s, no matter how poorly they managed their firms.

There was widespread and mostly angry publicity about the rapid increases in executive pay compared to worker earnings beginning in the early 1990s, yet CEO pay kept rising rapidly on average, despite a still high unemployment rate and slow-growing economy that did not turn up strongly until 1996. The rise in executive pay had become a major political issue during Bill Clinton's campaign for the presidency in 1991. As president, Clinton sought to cap CEO pay by denying companies the ability to expense the compensation as a deduction for taxes, as they would the salaries and wages of their workers. Compensation above $1 million a year was no longer to be tax deductible. The bill became law in 1993, but the cap made an exception of "performance-based" compensation, an exception requested by Robert Rubin—in other words, compensation earned from stock options. The exception led to the wholesale granting of such stock options. In the ten years since the law was passed, with no cap on stock options, the average compensation of CEOs of Fortune 500 companies rose from $3.7 million a year to $9.1 million.

Furthermore, stock options, unlike executive salaries, were not recorded as an expense on the income statement, only footnoted in the financial statements. They therefore did not reduce corporate earnings. Academic theoreticians insisted this didn't matter—that highly rational investors would count the options in their calculations of a company's profits and the stock's worth. But business executives knew better. When the Financial Accounting Standards Board proposed expensing stock options in

1994, Sandy Weill and others aggressively lobbied Congress against it. The high-technology executives were especially ardent opponents, because so much of their compensation was based on the stock options and the future rise of the share price. Led by the Democrats, Congress passed a bill in 1994 to block the proposal. The SEC's Levitt supported the Democrats' bill and later called it the "greatest mistake" of his tenure.

Economist Robert Shiller made a careful assessment of how high stock prices now were. He adjusted the Standard & Poor's 500 index for inflation and then compared it to reported corporate earnings of the 500 S&P companies over the preceding ten years, also discounted for inflation. In 1996, when Greenspan warned of "irrational exuberance," the price-earnings ratio was around its 1966 peak of 24 and well below its 1929 peak. But after a pause, stock prices took off compared to earnings, and by 1998, the average price-earnings ratio rose well above its pre-crash high in 1929 of nearly 33. In 2000, just before the crash, it reached 47. The Dow was about to lose 35 percent of its value, falling from approximately 11,700 in early 2000 to 7,673 in March 2003, only to rise to roughly 14,000 in 2007 before plunging again.

The summit of irrationality was reached with Internet company IPOs—initial public offerings, or, to repeat, the first sale of stock by a company to public investors. In this period, IPO stock prices soared to remarkable heights, supported by some of the most unscrupulous Wall Street research ever produced. So lucrative was owning shares in IPOs, they were allocated surreptitiously by the most prestigious investment bankers as a payoff to CEOs for their underwriting business.

The flamboyant leader of the IPO phenomenon was Frank Quattrone. He was born in 1955 and raised on the rough South Side of Philadelphia. He attended Wharton as an undergraduate, and then Stanford Business School. Quattrone began his career in Silicon Valley, working at Morgan Stanley in 1983. A bushy mustache his trademark, he was a lively, deliberately down-to-earth man who befriended the young new entrepreneurs of Silicon Valley well before others did. As their technologies matured, and markets for their products developed, Quattrone began taking them public.

The initiator of the IPO surge was Netscape. The company developed the first usable browser, enabling PC users to access the Web. In 1995, when Quattrone brought the company public, expectations for the potential of the Internet were high, but still unfulfilled. A simple browser would change that. The sudden groundswell of demand for Netscape shares caught even the ebullient Quattrone off guard. As brokers put in orders for shares of the IPO, demand so overwhelmed supply that Quattrone doubled the offering price and increased the number to be sold by half. He raised $1 billion for the company, tripling the amount anticipated. On opening day, the share price kept rising higher, from the $28 offering price—which had already been doubled, as noted—to nearly $60 a share by the market close.

Quattrone was now the stock promoter of the moment. Scores of high-technology IPOs were launched, and Quattrone handled most of the leading ones. Some IPOs rose by 200 to 300 percent or even more soon after their offering. The Linux IPO was priced at $30 per share in December 1999 and closed that day at a price of $239.25. The investment bank's fee on an IPO was typically 7 percent of the value of the deal, higher than for any other banking transaction.

Quattrone jumped from Morgan Stanley to Deutsche Bank, where he launched Amazon.com as a public company. He then moved to Credit Suisse First Boston, where he earned the firm hundreds of millions of dollars of underwriting fees. At his height in the late 1990s, he was reputedly paid $100 million a year, probably more than anyone else working for a securities firm in America, topped only by the hedge fund managers.

Netscape had a short life. Its future was quickly crushed by the introduction of Microsoft's Internet Explorer, released free as part of Windows, and many investors took serious losses as the stock fell. (AOL eventually bought Netscape, but the company could not be saved.)

With allocations of IPO shares in such demand, the unquenchable Quattrone saw a way to make still more money. He allocated IPO shares under the table to individual executives at client companies and at prospective client companies and demanded benefits in return, reminiscent of what Mike Milken had done a decade earlier. The executives were also violating their company duties, giving Quattrone investment banking business not primarily on the basis of what was good for their company but often for personal gain. Quattrone was not the only banker doing this, but he was the leader by far.

One of Quattrone's strategies was apparently to underprice IPOs deliberately, making an immediate price rise likely after the opening. This could benefit executives who got an allocation, not to mention the many money managers and other investors Quattrone sought to make happy with IPO allocations. But the company raised less money as a result than it otherwise could have.

Quattrone basically demanded kickbacks from clients who got IPO allocations. According to SEC documents, he and his traders allocated IPO shares to investing clients only on the condition they would do more stock trading with Credit Suisse First Boston, and, astonishingly, at as much as thirty times the normal commission rate. Thus, executives at pension or mutual fund management companies would benefit from owning and cashing in the IPOs while their funds traded shares at higher commissions, hurting their own investors. In 2000, the SEC investigated, subpoenaing countless e-mails from CS First Boston, many of which they made public (the National Association of Securities Dealers also investigated). To take part in the Linux IPO, for example, the SEC concluded that "customers that received at least 405,398 shares engaged in large transactions in highly liquid large capitalization securities at excessive commission rates." In some cases, clients were required to give back two thirds of their earnings on the IPOs in higher commissions. In a run-on sentence, a trader wrote in one e-mail: "Okay we got another screaming deal and I weaseled you guys some stock we've yet to see any leverage out of you guys for the free dough-re-me does it make sense for me . . . to continue to feed your guys with deal stock or should I take the stock to someone who will pay us direct for the allocation."

Under the pressure of the investigations, a new banker, John Mack, was brought in to run CS First Boston, and Quattrone, who had had a run-in with Mack when he was at Morgan Stanley, left the firm. Mack hired former SEC attorney Gary Lynch, who had successfully prosecuted Milken and Boesky—the last major convictions won by the government. Lynch worked out a highly beneficial deal for CS First Boston in which no criminal charges were brought. The firm was fined only $100 million, a small fraction of what it had earned over the years.

Quattrone was not pursued—to law professor Frank Partnoy another indication that the Justice Department feared modern fraud cases because they were difficult to prove. Partnoy believed there was clearly enough evidence to make a case against Quattrone that he gave IPO allocations to key clients at favorable prices. Years later, an e-mail was discovered that indicated Quattrone urged his employees to destroy documents while the investigation was under way. The government decided to prosecute on the basis of a flimsy case of tampering and obstruction of justice, rather than outright fraud, but after two trials ended in hung juries, Quattrone was acquitted in 2007 and back in the financial business.

Kickbacks and payoffs contributed to the stock market bubble. But after the 2000 crash, nearly all the thousands of IPOs issued in the late 1990s had fallen to below their initial offering prices. Half of the ones that hadn't gone out of business were selling for less than $1 a share. John Bogle, who had founded Vanguard Funds, estimated that the top executives of both old-line and newly public companies earned in total $1 trillion when they sold their shares during the bull market of the late 1990s. Fees and commission payments to investment banks, brokers, and mutual funds totaled another $1.275 trillion, he figured. "If the winners raked in what we can roughly estimate as at least $2.275 trillion, who lost all the money?" asked Bogle. "The losers of course were those who bought the stocks and who paid the intermediation fees . . . the great American public."

Sandy Weill's Salomon Smith Barney benefited handsomely from the bull market of the century, despite the trading losses of 1997 and 1998. The combination of bank lending, securities underwriting, and stock research was a potent way to make money even with the collapse of LTCM. Now, commercial banks, with their own trading desks and their securities subsidiaries, were central in the trading of derivatives that could be used to lend money to banking clients—these complex trades did not appear as liabilities on their books in contrast to conventional business loans. Derivatives could be used to circumvent regulations on capital requirements as well, and Citigroup was positioned to take full advantage.

The entry of commercial banks into lucrative derivatives trading began in the late 1980s with Bankers Trust Company, which was regulated by the Federal Reserve. The leader of BTC was Charles Sanford, a Wharton business school graduate who became its president in 1983 after making the bank a lot of money trading bonds. The choice of a trader as a commercial bank president was rare, and possibly unprecedented. *Fortune* editor Carol Loomis wrote that by the late 1980s, Sanford had transformed BTC into "a whole new way to run a bank," much like an investment bank, geared to making all the money it could every day, by trading in the markets, not by making loans. BTC's interest income from investing in government securities and making loans, the traditional commercial banking activities, was less than half the income derived from investing in and trading derivatives and other securities—and in 1987 and 1988 far less than half.

Sanford hired a young trader from Salomon to head the department, Andy Krieger, also a Wharton graduate, who had worked with John Meriwether at Salomon, where he specialized in currency options. Krieger was a catch. He was also discovered to be devious. Traders watched closely and often copied what others were doing, and Krieger sometimes made money by deliberately fooling competitors into thinking he was buying a certain currency while disguising how much he was in fact selling.

Krieger, trading currency derivatives, made enormous profits in 1987 and 1988. But in that frenetic world, traders like Krieger were loosely controlled. In 1988, Krieger misstated, perhaps accidentally, his trading earnings by a large amount, and the errors, once discovered, resulted in a loss of nearly $80 million at the bank. In the 1990s there would be more "rogue" traders who could alone bring down large institutions through highly risky trades that they adeptly covered up, until it was too late—most notably, Joe Jett, whose trading lost $350 million for Kidder Peabody, then owned by GE; and Nicholas Leeson, who lost $1 billion for Barings in England. (In 2008, a trader would lose $9 billion for Morgan Stanley.)

But in 1988, an $80 million error was huge. Sanford had already reported a gain to shareholders and the authorities, and now decided to cover up the loss by reducing a reserve set up to pay future bonuses. Through sleight-of-hand accounting, he took money from one pot to plug a hole in another and thus avoided publicly correcting the financial statements. However, within a few months, a Federal Reserve review caught the clumsy cover-up and forced the bank to restate earnings. Wall Street bank analysts were furious at the deceit, and Sanford never regained their trust. But the true reason for the restatement and Sanford's shenanigans was not made public until a 1992 article in *Fortune,* with author Loomis calling the activities "mind-boggling." Neither the SEC nor the Justice Department proceeded with a civil or criminal case against BTC, Sanford, or Krieger. Krieger had already been hired away to manage money by George Soros, and Sanford continued to run BTC. As Frank Partnoy complained, the message sent to the rest of the financial community was once again clear: derivatives-related wrongdoing was given a pass.

Sanford pursued derivatives trading more aggressively, and more outrageous behavior was to come. He hired traders in a variety of new derivatives markets to exploit opportunities. What it boiled down to was borrowing at the low rates fostered by Greenspan's Fed in the early 1990s—which were almost zero after inflation—and investing the funds in high-paying securities, especially the new kinds backed by mortgages and aggressively peddled by First Boston and Salomon Brothers, in particular, to mutual funds, pension funds, and some money market funds, as well as municipalities. For all the supposed hedging and sophisticated measures of risk, most of these trades were heavy bets that interest rates would stay low.

Another subsidiary of the bank, BT Securities, started creating complex ways for banking clients to borrow funds based on derivatives. BTC's clients, particularly Gibson Greetings and Procter & Gamble, used these derivatives-based transactions to reduce their borrowing costs, without fully understanding their risks. Under changing economic circumstances, the borrowing costs could rise sharply.

When Greenspan suddenly raised rates in 1994, this is exactly what happened. Gibson and P&G, which basically thought their debt payments were fixed—after all, they were dealing with a venerable commercial bank—were charged enormous liabilities, forcing P&G to take nearly $200 million in losses in one year. When the SEC investigated the Gibson case, it concluded that "from October 1992 to March 1994, BT Securities' representatives misled Gibson about the value of the company's derivatives positions by providing Gibson with values that significantly understated the magnitude of Gibson's losses. As a result, Gibson remained unaware of the actual extent of its losses from derivatives transactions and continued to purchase derivatives from BT Securities." The SEC uncovered gleeful e-mails about BT traders' ability to fool their clients and charge far more for derivatives trades—known as swaps—than they should have. "Lure people into the calm and then totally fuck 'em," said one e-mail. BTC earned $13 million in fees on the transactions for Gibson. The BTC traders assumed the market would turn around, but it did not in time.

Other bold borrowers in this period unwittingly took on risks they did not understand, usually based on complex derivatives strategies, including Orange County, California, and the highly regarded Fidelity mutual funds. Orange County lost more than $1 billion. But the SEC's punitive actions were again timid compared to the size of the losses. BTC paid only a $10 million settlement. NationsBank of North Carolina had a securities firm that sold dubious term trusts, another derivatives-based product, to unsuspecting investors who thought they were buying government bond funds. Despite big losses, NationsBank was fined only $4 million. Charles Sanford, the BTC rainmaker, left banking, dishonored but wealthy, never charged with wrongdoing.

The law was simply inadequate to the task of regulation, and the regulators failed to enforce strongly what laws there were. Fines were usually meaningless. The Commodities Futures Trading Commission had jurisdiction over formal futures contracts. The SEC had jurisdiction over exchange-traded options. But most of the options market was over-the-counter trading and fell entirely between the cracks; many new contracts—the swaps, for example—were simply written between the participants in the trade with no outside oversight. And trading in energy derivatives for petroleum and natural gas was, in fact, completely unregulated. Wendy Gramm, the former CFTC chairperson, and wife of Senator Phil Gramm, under George H. W. Bush, had exempted energy derivatives from CFTC oversight in 1993, and then took a seat on Enron's board of directors. Enron specialized in trading energy derivatives. Derivatives were a lawless island in which profits were easy to make off unsuspecting clients who had no idea of the risks they were taking,

In light of all the losses generated by derivatives trading in 1994, the Government Accounting Office published a study recommending regulation of over-the-counter derivatives in 1994. Jim Leach, the ranking Republican on the House Banking Committee, also had issued a report demanding regulation. But the International Swap Dealers Association, then new and composed of ten leading dealers including BTC, Citicorp, Goldman Sachs, and Merrill Lynch, succeeded with support from SEC chairman Arthur Levitt to block the legislation.

In 1995, more bills were proposed to regulate such practices, but the economy was recovering, the markets were now calm, and nothing significant was passed. Glass-Steagall was almost entirely dismantled, effectively so by 1996 when Greenspan's Fed let commercial banks do brokerage business, underwriting, and trading of securities up to 25 percent of their total revenues; in 1987, under Greenspan, the Fed had already formally allowed such business up to 10 percent of revenues, the first major crack in Glass-Steagall. "The lack of banking competition became an outrage," says Leo Hindery, former chairman of AT&T Cable. "You could no longer go across the street to get a competitive rate on a loan."

The aggressive trading and accounting practices, and the absence of serious watchdogs in the federal agencies, led directly to the 2001 debacle of Enron, a company that was largely the creation of accounting deception, culminating in the largest bankruptcy to date in the fall of 2001.

Enron was formed in 1985 as the combination of two staid natural gas and electricity companies, Houston Natural Gas and Internorth. It was run by a seemingly mild-mannered economist, Kenneth Lay, whose close relationships in Washington—he was especially friendly with George H. W. Bush—belied his diffident manner. In 1990, he hired a dazzling management consultant from McKinsey, Jeffrey Skilling, a Harvard MBA, whose ideas became the basis of the company's innovations. Enron was credible to investors because it could label itself as a quintessential New Economy company under Skilling's leadership, its central achievements seeming almost as remarkable as other purer high-technology successes of the time.

Traditionally, energy—oil, natural gas, and electricity itself—was bought and sold by regional utilities and local companies. It was Skilling's vision to use the new derivatives markets to unfetter energy from these physical limits. What was required for Enron to pursue its plan was that retail electricity prices, which were generally fixed by state governments, be deregulated. Enron executives worked hard at pushing deregulation, especially in the lucrative California market, where in 1996 they at last got their way. They argued that deregulation would enable energy providers to compete and lower prices to consumers. With deregulation, local utilities were required to transmit power owned by competitors over its utility lines for a fee should the customer request it. These other companies billed business and home users, often at prices lower than the local utility's.

Now Skilling could use derivatives to buy and sell energy in the future and supply it to local communities. Oil and gas futures had long been traded. Soon electricity was also traded as a future. The contracts enabled a buyer to place an order in the future at a set price, or a seller to arrange a sale in the future at a set price. For example, Enron could promise to guarantee a town in, say, Ohio electricity at a specified price up to thirty years into the future and then trade in futures contracts to reduce its risk and lock in the price of power when it was time to sell it to the Ohio town.

Enron traders were equal to and as sophisticated as those of any investment bank. The company had state-of-the-art technology and highly competent personnel, and were capable of manipulating the market. They made the California electricity shortage in 2000 far worse by selling electricity out of state to create the appearance of a shortage. As the price then rose rapidly for lack of available electricity, they sold electricity back to California at a huge profit. In fact, they made so much money that they sometimes had to hide it.

Arthur Andersen, their accountants, who were also, as usual, management consultants to the firm, approved this artificial reduction in earnings, which were simply pushed into the future. Traders can be seen in a documentary rejoicing over their trading profits as California electricity prices soared, shuttering countless businesses and forcing untold numbers of households to do without electricity.

Trading remained profitable until the end, generating nearly $3 billion in profit in the first three quarters of 2001, the year disaster struck Enron. Rather, it was unethical financial schemes, in partnership with the Wall

Street community and leading banks like Citigroup, that undid Enron. Because funds were so available at low rates, Enron made countless investments around the world in oil and natural gas pipelines and energy plants. It started a broadband unit to build cable capacity like WorldCom, whose stock was flying high on Wall Street. It made venture capital investments in high technology. All this activity was financed with borrowed funds, usually deliberately hidden by management off the financial statements with the active help of Citigroup, JPMorgan Chase, Merrill Lynch, and others. Skilling's financial officer, Andrew Fastow, a young Northwestern business school graduate, financed one venture after another, becoming with the help of banks a master of financial stealth.

Many of the dubiously financed ventures turned out to be disastrous. Fastow's job at first was to find new ways to finance these investments, but then he was forced to find ways to plug the holes as these companies ate up cash, produced business losses, and created rising, unsustainable levels of debt. At this task, Fastow was a charming wizard. He established partnerships (special purpose entities) with outside investors, which, through accounting loopholes, enabled Enron to sell bad assets into these partnerships. The partners participated only because their investments were collateralized by soaring Enron stock. Legally, the partnerships were supposed to be managed independently of Enron, but Fastow often ran them. The sales to the partnerships were recorded as Enron profits, even though it controlled the partnerships and determined what they would buy. The sales were financed through the debt of the partnerships, which Enron could keep off its balance sheet. Citigroup was a frequent investor in these partnerships, and as an underwriter also found other investors for its partnerships. Citigroup also lent money separately to Enron, the parent. The interlocking nature of the relationship was fraught with conflicts of interest. Some of the most sophisticated of Wall Street private investors became partners in these funds, many of them given names from the *Star Wars* movies.

Citigroup and JPMorgan Chase also devised an especially beneficial way to provide financing to Enron, and undertook the devious transactions with many other companies. These were known as prepay swaps, complex derivatives trades that were loans that never appeared on the balance sheet. Citigroup lent nearly $4 billion to Enron in this way. JPMorgan Chase undertook even more prepay transactions with Enron. As one analyst put it, prepays became the "quarter to quarter cash flow lifeblood" of the company.

Research analysts throughout Wall Street were touting Enron's stock.

If they were reluctant, they became victims of Enron's wrath; Enron was providing hundreds of millions of dollars in underwriting and loan fees to Wall Street banks and virtually called the shots. In 1998, Fastow withheld underwriting business from Merrill until the analyst, John Olson, who was less than enthusiastic about Enron stock, was forced by his bosses to reverse his negative views. Olsen was fired anyway. In 1999, Fastow demanded that Citigroup's Salomon fire its skeptical analyst, Don Dufresne, if it wanted to do underwriting business with Enron. Was there anything wrong with their underwriting capability? a Citigroup higher-up asked Fastow when Enron stopped giving them business. "Nothing like that," Fastow reportedly answered. "Dufresne is the one reason you guys don't have a big role."

Critical to the functioning of Fastow's partnerships was an ever higher Enron stock price since the stock was the collateral for the partnerships' loans. The pressure to push the stock price up was intense because any fall would require that more cash be put up in the partnerships and in other corporate investments. The strategy became a destructive circle. Money was borrowed against the stock to create artificial sales for Enron, the profit from which kept the stock price up. The higher stock price enabled Fastow to borrow still more to create further artificial sales, and so on.

In 2000, Enron claimed $100 billion in sales, twice the level of the year before, and $1.3 billion in earnings, 25 percent higher than the year before. Its stock price tripled in two years, reaching $90 in August 2000. At the annual analysts meeting in January 2001, Skilling attached much higher valuations to the various parts of the company that he did not bother to support with data. He claimed the stock was worth $126 a share. A Goldman Sachs analyst obligingly said he expected it to reach $110 a share. In October 2001, just before its collapse, sixteen of seventeen analysts who followed Enron awarded it a "buy" or "strong buy." Meanwhile, Lay, Skilling, and Fastow were selling their own shares and making a fortune. In 2000, Fastow made $18 million on his. Lay took in some $76 million over a similar period.

By mid-2000, however, there were more skeptics concerning Enron, and when the stock market began to fall, they were becoming credible. Some of the loans not recorded on the financial statements were buried in obscure footnotes that diligent analysts ferreted out. The broadband business was looking dubious—too much cable had been laid in the previous boom, and Enron had a major investment in it. Conventional measures of Enron's value, such as the return on equity, were low. Yet Enron's stock remained high.

As much of the high-technology and telecom market fell, Enron could not buck the tide of falling stock prices indefinitely. Then, in early 2001, *Fortune* published a piece questioning how Enron made its money. This was the first serious criticism from a mainstream journal, the reporting largely based on research done by the hedge fund manager Jim Chanos, who specialized in short selling. Six months later, in August, Skilling resigned as CEO and a midlevel accountant, Sherron Watkins, wrote Ken Lay a letter pointing out that Fastow's partnerships were about to sink the company. Over the preceding two years, the partnerships had hidden over $1 billion in losses through accounting gimmicks. Yet Arthur Andersen still insisted the accounting methods were fine. Enron's prestigious Texas lawyers, Vinson & Elkins, confirmed to Lay that the accounting was aboveboard and asserted that Watkins was simply wrong. Fastow had been compensated, apart from his Enron earnings and stock options, with millions of dollars from the partnerships, a clear violation of partnership rules requiring independence from the company. These were the violations that ultimately put Fastow in jail (Lay and Skilling may not have known about Fastow's violations).

Now Wall Street was demanding a more honest accounting and Enron had to take the losses from the partnerships onto its books. They claimed these charges were onetime events and irrelevant to their business. Fastow's extra payments from the partnerships also became public. As more information surfaced, Enron's stock price kept falling, which produced more claims against the partnership and the further selling of shares. Moody's, the credit rating agency, said it was reassessing its ratings on Enron's debt, and the SEC opened an investigation.

As Enron's stock price fell, its reportable losses rose. Investment banks would no longer roll over the day-to-day loans—commercial paper—that the company needed to stay in business. Now that the SEC investigation was under way, Arthur Andersen started shredding paperwork, stopping only when the SEC issued a subpoena. As the bleeding continued, Citigroup and JPMorgan Chase offered to make a substantial loan on the condition that Enron give them all its future underwriting business—a final example of such conflicts of interest inducing foolish, even absurd business decisions. Finally, Lay, who had taken over again when Skilling left the company, arranged merger talks with Dynegy, a seemingly healthy energy company. But when more bad earnings surprises surfaced that fall—Enron reported losses in the third quarter of $664 million—Dynegy became skeptical. What decisively ended the deal was that the credit ratings agencies downgraded Enron debt to junk status and Dynegy pulled out. Both JPMorgan and Citigroup, each with billions of dollars on the line, tried to influence the ratings agencies to postpone the downgrading. Robert Rubin, at the request of Mike Carpenter, who ran Citigroup's Salomon subsidiary, called a Treasury official in November to ask him to delay. Rubin claimed that the entire financial market could be jeopardized, but the Treasury refused to intervene. Rubin's call brought him a congressional investigation but four years later he was cleared of any wrongdoing. The downgrade was the last straw. Enron's share price fell to $1 from $3 that day. (It turned out, unsurprisingly, that Dynegy had established similar partnerships to those that doomed Enron—some through Citigroup—and they soon undid Dynegy as well.)

After the collapse, civil suits were brought against Enron and its executives, as well as its bankers. Over the years, Ken Lay sold his total $144 million of Enron stock, Jeff Skilling $76 million, and Andy Fastow $30 million. Fastow also earned at least $45 million and perhaps as much as $60 million from the devious partnerships he formed. The largest of the civil suits, a class action suit by shareholders, recovered $7 billion, not nearly enough to compensate fully the stunned Enron employees who had been induced to invest in the company. Citigroup paid $2 billion in claims for misleading shareholders, and JPMorgan Chase paid $2.2 billion. Separately, the SEC fined JPMorgan and Citigroup $300 million each. Several Enron executives pled guilty to crimes, notably Fastow and his wife. Fastow was forced to give up a large share of his earnings, the rest mostly spent on defense fees, and he received a sentence of six years because he cooperated against other defendants. Skilling made no such deal and went to jail, convicted of corporate fraud in 2006, for a term of twenty-four years (which is likely to be reduced and possibly overturned on a technical reinterpretation of the applicable law). Lay was also convicted but died of a heart attack before sentencing; few knew he had a history of heart problems. Arthur Andersen was found guilty of obstruction of justice for destroying evidence and the firm was ultimately dissolved. It had been earning $50 million a year in fees at Enron, mostly for consulting. Auditing standards became hostage to this conflict of interest.

Enron's October 2001 bankruptcy was the largest in American history. The company had $63.4 billion of assets on the books. In the following months, there were other major bankruptcies involving accounting frauds, many of these at large telecommunications companies. Global Crossing went bankrupt in January, Adelphia in June, and there were dozens of other less dramatic examples. Then, in July 2002, WorldCom, the second largest long-distance phone company after AT&T, filed for bankruptcy with $107 billion in assets on the books. Only nine months later, it had eclipsed Enron as the largest bankruptcy in American history.

The men who ran these companies were not brilliant, creative counterparts to Lay, Skilling, Fastow, and the others at Enron. They were pedestrian, as were their crimes, but their exploits were inflated to enormous scale by the Wall Street infrastructure of powerful, unethical financiers and complex, unregulated financial markets as well as by a remarkable display of self-aggrandizement on the part of the CEOs.

Key Salomon Smith Barney research analyst Jack Grubman was at the center of the telecommunications abuses, touting Global Crossing and WorldCom stock despite their increasingly visible failures—recommending WorldCom, in particular, as its stock collapsed. Before the fall, however, he earned hundreds of millions of dollars of underwriting and loan fees as a research analyst for Citigroup. His loose ethical standards almost brought Sandy Weill criminal charges.

There was no quicker way to build the investment banking presence Weill sought than to have star securities analysts promoting investment banking clients. Grubman was one of the early enthusiasts for telecommunications stocks—issued by those companies creating the cable and broadband capacity to manage the expected needs of the Internet and cable television. He became the leading telecom analyst of his time, probably earning more money than any other at a Wall Street securities firm except for Quattrone, who was an investment banker.

Grubman was born in 1953 and grew up in Philadelphia. He was an excellent math student at Boston University, where he earned his undergraduate degree before going on for a master's degree in probability theory at Columbia. He had planned to get a math Ph.D. and teach. But his ambitions shifted, and in 1977 he joined AT&T to do financial planning. There he uncovered an important computer error in the company's forecasting models, earning him praise and promotions. He also learned the telecommunications business in detail. Eight years later, he left to join the brokerage firm Paine Webber as an analyst. The telecom industry was almost as exciting in these years as the dot-coms. As the rapidly expanding Internet required that America and the rest of the world be wired, the Telecommunications Act of 1996 deregulated the telephone industry, allowing local phone companies, the survivors of the long-ago AT&T breakup, to compete in the long-distance market once reserved for AT&T alone. Grubman understood the industry and the new trends as thoroughly as anyone on Wall Street.

Always hardworking, Grubman early on developed a reputation for honesty when he downgraded AT&T as it faced new competition. On the other hand, when he applied at Salomon for a job, his résumé claimed that he had attended MIT as an undergraduate, not Boston University. He was hired by Salomon in the mid-1990s, and when Sandy Weill took the broker over, Grubman was already the leading analyst in the telecom field.

Early on, Grubman's word moved stocks. He picked astounding winners, and the market was ripe to believe. He recommended Qwest in the spring of 1998 and it doubled in less than a year. Through Salomon, he brought Global Crossing public in August 1998 and the stock tripled in price.

Global Crossing was another phenomenon of the age, built on a good idea and carried to extremes by the Wall Street juggernaut. It was created by Gary Winnick, one of Mike Milken's traders at Drexel Burnham, which he left in 1985 before the scandal broke. Granted immunity when Milken was under investigations, Winnick was one of the few who agreed to testify against Milken, but he was never called on to do so.

Global Crossing intended to develop an underwater cable between America and Europe, and other continents. The idea seemed a natural. Winnick started the business in 1997, and by the next year, owning more than 25 percent of the shares, he became a billionaire when Grubman launched his successful IPO. Winnick undertook one takeover after another with exchanges of the high-priced stock, paying fees, mostly to Salomon, of more than $400 million between 1998 and 2001.

But business was not nearly as good as Winnick had anticipated or claimed. Global Crossing engaged in dubious accounting practices, such as swaps of financial assets, some with Enron, others with Qwest, to inflate earnings. These and other such questionable accounting practices were again approved by Arthur Andersen (Winnick even hired Andersen's main auditor as his chief financial officer). Global went bankrupt a month after Enron. Its executives and other insiders had already sold $4.5 billion worth of stock, far more than the Enron executives did. Winnick sold $735 million. George W. Bush made a killing as did Bill Clinton's close friend and former chairman of the Democratic National Committee, Terry McAuliffe, who saw his $100,000 investment increase to $18 million. All along,

Jack Grubman advised on Winnick's deals for Salomon, sat in on board meetings, and kept giving Global Crossing shares his highest rating for most of its life as a public company. As a rule, securities analysts strictly stay away from the board meetings of their clients.

By 2000, Grubman's close ties to Salomon clients were being seriously questioned. Salomon Smith Barney took in $343 million in fees on telecom mergers and stock and bond underwritings in 1999, and, as long as stock prices moved up, Wall Street looked the other way. But *Money* magazine did a scornful piece titled "Is Jack Grubman the Worst Analyst Ever?" When *BusinessWeek* raised questions about Grubman, Sandy Weill, who gave *BusinessWeek* an interview, defended him strongly. "Jack probably knows more about the business than anybody I've ever met," he said. "The more knowledge and understanding an analyst has, the better job they can do in analysis. If they lose their objectivity, they will lose their credibility."

By late 2000, Grubman's claims were clearly just fantasies about the strength of cable, if moneymaking ones. By the time the telecom bubble burst, Salomon Smith Barney, mostly because of Grubman, had made $1.4 billion in telecom fees over four years. Earlier, Goldman Sachs tried to lure the rainmaking Grubman away, but Salomon raised his annual pay to $20 million to keep him.

Global Crossing was not Grubman's biggest mistake. He developed a similar relationship with Bernard Ebbers, the head of WorldCom. Ebbers had started a small long-distance phone services company in Mississippi, and expanded by acquiring other small phone companies. His strength was as a salesman; his weakness was numbers. Grubman noticed that the upstart firm, despite its small size, was expanding rapidly. He made contact with Ebbers and, as WorldCom grew, eventually convinced him to make a daring bid for the much larger MCI with Salomon's considerable help. MCI agreed to the acquisition, given Salomon's participation, and overnight Ebbers's WorldCom became the second largest long-distance phone company in the nation.

As recession coupled with overcapacity began to undo the telecommunications bubble in 2000, WorldCom's clever financial officer Scott Sullivan moved expenses off the profit and loss statement and into the company's capital account, keeping the earnings trajectory rising—outright accounting deception. With rising earnings, WorldCom could claim that it was unique in avoiding the plunging earnings of the rest of the sector and it was able to sell a $12 billion bond issue through Citigroup (Solomon) and JPMorgan Chase. As with all underwriting, the two investment bankers

were obliged by SEC rules to do due diligence, providing an opinion statement that all the financial reporting was in order and reflected the operations of the firm. Neither Citigroup nor JPMorgan Chase discovered the
major accounting deception, or if they had, they did not make it public.
The credit rating agencies also overlooked the obvious chicanery and gave
the new bond offering a high rating.

It turned out that WorldCom had overstated its $10.5 billion of earn-
ings in 2001 by at least $4 billion. Another $3 billion of false profits was
later found. The SEC discovered that WorldCom gave Ebbers more than
$400 million in personal loans, with which he bought more WorldCom
stock. Grubman maintained a buy recommendation until one month
before the formal bankruptcy and only a few days before the admission of
the accounting chicanery. The accounting restatements and the plunging
stock prices, plus ratings downgrades (again too late to save many investors), made WorldCom's end inevitable. Ebbers was ruined, but Global's
Winnick remained one of the richest men in Los Angeles.

In 2002, Grubman, at the peak of his influence, despite Global's bankruptcy and the similar fate awaiting WorldCom, denied to *BusinessWeek*
that he had conflicts of interest. It was just good business, he claimed.
"What used to be a conflict has now become synergy. Someone like me
who is banking-intensive would have been looked at disdainfully by the
buy side 15 years ago. Now they know that I'm in the flow of what's going
on. That helps me help them think about the industry. The notion that
keeping your distance makes you more objective is absurd. Objective? The
other word for it is uninformed." WorldCom went bankrupt in July 2002,
becoming the largest failure ever until Lehman Brothers a half dozen years
later.

Telecom was more profitable for Citigroup's Salomon than high-technology
stocks, but the two bubbles had a lot in common. Eliot Spitzer, who had
been elected New York state attorney general in 1998, did not attack the
extraordinary abuse of stock research until 2001, more than a year after
the crash had begun. But once he understood the nature and pervasive-
ness of these practices, he ignored Wall Street's self-serving logic and its
occasional threats, and moved effectively. The son of a wealthy New York
real estate investor, he grew up with the young men who would become
Wall Street leaders, attended college and Harvard Law School with them,
and said he understood how they rationalized their behavior. As attorney

general he had subpoena powers that the SEC did not and he sought inter-company e-mails as part of his investigations.

Henry Blodget of Merrill Lynch was a natural first target. Blodget was a Yale graduate who, at thirty-two years of age, while working for Oppenheimer, predicted in October 1998 that Amazon.com's stock price of $250 per share, already high, would rise to $400. It was an eye-catching call, as the stock rose to above $400 within a month. The accurate and striking forecast, three years after the Netscape IPO, was to launch a new stage of the speculative advance in technology stocks. Blodget, in the minds of investors and the media, apparently could do no wrong. He had been voted the top dot-com investment analyst several years in a row by *Institutional Investor* and Greenwich Associates, an investment consulting firm. He left Oppenheimer for a high-paying job at Merrill Lynch and started appearing regularly on CNBC, the television business network that inflamed optimism almost as its mission and encouraged individual investors to trade stocks at home. By one calculation, an investor who bought all the IPOs of 1999 would have tripled his investment in a year. Now when Blodget touted a stock, which he did often, it was bound to go up and brought Merrill Lynch an enormous underwriting business.

At the end of 2001, Spitzer began requesting Merrill e-mails and found that Blodget sometimes told the public one thing and those inside the firm another. His research reports were often fictions to promote companies' stock prices. Bad investment advice is one thing, lying to investors knowingly another. To take but one example of Blodget's willingness to write false recommendations, he gave a high rating to GoTo.com to get underwriting business for Merrill, but when the company took its business elsewhere, Blodget immediately lowered the rating. Merrill executives, the e-mails showed, also frequently pressured Blodget into making positive recommendations. Sometimes the demands were so outrageous even he resisted.

In 2002, Merrill agreed to a settlement with Spitzer, who demanded that Merrill alter its practices. It stopped rewarding research analysts for the investment banking business they brought in. Spitzer fined Merrill $100 million. In 2003, Blodget settled SEC fraud charges, paying a $2 million fine and handing over another $2 million in profits. He was barred from the financial industry for life.

Spitzer cast his net beyond Merrill and Blodget and came up with Grubman. On April 25, 2002, the attorney general subpoenaed Grubman's e-mails at Salomon. The SEC announced an investigation of Citigroup a day later. The SEC had also begun an investigation into Citigroup's dealings with Enron and Dynegy. Congressional committees were also investigating the events.

In July, Weill decided to write a letter of apology to his employees about the firm's activities with Enron. But it was more a defense than an apology. "I feel badly and truly regret the pain we caused," he wrote. But then he also said: "From everything we know, our activities with Enron were legal, met accounting standards, and reflected industry practices—and our people, relying on the advice of independent legal and accounting experts, believed they were doing the right thing."

That month, Weill was given a dinner by *Chief Executive* magazine for his award as Chief Executive of the Year. His fellow executives lavished praise on him, as did the magazine. The day of the award, however, Grubman faced a House investigating committee at a televised hearing and was caught off guard when a congressman asked him whether he had allocated IPO shares to WorldCom and other executives to get their underwriting business, just as Frank Quattrone had with his clients. Grubman was unconvincing in his own defense, and Weill, who saw the taping that night before the party, had a hard time enjoying his award reception.

Soon, the NASD, the National Association of Securities Dealers, the brokers' self-regulatory arm, started investigating Grubman's inflated research on another company, Winstar Communications. Congress started issuing subpoenas for e-mails from Citigroup as well.

While these investigations were pending, Spitzer had begun constructing a case against Weill for allegedly asking Grubman to upgrade his recommendation on AT&T back in 1999. As we have seen, Michael Armstrong, AT&T's CEO, also sat on the board of Citicorp, and Weill needed his vote to outflank John Reed.

In November, Spitzer came upon more incriminatory e-mails. One written by Grubman made it appear that he had agreed to change the rating on AT&T but, in return, asked Weill to donate $1 million to the 92nd Street Y to help get his twin children into a prestigious nursery school in Manhattan. Weill did indeed arrange the contribution and Grubman's children were admitted to the school. Grubman also upgraded AT&T, and Armstrong, as we have seen, voted for Weill rather than Reed.

Weill vehemently maintained he had not read Grubman's e-mails, and made the contribution only to help an employee. Spitzer said he found no evidence Weill had explicitly asked for Grubman to upgrade AT&T, but only to "take another look." Of course, such a request from a man as powerful as Weill could not be taken lightly. Spitzer had his top lawyer question Weill closely, and in the end, Spitzer did not believe Weill was guilty of an outright, actionable crime, but "Sandy knew what was going on," said Spitzer. "They all did."

When the investigations ended, the roster of questionable activities was staggering. The SEC, NASD, and the New York Stock Exchange (also a self-regulatory body), with Spitzer in the lead, got ten firms to agree to a settlement for their deceitful investment practices, resulting in a total fine of $1.4 billion. Citigroup was assessed the largest individual fine of the group, a total of $400 million. The SEC separately charged Citigroup with helping both Enron and Dynegy inflate profits and underreport debt. Citigroup agreed in July 2003 to pay $101 million for its Enron activities and $19 million for similar transgressions involving Dynegy. A class action suit by WorldCom investors cost Citigroup $2.6 billion in May 2004 and suits by Enron shareholders, as noted earlier, cost Citigroup more than $2 billion, settled in June 2005. The signing firms agreed to stop analysts' touting stock to get underwriting business, though the policy wasn't as well enforced in coming years as promised.

Overall, including all the civil and shareholder actions, Citigroup had to pay more in fines and penalties than any other financial company. Even so, in 2002, the company earned $16 billion and could easily absorb the fines and disgorgements. Only Grubman was fined personally, an almost trivial $15 million compared to his total income, but he was barred from the business for life.

Spitzer announced at the end of December 2002 that he was not going to charge Weill with a crime. Weill then embarked on a public rehabilitation project of his own image and Citigroup's. But even a $100 million gift to New York Hospital that year won him relatively few accolades.

A few months earlier, Weill had named his chief counsel, Chuck Prince, to run Salomon Smith Barney. Weill voluntarily adopted the guidelines to separate research and banking that Spitzer had imposed on Merrill Lynch and, also voluntarily, started recording as company expenses the hefty stock options he gave his executives, and most lavishly himself— a stricture he had vehemently resisted until this point. He raised Citigroup dividends significantly, though he had refused to do so in the past to keep cash in the company.

Weill completely escaped serious criticism by shareholders or his board, even as Citigroup shares fell by 25 percent in 2002. He escaped personal fines in civil suits as well. Robert Rubin escaped most public criticism, as did Chuck Prince—until the credit crisis several years later.

In the spring of 2003, Richard Grasso, head of the New York Stock Exchange, offered Weill a place on the stock exchange board as one of its public advocates, a position established to protect the interests of the investors as opposed to the firms. When Spitzer found out, he was furious. The man whose firm paid the largest fine for bilking the public was now being asked to be the public investors' advocate. Spitzer called Grasso and told him he would fight the appointment in the press. (He'd later fight Grasso's $190 million retirement pay package, unsuccessfully.) Weill declined the appointment and claimed he never sought the position anyway.

No one thought Weill would retire just because he turned seventy in March 2003. But that summer he announced he would do just that. The strains of 2002 perhaps took their toll. Chuck Prince replaced him. Weill remained chairman of the board.

A reason the scandals of the early 2000s did not cause even more damage was that the many billions of dollars of debt owed to Citigroup and JPMorgan Chase by Enron, WorldCom, and others were to some degree insured against losses through the derivatives market. Someone took the risk, however, mostly insurance companies and pension funds. But the existence of the insurance is also what encouraged these banks to lend so aggressively to Enron and WorldCom in the first place. For now, the cost of insurance was manageable, and the losses by those paying the insurance digestible. By the mid-2000s, that would no longer be the case.

After the scandals, Congress passed the Sarbanes-Oxley regulatory legislation to make executives and directors responsible for their financial reporting. Accounting standards were tightened. Companies restated earnings to meet the new requirements. And to some degree, the new legislation worked to improve standards. But this did not prevent banks and others from finding loopholes in accounting practices that enabled them to disguise or even conceal hundreds of billions of dollars of risky investments off their books.

Nothing was done about the ratings agencies' manifest errors in dealing with companies like Enron. Nor were over-the-counter derivatives brought under regulation, despite pleas by some government officials to do so. In fact, investment banks were given further license to borrow by the SEC, which ended formal restrictions on borrowing by broker-dealers in 2004. Even VAR, so disgraced as a measure of risk by the brilliant strategists of Long-Term Capital Management, escaped regulatory attention and was still used widely.

The outright losses borne by investors due to these activities during the 1990s and early 2000s are difficult to calculate, but they ran into the trillions of dollars. The money invested in high-technology companies, especially dot-coms, as well as the overextended telecom industry, that was entirely lost when these companies went under, amounted to nearly $3 trillion. Some of this was the winnings made during the speculative boom, but had a large portion been funneled into more productive activities, America would have gained immeasurably. Losses on the collapse of Enron, WorldCom, Global Crossing, and a few others like Tyco and Adelphia, all bankruptcies, alone amounted to another trillion dollars.

The overspeculation based so much on outright deception led to enormous amounts of wasted investment. Capital investment in telecom ventures was significantly overdone. The overselling of the industry led to at least $100–150 billion in superfluous investment of hard-earned dollars—not to mention the far greater amounts spent on buying the overinflated stocks of these companies. The $150 billion amounted to one third of spending on equipment and buildings in manufacturing and information services businesses in any single year.

By 2002, Weill was personally worth between $1.5 and $2 billion. By the time the stock market turned back up in the mid-2000s, taking Citigroup up with it, Weill had lost his contrition. He remained chairman of Citigroup until 2006. In 2007, he told *The New York Times* that the achievements of entrepreneurs like himself were similar to those of the first Gilded Age, when there was no income tax and government was much smaller. These new titans deserved their enormous fortunes, Weill had no doubt, and the diminished reach of government in the last quarter century was a key reason for the nation's current economic success. "People can look at the last 25 years and say this is an incredibly unique period of time," Weill said. "We didn't rely on somebody else to build what we built, and we shouldn't rely on somebody else to provide all the services our society needs." The *New York Times* reporter noted that among Weill's many trophies, a pen Clinton used to sign the repeal of the Glass-Steagall law was prominently displayed. Individual fortunes continued to speak loudly in America in the mid-2000s and overwhelmed vigilance in favor of private gain. Far bigger catastrophes were to come, but for essentially the same reasons. Weill had created the largest financial firm in the world; it had been involved with almost every major deception of the 1990s and 2000s. It remained at the forefront of deception in the mid-2000s as well, though now, given its sheer size, it could bring down the economy itself.

In the meantime, the foundation of the U.S. economy, threatened so often in the preceding twenty years, was beginning to crack. Just as Greenspan assured Clinton the economy had never been in better condition in his many years of experience as an economist, consumers were borrowing at an increasing rate to meet their expenses. The annual payments to meet interest and debt repayments reached new record highs as a share of consumer income by 2000, and the overall savings rate in the nation was falling rapidly. Even though worker compensation had risen fairly rapidly in the last few years of the 1990s, it had not made up for the preceding twenty years of virtual stagnation.

In the late 1990s, capital investment had reached new heights as a proportion of GDP at last, after a torpid decade and a half from the early 1980s to the mid-1990s. But its foundation about which so many had boasted was fragile. While there was a true technology boom based on falling computer chip prices and the spread of the Internet, much of the investment was wastefully built on deceit and corruption. As noted, in the early 2000s, the Nasdaq index, mostly dominated by new high-technology companies, lost 80 percent of its value. A large majority of the new high-technology companies had failed or were now trading in the stock market for pennies a share as the new decade began.

18

Angelo Mozilo

THE AMERICAN TRAGEDY

Without a high-technology boom, Alan Greenspan worried about what would lead to an economic resurgence in 2001. The stock market crash of 2000 and the tragedy of September 11, 2001, made real the risk that the moderate recession that had already started could turn into a deep and lasting one. Housing was a natural possibility for revival. An upturn in house prices could be achieved if Greenspan pushed mortgage rates down far enough. And if housing prices rose, American consumers were also likely to spend more, feeling wealthier and having high-value assets against which to borrow, to an even greater degree than they had in the late 1990s when stock prices rose so rapidly. Economists widely accepted that this "wealth" effect accounted for much of the Clinton boom. If housing strengthened too much, Greenspan was also confident he could handle the levers of the economy to slow it down. Most of the sophisticated Wall Street traders and analysts were convinced of this themselves, so they were more confident in making risky investments.

Greenspan cut rates even more in the first years of the new George W. Bush administration than in the early 1990s, eventually, as noted earlier, driving the target federal funds rate from 6 percent to 1 percent. The rate of interest on a conventional long-term mortgage fell from 8.5 percent in mid-2000 to 5.5 percent by mid-2004. Increasingly important, the teaser rates on increasingly popular adjustable rate mortgages over the first two years of the mortgage, typically set according to the rates on the three-month Treasury bill or a like instrument, plunged to as low as 3 percent. And the housing market took off.

But the mortgage market had radically changed. While the nation's thrifts had once funded most of the nation's mortgages with deposits

Countrywide CEO Angelo Mozilo being sworn in to testify before Congress

of savers, Wall Street was now channeling what became trillions of dollars from pensions and mutual funds, insurance companies, and wealthy individuals in the United States and around the world into individual mortgages through securitization. With so much funding, thousands of mortgage brokers started selling mortgages to homeowners, many to people with poor credit, known as subprime borrowers. Another industry took center stage in America: these mortgage writers, unregulated by a federal authority or even most state governments. The leader of the industry was Angelo Mozilo.

Greenspan remained oblivious to the dangers of the new abusive mortgages or the overheated housing market, even as the FBI warned in 2004 that there was an "epidemic" of fraudulent mortgages. When the Fed raised rates in 2004 to slow the economy, Greenspan was surprised to find that this time it didn't work. Rather than dampen speculation, the rising rates stimulated it all the more, as mortgage brokers like Mozilo and Wall Street securitizers financed riskier mortgages to make up for lower profit margins. Tens of billions of dollars of fresh capital flowed to the United States from China. Despite the rapid increase in rates by the Fed—the target federal funds rate rising from 1 percent to more than 5 percent—more subprime mortgages were written than ever before. In all, $7 trillion of mortgage debt was created between 2000 and 2007, more than the total debt of the federal government accumulated over fifty years.

Some economists blamed Greenspan for cutting rates to such low levels, and keeping them there for so long. But the low rates could have been a constructive way to revitalize the economy had they been accompanied by adequate regulatory oversight. On the contrary, in one of the most remarkable episodes of government irresponsibility, Greenspan and other Washington regulators looked the other way. Regulatory failure was the open valve through which bad debt flowed. This regulatory failure, like Wall Street excess, was the product of the ideology that first took root in the 1970s.

Ultimately, hundreds of billions of dollars of bad mortgage debt were bought by the world's largest investment institutions. All the while, the American people seemed to trust that even when they were taking mortgages they couldn't imagine qualifying for a decade earlier, the financial markets were working fairly and that federal overseers would see to it that Wall Street greed did no damage.

Angelo Mozilo, born in the Bronx in 1939, felt that as a son of Italian immigrants he would never be employed on Wall Street. Mozilo's father wanted him to follow in his footsteps at his successful butcher shop in the Bronx, but his mother was determined that all their children go to college. Mozilo went to public elementary school and Catholic high school in the 1940s and 1950s. He graduated from Fordham University in 1960.

In high school, he had worked as a messenger for a Manhattan mortgage company run by Jews, the only employee of Italian descent, but he ingratiated himself with the owner and eventually worked in every department of the firm, learning the intricacies of the mortgage business firsthand. Most mortgages being written were supported by the federal government in an effort to expand home ownership after the war, either the Federal Housing Authority (FHA), the agency established during the housing bust of the 1930s, or the Veterans Administration (VA), under a program for war veterans started in 1944. A housing boom started in the 1950s and was still under way in the 1960s.

The firm Mozilo worked for sold out to a larger mortgage company in a deal put together by another executive, David Loeb. Mozilo and Loeb, fifteen years older than he, became close friends and started their own mortgage company in 1968, Countrywide Credit Industries (later Countrywide Financial Services). At Loeb's insistence, Mozilo left New York to open mortgage offices in California, where the residential market was expanding most rapidly, while Loeb stayed in New York to raise "warehouse financing," money from brokerage firms and banks that would finance the mortgages. Then, when enough mortgages were gathered by Mozilo, Loeb sold them as a group to financial institutions, including savings and loan associations (thrifts), banks, money managers, and brokerage firms that wanted the interest income.

Countrywide was a simple mortgage broker in a simple but competitive business. The thrifts, which had federally insured savings deposits to lend, wrote by far the majority of mortgages in the country. To compete, companies like Countrywide had to be more aggressive. Mozilo knocked on the doors of countless home builders and Realtors to offer his services in hopes of winning the mortgage business of those who bought their homes. As Mozilo hired others, he demanded that his new salespeople do the same, get to know the Realtors in their territories and pressure them to use Countrywide to provide their customers with mortgages.

Countrywide then got lucky. In the beginning, it could sell only low-risk FHA/VA mortgages because they could be most readily financed on Wall Street; other mortgages were thought too risky. But in the late 1960s, Fannie Mae was revamped to broaden its role in the housing market. The agency had been created in the Depression to buy FHA mortgages in the open market when thrifts, then in financial trouble, had to sell them. But in 1968, a Federal Reserve governor and an LBJ economist came up with a plan, approved by Congress, to allow Fannie Mae to buy a wider range of mortgages and place them into a pool, pieces of which were to be sold to institutional investors—the beginning of securitization. The interest on the pooled mortgages was "passed through" to the investors. The mortgages Fannie Mae bought need not be guaranteed by the FHA or VA, and the pools were not guaranteed by the federal government, but they had to conform to standards for down payments, size of loans, and the income of the mortgage holders. These were called "A" or "conforming" mortgages, to be distinguished from nonconforming or nonprime loans, including subprime, which were graded A− through D.

No longer restricted to the FHA/VA mortgages, Countrywide's potential market expanded by many times. Not only was Fannie Mae, Federal National Mortgage Association—which also had been privatized in 1968—packaging a wider range of mortgages, but also another new agency, Ginnie Mae (the Government National Mortgage Association), was created to back mortgages with federal guarantees. Two years later, Freddie Mac (Federal Home Loan Mortgage Corporation) was created to supplement Fannie Mae, repackaging still more mortgages. Countrywide could now resell many more mortgages, as long as they were conforming mortgages, back to Fannie Mae or Freddie Mac, and suddenly the mortgage business was potentially a very good one. Mozilo, charming, energetic, and persuasive, carefully cultivated his relationships with the officers of Fannie Mae and Freddie Mac, and Countrywide now grew rapidly. In later years, two journalists wrote, Fannie Mae and Mozilo were joined at the hip, and, as a result, Mozilo was charged lower fees by the agency.

More good luck was to come. The thrifts, which up until then dominated the mortgage-making business, found themselves in Volcker's death grip as interest rates were pushed up in the 1970s and early 1980s. They couldn't get savers to deposit funds with them in order to write more mortgages because they were restricted by Regulation Q from paying the high rates now available at money market funds and other instruments. And they were losing money on existing mortgages, having written most of them at rates of 4 and 5 percent whereas the costs of funds were now much higher. So it was open season for Mozilo. He could write new mortgages at higher rates with no competition from the thrifts, and sell them to Fannie and Freddie (known as government sponsored enterprises, or GSEs), which securitized them and passed them on to institutional investors. After chasing down home buyers for years, Mozilo had Realtors coming to him. "AC" was Mozilo's motto—"always closing."

In the early 1980s, the thrifts, most teetering on the brink of insolvency, were bailed out by Congress. First, in 1981, Congress passed a tax break allowing them to write off the losses against past profits that they had to take to sell their low-yield mortgages to investors. It thus cost them far less to get them off their books. In 1982, as noted, Congress passed the Garn-St. Germain bill, which removed the Regulation Q cap on interest rates that the thrifts could pay to savers. It also allowed them to invest 40 percent of their funds in nonresidential real estate and other investments, from Southwest resorts to golf courses to junk bonds.

Soon, the more aggressive thrifts were paying very high rates to attract savers and making billions of dollars of bad investments. It was not the thrift executives' money, after all; it was ultimately the federal government's through deposit insurance. So attractive were the high rates on insured accounts that a new brokered-deposit business was created by Merrill Lynch among others to channel clients' money in bulk into the thrifts around the country that paid the highest interest.

Now the thrifts were momentarily in clover, or so many thought. But later in the 1980s, when rates rose again and real estate, junk bonds, and other speculative investments turned down, thrift after thrift went out of business or was paralyzed by losses, and the field was left open for brokers like Mozilo. He not only sold mortgages but also signed up as independent brokers many of the well-trained salespeople who lost their jobs at the thrifts. It was much cheaper than opening new offices and staffing them with employees earning annual salary; these brokers worked out of their cars or homes or from phone booths and were paid a commission only if they sold a mortgage.

His partner, David Loeb, was opposed to using independent brokers, who he thought were typically unscrupulous and hard to monitor. There was no federal regulation of mortgage brokers and only weak state oversight. Who knew what promises they made to home buyers or deceptive tactics they used? But Mozilo saw only opportunity and the eager younger man opened a new division for independent loan brokers who were not direct employees of the company.

Wall Street, in turn, took some of the new mortgage firms public, including Countrywide, whose first public offering had raised only $450,000 during the stock market slide in 1969. Happily for Mozilo, the next fifteen years saw profits rise rapidly and the company expanded across the nation. In the 1980s, the firm was able to raise $11 million in fresh capital.

When Mozilo and other brokers were building their sales forces, especially in fast-growing regions like California, the Southwest, and Florida, Wall Street had begun to privatize the mortgage securitization pioneered by Fannie Mae. Salomon was the first to do so, predictably enough because it had dominated government bond trading for so long, and now, in the 1970s, as federal budget deficits grew, and interest rates became more volatile, trading in and underwriting Treasury securities grew more profitable. Once the bond trading desks had been run by proven, savvy, hard-nosed traders, like William Simon, the former treasury secretary, who was proud that he never hired a trader with an MBA or an intellectual idea. "If you weren't trading bonds, you'd be driving a truck," Simon supposedly told his employees. Simon himself hadn't finished college. At the time, there were twenty-eight partners at Salomon, and only fifteen had finished college. Mike Bloomberg, the future New York City mayor, was the rare Salomon trader who had an MBA, but he was forced out after John Gutfreund took over, only to start his own company, Bloomberg, the maker of the ubiquitous trading information terminals that eventually made him far richer than any Salomon partner.

Despite the proud blue-collar tradition of traders, the uneducated trader soon became a relic of a former age. One of Simon's traders, Bob Dall, did have the sort of smart idea Simon discouraged. Dall was a traditional bond trader who had also begun to trade Ginnie Maes, the federally guaranteed pass-throughs, but it was a small sideline for Salomon. Based on analysis by the firm's economist, Henry Kaufman, Dall was convinced that as baby boomers grew older, and many Americans moved to the West and Southwest, demand for housing would likely grow rapidly, radically raising the need for financing.

The ever cynical Simon thought Ginnie Maes could at best become a minor profit center for Salomon, and for several years, they were, but Dall thought he saw the future. In 1978, with Simon long gone into government, Dall and another Salomon partner decided to try to underwrite a mortgage bond privately. As discussed, before this, Fannie Mae and the other GSEs packaged these bonds themselves, using Wall Street only as a sales force to distribute them to investors. Dall's innovation made history. He convinced Bank of America to pool its mortgages and let Salomon create a security based on them that it then sold to its large investment clients, including pension funds, trust companies, and other investors. Salomon was doing on its own what Fannie Mae had been doing with government support—and a window opened on an entirely new world of profit-making opportunity.

The mortgage-backed security (MBS) sold well. Dall correctly thought it was a breakthrough, a privately created pass-through. In that year, he persuaded Gutfreund, newly named as Salomon's managing partner, to create a separate department and trading desk for mortgage bonds. Now manager of the new department, Dall needed a talented trader to replace himself, and chose one of Salomon's best, Lewis Ranieri, another free-wheeling college dropout. Gutfreund agreed to the transfer. Ranieri was a coarse, overweight, poorly dressed loudmouth who never let anyone forget he was a poor Italian boy from Brooklyn. He had started in the mailroom at Salomon and, through his wits and aggressiveness, worked his way to the trading floor. The best traders were often rogues who sometimes didn't let management know the extent of the risks they took. Some of these would lose tens of millions of dollars, and a few much more. Ranieri was a rogue who made money. Financial writer Michael Lewis, then a Salomon novice, in his first-person account of working at Salomon Brothers in these years, quoted Dall as saying of Ranieri, "He was tough-minded. He didn't mind hiding a million-dollar loss from a manager, if that's what it took. He didn't let morality get in his way. Well, morality is not the right word, but you know what I mean." Trading was the key to profits in the new mortgage department. Ranieri, the man in the middle, had the information about supply and demand and also the deep financial pockets of a house like Salomon.

Ranieri was not merely aggressive and willing to cut corners; he was by every account smart. "I have never seen anyone, educated or uneducated, with a quicker mind," said Dall, whom Ranieri eventually forced out of the department. But it was the struggles of the thrifts in the late 1970s and early 1980s that made his trading desk Salomon's most profitable operation for several years. As thrifts went out of business when interest rates soared, many at Salomon wanted to close down the mortgage desk because there was little trading. But Ranieri fought them off, never forgetting later how shabbily he was treated by his colleagues. When Congress passed the tax subsidy for the dying thrifts, the thrifts rushed to sell the mortgages on their books, even at deep discounts, and Salomon bought them up at the bargain price, often able to resell them at enormous profits or, if not, simply hold them on the books. Some at Salomon thought Ranieri was taking dangerous levels of risk by buying mortgages for Salomon's own inventory. But with the deep recession of 1982, interest rates started at last to fall, and the prices of Ranieri's purchases rose handsomely.

When rates fall, bond prices rise. If Ranieri paid $600 for a $1,000 bond paying 5 percent interest, for example, he earned more than 8 percent on his payment. If interest rates on comparable securities then fell to 7 percent, his bond was worth more—he could sell it for $700, a handsome gain. The mountain of mortgages that Ranieri bought on the cheap made Salomon a fortune. Ranieri's team made roughly $150 million for Salomon in 1982, $200 million in 1983, $175 million in 1984, and $275 million in 1985. This may have been as much as all the rest of Wall Street made all together, or so Ranieri claimed.

There was still a serious obstacle to overcome if more institutional investors were going to buy pools of mortgages. To be attractive, mortgages required a predictable rate of return and maturity date, but because homeowners could pay them off early, mortgages didn't offer such security. Early prepayments might have to be invested at a lower interest rate, for example, resulting overall in a less profitable investment. Laurence Fink of First Boston, a mortgage trader who was building a mortgage operation to rival Ranieri's, developed with his colleagues a novel idea. A few years younger than Ranieri, Fink was part of the new class of Wall Street traders, with an MBA from UCLA, a serious demeanor, and a highly analytical approach to the market.

Fink's innovation, developed with his colleagues at First Boston, was to pool perhaps ten thousand mortgages into an investment vehicle and sell bonds to investors with the mortgages as collateral. The new security was called a collateralized mortgage obligation (CMO), and the bonds were divided into pieces, or as they were called, "tranches," according to their seniority. The first piece or tranche, the French word for slice, was usually called Class A, and consisted of 75 to 80 percent of the bonds. It was thus most senior and was entitled to all the mortgage interest payments from the pool until the Class A investors received their full bond interest. Even if some mortgage holders prepaid sooner than expected, the interest from the rest of the mortgages would almost always be enough to cover the payments to these investors. Thus, investors in the first tranche could be almost entirely protected from the prepayment risk, and provided a reliable rate of return.

After Class A was paid off, Class B, the next tranche, received the next round of cash flows, which were more susceptible to high levels of prepayment but still fairly reliable. The third group, Class C, perhaps 15 percent of investors, and known as the mezzanine financing, would get paid off last, and was most likely to suffer the prepayment risk. There was a tiny sliver near the bottom, usually known as the equity, which bore any prepayments immediately and was most risky.

In 1983, Fink and his team devised such a tranche structure for an issue sponsored by Freddie Mac, which agreed to go along with the idea. More important, Fink convinced the ratings agencies to rate each tranche separately. The most senior tranche was rated triple-A, just like a Treasury bond or the bond of a first-rate corporation. The next tranche was awarded a double-A or single-A rating. In future deals, there may have been one or two more tranches before reaching the mezzanine, which was typically awarded a triple-B or triple-B−. The equity was too speculative to warrant a rating.

Because they took less risk, investors were paid a lower interest rate for the Class A tranches, and then gradually higher rates down the line. But because mortgage interest was higher than interest on government or quality corporate bonds, the triple-A tranches of mortgage-backed securities paid a higher rate than government or corporate bonds with comparable ratings. This was the magic of securitization and why so many investors around the world were ultimately attracted to it. For the same credit rating, an investor collected more interest. Freddie Mac went along with Fink's idea because it would more easily sell the package of loans his way than with a traditional pass-through, and perhaps at a higher interest rate than it would otherwise get. With several tranches paying more enticing rates, and with prepayment risks controlled, many more investors would be willing to buy.

In the early 1980s, Fink and the others did not as yet worry about higher levels of defaults on the mortgages. But when defaults started to become a serious issue, especially in the 2000s, the tranche structure provided a similar protection. The Class A investors were almost assuredly protected from such unexpected default risk, the Wall Street securitizers argued, because they got their money first—an assumption that turned out to be wrong as securitization techniques grew more complex.

And so "structured" finance in mortgages was born. As computer power increased, more tranches could be calculated and carved out of a collateralized mortgage obligation almost overnight. Soon, there were as many as ten tranches (and occasionally many more). There were also newer ways to divide the mortgage-backed securities. Some investors would want only interest income, for example, some wanted the principal of the bond, which rose and fell with changes in interest rates. As Wall Street packaged diversified mortgages to investors with different objectives, it could sell more of them. When working ideally, this practice reduced mortgage rates across the country as more money became available. It also made Wall Street enormous profits, however, as they took substantial fees on every deal they put together. It was soon no longer clear that the benefits of securitization were truly flowing to borrowers. Wall Street firms were taking a big cut of the profits.

First Boston and Salomon quickly became the leaders in underwriting the CMOs for the government agencies. They then began packaging nonconforming loans, including jumbos (now classified as above roughly $400,000) and adjustable rate mortgages, ARMs, that were typically outside the boundaries of Fannie, Freddie, and Ginnie. Eventually, they also packaged subprime mortgages as well, the category of the nonconforming loans sold to home buyers with unusually low credit scores and histories of late payments or defaults.

The expansion of the business required legislative help, on both state restrictions and tax concerns. The most important change was Jimmy Carter's deregulatory legislation in 1980, the Depository Institutions Deregulation and Monetary Control Act of 1980, which aside from formally abolishing Regulation Q (over time), also as noted preempted the many state usury laws that placed a ceiling on mortgage and credit card rates. Now, mortgage originators could charge much higher rates, making it possible to write subprime mortgages. Ranieri pressed Congress for further friendly legislation, in particular the Secondary Mortgage Market Enhancement Act, passed by Congress in 1984, that largely ended key state restrictions on the sale of mortgage-backed securities as long as the private ratings agencies gave the securities a high rating. As usual, Ranieri argued that securitization reduced mortgage rates for homeowners (he later expressed doubts, admitting that Wall Street took too much of the benefit in fees and trading profit), and that the ratings agencies were competent enough to provide a trustworthy assessment of risk. Congress in turn enthusiastically supported securitization by Wall Street as a way to expand home ownership. Reagan was an advocate as well, the promise that perhaps private securitization would one day eliminate the government's role in subsidizing housing through Fannie Mae and Freddie Mac in particular appealed to him ideologically.

The CMOs transformed the market. By the second half of the 1980s, pension funds, trusts, and investors were eagerly buying them. Michael Lewis figured that $60 billion of CMOs were sold privately by Wall Street between 1983 and 1988. As early as 1986, 25 percent of all mortgages were being securitized, both directly by the GSEs or privately through Wall Street. Salomon and First Boston made a fortune, as did Ranieri and Fink personally. According to Lewis, Ranieri earned $2–5 million a year between 1982 and 1986, making him one of the highest-paid Wall Street professionals at the time.

The easy moneymaking environment did not last. Both Ranieri and Fink, by now angry, griping rivals, were caught off guard by the stock market crash in 1987, and then by the higher interest rates later imposed by Greenspan once the economy seemed out of danger. Both took major losses on their portfolio of bonds. Ranieri was fired by Gutfreund, supposedly because the brash man had made too many enemies, which of course would have been fine were he making money for the firm. The younger Fink, who had been a candidate to run First Boston, was now being ostracized. In 1988, he left to run BlackRock, a private investment firm specializing in distressed mortgages and other debt, for Pete Peterson and Stephen Schwarzman, who had a few years earlier left Lehman Brothers to found the investment firm Blackstone Group.

The setback of the late 1980s was temporary, however. By the early 1990s, the mortgage market had been transformed from the one dominated by thrifts, savings banks, and commercial banks, which were financed by depositor savings, to a decentralized marketplace where mortgage brokers (and a dwindling number of thrifts) wrote mortgages and immediately sold them off to the GSEs and increasingly directly to Wall Street securitizers like Salomon. Fannie Mae and the other GSEs retained high standards for their loans. But the mortgages sold to Wall Street had no such screen. Because they were quickly sold off, their quality was of less concern to mortgage companies, which once had to monitor and assess the creditworthiness of home buyers because they held their mortgages on their books for a generation. The Wall Street packagers were also not interested in the credit quality of individual mortgages. They were convinced that, like life insurance companies, they could diversify such risk away in large pools of mortgages from all over the country and from varieties of homeowners—all accomplished with sophisticated computer models. Now, no one was minding the store. The radically new mortgage model was called "originate to sell."

For Countrywide—and other fast-growing mortgage originators—the transformation of the industry to securitization of mortgages was a miracle. Mozilo now had a constant flow of finance and the only limit to profits was how many mortgages he could write. The groundwork laid, securitization advanced rapidly after the troubles of the 1980s and the recession of 1990–1991. Overall, home (and multi-residence) mortgages outstanding rose by from $2.4 trillion to $3.5 trillion over the period between 1988 and 1993. Securitization increased from $800 billion in 1988 to $1.1 trillion in 1993. The annual lending by the increasingly outdated thrifts shrank by $200 billion, as the deposit-taking institutions were displaced by brokers like Mozilo with direct access to Wall Street financing. In 1992, Countrywide was already the largest originator of residential mortgages in the United States, selling a total of $30.5 billion worth. There were other new giant competitors, led by executives more aggressive than Mozilo, who ran Southern California companies like New Century and Fremont. Mozilo was the industry leader, however, and he was named president of the Mortgage Bankers Association that year, a position of which he was immensely proud.

By the mid-1980s and especially the 1990s, the mortgage business was seen by most of the major commercial and investment banks as the gold mine it truly was, and they began increasing the funds they raised by tens of billions of dollars a year. In the mid-1980s, traders trained on Ranieri's desk were leaving for big compensation packages at new mortgage desks across Wall Street, as old-line firm after firm joined the new mortgage business. All these firms would eventually founder in the 2000s.

The Salomon mortgage department grew, but several traders made it especially profitable. A standout was Howie Rubin, who learned the business under Ranieri. Ranieri hired the mathematically trained engineer right out of Harvard Business School, and later called him the most talented trader he had ever seen. Unlike Ranieri, Rubin applied mathematical techniques to trading that were similar to those Meriwether was using just across the Salomon trading floor. But he also had a special taste for gambling. When still an engineer, he had taught himself how to count cards and regularly beat the house at blackjack in Las Vegas. Ironically, the dropout Ranieri respected the new quants, and recognized their techniques as key to the mortgage market and its complexities, particularly calculating reliable estimates of prepayment schedules. Rubin made Salomon $25 million in his first year, but still unaccustomed to paying large bonuses, Gutfreund refused to give him a seven-figure compensation package. Merrill Lynch lured Rubin away with a $1-million-a-year offer in 1985 to work on its new mortgage desk.

Rubin did very well in 1985 and 1986, bringing Merrill's mortgage business almost to the level of Salomon's and First Boston's. But then he gambled heavily that interest rates would continue to fall, without informing his bosses of the major trades he was undertaking, because the size of the risk he took—potential losses—violated the in-house rules. He merely hid the paperwork in a desk drawer. When rates turned up in 1986 and 1987 under both Volcker and his successor, Greenspan, Rubin lost between $250 million and $377 million for Merrill, according to estimates, well more than half of the company's profits that year. Merrill immediately fired him, claiming he had far exceeded his authorization. (The SEC eventually brought charges against him that were settled in 1990.) It is likely, however, that Merrill was aware that its traders, especially stars like Rubin, exceeded their authorization. It was expected of them, as long as management didn't know the details.

Rubin's trades were typical of how incentives on Wall Street favored taking risk more than managing risk. The traders almost always landed on their feet again—and of course almost never had to pay back what they lost. Trading began to dominate Wall Street, and the profits to be made in turn by daredevils, now well-educated ones, fueled the mortgage market.

Adding to the taste for more risk taking, by the late 1980s many of the major firms were public, no longer partnerships risking their own money but rather the shareholders' money. By the end of the 1990s, all the major firms were public, Goldman the last holdout selling an IPO in 1999. Like the traders, the partners were rarely if ever personally responsible for the firm's losses. Before the 1980s, this was not so. Felix Rohatyn, who as a board member of the New York Stock Exchange was often involved in rescuing brokerage firms in the late 1960s, was assigned to the task by Lazard's managing partner, André Meyer, precisely to help avoid any liability he and his partners might have for the assets of the clients of other brokers who went out of business. The Securities Investor Protection Corporation hadn't been formed until 1970 to insure these assets.

After being fired, Rubin quickly got a job offer from Bear Stearns. Bear was among the earliest of the old-line investment banks to enter the mortgage business aggressively. It was a freewheeling, risk-oriented house that specialized in bond trading and was among the first to risk capital liberally. Bear had always been trying to catch up to the far bigger investment banks, which were more diversified or had much more capital. Seeing an opportunity and fearlessly taking advantage of it was part of Bear's competitive, fast-moving culture. It had opened a mortgage desk in 1981, designed to emulate Salomon.

Bear's CEO, Alan "Ace" Greenberg, in justifying hiring the controversial Howie Rubin, claimed everyone deserved a second chance, but Greenberg was more risk-conscious than most and placed Rubin under close watch. With Greenberg's oversight, Rubin made Bear Stearns a leader in the mortgage securitization boom. In 1987, when Rubin was hired, Bear Stearns ranked seventh among Wall Street firms as an underwriter of mortgage-backed securities. By early 1989, it was number one, pulling ahead of the major competition, including Salomon, First Boston, Merrill, and Lehman. Rubin stayed with the firm until 1999, making it enormous profits. (In 2008, George Soros hired him to run a distressed mortgage securities fund.)

In the late 1980s, most of Wall Street did poorly. The 1987 crash was soon followed by the federal bailout of the thrifts and the junk bond market failures. The housing market slowed its growth and the mortgage business slowed with it. Then recession descended upon the nation. Merrill Lynch lost $1 billion between 1987 and 1989. But Bear Stearns bucked the trend. Greenberg had kept Bear Stearns' risks in check, unlike most other firms, and did not post a quarterly loss from the 1987 crash through the 1990–1991 recession. By 1991, it was one of the most profitable firms on Wall Street, mostly because of its mortgage operation. Greenberg was paid $5 million and his number two man, Jimmy Cayne, just a little less. In 1992, the economy recovered, and with the housing market thriving, Bear Stearns earned $275 million. Greenberg paid himself $15.8 million and Cayne $14.7 million, the two making as much or more than peers in far bigger firms like Merrill.

Yet Bear Stearns was not the largest mortgage house on the Street at the time. A mortgage trader, Michael Vranos, had produced enormous profits at Kidder Peabody, now owned by GE. Also, Lehman Brothers expanded rapidly in mortgage securitization.

But when Greenspan suddenly pushed up rates in 1994, traders, stretched thin by major investments and high levels of debt, were flattened. Vranos in particular sustained losses in the hundreds of millions of dollars at Kidder as his investment sharply reversed, stunning Jack Welch of GE, who had bought the firm the year before. Then Joe Jett almost bankrupted the firm when he hid losses on enormous trades. Traders like Rubin and Vranos could single-handedly make a fortune for a firm but they could also break it. This was new on Wall Street.

Wall Street was more devastated than was realized or widely reported in 1994. Salomon lost hundreds of millions of dollars. Lehman Brothers, Bear Stearns, and Morgan Stanley were only marginally in the black. Major hedge funds went under. But by mid-1995, interest rates were falling again, as Greenspan started loosening policy. Soon the high-technology IPO wave was fully under way, with Netscape coming to market that year. Less noticed by the media, the mortgage market started to improve rapidly, as mortgage originations again grew quickly and housing starts rose. So rapidly did the housing market grow that at last home ownership rates also began to climb after languishing for years at 64 percent or less of the potential market. Home prices also began to climb and housing became a key pillar of the economy, based on securitization, even as high technology and the so-called New Economy attracted all the attention. Firms like Bear Stearns, Lehman, and Morgan again made enormous profits on the soaring housing market and mortgage securitization.

For Mozilo at Countrywide, circumstances could not have been better in the 1990s. The aggressive entry of securitizing firms like Bear Stearns and Lehman, as well as other commercial and investment banks, meant he could open offices anywhere in the nation, sell his mortgages to Wall Street, whose appetite was now insatiable, and use the money to write more mortgages. As Wall Street developed a base of investors around the world willing to buy the mortgage-backed securities, Mozilo was able to make his own capital markets operation successful, securitizing the mortgages he wrote. He also opened an operation at Countrywide to trade jumbo loans (which did not conform to Fannie Mae standards), stepping on the toes of the Wall Street firms that he always disliked, which specialized in such trading. But Mozilo had thus far largely avoided subprime mortgages.

Mozilo's competitors were expanding rapidly into subprime loans, however, and some Wall Street firms had also begun to securitize the lower-quality issues. In the 1990s, the forerunners of subprime mortgages (the term was not yet in wide use) were second liens offered by consumer finance companies like Beneficial Trust or the Money Store, which Phil Rizzuto, the former New York Yankee shortstop, promoted on TV. A mortgage was almost always at first less than the value of a house (homeowners put up a down payment), and firms like Beneficial and the Money Store liberally lent the mortgage holder more money using the remaining equity as collateral. But the rates charged were usually high, and sometimes these loans were greater than the value of the house. When a change in the tax laws in 1986 ended the deductibility of interest on car loans and credit cards, the second liens became all the more attractive, since interest on second liens remained tax deductible. Companies like Beneficial and the Money Store started to push the high-interest second liens to finance college education, cover health care expenditures, purchase a new car, or just meet the weekly food bill. Ames, a Southern California company, where most of the large originators were domiciled, wrote second liens on homes—in effect, a home equity loan—at interest rates of up to 14 percent a year. By 1996, another company, First Plus, was writing second liens worth up to 125 percent of the value of the house. These successful loan companies were going public, with Bear and other major bankers as their underwriters.

Mozilo eventually couldn't stand seeing the profits go to the competition, like First Plus, which earned as much as Countrywide but wrote only 10 percent as many mortgages. In 1995, Mozilo started writing subprime mortgages as well, tentatively, prodded on by David Sambol, his young aggressive national sales manager.

By 2000, the overheated economy headed for recession as the stock market bubble burst. Mozilo, whose partner, Loeb, had now retired, considered selling Countrywide, but could not bring himself to give up control. His decision to hold on proved a good one. As Greenspan pushed down rates, the housing market again took off, fueled by more Wall Street securitizations than ever before. And ARMs proliferated. With ARMs, there was the risk to the homeowner that the lower teaser rate could be reset upward. But if house prices kept rising, homeowners could simply refinance and get a new ARM or pay off some of the principal with the proceeds. In 2003, as we saw earlier, Greenspan himself tacitly encouraged homeowners to take out ARMs.

Now Mozilo's business, energized by subprime mortgages, was growing rapidly again. Mortgage originations set a record, reaching $3.8 trillion in 2003, as did Countrywide's earnings, reaching $2.4 billion, astoundingly tripling their level two years earlier. Its stock price stood at four times its 2000 level.

As competition geared up and the prime mortgage market became saturated, the true boom in subprime mortgages began. The securitization business at Bear Stearns and Lehman as well as Merrill Lynch, Morgan Stanley, and Goldman Sachs, and at the commercial banks like Citigroup, JPMorgan Chase, and Wells Fargo, soared. Most major banks also had giant mortgage writing subsidiaries that actively originated subprime mortgages, a fact often neglected by the media. The annual volume of subprimes was $35 billion in 1994, and $625 billion in 2005. Three out of five subprimes were now securitized—that is, funded by Wall Street investors. There was also a sharp increase in other loans like the Alt-As, which do not require that homeowners provide information about their income, and the jumbos.

Mozilo, seeing his competitors growing so quickly, abandoned his former caution. He craved an ever larger market share—in fact, he aimed to more than double it to 30 percent of the market, an ambition almost impossible to achieve without adopting unscrupulous practices. He had a large personal stake in Countrywide, multiplied by generous stock options he paid himself; the experience of owning so many shares as Countrywide's stock price soared was heady. Encouraged by his second in command, the aggressive David Sambol, Mozilo now offered any and all products that the competition did, including the aggressive sorts of subprime mortgages that he once had disparaged.

Mozilo became every bit as deceptive as he had long claimed those on Wall Street were. He was no longer writing mortgages to earn fees when he sold them to securitizers. He was writing them for his own voracious securitization department, which he had established years earlier and through which he now made huge fees by selling the packages to institutional investors. He was under constant pressure to write more and more mortgages as investor money flooded in, and he profited from every corner of the business. Meantime, major commercial banks like Citigroup and investment banks like Bear Stearns had their own mortgage broker subsidiaries, which were in direct competition with Mozilo.

At the beginning of 2004, Countrywide's market share was 11.4 percent of the U.S. mortgage market; by the end of 2006 it was 15.7 percent. Over the same period, Countrywide's stock price rose by 68 percent, from $25.25

to $45.50, raising Mozilo's wealth on paper by several hundred million dollars. As the market rose, he started aggressively selling his Countrywide shares.

Mozilo's record was stunning. The volume of industry-wide residential mortgages written tripled to $2.9 trillion between 2000 to 2006. But at Countrywide, annual mortgage originations rose by almost eightfold from $62 billion to $463 billion. Almost overnight, Countrywide was writing more subprime loans, jumbo loans, interest-only loans, and more Alt-A loans with little or no income verification than the prime conforming loans that had been its bread and butter in the past. Sixty percent of mortgages Countrywide wrote in the 1990s through 2004 were conforming loans, as defined by Fannie Mae—those going to good credit risks, with reported incomes and adequate down payments. In both 2006 and 2007, only 30 percent were. In this environment, home prices soared, almost doubling on average from 2003 to 2006, and the U.S. home ownership rate reached nearly 70 percent.

The mortgage products sold by Countrywide were increasingly abusive, luring homeowners into debt they could not possibly afford to pay over time, and Mozilo knew it. At the top of the list of abusive products in the 2000s was the pay option adjustable rate mortgage (POA), sold with an annual teaser rate as low as 1 percent. After two years (typically), the rate then rose according to a formula linked to market interest rates. The mortgage holder was offered the enticing option of continuing to pay the low interest rate, but the unpaid interest was added to the amount of the loan. This was aptly called negative amortization—instead of writing down the principal owed, as in a typical mortgage, the principal increased. When the total amount of the loan rose to 115 percent of the original loan, the interest rate to be paid was sharply raised.

The holder of a POA could also choose to pay only the interest not the principal, thus keeping monthly payments down. But in the fifth year, the loan was transformed into a conventional mortgage, with principal and interest payments. The increases in monthly payments could be brutal. In one example, according to the state of California, whose attorney general, Jerry Brown, sued Mozilo and two key executives in 2008, an original monthly payment of $1,480 could be raised to $3,748 in the fifth year. Mozilo paid his salespeople higher commissions if they wrote such loans.

To avoid the need for a down payment, Countrywide also sold piggyback loans, a regular mortgage plus a piggyback to cover the down payment. The mortgage holder thus borrowed 100 percent of the equity of the house. Without a down payment, it was easy to attract poorer credit risks to take the loan and even better credit risks to buy larger homes that otherwise would have been out of reach. Countrywide also sold many more Alt-As, as noted.

Ultimately, many of the mortgage holders could not meet the higher monthly payments and defaulted, often losing their homes. They simply were not adequately informed that their monthly payments could go higher. This charge was the gist of many future lawsuits against Mozilo. And much of the rest of the mortgage brokerage industry was selling seamy products without checking borrowers' credit. New Century boasted it could approve a mortgage in just twelve seconds, given its computer technology.

The risk of the POAs was not lost on Countrywide's own risk management department, which continually warned Mozilo and Sambol about the dangers. But the two were sweeping future problems under the rug. Sambol realized, and so probably did Mozilo, that these aggressive subprime mortgages were the only ones that could make a profit—at least in the short run—and drive the stock price up. They hoped that house prices would keep rising and allow enough home buyers to refinance, borrow more, reduce monthly payments, or sell out.

In 2006, Mozilo was waking up to the disaster in the making and wrote Sambol a series of e-mails about the need to reduce exposure to these loans and sell them as soon as possible. By then, Countrywide was unable to securitize all the mortgages they were making, especially the subprimes, as pensions and other investors began to shy away from buying the mortgage securities. House prices had begun to fall that year as well. Though Mozilo seemed sincerely alarmed, Sambol disregarded him, perhaps a sign that Mozilo, approaching seventy, was losing control of his subordinates. Mozilo demanded that Countrywide begin to sell its portfolio of bad mortgages, but his subordinates either did not carry out his requests or were unable to find buyers at a reasonable price.

Despite Mozilo's worried e-mails, he repeatedly told shareholders from 2006 and 2007 that the credit risk taken on by Countrywide was under control. In reality, the company had explicitly lowered its credit standards, and never informed shareholders. It also failed to mention the reduction in the loan standards in its filings with the SEC, though disclosure of such material changes was required by law. From 2005 to 2007, as prospects dimmed for the company, Mozilo executed stock options and sold shares worth a total of $260 million, according to an SEC lawsuit brought in 2009. Sambol cashed in $40 million of stock. In 2006 and 2007, Mozilo also executed a plan to sell stock on a regular basis totaling another $139 million, for a total of $400 million he had in trust for his family.

Two years after the Greenspan Fed started to raise rates, the rates on ARMs were being reset higher. Because house prices had at last cracked in 2006, homeowners found it almost impossible to refinance. As feared, by 2007, defaults by mortgage holders shot up at Countrywide and the company was forced to report large losses.

Mozilo's competitors were falling fast. New Century and Fremont were now out of business. In 2007, Countrywide was almost the last big man standing. As Mozilo's stock price plunged, he announced to the world that the housing market was worse than he had ever seen it. Though he raised $2 billion from Bank of America in August 2007, it wasn't enough. As house prices fell further, defaults inevitably rose still more. At the end of the year, 27 percent of the nonprime mortgages on Countrywide's books were delinquent. For a few years, Mozilo was rich as Croesus based on his shares in Countrywide, ensconced in a large Beverly Hills mansion, on top of the world. In January 2008, he sold Countrywide to Bank of America for $4 billion; the company had been worth roughly $25 billion about a year earlier. He soon retired from his firm, but faced countless civil suits from shareholders and mortgage holders, a state of California lawsuit, and an SEC civil suit for fraud and insider trading, which he settled in 2010 for $67.5 million, a relatively small portion of his $400 million fortune. In addition, the Justice Department was now investigating reduced rate mortgages Mozilo allegedly sold to Senators Chris Dodd of Connecticut and Kent Conrad of North Dakota, as well as two former heads of Fannie Mae, Jim Johnson and Franklin Raines. They were known as "Friends of Angelo."

One irony about Mozilo was how fiercely he had once criticized traditional Wall Street bankers for their greed. He, for one, would not exploit homeowners with subprime mortgages. But when the opportunity to get very rich presented itself—or more precisely, when his competitors were taking his market share—Mozilo cast his scruples aside. He exploited homeowners, but also investors in the complex mortgage securities his firm underwrote. And regulators were nowhere to be found. Even in these most complex of financial products, Greenspan argued that investors, and even home buyers, were able to fend for themselves.

Jimmy Cayne, Richard Fuld, Stan O'Neal, and Chuck Prince

COLLAPSE

The bursting of the housing bubble and the failure of Mozilo's Countrywide and the other giant mortgage brokers did not alone nearly bring the nation to the cusp of full-fledged depression. The decline in housing prices would have resulted in reduced consumer spending and a substantial recession in the United States, as many economists had warned, but not the economic catastrophe of late 2007 and 2008. It was the house of cards built on Wall Street greed, unchecked by Washington regulators, that created the nation's credit crisis—the sudden drying up of lending to consumers, business, and homeowners—and caused the most severe recession in the United States since the Great Depression.

Some participants blamed the Wall Street collapse of 2008 on a rare "tsunami"—common parlance at the time—that no one could have anticipated. These panics and collapses just happen from time to time, they often claimed. Former treasury secretary Robert Rubin, who would later become chairman of Citigroup's executive committee, urged Chuck Prince, successor to Sandy Weill at Citigroup, to make the risky investments in mortgage securities, told an investigating committee that almost everyone was responsible for the market failure. Another favorite line was that it was a systematic failure. But to blame everyone was to blame no one.

Some took refuge in the claim that few had anticipated what would happen. Warren Buffett, who owned a large stake in Moody's, the ratings agency, said at an investigatory hearing that almost no one had anticipated the problems. Alan Greenspan made similar comments in interviews. John Mack, head of Morgan Stanley, whose key mortgage trader lost $9 billion in a single trade, wiping out all the annual profits of the company in 2007, insisted the crisis was one of those events so rare it barely showed up statistically—a "tail risk" as it was now called.

Bear Stearns CEO Jimmy Cayne

Richard Fuld, CEO of Lehman
Brothers, about to testify before
Congress

None of these claims was correct. Even if the housing market had only stopped rising rapidly, rather than plunging, Wall Street would have lost enormous amounts of money, jeopardizing the world credit markets. Bad mortgage loans had been pushed to the limit by Mozilo, and big banks' lending was so excessive on Wall Street based on collateral so risky that financial failure of one firm could lead to financial failure across the entire landscape. Meantime, Greenspan's low interest rates fed ever-rising levels of debt at investment banks that aggressively expanded trading and other speculative activities. The low rates also fueled a revival of hedge funds. In fact, now much of Wall Street was run like a hedge fund, making hugely leveraged bets in all levels of markets but especially in mortgage securities.

In the 2000s, four CEOs, in particular, ordered their firms to take on reckless amounts of debt to invest in risky mortgage securities in a head-long rush to make profits and achieve glory for their companies and themselves. Jimmy Cayne of Bear Stearns and Richard Fuld of Lehman Brothers borrowed so heavily, and with the loans bought such risky assets, that when prices turned down the old-line firms could not survive. Even as warning signs rose all around them, they doubled down on risky investments, and their firms were the first large investment banks to fail. Stan O'Neal of Merrill Lynch and Chuck Prince of Citigroup, both taking the helms of their firms in 2003, were latecomers to the rush to invest in mortgage securities, and then all the more determined to prove themselves by making more profits than any other firm. They pushed their firms especially

Merrill Lynch's CEO Stan O'Neal leading
a group of his executives

Chuck Prince, left, successor to Sandy Weill as
Citigroup CEO, with Robert Rubin, testifying before
the Financial Crisis Inquiry Commission

aggressively into the mortgage business just as it was starting to fall apart. In a few years, Citigroup and Merrill became the largest issuers of the riskiest mortgage securities, surpassing earlier leaders including Bear and Lehman, reaping huge fees in the process, making stars of their CEOs, who were all the while oblivious to the high risks they were taking. Together they ultimately lost as much as $100 billion in mortgage securities, perhaps more.

There were others. Joe Cassano, an executive at AIG, the giant insurance company, made inexplicably outsize bets that made the company liable for $80 billion should mortgage securities go bad. Cassano, a graduate of

Brooklyn College and trained in Michael Milken's junk bond department at Drexel Burnham in the 1980s, was a managerial tyrant consumed by his mini-empire and easy profits. In the 2000s, he effortlessly generated millions of dollars a year by selling what were known as credit default swaps—an insurance policy of sorts that guarantees to pay the value of a bond if it fails—for Hank Greenberg, the hard-nosed AIG chief executive, who was forced out in early 2005 in an accounting scandal. When Greenberg left, Cassano became temporarily even more aggressive, though he soon after halted his buying. It cost the U.S. Treasury more than $180 billion to bail out AIG in 2008 and 2009, due to both AIG's insurance and also aggressive purchases of mortgage securities.

UBS, the Swiss firm, gave its U.S. traders in the New York office license to invest freely and they turned in extraordinary losses on mortgage securities—ultimately almost $38 billion. Banks across Britain and Europe invested in U.S. mortgage securities as well, emulating the American bankers they had come to admire. Fannie Mae and Freddie Mac, turned into profit-making companies years earlier by Congress, bought subprime mortgages voluminously in 2004 and 2005 to make up for lost market share during a scandal in earlier years. Still, their ownership of subprimes came to only 10 percent of their portfolios, and they bought only a minority of all subprime purchases even in the years of their most aggressive purchases. They contributed to the market frenzy nevertheless, if far less so than did the private entities, pushed on by their private-enterprise-oriented CEOs, whose compensation as a result reached many millions of dollars a year.

Cash eventually ran out at several of the Wall Street firms, and when the firms sold their assets in a panic, they threw those who acted less recklessly into danger of financial ruin as well. All sold their assets at the same time to stay solvent, and as a result the value of all kinds of financial assets plummeted in a massive replay of the calamity caused by the failure of Long-Term Capital Management in 1998. A bottom was found only when the federal government made hundreds of billions of dollars available to the firms to shore up their collapsing finances. Contrary to claims that few anticipated the crisis, many Wall Street traders and analysts within these firms—though very few economists—had warned their top managers that their strategies were far too risky. The collapse was the product of decisions by individuals, set upon making fortunes and becoming one of the kings of the mountain, not an inevitable failure of a system.

Throughout history, financial crises have generally been similar to each other. An asset—land, housing, stocks, bonds, and so on—rises in price, financial institutions lend to investors to buy more, and prices are driven to unsustainable levels. When the bubble bursts, investors sell assets to repay their loans and prices fall further, often in panic. Bad debts rise on the books of the financial institutions, credit stops flowing, businesses and consumers sharply reduce spending, and the economy slides into serious recession.

Usually each crisis is different in detail. The 2008 credit crisis was not merely a repetition of the financial crises of which there have been many since the early 1980s; it was by far the worst since the 1930s. It is worth summarizing the list of such crises we have already discussed: the defaults on Third World debt in 1982; the stock market crash of 1987; the thrifts failures and junk bond collapse culminating in 1989 and 1990; the Mexican debt crisis in 1994; the Asian financial crisis in 1997; the Russian default in 1998; the collapse of Long-Term Capital Management, also in 1998; and the bursting of the high-technology bubble beginning in 2000.

Even given this list, the 2008 crisis, as noted, was much worse. Partly it had to do with excess dollars around the world. There was a rapidly rising flow of capital from overseas countries like China, which had increased its reserves of dollars to several trillion dollars, making funds available for borrowing in the United States at low rates. A high savings rate in China and several other nations, where business and consumers spent less than they could on goods from outside their borders, contributed to huge trade surpluses as local companies took more dollars in than they paid out. The growing dollar flow was also made possible by a Clinton administration policy to keep the value of the dollar high, giving foreigners confidence to buy debt in dollars. But the high dollar in turn persistently put American manufacturers at a cost disadvantage, hastening manufacturing decline in America and costing countless good jobs. It completed the circle: the high dollar contributed to a massive trade deficit, putting dollars in the hands of foreigners, who in turn bought American securities with their excess reserves. As earlier discussed, China and others also built reserves of dollars to protect them against a repetition of the 1997 Asian crisis, when their currencies collapsed. The upshot was an injection of highly potent and cheap fuel for speculation on Wall Street.

But a flow of lending at low interest rates, even a flood, could have been used productively as well. Why this crisis was the worst since the Depression requires other explanations. The growth of mortgage securitization was a key factor, as earlier noted, turning packages of mortgages into debt that institutional investors like pension funds and private investors around the world could buy just like they bought Treasury or corporate bonds—but often at higher interest rates. Washington failed to notice how much more risky the debt was becoming, portions of this debt retaining high ratings from the credit ratings agencies who were paid by the issuers of the debt.

But in the 2000s, a still more influential and dangerous security was developed. Complex computer models were used to create the collateralized debt obligation, or CDO, that was at the center of the rising levels of risk. Adapted from a junk bond innovation of the late 1980s, it was a provocative step in the evolution of securitization. The CDO was to Wall Street what radium was to Madame Curie, intriguing, seemingly harmless, but highly radioactive. It effectively disguised risk and enabled Wall Street to mislead investors and often even itself.

The original mortgage-backed securities, as discussed earlier, were a package of both good and potentially bad mortgages against which new bonds were issued. About 80 percent of the bonds, the top tranche or senior tranche, was usually awarded a rating of triple-A or at worst double-A. These bondholders were paid all the mortgage interest until they got what was due them, and accordingly, this tranche paid the lowest interest rate. The tranches that followed received the rest of the income in descending order. The lowest tranche, rated triple-B, received what remained of the mortgage payments after all other obligations were met and was most likely to be adversely affected by a rise in the default rates (except for a still more risky equity sliver at the very bottom of the line, which usually got no rating).

A CDO looked like a mortgage-backed security, but it was a package of these tranches, not of mortgages themselves. (Many CDOs were also actively managed, like a mutual fund, in which the manager could buy and sell securities as market conditions changed.) Triple-A and triple-B tranches were mixed together and most—up to 80 percent—were turned into new triple-A bonds, according to the ratings agencies, through another round of tranching. The idea was the same: the senior tranche holders of the CDO would get paid first from the package of mortgage bonds (to repeat, these were the tranches of original mortgage-backed securities), so it seemed the risk was minimized for 80 percent or so of the investors.

Soon, the bankers were building the CDOs entirely of triple-B bonds, however. A senior tranche was created whose investors received their interest first for the package of triple-B mortgage bonds. It was a superbly profitable idea, turning 80 percent of the low-rated mortgage bonds, which paid high interest rates, and were increasingly composed of subprime mortgages, into high-rated bonds, as long as the ratings agencies agreed, which they did.

It was apparently magic, except that the concept was flawed. Triple-B bonds were not like triple-B mortgages. They were the tranches that took the losses first if default rates rose even moderately. A portfolio of all triple-B tranches was highly vulnerable to problems in the housing market. In a traditional mortgage-backed security, some mortgages may become delinquent but most won't. In a CDO of triple-B tranches, most can go bad if default rates rise moderately. The bankers, and the rating agencies that provided the high ratings, claimed, with the help of their ever more complex models, that by picking triple-B tranches from across the country, even when replete with subprime mortgages, such diversification could assure investors that only a smaller portion of them would go bad in a deteriorating housing market. As one investor put it, when the bankers start using a lot of Greek letters to explain the mathematics that go into the models, you know there is a problem. The triple-A tranches of the CDOs were considered supersafe.

But it turned out there was no magic and a lot of wishful thinking. The triple-B tranches did in fact almost all go down together once the housing market soured. When one collapsed, "most would go bad," wrote Michael Lewis. The only way to avoid a collapse was if the housing boom continued forever. One hedge fund manager figured the defaults on subprime mortgages needed to rise only to 7 percent to sink many CDOs, including those rated triple-A, and a default rate of 8 to 10 percent would surely cause enormous damage. The default rate on subprime mortgages soon rose to 15–30 percent.

The credit boom between 2003 and mid-2007 was built on sand. So stretched and risky were these mortgage-backed securities that the mere end of the rapid rise in housing prices, not even a downturn, endangered Wall Street. Most of the losses in 2007 and 2008 that nearly brought down the Street were not on low-rated securities, but on the CDOs that Moody's and Standard & Poor's rated triple-A and double-A. The Federal Reserve and the SEC were caught completely by surprise.

Jimmy Cayne was named CEO of Bear Stearns in 1993, sixteen years after he joined the firm as a retail broker. Son of a patent attorney, Cayne went to Purdue but spent most of his time playing bridge, becoming a national champion. Cayne's first major coup as a broker was a risky one. He bought New York City bonds in the mid-1970s when few wanted them, the city then on the verge of bankruptcy with the bonds selling at distress levels. When the city's finances turned around, after a rescue led by Felix Rohatyn, the bonds rose handsomely.

Bridge created a bond between him and Ace Greenberg, who later became head of the firm, and who was also a first-rate bridge player, if not of Cayne's caliber. As Cayne rose at Bear Stearns, he ingratiated himself with Greenberg, driving him to work every morning. Many thought him especially talented at maneuvering within the organization. Greenberg was the consummate trader, and prided himself on watching costs and taking closely measured risks. Cayne was a retail man with less understanding of the trading floor and an ambition to make it to the top.

In the early 1980s, Bear Stearns, emulating the success Salomon and First Boston had in mortgage securities, became the first of the other major investment banks to enter the market. Warren Spector, another bridge player but more introspective than either Greenberg or Cayne, managed the business to immense profitability—in large part by hiring and then controlling traders like Howie Rubin.

Cayne and Greenberg began to clash, and, in a coup, Cayne was chosen to succeed his mentor when Greenberg turned sixty-five (Greenberg stayed at the firm). Cayne launched few new businesses at Bear Stearns, riding its existing expertise in the mortgage market and securities trading to profits. When stocks crashed in 2001, leveling most other Wall Street firms, Bear Stearns' mortgage business shone. It became the hottest investment bank on the Street, the stock price soaring to more than $170. In 2005, Cayne was worth nearly $1 billion based on his stock holdings, the only bank CEO listed on the Forbes 400. The very rich man became aloof and arrogant, protecting senior management from any encroachment by up-and-coming bankers.

Cayne was a man of uncontrollable appetites, and lacked the grace of a Wall Street CEO. He smoked cigars incessantly and reporters broke stories about his pot habit as well. He left Thursdays in the summer to play golf all weekend. He was often off at bridge tournaments, even in the heat of crises. Bear was all about Jimmy, his underlings would say. He fired Warren Spector, his most threatening rival, when he needed his expertise most. The top management became more distant from the firm. Many felt Cayne wanted no competition. "I really do believe that ironically one of the things that hurt the firm most was that the stock price did so well," said an executive at the firm. "It emboldened Jimmy to stop listening, and that [listening] was the one thing he was really good at."

The downfall of the firm began with two hedge funds started under Cayne that perfectly reflected the excesses of the mortgage business. In 2003, Cayne put a star mortgage salesman, Ralph Cioffi, in charge of the new funds. The objective was simple: to buy mortgage securities—mostly CDOs—for their high yields with funds borrowed from other banks (usually simple loans of securities for an interest rate that banks agreed to take back, known as repurchase agreements, or repos) or from money market funds at the exceptionally low rates put in place by Alan Greenspan.

Cioffi and his number two, Matthew Tannin, assured investors they bought only triple-A or double-A securities. This was true, but they were the far riskier CDOs made up of many subprime mortgages, not simple mortgage bonds, a fact they sometimes disguised. Moreover, Cioffi and Tannin knew the ratings on the CDOs were not trustworthy. Many subsequently blamed the ratings agencies for deceiving investors. The agencies had blatant conflicts of interest, being paid handsomely by the issuers of the CDOs themselves, and their ratings were scandalously misleading. But sophisticated investors had been skeptical of such ratings. In an April e-mail, Tannin wrote Cioffi, "There are good AAAs and not so good ones and that is our job to find those ones that are good." The fact that a triple-A CDO paid significantly more interest than a triple-A corporate bond was in itself a clear indication that something was amiss—the security was not priced like a triple-A. The press rarely asked about the contradiction, nor apparently did the regulators.

As subprime defaults started to rise, Cioffi assured investors the funds had very few such subprime mortgages in their portfolio. This was decidedly not true. Cioffi may not have bought subprimes directly but he bought plenty of the complex CDOs that ultimately had large amounts of subprime mortgages as collateral. He claimed only 6 percent of their portfolios had exposure to subprime mortgages but others estimated that up to 60 percent of Bear's $1.5 billion in assets were in reality backed by subprimes.

A still newer CDO product had also been created, a synthetic CDO, which added more risk to the mortgage market and which Cioffi and Tannin bought enthusiastically. They were created out of the credit default swaps (CDSs) that AIG and soon others were liberally selling across Wall Street—the insurance on the CDOs.

The great advantage of the synthetic CDOs is that their issuance was not restricted to the number of mortgages that could be sold to prospective homeowners. There was no collateral. There was one requirement, however: someone had to be willing to buy the CDSs—the insurance was the basis of the synthetic, "collateral-less" CDOs. Because someone had to be willing to bet that mortgage securities were overvalued, investment banks that wanted to create synthetic CDOs for their clients to buy also had to find others to sell them. This led to unusual conflicts of duties within firms—some urging investors to buy mortgage-backed securities, others to sell them.

The development of the CDSs on mortgages came about when some investors were exploring how to sell mortgage securities short in 2003—that is, they would sell what they were certain were overvalued CDOs without owning them. As told by Michael Lewis, one of them, a medical doctor, Michael Burry, convinced Goldman Sachs and Morgan Stanley to let him buy insurance—CDSs, which already existed for other kinds of loans—on triple-B bonds. He paid $2 or $2.50 for every $100 of mortgage bonds, and if the bonds failed, Goldman and Morgan would pay him the full $100. Otherwise, Goldman and Morgan pocketed the $2.50—potentially $20–25 million on $1 billion of securities. The odds the bonds would fail were low, it seemed at the time, but Goldman in particular took few chances, probably understanding better than most that the CDOs were riskier than they were widely believed to be. It unloaded the insurance liabilities on AIG's eager Cassano by buying the equivalent insurance from him on the CDOs, which it had agreed to sell to Burry.

AIG's Cassano could hardly believe how simple it was to take the Street's money. In fact, he got taken for a ride. Goldman paid only 12 to 20 cents on $100 of CDOs to Cassano for his insurance but collected $2.50 from Burry and others for insurance Goldman sold. It did this by transforming Burry's triple-Bs into the triple-As of a new CDO.

Then came the synthetic CDO. Goldman Sachs bankers realized that the CDSs on triple-B tranches provided a way to re-create a CDO without bothering to find triple-B mortgage bonds themselves. If that could be done, it would be a bonanza. What limited the creation of even more CDOs was the lack of mortgages for collateral. Goldman took the cash flow from insurance bought by investors like Burry and treated it as if it were mortgage interest. With this key piece in place, they could pay investors the interest and replicate the investment characteristics of a normal CDO. These new synthetic CDOs were tranched just like the conventional ones. The ratings agencies awarded the top 80 percent of the new bonds a senior rating of triple-A or double-A.

The creation of CDOs raised the risk on Wall Street substantially. Soon after, half of CDOs issued were synthetic, but the funds never reached the real housing economy; they were contracts to pay based on future movements in the prices of existing mortgage bonds. There were no new mortgages, but there was added debt, and a lot of profit for the banks.

Clearly, it was now in the interest of investment bankers and other securitizers to get investors to buy insurance—that is, short the mortgage market. The more CDSs short sellers bought, the more synthetic CDOs could be issued, generating handsome fees like regular CDOs of 1 percent to 2 percent for the bankers. Deutsche Bank had an active sales program to persuade investors to sell short the very CDOs their investment bankers were issuing to clients. Goldman welcomed short sellers like Burry and the hedge fund manager John Paulson.

Even if the bankers could not find buyers for all the securities in a deal, the fees were so high that they often bought large pieces of the traditional and synthetic CDOs for their own portfolios to complete the deal; they satisfied themselves that they only held on to the highest-rated tranches, which became known as super-senior securities. To make a CDO work, the entire package usually had to be bought. Now aggressive latecomers to the mortgage securitization market, notably Merrill and Citigroup, bought tens of billions of dollars of the highly rated CDOs for their own portfolios so that they could securitize and issue CDOs and make high fees. Bear, partly because of Cioffi and Tannin, and Lehman, among others, also had billions of dollars of CDOs on the books. The high-rated securities turned out to be far from secure.

When John Paulson proposed buying insurance on a number of triple-B bonds he thought likely to fail, Goldman packaged them into one of a series of synthetic CDOs it called Abacus. The SEC brought a suit against Goldman in 2010 for not telling investors that Paulson chose the triple-B securities because he believed they would go bad. The SEC believed this failure to divulge Paulson's role was a clear violation of the law, but in fact the suit diverted attention from a more disturbing issue. Goldman was also shorting CDOs itself, by then convinced the market was overvalued. Goldman may have been creating new CDOs filled with tranches the firm itself wanted to get rid of, or similar to ones it held. In 2010, a hedge fund sued Goldman over another CDO called Timberwolf, claiming just that. According to the hedge fund's lawyer, "Goldman was pressuring investors to take the risk of toxic securities off its books with false sales pitches." There were reports the SEC was investigating other Goldman deals, as well as deals put together by Morgan Stanley. Goldman argued that its sophisticated investors knew what they were buying and were not deceived. But were Goldman and others selling CDOs rated triple-A that they knew were far less secure? Despite a rating of triple-A on the senior securities, the Abacus deal involving Paulson fell to zero within six months of its issuance. Paulson's firm earned $1 billion on the Abacus short sales, and the Abacus investors lost $1 billion. As noted, Paulson personally earned $4 billion in total that year, based on several of these kinds of trades, the most any hedge fund manager had earned to date. Soros also shorted the market, earning himself $3 billion.

Cioffi and Tannin were among Wall Street's big buyers of CDOs, and the first fund the Bear Stearns duo started turned in an excellent performance for the forty months since its inception in 2003. (Cioffi was the major buyer of Merrill's many new CDO issues once Stan O'Neal took over.) But by early 2007, the good times were over. Housing indices showed that home prices were starting to fall, mortgage defaults were rising, major mortgage brokers like New Century were going under, and a new trading index showed that the value of mortgage bonds was sinking.

The mortgage bond markets were now cracking. By all rights, the value of the CDOs should have fallen also. But they were holding up—to the annoyance of those like Burry and others who had sold them short. Because CDOs were not publicly traded, Wall Street firms could set the prices themselves, a gray area that left room for enhancing earnings by overstating the value of assets or sweeping what they hoped were temporary problems under the rug by refusing to concede a decline in the value of their securities.

Those that had owned billions of dollars of CDOs themselves, like Citigroup and Merrill, were especially hesitant to downgrade the value of their CDOs because it would have meant they would have to take losses on their income statement. For a while, there was a kind of limbo regarding the true value of the CDOs. Investors who were short believed the firms were rigging the market—and they were. "Either the game was rigged or we had gone totally fucking crazy," said one.

But the Street was no longer buying the CDOs with abandon. Cioffi and Tannin started reporting losses to their investors in early 2007, unable to sell their assets at reasonable prices. Several surprised investors, remembering they had been told they were invested in triple-A securities with little exposure to subprimes, wanted to withdraw their investments. As requests for redemptions rose, banks that lent the Bear Stearns managers money in the repo market also started to demand collateral on their debt. Because the funds were so highly leveraged, there was little room for losses, and they were running out of cash. They halted redemptions, creating panic, so the parent company, Bear Stearns, made $3 billion of its own capital available to cover commitments in order to keep the funds alive. It wasn't enough. Markets continued to deteriorate and in July the funds were shut down.

The closing of the funds came as a shock to much of Wall Street. In the first half of 2007, the large U.S. and European banks earned $425 billion and their capital easily exceeded the requirements established by the Bank for International Settlements in Basel. The Dow Jones Industrials were trading near all-time highs, well above 13,000, even occasionally topping 14,000, and investors were oblivious to the risks in the market. The nation's unemployment rate was still well below 5 percent. All seemed fine.

The regulators also failed to scratch the surface. In a speech in May at the Chicago Federal Reserve Bank, Ben Bernanke, the Princeton professor who had succeeded Alan Greenspan as chairman of the Federal Reserve in 2005, assured his listeners that rising subprime default rates would have no "serious broader spillover to banks or thrift institutions." As late as July, he still doubted that the subprime default rate would have widespread ramifications. He figured subprime losses would come to only $100 billion, against which banks had ample cushion. Another Fed official, William Dudley, said the crisis could be over "in a matter of weeks."

It was a remarkable miscalculation. Both Moody's and Standard & Poor's, for example, had already downgraded billions of dollars of subprime mortgage bonds, at last recognizing something was wrong with their models (they announced as much in May). The Fed had measured the size of the subprime market compared to the entire mortgage market, conservatively estimated the likely rise in defaults, and looked no further. It was unaware of the severely shaky foundation of the CDOs, despite the enormous volume outstanding, or how much of the CDOs the banks it oversaw were holding on their own books. The subprime mortgages were collateral for a huge proportion of the CDOs.

Then, in August, the money market funds that bought commercial paper from the investment banks rightly got nervous and sharply reduced their purchases, driving up interest rates. No one expected this. It was like an old-fashioned run on banks, ordinary savers losing trust that banks would be able to pay them back their money. Without access to commercial paper financing, some firms might fold. Later that month, the European Central

Bank announced it had made nearly E100 billion available to banks that it found were suddenly unable to meet their cash needs. Within hours of that ECB announcement, Bernanke at last reduced interest rates. Credit conditions in the United States were freezing up as investors stopped buying corporate and other bonds and bought U.S. Treasurys for safety. The Fed kept reducing the Fed funds rate until it reached almost zero at the end of 2009.

That fall, the rating agencies downgraded mortgage bonds, and later that fall they started downgrading CDOs themselves. In September, Northern Rock, a giant British bank, was bailed out by its government. The two major insurers of mortgages, Ambac Assurance Corporation and MBIA Insurance Corporation, were also put on a credit watch list by the rating agencies.

In early October, having recently assured investors all was fine, Merrill announced that it had to write down $5.5 billion of its assets, probably mostly mortgage securities. By late October, it raised the estimate to more than $8 billion. Citigroup announced that it would take a loss of nearly $6 billion in the value of its assets, most of it in mortgage securities, and a month later raised the estimate to $11 billion. UBS announced write-downs of $10 billion. Most of the bad assets at all three banks were in triple-A- or double-A-rated CDOs.

Although Bernanke was cutting rates sharply and kept adding liquidity to the markets, the financial markets continued to fall apart. Bear Stearns' large investment positions in mortgage securities and its high leverage in general made its battle for survival almost impossible. By this point it was borrowing $44 for every dollar of capital, when only ten years earlier Long-Term Capital's leverage ratio of 25 to 1 was considered dangerous. Cayne's faint hope was to ride it out until the markets revived and default rates stopped rising. Little new business was being done and Bear posted its first loss—nearly $2 billion in the final quarter of 2007. Cayne, now seventy-three, was asked to step aside to allow Alan Schwartz, the president, to take over. Schwartz had no new strategy to save the company. Cayne and Schwartz had been urged to raise fresh equity through a stock offering for months and refused to do so, partly because the stock price was falling and, partly, according to financial writer William Cohan, because it would have diluted their ownership and therefore their bonuses. They then sought merger partners, but could not come to terms with any. Market conditions continued to deteriorate in early 2008, and Bear Stearns' lenders stopped the flow of funds to them.

In March, Bear Stearns was essentially out of cash, and told the Fed it might face bankruptcy. Bernanke, Timothy Geithner, the president of the New York Federal Reserve branch, and Henry Paulson, the Bush treasury secretary, agreed that Bear Stearns should not be allowed to go bankrupt because a domino effect could bring down other firms. They sought a buyer to avoid the turmoil among creditors if there were a bankruptcy. Jamie Dimon, whom Sandy Weil had let go years earlier, had avoided much of the overinvestment in mortgage securities at JPMorgan Chase, where he was now chairman. He agreed to make an offer only if the Fed guaranteed some $30 billion of Bear Stearns' assets. Under pressure, the Fed did so, and Dimon bought Bear for a mere $2 a share, down from the $170 it was trading at fifteen months earlier. Bear employees, many of whom had their pensions invested in Bear shares, were devastated. They lost their jobs and their retirement security. In an unprecedented action, the Fed opened its discount window (which lent Treasury securities at low interest rates) to all financial firms, not just commercial banks, to make sure they had the funds they needed to meet their obligations and to stop the possible contagion.

Even Dimon was surprised at the low price the Fed was willing to accept for Bear. Dimon, under criticism for getting a bargain, raised the purchase price to $10 a share.

Stock prices rose somewhat after the Bear buyout, having fallen by about 10 percent in the preceding six months. Now that investment banks had access to the discount window, perhaps confidence would return. Credit market conditions were relaxing as banks began to lend to each other. Some investment firms even reported profits. In July, Paulson announced the Treasury would bail out struggling Fannie Mae and Freddie Mac, calming the markets further. The subprime mortgages on the books of Fannie Mae and Freddie Mac, mostly added in 2004 and 2005, had created losses there, though even at their highest level their purchases came to substantially less than in the private markets.

But the stock of Lehman Brothers plunged after the Bear Stearns rescue. To Wall Street, the once legendary Lehman was simply a bigger version of Bear Stearns, highly leveraged with a lot of questionable assets on its books—perhaps even more questionable than Bear Stearns' given that it recently made large purchases of commercial and residential real estate and financed new privatizations of public companies at high prices.

Richard Fuld, the CEO, was also even more aloof than Cayne and showed little capacity to understand fully the crisis that threatened the firm's survival. The son of a wealthy manufacturer, his father got him a job with a friend at Lehman in 1966 while he was at the University of Colorado. He later earned his MBA from NYU at night. Lehman was an investment banking legend and one of the largest firms on the Street. Fuld, a natural battler who had a couple of fistfights as an adult, became a commercial paper trader, and an intimate of the gruff man who eventually ran the firm, Lewis Glucksman.

Glucksman won a power struggle against the investment banker Pete Peterson for control of the firm in the early 1980s and sold it (see Chapter 16) to Sandy Weill's former protégé at American Express, Peter Cohen, who merged it with Shearson, Weill's old firm. When the American Express CEO, Harvey Golub, let Cohen go after the RJR Nabisco battle with KKR, he named Fuld head of the Lehman subsidiary. Then he spun Lehman off. Fuld's dream had come true, to run his own independent firm.

Fuld's ambition could now be fully unleashed. He wanted to invest aggressively in mortgage underwriting and securities trading to catch up to Goldman or Morgan in size and influence. His inattention to risk drew internal criticism. As early as 2005, Mike Gelband, the respected head of fixed income securities at the firm, warned him to reverse exposure in mortgages. Fuld thought Gelband was a naysayer, ignored him, and Gelband eventually left the firm. At a management meeting, Madelyn Antonic, the firm's risk manager, criticized the aggressive risk being taken by the mortgage department and Fuld told her outright to shut up. She, too, soon left the firm. Those who disagreed were thought disloyal and dissent was stifled. In the face of growing risk, Fuld raised the stakes further and earned a $35 million bonus that year. In 2007, he went on a real estate buying spree, buying buildings in the United States and overseas, even as markets were weakening. He kept issuing CDOs as well. As the markets became nervous, he chose to double down.

There were still more foolishly optimistic shows of bravado than Fuld's toward the end of 2006 and into 2007. Howie Hubler, a trader for Morgan Stanley, wrote insurance—CDSs—on $16 billion of triple-A CDOs, convinced they were not dangerous, just as the market was cracking. Hubler apparently believed the conventional fiction that not all the tranches would fail even if default rates rose substantially. He had many opportunities to sell in the first half of 2007 at only moderate losses, and refused to take them. By the time the trade was unwound nine months later, he lost Morgan Stanley a stunning $9 billion, which CEO John Mack essentially attributed to a very rare, unpredictable set of circumstances. Mack didn't know what he was talking about. The true riskiness of the CDOs was simply minimized by much of Wall Street, not least Hubler. Meantime, the investment firm Cornwall Capital was buying insurance on the highly rated CDOs—unlike Burry, who bought insurance on the low-rated tranches. The Cornwall managers realized the high-rated CDOs would also collapse. It was probably the most brilliant trade of the time, costing Cornwall a dime or so per $100 of bonds compared to Burry's $2 to make the same gain when the market fell apart.

There were other warnings across Wall Street, besides those at Lehman and a handful of short sellers. Karen Weaver, in charge of securitization for Deutsche Bank in New York, warned her firm against the investments in late 2005, and Deutsche Bank started shorting the market in 2006. Lewis Ranieri himself, the Salomon pioneer, warned in mid-2006 that securitization had become reckless. Economists at the Bank for International Settlements were also actively warning about the fragility of the mortgage products. These concerns had in fact been expressed several years earlier but they were condescendingly ignored by Greenspan and others. Even Angelo Mozilo had announced a few months earlier that it was the worst housing market of his lifetime. Goldman had begun selling short either in late 2006 or early 2007, as did Deutsche Bank. Neither had a large quantity of CDOs on their books any longer. JPMorgan had started to remove itself from the securitization market far earlier, but its consumer loan subsidiary continued to write mortgages.

After Bear Stearns' demise, Fuld started looking for equity partners or merger possibilities. In the late summer, with leverage high and defaults rising, Lehman was about to run out of cash. To make its balance sheet look stronger than it was, Lehman cooked the books, temporarily hiding $50 billion in loans it took at the end of each of the first and second quarters of 2008, a tactic similar to the one used by Enron to minimize its debt. The hidden loans, condoned by its auditor, Ernst & Young, were not then uncovered by federal regulators, even though they combed the books in late 2008, but by a special bankruptcy examiner in early 2010. Despite the ruse, Lehman's capital levels were falling far short. There was no time left.

The Fed gathered bankers together in lower Manhattan to try to work out a deal to save Lehman in September. All were worried that if Lehman fell and asset prices were driven down further, because of the intertwined nature of the Street, all lending and borrowing from one another, it would take down other firms. The collective debt of financial firms had risen from half of GDP in 1990 to about 120 percent of GDP in 2008—some $17 trillion. That was two and a half times the amount of outstanding federal debt at the time, and some 70 percent more than all the mortgages in the United States.

Bernanke, Geithner, and Paulson later said that Washington had no authority to shut down or take over Lehman, since it was not a commercial bank; all they could do was sell it to a solvent buyer. This time the Fed and the Treasury did not guarantee Lehman's bad assets, as they had done for Bear Stearns, and therefore no deal could be reached among the still healthy American firms. Only Britain's Barclays Bank came forward, but the British financial regulator refused to approve the purchase.

Few accepted the claim that Washington could not have taken over the firm if it had wanted to. Bernanke, Geithner, and Paulson were becoming confident in August that the markets might be able to withstand a Lehman bankruptcy, and Paulson particularly feared creating moral hazard—overconfidence that the government would always bail out firms in trouble, thereby encouraging them to take risks. There was rising public anger about bailouts and conservative anger about the creation of moral hazard.

In letting Lehman fail, however, the Fed and Treasury were largely flying blind. They presumed that the securitized mortgage products had been distributed among investors around the world—and therefore losses would be dispersed and readily manageable. In fact, much of the risk had been taken on by Joe Cassano at AIG, even though that had stopped by late 2005. Now the banks like Citigroup and Merrill Lynch were taking on tens of billions of dollars of risk themselves. It was a handful of individual men making bad, self-serving decisions that placed the entire credit system at risk. Only one such giant need topple to take the global credit system down.

CDO issuance soared in 2006, led by Merrill and Citigroup. Money flowed to the individual bankers like water. That year, the CDOs produced a total of $8.6 billion in underwriting and management fees for Wall Street. In a year when more bad investment decisions were made than in any year since 1929, Lloyd Blankfein of Goldman earned $53 million, Cayne $40 million, Fuld $28 million, Mozilo $43 million, and Mack of Morgan $41 million. In 2006, *The New York Times* reported, more than fifty Goldman Sachs employees earned $20 million or more each. Merrill and Citigroup kept issuing CDOs and adding CDO assets to their own balance sheets, digging themselves into deeper holes, as did UBS, while all reported huge profits, much of it merely on paper—and the bankers expected to take home personal fortunes.

Merrill's CEO Stan O'Neal made Fuld's excesses seem measured. A successful investment banker who was widely considered among the most intelligent of his peers, he was named CEO in 2002, when Goldman, Lehman, Bear Stearns, and the mortgage brokers were making enviable profits in housing and their stock prices were rising commensurately. He was also known as arrogant and unable to listen to subordinates.

O'Neal was determined to catch up with the competition, wanting to recast his firm—in his mind, a mediocre one too focused on retail stock brokerage—into another Goldman Sachs. By 2006, through aggressive borrowing and new hires, he made Merrill the largest issuer of CDOs on the Street, producing $700 million in fees for the firm, raising overall earnings by 50 percent over the year before. He bought a mortgage originator, First Franklin, a competitor of Countrywide's, as late as September 2006, as defaults started rising. That year, Merrill paid $500 million in bonuses to just one hundred employees. As the markets weakened, the company kept selling CDOs well into 2007, and taking chunks of them onto its own books.

Under Chuck Prince, the Citigroup mortgage securities operation was also unleashed to restore profits after the high-technology stock crash early in the decade, the lost loans to Enron and WorldCom, and the costly fines paid in settlement of various charges by Eliot Spitzer and the SEC. Prince, a lawyer, who rose in the organization through loyalty to Sandy Weill, not financial experience, gave one of Weill's star Salomon traders, Tommy Maheras, a free hand to generate mortgage business. Maheras was a close friend to the bank's risk manager, whose job was to check his excesses. With Weill gone and Prince inexperienced, Bob Rubin, now the company's senior consultant, pressed the company to take more risk, and Maheras, an especially aggressive trader, obliged. Citigroup's rapid growth in CDO sales put it in second place behind Merrill.

As noted, the SEC, which regulated how much capital had to be kept against brokers' assets, including CDOs, had loosened the restraints in 2004—in fact, largely did away with any ceiling on leverage at all. It was one of the more extraordinary derelictions of regulatory duty in a long list under Christopher Cox, Bush's appointee to run the SEC. The investment banks argued they could manage the risk themselves, and Cox, an ideological deregulationist, agreed.

Goldman Sachs immediately started borrowing aggressively at Greenspan's low rates to support its profitable trading operations, and others followed their lead. As noted, they were now more like hedge funds than ever before, but playing with shareholders' money, not the capital of partners or much of their own. Merrill could add virtually all the CDOs to its balance sheet that it cared to, as Lehman and Bear Stearns had done. Leverage ratios shot up to $35 and $40 to $1 of capital, and sometimes higher.

It should be restated that the firms bought the CDOs' tranches to facilitate their selling to their investor clients; they had to take some, usually the highest rated, which they therefore thought the safest, to make the deal work. But the fees in selling the entire CDO, even when the bank bought part of it, were enormous. In the rush to make profits, they gobbled up far more of the CDOs than they could handle, suppressing any doubts they might have had about their riskiness.

Citigroup could not as simply place the rising volume of CDOs it kept on the balance sheet as could Merrill because it was regulated by the Federal Reserve, which imposed stricter leverage restrictions. It hid them instead in structured investment vehicles and similar "conduits"—basically partnerships with outside investors, which borrowed heavily in the repo and commercial paper markets to finance the purchases of the CDOs. Citi sold the obligations to the SIVs, with the proviso it would buy them back should they fall in value, a legally dubious agreement. The Fed did not stop them nor was it even fully aware of the circumvention of the rules.

In late 2007, as the housing market cracked and mortgages started going bad, Merrill and Citigroup had at last to start taking their first major losses on their high-rated CDOs. In light of the mounting losses, O'Neal tried to sell the firm, but failed. In November, he was forced out, taking a $161 million settlement package with him. Prince was also forced out that month, with a settlement of $80 million. The questionable CDOs sat on the books of these institutions, and no one knew when the bleeding would stop. Early in 2008, Merrill, Citigroup, and UBS were forced to take another $50 billion in write-downs, most of it high-rated CDOs. How much more was left? Residential foreclosures were doubling from 147,708 to 303,879 between April 2007 and August 2008. When Lehman went bankrupt, no one knew how vulnerable Wall Street was. Hundreds of billions of dollars of assets could plunge in value. Many of them were rated triple-A.

By late summer, Lehman needed some $40 billion in fresh capital to stay alive. In 1998, LTCM required only several billion dollars to stabilize the financial markets. The difference now was the sheer size of the pool of debt—$7–8 trillion of mortgages had been written, from which several trillion dollars of mortgage-backed securities had been created, and massive amounts of credit default swaps as well. Tim Geithner, president of the New York Fed, Ben Bernanke, chairman of the Fed, and Hank Paulson, treasury secretary, claiming helplessness, let Lehman go bankrupt.

When the Lehman bankruptcy was announced on Sunday, September 14, a financial editor turned to me at a dinner party and said the crisis was now over. But it was merely the beginning of the most tumultuous financial period since early in the Great Depression. Lehman owed $600 billion worldwide. It handled 14 percent of the trading in stocks in London, 12 percent of bond trading in New York, and billions of dollars a year of brokerage business for hedge funds. If it didn't pay, its creditors in turn would find it difficult to meet their obligations. AIG had written billions of dollars of insurance—credit default swaps—to guarantee losses if Lehman failed, for which mammoth amounts of money from the insurance company were now due.

When the stock market opened the day after Lehman's demise, the Dow Jones Industrials dropped 500 points. The money markets—short-term lending markets of commercial paper and bank repos—stopped functioning. Paulson had not expected it to be that bad. Interest rates on bank borrowing and short-term corporate debt soared, as investors fled to relatively safe U.S. Treasury securities. The key indicator of the failure of the credit markets is the spread between the rates paid on such Treasury bills, which fell rapidly, and the rates paid on a proxy for corporate debt (literally, on three-month Eurodollar debt), which rose in these risky times as investors refused to buy it. Ordinarily, the spread, called the TED spread, was half a percentage point or less; in mid-October it was 3.5 percentage points.

At those rates, no one on Wall Street could afford to borrow to maintain liquidity. If the market did not unfreeze and rates come down, more firms would be forced to sell assets to raise cash, falling asset prices would generate more losses, and the stock market itself would collapse.

Paulson, Geithner, and Bernanke now moved rapidly. On Monday, Merrill, by now also on the brink, was sold, at their insistence, to Bank of America. AIG's stock fell by 60 percent. AIG was short tens of billions of dollars of cash on its insurance commitments. On Tuesday morning, the credit agencies announced a downgrading of AIG, once considered an indomitable triple-A credit. The insurance company was not only buried in CDS commitments, but had also invested in bad CDOs. The worst of all the holes in the nation's regulatory system was the lack of capital requirements on those who traded in derivatives like CDSs to make sure they could meet their commitments. Literally no one regulated AIG's sales of the credit default swaps. Later that day, the Treasury announced that it had injected $85 billion of capital into AIG, taking 80 percent of the company's stock in return. If AIG failed, with its liabilities to the rest of the Street unpaid, the devastation, the Treasury and the Fed believed, would be incalculable.

With that money and several more injections of capital, all of AIG's customers—its counterparties—were made whole by federal bailouts, none required to take even a modest loss. Goldman Sachs, Paulson's old firm, was one of the largest creditors. Paulson, the former CEO of Goldman, had been on the phone with Lloyd Blankfein several times during the negotiations, though he had later claimed he had nothing to do with the Fed's bailout of the firm. The creditors absorbed little of the losses, only the U.S. taxpayers did.

Money market funds were also in crisis, perhaps the most dangerous problem of all. They were generally considered as safe as U.S. Treasury bills by their investors, even when their charters allowed them to invest in bank CDs, which many now did. But some had bought Lehman CDs for the higher yield. On Monday, the Reserve Primary Fund, run by the once highly cautious founders of the very first money market fund (see Chapter 6), announced that it had more than 1 percent of its assets in Lehman commercial paper. Its investors, stunned they could lose money at all, immediately began to withdraw what could have amounted to $5 billion from the fund. If investors in other money market funds followed, the consequences were unimaginable. Money market funds would sell their commercial paper willy-nilly. No Wall Street firm might survive. By the end of the week, the Treasury decided to guarantee the funds in all money market funds and stemmed the tide—what could have been a true bank run every bit as frightening as the bank runs of the early 1930s.

Geithner and Paulson tried to get the stronger banks to merge with weaker ones, in particular, Goldman with Citigroup and JPMorgan Chase with Morgan Stanley, but the deals did not work out. To shore up its capital, Goldman separately lined up a $5 billion investment for preferred stock and warrants (rights to buy common stock in the future) from Warren Buffett. JPMorgan Chase raised $9 billion in preferred shares from Mitsubishi Bank.

Given the crisis, Bernanke, Paulson, and Geithner believed Washington had to make a massive amount of money available to the financial community. Bernanke did not want to take the weight of a future bailout entirely on the Fed's own back and demanded the Treasury put up the funds. Paulson, with help from Geithner and Bernanke, put together a $700 billion relief package, called the Troubled Asset Relief Program (TARP), to buy up the failing assets of the banks—the so-called toxic assets.

TARP required congressional approval, but anger was high, and the House of Representatives voted the proposal down on September 29. The next day, the Dow Jones Industrials plunged 777 points. President Bush got on the phone to apply political pressure on the legislators, and the TARP bill passed both houses of Congress a few days later.

But calm did not return to the credit markets and stock prices remained weak. In an indication of the shaky finances of the old-line investment banks, both Morgan and Goldman now applied to become bank holding companies, so they would if necessary be able to borrow fresh reserves instantaneously from the Fed. The Fed by now was also guaranteeing the commercial paper of the banks. Meanwhile, the unemployment rate was rapidly rising toward 7 percent, pushing the nation's economy into a deep recession as credit dried up and consumer and business spending fell.

Paulson, Bernanke, and Geithner quickly reworked TARP, giving up the idea of buying the toxic assets. It was simply too hard to determine workable prices and might even cause more losses by forcing the banks to write down more assets. In mid-October, the trio decided to do what the British authorities had done in response to their crisis, and inject capital directly into the banks in return for shares in the company—in this case, preferred shares rather than common shares, which paid little but conferred shareholder voting rights. Through the FDIC, the new TARP would also guarantee all the liabilities of some of the troubled banks to restore complete confidence in the institutions and stop any flight of capital.

The trio decided to provide up to $250 billion in capital to the nine largest banks in the country. Mostly at Geithner's insistence, they demanded that all the major banks take rescue money for fear that if only a few did, those banks would be seen as particularly endangered. Though it was unlikely the markets could be so easily fooled, Geithner, feeling the pressure, wanted to take no chances.

On October 14, nine bankers attended a meeting at the Treasury—including the CEOs of Bank of America, Citigroup, JPMorgan Chase, Goldman Sachs, Morgan Stanley, State Street, and Wells Fargo. Paulson told them that in return for preferred shares, he would give $25 billion to each of the major commercial banks—Citigroup, Bank of America, JP Morgan Chase, and Wells Fargo—and $10 billion to each of the smaller commercial banks and the investment banks. They would have the option of redeeming the shares owned by the government within three years. The federal government also demanded warrants for common shares and a direct say in compensation practices of the companies. Most important, as noted, some of their liabilities would be guaranteed by the federal government. Several of the banks momentarily balked, but all signed.

Citigroup was the company most in need of the capital, and received another $20 billion in aid, a total of $45 billion. The government also guaranteed more than $300 billion of its liabilities. The house that Wriston and Weill built was now a flimsy and dangerous if gigantic construction. Bank of America now had billions of dollars of Merrill's bad assets it may not have fully known about when it made the purchase. It received a total of $45 billion and had liabilities guaranteed. AIG received additional injections of funds, a total of $182 billion.

TARP eventually calmed the markets. The TED spreads between Treasury securities and corporate debt fell rapidly by the end of 2009 to pre-crisis levels. All those receiving aid eventually paid the government back by 2010, with interest, except AIG, whose future remained uncertain.

The federal government, however, having rescued the firms, should have recovered far more money. A formal analysis by a congressional commission appointed to be the TARP watchdog concluded that the Treasury paid two thirds more than the securities it received were worth. Warren Buffett got a far better deal from Goldman Sachs, for example. The federal government, cowed by thirty years of ideological claims that government was too interventionist, had provided Wall Street a sweet deal even if losses were ultimately minimized. Any private investor that took all the risk when markets were plummeting deserved a major piece of the upside, as the Street puts it. In panic, Paulson, Geithner, and Bernanke did not see very far ahead.

More important, because the federal government did not make adequate demands, the financial institutions did not use the money to restart lending to homeowners or businesses. Most of the banks came out whole, and went on, with only a couple of exceptions, to generate enormous profits in 2009. But lending to American business, large and small, fell in 2009 from the year before. At the banks that got the largest bailouts, business lending at the end of 2009 was down nearly 14 percent from 2008. Lending to consumers also fell.

Had Washington removed some of bank management, as it had with General Motors, when it received far less in TARP funds, it could have devised firmer plans to restore business lending. It had also refused to put any of the banks in conservatorship and take over their finances, which would also have given it more control over the allocation of the bank funds.

Much of the rescue was, however, undertaken by aggressive purchase of securities by the Federal Reserve in 2008, including Treasury bonds in 2009. The Treasury had also guaranteed for a time, with help from the Fed, commercial paper and money market liabilities, again amounting to trillions of dollars. The FDIC guaranteed bank debt. In total the federal government had more than $12 trillion on the line, a number hard to assimilate. Because of such backstops, the federal bailout, and the Obama stimulus that was passed in early 2009, the recession did end in mid-2009.

In the collapse, Americans lost nearly $13 trillion in the value of their homes and fallen stocks. By late 2010, only some $2–3 trillion was recovered in the stock market and none on average in the housing market. Perhaps three million Americans would lose their homes. The unemployment rate rose to more than 10 percent, and when discouraged and involuntary temporary workers are included, the rate was more than 17 percent in 2010. Wages fell and family incomes were below the levels reached more than ten years earlier. Capital investment was tepid.

President Obama's economic team put together the $800 billion stimulus package, but it did not reshape TARP. To the contrary, it appointed one of the creators of TARP, Tim Geithner, as treasury secretary. No new financial regulations were proposed until June 2009, when a perfunctory white paper without clearly stated objectives was published by the Treasury Department, mostly reiterating ideas already developed by the Bush administration, and providing little useful discussion of the causes of the crisis. A bill was passed by Congress in 2010 with one refreshing proposal, a plan for an independent Financial Product Safety Commission. Even when a bill was finally passed by Congress in 2010, known as the Dodd-Frank bill, named for its sponsors, Senator Christopher Dodd and Congressman Barney Frank, most of the harder decisions were left to the future. The new Financial Product Safety Commission was not made independent but housed in the Fed.

One of the reasons so much risk was taken on by Wall Street was straightforward: the individual bankers made personal fortunes. They were paid when the assets they bought went up in value, even if they were not sold, but when they fell, they were not required to return the money. They were also paid out of fees generated by the issuance of CDOs and other securities for which they had no personal liability. Sometimes they were paid in the firm's stock, but much of their compensation was outright cash. They thus had strong incentives to take maximum risk and little incentive to be concerned about losses. Proposed regulations did not deal firmly with the skewed compensation programs though recipients of TARP were temporarily subject to restrictions. The bankers made enormous sums personally when they issued CDOs. By 2008, the banks lost at least $100 billion on the CDOs, perhaps more, and endangered the health of the world financial system as credit markets closed down, but few bankers were required to give back any money.

In the 2000s, Wall Street had misallocated hundreds of billions of dollars of capital, even trillions of dollars, on investments in an inflated housing market. Ten years earlier, it had misallocated hundreds of billions of dollars on fantasy high-technology and telecom projects. Even when corporate profits rose in the 2000s, capital investment was disappointing as American corporations bought back their shares instead of making valuable investments in the nation's productive capacity. In fact, investment as a proportion of the economy, the GDP, was lower in the 2000s than in any other decade since World War II. Meanwhile, the foundation of the American economy was neglected: government investment in transportation infrastructure, education, health care, and energy technologies was not raised to the levels needed.

In 2010, the top four banks in America had a higher market share than they did in 2005. Banks that were considered too big to fail then were bigger now, though some of their more risky trading was to be restricted by the new financial regulations. A new group was established, made up of financial regulators, to oversee the giant banks but none of the banks was broken up.

On the other hand, there were few new restrictions on what Wall Street investment banks could do with their money. Mortgage brokers had never been regulated and were still not. There would be higher capital requirements for most financial firms, set by international regulators, but these would be implemented slowly. There were restrictions on how much speculative trading banks could do—a rule proposed by former Fed chairman Paul Volcker, but they were ambiguous. The new consumer protection agency was established, but how much power it had was yet to be determined.

Weill retired a billionaire from Citigroup. Until 2009, Rubin earned $15 million a year for part-time work, admitting that he did not even know about the $43 billion of shaky CDOs on Citigroup's books until they were publicly written down as losses in late 2007. O'Neal and Prince were fantastically rich. Even Mozilo still had most of his money. Howie Hubler, who lost $9 billion for Morgan, was allowed to quit with millions of dollars of bonuses and soon reentered Wall Street. Ralph Cioffi and Matthew Tannin were found innocent of fraud and insider trading charges by a jury for their misleading management of the Bear Stearns hedge funds and suffered no financial penalties. Many thought that the personal fortunes Cayne built at Bear Stearns and Fuld built at Lehman were wiped out when their companies' stock prices fell. But between 2000 and 2008, Harvard Law School researchers found that the top five executives at each firm drew out cash and stock of $1.4 billion from Bear and $1 billion from Lehman. It is fair to estimate that both Cayne and Fuld had put away $300–400 million each.

For 2009, a year in which one out of six Americans who wanted a job couldn't find one, Wall Street paid its high-level workers $140 billion in bonuses, the second largest bonus pool in its history. The crash of 2008 was not a systemic failure. It was a function of the unchecked greed of a handful of individuals, the culmination of forty years of growing power and weakened government. And the same individuals were essentially still in charge. The age of greed continued.

Epilogue

I n an op-ed piece published in the *Financial Times* in mid-2010, Sheila Bair, the Republican-appointed chairman of the FDIC, wrote that Wall Street had channeled hundreds of billions of dollars of capital into foolish speculation in housing in the 2000s. "The bust that followed is clear evidence," she wrote, "that capital was misallocated and could have been put to better use in areas such as energy, infrastructure, or the industrial base."

The same complaint would have been appropriate in each decade of the age of greed. In the 1970s, tens of billions of petrodollars were channeled into bad loans in Latin America. In the 1980s, hundreds of billions of dollars of dubious corporate acquisitions were made with junk bond financing and loans from banks. That same decade, thrifts, released from restraints by the Garn-St. Germain bill, spent savers' money, guaranteed by federal insurance, on one foolish fantasy after another, including investing in junk bonds that were soon to collapse.

In the 1990s, an era of deceit helped promote the speculative bubble in high-technology and telecom stocks that carried forward from 1995 to 2000. Good money was invested after bad in one absurdist dream after another, justified by Wall Street analysts who were paid handsomely to exaggerate or deceive investors outright about company prospects. Accounting fraud reached new heights across corporate America, with the help and approval of the most prestigious accounting firms. Questionable compensation to high-technology executives and institutional investors promoted still higher prices. The Nasdaq Composite Index reached a high of about 5,000 in March 2000 only to fall to just above 1,000 thirty months later. Enron and WorldCom went bust, the soaring early success of both due to accounting fraud and misleading Wall Street analysis. Several trillion dollars of value was lost overall. As late as the fall of 2010, the Nasdaq was still 50 percent below its 2000 high. Overall, capital investment rose in the 1990s as a proportion of GDP, but many hundreds of billions of dollars of it turned out to be wasted.

The collapse of housing eight years later followed the same pattern, but the bubble in terms of actual dollars was far bigger and the collapse of greater consequence. Six to seven trillion dollars of new mortgages had been written that decade; mortgage debt was now much greater in total than federal debt. Wall Street firms learned how to raise capital for new mortgages around the world by creating attractive securities that in fact disguised the real risk of the mortgages. The major banking firms not only "securitized" these mortgages but had consumer loan subsidiaries that wrote subprime and other risky mortgages aggressively. Citigroup was every bit as aggressive at originating subprime mortgages as was Countrywide; Bear Stearns, Lehman, Merrill, and JPMorgan Chase had subsidiaries that were subprime leaders as well.

For all these endeavors, Wall Street professionals got fabulously rich. They channeled hundreds of billions of dollars into wasteful investments that could have been spent on energy, transportation, and communications infrastructure, health care and medical research, education, technical and business R&D, and new, truly innovative consumer products and business equipment. The question was not whether Wall Street bankers contributed enough to the economy to warrant their compensations, but how much they cost the economy in the damage done.

In fact, in the 2000s, capital investment was notably weak, even as corporations made enormous profits and built up coffers of cash of $2 trillion. Many bought back the shares of their own company to drive up their stock prices. Academic finance theory supported such strategies. Buying back stock was sensible if there were no better alternatives. Stock prices would rise and investors would sell, take their profits, and themselves supposedly invest in more attractive corners of the economy, contributing to prosperity. This claim was made time and again over the course of three decades, offered as justification for the aggressive corporate takeovers of the 1980s as well. If the acquiring companies did not do better, as was typical, or even did worse after their acquisitions, at least they pushed up stock prices of the firms acquired, and supposedly distributed money to investors who then invested it wisely.

In fact, there are many flaws in this theoretical argument. Capital investment in new ideas has always been risky; therefore there has been a bias to take the safe way out, such as buying up shares instead. Another flaw is the assumption that business executives make decisions to benefit their firms in the long run, when in fact, under the tutelage of Wall Street, they often make decisions to make themselves rich by driving up the value of their stock options in the short run. As discussed, efficient markets theory holds that the stock price rationally reflects the long-term prospects of the company at any point in time; this was the extremist theoretical argument that was widely endorsed by a dominant school of economists. But too often what drove stock prices were short-term profits, not long-term projects or high-risk investments in new ideas. Short-term profits were easy to achieve by cutting labor costs or R&D. As noted, overall capital investment was relatively weak in the 1980s and 2000s, and the boom of the 1990s was built on a dubious speculative bubble.

The amount of federal money spent to bail out failing financial institutions after a crisis was not the only cost of overspeculation. To save the depositors in the failed thrifts of the 1980s, for example, the federal government spent $150–200 billion. Hundreds of billions of dollars of bad investments had been made by the thrifts in golf resorts, shopping malls, and junk bonds. The money should have been invested more intelligently and productively. The collapse of the thrifts weakened the economy and helped precipitate a credit crisis and the 1990 recession, reducing total income in the nation as well as federal tax revenue.

Similarly, the cost of the $700 billion TARP bailout was small. The federal government was paid back by financial institutions, sometimes with interest, and in the final tally may even make a small profit. In fact, the Treasury should have made a much better deal—even made a substantial profit—having supplied the risk money that saved the system. More important, it should have demanded that the firms that got the money lend much of it out. Lending remained weak.

But the largest cost of the crisis was the steepest recession since the 1930s. GDP fell sharply. Eight million jobs were lost. And recovery in the subsequent year and a half beginning in mid-2009 was slow, and will likely stay slow, resulting in considerably higher unemployment and lower national income for many years than otherwise could have been realized. Federal tax revenues were and will continue to be reduced accordingly, and the budget deficit will be much higher as a result. None of this counts the several trillion dollars of debt or loan guarantees made by the Federal Reserve, whose future costs cannot yet be computed.

Over the four decades of the age of greed, financial assets as a percentage of GDP more than doubled. Revenues of financial firms rose from 3 percent of GDP to 6 percent, and profits of those financial firms soared from 13 percent of all profits to 30–40 percent. Average compensation per employee at financial firms started growing far faster by 1978 than the average of other U.S. business, and was well more than double the average compensation elsewhere by 2008.

Few with influence in Washington seriously criticized the growth of the financial community until the crisis that began in 2007. Finally, at least some economists started analyzing the issues. Using conventional economic methods, Thomas Philippon found that the size of the financial community grew far faster in the 2000s than did the amount of capital it raised for nonfinancial businesses, supposedly its main function. Philippon probably understated the case, assuming, for example, that the financings and IPOs of the 1990s were generally worthwhile. As we have seen, the high-technology IPOs then were highly speculative, and the vast majority of businesses financed by them failed. It is likely a strong statistical case will someday be made that the financial community grew too fast in the 1990s as well, and likely in the 1980s. Economist Paul Wachtel found after extensive research of the experience in other nations, as well as in the United States, that rapid expansion of financial firms does not lead to more rapid economic growth.

In retrospect, recent economic research finds that the high levels of personal compensation paid to bankers and traders were also not remotely deserved. Philippon and his co-author, Ariell Reshef, showed that, even adjusting for education levels and other factors such as demands for innovative techniques, individual ability wasn't able to account for the high compensation since the mid-1990s. A more interesting study by economists Lawrence Katz and Claudia Goldin compared the future salaries of successive graduating classes from Harvard College, adjusted for many factors, such as grades, College Board scores, time out of the workforce, and many other measures. They found that those who went into finance earned three times as much as their peers with identical measures of talent or ability.

It was not as if there were no precedents for these excesses. Much the same level of speculation, often reaching absurd proportions, took place in the 1920s and set in place some of the conditions for the Great Depression. Over the years, these concerns were minimized and then forgotten. The writings of economists like John Kenneth Galbraith, Charles Kindleberger,

and Hyman Minsky were neglected in favor of explanations more congenial to those who believed that unfettered free markets worked best.

Fortunately, one major lesson of the 1930s was not entirely forgotten—
the Keynesian lesson that government must intervene in times of crisis like
the one that overwhelmed the nation in 2007 and 2008. The only reason
a far worse recession did not occur was the expensive government rescue
package, including not only TARP but trillions of dollars of loan guarantees and Federal Reserve purchases of debt, as well as President Obama's
nearly $800 billion of government spending and tax cuts, most of which
was spent in 2009 and 2010.

The true cost of the financial excesses of Wall Street and what would
have happened to the economy were mooted by the federal government's
rescue. But one mainstream analysis by Alan Blinder and Moody's analyt-
ics chief economist, Mark Zandi, estimated the damage that would have
been done. In all, federal guarantees and loans came to more than $12 tril-
lion. These included guarantees of money market funds and commercial
paper, as well as TARP and other matters. These also included the guarantees and loans by the Federal Reserve, which came to some $2 trillion.

Most of these guarantees were ultimately not called upon. But had nothing been done by Washington—no TARP, federal guarantees, or Federal
Reserve purchases and loans—Blinder and Zandi estimated that the recession would have continued through 2011, and GDP would have fallen
by 12 percent from its high rather than by the substantial 4 percent it did
fall, which itself was greater than any other recession in the post–World
War II period. About twice as many jobs would have been lost, some
16.5 million compared to the already high eight million. The unemployment rate would have reached 16.5 percent. It would have been a full-fledged
depression. One in four Americans looking for a full-time job would not
have been able to find one. Average wages may have fallen sharply for those
with a job.

Some economists argued that because bankers knew the federal government would bail them out, they took undue risks that led to speculative excess—such moral hazard, these economists argue, meant that the
crisis was government's fault. But this argument is exaggerated, implying
that speculative bubbles are more rational than they are. Damaging financial crises occurred throughout nineteenth-century and early-twentieth-
century America when no government entity could genuinely be counted
on to bail out big lenders. To take a contemporary example, when Mexico was bailed out in 1994 with a $40 billion rescue package of loans and

guarantees from the U.S. Treasury, many economists argued that this only made future crises inevitable because outside investors would invest recklessly in such countries again, knowing they would be bailed out if necessary. In fact, investment in Mexico not only failed to revive, but fell and stayed low in Mexico and other developing countries at the time. There are many other examples of nations that got government bailouts without a revival in investment.

The nature of herd behavior is to cast common sense aside, whether a lender of last resort exists or not. Moral hazard is among the causes of overspeculation but not likely the determining part. Herd behavior is hardly rational. And the extent of federal activity in 2008 and 2009 was far greater than ever before. No one on Wall Street could have anticipated such aggressive responses. The larger concern by far is what would have happened had government not taken the actions it did. Blinder and Zandi may well have understated the consequences.

Given the federal government's future guarantees, the costs in higher federal budget deficits will be substantial. Moreover, economic growth will likely continue to be slow. Nevertheless, TARP, the fiscal stimulus, and the Federal Reserve's aggressive loans and guarantees, known as quantitative easing, it should be reemphasized, did stop the collapse and shorten the recession. The Keynesian response did work. By 2009, Wall Street was back and operating, and the recession was declared ended by the summer of that year, having formally started in late 2007. As 2010 came to a close, the question was whether the lesson of government stimulus was learned well enough. Business lending remained weak, consumer spending did not revive strongly, and the number of new jobs created was not nearly what was needed to absorb a growing workforce. That the economy did not recover more rapidly was the consequence of the federal government not doing enough. As the nation entered 2011, still more federal spending and further aggressive Federal Reserve action to reduce rates and stimulate lending were needed. Adequate medicine was not forthcoming.

In 2010, Congress passed a financial reregulation bill, supported by President Obama. It is by no means clear it will prevent future catastrophe. Many of the difficult decisions regarding capital requirements, limitations on leverage, restrictions on investing, and the power of the consumer protection agency have yet to be made. The huge financial institutions once declared too big to fail, if subject to more oversight and potentially higher capital requirements, were left in place. The effectiveness of the new regulations will depend on how vigorously the new rules are enforced, and there is a great deal of leeway regarding that. In coming years, once the 2008 crisis is forgotten, regulators may again neglect the dangers of financial speculation in favor of a set of dubious economic principles similar to those that have influenced them since the 1970s.

Preventing catastrophe should not be the only objective of reregulation—a point Washington, including the Obama administration, has barely discussed. The financial community has to be remade to allocate resources effectively again. This requires more regulation of compensation and conflicts of interest, more transparency of trading, and more outright prohibition of activities that distort markets and promote speculation. The regulation work of the Obama administration and Congress did not go far enough in these critical areas.

It bears repeating one last time that average compensation never grew as slowly in American industrial history than it did over the course of the age of greed. One commonplace assumption was that as productivity rose—the corporate income generated by each worker—wages and salaries should rise. Over this period, productivity rose significantly faster than worker compensation. In the 2000s, typically household incomes actually fell. Productivity gains flowed to corporate profits.

Washington has not come forward with a well-developed plan for long-term growth and a reoriented financial industry that would do what it is supposed to do: channel savings to productive uses. Wall Street has continued to complain about how new regulations would undermine its profitability and has threatened to leave those financial capitals that impose restrictions they deem damaging. America has not yet turned the page.

Notes

PROLOGUE

3 THE ECONOMY GREW AT PRODIGIOUS RATES: Mike Davis, *City of Quartz* (New York: Random House, 1990), pp. 15–40.

3 THE SEEDS OF AMERICA'S FUTURE: In general, see Rick Perlstein, *Before the Storm* (New York: Hill & Wang, 2001), Chapter 7.

4 "MY FATHER WAS A POLITICAL ANIMAL": Author interview with Lewis Uhler, October 2003.

4 ULTIMATELY, THE TYPICAL WHITE AMERICAN: See for example Isabelle Sawhill and John E. Morton, *Economic Mobility: Is the American Dream Alive and Well?*, Pew Charitable Trusts, http://www.economicmobility.org/assets/pdfs/EMP%20American%20Dream%20Report.pdf.

4 THERE WERE POVERTY AND NEED: Davis, *City of Quartz*, p. 17.

4 THEY PARTICIPATED IN THE REAL AND RELIABLE: This actually characterized the history of the American economy since before the Civil War.

5 IN SOUTHERN CALIFORNIA: Perlstein, *Before the Storm*, pp. 608–16.

5 THEY FOUND POWERFUL ALLIES: A particularly useful history of the development of business political interest is Kim Phillips-Fein, *Invisible Hands: The Making of the Conservative Movement from the New Deal to Reagan* (New York: W. W. Norton, 2009).

6 "WE THOUGHT OF OURSELVES": Author interview with Lewis Uhler, June 2004.

6 THE SOCIETY SOON DREW: Perlstein, *Before the Storm*, pp. 120–22; "Orange County had caught anti-communism fever," he writes.

6 UHLER JOINED THE BIRCHERS: Lou Cannon, *Governor Reagan: His Rise to Power* (New York: PublicAffairs, 2003), p. 369.

8 UHLER WROTE A REPORT: Author interview with Lewis Uhler, October 2003.

8 THE INVESTIGATION CONCLUDED: Andy Furillo, "The Front Man for Proposition 75," *Sacramento Bee*, August 15, 2005, p. A1.

9 "TO MY LATE FATHER": Lewis K. Uhler, *Setting Limits: Constitutional Control of Government* (Washington, D.C.: Regnery Gateway, 1989), p. v.

CHAPTER 1: WALTER WRISTON

10 APPLETON, WISCONSIN: Phillip L. Zweig, *Wriston: Walter Wriston, Citibank, and the Rise and Fall of American Financial Supremacy* (New York: Crown, 1995), p. 14.

11 "I KNEW I WOULDN'T DO THAT": Unless otherwise indicated, all Walter Wriston quotes in this chapter are from the author's interview with Walter Wriston, July 2004.

11 HOSTILITY TOWARD HIS FATHER: Zweig, *Wriston*, p. 53.

11 "IF I STAYED UP ALL NIGHT": Author interview with Walter Wriston, July 2004.

12 BANKS WENT OUT OF BUSINESS BY THE HUNDREDS: Charles P. Kindleberger, *Manias, Panics and Crashes: A History of Financial Crises* (New York: John Wiley, 1978), remains the leading history of the period. For an early if ideological history, see Murray Rothbard, *The Panic of 1819: Reactions and Policies* (New York: Columbia University Press, 1962). For more up-to-date histories, see Edward Chancellor, *Devil Take the Hindmost: A History of Financial Speculation* (New York: Farrar, Straus & Giroux, 2000); and Peter M. Garber, *Famous First Bubbles* (Cambridge, Mass.: MIT Press, 2000).

12 BUT A BALANCE BETWEEN ADEQUATE CREDIT: Gordon S. Wood, *Empire of Liberty: A History of the Early Republic, 1789–1815* (Oxford: Oxford University Press, 2010).

13 SUCH A CREDIT BOOM AND BUST ALONE: John Kenneth Galbraith, *The Great Crash, 1929* (Boston: Houghton Mifflin, 1978), pp. 186–88. A contemporary, mainstream assessment that acknowledges an important role for financial speculation and excess as a cause of the Depression is Barry Eichengreen and Kris Mitchener, "*The Great Depression as a Credit Boom Gone Wrong*" (working paper, Department of Economics, University of California, Berkeley, August 2003), http://www.econ.berkeley.edu/~eichengr/research/bisconferencerevision5jul30–03.pdf.

14 "THERE WAS SOMETHING EMOTIONAL": Author interview, Albert Wojnilower, July 2004.

15 WHILE MOORE ALONE WOULD NOT HAVE BEEN ABLE: Zweig, *Wriston*, p. 126.

15 "THE REST AS THEY SAY": Author interview with Walter Wriston, July 2004.

15 BANKS, IN CONTRAST, HAD TO MEET: A short-term note is repaid by the borrower within months or even days; a long-term bond is repaid in years, often as long as thirty years.

16 IT WAS TOO BOLD: Zweig, *Wriston*, p. 778.

16 "ONE TIME I BROUGHT HIM A LOAN": Author interview with Walter Wriston, July 2004.

16 "WE LOOKED AT THE DATA": Ibid.

16 THE GOVERNMENT REPORTED: Board of Governors, *The Flow of Funds Accounts*, The Federal Reserve, 1986, p. 74.

17 "BUT AT THE SAME TIME": Author interview with Walter Wriston, July 2004.

18 WITHIN A YEAR, OUTSTANDING CDS: Timothy Q. Cook and Robert K. Laroche, eds., *Instruments of the Money Market*, Federal Reserve Bank of Richmond, 1998, p. 38.

18 THERE WERE STILL RESTRICTIONS: Jerry W. Markham, *A Financial History of the United States*, vol. 2 (Armonk, N.Y.: M. E. Sharpe, 2002), p. 338.

18 "BANKS BEGAN TO BID": Henry Kaufman, *Of Money and Markets: A Wall Street Memoir* (New York: McGraw-Hill, 1999), p. 253.

18 "THE YEAR 1966": Sidney Homer and Richard Sylla, *A History of Interest Rates* (New Brunswick, N.J.: Rutgers University Press, 1991), p. 379.

19 INSTEAD, THE LOWER-KEYED WRISTON: Zweig, *Wriston*, p. 216.

21 THE AMOUNT OF COMMERCIAL PAPER OUTSTANDING: Jerry W. Markham, *A Financial History of the United States*, vol. 3 (Armonk, N.Y.: M. E. Sharpe, 2002), p. 5.

21 THE RAILROAD HAD BEEN GIVEN A HIGH RATING: Ibid.

21 WRISTON BLAMED PENN CENTRAL: Zweig, *Wriston*, pp. 314–16.

22 UNDER PRESSURE, BURNS ALSO ELIMINATED: Donald D. Hester, *The Evolution of Monetary Policy and Banking in the U.S.: Arthur Burns and William G. Miller* (Berlin: Springer, 2008), pp. 41–56.

22 THE CRISIS PASSED: Cook and Laroche, *Instruments of the Money Market*, p. 38.

22 "IT WAS THE BEGINNING OF THE END": William Greider, *Secrets of the Temple: How the Federal Reserve Runs the Country* (New York: Touchstone, 1987), p. 319.

23 EVENTUALLY WRISTON PUBLISHED: Walter B. Wriston, *Risk and Other Four-Letter Words* (New York: Harper & Row, 1986).

23 "THESE NEW MONEY MARKET INSTRUMENTS": Kaufman, *Of Money and Markets,* p. 253.

24 ONLY A CREDIT CRUNCH TRULY SLOWED: Albert Wojnilower, "The Central Role of Credit Crunches in Recent Financial History," Brookings Papers on Economic Activity, vol. 2, 1980.

24 "I THOUGHT THE OLD REGULATIONS": Author interview with Albert Wojnilower, July 2004.

CHAPTER 2: MILTON FRIEDMAN

26 AFTER HE HAD GAINED WORLDWIDE FAME: Milton Friedman, *Capitalism and Freedom* (Chicago: University of Chicago Press, 1962), Preface, 1982 edition, p. xiv.

26 HIGH UNEMPLOYMENT OF 9 PERCENT: In fact, as we shall see, there was a major error in computing mortgage costs back then. Later corrected by federal data gatherers, as we shall see in a later chapter, consumer inflation reached no higher than 11 percent in these years.

28 HIS MAIN COMPETITOR: See a workmanlike biography, Anne C. Heller, *Ayn Rand and the World She Made* (New York: Nan A. Talese, 2009).

28 "MONEY WAS ALWAYS A CONCERN": Friedman gives an account in the book he co-authored with his wife, Rose, *Two Lucky People: Memoirs* (Chicago: University of Chicago Press, 1998), pp. 20–32.

28 YET THE FAMILY WAS ABLE TO BUY: Author interview with Milton Friedman, November 2003.

29 "FANATICALLY RELIGIOUS": Ibid.

29 IF HIS FATHER HAD ANY POLITICAL INFLUENCE: Ibid.

30 "SAVE FOR MY PARENTS": Friedman and Friedman, *Two Lucky People,* p. 30

30 FRIEDMAN THOUGHT MARSHALL'S MODEL: Friedman's early devotion to Marshall is evident in an essay, "Marshall's Demand Curve," in his book *Essays in Positive Economics* (Chicago: University of Chicago Press, 1953).

31 "LIKE HIS MENTOR": Friedman and Friedman, *Two Lucky People,* p. 32.

31 JONES WAS THE REASON: Ibid., p. 33.

31 IT EMPHASIZED, AS SIMONS PUT IT: Henry Simons private papers, cited by Rob Van Horn and Philip Mirowski, "The Rise of the Chicago School of Economics and the Birth of Neoliberalism," in *The Road from Mont Pelerin: The Making of the Neoliberal Thought Collective,* ed. Philip Mirowski and Dieter Plehwe (Cambridge, Mass.: Harvard University Press, 2009), p. 145.

31 THIS APPROACH IN A TIME: H. L. Miller, "On the Chicago School of Economics," *Journal of Political Economy* 70 (February 1962): 64–69.

31 "MY TEACHERS REGARDED THE DEPRESSION": Milton Friedman, "Comments on the Critics," *Journal of Political Economy* (September-October 1972): 906–50.

32 "SIMONS FOR EXAMPLE DID NOT EQUATE": Miller "On the Chicago School of Economics," p. 70.

32 "ONCE A DEFLATION HAS GOTTEN UNDER WAY": Henry Simons, *Personal Income and Taxation: The Definition of Income as a Problem of Fiscal Policy* (Chicago: University of Chicago Press, 1938), p. 222, cited by Esteban Pérez Caldentey and Matías Vernengo, "Fiscal Policy for the Global Economic Crisis," *Challenge,* May-June 2001.

32 HE WAS, IN FACT, A MILD PROPONENT: Author interview with Milton Friedman, November 2003; Lanny Ebenstein, *Milton Friedman: A Biography* (London: Macmillan Palgrave, 2007).

33 FEW INVITATIONS CAME HIS WAY: Friedman did get an offer from the University of Wisconsin, but became embroiled in what he said was an anti-Semitic battle between the economics department and the business school, and he had to leave. Academy of Achievement interview, January 31, 1991, http://www.achievement.org/autodoc/page/frioint-6.

33 MOREOVER, IT WAS PUBLISHED BY: Milton Friedman and George J. Stigler, *Roofs or Ceilings?* (New York: Foundation for Economic Education, 1946).

33 ONE CONSERVATIVE STAFFER: Van Horn and Mirowski, "The Rise of the Chicago School of Economics and the Birth of Neoliberalism," p. 173n58.

33 THERE, PARTLY UNDER THE INFLUENCE: Obituary on his death, 2004, University of Chicago Press Office, http://eh.net/pipermail/hes/2004-September/002496.html.

34 THE FUND ALSO HELPED FINANCE: In the Foreword to *Capitalism and Freedom*, Friedman acknowledges the Volker Fund's financing of his book, which many considered the American version of *The Road to Serfdom,* despite obvious differences.

35 HAYEK WROTE THE PROPOSAL: From Theodore Schultz (a Chicago economist) papers, cited by Van Horn and Mirowski, "The Rise of the Chicago School of Economics and the Birth of Neoliberalism," p. 152.

35 HE HAD WRITTEN IN 1948: Ibid. See also J. Bradford DeLong, "In Defense of Henry Simons' Standing as a Classical Liberal," *Cato Journal* 9, no. 1 (1990): 601–18.

35 BUT THE MEN WHO RAN: Van Horn and Mirowski, "The Rise of the Chicago School of Economics and the Birth of Neoliberalism," p. 152.

35 COMPETITION WOULD OFTEN NATURALLY UNDERMINE MONOPOLY: Rob Van Horn, "Reinventing Monopoly and the Role of Corporations: The Roots of Chicago Law and Economics," in Mirowksi and Plehwe, eds. *The Road from Mount Pelerim,* pp. 217–19.

35 BY 1951, MILTON FRIEDMAN HAD ALSO SHIFTED: Ibid., pp. 219–20.

36 THE POWER TO SET PRICES: Friedman, *Capitalism and Freedom,* p. 28; see Chapter 8 in general, pp. 119–36.

36 FRANK KNIGHT, THE MOST HIGHLY REGARDED: Frank Knight to W. H. Rappard, in Angus Burgin, "The Radical Conservatism of Frank H. Knight," *Modern Intellectual History* 6, no. 3 (2009): 536–37.

36 "COLLEAGUES SPOOF AT [GALBRAITH]": The Knight papers, cited by Burgin, "The Radical Conservatism of Frank H. Knight," p. 537.

36 CLAIMS THAT THE "NEO-LIBERALISM" OF FRIEDMAN: Van Horn and Mirowski, "The Rise of the Chicago School of Economics and the Birth of Neoliberalism," pp. 157–58.

37 ECONOMISTS REFER TO THIS: The latter is known as general equilibrium analysis, referring to how the entire economy stabilized, not just a single market. It was too abstract and theoretical for Friedman's taste, and largely derived from the work of the French economist Léon Walras, who died just before Friedman was born. While many of his colleagues worked the more theoretical territory of Walrasian economics, especially in later years, Friedman preferred the more concrete world of Marshall's partial analysis. Both were integral parts of twentieth-century neoclassical economics.

38 KEYNES ARGUED THIS WAS EXACTLY THE WRONG APPROACH: A nation's savings, composed of profits and personal savings, was in the short run reduced by government deficits. Older-school economists held that the savings released by balancing a budget would be invested.

38 IN OTHER WORDS, EVEN AS DEFICITS MAY RISE: By this point, a school of thought had gained wide acceptance (in fact, it was first proposed earlier in the twentieth century) that damaging social costs, so-called externalities such as pollution, could be caused in markets and required government intervention to mitigate. Friedman acknowledged this concept but minimized its importance.

38 MANY AMERICAN ECONOMISTS: Mark Blaug, *Economic Theory in Retrospect* (Cambridge: Cambridge University Press, 1962), pp. 641–51.

38 THE CONVERTS INCLUDED: Economists like future Nobelists Samuelson and Franco Modigliani of MIT and James Tobin of Yale advocated fiscal stimulus as a necessary and aggressive correction, after which the economy would find its ideal operating level again without government intervention. In other words, neoclassical forces would operate again. This became known as the neoclassical synthesis, combining moderate Keynesianism with neoclassical principles. Some British followers of Keynes, including several prominent students such as Joan Robinson of Keynes's university, Cambridge, however, believed that neoclassical principles did not as readily take hold once an economy was stimulated to full employment and more or less constant government policy intervention was required to keep economies efficient and unemployment low. Other so-called post-Keynesian schools of thought arose in America that had more in common with Cambridge, England, than Cambridge, Massachusetts, but the neoclassical synthesis dominated the major academic institutions in America.

39 "EVER SINCE THE NEW DEAL": Friedman, *Capitalism and Freedom*, p. 75.

39 FRIEDMAN'S EARLY EFFORTS: For example, see Carl Shoup, Milton Friedman, and Ruth Mack, *Taxing to Prevent Inflation: Techniques for Estimating Revenue Requirements* (New York: Columbia University Press, 1943).

39 THE THEORY HELD THAT THE QUANTITY: The famous equation is $MV = PQ$, where M equals the money supply, V the velocity, P, the price of goods, and Q the quantity of goods. It was later Friedman's license plate.

40 IT WAS PROBABLY FRIEDMAN'S MOST EFFECTIVE USE: Milton Friedman, *A Theory of the Consumption Function* (Chicago: University of Chicago Press, 1957). Keynesians like Franco Modigliani of MIT developed similar theories.

40 BUT IT ONLY DENTED THE SURFACE: He readily admitted this in an interview. His successors, however, have made this a major area of disagreement, producing models that show there is no multiplier effect. On balance, however, the majority of such analyses do show a positive multiplier.

40 HE HAD NOT YET COME UP WITH A DEFINITIVE STATISTICAL FOUNDATION: For example, Milton Friedman, *A Program for Monetary Stability, Milan Lectures of 1959* (New York: Fordham University Press, 1960).

41 "THE FACT IS THAT THE GREAT DEPRESSION": Friedman, *Capitalism and Freedom*, p. 38.

41 "SO LONG AS THE FREEDOM": Ibid., pp. 14–15.

41 ECONOMIC FREEDOM IS: Ibid., p. 8.

43 IN 1963: Milton Friedman and Anna Jacobson Schwartz, *A Monetary History of the United States, 1867–1960* (Princeton, N.J.: Princeton University Press, 1963).

44 IN 1953, HE MAINTAINED: This contention was a simplified version of American philosophical pragmatism, which by and large asserted that complete explanations were hard to come by and an answer to a question should be judged by its usefulness. If an economic model passed statistical test, it was good enough, argued Friedman, but the central flaw was that such statistical tests were based on history. Without a cogent theory about what truly caused the results, it would be hard to assess how departures from history affected economic relationships. Abraham Hirsch and Neil De Marchi, *Milton Friedman: Theory and Practice* (New York: Harvester Wheatsheaf, 1990), pp. 138–45.

44 MONEY CREATION IN A MODERN ECONOMY: Robert J. Gordon, ed., *Milton Friedman's Monetary Framework: A Debate with His Critics* (Chicago: University of Chicago Press, 1970).

44 YET FRIEDMAN HIMSELF WROTE: Hirsch and De Marchi, *Milton Friedman*, pp. 229, 230.

44 IF THE SAME AMOUNT OF MONEY: Velocity equaled GDP divided by the money supply; in the general Friedman-Schwartz case, GDP divided by currency and checking accounts.

45 "TO ME IT SEEMS STRANGE": The late James Tobin was and remains the most perceptive and diligent critic of the work. James Tobin, "The Monetary Interpretation of History," *American Economic Review,* 55 no. 3 (June 1965): 464–85. Tobin was effusively complimentary of their data gathering, however.

45 AND THE FED FAIRLY QUICKLY REVERSED ITSELF: He claimed the Fed withdrew reserves in 1932 in his 1967 presidential speech for the American Economics Association.

45 WHEN RESERVES WERE ADDED IN 1932: Nicholas Kaldor, "The New Monetarism," *Lloyd's Bank Review,* March 1970.

45 IN THE TWO PRECEDING YEARS: Peter Temin, *Did Monetary Forces Cause the Great Depression?* (New York: W. W. Norton, 1976), p. 169.

45 THE MONEY SUPPLY PROBABLY WOULD NOT HAVE RISEN: Simply put, the Federal Reserve requires banks to set aside securities as reserves against loans, known as the reserve requirement, and the central banks can control how much in reserves they have. But it cannot induce them to lend as much as they can. This depends on economic and financial conditions. Even those who still support Friedman's broad contention that the Fed caused the Depression take largely different approaches that are related, not directly to the money supply, but to the enormous numbers of bank failures in this period and the collapse of credit, to which Friedman paid little attention. In general, Ben S. Bernanke, *Essays on the Great Depression* (Princeton, N.J.: Princeton University Press, 2000).

46 THE MONETARY HISTORY, THEY WROTE: Hirsch and De Marchi, *Milton Friedman,* p. 264.

48 EVEN HE EVENTUALLY ALLOWED: Milton Friedman, "Perspective on Inflation," *Newsweek,* June 1974.

49 "THE GREAT INFLATION OF 1973–74": Alan S. Blinder, *Economic Policy and the Great Stagflation* (New York: Academic Press, 1979), p. 103.

49 THERE HAS BEEN SO MUCH CORROBORATING RESEARCH: Alan S. Blinder and Jeremy B. Rudd, "The Supply Shock Explanation of the Great Stagflation Revisited," Center for Economic Studies Working Paper, No. 176, Princeton, November 2008, p. 49.

49 MANY ECONOMISTS HAILED: Ben S. Bernanke, "The Great Moderation," Speech, February 2004, http://www.bis.org/review/r040301f.pdf.

49 THERE HAD BEEN DISSENTERS: George A. Akerlof, William T. Dickens, and George L. Perry, "Near-Rational Wage and Price Setting and the Optimal Rates of Inflation and Unemployment," Brookings Papers on Economic Activity, Economic Studies Program, The Brookings Institution, vol. 31 (2000–2001), pp. 1–60.

49 "NOBODY KNOWS THE COST": On Blanchard's inflation targeting, see Chris Giles, "IMF Experts Spell Out Policy Flaws," *Financial Times,* February 12, 2010, p. 3; Akerlof, Dickens, and Perry, "Near-Rational Wage and Price Setting and the Optimal Rates of Inflation and Unemployment," p. 1.

49 RATHER, HIS SOCIAL POLICY WAS DRIVEN: Friedman, *Capitalism and Freedom,* p. 169.

50 "THE GREAT ADVANCES OF CIVILIZATION": Ibid., p. 5.

50 "THE GREAT ACHIEVEMENT OF CAPITALISM": Ibid., p. 169.

51 "I HAVE ALWAYS BEEN IMPRESSED": Friedman and Friedman, *Two Lucky People,* pp. 217–18.

CHAPTER 3: RICHARD NIXON AND ARTHUR BURNS

53 HE BOUGHT A SMALL: Richard M. Nixon, *The Memoirs of Richard Nixon* (New York: Grosset & Dunlap, 1978). Nixon started his book: "I was born in a house my father built."

53 FRANK WAS STERN: Garry Wills, *Nixon Agonistes: The Crisis of the Self-Made Man* (Boston: Houghton Mifflin, 1969), pp. 176–77.

53 RICHARD'S MOTHER: Nixon, *Memoirs*, pp. 8–9.

54 FRANK HAD CONVERTED: Ibid.

54 THE RICHFIELD GAS STATION: Stephen A. Ambrose, *Nixon: The Education of a Politician, 1913–1962* (New York: Simon & Schuster, 1987), p. 34.

54 IN LATER YEARS: Fawn M. Brodie, *Richard Nixon: The Shaping of His Character* (New York: W. W. Norton, 1981), p. 51.

54 WITH A THRIVING STORE: Ambrose, *Nixon*, p. 114.

54 "FOR NIXON, THE THIRTIES": Wills, *Nixon Agonistes*, p. 79.

54 AS PRESIDENT, HE FOUND OUT: Brodie in general on this subject, *Richard Nixon*, p. 132.

55 HIS MOTHER VOTED FOR WOODROW WILSON: Ambrose, *Nixon*, p. 70.

55 IN HIS MEMOIRS, HE CLAIMED: Nixon, *Memoirs*, p. 41.

55 NIXON BECAME THE MOST VOLUBLE: Hiss's guilt, if not implausible, has ever after been a source of debate and controversy. He was sent to jail for perjury, always denying accusations.

55 "A PASSION FOR TAKING ON ENEMIES": Brodie, *Richard Nixon*, p. 173.

57 THE ECONOMY FOUNDERED AGAIN: See Herbert Stein for a good summary of the issues, especially the ongoing war on inflation in the 1950s: *Fiscal Revolution in America: Policy in Pursuit of Reality* (Chicago: University of Chicago Press, 1984), pp. 325–36 for the decisions of 1958; pp. 366–71 for 1960.

57 IN HIS 1962 MEMOIR: Richard M. Nixon, *Six Crises* (New York: Doubleday, 1962), pp. 310–11.

58 AT THE REPUBLICAN CONVENTION: Ibid., pp. 261–63.

58 "DEFEAT OF THE NEW ECONOMICS": John W. Sloan, "President Johnson, the Council of Economic Advisers and the Failure to Raise Taxes in 1966 and 1967," Center for the Study of the Presidency and Congress, www.jstor.org/pss/27550166.

58 "IT APPEARS KEYNESIAN POLICY": William Greider, *Secrets of the Temple: How the Federal Reserve Runs the Country* (New York: Touchstone, 1987), p. 333.

59 "A MAJOR EVENT": Stein, *Fiscal Revolution in America*, p. 413.

59 WHEN PASSED UNDER JOHNSON: Steven R. Weisman, *The Great Tax Wars* (New York: Simon & Schuster, 2002), p. 356. Some economists, notably Galbraith of Harvard, advocated more government spending on public goods like education and antipoverty programs. Cutting taxes would come back to haunt the administration, he believed. Richard Parker, *John Kenneth Galbraith* (New York: Farrar, Straus & Giroux, 2008).

59 AND THE ECONOMY GREW STRONGLY: Kennedy did not rely fully on the Keynesian defense, reflecting the strong hesitation to accept Keynesianism fully and abandon faith in balancing budgets—and perhaps Kennedy's own lingering doubts about the New Economics. In a key speech to the New York Economics Club that year, he sold the tax cut as an orthodox boon to business to improve incentives to invest, which infuriated Galbraith, then ambassador to India.

59 NIXON'S TEAM WAS OPEN: They developed their budget assuming tax revenues based on full employment—the full employment budget.

59 MCCRACKEN, A POLITICAL CONSERVATIVE: Herbert Stein, *Presidential Economics:*

The Making of Economic Policy from Roosevelt to Clinton (Washington, D.C.: American Enterprise Institute, 1994), pp. 141–42; author interview with Paul McCracken, June 2004.

60 IF CONSUMERS EXPECTED PRICES TO RISE: Frank Levy and Peter Temin, "Inequality and Institutions in the 20th Century," MIT Working Paper 07–17, May 1, 2007.

60 MANUFACTURING AND SERVICE GIANTS: Stein, *Presidential Economics*, pp. 159–60.

60 "AS CHIPS FLOATING": Ibid., p. 141.

61 "NOW I AM A KEYNESIAN": Stein, *Fiscal Revolution in America*, p. 548.

61 YET NIXON ATTACKED MANY OF JOHNSON'S PROGRAMS: Arthur J. Blaustein, Letter to the Editor, *New York Times*, February 22, 2008, p. A22.

61 AS RALPH NADER SAID: Ralph Nader, *Meet the Press*, NBC News, February 24, 2008.

61 WHEN THEY WERE LIFTED AFTER THE KOREAN WAR: Hugh Rockoff, *A History of Wages and Price Controls in the United States* (Cambridge: Cambridge University Press, 1984), p. 114.

62 NIXON WANTED TO RESPOND STRONGLY: Stein, *Presidential Economics*, p. 162.

62 "I REALLY LOVED THE GUY": Author interview, Arthur Laffer, March 2004.

63 HE REPORTED TO VOLCKER: Author interview, Murray Weidenbaum, July 19, 2004.

63 "WE PUSHED CONTROLS STRONGLY": Ibid.

63 BOTH STEIN AND SHULTZ: Stein, *Presidential Economics*, p. 163.

64 INVESTORS ON WALL STREET: The new agreement also allowed a wider range of fluctuation around the fixed value of the currency than under the Bretton Woods agreement. A currency could shift by 2.5 percent rather than the former 1 percent, before a nation was required to intervene to stabilize it.

64 IN THE REMAINING MONTHS OF 1971: Blinder, *Economic Policy and the Great Stagflation*, pp. 142–43; Stein, *Presidential Economics*, pp. 183–84.

64 HE INSTRUCTED HIS CABINET: Stein, *Fiscal Revolution in America*, p. 559.

64 BUT THE EVIDENCE SUGGESTS BURNS: Burton D. Abrams, "How Richard Nixon Pressured Arthur Burns: Evidence from the Tapes," *Journal of Economic Perspectives* vol. 20, no. 4 (Fall 2006): 177–188.

65 THIS EVENTUALLY LED TO FURTHER DECLINES: Greider, *Secrets of the Temple*, p. 338.

66 CROPS FAILED AGAIN: Blinder, *Economic Policy and the Great Stagflation*, p. 36; updated: Alan S. Blinder and Jeremy B. Rudd, "The Supply Shock Explanation of the Great Stagflation Revisited," Center for Economic Studies Working Paper, No. 176, Princeton, N.J., November 2008, p. 31.

66 THUS, INFLATION ITSELF: The most cogent advocate of this view is Bradford J. De-Long, "America's Peacetime Inflation: The 1970s," in *Reducing Inflation: Motivation and Strategy*, ed. Christina D. Romer and David H. Romer (Chicago: University of Chicago Press, 1997), pp. 247–80. For persuasive rebuttals, see Blinder and Rudd, "The Supply Shock Explanation," pp. 56–58.

66 THE HIKE ADDED: Blinder and Rudd, "The Supply Shock Explanation," pp. 28–29.

66 AT THE TIME, OIL EXPENDITURES: Ian H. W. Parry and Joel Darmstadter, "The Costs of U.S. Oil Dependency," Discussion Paper 03–59, Resources for the Future, Washington, D.C., December 2003.

66 ALAN BLINDER COMPUTED: Blinder, *Economic Policy and the Great Stagflation*, pp. 126–30.

67 IN THE SECOND HALF OF 1973: Milton Friedman argued vehemently that a hike in oil prices could not raise inflation on average because it would be offset by decreases in prices elsewhere unless it was accommodated by rapidly rising money supply. This criticism is perhaps the purest example of Friedman's assumption that the real world works in a purely competitive way. Prices are of course "sticky," as economists say, and

don't immediately rise and fall as they would in the Friedman laboratory. He eventually admitted that it could cause a temporary increase on average, the debate then over how long temporary was. See Milton Friedman, "Perspective on Inflation," *Newsweek*, June 24, 1974.

68 BEFORE STEIN LEFT: Stein, *Fiscal Revolution in America*, p. 573.

68 "AS MUCH AS POSSIBLE": Ibid., p. 574.

68 BURNS AND SIMON EVEN MORE VIGOROUSLY URGED: Ibid., p. 574.

68 AS FOR UNEMPLOYMENT: Ibid, p. 569.

69 AFTER THE AUGUST MEETING: Stein, *Presidential Economics*, p. 212.

69 A COUPLE OF MONTHS LATER: Blinder, *Economic Policy and the Great Stagflation*, p. 149.

CHAPTER 4: JOE FLOM

72 THE BUBBLE BURST: See for example, Adam Smith, *The Money Game* (New York: Vintage, 1977); Andrew Tobias, *The Funny Money Game* (New York: Playboy Press, 1970).

73 SOME MERGERS WERE SENSIBLE: Dennis C. Mueller and Mark L. Sirower, "The Causes of Mergers: Tests Based on the Gains to Acquiring Firms' Shareholders and the Size of Premia," http://homepage.univie.ac.at/Dennis.Mueller/GAINSMS.PDF.

74 "IT IS MORE LIKELY THAN NOT": Mark L. Sirower, *The Synergy Trap: How Companies Lose the Acquisition Game* (New York: Free Press, 1997), p. 141.

74 "SO EAGER WERE THEY": David Henry, "Mergers: Why Most Big Deals Don't Pay Off," *BusinessWeek*, October 14, 2002. Sirower further found that falling stock prices in the year after a merger are a good indication of poor performance over five years. Mark L. Sirower and Sumit Sahni, "Avoiding the Synergy Trap: Practical Guidance on M&A Decisions for CEOs and Boards," *Journal of Applied Corporate Finance* 18, no. 3 (2006): 83–95.

74 "SUDDENLY, EVERY CEO": Walter Kiechel III, *The Lords of Strategy: The Secret Intellectual History of the New Corporate World* (Boston: Harvard Business Press, 2010), pp. 207–8.

75 "MY FATHER WAS A UNION ORGANIZER": Author interview, Joe Flom, September 2004. Also see Jeff Madrick, *Taking America* (New York: Bantam, 1987).

77 THE TRADITIONAL EQUITY BUSINESS WAS FOUNDERING: Barrie A. Wigmore, *Securities Markets in the 1980s* (Oxford: Oxford University Press, 1997), p. 80.

77 THE AVERAGE P-E MULTIPLE: Companies issue shares to investors, which vary in quantity by company. Earnings per share are total earnings divided by the shares outstanding.

77 IN OTHER WORDS, ONE COULD OFTEN SELL OFF: This is known as the Q-ratio, an analytical concept developed by Nobel Prize–winning economist James Tobin.

77 IN 1974, THE AVERAGE PRICE OF A STOCK: Wigmore, *Securities Markets in the 1980s*, p. 93.

78 "I HAD THE FASTEST HANDS": Madrick, *Taking America*, p. 25.

78 INCO APPROACHED MORGAN STANLEY: Based on author interviews with Charles Baird, Joe Flom, Robert Greenhill, Milton Friedman, Robert Rubin, and William Sword. See Madrick, *Taking America;* Lansing Lamont, "Inco: A Giant Learns How to Compete," *Fortune*, January 1975.

82 BY THE LATE 1970S AND EARLY 1980S: Wigmore, *Securities Markets in the 1980s*, p. 314.

82 GENERAL ELECTRIC SOLD UTAH INTERNATIONAL: Malcolm Salter and Wolf Weinhold, "Merger Trends and Prospects for the 1980s," in *The Law and Finance of Corporate Acquisitions,* 2nd ed., eds. Ronald J. Gilson and Bernard S. Black (Westbury, N.Y.: Foundation, 1995).

83 "IN 1975, THE YEAR AFTER": W.T. Grimm & Co., Annual Reviews, Chicago.

83 ACADEMIC STUDIES OF LBOS ALONE: Economic researchers never reach unanimity on such subjects, but the preponderance of studies is clear. David J. Ravenscraft and William F. Long, "The Financial Performance of Whole Company LBOs," Working Paper, Economic Studies Series, U.S. Census Bureau, 1993. As for R&D cuts, they do result in short-term profit increases. Long-term performance remains questionable. See "Do LBOs Profit after R&D Cuts?" Census Bureau, http://www.census.gov/apsd/www/statbrief/sb95_14.pdf.

CHAPTER 5: IVAN BOESKY

89 "UNRIVALED SELF-DISCIPLINE": Conversation with friend of Ivan Boesky, 1980.

89 BOESKY, THOUGH, WAS NOT INTERESTED: The author edited Boesky's book, originally a textbook, later changed with new material to *Merger Mania* (New York: Holt, Rinehart and Winston, 1985).

90 HE FOUND HIS WAY: Madrick, *Taking America* (New York: Bantam, 1987), p. 99.

90 HE AND SEEMA WENT: Author interview with Seema Boesky, July 1989.

90 BOESKY HAD FOUND AN EXPERT: Madrick, *Taking America*, p. 108.

94 IF THE MERGER FELL THROUGH, LEVINE WOULD PAY BACK: James Stewart, *Den of Thieves* (New York: Touchstone, 1991), p. 159.

94 HE MADE A DEAL TO NAME: Ibid., p. 318.

94 FREEMAN PLEADED GUILTY: Ibid., p. 495.

95 BOESKY'S PENALTIES CAME TO $100 MILLION: Peter Kilborn, "Big Trader Agrees to Pay $100 Million for Insider Abuses," *New York Times,* November 15, 1986, http://www.nytimes.com/1986/11/15/us/big-trader-to-pay-us-100-million-for-insider-abuses.html?&pagewanted=3.

95 FINALLY, HE TOLD HIS CONCERNED WIFE: Author interview with Seema Boesky, July 1989.

CHAPTER 6: WALTER WRISTON II

96 THESE SECURITIES WERE CALLED DERIVATIVES: A futures contract is a promise by an investor to buy, for example, gold, a bushel of wheat, a barrel of petroleum, or the German mark for a set price at a given time in the future for only a small down payment. Conversely, a counterparty—another investor—promises to sell at these prices by these dates. Usually, these contracts rise and fall with the prices of the underlying assets and are sold before the actual asset is due. The futures contracts had long existed in agricultural markets to help farmers and food processors lock in prices that were volatile due to unpredictable weather.

Options are a version of the same concept, usually applied only to financial securities like stocks or bonds. They are a contract that enables investors to buy or sell a stock or bond at a future date for a set price, but do not require them to do so. The contract costs much less than the actual purchase of the underlying asset.

97 IN 1973, A SEAT ON THE MERC: Jerry W. Markham, *A Financial History of the United States,* vol. 3 (Armonk, N.Y.: M. E. Sharpe, 2002), p. 43.

98 "I SAID TO MY PARTNER": Author interview with Bruce Bent, April 2006.

98 WITHIN A WEEK OF THE *TIMES* ARTICLE: Ibid.

99 STATE BANKING AUTHORITIES: Markham, *A Financial History of the United States,* vol. 3, pp. 8–10.

100 ALTHOUGH SOME OBSERVERS WERE ALREADY WORRIED: Phillip L. Zweig, *Wriston:*

Walter Wriston, Citibank, and the Rise and Fall of American Financial Supremacy (New York: Crown, 1995), p. 383.

101 INVESTMENT BANKERS DID NOT FAIL TO NOTICE: Ibid., pp. 454–65.

101 EVEN GERALD FORD'S CHIEF OF STAFF: Zweig presents an excellent review of these issues in *Wriston*, pp. 390–96.

102 "RECYCLING. BLAH.": Ibid., p. 397.

102 THE U.S. BANKS ALSO BELIEVED: Michael Mussa, "LDC Debt Policy," in *American Economic Policy in the 1980s,* ed., Martin Feldstein (Chicago: University of Chicago Press, 1994), p. 738.

102 "AFTER THAT, YOU COULD HARDLY FIND": Zweig, *Wriston,* p. 388.

102 "WE WERE READY TO GO": Ibid., p. 387.

103 FOREIGN LENDING ACCOUNTED FOR AN EVEN HIGHER PROPORTION: Silfen Glasberg Davita, *The Power of Purse Strings: The Effects of Bank Hegemony on Corporations and the State* (Berkeley: University of California Press, 1989), p. 149.

103 AS COMPETITION IN LDC LOANS INCREASED: Paul Volcker and Toyoo Gyohten, *Changing Fortunes* (New York: Times Books, 1992), p. 197.

104 WRISTON INSISTED THAT SOVEREIGN NATIONS: Walter Wriston, "Banking Against Disaster," *New York Times,* September 14, 1982.

104 TREASURY SECRETARY SIMON PRAISED: Zweig, *Wriston,* p. 574.

104 BY THE END OF 1979: Volcker and Gyohten, *Changing Fortunes,* p. 190.

104 THE RECORD OF REPAYMENT: Ibid., pp. 194–95.

104 FEW, INCLUDING WRISTON: Zweig, *Wriston,* p. 637.

105 "WE HAD SET LIMITS" AND FOLLOWING: Ibid., pp. 639, 642.

105 MOODY'S FOLLOWED SUIT: Ibid., p. 747.

106 THEY HAD LITTLE CHOICE: Volcker and Gyohten, *Changing Fortunes,* pp. 189–200.

106 SEARS BOUGHT THE REALTOR: Zweig, *Wriston,* pp. 724–75.

107 ACCORDING TO JOURNALIST PHILLIP ZWEIG: Ibid., pp. 523–24. In contrast, Wriston favored marking stocks to market because there was a true market for them.

108 HE TURNED AGAINST VOLCKER: Ibid., pp. 737, 760.

108 LEAST NOTICED WAS THE PLIGHT: Paul Krugman, "LDC Debt Policy," in Feldstein, ed., *American Economic Policy in the 1980s,* p. 719.

CHAPTER 7: RONALD REAGAN

111 HIS PROTESTANT MOTHER, THE DO-GOODER: Ronald Reagan with Richard G. Hubler, *Where's the Rest of Me?: The Ronald Reagan Story* (New York: Duell, Sloan & Pearce, 1965), pp. 7–8.

111 ACCORDING TO RONALD REAGAN: Ibid., pp. 8–9. Also on Jack's anger, see Robert Dallek, *Ronald Reagan, The Politics of Symbolism* (Cambridge: Harvard University Press, 1984), Chapter 1 in general. Dallek also makes much of Reagan's fear of a loss of self-control, a more spurious claim, at least to the degree Dallek stresses it.

112 "HE SUCCEEDED IN EVERYTHING HE TRIED": Lou Cannon, *President Reagan: The Role of a Lifetime* (New York: Simon & Schuster, 1991), p. 33.

112 HE SHOWED LITTLE OF THE DEEPER EMOTION: Garry Wills, *Reagan's America: Innocents at Home* (New York: Doubleday, 1987), pp. 305–6.

112 REAGAN RETAINED: Edmund Morris, *Dutch: A Memoir of Ronald Reagan* (New York: Random House, 1999), pp. 157–60.

113 "THE PROFITS OF CORPORATIONS HAVE DOUBLED": Dallek, *Ronald Reagan,* p. 27.

113 GARRY WILLS ARGUES PERSUASIVELY: Wills, *Reagan's America,* pp. 288–97.

113 "THE COMMUNIST PLAN": Reagan and Hubler, *Where's the Rest of Me?,* p. 162. See also

Lou Cannon, *Governor Reagan: His Rise to Power* (New York: PublicAffairs, 2003), pp. 85–90.

114 IT WAS LATER DISCOVERED: On the code name, T-10: Wills, *Reagan's America*, pp. 290–99. Also see Morris, *Dutch*, p. 288.

114 BUT REAGAN HAD SAG: Cannon, *Governor Reagan*, pp. 103–5.

114 REAGAN WAS CALLED TO TESTIFY: Cannon, *Governor Reagan*, pp. 103–5.

115 "SINCE THE BEGINNING OF THE CENTURY": Ibid., p. 123.

115 "NEAR HOPELESS HEMOPHILIC LIBERAL": Reagan and Hubler, *Where's the Rest of Me?*, p. 139.

115 IF AMERICA DID NOT RETURN: Ibid., p. 312.

115 "I, IN MY OWN MIND": Commencement address, Williams Woods College, June 1952.

115 MARTIN ANDERSON, A PRINCIPAL ECONOMIC ADVISER: Martin Anderson, *Revolution: The Reagan Legacy* (New York: Harcourt Brace Jovanovich, 1988), p. 164.

115 BUT LOU CANNON WROTE: Cannon, *President Reagan*, p. 202.

116 "TODAY," REAGAN SAID IN A SPEECH IN 1959: Ibid., p. 121.

116 "TO REAGAN . . . THERE ARE": Dallek, *Ronald Reagan*, p. 132.

116 AS FOR COMMUNISM: Cannon, *President Reagan*, p. 292; John Patrick Diggins, *Ronald Reagan: Fate, Freedom and the Making of History* (New York: W. W. Norton, 2007), pp. 7–12.

116 REAGAN MENTIONED HIS FELLOW CONVERT: Reagan and Hubler, *Where's the Rest of Me?*, p. 268.

116 "AT HEART," WROTE CHAMBERS: Whittaker Chambers, Jr., *Witness* (New York: Random House, 1952), p. 4.

116 "WE ARE FACED WITH": Reagan and Hubler, *Where's the Rest of Me?*, p. 311.

116 IT SHOULD NOT HAVE COME AS A SURPRISE: Morris, *Dutch*, pp. 472–73.

117 THE STORY HE TOLD AMERICANS: In general, Wills, *Reagan's America*, and in particular, p. 338.

117 "THE BASIS OF THE DRAMATIC FORM": Reagan and Hubler, *Where's the Rest of Me?*, p. 294.

117 "REAGAN'S CAPACITY FOR SELF-DENIAL": Cannon, *President Reagan*, p. 190.

117 CANNON BELIEVED REAGAN SIMPLY THOUGHT: Cannon, *Governor Reagan*, pp. 116–17.

117 HE WROTE IN A LATER MEMOIR: Kiron K. Skinner, Annelise Anderson, and Martin Anderson, eds., *Reagan in His Own Hand: The Writings of Ronald Reagan That Reveal His Revolutionary Vision for America* (New York: Free Press, 2001), p. 67.

117 GARRY WILLS, HOWEVER: Wills, *Reagan's America*, p. 339.

118 CANNON LEANS TOWARD: Cannon, *Governor Reagan*, pp. 112–13.

118 "A TIME FOR CHOOSING": For the speech actually made, with a different opening paragraph, see http://www.nationalcenter.org/ReaganChoosing1964.html.

119 "GOLDWATER HAD BECOME A CAUSE": Morris, *Dutch*, p. 333.

119 IT WAS MORE LIKELY A STANCE: For example, Wills, *Reagan's America*, p. 367.

119 THEIR ADVICE WAS PREDICTABLE: Cannon, *Governor Reagan*, pp. 136–40; Wills, *Reagan's America*, pp. 346–54.

119 WHEN FOX WENT TO SELL IT SOON AFTER: Cannon, *President Reagan*, p. 354; Dan Moldea and Jeff Goldberg, "Film Company Paid the Candidate a Steep Price for Some Steep Land to Make Him a Millionaire," *Wall Street Journal*, August 1, 1980.

120 WELFARE POLICIES WERE RESULTING: Cannon, *Governor Reagan*, p. 350.

120 "WE MUST RETURN": Ibid., p. 216.

120 REAGAN HAD A PERFECT CAMPAIGN ISSUE: Ibid., pp. 338–39.

120 "WELFARE IS THE GREATEST DOMESTIC PROBLEM": Ibid., p. 342.

120 LOU CANNON INSISTED REAGAN: Ibid., p. 122.

120 "WE NEVER THOUGHT": Author interview with Walter Shorenstein, July 2004.

121 HE AND THE DEMOCRATS JOINTLY AGREED: Cannon, *Governor Reagan*, p. 359.

121 GOVERNMENT SPENDING KEPT RISING UNDER REAGAN: Wills, *Reagan's America*, p. 373.

121 REAGAN FORMED THE TAX REDUCTION TASK FORCE: Author interviews with Lewis Uhler, January 12, 2004, and February and March 2004. All subsequent quotes from interviews. Also, Cannon, *Governor Reagan*, p. 369.

121 MILTON FRIEDMAN IMMEDIATELY AGREED: Friedman remembered the dinner. Author interview with Milton Friedman, November 11, 2003.

122 A CONSTITUTIONAL CEILING: For the details, see Lewis K. Uhler and Barry Poulson, *Tax Expenditures and Limits: From Roots to Current Realities*, National Tax Limitation Foundation, 2003.

122 "WHEN HE HAD SOMETHING IMPORTANT": Author interview with Lewis Uhler, January 2004.

122 UHLER NOT ONLY WON REAGAN: Cannon, *Governor Reagan*, p. 372.

122 A GALLUP POLL FOUND: William Watts and Lloyd A. Free, *State of the Nation* (New York: Universe, 1973), pp. 138–39.

123 FEDERAL WELFARE PROGRAMS FOR THE POOR: Ibid., pp. 295–96.

123 THE DEFEAT OF PROPOSITION 1 WAS DECISIVE: Cannon, *Governor Reagan*, p. 378.

123 TO THE CONTRARY: Ibid., p. 380.

124 "THE WORLD'S TRULY GREAT THINKERS": Eureka College Library Dedication, Eureka, Illinois, September 28, 1967, http://www.ibiblio.org/sullivan/CNN/RWR/album/speechmats/eureka.html.

124 "FREE ENTERPRISE IS NOT": Ronald Reagan, "Ours Is Not a Sick Society," (speech, Sacramento, California, September 4, 1970).

124 "I WANT TO HELP GET US BACK": Dallek, *Ronald Reagan*, p. 132.

CHAPTER 8: TED TURNER, SAM WALTON, AND STEVE ROSS

125 IRONICALLY, THIS OCCURRED: James Hoopes, "Growth Through Knowledge: Wal-Mart, High Technology, and the Ever Less Visible Hand," (unpublished paper, Babson College, April 2004).

127 "I HAVE BEEN OVERBLESSED": Sam Walton with John Huey, *Sam Walton: Made in America* (New York: Bantam, 1992), p. 14.

127 SAID SAM'S BROTHER: Ibid.

127 IT WAS 1945: Bob Ortega, *In Sam We Trust: The Untold Story of Sam Walton and Wal-Mart, the World's Most Powerful Retailer* (New York: Three Rivers, 2000), pp. 25–27; Charles Fishman, *The Wal-Mart Effect: How the World's Most Powerful Company Really Works—and How It's Transforming the American Economy* (New York: Penguin, 2006), p. 29.

128 WALTON'S PERSONAL SHARES: Ortega, *In Sam We Trust*, pp. 57–71.

129 THE LABOR DEPARTMENT ORDERED HIM: Ibid., pp. 86–87.

129 EVEN HIS WIFE COMPLAINED: Walton, *Sam Walton*, p. 165.

129 WALTON WAS A TALENTED, COMMITTED CHEERLEADER: Ibid., pp. 167–70.

130 FEW FAMILIES, NO LESS INDIVIDUALS: Fishman, *The Wal-Mart Effect*, p. 232.

130 TURNOVER RATES: Ellen Israel Rosen, "Technology, 'People Policy' and the Quality of Work at Wal-Mart," 2004, http://www.brandeis.edu/centers/wsrc/scholars/profiles/Rosen.html.

130 AS WAL-MART BOUGHT MORE GOODS FROM CHINA: Steven Greenhouse, *The Big Squeeze: Tough Times for the American Worker* (New York: Alfred A. Knopf, 2008), pp. 149–51.

131 CONGRESS ALSO DELIBERATELY: See ibid. in general for an excellent summary of labor

practices and violations. Also, Jeff Madrick, "Time for a New Deal," *New York Review of Books,* September 25, 2008.

131 MANY CLAIMED, DESPITE THE LOW WAGES: See, for example, economist Jason Furman, http://www.slate.com/id/2144517.

132 SUCH AS COSTCO: See, for example, Christine Fey, "Costco's Love of Labor," *Seattle Post-Intelligencer,* March 29, 2004, http://www.seattlepi.com/business/166680_costco29.html.

132 MCKINSEY, THE CONSULTING FIRM: James Hoopes, "Tear Down This Wall," *The American Prospect,* June 4, 2004, Web only, http://www.prospect.org/cs/articles?articleId=7812.

132 IT WAS NOT A MODEL: Fishman, *The Wal-Mart Effect,* pp. 102–8.

133 SOON, KINNEY WAS GENERATING ENOUGH PROFIT: Connie Bruck, *Master of the Game* (New York: Penguin, 1994), pp. 48–58.

134 THEY IN TURN RESPONDED TO HIS CHARM: Ibid., p. 129.

134 "HE WAS A GUY": Ibid., p. 363.

134 HE EVEN CLAIMED: Ibid., p. 84.

135 WITH SO MUCH MONEY COMING IN: Ibid., p. 104.

135 BY THE END OF THE 1970S, ROSS WAS AT THE TOP: The following information is based on press releases and media reports of the periods cited.

139 TURNER WAS BORN IN 1938: What follows is based on several books about Ted Turner, many of which corroborate the same facts. Robert Goldberg and Gerald Jay Goldberg, *Citizen Turner: The Wild Rise of an American Tycoon* (New York: Harcourt Brace, 1995); Porter Bibb, *It Ain't as Easy as It Looks* (New York: Crown, 1993); Ken Auletta, *Media Man: Ted Turner's Improbable Empire* (New York: W. W. Norton, 2004); Harry Evans with Gail Buckland and David Lefer, *They Made America: From the Steam Engine to the Search Engine: Two Centuries of Innovators* (Boston: Little, Brown, 2004).

140 WHAT THEY NEEDED WAS PROGRAMMING: Auletta, *Media Man,* p. 34.

141 CNN KEPT GROWING: Bibb, *It Ain't as Easy as It Looks,* pp. 154–75.

142 "YOU NEEDED TO CONTROL EVERYTHING": Auletta, *Media Man,* pp. 63–64.

142 "I'M TIRED OF BEING LITTLE": Mark Landler, "Turner to Merge into Time Warner; A $7.5 Billion Deal," *New York Times,* September 23, 1995.

CHAPTER 9: JIMMY CARTER

144 HIS IMAGE OF FRANKNESS AND HONESTY: *Time,* May 31, 1971.

146 WHEN *BUSINESSWEEK* ASKED HIM: W. Carl Biven, *Jimmy Carter's Economy* (Chapel Hill: University of North Carolina Press, 2002), p. 59.

147 CARTER DELIBERATELY DIVERSIFIED HIS TEAM: Author interviews with Charles Schultze and Barry Bosworth, June 2004.

148 HIS FIRST ECONOMIC POLICY INITIATIVE: Biven, *Jimmy Carter's Economy,* p. 40.

149 "INFLATION HAS CONTINUED": Ibid., p. 127.

149 AS THE SCHULTZE CEA: Economic Report of the President, 1978, p. 142, http://fraser.stlouisfed.org/publications/erp/issue/1381/download/5772/ERP1978_Chapter4.pdf.

150 "BERT, MIKE BLUMENTHAL AND I": Biven, *Jimmy Carter's Economy,* p. 78.

150 CARTER MAINTAINED HIS POSITION: Anthony Campagna, *Economic Policy in the Carter Administration* (Westport, Conn.: Greenwood, 1995), p. 65.

150 SCHULTZE, HOWEVER, DID NOT YET THINK THE LOW: Biven, *Jimmy Carter's Economy,* p. 201.

150 STILL, EVEN 6 PERCENT WAS A SERIOUS IMPROVEMENT: Herbert Stein insisted that Ford was succeeding in reducing inflationary expectations by doing just this. But

Ford's economy had just come out of the worst recessions since the Great Depression, and its dampening effects were no doubt still lingering.

152 OIL EXPORTS WERE CUT OFF: Barrie A. Wigmore, *Securities Markets in the 1980s* (Oxford: Oxford University Press, 1997), p. 17.

152 IN EARLY 1980, REPORTED CONSUMER INFLATION: The Carter administration also inherited a cumbersome set of price controls on oil that it was determined to dismantle. Domestic oil prices had been kept low by the controls, stimulating demand and contributing to the trade imbalances. But phasing out the controls on oil would also add immediately to inflation. Thus, Carter again faced contradictory forces. Having promised the Europeans to end the controls, he would start to decontrol oil prices but not until April 1979.

152 ACCORDING TO BLINDER'S ESTIMATES: Alan Blinder, "Anatomy of Double-Digit Inflation in the 1970s," in *Inflation: Causes and Consequences,* ed. Robert E. Hall (Chicago: University of Chicago Press, 1982), p. 269.

153 CARTER'S OVERALL APPROVAL RATING: William Greider, *Secrets of the Temple: How the Federal Reserve Runs the Country* (New York: Touchstone, 1987), p. 14.

153 BUT WITH INFLATION SO HIGH: Biven, *Jimmy Carter's Economy,* p. 144.

153 "IT IS A CRISIS OF CONFIDENCE": "The Crisis of Confidence," July 15, 1979, http://www.pbs.org/wgbh/amex/carter/filmmore/ps_crisis.html.

CHAPTER 10: HOWARD JARVIS AND JACK KEMP

155 MEN'S WAGES IN PARTICULAR GREW EXTREMELY SLOWLY: Douglas A. Hibbs, Jr., "Public Concern About Inflation and Unemployment in the United States: Trends, Correlates, and Political Implications," in *Inflation: Causes and Consequences,* ed. Robert E. Hall, (Chicago: University of Chicago Press, 1982), pp. 211–26.

155 EVENTUALLY THE SENIOR JARVIS BECAME A RESPECTED UTAH JUDGE: Howard Jarvis, *I'm Mad as Hell* (New York: Times Books, 1979), p. 195.

156 COMPARING SALT LAKE CITY TO DETROIT: Ibid., p. 233.

157 HE HAD SWITCHED: "Generals of a Rebellion by California Taxpayers," *New York Times,* June 8, 1978, p. A25.

157 "DURING OUR FIFTEEN YEAR STRUGGLE": Jarvis, *I'm Mad as Hell,* p. 8.

157 FOR EXAMPLE, HOME PRICES: Jack Citrin and Frank Levy, "From 13 to 4 and Beyond: The Political Meaning of the Ongoing Tax Revolt in California," in *The Property Tax Revolt,* eds. George G. Kaufman and Kenneth T. Rosen (Cambridge, Mass.: Ballinger, 1981), p. 4.

158 TWO SOCIAL SCIENTISTS DEVISED AN INDEX: Seymour Martin Lipset and William Schneider, "The Decline of Confidence in American Institutions," *Political Science Quarterly* 98, no. 3 (Fall 1983): 379–402.

158 IN 1978, PERSONAL INCOME TAXES WERE LOWERED: Thomas E. Mullaney, "The California Tax Vote," *New York Times,* p. F15.

158 "CALIFORNIA VOTE SEEN AS EVIDENCE": Adam Clymer, *New York Times,* June 8, 1978, p. A23.

159 KEMP HAD BEEN WORKING ON A TAX REDUCTION BILL: Bruce Bartlett, "Revolution of 1978," *National Review,* October 27, 1978.

CHAPTER 11: PAUL VOLCKER, JIMMY CARTER, AND RONALD REAGAN

161 VOLCKER VEHEMENTLY WARNED AGAINST: The real interest rate is what usually matters—the rate discounted for inflation—and it was high in the 1980s as inflation

fell, suppressing capital investment, which remained historically low throughout the decade.

162 THE CHAMBER OF COMMERCE FOCUSED ITS ACTIVITIES: In general, Kim Phillips-Fein, *Invisible Hands: The Making of the Conservative Movement from the New Deal to Reagan* (New York: W. W. Norton, 2009).

162 HE FOUND THE BRITISH CULTURAL ATMOSPHERE CONGENIAL: Joseph B. Treaster, *The Making of a Financial Legend* (Hoboken, N.J.: John Wiley & Sons, 2004), pp. 108–9.

163 "HE WAS AN INTELLECT": Paul Volcker and Toyoo Gyoten, *Changing Fortunes* (New York: Times Books, 1992), p. 24.

163 IT WAS AN IDEA THAT A MARKET PURIST: Ibid., p. 33.

163 BY THIS TIME, HE WAS CARING FOR A WIFE: William Greider, *Secrets of the Temple: How the Federal Reserve Runs the Country* (New York: Touchstone, 1987), p. 68.

164 CARTER PUT WALTER MONDALE: Ibid., p. 34.

164 "AS LONG AS PEOPLE BELIEVED": Ibid., p. 76.

164 EVEN BERT LANCE: Ibid., p. 216.

164 CARTER CALLED VOLCKER: Ibid., p. 122.

165 IN DISCUSSIONS MORE THAN TEN YEARS LATER: Paul Volcker, "Monetary Policy," in *American Economic Policy in the 1980s*, ed. Martin Feldstein (Chicago: University of Chicago Press, 1995), p. 159. William Greider had a more critical theory. He wrote that Volcker's harder-nosed monetarist approach was more or less dictated by the advisory group of bankers who met with the Fed regularly. Greider, *Secrets of the Temple*, p. 145.

165 OVERSIMPLIFICATION WAS PRECISELY WHY: Volcker later wrote, with what became characteristic ambiguity, "I was as skeptical of the extreme claims of that school about the virtues of constant money growth as I had been about the efficacy of floating exchange rates. . . . But shorn of some of those extreme claims, the approaches that had been debated (and half forgotten) seemed worth looking at again." Volcker and Gyohten, *Changing Fortunes*, p. 167.

165 IN THE SAME BROOKINGS DISCUSSION: Volcker, "Monetary Policy," in Feldstein, ed., *American Economic Policy in the 1980s*, p. 160.

165 VOLCKER FACED A DIFFICULT TASK: Greider, *Secrets of the Temple*, p. 105.

165 VOLCKER RETURNED EARLY: Schmidt and others wanted higher rates in the United States partly because the value of the U.S. dollar was falling against their currencies, reducing their exports to the U.S.

166 THE MONEY SUPPLY GREW MORE SLOWLY: There is typically a lag, but its duration is debatable.

166 "THE OCTOBER [1979] SPURT": Greider, *Secrets of the Temple*, p. 140.

167 THE CREDIT CONTROLS WERE STRONGLY SUPPORTED: W. Carl Biven, *Jimmy Carter's Economy* (Chapel Hill: University of North Carolina Press, 2002), pp. 246–49.

167 ANOTHER COMMENT WAS POSSIBLY MORE INFLUENTIAL: Greider, *Secrets of the Temple,* p. 218.

168 BUT MORE CONVENTIONAL REAGAN ADVISERS: Charls Walker, "Tax Policy," in Feldstein, ed., *American Economic Policy in the 1980s*, pp. 224–25.

169 THE LARGEST TAX CUT OF THE POST–WORLD WAR II ERA: William Ahern, "Comparing the Kennedy, Reagan and Bush Tax Cuts," The Tax Foundation, Washington, D.C., August 24, 2004.

171 THE RATE OF ACTUAL FEDERAL TAXES: Lawrence Mishel, Jared Bernstein, and Heidi Shierholz, *The State of Working America 2008/2009*, The Economic Policy Institute (Washington, D.C.: ILR Press, 2009), pp. 71–76. (The better-off paid a higher proportion of total American taxes because they were far richer. Income inequality expanded sharply in the 1980s and the better-off enjoyed much more rapid increases in income than the rest. They paid a lower rate, in other words, on a higher level of income.)

171 THE OTHER MAJOR FEDERAL SPENDING INCREASE: James M. Poterba, "Budget Policy," in Feldstein, ed., *American Economic Policy in the 1980s*, pp. 238–40.

171 MEANTIME, BUSINESS DID NOT SPEND: Benjamin M. Friedman, *The Moral Consequences of Economic Growth* (New York: Alfred A. Knopf, 2005), pp. 405–7. While nominal interest rates fell rapidly, real interest rates (nominal rates less inflation), remained high, partly as a consequence of the high deficits. When inflation is running at 12 percent, it may make sense to borrow at an interest rate of 14 percent in order to buy equipment. But when inflation is running at 4 percent, it may not make sense to borrow at 8 percent to invest. Partly as a consequence, capital investment remained historically weak throughout Reagan's tenure.

171 IN FISCAL 1983, THE BUDGET DEFICIT: Technically measured as Gross National Product at this point, or GNP. The two measures are close enough to make comparisons valid.

172 "AN ANTIREGULATION APPROACH": W. Kip Viscusi, "Health and Safety Regulation," in Feldstein, ed., *American Economic Policy in the 1980s*, p. 510.

172 THE STAFF AND FINANCIAL APPROPRIATIONS: Harry M. Reasoner, "Antitrust Policy," in Feldstein, ed., *American Economic Policy in the 1980s*, p. 617.

172 "ANTITRUST BASHING": Ibid.

173 SOME TWO THOUSAND SUCH BANKS: Simon Johnson and James Kwak, *13 Bankers: The Wall Street Takeover and the Next Financial Meltdown* (New York: Pantheon, 2010), p. 74.

173 ANNUAL CONSUMER INFLATION REMAINED: Velocity remained variable and unpredictable, contrary to Friedman's claims. Now it fell sharply.

173 HIGH RATES ALSO PUSHED THE VALUE OF THE DOLLAR UP SHARPLY: Robert Brenner, *The Boom and Bubble: The U.S. in the World Economy* (London: Verso, 2009).

174 "OH, BY AND LARGE": Greider, *Secrets of the Temple*, p. 179.

175 MOST IMPORTANT, ADJUSTED FOR THE BUSINESS CYCLE, PRODUCTIVITY: Productivity grew especially rapidly in the 1950s and 1960s, but the rate of productivity growth, cyclically adjusted, in the 1980s also did not rise to pre–World War I levels or certainly the rates of growth of the 1920s.

175 UNDER REAGAN, INVESTMENT IN PUBLIC TRANSPORTATION: Poterba, "Budget Policy," in Feldstein, ed., *American Economic Policy in the 1980s*, p. 240.

CHAPTER 12: TOM PETERS AND JACK WELCH

179 "THE STORM THAT FLICKERED": Robert H. Hayes, Steven C. Wheelwright, and Kim B. Clark, *Dynamic Manufacturing* (New York: Free Press, 1988), p. 1.

180 "WHEN DETROIT CHANGES ITS MANAGEMENT SYSTEM": Thomas J. Peters and Robert H. Waterman, Jr., *In Search of Excellence: Lessons from America's Best-Run Companies* (New York: Harper & Row, 1982), pp. 34–35; Louis Kraar, "Japan's Automakers Shift Strategies," *Fortune*, August 11, 1980, p. 109.

180 "THERE WAS SIMPLY A PROFOUND HUNGER": Author interview with Jay Lorsch, Harvard Business School, June 2006.

181 AMERICA'S SEEMING BUSINESS FAILURE: Jean-Jacques Servan-Schreiber, *The American Challenge* (New York: Atheneum, 1967).

181 TAYLOR'S MAJOR WORK: Robert Kanigel, *The One Best Way: Frederick Winslow Taylor and the Enigma of Efficiency* (New York: Penguin, 1997).

181 IN THE PAST, THE CEOS OF MAJOR: As a twenty-four-year-old business reporter, I did my first cover story for *BusinessWeek* on the subject back in 1971. I did not fully anticipate the dangers of the trend I perceived. "The Rise of the Financial Man," *Business Week*, September 14, 1971.

183 IF WORK COULD PROVIDE SUCH SELF-ESTEEM: Douglas McGregor, *The Human Side of Enterprise* (New York: McGraw-Hill, 1960).

183 "BUT THE MILITARY MODEL": Author interview with Tom Peters, June 11, 2007.

184 GENERAL INTELLIGENCE, BCG BELIEVED: Walter Kiechel III, *The Lords of Strategy: The Secret Intellectual History of the New Corporate World* (Boston: Harvard Business Press, 2010), in general, pp. 13–30.

184 PETERS AND WATERMAN WERE SKEPTICAL: Tom Peters, "Tom Peters' True Confessions," *Fast Company*, November 2001.

184 "PROFESSIONALISM IN MANAGEMENT": Peters and Waterman, *In Search of Excellence*, p. 29.

184 AMERICAN MANAGEMENT HAD TO GET OUT: Robert H. Hayes and William J. Abernathy, "Managing Our Way to Economic Decline," *Harvard Business Review*, July–August, 1980.

184 THE JAPANESE WORKERS WERE CENTRAL: W. Edwards Deming, *Quality, Productivity, and Competitive Position* (Cambridge, Mass.: MIT Center for Advanced Engineering, 1982).

185 SOME LIKE HARVARD PROFESSOR JAY LORSCH: Author interview with Jay Lorsch, 2006.

185 "SEEN AS A SOURCE OF IDEAS": Peters and Waterman, *In Search of Excellence*, pp. 13–19.

185 FOR HIM, THE GOOD COMPANIES SEEMED: Ibid., pp. 270–74.

185 "THE NUMERATIVE ANALYTICAL": Ibid., p. 44.

186 "YOUNG JACK WELCH WAS THE CLASSIC CHAMPION": Ibid., p. 206.

186 "THE FLIP": Author interview with Tom Peters.

187 "WHAT'S STRIKING ABOUT": Kiechel, *The Lords of Strategy*, p. 205.

187 "THE GOAL FOR COPORATE MANAGERS": Ibid., p. 211.

188 WELCH HAD A BAD STAMMER: Jack Welch with John Byrne, *Jack: Straight from the Gut* (New York: Warner Business, 2001), Chapter 1; "Robert Goizueta and Jack Welch: The Wealth Builders," *Fortune*, December 11, 1995, p. 83.

189 "YOU BUILD STRONG TEAMS": Welch, *Jack*, p. 25.

190 HE WAS THE YOUNGEST GENERAL MANAGER: Ibid., p. 36.

191 "THESE AMBITIOUS PLANS": Ibid., p. 69.

191 "THESE DOWNSIZINGS ARE AWFUL": Ibid., p. 70.

191 "MY GUT TOLD ME": Ibid., p. 71.

192 "WHAT WE HAVE TO SELL": Ibid., p. 84.

193 "HE WAS WITH ME": Ibid., p. 130.

193 "HE NEVER STOPS BOTHERING US": Remark at a dinner party, November 1993.

194 TIMES WERE NEVER BETTER FOR CEOS: Eugene F. Fama and Michael C. Jensen, "Organizational Forms and Investment Decisions," *Journal of Financial Economics* 14, no. 1 (March 1985); also appeared in Michael C. Jenson, *Theory of the Firm: Governance, Residual Claims, and Organizational Forms* (Cambridge, Mass.: Harvard University Press, 2000).

194 "AND IF THE ANSWER IS NO": Thomas F. O'Boyle, *At Any Cost: Jack Welch, General Electric and the Pursuit of Profit* (New York: Random House, 1998), p. 69.

194 "THE $2 BILLION DIVESTITURE": Welch, *Jack*, p. 120.

195 BUT WITH THE STOCK MARKET IN MIND: Ibid., p. 71.

195 CONSUMERS WAS NOW ONE OF AMERICA's: O'Boyle, *At Any Cost*, pp. 87–88.

196 WELCH DID NOT WRITE ABOUT THE EPISODE: Ibid., pp. 90–101.

196 "I KEPT ASKING": Welch, *Jack*, p. 142.

197 WRIGHT, WHEN HEAD OF GE CAPITAL: O'Boyle, *At Any Cost*, p. 337–38.

198 VRANOS, SEEMINGLY INVULNERABLE: Charles R. Morris, *The Trillion Dollar Melt-down: Easy Money, High Rollers, and the Great Credit Crash* (New York: PublicAffairs, 2008), pp. 56–88; O'Boyle, *At Any Cost*, p. 346.

198 BUT DISDAIN WOULD BE SHORT-LIVED: O'Boyle, *At Any Cost*, pp. 355–56.

199 DESPITE IMMELT'S MORE SINCERE EFFORTS: Ibid., pp. 183–91; Welch, *Jack*, pp. 283–94.

199 "IN 1980": Welch, *Jack*, p. 250.

199 "THOUGH EARNINGS MANAGEMENT": Geoffrey Colvin and Katie Benner, "GE Under Siege," CNNMoney.com, October 15, 2008.

199 GE WAS NOW THE MOST HIGHLY VALUED: "GE Seen Regaining Historical Premium," Forbes.com., January 18, 2005.

199 WELCH HAD PRODUCED EARNINGS INCREASES: Robert M. Grant, "Life After Jack," in Robert M. Grant, ed., *Cases to Accompany Contemporary Strategy Analysis* (Maldin, Mass.: Blackwell Publishing, 2005), pp. 336–53.

199 OVER HIS TENURE: O'Boyle. *At Any Cost*, p. 136.

199 "WE FEEL THAT WE CAN GROW": Ibid., p. 139.

199 "CONSIDER FIRST WHAT THE COMPANY REALLY IS": Colvin and Benner, "GE Under Siege."

200 "JACK ALWAYS ARGUED HE WAS A GREAT INNOVATOR": Author interview with Tom Peters, 2007.

200 IN THE FERVOR OF THE BULL MARKET: *Fortune*, http://www.timewarner.com/corp/newsroom/pr/0,20812,667526,00.html.

CHAPTER 13: MICHAEL MILKEN

202 BY 1988, JUNK BONDS: Sam Ramsey Hakim and David Shimko, "The Impact of Firm's Characteristics on Junk Bond Default," *Journal of Financial and Strategic Decisions* 8, no. 2 (Summer 1995).

202 THREE FIFTHS OF IT: D. Anthony Plath, "Financing Takeovers: Junk Bonds and Lever-aged Buyouts," *Managerial Finance* 17, no. 1 (February 1993).

203 "THE FIRST THING YOU NOTICED": Author conversation with Martin Siegel, 1985.

204 IN FACT, MILKEN MAY HAVE MISINTERPRETED: Riskier assets should return a higher yield over time *on average* or they would not be bought at all; the higher yield justifies the risk. The problem is that an investor cannot know which companies will perform well and which will not, and will often lose a lot of money if invested in only a handful of companies, one or two of which may go bankrupt. A large, diversified portfolio likely reduces the penalties of choosing the wrong bonds, however, because the high yields offered by all the bonds more than compensate for the small handful of big los-ers. The same principle holds for a portfolio of stocks. The average return on stocks should be higher over time; but owning any individual stock is riskier.

205 HE THEN WENT EAST: Howard Rudnitsky, Allan Sloan, Richard L. Stern, and Matthew Heller, "A One-Man Revolution," *Forbes*, August 25, 1968, pp. 34–37.

205 EVENTUALLY HE DID DO THE PAPER: A Wharton School economist, A. T. Atkinson, updated research on the subject. Connie Bruck, *The Predator's Ball: The Inside Story of Drexel Burnham and the Rise of the Junk Shop* (New York: Penguin, 1988), pp. 23–27.

205 THERE WERE FEW EMPLOYEES OF JEWISH DESCENT: Ibid., p. 31.

205 "THE OPPORTUNITY TO BE TRUE": Ibid., pp. 28–29.

206 MILKEN DEMANDED AUTONOMY: Rudnitsky et al., "A One-Man Revolution"; Bruck, *The Predator's Ball*, pp. 31–32.

207 IN 1979, LINDNER SETTLED: Dan Mong, "Lindner Legacy," *Cincinnati Business Cou-rier*, March 4, 2005.

208 OFTEN HE BOUGHT PART OF THE OFFERING: Rudnitsky et al., "A One-Man Revolution."

208 ONE MAN, MICHAEL MILKEN: Bruck, *The Predator's Ball*, pp. 46–49.

209 BY ONE ESTIMATE IN THE LATE 1970S: Ibid., p. 54. Bruck does not provide the source for this estimate.

210 MILKEN DID NOT ALWAYS TELL HIS CLIENTS: Ibid., p. 74.

210 TEDDY FORSTMANN, WHO RAN AN LBO FIRM: Ibid., pp. 74–77.

211 WHEN A WHITE KNIGHT BID MUCH MORE: Jeff Madrick, *Taking America* (New York: Bantam, 1987), p. 112.

213 MOST OFTEN, THIS HIGHER-RISK JUNIOR FINANCING: Barrie A. Wigmore, *Securities Markets in the 1980s: The New Regime, 1979–1984* (Oxford: Oxford University Press, 1997), pp. 339–45.

213 IN 1976, HE LEFT BEAR STEARNS: George Anders, *Merchants of Debt* (New York: Basic Books, 1992), pp. xv–xx.

213 IN 1979, AFTER COMPLETING: Ibid., pp. 181–84.

213 IN 1981, THERE WERE 99 SUCH LBOS: Ibid., p. 37.

213 IN 1984, A KKR BUYOUT: Plath, "Financing Takeovers: Junk Bonds and Leverage Buyouts."

214 THE KKR PARTNERS WERE STUNNED: Anders, *Merchants of Debt*, p. 89.

214 TO DEFENDERS OF THE LBOS: A classic defense is Michael C. Jensen, "Agency Costs of Free Cash Flow, Corporate Finance, and Takeovers," *AEA Papers and Proceedings*, May 1986, pp. 323–29.

215 THE ICAHN GROUP: Bruck, *The Predator's Ball*, pp. 166–69.

215 THOUGH ENTREPRENEURIAL OWNERS: Alfred Chandler, *The Visible Hand: The Managerial Revolution in American Business* (Cambridge, Mass.: Harvard University Press, 1993).

216 PERELMAN WON THE BIDDING CONTEST: Bruck, *The Predator's Ball*, pp. 225–27.

216 THE INCENTIVES FOR EVER LARGER TAKEOVERS: Ibid., p. 231.

216 IN THESE YEARS, KKR DID: Anders, *Merchants of Debt*, pp. 92–95.

217 ON ITS TAKEOVER OF RJR NABISCO: Ibid., p. 75.

217 IT DISCUSSED MILKEN'S CENTRAL PLACE: Cary Reich, "Milken the Magnificent," *Institutional Investor*, August 1986.

217 MILKEN'S TOTAL PERSONAL TAKE: Bruck, *The Predator's Ball*, pp. 246–47.

217 IN 1986, *FORBES* FIGURED: http://www.forbes.com/lists/2005/54/SSM6.htm.

218 EVEN AFTER FINES: James Stewart, *Den of Thieves* (New York: Touchstone, 1991), pp. 523–25.

218 RATINGS ON JUNK BONDS HAD FALLEN SHARPLY: John Paul Newport, Jr., "Junk Bonds Face the Big Unknown," *Fortune*, May 22, 1989, http://money.cnn.com/magazines/fortune/fortune_archive/1989/05/22/72000/index.htm.

219 CONTRARY TO MILKEN'S REPUTATION: Anders, *Merchants of Debt*, p. 272.

220 DOING REAL BUSINESS AT RJR NABISCO: Ibid., pp. 272–74.

221 ONLY A WATERED-DOWN VERSION: Bruck, *The Predator's Ball*, pp. 264–65.

221 ACTIVE LOBBYING BY BUYOUT LENDERS: The Center for Private Equity and Entrepreneurship, Tuck School of Business at Dartmouth, "Private Equity Valuation and Reporting," June 2003, http://mba.tuck.dartmouth.edu/pecenter/research/pdfs/conference_proceedings.pdf.

CHAPTER 14: ALAN GREENSPAN

222 LATER IMPRISONED FOR SECURITIES FRAUD: The verdict was overthrown on technicalities due to improper behavior of the judge.

222 DANNY WALL: Nathaniel C. Nash, "Savings Executive Won't Testify and Blames Regulators for Woes," *New York Times*, November 22, 1989, http://www.nytimes.com/1989/11/22/business/savings-executive-won-t-testify-and-blames-regulators-for-woes.html.

222 "IF THE ALLEGATIONS": Margaret Carlson, "Keating Takes the 5th," *Time*, December 4, 1989.

223 GREENSPAN WROTE THE FHLB: Nathaniel C. Nash, "Greenspan's Lincoln Savings Regret,"; *New York Times*, November 20, 1989, http://www.nytimes.com/1989/11/20/business/greenspan-s-lincoln-savings-regret.html.

223 ONE REGULATOR LATER WROTE: L. William Seidman, *Full Faith and Credit: The Great S&L Debacle and Other Washington Sagas* (New York: Random House, 1993), pp. 233–35.

224 IN HIS MEMOIR: Alan Greenspan, *The Age of Turbulence: Adventures in a New World* (New York: Penguin, 2007), pp. 115–16.

224 HE REPORTEDLY RECEIVED $30,000–40,000: Justin Martin, *Greenspan: The Man Behind the Money* (New York: Perseus, 2000), p. 192.

227 HE TOOK LITTLE NOTICE: Federal Reserve Statistical Release, *Flow of Funds Accounts of the United States*, Board of Governors of the Federal Reserve System, Washington, D.C., quarterly releases.

227 A COMPREHENSIVE ACADEMIC ANALYSIS: Jeffrey Frankel and Peter Orszag, eds., *American Economic Policy in the 1990s* (Cambridge, Mass.: MIT Press, 2002).

227 HE QUIT THE DEMANDING PROGRAM: Martin, *Greenspan*, pp. 11–22.

228 "IT IS PRECISELY THE 'GREED' ": Ibid., pp. 48–49.

228 RAND WELCOMED AND ADMIRED: In general, Anne C. Heller, *Ayn Rand and the World She Made* (New York: Nan A. Talese, 2009).

229 TOWNSEND-GREENSPAN . . . PROSPERED: Greenspan, *The Age of Turbulence*, p. 55.

229 BUT WHEN NIXON WON: Ibid., pp. 56–60.

230 WHEN CHALLENGED IN OCTOBER 1976: Martin, *Greenspan*, pp. 133–34.

230 IN THE LATE 1970S, HE EARNED: Ibid., p. 89.

231 HE EXPANDED HIS TIES TO THE MEDIA: The author had several long and always courteous conversations with Greenspan on a variety of issues, when he was a journalist with *BusinessWeek* and also a cable TV business journalist. One in particular on contract law stands out.

231 THE TARGET FEDERAL FUNDS RATE: Bob Woodward, *Maestro: Greenspan's Fed and the American Boom* (New York: Simon & Schuster, 2000), p. 18.

231 IT WAS CLEAR THAT THE REAGAN ADMINISTRATION: William Greider, *Secrets of the Temple: How the Federal Reserve Runs America* (New York: Touchstone, 1987), pp. 713–14.

232 SENATOR BILL BRADLEY WORRIED: Martin, *Greenspan*, p. 157.

232 GREENSPAN BECAME CHAIRMAN: Friedman's natural rate of unemployment now held sway. The formal term was the Non-Accelerating Inflation Rate of Unemployment, or NAIRU.

233 HERE AGAIN, FRIEDMAN'S IDEAS WON OUT: Greenspan, *The Age of Turbulence*, pp. 102–3.

234 "THOSE WHO ARGUE THAT WE ARE IN A RECESSION": Martin, *Greenspan*, p. 195.

234 BOND TRADERS WERE WRONG TOO OFTEN: N. Gregory Mankiw, "U.S. Monetary Policy During the 1990s," in Frankel and Orszag, eds, *American Economic Policy*, pp. 19–40.

235 IN HIS MEMOIR: Greenspan, *The Age of Turbulence*, pp. 144–45.

235 IT WAS ONE OF THE MOST SIGNIFICANT DECISIONS: Robert B. Reich, *Locked in the Cabinet* (New York: Random House, 1997), pp. 60–66.

236   ROBERT SAMUELSON, A *NEWSWEEK* COLUMNIST: Woodward, *Maestro*, p. 140.

236   GREENSPAN HAD FEARED: Alan Blinder and Janet Yellen, *The Fabulous Decade: Macroeconomic Lessons from the 1990s* (New York: Century Foundation Press, 2001), p. 90.

236   MAYBE MORE IMPORTANT TO GREENSPAN: The interest rate on the ten-year Treasury bond, for example, had risen to 8 percent by the end of 1994 from a low of 5.75 percent in 1993.

236   HE WAS PRIVATELY FURIOUS: Blinder and Yellen, *The Fabulous Decade*, p. 26. The authors were members of the Fed board at the time.

236   BUT RUBIN CONVINCED HIM: Robert E. Rubin, *In an Uncertain World: Tough Choices from Wall Street to Washington* (New York: Random House, 2003), p. 193.

236   BLINDER ALSO VOTED FOR THE INCREASES: Alan Blinder, "Monetary Policy," in Frankel and Orszag, eds., *American Economic Policy*, p. 45.

237   BUT CLINTON, UNDER RUBIN'S STRONG INFLUENCE: Martin, *Greenspan*, pp. 211–12.

238   "POISED" TO RAISE RATES IN 1997: Blinder and Yellen, *The Fabulous Decade*, p. 54.

239   THIS POLICY ONCE AGAIN REFLECTED: Lawrence Summers, "Comments," in Frankel and Orszag, eds., *American Economic Policy*, pp. 218–220, and 260–64.

239   HE AND RUBIN HAD A WEEKLY MEETING: Rubin, *In an Uncertain World*, p. 194.

239   HE SAID THAT INVESTORS SIMPLY MADE MISTAKES: Testimony of Alan Greenspan, House Banking and Financial Services Committee, November 13, 1997, http://www .federalreserve.gov/boarddocs/testimony/1997/19971113.htm.

239   THE ASIAN ECONOMICS COLLAPSED INTO SEVERE RECESSION: Joseph E. Stiglitz, *The Roaring Nineties: A New History of the World's Most Prosperous Decade* (New York: W. W. Norton, 2003), pp. 217–19.

239   THE GREENSPAN FED: Blinder and Yellen, *The Fabulous Decade*, pp. 54–55; J. Bradford DeLong and Barry Eichengreen, "Between Meltdown and Moral Hazard," in Frankel and Orszag, eds., *American Economic Policy*, p. 230.

239   "REGULATED THOSE WHO LEND MONEY": Anita Raghavan and Michtell Pacell, "A Hedge Fund Falters, so the Fed Beseeches Big Banks to Ante Up," *Wall Street Journal*, September 24, 1998.

240   "NO ONE SHOULD THANK THE FOMC'S": Blinder and Yellen, *The Fabulous Decade*, p. 53.

240   "LARRY THOUGHT I WAS OVERLY CONCERNED": Rubin, *In an Uncertain World*, p. 288.

240   AS DIRECTOR OF THE CFTC: Author interview with Michael Greenberger, an attendee and former CFTC counsel, December 2009.

240   "I KNOW OF NO SET": "The Warning," *Frontline*, PBS, October, 29, 2009, http://www .pbs.org/wgbh/pages/frontline/warning/.

240   AS BORN WARNED BACK THEN: Ibid.

241   "THIS IS THE BEST ECONOMY I HAVE EVER SEEN": Woodward, *Maestro*, p. 195.

241   "THE SIZE OF THE POTENTIAL MARKET": E. Ray Canterbery, *Alan Greenspan: The Oracle Behind the Curtain* (Singapore: World Scientific, 2006), p. 99.

242   WALL STREET, THEREFORE, HAD FAR MORE MONEY: DeLong and Eichengreen, "Between Meltdown and Moral Hazard," in Frankel and Orszag, eds., *American Economic Policy*, pp. 200–202.

242   "WAY DOWN ON THE LIST": Greenspan, *The Age of Turbulence*, p. 375.

242   GREENSPAN WAS AT LAST ALSO APPARENTLY WORRIED: Blinder and Yellen, *The Fabulous Decade*, p. 70.

243   "I CAME TO A STARK REALIZATION": Greenspan, *The Age of Turbulence*, p. 218.

243   GREENSPAN PROFESSED BEING CAUGHT: Ibid., p. 224.

244   AS ECONOMIST MARK ZANDI SAID: Mark Zandi, *Financial Shock: A 360 Degree Look at the Subprime Mortgage Implosion, and How to Avoid the Next Financial Crisis* (Upper Saddle River, N.J.: FT Press, 2009), pp. 72–73.

244 EVEN THE FBI WARNED: Terry Frieden, "FBI Warns of Mortgage 'Fraud' Epidemic," September 17, 2004, CNN.com, http://www.cnn.com/2004/LAW/09/17/mortgage .fraud/AboutFraud.

244 GREENSPAN KNEW ABOUT THESE LOANS: Edward M. Gramlich, Financial Services Roundtable Annual Housing Policy Meeting, May 21, 2004, http://www.federalreserve .gov/boarddocs/speeches/2004/20040521/default.htm; Greg Ip, "Did Greenspan Add to Subprime Woes? Gramlich Says Ex-Colleague Blocked Crackdown on Predatory Lenders Despite Growing Concerns," *Wall Street Journal*, June 9, 2007.

244 "MANY HOMEOWNERS MIGHT HAVE SAVED": Zandi, *Financial Shock*, p. 67.

246 "MADE A MISTAKE IN PRESUMING": Brian Knowlton and Michael M. Grynbaum, "Greenspan's Shocked That Free Markets Are Flawed," *New York Times*, October 23, 2008, http://www.nytimes.com/2008/10/23/business/worldbusiness/23iht-gspan.4.17206624 .html.

246 "ASSISTED BY THE WAVE": Greenspan, *The Age of Turbulence*, pp. 279, 373.

CHAPTER 15: GEORGE SOROS AND JOHN MERIWETHER

249 ACCORDING TO AN ESTIMATE BY *FINANCIAL WORLD* MAGAZINE: Alison Leigh Cowan, "Where the Money Is: Wall Street's Best Paid People," *New York Times*, June 4, 1988.

249 BY 2007, HEDGE FUND MANAGER JOHN PAULSON: Stephen Taub, "Best Paid Hedge Fund Managers," AR, April 15, 2008, http://www.absolutereturn-alpha.com/Article/ 1914753/Search/Best-Paid-Hedge-Fund-Managers.html?Keywords=2007+paulson +earnings.

250 "SPECULATION CAN BE VERY HARMFUL": Anatole Kaletsky, "How Mr. Soros Made a Billion," *The Times* (London), October 26, 1992. It is worth citing the entire passage: "Speculation can be very harmful, especially in currency markets. But measures to stop it, such as exchange controls, usually do even more harm. Fixed exchange-rate systems are also flawed, because they eventually fall apart. In fact, any exchange-rate system is flawed and the longer it exists the greater the flaws become. The only escape is to have no exchange-rate system at all, but a single currency in Europe, as in the U.S. It would put speculators like me out of business, but I would be delighted to make that sacrifice."

251 "I CONSIDER [SPECULATION]": George Soros with Byron Wien and Krisztina Koenen, *Soros on Soros: Staying Ahead of the Curve* (New York: John Wiley, 1995), pp. 83–84.

251 "I BELIEVE OUR CONCEPT OF FREEDOM CHANGED": Ibid., pp. 181–82.

252 HE ODDLY ADMITTED: Robert Slater, *Soros: The World's Most Influential Investor* (New York: McGraw-Hill, 2009), p. 17.

252 "THE RUSSIAN EXPERIENCE SHAPED": Author interview with George Soros, April 14, 2009.

252 TIVADAR SOROS WROTE A BOOK: Tivadar Soros, *Masquerade: Dancing Around Death in Nazi-Occupied Hungary* (New York: Arcade, 1965).

253 "AS WITH ANYONE WHO WENT THROUGH": Author interview with Gerard Mano-lovicci, April 16, 2009.

253 GEORGE SOROS WAS BORN: Slater, *Soros*, p. 19.

253 HE CREATED FORMAL PAPERS: Ibid., p. 30.

255 "IT WAS SIMPLE": Author interview with Jim Rogers, April 10, 2009. All subsequent quotes are from this interview.

255 "THE ATTRACTION OF HEDGE FUNDS": Author interview with George Soros, April 14, 2009. All subsequent quotes, unless otherwise noted, are from this interview.

256 "HIS GREATEST KEY TO SUCCESS": Slater, *Soros*, p. 62.

257 BUT BARTON BIGGS, LATER A PROMINENT: Barton Biggs, *Hedge Hogging* (Hoboken, N.J.: John Wiley, 2006), pp. 82–85.

257 "LUCKY ELIOT SPITZER": Ibid., p. 85.

258 "WE HAD A GENTLEMAN'S AGREEMENT": Anonymous author interview, May 2009.

258 IN ONE OF THE PREDICTIONS: These successful predictions also included timely investments in Japanese and European energy companies and food stocks, and selling short the overly popular growth stocks, known as the Nifty Fifty, such as Xerox. They also invested in defense company stocks when few were interested after the Vietnam War, anticipating there would again be an arms race with Russia, and that Israel would step up its armaments purchases after the Yom Kippur War. Slater, *Soros*, pp. 76–77.

259 SOROS SOLD BRITISH GILTS: Ibid., p. 84.

259 THE SOROS FUND ROSE: George Soros, *The Alchemy of Finance*, p. 146; Slater, *Soros*, pp. 80–84.

260 BONDS COLLAPSED IN VALUE: Slater, *Soros*, pp. 90–92.

261 HE POSITIONED THE QUANTUM FUND: He documented the ensuing trades between 1985 and 1986 in *The Alchemy of Finance*, in which he published a real-time diary of his strategy.

261 AND HE DID ALL THIS AGGRESSIVELY: Ibid., Chapters 12–14, pp. 196–296.

261 HE EARNED HIMSELF NEARLY $95 MILLION: Slater, *Soros*, p. 143.

261 "MARKETS ARE ALWAYS BIASED": Soros, *The Alchemy of Finance*, p. 49.

261 SOROS, FOR EXAMPLE, WAS ACCUSED: Slater, *Soros*, p. 83.

262 BUT HE WAS FOUND GUILTY: John Tagliabue, "Soros Is Found Guilty in France on Charges of Insider Trading," *New York Times*, December 21, 2002, http://search.aol.com/aol/search?query=George+aSoros+and+Computer+Science+stock&s_it=keyword_rollover.Slater, p. 268.

262 ONE LARGE HEDGE FUND MANAGER: Anonymous author interview, December 2009.

262 FINANCIAL WRITER SEBASTIAN MALLABY: Sebastian Mallaby, *More Money Than God: Hedge Funds and the Making of a New Elite* (New York: Penguin, 2010), pp. 56–57.

263 STEINHARDT REMINISCED: Ibid., p. 58.

263 AGREED TO PAY $76 MILLION: SEC press release, December 16, 1994, http://www.justice.gov/opa/pr/Pre_96/December94/711.txt.html; Peter Temple, *The Hedge Funds: Courtesans of Capital* (New York: John Wiley & Sons, 2001), p. 87.

263 PAUL TUDOR JONES, WITH ENORMOUS BUYING POWER: Mallaby, *More Money Than God*, pp. 144–46.

264 "GEORGE USED TO SAY": Steven Drobny, *Inside the House of Money: Top Hedge Fund Traders on Profiting in the Global Markets* (Hoboken, N.J.: John Wiley, 2006), quoting Scott Bessent, p. 285.

264 OVER THE COURSE OF HIS LIFE: Author interview with George Soros, April 14, 2009.

264 BETWEEN $100 AND $200 BILLION: Center for International and Securities Derivatives Markets, *The Benefits of Hedge Funds*, May 2006.

264 SOME THREE THOUSAND: Mallaby, *More Money Than God*, p. 174.

264 "THEY COULD EVEN OVERPOWER GOVERNMENTS": Mallaby, *More Money Than God*, pp. 174, 92.

266 SOROS WAS NOW AN INTERNATIONAL CELEBRITY: Slater, *Soros*, p. 178.

266 "I DIDN'T DO IT TO HURT ENGLAND": *The Guardian* (London), December 19, 1993.

266 A SIMILAR INVESTMENT: Slater, *Soros*, pp. 185, 209.

267 QUANTUM COULD NOT EVEN KEEP UP: Phillip L. Zweig, "The Rich Get Richer, but Hedge Funds Still Can't Bet the S&P 500," *BusinessWeek*, August 7, 1997.

267 WHEN RUSSIA, ITS CITIZENS: Slater, *Soros*, pp. 255–56.

267 MOST HEDGE FUNDS PROFITED: Ibid., pp. 246–57; "The Hedge Funds: The Rich Get a

Little Richer," *BusinessWeek,* August 25, 1997, http://www.businessweek.com/1997/34/b3541191.htm.

269 TO THOSE WHO HAD FAITH IN EFFICIENT MARKETS: These were the arguments government policymakers like Greenspan and even Lawrence Summers (who ironically wrote academic pieces that were skeptical of claims made about market efficiencies before he joined the Clinton administration) used to suppress attempts to regulate derivatives.

270 GUTFREUND, THE FIRM'S RELATIVELY NEW: Roger Lowenstein, *When Genius Failed: The Rise and Fall of Long-Term Capital Management* (New York: Random House, 2000), pp. 3–5.

270 "THE PRIEST OF THE CALCULATED GAMBLE": Ibid., p. 10.

270 MISPRICING IN THE MARKETS: Perry Mehrling, *Fischer Black and the Revolutionary Idea of Finance* (Hoboken, N.J.: John Wiley, 2005).

270 "MERIWETHER CAST A SPELL": Michael Lewis, *Liar's Poker: Rising Through the Wreckage on Wall Street* (New York: W. W. Norton, 1989), p. 15.

271 BY CONTRAST, HIGH INFLATION: Moreover, Salomon had been doing specialized research in bonds before it became lucrative to do so. An early partner, the economist Sidney Homer, who had written extensively about the history of bonds and interest rates, hired in 1969 an NYU mathematician, Martin Leibowitz, to do sophisticated quantitative research into the behavior of bonds. Leibowitz was the first of the academically oriented bond researchers on Wall Street. Homer had also hired Henry Kaufman, then a young economist at the New York Federal Reserve, when it was still rare to do so. Leibowitz deepened the understanding of bonds, how they functioned and how they were related to each other. He also began to hire young intellectuals to do mathematically oriented research, and Meriwether naturally extended the role. See Sidney Homer, *A History of Interest Rates* (New Brunswick, N.J.: Rutgers University Press, 1963).

271 WHEN INTEREST RATES RISE: To repeat, when general interest rates rise, the price to buy a bond falls because investors can buy other bonds with higher interest rates. Keep in mind, each bond's interest payment is set when the bond is issued. The price only changes in the aftermarket, not the amount the bond issuer pays on each bond. Conversely, when general interest rates fall, bond prices rise.

272 MERIWETHER WAS PUT IN CHARGE: Nicolas Dunbar, *Investing Money: The Story of Long-Term Capital Management and the Legends Behind It* (Hoboken, N.J.: John Wiley, 2000), pp. 99–100.

272 AS MERIWETHER MADE A LOT OF MONEY: In general, Lewis, *Liar's Poker;* also, Lowenstein, *When Genius Failed.*

272 ONE OF MERIWETHER'S STAR TRADERS: Dunbar, *Investing Money,* p. 106.

272–73 THE MANAGERS COULD ALSO BUY HEDGES: Ibid., pp. 137–41.

275 SALOMON HAD TO PAY FINES: Richard Bookstaber, *A Demon of Our Own Design* (New York: John Wiley, 2007), pp. 195–98; Dunbar, *Investing Money,* pp. 109–12; Carol J. Loomis, "Warren Buffett's Wild Ride," *Fortune,,* October 27, 1997.

275 BETWEEN 1990 AND 1993: Dunbar, *Investing Money,* p. 123.

276 THE FUND OPENED ITS DOORS: Ibid., pp. 130–31.

276 IN 1994, A BAD YEAR: Frank Partnoy, *Infectious Greed: How Deceit and Risk Corrupted the Financial Markets* (New York: Henry Holt, 2003), pp. 251–53.

277 IN PARTICULAR, IT HAD LEARNED: Dunbar, *Investing Money,* p. 153.

277 MANY WERE TRYING TO FIND OUT: Interviews with Christian Siva-Jothy, in Drobny, *Inside the House of Money,* pp. 72–101.

277 IN 1997, BY CONTRAST: Dunbar, *Investing Money,* p. 180.

277 AT THIS POINT: Lowenstein, *When Genius Failed*, p. 127.

277 SUCH FORECASTING HAD BEEN SCORNED: Bookstaber, *A Demon of Our Own Design*, p. 98.

278 ANY WARNINGS FROM THEIR NOBEL PRIZE: Dunbar, *Investing Money*, pp. 120–21.

278 THEY BECAME KNOWN AS: Lowenstein, *When Genius Failed*, pp. 123–26. Dunbar, *Investing Money*, p, 178.

278 IT PREDICTED THAT A LOSS OF: Dunbar, *Investing Money*, pp. 184–86.

278 AT THE TIME, THEIR CAPITAL: Joe Kolman, "LTCM Speaks," DerivativesStrategy .com, April 1999, www.derivativesstrategy.com/magazine/archive/1999/049.

279 IN FIVE WEEKS, THEY WOULD LOSE: Lowenstein, *When Genius Failed*, p. 143.

279 ALL THE SELLING FORCED PRICES: Dunbar, *Investing Money*, pp. 204–5.

280 ON AUGUST 21 ALONE: Ibid., p. 205; Lowenstein, *When Genius Failed*, pp. 147, 159.

280 BUFFETT DID ULTIMATELY PUT TOGETHER: Buffett had persuaded Hank Greenberg of AIG to put up $700 million and Jon Corzine of Goldman Sachs to put up another $300 million, while Buffett put up $3 billion. But it required Meriwether and his partners to leave the firm. Meriwether essentially turned it down. Dunbar, *Investing Money*, pp. 220–22. Lowenstein, *When Genius Failed*, disputes that Meriwether rejected the offer, pp. 202–4.

280 THE FED DID NOT WANT TO TAKE THE CHANCE: Lowenstein, *When Genius Failed*, pp. 188–89, 194–95, 201.

281 MERIWETHER AND HIS TEAM: Dunbar, *Investing Money*, p. 224.

281 MERIWETHER TOLD THE FED: Lowenstein, *When Genius Failed*, p. 173. In general, Michael Lewis, "How the Eggheads Cracked," *New York Times Magazine*, January 24, 1999.

281 HAD LTCM DEEPER POCKETS: Bookstaber, *A Demon of Our Own Design*, p. 105; Kolman, "LTCM Speaks," p. 7.

282 "WHAT IS REMARKABLE": Dunbar, *Investing Money*, p. 227.

282 NEITHER THE CLINTON ADMINISTRATION NOR GREENSPAN: Lowenstein, *When Genius Failed*, p. 231.

283 THESE EARNED BILLIONS OF DOLLARS: In general, Michael Lewis, *The Big Short: Inside the Doomsday Machine* (New York: W. W. Norton, 2010).

283 OVER THE YEARS, EVEN IN THE 2000S: The principal work is Roger G. Ibbotson, Peng Chen, and Kevin X. Chu, "The ABCs of Hedge Funds: Alphas, Betas, and Costs," Social Science Research Network Working Paper, March 30, 2010, http://papers.ssrn .com/sol3/papers.cfm?abstract_id=1581559.

283 "POWER TO CAUSE AVALANCHES": Mallaby, *More Money Than God*, p. 145.

284 "I REMEMBER IN THE 1990S": Drobny, *Inside the House of Money*, pp. 72–101.

284 ONE ACADEMIC STUDY: Ilia D. Dichev and Gwen Yu, "Higher Risk, Lower Returns: What Hedge Fund Investors Really Earn," *Journal of Financial Economics*, http://papers .ssrn.com/sol3/papers.cfm?abstract_id=1354070.

CHAPTER 16: SANDY WEILL

286 HE COULD NOT HAVE IMAGINED THAT HE COULD HAVE A BRANCH: The Interstate Banking and Branching Efficiency Act of 1994.

288 "HE WAS SO WEAK": Anonymous author interview, August 14, 2009.

289 WEILL SHOWED LITTLE SYMPATHY: Sandy Weill and Judah S. Kraushar, *The Raw Deal: My Life in Business and Philanthropy* (New York: Warner Business, 2006), pp. 20, 30.

289 A MORE CREDIBLE ACCOUNT: Monica Langley, *Tearing Down the Walls: How Sandy*

Weill Fought His Way to the Top of the Financial World . . . and Then Nearly Lost It All (New York: Free Press, 2003), p. 11.

290 EACH CONTRIBUTED $60,000: Ibid., p. 16.

290 THIS VENTURE REQUIRED: Weill, *The Raw Deal*, p. 40.

291 CBWL HAD ALREADY ABSORBED THE OLD-LINE: Institutional Investor, *The Way It Was: An Oral History of Finance, 1967–1987* (New York: William Morrow, 1988), p. 368.

291 HAYDEN STONE WAS NEARLY EIGHTY YEARS OLD: Amy Stone and Mike Brewster, *King of Capital: Sandy Weill and the Making of Citigroup* (New York: John Wiley, 2002), pp. 80–81.

292 WITH THEIR SUDDEN RICHES: Langley, *Tearing Down the Walls*, p. 43.

293 WEILL "WOULD TAKE ALMOST ANYTHING": Stone and Brewster, *King of Capital*, p. 100.

293 FINALLY, WEILL'S FIRM SETTLED: Weill and Kraushar, *The Raw Deal*, pp. 84–86.

293 THOSE CO-WORKERS WHO STAYED: Langley, *Tearing Down the Walls*, pp. 44, 53.

294 HE AND A COUPLE OF COLLEAGUES: Ibid., p. 45.

294 "THE TURNING POINT OF MY CAREER": Jon Friedman, "Sandy Weill Roars Back," *BusinessWeek*, December 4, 1989, p. 88.

295 HE CUT SALARIES BY 40 TO 50 PERCENT: Weill and Kraushar, *The Raw Deal*, p. 84.

295 WEILL HAD BECOME THE MANAGER OF ADVERSITY: Stone and Brewster, *King of Capital*, p. 107.

296 AT COHEN'S FAREWELL PARTY: Langley, *Tearing Down the Walls*, p. 106.

297 WITH THE LOEB RHOADES MERGER: Stone and Brewster, *King of Capital*, pp. 116–20; Langley, *Tearing Down the Walls*, pp. 56–60.

298 "VISIONS OF BROKERS SELLING": Weill and Kraushar, *The Raw Deal*, p. 117.

298 MOREOVER, AMERICAN EXPRESS HAD $20 BILLION: Langley, *Tearing Down the Walls*, p. 65.

298 BACHE FEARED AN UNFRIENDLY ACQUISITION: Robert J. Cole, "A Prudential Offer for Bache Accepted," *New York Times*, March 19, 1981.

298 "THIS WILL CHANGE": Weill and Kraushar, *The Raw Deal*, p. 120.

299 ON PAPER, WEILL'S SHARES: Stone and Brewster, *King of Capital*, p. 137.

299 THE IDS PEOPLE: Langley, *Tearing Down the Walls*, p. 78.

300 "SANDY WAS NOT A DETAIL GUY": Stone and Brewster, *King of Capital*, p. 164.

300 WEILL DID WHAT HE KNEW HOW TO DO BEST: Langley, *Tearing Down the Walls*, pp. 82–89; Stone and Brewster, *King of Capital*, p. 148.

300 AMERICAN EXPRESS SOLD FIREMAN'S FUND: Stone and Brewster, *King of Capital*, pp. 149–51.

301 "WHATEVER I DO NEXT": Langley, *Tearing Down the Walls*, pp. 87–89.

301 AN ARTICLE IN *FORTUNE*: Ibid., p. 109.

302 TO SHOW HIS CONFIDENCE IN CCC'S FUTURE: Weill and Kraushar, *The Raw Deal*, p. 186.

303 HE COMMANDEERED THE $50 MILLION SURPLUS: Langley, *Tearing Down the Walls*, pp. 131–32.

303 "THE WORK ETHIC OF EMPLOYEES": Weill and Kraushar, *The Raw Deal*, p. 94.

303 WEILL HAD GAINED THE TRUST OF SHAREHOLDERS: Stone and Brewster, *King of Capital*, p. 178.

304 PRIMERICA HAD 25,000 EMPLOYEES: Ibid., p. 188.

304 "A BUNCH OF GODDAMN BABIES": Langley, *Tearing Down the Walls*, p. 173.

304 BUT THE A.L. WILLIAMS SALES FORCE REACTED BADLY: Mark L. Sirower, *The Synergy Gap: How Companies Lost the Acquisition Game* (New York: Free Press, 1997), p. 41. A.L. Williams eventually had a serious scandal, its founder having to leave the firm.

304 ACCORDING TO ONE BIOGRAPHER: Langley, *Tearing Down the Walls*, p. 190.

305 *FORTUNE* REPORTED THAT WEILL: Ibid., pp. 185–90.

305 ONE OF WEILL'S EXECUTIVES: "Primerica: Sandy Weill and His Corporate Entrepreneurs," *Harvard Business Review*, November 20, 1962, p. 5.

305 "HE ALWAYS WANTED TO BE KING OF THE WORLD": Stone and Brewster, *King of Capital*, p. 200.

305 IN 1992, EVEN AS THE COMPANY: Ibid., p. 199.

306 IN THE SPRING OF 1993: Weill and Kraushar, *The Raw Deal*, pp. 246–47.

306 WEILL'S SHARES IN PRIMERICA: Allen R. Myerson, "Building an Empire, Again," *New York Times*, March 13, 1993.

308 THUS, A PERMANENT WEDGE: Stone and Brewster, *King of Capital*, pp. 205–9.

308 WEILL LATER TRIED TO MINIMIZE: Weill and Kraushar, *The Raw Deal*, p. 285.

309 TRAVELERS WAS MISSING OUT: Langley, *Tearing Down the Walls*, p. 247.

309 "THE ANNOUNCEMENT SHOOK ME THOROUGHLY: Weill and Kraushar, *The Raw Deal*, p. 270.

309 IT WAS OPENING ENOUGH: Ibid., pp. 269–72.

310 "I AM NOT SURE WE EVER": Ibid., p. 291.

310 EVEN WITH SALOMON'S LOSSES: Stone and Brewster, *King of Capital*, pp. 289–90; Langley, *Tearing Down the Walls*, pp. 263–71; Weill and Kraushar, *The Raw Deal*, pp. 291–92.

311 BUT WITH THE ECONOMIC EXPANSION: Brett D. Fromson, "For Citicorp's Reed, a Dicey Board Game; Directors' Support as Chairman Faces More Flak," *Washington Post*, September 13, 1992; Peter Alan Harper, "Reed Steered Citicorp from Depths to Heights," Associated Press, April 6, 1998.

311 REED'S NEXT GOAL: Pearl Bosco, "Citicorp's Reed Cast Eclectic Talent to Lead Retail Banking Charge," *American Banker*, October 20, 1997.

311 "I LAUNCHED INTO A MONOLOGUE": Weill and Kraushar, *The Raw Deal*, pp. 302–3.

312 IN TERMS OF GEOGRAPHICAL REACH": Langley, *Tearing Down the Walls*, pp. 273–74.

312 SINCE THE 1980S, BANKERS TRUST: See, as examples, Gary Hector, "Bankers Trust: Leaner, Meaner, Keener," *Fortune*, January 9, 1984, p. 104; Sarah Bartlett, "Bankers Trust Could Beat the Street at Its Own Game," *BusinessWeek*, August 11, 1988, p. 86.

312 WEILL WAS A KEY SUPPORTER: Frank Partnoy, *Infectious Greed* (New York: Henry Holt, 2003), pp. 45–48.

313 "I HAVE NOTHING AGAINST SIZE": "Weill and Kraushar, *The Raw Deal*, p. 312; Langley, *Tearing Down the Walls*, pp. 279–81.

313 "THIS IS REALLY ABOUT CROSS MARKETING": Stone and Brewster, *King of Capital*, p. 230.

313 *THE WALL STREET JOURNAL* CREDULOUSLY REPORTED: Steven Lipin and Stephen E. Frank, "The Big Umbrella: Travelers/Citicorp Merger—One-Stop Shopping Is the Reason for the Deal," *Wall Street Journal*, April 7, 1998.

313 SALOMON'S QUANT TRADING OPERATIONS: Weill and Kraushar, *The Raw Deal*, pp. 330–32.

314 CITIGROUP REPORTED A DECLINE: Stone and Brewster, *King of Capital*, p. 200.

314 REED INCREASED THE FRICTION: Ibid., p. 250.

314 WEILL, STUNNED BY REED'S CANDOR: Langley, *Tearing Down the Walls*, pp. 328–30.

315 "CONGRESS DITHERS": Editorial, "Monster Merger," *New York Times*, April 8, 1998.

316 "HE TALKED ABOUT RELOADING ALL THE TIME": Anonymous interview, May 2009.

316 IN THAT YEAR, HIS TOTAL COMPENSATION: Stone and Brewster, *King of Capital*, p. 240.

316 HE AND OTHERS LIKE HIM: Louis Uchitelle, "The Richest of the Rich, Proud of a New Gilded Age," *New York Times*, July 15, 2007.

317 THE BIOGRAPHERS MERELY REFLECTED: Stone and Brewster, *King of Capital*, p. 279.

317 IN AN INTERVIEW IN 2004: Author interview with Walter Wriston, July 2004.

317 BY 1999, WHEN WEILL CREATED: Kevin J. Stiroh and Jennifer Poole, "Explaining the Rising Concentration of Banking Assets in the 1990s," Federal Reserve Bank of New York, *Current Issues in Economics and Finance* 6, no. 9 (August 2000), cited by Simon Johnson and James Kwak, *13 Bankers: The Wall Street Takeover and the Next Financial Meltdown* (New York: Pantheon, 2010), p. 85.

317 "THE GOAL WAS TO BE BIG": Johnson and Kwak, *13 Bankers*, p. 86.

CHAPTER 17: JACK GRUBMAN, FRANK QUATTRONE,
KEN LAY, AND SANDY WEILL

318 "THE HISTORY OF ONE-STOP SHOPPING": Amy Stone and Mike Brewster, *King of Capital: Sandy Weill and the Making of Citigroup* (New York: John Wiley, 2002), p. 124.

318 "THE ONE YOU READ ABOUT": Ibid., p. 124.

318 "CROSS-SELLING DOESN'T WORK": Ibid., pp. 124–25.

320 A FIRST MARKER: Michael Siconolfi, "Under Pressure: At Morgan Stanley, Analysts Were Urged to Soften Harsh Views," *Wall Street Journal*, July 14, 1992, p. A1.

321 THE LOW PERCENTAGE REMAINED UNCHANGED: D. Quinn Mills, *Wheel, Deal and Steal: Deceptive Accounting, Deceitful CEOs, and Ineffective Reforms* (Upper Saddle River, N.J.: Prentice Hall/Financial Times, 2003), pp. 113–15.

321 "NOW THE JOB OF ANALYSTS": Quoted by ibid., pp. 122–23; testimony to the House Financial Services Subcommittee, July 31, 2001.

322 "THE BIGGEST HISTORICAL EXAMPLE": Robert J. Shiller, *Irrational Exuberance*, 2nd ed. (Princeton, N.J.: Princeton University Press, 2005), p. 2.

322 "I HAVE TWELVE OR FOURTEEN": Author interview with Albert Vilar, May 2000.

322 AMERINDO FOLDED AND VILAR, CONVICTED: http://topics.nytimes.com/topics/reference/timestopics/people/v/alberto_w_vilar/index.html.

323 IN 1990, THE TEN LARGEST COMPANIES: Frank Partnoy, *Infectious Greed: How Deceit and Risk Corrupted the Financial Markets* (New York: Henry Holt, 2003), p. 2.

323 "STOCKS FOR A NEW INDUSTRY": Mary Meeker, *U.S. News & World Report*, April 3, 2000.

323 "A NEW ERA ECONOMY": Partnoy, *Infectious Greed*, p. 107.

323 YET THERE WERE MANY HISTORICAL ANALOGIES: See, for example, Murray N. Rothbard, *The Panic of 1819* (New York: AMS, 1962).

323 THE ECONOMIST WROTE IN 1999: *The Economist*, September 29, 1991, quoted by Jeff Madrick, *The Business Media and the New Economy*, Joan Shorenstein Center, Harvard University, December 2001, p. 13.

323 AS LATE AS 2000: Peter Schwartz and Peter Leyden, "The Long Boom: A History of the Future, 1980–2020," *Wired*, July 1997.

324 THERE WAS BROAD SUPPORT: "Question: Is There a New Economy?," Speech by Alan Greenspan at the University of California, Berkeley, September 4, 1998.

324 THE MEDIA PAID GROWING ATTENTION: Madrick, *The Business Media and the New Economy*.

324 FORTUNE ANALYZED HOW JACK WELCH: Betsy Morris, "Tearing Up the Jack Welch Playbook," *Fortune*, July 11, 2006.

324 CORPORATIONS WILL NORMALLY MINIMIZE: Alan Murray, "Inflated Profits in Corporate Books Is Half the Story," *Wall Street Journal*, July 2, 2002, cited by Partnoy, *Infectious Greed*, p. 210.

324 THE SUPREME COURT RULED: *Central Bank of Denver v. First Interstate Bank of Detroit*.

325 "IT WAS A RADICAL DECISION": Partnoy, *Infectious Greed*, p. 172.

325 IN CONGRESSIONAL TESTIMONY: Ibid., p. 172.

325 THE MERGED GARBAGE COMPANY: *Securities and Exchange Commission v. Dean L. Buntrock, Phillip B. Rooney,* et al., No. 02C2180, Northern District, Illinois.

325 IT WAS ALSO SUED: See in general, David Young, "Waste Firm Still Hauling Image Woes," *Chicago Tribune,* October 6, 1991; and Partnoy, *Infectious Greed,* pp. 196–98.

326 IT WAS A MODEST FINE: Securities and Exchange Commission, Litigation Release, No. 19351, August 29, 2005.

326 BETWEEN 1990 AND 1994: John C. Bogle, *The Battle for the Soul of Capitalism* (New Haven, Conn.: Yale University Press, 2005), p. 111.

327 SECURITIES LAW PROFESSOR FRANK PARTNOY ARGUED: Partnoy, *Infectious Greed,* pp. 33, 166–68, 269.

327 BY 1996, AVERAGE CEO COMPENSATION: Kevin J. Murphy, "Executive Compensation," April 1998, p. 90, http://ssrn.com/abstract=163914 or doi:10.2139/ssrn.163914.

327 AT THE HEIGHT OF THE BULL MARKET: Bogle, *The Battle for the Soul of Capitalism,* p. 17.

327 IN THE MID-1990S ALONE: Murphy, "Executive Compensation," p. 6. In general, Lucian Bebchuk and Jesse Fried, *Pay Without Performance: The Unfulfilled Promise of Executive Compensation* (Cambridge, Mass.: Harvard University Press, 2004).

328 INCREASED STOCK OPTION INCENTIVES: Murphy, who found these results, is largely a supporter of the efficient markets thesis, and a defender of higher CEO compensation, but in the 1990s he could not find a relationship between pay and performance. He attributed it partly to the difficulty of the task. Murphy, "Executive Compensation," pp. 41–42. Later work was very persuasive that the incentives did not improve performance and that compensation was basically set by those sympathetic to the CEOs. Lucian Bebchuk and Yaniv Grinstein, "The Growth of Executive Pay," *Oxford Review of Economic Policy* 21, no. 2 (2005); Bebchuk and Fried, *Pay Without Performance.*

328 TWO LAW SCHOOL PROFESSORS: Bebchuk and Fried, *Pay Without Performance.*

328 THERE WAS WIDESPREAD: Stock and home prices were rising in this period, which may have satisfied some workers.

328 IN THE TEN YEARS: "How Bill Clinton Helped Boost CEO Pay," *BusinessWeek,* November 27, 2006.

329 THE SEC'S LEVITT: Partnoy, *Infectious Greed,* p. 156.

330 THE INVESTMENT BANK'S FEE: Ibid., pp. 266–67.

330 AT HIS HEIGHT: Ibid., p. 267–68.

330 WITH ALLOCATIONS OF IPO SHARES: Ibid., p. 279.

331 IN 2000, THE SEC INVESTIGATED: *Securities and Exchange Commission v. Credit Suisse First Boston Corp.,* United States District Court, District of Columbia, January 22, 2002, http://www.sec.gov/litigation/complaints/complr17327.htm.

331 THE GOVERNMENT DECIDED TO PROSECUTE: Partnoy, *Infectious Greed,* pp. 409–12.

332 HALF OF THE ONES THAT HADN'T GONE OUT OF BUSINESS: "That Was Then," *The Economist,* January 26, 2002, cited by Partnoy, *Infectious Greed,* p. 267.

332 "IF THE WINNERS RAKED IN": Bogle, *The Battle for the Soul of Capitalism,* pp. 11–12.

332 FORTUNE EDITOR CAROL LOOMIS: Carol J. Loomis, "A Whole New Way to Run a Bank," *Fortune,* September 7, 1992.

332 BTC'S INTEREST INCOME: Gene D. Guill, "Bankers Trust and the Birth of Modern Risk Management," Loan Exposure Management Group, Wharton and Deutsche Bank, May 21, 2009, http://www.fields.utoronto.ca/programs/cim/08–09/PRMIA/BankersTrustPresentation.pdf.

333 BUT THE TRUE REASON: The story was largely uncovered and later recounted in *Fortune.* See Carol D. Loomis, "How Bankers Trust Lied About $80 Million," *Fortune,* September 7, 1992.

333 AS FRANK PARTNOY COMPLAINED: Partnoy, *Infectious Greed*, p. 32.

334 WHEN THE SEC INVESTIGATED: *The Securities Exchange Commission in the Matter of BT Securities Corp.*, Release No. 7124, December 22, 1994.

334 BTC PAID ONLY: NationsBank of North Carolina also created securities that resulted in large losses for clients. The SEC concluded that they were sold as "straightforward U.S. Government bond funds, when, in fact, they were highly leveraged and invested in interest-rate-sensitive derivatives." *The Securities and Exchange Commission in the Matter of NationsSecurities and NationsBank, S.A.*, Release No. 7532, May 4, 1998.

335 "THE LACK OF BANKING COMPETITION": Author interview with Leo Hindery, October 23, 2010.

336 THEY MADE THE CALIFORNIA ELECTRICITY SHORTAGE: Partnoy, *Infectious Greed*, pp. 326–27; Bethany McLean and Peter Elkind, *The Smartest Guys in the Room: The Amazing Rise and Scandalous Fall of Enron* (New York: Penguin, 2003), pp. 270–71.

336 ARTHUR ANDERSEN, THEIR ACCOUNTANTS: David Barzoa, "Former Officials Say Enron Hid Gains During Crisis in California," *New York Times*, June 23, 2002.

336 TRADERS CAN BE SEEN: Alex Gibney, *The Smartest Guys in the Room*, 2005. Documentary based on McLean and Elkind.

336 TRADING REMAINED PROFITABLE UNTIL THE END: Partnoy, *Infectious Greed*, p. 321.

336 RATHER, IT WAS UNETHICAL FINANCIAL SCHEMES: McLean and Elkind, *The Smartest Guys in the Room*, pp. 327–31.

337 AS ONE ANALYST PUT IT: Ibid., p. 159.

338 OLSON WAS FIRED ANYWAY: Kurt Eichenwald, *Conspiracy of Fools: A True Story* (New York: Broadway, 2005), p. 184.

338 IN 1999, FASTOW DEMANDED THAT CITIGROUP'S SALOMON: Ibid., p. 220.

338 A GOLDMAN SACHS ANALYST: McLean and Elkind, *The Smartest Guys in the Room*, pp. 313, 314.

338 IN OCTOBER 2001: Jeff Madrick, "Enron: Seduction and Betrayal," *New York Review of Books*, March 14, 2002.

338 IN 2000, FASTOW MADE: McLean and Elkind, *The Smartest Guys in the Room*, p. 366.

338 LAY TOOK IN SOME: Ibid., p. 344.

339 THIS WAS THE FIRST SERIOUS CRITICISM: Bethany McLean, "Is Enron Overpriced?" *Fortune*, February 13, 2001.

339 ENRON'S PRESTIGIOUS TEXAS LAWYERS: Kurt Eichenwald and Diana B. Henriques, "Enron's Many Strands: The Company Unravels; Enron Buffed Image to a Shine Even as It Rotted from Within," *New York Times*, February 10, 2002.

339 MOODY'S, THE CREDIT RATING AGENCY: McLean and Elkind, *The Smartest Guys in the Room*, p. 371.

340 RUBIN'S CALL BROUGHT HIM: Richard A. Oppel, Jr., "Senate Report Says Rubin Acted Legally in Enron Matter," *New York Times*, January 3, 2003.

340 ENRON'S SHARE PRICE FELL: Partnoy, *Infectious Greed*, p. 338.

340 OVER THE YEARS, KEN LAY SOLD: Ibid., pp. 341–43.

341 ONLY NINE MONTHS LATER: After an investigation, the SEC also forced Xerox to restate its earnings over the preceding five years by $2 billion. The once respected firm, a charter member of the Nifty Fifty, was inflating earnings per share in the late 1990s to support its rising stock price, with the approval of its auditors, KPMG.

342 ON THE OTHER HAND, WHEN HE APPLIED AT SALOMON: Peter Elstrom, "Jack Grubman, the Power Broker," *BusinessWeek*, May 15, 2000, http://www.businessweek.com/archives/2000/b3681212.arc.htm.

342 WINNICK UNDERTOOK ONE TAKEOVER: Partnoy, *Infectious Greed*, p. 354.

343 AS A RULE, SECURITIES ANALYSTS: Ibid., p. 355.

343 BUT *MONEY* MAGAZINE DID A SCORNFUL: Amy Feldman and Joan Caplin, "Is Jack Grub-

man the Worst Analyst Ever?," *Money*, April 25, 2002, http://money.cnn.com/2002/04/25/pf/investing/grubman/.

343 "JACK PROBABLY KNOWS MORE": Ibid.

344 THE CREDIT RATING AGENCIES: Partnoy, *Infectious Greed*, p. 367.

344 "WHAT USED TO BE A CONFLICT": Elstrom, "Jack Grubman, the Power Broker."

345 BY ONE CALCULATION: Mark Hulbert, "The Fantasy and the Fact of New Stock Offerings," *New York Times*, March 15, 2000, p. 8, cited by Partnoy, *Infectious Greed*, p. 274.

346 "I FEEL BADLY": Rick Weinberg, "While Denying Wrongdoing, Sandy Apologizes for Enron Relationship," *Registered Rep.*, July 25, 2002, http://registeredrep.com/news/finance_denying_wrongdoing_sandy/.

346 CONGRESS STARTED ISSUING SUBPOENAS: An excellent summary of the demands by government agencies is Bruce Mizrach and Susan Zhang Weerts, "Does the Stock Market Punish Corporate Malfeasance?" *Corporate Ownership & Control*, Summer 2006, http://snde.rutgers.edu/pubs/%5B25%5D-2006_COO.pdf.

347 "SANDY KNEW WHAT WAS GOING ON": Author interview with Eliot Spitzer, June 12, 2009.

347 THE SIGNING FIRMS: Susanne Craig, Kara Scannell, and Randall Smith, "SEC Didn't Expand Upon Stock-Abuse Settlement," *Wall Street Journal*, March 19, 2010, p. C1.

347 BUT EVEN A $100 MILLION: Monica Langley, *Tearing Down the Walls: How Sandy Weill Fought His Way to the Top of the Financial World . . . and Then Nearly Lost It All* (New York: Free Press, 2003), p. 388.

348 SPITZER CALLED GRASSO: Author interview with Eliot Spitzer, June 12, 2009.

348 WEILL DECLINED THE APPOINTMENT: Langley, *Tearing Down the Walls*, pp. 426–27.

348 A REASON THE SCANDALS OF THE EARLY 2000S: Partnoy, *Infectious Greed*, pp. 371–83.

349 THE $150 BILLION AMOUNTED TO ONE THIRD: M. Hosein Fallah and Rishi Herwadkar, "Telecommunications Industry Overinvestment: Defying Rational Economics," Stevens Institute of Technology, http://howe.stevens.edu/fileadmin/Files/research/Telecom/publications/Telecommunications_Industry_Overinvestment.pdf; "U.S. Capital Spending Patterns, 1999–2007," Census Bureau, http://www.census.gov/econ/aces/report/2009/capitalspendingreport2009.pdf.

349 "PEOPLE CAN LOOK AT": Louis Uchitelle, "Age of Riches: The Richest of the Rich, Proud of a New Gilded Age," July 15, 2007, *New York Times*, Sunday Business, p. 1.

CHAPTER 18: ANGELO MOZILO

351 WITHOUT A HIGH-TECHNOLOGY BOOM, ALAN GREENSPAN: There was also fear that the resetting of computerized calendars in 2000—Y2K—could cause some economic turmoil.

352 SOME ECONOMISTS BLAMED GREENSPAN: In particular, John B. Taylor, *Getting Off Track: How Government Actions and Interventions Caused, Prolonged, and Worsened the Financial Crisis* (Stanford, Calif.: Hoover Institution Press, 2009).

354 AS MOZILO HIRED OTHERS: Connie Bruck, "Angelo's Ashes," *The New Yorker*, June 29, 2009.

354 BUT IN THE LATE 1960S: For a fine brief summary of the history of Fannie, Freddie, and related instititions, see Sarah Quinn, "Securitization and the State" (working paper, University of California, Berkeley, 2008), http://www.sarahquinnsociology.com/documents/SecuritizationandtheStateASA2008.pdf.

354 MOZILO, CHARMING, ENERGETIC: Paul Muolo and Mathew Padilla, *Chain of Blame: How Wall Street Caused the Mortgage and Credit Crisis* (Hoboken, N.J.: John Wiley, 2008), p. 113.

354 FANNIE MAE AND MOZILO WERE JOINED AT THE HIP: Ibid.

355 "AC" WAS MOZILO'S MOTTO: Muolo and Padilla, *Chain of Blame*, p. 58.

355 IT THUS COST THEM: Michael Lewis, *Liar's Poker: Rising Through the Wreckage on Wall Street* (New York: W. W. Norton, 1989), p. 103.

355 SO ATTRACTIVE WERE THE HIGH RATES: As a young TV business analyst on *Business Times on ESPN*, I did a weekly report on the thrifts paying the highest interest, based on information from a news service then, the Bank Rate Monitor.

356 HAPPILY FOR MOZILO: Quinn, "Securitization and the State," p. 1.

356 "IF YOU WEREN'T TRADING BONDS": Lewis, *Liar's Poker*, p. 86.

356 ONE OF SIMON'S TRADERS, BOB DALL: Ibid., pp. 86–90.

357 "HE WAS TOUGH-MINDED": Ibid., p. 90.

357 "I HAVE NEVER SEEN ANYONE": Ibid., p. 90.

358 THE MOUNTAIN OF MORTGAGES: Ibid., pp. 105–6.

358 THIS MAY HAVE BEEN AS MUCH AS: Ibid., p. 108.

360 IT WAS SOON NO LONGER CLEAR: Investors paid slightly more—that is, accepted lower interest income—because the different structures met their specific needs and the varieties of risk they could take over differing periods of time.

360 EVENTUALLY, THEY ALSO PACKAGED SUBPRIME MORTGAGES: Charles R. Morris, *The Trillion Dollar Meltdown: Easy Money, High Rollers, and the Great Credit Crash* (New York: PublicAffairs, 2008), p. 41.

360 AS USUAL, RANIERI ARGUED: Quinn, "Securitization and the State," p. 6.

361 REAGAN WAS AN ADVOCATE AS WELL: Ranieri also had an influential hand in rewriting tax laws that were until this point obstacles to the creation of the trusts required by the MBSs and new CMOs; the new tax rules were passed as part of the Tax Reform Act of 1986. Alyssa Katz, "The Dubious Birth of Mortgage-Backed Securities," *Slate*, June 25, 2009, http://www.thebigmoney.com/articles/history-lesson/2009/06/25/dubious -birth-mortgage-backed-securities?page=0,2.

361 RANIERI WAS FIRED: Charles Gasparino, *The Sellout: How Three Decades of Wall Street Greed and Government Mismanagement Destroyed the Global Financial System* (New York: HarperCollins, 2009), p. 75.

361 IN 1988, HE LEFT TO RUN: Ibid., pp. 66–69, 82.

362 THE ANNUAL LENDING BY THE INCREASINGLY OUTDATED THRIFTS: "Mortgage debt outstanding," U.S. Census Bureau, http://www.census.gov/compendia/statab/2010/ tables/10s1155.xls. The amount of mortgages outstanding at the thrifts contracted by $200 billion but expanded by nearly $300 billion at commercial banks. The GSEs increased their portfolio holdings by $100 billion.

363 WHEN STILL AN ENGINEER: Lewis, *Liar's Poker*, p. 124.

363 TRADING BEGAN TO DOMINATE WALL STREET: Associated Press, "Ex-Merrill Trader Cited," *New York Times*, April 11, 1989, http://www.nytimes.com/1989/04/11/business/ ex-merrill-trader-cited.html?pagewanted=1.

364 THE SECURITIES INVESTOR PROTECTION CORPORATION: Author interview with Felix Rohatyn, January 22, 2010.

364 THEN RECESSION DESCENDED: Gasparino, *The Sellout*, p. 77.

364 BUT BEAR STEARNS BUCKED THE TREND: Ibid., pp. 76–77.

364 GREENBERG PAID HIMSELF $15.8 MILLION: William D. Cohan, *House of Cards: A Tale of Hubris and Wretched Excess on Wall Street* (New York: Doubleday, 2009), pp. 219–20.

365 AS WALL STREET DEVELOPED A BASE: Muolo and Padilla, *Chain of Blame*, p. 115.

365 HE ALSO OPENED AN OPERATION: In addition, he saw an opportunity in trading CRA loans. The Community Reinvestment Act (CRA), first passed in 1977, required thrifts and commercial banks to write a certain proportion of mortgages in their local com-

munity to undercut the discrimination that was widely found to occur in granting mortgages. Mozilo started trading the CRA loans that banks often had to buy to meet the law's minimum requirements. The CRA loans, according to well-documented research from the San Francisco Federal Reserve Bank, the FDIC, were seldom subprime loans and performed relatively well. The ideological criticism of the program continued, nevertheless. Robert B. Avery, Kenneth P. Brevoort, and Glenn B. Canner, "The 2006 HMDA Data," *Federal Reserve Bulletin* 94 (2007), p. A89; speech of Janet Yellen, president, Federal Reserve Bank of San Francisco, March 31, 2008, http://www.frbsf .org/news/speeches/2008/0331.html.

366 IN 1995, MOZILO STARTED WRITING: Muolo and Padilla, *Chain of Blame*, pp. 37–42, 117.

366 IN 2003, AS WE SAW EARLIER, GREENSPAN: Morris, *The Trillion Dollar Meltdown*, p. 68.

367 ITS STOCK PRICE STOOD: Muolo and Padilla, *Chain of Blame*, pp. 120–21; *Securities and Exchange Commission v. Angelo Mozilo, David Sambol, Eric Sieracki*, p. 7, http://www.sec.gov/litigation/complaints/2009/comp21068.pdf.

368 AS THE MARKET ROSE: SEC complaint, pp. 9–10, http://www.sec.gov/litigation/ complaints/2009/comp21068.pdf.

368 IN THIS ENVIRONMENT: The twenty-city composite index was 200 percent higher than it was in 1997, 125 percent higher than in 2000. S&P, Case-Shiller Home Price Indices: 2008, http://www.standardandpoors.com/servlet/BlobServer?blobheadername3 =MDT-Type&blobcol=urldata&blobtable=mungoBlobs&blobheadervalue2 =inline%3B+filename%3DCase-Shiller_Housing_Whitepaper_YearinReview%2Co .pdf&blobheadername2=Content-Disposition&blobheadervalue1=application%2Fpdf &blobkey=id&blobheadername1=content-type&blobwhere=1243618038238&blobheader value3=UTF-8.

368 IN ONE EXAMPLE, ACCORDING TO THE STATE OF CALIFORNIA: SEC complaint, pp. 42–46, http://www.sec.gov/litigation/complaints/2009/comp21068.pdf.

368 MOZILO PAID HIS SALESPEOPLE HIGHER COMMISSIONS: *The People of the State of California v. Countrywide Financial Corp.*, http://ag.ca.gov/cms_attachments/press/pdfs/ n1582_draft_cwide_complaint2.pdf, pp. 12–13.

370 AT THE END OF THE YEAR: Ibid., p. 45.

370 THEY WERE KNOWN AS: Dodd claimed he did not know he was getting a discounted rate or reduction in fees.

CHAPTER 19: JIMMY CAYNE, RICHARD FULD, STAN O'NEAL, AND CHUCK PRINCE

371 THESE PANICS AND COLLAPSES: One among many was Richard Parsons, chairman of the board of Citigroup, comments made at the New School, the Milano School Lecture, September 14, 2010.

371 FORMER TREASURY SECRETARY ROBERT RUBIN: April 8, 2010, Financial Crisis Inquiry Commission, http://online.wsj.com/public/resources/documents/Rubintestimony408 .pdf.

371 JOHN MACK, HEAD OF MORGAN STANLEY: Michael Lewis, *The Big Short: Inside the Doomsday Machine* (New York: W. W. Norton, 2010), pp. 216–19.

373–74 CASSANO, A GRADUATE OF BROOKLYN COLLEGE: Gillian Tett, *Fools' Gold: How the Bold Dream of a Small Tribe at J.P. Morgan Was Corrupted by Wall Street Greed and Unleashed a Catastrophe* (New York: Free Press, 2009), pp. 62–63.

375 THE UPSHOT WAS AN INJECTION: See, for example, Paul Krugman and Robin Wells, "The Slump Goes On: Why?," *New York Review of Books*, September 30, 2010.

377 AS ONE INVESTOR PUT IT: Author interview with a hedge fund manager, May 4, 2010.

377 WHEN ONE COLLAPSED: Lewis, *The Big Short*, p. 129.

377 THE DEFAULT RATE ON SUBPRIME MORTGAGES: Ibid., pp. 128–29.

377 THE FEDERAL RESERVE AND THE SEC: Tett, *Fools' Gold*, p. 202; William D. Cohan, *House of Cards: A Tale of Hubris and Wretched Excess on Wall Street* (New York: Doubleday, 2009), p. 326; Lewis, *The Big Short*, pp. 128–29, 225.

378 WHEN THE CITY'S FINANCES TURNED AROUND: Charles Gasparino, *The Sellout: How Three Decades of Wall Street Greed and Government Mismanagement Destroyed the Global Financial System* (New York: HarperCollins, 2009), pp. 41–47.

378 WARREN SPECTOR, ANOTHER BRIDGE PLAYER: Cohan, *House of Cards*, p. 210.

378 THE VERY RICH MAN BECAME ALOOF: Ibid., p. 314.

378 HE WAS OFTEN OFF AT BRIDGE TOURNAMENTS: Kate Kelly, *Street Fighters: The Last 72 Hours of Bear Stearns, the Toughest Firm on Wall Street* (New York: Penguin, 2009), pp. 155–56.

378 "I REALLY DO BELIEVE": Cohan, *House of Cards*, p. 316.

379 "THERE ARE GOOD AAAS": Ibid., p. 326.

379 HE CLAIMED ONLY 6 PERCENT OF THEIR PORTFOLIOS: Ibid., p. 355.

380 AIG'S CASSANO COULD HARDLY BELIEVE: Lewis, *The Big Short*, pp. 70–80.

380 THEN CAME THE SYNTHETIC CDO: Ibid., pp. 74–75. What's more, the issuers only had to set a small amount of capital to back the CDOs, according to the regulators.

381 SOON AFTER, HALF OF CDOS ISSUED WERE SYNTHETIC: Roger Lowenstein, *The End of Wall Street* (New York: Penguin, 2010), p. 56.

381 THERE WERE NO NEW MORTGAGES: Cassano thought he was selling insurance on triple-A CDOs and to justify the low price he charged had a fancy computer model from respected academic economist Gary Gorton of Wharton, later of Yale Management School. But they were far riskier than he realized. When asked, Gorton said he never knew the CDOs were composed completely of triple-B tranches. Thus, Goldman sold insurance for, say, $20 million on a $1 billion package of bonds but transferred its liability to AIG for only $2 million, simply pocketing the $18 million difference and getting rid of any risk. In total, Cassano earned perhaps $20 million over a couple of years but took responsibility for $20 billion of losses should the market go bad. Cassano underwent the same transactions with other firms, taking on in total about $80 billion in risk.

381 "GOLDMAN WAS PRESSURING INVESTORS": Joe Bel Bruno and Joseph Checkler, "Goldman Hit with a Suit for $1 Billion," *Wall Street Journal*, June 10, 2010, p. C3.

381 THERE WERE REPORTS: Ibid.

382 CIOFFI WAS THE MAJOR BUYER: Lowenstein, *The End of Wall Street*, p. 90.

382 "EITHER THE GAME WAS RIGGED": Lewis, *The Big Short*, p. 166.

383 MARKETS CONTINUED TO DETERIORATE: Lowenstein, *The End of Wall Street*, p. 90.

383 THE CLOSING OF THE FUNDS: Tett, *Fools' Gold*, p. 208.

383 IN A SPEECH IN MAY: The Federal Reserve Bank of Chicago's 43rd Annual Conference on Bank Structure and Competition, Chicago, Illinois, May 17, 2007, http://www.federalreserve.gov/newsevents/speech/bernanke20070517a.htm.

383 ANOTHER FED OFFICIAL: Tett, *Fools' Gold*, p. 181–82.

383 BOTH MOODY'S AND STANDARD & POOR'S: Ibid., p. 177.

384 THAT FALL, THE RATINGS AGENCIES: Ibid., pp. 199–207.

384 BY THIS POINT: Cohan, *House of Cards*, p. 382.

384 CAYNE AND SCHWARTZ HAD BEEN URGED: Bonuses were based on return to equity and if equity was increased, that rate of return would be reduced. Ibid., p. 398.

385 DIMON, UNDER CRITICISM: Tett, *Fools' Gold*, p. 221.

385 BAIL OUT STRUGGLING FANNIE MAE AND FREDDIE MAC: The GSEs took on a lot

of subprime mortgages in 2004 and 2005 to compensate for accounting scandals that kept them out of the markets for a while. In 2003, Fannie Mae, for example, reported more than $6 billion of earnings overstatements. The private GSE, led by Franklin Raines, who made $90 million in compensation over several years, had become a scandal-ridden and troubled company, inflating profits in an attempt to keep its stock price up as a private company with an implied federal guarantee. Once the accounting misstatements were investigated and adjusted, the profit-making GSEs resumed normal activities, but now sought to catch up with the private mortgage industry's purchases and securitization of subprime mortgages, both to meet their government mandate to buy mortgages and to rebuild profits. Fannie and Freddie took on far too many loans that went bad, but they were the cart, not the horse, of the subprime catastrophe. Their highest total purchases of subprime mortgages by far reached 44 percent of the market in 2004 and 33 percent in 2005, before falling back to 20 percent of subprime purchase in 2006, when the frenzy became extreme.

386 FULD'S DREAM HAD COME TRUE: Andrew Ross Sorkin, *Too Big to Fail: The Inside Story of How Wall Street and Washington Fought to Save the Financial System—and Themselves* (New York: Viking, 2009), pp. 19–23.

386 FULD'S AMBITION COULD NOW BE FULLY UNLEASHED: Lawrence G. McDonald with Patrick Robinson, *A Colossal Failure of Common Sense: The Inside Story of the Collapse of Lehman Brothers* (New York: Crown, 2009), pp. 136–38.

386 AT A MANAGEMENT MEETING: Ibid., pp. 268–69.

386 IN THE FACE OF GROWING RISK: Ibid., pp. 274–75.

387 IT WAS PROBABLY THE MOST BRILLIANT TRADE: Lewis, *The Big Short*, pp. 206–14, 128.

387 LEWIS RANIERI HIMSELF . . . WARNED: Paul Muolo and Mathew Padilla, *Chain of Blame: How Wall Street Caused the Mortgage and Credit Crisis* (Hoboken, N.J.: John Wiley, 2008), pp. 223–25.

387 ECONOMISTS AT THE BANK FOR INTERNATIONAL SETTLEMENTS: Tett, *Fools' Gold*, p. 154.

387 DESPITE THE RUSE: Michael J. de la Merced, "Findings on Lehman Take Even Experts by Surprise," *Wall Street Journal,* March 13, 2010, p. B1.

388 FEW ACCEPTED THE CLAIM: Congressional Oversight Committee, *December Oversight Report, Taking Stock: What Has TARP Achieved?,* December 9, 2009, http://cop.senate.gov/documents/cop-120909-report.pdf, p. 14.

388 THAT YEAR, THE CDOS PRODUCED: "Collateralized Debt Obligations Face Funding Woes," *New York Times,* July 24, 2007, http://www.nytimes.com/2007/07/24/business/worldbusiness/24iht-mortgage.1.6798554.html.

388 IN A YEAR WHEN: Among other sources, Lowenstein, *The End of Wall Street,* p. 75.

388 IN 2006, *THE NEW YORK TIMES* REPORTED: Louise Story, "On Wall Street, Bonuses, Not Profits, Were Real," *New York Times,* December 17, 2008, http://www.nytimes.com/2008/12/18/business/18pay.html.

389 BY 2006, THROUGH AGGRESSIVE BORROWING: Tett, *Fool's Gold,* pp. 133–36; "Collateralized Debt Obligations Face Funding Woes."

389 AS THE MARKETS WEAKENED: Louise Story, "On Wall Street," *New York Times,* http://www.nytimes.com/2008/12/18/business/18pay.html.

389 WITH WEILL GONE: Gasparino, *The Sellout,* p. 146.

390 LEVERAGE RATIOS SHOT UP: McDonald and Robinson, *A Colossal Failure of Common Sense,* p. 287.

390 IN NOVEMBER, HE WAS FORCED OUT: Lowenstein, *The End of Wall Street,* p. 110.

390 EARLY IN 2008: Tett, *Fools' Gold,* p. 210.

390 RESIDENTIAL FORECLOSURES WERE DOUBLING: RealtyTrac, *Foreclosure Activity*

Increases 12 Percent in August (September 12, 2008, www.realtytrac.com/content management/pressrelease.aspx?channelid=9&accnt=0&itemid=5163.

390 MANY OF THEM WERE RATED TRIPLE-A: Laurie S. Goodman, "Synthetic CDOs: An Introduction," *Journal of Derivatives* (Spring 2002): 60–72.

391 GEITHNER . . . BERNANKE . . . AND . . . PAULSON . . . CLAIMING HELPLESSNESS: Tett, *Fool's Gold*, p. 233.

391 ORDINARILY, THE SPREAD: TED is an acronym for the Treasury bill rate and the rate on Eurodollar futures, the latter symbolized as ED.

392 BY THE END OF THE WEEK: Lowenstein, *The End of Wall Street*, pp. 206–7.

392 GEITHNER AND PAULSON TRIED: Congressional Oversight Panel, *April Oversight Report*, p. 17.

392 BERNANKE DID NOT WANT: Gasparino, *The Sellout*, p. 469.

393 IT WAS SIMPLY TOO HARD: If the banks sold their troubled assets to the government at the low prevailing price, they would have to write down billions of dollars of similar assets on their books, taking enormous losses and wiping away capital. This was required by what was known as the mark-to-market rule. They wouldn't voluntarily sell under those conditions.

394 ALL THOSE RECEIVING AID: Serena Ng, "Panel: U.S. Risks 'Severe' AIG Losses," *Wall Street Journal*, June 10, 2010, p. C3.

394 A FORMAL ANALYSIS: Congressional Oversight Panel, *February Oversight Report: Valuing Treasury's Acquisitions*, February 6, 2009, cop.senate.gov/documents/cop-020609-report.pdf.

394 AT THE BANKS THAT GOT: Congressional Oversight Panel, *December Oversight Report*, December 2009, p. 38. Also, lending was down 1 percent from 2008.

395 BECAUSE OF SUCH BACKSTOPS: Mark Zandi, "Assessing the Federal Response to the Economic Crisis," testimony before the Senate Budget Committee, Table 1, September 22, 2010.

395 BY LATE 2010: Congressional Oversight Panel, *April Oversight Report*, p. 17.

395 A PERFUNCTORY WHITE PAPER: The U.S. Treasury, *A New Foundation: Rebuilding Financial Supervision and Regulation*, http://www.financialstability.gov/docs/regs/FinalReport_web.pdf.

396 UNTIL 2009, RUBIN EARNED: Rubin testimony, ibid.

397 HOWIE HUBLER, WHO LOST: A French trader who lost $6 billion for Société Générale in early 2008 was put on trial. Paul Betts, "The Rogue Trader, the Bank, the System: Who's on Trial?," *Financial Times*, June 9, 2010, p. 1.

397 IT IS FAIR TO ESTIMATE: Lucian A. Bebchuk, Alma Cohen, and Holger Spamann, "The Wages of Failure: Executive Compensation at Bear Stearns and Lehman 2000–2008," *Yale Journal on Regulation*, forthcoming.

EPILOGUE

398 "THE BUST THAT FOLLOWED": Sheila Bair, "The Road to Safer Banks Runs Through Basel," *Financial Times*, August 24, 2010.

400 FINANCIAL ASSETS AS A PERCENTAGE OF GDP: Johnson and Kwak, *13 Bankers: The Wall Street Takeover and the Next Financial Meltdown* (New York: Pantheon, 2010), p. 85.

401 AVERAGE COMPENSATION PER EMPLOYEE AT FINANCIAL FIRMS: Ibid., p. 115.

401 THE FINANCIAL COMMUNITY GREW FAR FASTER: In general, Thomas Philippon, *The Evolution of the U.S. Financial Industry from 1860 to 2007: Theory and Evidence*, http://pages.stern.nyu.edu/~tphilipp/papers/finsize.pdf.

401 PERSONAL COMPENSATION PAID TO BANKERS: Johnson and Kwak, *13 Bankers,* p. 115. For a simple summary, see Thomas Philippon, "Are Bankers Overpaid?," Stern on Finance, http://sternfinance.blogspot.com/2008/11/are-banker-over-paid-thomas -philippon.html; Claudia Goldin and Lawrence Katz, "Transitions: Career and Family Life Cycles of the Educational Elite," *American Economic Review* 98, no. 2 (May 2008): 363–69.

402 BUT ONE MAINSTREAM ANALYSIS: Alan S. Blinder and Mark Zandi, *How the Great Recession Was Brought to an End,* July 27, 2010, http://www.economy.com/mark-zandi/ documents/End-of-Great-Recession.pdf.

402 TO TAKE A CONTEMPORARY EXAMPLE: Ricardo Hausmann and Andrés Velasco, "The Causes of Financial Crisis, Moral Failure Versus Market Failure," December 2004, http://www.hks.harvard.edu/fs/rhausma/new/causes_of_fin_crises.pdf.

404 THREATENED TO LEAVE: Patrick Jenkins and Megan Murphy, "Goldman in Europe Warning," *Financial Times,* Thursday, September 30, p. 13.

Acknowledgments

The esteemed editor Jim Silberman shepherded this project since the beginning, offering countless insights and sharp, persistent editing every step of the way. The indefatigable literary agent Charlotte Sheedy started this ball rolling years ago, and her optimism about the project never flagged. Alfred A. Knopf's consummate pro Jon Segal added valuable editorial insight and enlightened editing, making the package tight, complete, and that much wiser. Knopf's editor-in-chief, Sonny Mehta, showed faith in this project years ago. Remarkably, he retained his faith in this project and this writer over the many years it took to complete the book. Without these people, this book would simply not have been what it became.

Over the course of the age of greed, there have been dozens of fine books written about aspects of this story. They now amount to hundreds, in fact. I am grateful to all the authors I cite for their efforts—and the daily and weekly journalists who have covered the dozens of stories that make up this history.

I have had many conversations with journalists, economists, policymakers, and astute friends and colleagues at *Challenge* magazine, the New School, the Roosevelt Institute, and elsewhere about the issues raised here. They should know I am grateful for their ideas and criticism.

I must also thank my brother, Rob Madrick, an editor, and my daughter, Matina Madrick, a government consultant, for their ready willingness to read parts of the manuscript and their always constructive and valued criticism. My mother, Corazon, also must be thanked. She has always been the family motivator. She rarely let a week go by without asking me whether I had finished the book. That turned into many, many weeks.

Finally, there is the principal emotional and intellectual support in my life, my wife, Kim Baker, who read every page of this book, often several times. She knows only one direction, straight ahead.

Index

Page numbers in *italics* refer to illustrations.

ILLUSTRATION CREDITS

LEWIS UHLER: Terry Ashe / TIME LIFE Pictures / Getty Images
WALTER WRISTON: Ralph Morse / TIME LIFE Pictures / Getty Images
MILTON FRIEDMAN: AP Photo
RICHARD NIXON: Bettmann / CORBIS
JOE FLOM: Rob Rich / Getty Images
IVAN BOESKY: Misha Erwitt / NY Daily News Archive via Getty Images
WALTER WRISTON: Bettmann / CORBIS
RONALD REAGAN: Courtesy Ronald Reagan Library
TED TURNER: Cynthia Johnson / Liaison / Getty Images
SAM WALTON: Eli Reichman / TIME LIFE Pictures / Getty Images
STEVE ROSS: Richard Corkery / NY Daily News Archive via Getty Images
JIMMY CARTER: AP Photo / Harvey Georges
HOWARD JARVIS: AP Photo / Lennox McLendon
PAUL VOLCKER: AP Photo / Stf
TOM PETERS: Roger Ressmeyer / CORBIS
JACK WELCH: Reuters / Landov
MICHAEL MILKEN: Ed Molinari / NY Daily News Archive via Getty Images
ALAN GREENSPAN: Paul J. Richards / AFP / Getty Images
GEORGE SOROS: AP Photo / Wilfredo Lee
JOHN MERIWETHER: James Leynse / CORBIS
SANDY WEILL: Susan Steinkamp / CORBIS
JACK GRUBMAN: Shawn Thew / AFP / Getty Images
FRANK QUATTRONE: AP Photo / Louis Lanzano
KEN LAY: AP Photo / Kenneth Lambert
ANGELO MOZILO: AP Photo / Susan Walsh
JIMMY CAYNE: Sarah A. Friedman / Contour by Getty Images
RICHARD FULD: Karen Bleier / AFP / Getty Images
STAN O'NEAL: AP Photo / Kathy Willens
CHUCK PRINCE: Chip Somodevilla / Getty Images